The Experimental Earthwork Project, 1960–1992

edited by
M Bell , P J Fowler and S W Hillson

with principal contributions by
P Andrews, H M Appleyard, M Armour-Chelu,
S R Band, J Beavis, M Bell, R Blanchette, S Bond,
T and K Brown, C Calnan, W Carruthers, A Clark, K Crabtree,
J Crowther, G M Cruise, G W Dimbleby, G Edwards, N Evans,
P J Fowler, S Hardman, J G Hather, J Hemsley, R Hedges,
G Hendry, S Hillson, R Janaway, S Johnson, C Keepax,
J Kelley, S Limbrey, G MacLeod, R Macphail, J Moore,
R G Newton, K O'Donoghue, P J Reynolds,
M B Richards, A Rouse, M Ryder,
V Straker, G Swanton, B C Sykes,
K Thompson and P Wiltshire

and based on work by many others

on behalf of
The Experimental Earthworks Committee
British Association for the Advancement of Science

1996

CBA Research Report
Council for British Archaeology

Published 1996 by the Council for British Archaeology
Bowes Morrell House, 111 Walmgate, York YO1 2UA

British Library Cataloguing in Publication Data
A catalogue for this book is available from the British Library

ISSN 0141 7819

ISBN 1 872414 64 8

Typeset from authors' disks by Archetype, Stow-on-the-Wold

Printed in Great Britain at Adpower, Halifax

The publishers acknowledge with gratitude a grant from
English Heritage towards the publication of this report.

Front cover Overton Down, Experimental Earthwork excavation 1992 (photo Ed. Yorath, Experimental Earthworks Committee).
Back cover Construction of the Overton Down Experimental Earthwork in 1960 (photo: Peter Jewell, Experimental Earthworks Committee).

The Experimental Earthwork Project, 1960–1992

This report is dedicated to the founders of the Experiment. Top left – Paul Ashbee (hat A) reaches the bottom of the Wilsford shaft in 1962 (photo: Reuter, Press Association). Top right – Richard Atkinson. Middle right – Ian Cornwall. Bottom left – Geoffrey Dimbleby. Bottom right – Bruce Proudfoot and Peter Jewell. For other founders see Table 1.2.

Contents

vi

List of figures

List of tables

Contributors' names and addresses

Mr H Appleyard
14, Greenacres
Shelf
Halifax
HX3 7QT

Dr M Armour-Chelu
2415, 20th Street NW
No 12 Washington DC
20009 USA

Dr P Andrews
Human Origins Group
Dept of Palaeontology
Natural History Museum
Cromwell Road
London
SW7 5BD

Dr S R Band
Unit of Comparative Plant Ecology
Dept of Animal and Plant Sciences
University of Sheffield
Sheffield
SIO 2TN

Dr J Beavis
Dept of Tourism and Heritage Conservation
Dorset House, Fern Barrow
Poole
Dorset
BH12 5BB

Dr M Bell
Dept of Archaeology
University of Wales: Lampeter
Lampeter
Dyfed
SA48 7ED

Professor R A Blanchette
Dept of Plant Pathology
University of Minnesota
495, Borlaug Hall
1991 Upper Buford Circle
St Paul
MN 55108, USA

Ms S Bond
Institute of Archaeology
University College, London
31–4, Gordon Square
London
WC1H OPY

Dr T Brown and Dr K Brown
Dept of Biochemistry and Applied Molecular
Biology
UMIST
PO Box 88
Manchester
M60 1QD

Dr C N Calnan
Leather Conservation Centre
34, Guildhall Road
Northampton
NN1 1EW

Dr A J Clark
19, The Crossways
Onslow Village
Guildford
Surrey

Ms W Carruthers
Sawmills House
Castellau
Llantrisant
Mid Glamorgan
Wales
CF7 8LP

Dr J Crowther
Dept of Geography
University of Wales: Lampeter
Lampeter
Dyfed
SA48 7ED

Dr K Crabtree
Dept of Geography
University Road
Bristol
BS8 1SS

Professor G W Dimbleby
Institute of Archaeology
University College, London
31–4, Gordon Square
London
WC1H OPY

Ms G Edwards
Conservation Section
Ancient Monuments Lab
Fortress House
23, Savile Row
London
WIX 1AB

Ms N Evans
Archaeology Department
University of Wales: Lampeter
Lampeter
Dyfed
SA48 7ED

Professor P J Fowler (Committee Chair)
Dept of Archaeology
University of Newcastle upon Tyne
Newcastle upon Tyne
NE1 7RU

Dr S Hardman
School of Chemistry and Applied Chemistry
University of Wales: Cardiff
PO Box 912
Cardiff
CF1 3TB

Dr J Hather
Institute of Archaeology
University College, London
31–4, Gordon Square
London
WC1H OPY

Dr R Hedges
Research Lab. for Archaeology and the
History of Art
6, Keble Road
Oxford
OX1 3QJ

Dr G Hendry
Unit of Comparative Plant Ecology
Dept of Animal and Plant Sciences
University of Sheffield
Sheffield
SIO 2TN

Mr J Hemsley
2, Littlecourt Cottages
West Bayborough
Taunton
Somerset
TA4 3EH

Dr S Hillson
Institute of Archaeology
University College, London
31–34, Gordon Square
London
WC1H OPY

Dr R Janaway
School of Archaeological Sciences
The University
Bradford
BD7 IDP

Mrs S Johnson
Archaeology Department
University of Wales: Lampeter
Lampeter
Dyfed
SA48 7ED

Dr C Keepax
Auchravie
Monymusk
Aberdeenshire
Scotland
AB3 75Q

Dr J Kelley
International Mycological Institute
Bakeham Lane
Egham
Surrey
TW20 9TY

Dr S Limbrey
Department of Ancient History and
Archaeology
University of Birmingham
Edgbaston
Birmingham
B15 2TT

Dr G MacLeod
Dept of Tourism and Heritage Conservation
Dorset House
Fern Barrow
Poole
Dorset
BH12 5BB

Dr R Macphail
Institute of Archaeology
University College, London
31–4, Gordon Square
London
WC1H OPY

Ms J Moore
Dept of Archaeology and Prehistory
University of Sheffield
S1O 2TN

Professor R G Newton
Flat 3
20 Hardwick Crescent
Sheffield
S11 8WB

Dr K O'Donoghue
Dept of Biochemistry and Applied Molecular Biology
UMIST
PO Box 88
Manchester
M60 1QD

Dr P Reynolds
Ancient Farm Project
Nexus House
Gravel Hill
London Road
Horndean
Hampshire
PO8 OQE

Dr M B Richards
Research Lab. for Archaeology and the History of Art
6, Keble Road
Oxford
OX1 3QJ

Ms A Rouse
School of History and Archaeology
University of Wales: Cardiff
PO Box 909
Cardiff CF1 3XU

Dr M Ryder
4,Osprey Close
Southampton
SO1 8EX

Ms V Straker
Dept of Geography
University Road
Bristol
BS8 ISS

Mrs G Swanton (Committee Secretary)
North Farm
West Overton
Marlborough
Wiltshire
SN8 1QE

Dr B C Sykes
Research Lab. for Archaeology and the History of Art
6, Keble Road
Oxford
OX1 3QJ

Dr K Thompson
Unit of Comparative Plant Ecology
Dept of Animal and Plant Sciences
University of Sheffield
Sheffield
SIO 2TN

Dr P Wiltshire
Institute of Archaeology
University College, London
31–4 Gordon Square
London
WC1H OPY

Summary

This monograph reports on, provides a synthesis of, and assesses the results from the first 32 years of the Experimental Earthworks Project. The project has its origins in the Charles Darwin centenary meeting (1958) of the British Association for the Advancement of Science which resulted in the formation of a research committee 'to investigate by experiment the denudation and burial of archaeological structures.' The experiment is designed to last for over a century. It is principally concerned with two earthworks, one on Overton Down, Wiltshire, the other on Morden Bog, near Wareham, Dorset, England. Reference is also made to other earthwork experiments. The Committee has from the start drawn on two major strengths. It has always believed in the virtues of thinking long-term; and it has always thought in interdisciplinary terms. This report not unnaturally, therefore, focuses on the nature of the data from field experiment over decades and on the ambitious research programme centred around the thirty-second year excavation of the Overton Earthwork in 1992.

The Overton Earthwork was built in 1960; that on Morden Bog in 1963. Both have been monitored throughout their lives and excavated in sections cut through them at intervals on a progressive scale of years. Thus the Overton Earthwork was sectioned in 1962, 1964, 1968, 1976 and 1992, that on Morden Bog in 1965, 1967, 1972 and 1980. A basic manual described the project, its design and expectation (Jewell 1963). The early work on the Overton Earthwork was published by Jewell and Dimbleby (1966).

This new monograph reviews the project's history over its first 32 years in the particular context of excavations at Overton in 1968, 1976 and 1992 and at Wareham in 1980. Results from the latter are reported and related to the earlier history of that earthwork. For Overton, this report draws on, in part summarizes, and constantly refers to the basic manual and the first report (Jewell 1963, Jewell and Dimbleby 1966). It reports from the excavations at the eight and sixteen-year intervals and takes an overview of the first 32 years in this earthwork's life.

In particular, it records the more detailed programme of analytical work which it was possible to implement at Overton in 1992. This concentrated on the preservation of biological and environmental evidence in the 32 year old buried soil as analogues for archaeological buried soils, and on the analysis of a range of organic and inorganic materials which had been buried in 1960. Included here is work on vegetation history, a linked study of soil micromorphology and chemistry, seeds and pollen, Scanning Electron Microscope studies of bone, wood and textiles, and a microbiological study.

The history of the project reflects in some ways several currents in contemporary archaeology with considerable accuracy, for example in theory and method, in organization and personnel, and in changes externally in the climate of research and internally in the growth of professionalism. The development of science-based archaeology in particular has coincided with the early decades of the experiment and has very strongly influenced its conduct. There may be a reciprocal effect. Results from the first 32 years provide the opportunity to consider the strengths and weakness of experimental methodology in archaeology, especially with reference to issues of timescale, pattern and chance.

Sommaire

La présente monographie présente un compte-rendu des résultats des 32 premières années du Projet des Terrassements Expérimentaux, en fournit une synthèse et les évalue. Ce projet démarra durant la réunion du centenaire de Charles Darwin (1958) de l'Association britannique pour le Progrès de la Science, dont le résultat fut la formation d'un comité de recherches 'pour effectuer une enquête expérimentale sur la dénudation et l'ensevelissement des structures archéologiques'. En principe, l'expérience doit durer plus d'un siècle. Elle se rapporte principalement à deux terrassements, dont l'un se trouve à Overton Down, Wiltshire, et l'autre à Morden Bog, près de Wareham, Dorset, en Angleterre. On mentionne également d'autres expériences sur les terrassements. Dès le début, le comité a bénéficié de deux grands atouts: il a toujours cru à la valeur des objectifs à long terme et il a toujours pensé en termes interdisciplinairs. Il est donc naturel que ce rapport se concentre donc sur la nature des données tirées de décennies d'expériences pratiques sur le terrain et sur l'ambitieux project de recherche qui tourne autour de la trente-deuxième année de fouilles du terrassement d'Overton en 1992.

Le terrassement d'Overton fut édifié en 1960, celui de Morden Bog en 1963. Tous deux ont fait l'object d'une surveillance suivie pendant toute leur vie et des fouilles ont été effectuées par intervalles dans des sections coupées au travers des terrassements sur une échelle d'années progressive. C'est ainsi que le terrassement d'Overton a été sectionné en 1962, 1964, 1968, 1976 et 1992 et celui de Morden Bog en 1965, 1967, 1972 et 1980. Un manuel de base décrivit le projet, sa conception et ce qu'on en attend (Jewell 1963). Les premiers résultats concernant le terrassement d'Overton ont été publiés par Jewell et Dimbleby (1966).

Cette nouvelle monographie passe en revue l'histoire du projet durant ses 32 premières années dans le contexte spécifique des fouilles effectuées à Overton en 1968, 1976 et 1992 et à Wareham en 1980. On trouvera un compte-rendu sur les résultats de ces dernières ainsi que leurs liens avec les débuts de ce terrassement. En ce qui concerne Overton, ce rapport fait appel au manual de base et au premier rapport (Jewell 1982, Jewell et Dimbleby 1966), les résume en partie et y fait constamment référence. Il fournit un compte-rendu des fouilles aux intervalles de huit et de seize ans ainsi qu'un panorama des 32 premières années de la vie de ce terrassement.

En particulier, il décrit le programme plus détaillé de travail analytique qu'il fut possible de mettre en oeuvre à Overton en 1992. Ceci se concentrait sur la conservation de documents biologiques et de documents concernant l'environnement dans les sols ensevelis depuis 32 années en tant qu'analogues pour les sols archéologiques ensevelis et sur l'analyse d'un éventail de matériaux organiques et inorganiques qui avaient été ensevelis en 1960. Il inclut également des travaux sur l'histoire de la végétation, une étude qui s'y relie sur la micromorphologie et la chimie du sol, les graines et le pollen, des études d'os, de bois et de textiles par microscope électronique à balayage, et une étude microbiologique.

A certains points de vue, l'histoire du projet reflète avec une grande précision plusieurs tendances de l'archéologie contemporaine, par exemple en ce qui concerne le théorie et le méthode, l'organisation et le personnel et les changements externes des courants de la recherche, et les changements internes liés à la croissance du professionnalisme. En particulier, le développement de l'archéologie basée sur la science a coïncidé avec les premières décennies de l'expérience et a beaucoup influencé la manière dont elle a été menée. Il pourrait y avoir en effet réciproque. Les résultats des 32 premières années donnent l'occasion de considérer la force et les points faibles de la méthodologie expérimentale en archéologie, particulièrement en ce qui concerne les quesions d'échelle de temps, de modèle et de hasard.

Übersicht

Diese Monographie liefert eine Synthese, beurteilt die Ergebnisse und berichtet über die ersten 32 Jahre des Experimentalprojektes der Erdhügel. Diese Projekt entstand 1958 anläßlich de Charles Darwin Hundertjahreskonferenz des Britischen Vereines für die Förderung der Wissenschaft (British Association for the Advancement of Science) aus dem sich ein Forschungskommite bildete 'um versuchsweise das Maß der Abnützung vergrabener archäologischer Strukturen zu erkunden'. Die Dauer des Experimentes soll sich über ein Jahrhundert hinausstrecken. Es beschäftigt sich hauptsächlich mit zwei Erdhügeln, der eine befindet sich in den Overton Down (eine Hügellandschaft) in Wiltshire, der andere in Morden Bog, in der Nähe von Wareham, Dorset, England. Andere Erkhügel – Experimente werden auch erwähnt. Van Anfang an hat sich das Kommittee auf zwei bedeutende Stärken bezogen: auf den Vorzug langfristig vorauszuplanen und auf interdisziplinäre Zeitspannan. Deshalb überrascht es nicht, daß such dieser Bericht auf die Beschaffendeit der Daten van Fachexperimenten, die Jahrzehnte lang notiert wurden, konzentriert. Im gleichen Maß konzentriert er sich auf das ehrgeizige. Forschungsprogramm, das sich mit dem zweiunddreißigsten Jahr der Ausgrabumg des Overton Erdhügel befaßt.

Der Overton Erdhügel wurde 1960 gebaut, der in Morden Bog in 1963. Beide wurden seit ihrum Bestehen überwacht und in Streckenabschnitten in immer zunehmenden Jahresabständen ausgegraben. In deiser Weise wurder der Overton Erdhügel 1962, 1964, 1968, 1976 und 1992 und der Erdhügel in Morton Bog 1965, 1967, 1972 und 1980 ausgegraben. Ein Handbuch beschreibt das Projekt, seine Absicht und seine Ziele. (Jewell 1963). Die ersten

Studien über den Overton – Erdhügel wurden 1966 von Jewell und Dimbleby veröffentlicht.

Diese neue Monographie gibt eine Überblick über das Projekt in den ersten 32 Jahren seines Bestehens, insbesondere im Kontext der Overton – Erdhügel in 1968, 1975 und 1992 und den Wareham – Erdhügeln in 1980. Die Ergebnisse der letzteren wurden niedergeschrieben und mit dem früheren Bestehen dieser Erdhügel verglichen. Hinsichtich der Overton – Erdhügel stützt sich dieser Bericht auf das Handbuch und den ersten Bericht. Er faßt ihn auch teilweise zusammen und bezieht sich fortwährend auf ihn und den ersten Bericht. (Jewell 1963, Jewell und Dimbleby 1966). Dieser Bericht befaßt sich mit den Ausgrahungen, die in einem achtjährigen und sechzehnjährigen Abstand durchgeführt wurden und gibt einen Überblick über das Bestehen der ersten 32 Jarhe dieses Erdhügels.

Im besonderem verzeichnet diese Monographie ein gründlichere Durchführungsprogramm der analytischen Arbeitsvorgänge, die man 1992 in Overton durchführen konnte. Diese Monographie konzentriert sich auf das Erhaltungprogramm der biologischen und auf in der Umwelt gefundene Beweise der 32 jährigen vergrabenen Erde, die der vergrabenen archäologischen Erde gegenüber-gestellt wird. Weiterhin konzentriert sich dieser Bericht auf die Analyse einer Reihe von organischen und unorganischen in 1960 vergrabenen Materialien, Dazu gehört ein Werke über Pflanzengeschichte, eine verwandte Studie der Erdmikromorphologie und Chemie, Samen und Pollen, Scanning – elektronische – Mikroskope – Studien der Gebeine, Holz und Textilien und einer mokrobiologischen Studie.

Die Geschichte dieses Projekts refektiert einigermaßen mit beachtenswerter Genauighkeit eine Anzahl von Trends in der gegenwärtigen Archäologie. Beispiele dafür sind Theorie und Methode, Organization und Personell, äußerlich, die Atmosphäre der Forschung und innerlich, die Zunahme an Perfektion. Die Entwicklung der auf Wissenschaft basierte Archäologie im besonderem findet zur gleichen Zeit wie die ersten Jahrzehnte des Experimentes statt und übte einen sehr starken Einfluß auf dessen Fortführung aus. Vielleicht gab es eine gegenseitige Wirkung. Mit den Resultaten der ersten 32 Jahre wird die Möglichkeit geboten, die Stärken und die Schwächen dieser Experimentalmethodik in der Archäologie, im besonderem im Bezug auf Zeitmaßstab – Vorlagen und Zufallprobleme – zu überlegen.

Acknowledgements

1960 – c 1990

The excavations of 1968 and 1976 were only possible with the help of several organizations and many people. We were extremely indebted to the then Ministry of Public Buildings and Works, which, from its Avebury depot, lent us tools and equipment through the good offices of first Leo Biek and then John Musty, both of the Ancient Monuments Laboratory of the Inspectorate of Ancient Monuments. Members of the same laboratory and Inspectorate have always shown an interest in the project and, perhaps unofficially, have helped considerably. We have also benefitted in a similar institutional and personal way from what was when we began the Nature Conservancy and its officers. Our debts are legion to Jim Hemsley, who was initially responsible in the 1950s for work in designating the National Nature Reserve, and to the two early wardens of Fyfield Down NNR, Inigo Jones (in the 1960s, not the 1660s) and Noel King.

Both excavations were organized from the Department of Extra-Mural Studies, Bristol University; neither would have been possible without the logistical and modest but crucial financial support provided by them. The Wiltshire Archaeological and Natural History Society also helped, with equipment and the interest and help of its staff and members. We could not have operated without the consent of the various landowners, initially George Todd followed by John Bloomfield and Robert Sangster, but of course the key practical help throughout has been from the tenant farmers, and amazingly friends still, the Swantons. At first it was the late Frank Swanton and his wife, then son Robin and wife Gillian, and now their children, especially PJF's godson James, who, too young to be of much assistance in 1976, put in sterling work in 1992. PJF's own family grew up on and between the '68 and '76 earthwork excavations and he would thank them for their assistance and Elizabeth Fowler for her hard work on the recording front. Figs 4.4 and 5.3 are by S. Hooper.

Many of those who helped on site are mentioned in the text, with gratitude. PJF's particular debt is to Richard Atkinson and Geoffrey Dimbleby, and then Susan Limbrey and John Evans, who not only did such a splendid job for the Committee but taught him so much about what he did not know. He is also extremely indebted, both as Chairman of the Committee and personally, to Gillian Swanton, who has kept the show on the road. It has been a privilege personally to benefit both from the wisdom of my elders in the 1960s and the energies and widening perspectives of my younger colleagues in the 1980s and '90s. I am grateful for the experience, and the friendship.

Peter Fowler

1980 Wareham Report

The 1980 Wareham excavation was directed by Peter Fowler, and carried out over one very full week almost entirely by him, Gillian Swanton and Carole Keepax. The Committee owes them a real debt of gratitude for stepping in at short notice. Collection of buried materials and dispersal of samples to specialists was also carried out by Carole Keepax. After some years, I was asked to assemble the results and write them up into the report which is published here. I am very grateful for the contributions and advice of Jim Hemsley, Keith Crabtree, Richard Macphail, H M Appleyard, Jon Hather, Roy Newton, Christopher Calnan, Carole Keepax, Gillian Swanton and Susan Limbrey

Simon Hillson

1992 Overton Excavation

Funding for the 1992 stage of the project was provided by the Science Based Archaeology Committee of the Science and Engineering Research Council (from 1.4.94 part of Natural Environment Research Council); English Heritage, Society of Antiquaries of London and the Prehistoric Society. The last award carries the name of the late Dr Bob Smith who had a particular interest in the archaeology of the chalk and the Avebury area (Smith 1984). Dr Smith died young when he still had so much to offer to archaeology and we are grateful for his friendship and memory. Support at a crucial stage by Dr G J Wainwright, Chief Archaeologist of English Heritage, is particularly acknowledged.

That the project went so smoothly and was so enjoyable is particularly due to the kindness of Robin and Gillian Swanton who provided accommodation and hospitality for the whole team. In addition Gillian made many of the administrative arrangements for the excavation. It is good to record that two of the project's founders joined us for the fieldwork: Professor Bruce Proudfoot for the whole time and Professor Peter Jewell for a day (frontispiece). Professor Peter Fowler, who has chaired the project for the greater part of its life, was also with us for the whole time and his experience, advice and support was very much appreciated. Equipment was kindly loaned by Robin Swanton; Devizes Museum; the School of Archaeological Sciences, Bradford; the University of Wales: Lampeter; and Wessex Archaeology, who through the good offices of Andrew Lawson, both loaned equipment and Liz James to draw the section. Other key members of the field team were Dr Simon Hillson (bones) and Rob Janaway (excavation and stabilization of the buried materials). The excavation staff were Nicky Evans (excavation and documentation); Kath Dowse (sieving); Chantelle Hoppe (excavation); Dave Lucy (conservation); Jenny Moore (excavation); Dr Becky Roseff (excavation); Amanda Rouse (sampling); Bill Timmins (excavation); Ed Yorath (photography). Ed's contribution in taking many of the 1992 field photographs is acknowledged. We are grateful to the following specialists who found time to visit the excavation and discuss with us their sampling requirements and the project as a whole: Dr Miranda Armour-Chelu, Dr Dennis Allsopp (IMI), Dr K Brown, Dr T Brown, Ms W Carruthers, Dr A J Clark, Dr K Crabtree, Dr J Crowther, Ms G Edwards, Dr R Hedges, G Macleod, Dr R Macphail, Dr M Ryder, Ms V Straker, and Dr P Wiltshire.

With regard to post excavation aspects I am especially grateful to Ms N Evans who has made a major contribution to the smooth running of the programme as part-time post excavation assistant. Gillian Swanton has also provided a great deal of help at the post excavation stage. Mrs Barbara Garfi has done most of the drawings for Chapter 7 and several drawings for other chapters. Mrs Maureen Hunwicks has helped with word processing. Dr Jennifer Foster has provided great help and support during the editorial stages. The final thanks must go to all the 1992 specialists whose hard work and dedication have made possible the prompt publication of the results

Martin Bell

Preface

It is still a little too soon to judge whether the Experimental Earthworks Project is worthwhile. It has been running since 1960, but that is only 25% of its intended life. Some early results, however, look promising.

The idea of field experiment was not entirely new in the archaeology of Britain in the late 1950s, but it was innovative to undertake such a long-term experiment on interdisciplinary lines. The founders of this experiment nevertheless knew what they were about. They themselves wrote: 'The building of this [Overton Down] experimental earthwork is an innovation that stems from a synthesis of ideas out of both archaeology and the natural sciences' (Jewell 1963, 1). It was also interesting that they proposed to implement their innovation through a committee.

In three senses, then, the proposers in 1959 of the Committee 'to investigate by experiment the denudation and burial of archaeological structures' were pioneers and we are happy to acknowledge the 'blue skies research' ideal of Richard Atkinson, Ian Cornwall, Geoffrey Dimbleby, Peter Jewell, Bruce Proudfoot and Paul Ashbee (Frontispiece). As we have often had cause to remark in the three decades and more since their innovation, they, and what they were trying to do was, both in its thinking and in its interdisciplinarity, at least half a generation, perhaps even a full one, ahead of its time. Yet, in another sense, experiment in the field already had a long and respectable history in archaeological affairs, and the idea of doing things by committee was very much in vogue in a positively socialist intellectual climate of a post-War society still innocently believing that 'things' could be improved, including society itself.

Sadly as this report was in its final editorial stages we learnt of the death of two of the experiment's founders. Professor Richard Atkinson died on 10.10.94 and an obituary appeared in *The Independent* (Aldhouse-Green 1994). Dr Ian Cornwall also died during 1994.

The development of an experimental strain in archaeology's historical background was outlined in chapter 1 in the Committee's first major publication (Jewell 1963, 1-17). The chapter was called 'Nature, Science and Experiment in Field Archaeology.' This was not altogether too distant from *Archaeology, History and Science,* the title of the inaugural professorial lecture by one of the Committee's founders, Richard Atkinson (1960). We see here a reaching out into multi-disciplinarity, not just a recognition that Atkinson's archaeological approach, Cornwall's (1956, 1958) burgeoning knowledge of bones and soils, Dimbleby's journey from forestry to environmental science (1965) and Jewell's (1958) ecological sense could be applied together to History

and Science; but also that the results of such research would be better History and Science. Indeed, surely here are seeds of something to be called interdisciplinary knowledge.

Yet in the implicit rejection of C P Snow's contemporary (1959) categorization of the 'two cultures' of Arts and Science, we can detect simultaneously almost a reaching back to times when knowledge was, as we would now say, holistic. There is in fact an ambivalence here. On the one hand the Committee was innovating in consciously seeking not just to link different specialisms in an harmonious project but to bridge the gap between them with a new sort of archaeologically-led, science-based interdisciplinarity. On the other hand, however, the very specialisms, particularly within the Natural Sciences, which it sought to exploit and blend precisely reflected that compartmentalization of knowledge in the second half of the 19th century which, half-way through the next, this project sought to circumvent.

Though advanced and prescient in many ways, that chapter 1 nevertheless could not of course escape from its own time and it very much reflected the contemporary academic and scientific world as seen through the eyes of the project's founders. Another major influence here, combining pragmatism with a strong sense of archaeology's own history, was an early member of the Committee, Paul Ashbee, at the time a prolific excavator of barrows, mainly on chalk, in Wessex (and now, to his credit, the author of many reports publishing those excavations). Experimental archaeology has subsequently twice been surveyed by Coles in book form (1973 and 1979) and, it would be nice to say, has subsequently come of age; but of course, that is the point, for it has not done so. In pondering why this should be so we cannot help wondering whether the experimental earthworks have had something to do with the persistence of an unexpected immaturity in this field. Nevertheless, as a result of these publications we need not repeat most of the background to the Committee's origins (which in any case is discussed in Fowler 1988 and Jewell 1993), though it seems to us worthwhile just to pause briefly at what is still, in 1994, relevant to our endeavours.

Three major factors immediately stand out. One is the personal and humane, the historical and individual. That chapter 1 is full of great names in the development not just of experimental field archaeology, not just of a discipline, but of Western society's increasingly successful attempts to grapple with the concept of 'antiquity'. John Aubrey and William Stukeley on page 1, Gilbert White, Dr Plott and Sir Richard Colt Hoare on page 2 (together with, in a prescient example of the Committee's own philosophy 140 years later, 'two of the most able chymists of the day, Mr Hatchettt, and Dr Gibbes'), and, on p 3, William Cunnington, Archbishop Ussher and our true intellectual progenitor, Charles Darwin: these are humbling names that a project is privileged to have in its intellectual genealogy. Furthermore, it is somewhat awesome to think that the Committee's own small endeavours are directly within both a mainstream scientific tradition and European culture's rationalization of two concepts, the passage of time and change through time. We can remark unselfconsciously that a sense of Darwinian presence, of big people wrestling with big issues, has been with us, as inspiration and provider of a sense of perspective, as background to the Committee's endeavours since the start. Nor has such influence only been remote. While that 'Darwinian presence', for example, was certainly a motor in the conceptualization of the project's purpose and the formation of the Committee, so was it also in mind every time we saw a worm in the Overton Earthwork (none inhabit that at Morden Bog). It is not everywhere appreciated that, in addition to his achievements in evolutionary theory arising from his travels and studies overseas, Darwin studied by experiment in England the humble earthworm throughout his life. As early as 1837, he published a paper on worms and their part in the formation of humus. His (other) great work with the unforgettable title, *The formation of vegetable mould through the action of worms with observations on their habits,* was published 44 years later (1881). He wrote from direct observation of *The degradation of ancient encampments and tumuli, of the preservation of ancient remains, of worms' abilities to bury small objects, and the part which worms have played in the burial of ancient buildings* (Jewell 1963, p 4). In appreciating the project's origins, we can now appreciate more than its originators how central Darwin's concerns are to understanding much of what has happened in the Overton Earthwork over 32 years

The basic manual (p 4) noted with admiration also that 'Darwin inititated experiments to measure precisely the rates at which large stones are buried by worms.' Measurement, in other words, is the method, and control is the unspoken principle. It may seem a commonplace now but it was at the very least unusual in the 1950s to set up a field experiment in archaeology in which it is stated that (p 1) 'controlled conditions had been created whereby the process of weathering could be precisely observed and quantitatively assessed'. Our originators were quite clear about the need for control and precision, not least because they were both encouraged by and well aware of contemporary developments in embryonic experimental archaeology in Denmark (Jewell 1963, 12–13, quoting Klindt-Jensen 1957 but also at the time seriously reviewed and academically available in English in Steensberg 1957). Simultaneously, again strongly influenced by Danish example, attempts at experimentation in prehistoric agriculture were also starting in England (Jewell 1963, 12, quoting Aberg and Bowen 1960; see also Bowen

1961). Hardly surprisingly, there was an overlap of personnel and interests between the two committees respectively and simultaneously promoting experimental earthworks and experiment in ancient agriculture (which still continues, see Reynolds below p. 225).

In 1959–60, nevertheless, the Earthworks Committee very consciously attempted something new. It deliberately tried to set up a controlled archaeological experiment in the field, of course to study the unknown but one in which a set of parameters was clearly defined by the project's own agenda. It seems not unreasonable now for it to have claimed that 'With the building of the experimental earthwork ... a new phase of archaeological fieldwork began.' It was the concept of control, allied to the concept of long-term research (far exceeding the life-expectation of any of the originators), which needs to be acknowledged now as of great significance in experimental field archaeology. As Jewell remarked (1963, 17), 'The co-operation of field archaeologists with natural scientists ... where it has occurred ... is nearly always temporary, that is for the duration of a single operation.'

It may well be that (to pick up a point above), by setting such standards of control, co-operation and longevity under the auspices of an originally 'big-name committee', the Committee itself inadvertently deterred others from serious experimentation. Certainly much of that which was subsequently claimed to be experimental field archaeology was qualitatively reduced to being what it actually so often was: weekend fun, uncontrolled, unrepeatable, short-term and scientifically nugatory.

The originals took their self-imposed task very seriously but they were not obliged to set up a committee to pursue it. Early experimenters, notably Darwin (1881), Pitt Rivers (1898) and the Curwens (eg 1930) (Jewell 1963, pp 8–10), were indeed often individualists. Committees nevertheless had already provided a model of how to get things done archaeologically in some circumstances. Relevant examples included the Society of Antiquaries' Earthworks Committee early in the 20th century, discussed in his history of field archaeology in England by Ashbee (1972). Paradoxically, in a way, that Committee's main successes in terms of publication were by three highly individual persons, Hadrian Allcroft (1908), Williams-Freeman (1915), and Heywood Sumner (1913, 1917). The last-named's two geologies in those books, incidentally, exactly anticipated the Committee's interests in chalk and Tertiary deposits. Nearer in time and spirit to the Experimental Earthwork Project's thinking, the Fenland Research Committee had from the 1930s effectively pursued a long-term, multi-disciplinary research project, reflected generally in publications by Professors Graham Clark (eg Clark *et al* 1935) and Harry Godwin (1978) and specifically in Phillips (1970).

Strange though it may read to competitors in the academic rat races of the 1990s, the later '50s and 1960s were a time of corporate endeavour in which it was normal, and seemed natural, to combine to try to achieve a common, agreed objective. The Council for British Archaeology in particular, itself based on the democratic exercise of such a principle, was spawning committees, not just centrally to look after various time-periods nationally but also locally for specific purposes. Rescue work in the Nene and Welland Valleys was a case in point (Thomas 1966). Here, as in the Fens and elsewhere, the environmental dimension of investigation into the past was becoming increasingly important. Indeed, precisely that message was being promoted in their teaching and writings by the Committee's own founder-members and their associates eg Ashbee 1960, Atkinson 1956 and 1957, Biek 1963, Cornwall 1956 and 1958, Dimbleby 1962, Jewell 1958 and, from the Committee's Honorary Treasurer, Pyddoke 1961. In a sense, therefore, the Experimental Earthwork Committee, in both its format and its self-given remit of interrelationships between time, people and environment, was a child of its time. It was pioneering but can also be seen as taking the next logical step in a conceptual progression.

By building the environmental dimension into its thinking from the start, the Committee was aware that it was keying into an aspect of palaeo-study which was likely to become more important. What it cannot have been aware of, however, was another facet of the environmental interest which gives the whole project an entirely serendipitous significance on a time-scale even grander than that originally envisaged. It must be stressed that the earthworks were always intended to be monitored in order to observe and measure change, but no-one could possibly have known in the early sixties that two very big environmental changes were about to happen – perhaps were about to be perceived would be more accurate. The earthworks happened to have been built at the start of both a growth in environmental concern and, as we can now see from the vantage point of 1994, a period of environmental change most noticeably expressed by rapid climatic variation.

At the global level, that concern was articulated by Rachel Carson in her *Silent Spring* (1965); and it was there locally too, finding expression even in Wiltshire (for example in Fowler 1968). Since the earthworks were built, they have enjoyed remarkable weather fluctuations and seasonal extremes which may or may not be part of a trend or trends; but whether 'global warming' is occurring or not, the fact that such suspicions exist gives a quite unexpected relevance of the experimental earthworks project to late 20th century environmental concerns. There, after all, the earthworks stand, conceived and constructed *c* 1960 to monitor change over a century and more; and the century in question just happens to be the one in which humanity may well simply have to come to terms not just with its environment but with itself. No project could ask for a role, however minor, in a drama more basic than that.

1 Introduction *by Peter Fowler and Gillian Swanton*

1.1 The nature of the experiment

The experimental earthwork on Overton Down, between Marlborough and Avebury, Wiltshire, England, was built in 1960 (Jewell 1963). A similar earthwork was built on Morden Bog near Wareham, in Dorset, in 1963 (Evans and Limbrey 1974). Both form the core of a long-term field experiment devised in 1958–60 by a group of archaeologists and scientists under the auspices of the British Association for the Advancement of Science.

The overall objective of the project is to study short and medium-term changes in order to help bridge the gap between contemporary observations of environmental processes and the much longer timescales with which archaeologists are concerned. In this way, it was originally envisaged that new understanding could be brought to the way in which the archaeologi-

cal record is formed, preserved and recovered. Such is proving to be the case.

Essentially, each part of the experiment consists of building an earthwork and monitoring it through time, in particular by cutting sections through it at intervals on a progressive scale of 1, 2, 4, 8, 16, 32, 64 and 128 years. Each bank and ditch (Figs 1.1 and 1.3) included structural details commonly found in archaeological monuments, such as a turf core in the centre of the bank, though neither set out to replicate any one particular type of ancient structure. The two sets of bank and ditch were built to precise specifications so that changes in their size and shape could be monitored over the years. Various markers were also placed in known positions so that, through their individual movements, the results of erosion and compaction could be measured. Over the years and through the excavated sections in particular, meticu-

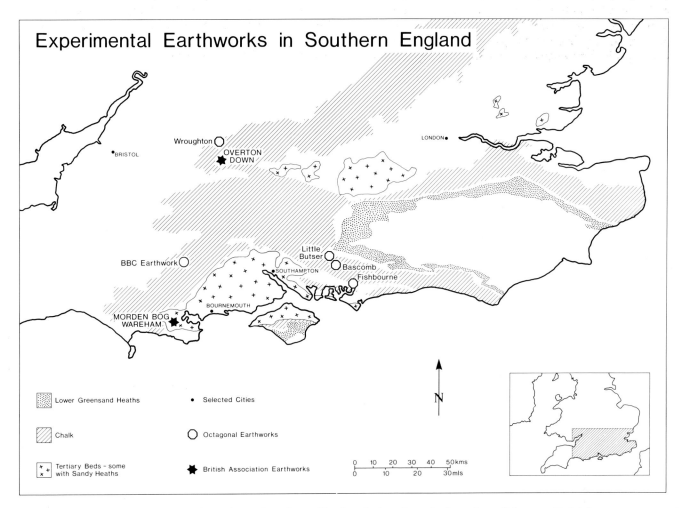

Figure 1.1 Experimental earthworks in Southern England showing the location of the two British Association earthworks with which this monograph is largely concerned; the octagonal earthworks discussed in Chapter 13 and the earthwork made for a BBC television programme 'Living in the Past' (Percival 1980)

2

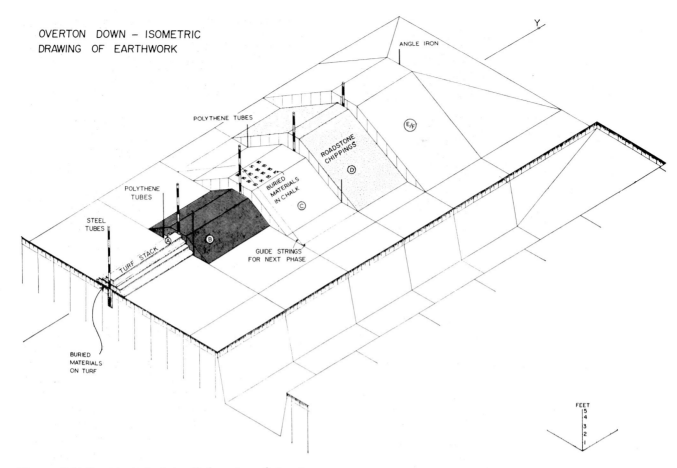

OVERTON DOWN – ISOMETRIC
DRAWING OF EARTHWORK

Figure 1.2   Isometric (original) drawing of structure

Figure 1.3   The Overton Down Earthwork under construction, 1960

Figure 1.4 Material before burial under the turf core, Overton Down 1960

Figure 1.5 Material before burial in the chalk mound, Overton Down 1960

lous recording of structural changes in the earthwork is assembling, as intended, a unique morphological record.

The experiment is also studying another aspect of change through time. Inside and beneath each bank, carefully placed in two different contrasting environments (Figs 1.4 and 1.5), a range of materials was buried at positions where the future excavations would occur. Materials included charred and uncharred oak and hazel, human and animal bone, leathers, textiles, flints and pottery. At Wareham metals and glass were additionally included. Recovering this material, if it still exists, is the second main purpose of the excavations.

The 32nd year excavation at Overton Down was undertaken in 1992 in the equivalent week to that in which construction took place in July, 1960. Another 32 years stretch ahead before another excavation will

occur there, in July 2024, sixty-four years after construction. The final excavation is planned for July 2088, a further sixty-four years later when the earthwork is 128 years old. The Wareham Earthwork follows an identical pattern, three years in arrears throughout and thus seeing its last planned excavation in 2091. The present Committee will attend to its 32nd year excavation in 1996 but will expect another generation to see to matters thereafter. Reflecting that the director of the 64 year excavations may well be starting school somewhere about now, original and current members of the team do not expect to write even that half-time, never mind the final, report. Table 1.1 summarizes the programme of earthwork excavations, including those excavations which have taken place, where they are published and the dates of planned future excavations.

Table 1.1 The timescale and progress of the experimental earthworks project to date

Timescale	Overton	Publication	Wareham	Publication
Constructed	July 1960	Jewell 1963	7–29 July 1963	Evans & Limbrey 1974
7½ months	March 1961	Jewell & Dimbleby 1966	–	–
13½ months	–	–	11–15 Sept 1964	Evans & Limbrey 1974
2 years	Sept 1962	Jewell & Dimbleby 1966	Sept 1965	Evans & Limbrey 1974
4 years	July 1964	Jewell & Dimbleby 1966	–	–
5 years	–	–	20–22 Sept 1968*	Evans & Limbrey 1974
8 years	1968	This volume, Chap 4	–	–
9 years	–	–	14–18 Sept 1972*	Evans & Limbrey 1974
16 years	1976	This volume, Chap 5	–	–
17 years	–	–	10–13 Sept 1980*	This volume, Chap 12
32 years	1992	This volume, Chap 7–11	Proposed 1996*	Proposal *Journal Arch Sci*
64 years	Proposed 2024	–	Proposed 2027	–
128 years+	Proposed 2088	–	Proposed 2091	–

*From 1968 onwards unforeseen circumstances have meant that the Wareham excavations have been done a year late.
+ The decision has been made to cut the final sections after 128 years not 100 years as noted in Jewell (1963).

1.2 Nature of this report

The Committee's early work was published principally in Jewell (1963), Jewell and Dimbleby (1966) and Evans and Limbrey (1974). Other publications are listed in the Bibliography. A considerable amount of data has accumulated over the last 25 years or so, however, and the 32 year excavation at the Overton Down Earthwork in 1992, with its own need for rapid publication, provided a suitable opportunity to pull together the whole Project over it first 32 years. During that time, Jewell (1963) has been the textual bedrock of the Experimental Earthwork Project. This report attempts to be the equivalent for the next 32 years.

The basic manual, as Jewell 1963 came to be called, has long been out of print. The chances of acquiring one are slight for any in the new audience for experimental archaeology which has emerged over the last generation since the experiment was conceptualized. We therefore repeat a small part of the fundamental data here. We also summarize early results so that, to an extent, this volume is free-standing, able to hold the line for the next 32 years in the way that the basic manual has since 1963. We would emphasize that, to that end, this monograph is supported now, in a way never enjoyed by Jewell 1963 (despite the statement in it, p iv), by a reasonably organized and accessible archive of data, graphics and materials (p 7).

This report's main thrust is, nevertheless, to present in some detail data acquired from the two earthworks: at Overton Down in the 8, 16 and 32 year sections in 1968, 1976 and 1992, and at Morden Bog at the sixteen year section which should have been executed in 1979 but was actually executed in 1980. Drawing in no small measure on the Project's archive which has been built up since the late 1950s, over and above the excavation records, we also look at some aspects of the three decades as a whole. These include matters as diverse as the specifics of on-site vegetational change, changing archaeological methodology and theory, the development of archaeological science which is at the core of differing approaches to the experiment as a scientific resource, and the relevance of the experiment to the late-twentieth century conservation concerns.

The Committee hopes that this monograph will lay the foundations for a new generation of research. It is already immensely encouraged that its lead has inspired other earthworks, notably those built under the aegis of the Butser Ancient Farm Project in the 1980s (p 225). Others will have to judge whether, in the light of the work presented here, further earthworks are worth constructing. We would merely observe that once the 32 year excavation is completed at the Morden Earthwork in 1995, another twenty-nine years will pass before the next, 64 year section at Overton in 2024. So there is plenty of time for more earthworks to be built. Meanwhile this Report is a 'one off', by definition unrepeatable and with the sequel unavailable until the second quarter of the 21st century.

Editorial notes

a. On the composition and authorship of this report

Clearly, the creation of this report has been a complex task involving many people in planning, research and writing. Many of them have drawn on yet other expertises and resources. Nevertheless, the three named authors have basically put the report together, writing much of it themselves and also acting editorially both as individuals and collectively. In large part the prefatory material and Chapters 1–2 and 4–6, mostly Overton Down up to and including 1976, were written by Fowler; Chapter 7, Overton Down in 1992, by Bell, who likewise edited chapters 8 to 11. Hillson wrote Chapter 12 on Wareham.

All three parts include, however, substantial passages by others where authorship is gladly acknowledged and where the role of the three overall authors has been mainly editorial. The survey of the vegetation over the decades by Hemsley is sufficiently large and substantial to command a Chapter, 3, of its own, and other weighty contributions occur within chapters; Crabtree and Limbrey, for example, in Chapters 5 and 6, and several major contributions by specialists on the 1992 evidence in later Chapters. Chapter 14 was written by Bell but it, like all parts of the report whoever initiated them, has been read and modified by all three principal authors and by other collaborators too.

The result overall may well appear like a hotpotch report written by a committee or as a reasonably integrated work of interdisciplinary collaboration. The authors suspect it contains elements of both. Any worth in it owes a great deal to Gillian Swanton, the Committee honorary secretary for nearly twenty years who, while contributing here as author in her own right, has been of the greatest editorial support to the principal authors, especially 1992–4. All of us would emphasize that, whoever initially drafted whichever part, the whole has been created only by the expertises and co-operative endeavours of a generation of interdisciplinarians.

b. Mensuration

During the generation marked by the experimental earthworks project so far, Britain, and particularly British archaeology, changed from the imperial to the metric system of measurement. Both the Overton Down and the Morden Bog Earthworks were conceived, laid out and excavated during their first 16 years in imperial. Nevertheless, by 1992 the reality of metrication had to be faced and the Overton Down work of that year was carried out in metric. This report is also primarily metric. Figure keys relating to the earthworks (but not to the microscopic examination of buried materials) use both scales and so too does the text, with the imperial equivalent in brackets following a metric measurement. It must be stressed, however, that before 1992 all measure-

Table 1.2 Committee membership 1959–1994

Name	59	60	61	62	63	64	65	66	67	68	69	70	71	72	73	74	75	76	77	78	79	80	81	82	83	84	85	86	87	88	89	90	91	92	93	94
ARMITAGE P																				■	■	■	■	■	■	■	■	■								
ASHBEE P		■	■	■	■	■	■	■	■	■	■	■	■	■	■	■	■	■	■	■	■	■	■	■	■	■	■	■	■	■	■	■	■	■	■	■
ATKINSON RJC	■	■	■	■	■	■	■	■	■	■	■	■	■	■	■	■	■	■	■	■	■	■	■	■	■	■	■	■	■							
BELL M																														■	■	■	■	■	■	■
CHADBURN A																																		■	■	■
CLEERE H														■	■	■	■	■	■	■	■	■	■	■	■	■	■	■	■	■	■	■	■	■	■	■
CORNWALL IW	■	■	■	■	■	■	■	■	■	■	■	■	■	■	■																					
CRABTREE K														■	■	■	■	■	■	■	■	■	■	■	■	■	■	■	■	■	■	■	■	■	■	■
DARVILL T																																		■	■	■
DIMBLEBY GW		■	■	■	■	■	■	■	■	■	■	■	■	■	■	■	■	■	■																	
DURY G	■	■																																		
EVANS JG														■	■	■	■	■	■	■	■	■	■	■	■	■	■	■								
EVERARD CE		■	■	■	■	■	■	■	■	■	■	■	■	■	■																					
FOWLER PJ		■	■	■	■	■	■	■	■	■	■	■	■	■	■	■	■	■	■	■	■	■	■	■	■	■	■	■	■	■	■	■	■	■	■	■
HEMSLEY																						■	■	■	■	■	■	■	■	■	■	■	■	■	■	■
HILLSON SW																				■	■	■	■	■	■	■	■	■	■	■	■	■	■	■	■	■
HUBBARD R														■	■	■	■	■	■	■	■	■	■	■	■	■	■	■	■							
JANAWAY R																																	■	■	■	■
JEWELL PA	■	■	■	■	■	■	■	■	■	■	■	■	■	■	■	■	■	■	■	■	■	■	■	■	■	■	■	■	■	■	■	■	■	■	■	■
JONES M																																	■	■	■	■
KEEPAX C																						■	■	■	■	■	■	■	■	■	■	■	■	■	■	■
LAWSON AJ																						■	■	■	■	■	■	■	■	■	■	■	■	■	■	■
LIMBREY S														■	■	■	■	■	■	■	■	■	■	■	■	■	■									
MACPHAIL R																																	■	■	■	■
MALONE C																											■	■	■	■	■					
PATTERSON A																										■	■	■	■	■	■	■				
PROUDFOOT B	■	■	■	■	■	■	■	■																							■	■	■	■	■	■
PUTNAM WG																				■	■	■	■	■	■	■	■	■	■	■	■	■	■	■	■	■
PYDDOKE E			■	■	■	■	■	■	■	■	■	■	■	■	■																					
REYNOLDS PJ																						■	■	■	■	■	■	■	■	■	■	■	■	■	■	■
SWANTON GR																				■	■	■	■	■	■	■	■	■	■	■	■	■	■	■	■	■
WILSON PM		■	■	■	■	■	■	■	■	■	■	■	■	■	■																					

In addition the British Association has always been represented. Specialists and other interested parties have attended meetings by invitation.

ments were actually made in imperial so that metric measurements here from before that date are conventions. The following conversion factors were used here and can be used to compare measurements with those given in earlier publications:

$$1 \text{ inch} = 25.4 \text{ mm.}$$
$$1 \text{ metre} = 39.370113 \text{ inches} = 3.280843 \text{ feet}$$

1.3 Organization and personnel

The original organization and personnel are detailed by Jewell (1963, iii–iv, 18–21, 92–93). Some aspects of the early history of the Committee and its work are outlined by Fowler (1989) and autobiographically, by Jewell (1993). The membership of the Committee is covered in Table 1.2. Essentially, those involved on and with the Committee and its Project were kept very busy, it becoming quite clear by the mid-60s that the amount of work had been seriously underestimated.

The programme actually executed, to a relentless timetable, over the first dozen years or so appears daunting in retrospect. Certainly Committee members increasingly found it so at the time, especially as the task was undertaken entirely by people with full-time employment elsewhere. All this was in a real sense voluntary effort, professional maybe in concept and execution but nevertheless something which was fitted in between other commitments:

1958: Darwin centenary meeting: experimental project proposed, Committee formed

1959: Day-long extended Committee meeting for wide consultation under chairmanship of G W Dimbleby; additions to Committee membership including P Ashbee and V B Proudfoot; detailed planning of Overton Down Earthwork

1960: Construction of Overton Earthwork with Dr P Jewell as its secretary

1961: Section of ditch of Overton Earthwork

1962: Section of Overton Earthwork plus planning of second earthwork and preparation of basic manual (Jewell 1963)

1963: Construction of Wareham Earthwork, with Professor R J C Atkinson as its secretary; Jewell (1963) published

1964: Four-year section of Overton Earthwork; Wareham Earthwork sectioned

1965: Second year section of Wareham Earthwork

1966: In the first 'lull' in the Committee's activities, much time was spent considering a third earthwork, including site visits and wide consultation, resulting in a decision not to proceed *pro tem* in view of the workload so far, unavoidable commitments already built into the project and the lack of 'new blood' to take a further initiative

1968: 8th year section of Overton; '4th' year section of Wareham, in fact after 5 years, highlighting the problems a voluntary Committee was facing over a Project of this scale

1969–71 Exhausted and in some disarray through increased responsibilities of its senior members, the Committee almost disintegrated, a crisis signalled by the failure once again to section the Wareham Earthwork on its due date (1971)

1972: Major changes in the Committee personnel saw Professor Dimbleby succeeded as Chairman by P J Fowler, joined by a 'new generation' of Drs K Crabtree, J G Evans, R Hubbard and S Limbrey; Dr P Jewell continued as secretary for the Overton Earthwork, with Dr Evans becoming responsible for the Wareham Earthwork which was sectioned later in the year.

In 1974 it was decided that, with the kind permission of the authorities, the Committee archive should be housed at the Institute of Archaeology, London University. Dr Hubbard was appointed archivist. Planning the 1976 Overton Down section began early. Included in the arrangements was to be a longer period set aside for the work (previous sections had been completed in six days).

1975 saw the proposal that new techniques such as biochemical and microbiological investigation should form part of the analyses of the buried materials. The workforce for the 1976 section was to be drawn from University College, Cardiff students. In 1976 Mrs Gillian Swanton joined the Committee; living close to the Overton site at North Farm she was able to undertake a monthly photographic monitoring of the site following the excavation. Storage for bulky archive material would also be provided at North Farm. It was proposed that a member of the Dorset Institute of Higher Education Archaeology Department be invited to join the Committee and set up a similar monitoring project for the Wareham site. The Committee recognized the importance and urgency of attracting new young blood into its membership. Over the previous few years the Committee had been discussing with the British Association for the Advancement of Science their relationship; by the end of 1976 this had been satisfactorily resolved.

In 1977 W G Putnam of the Dorset Institute was co-opted onto the Committee, beginning a relationship which continues to this day though the Archaeology Department has metamorphosed into the Department of Conservation Science, Bournemouth University (via Bournemouth Polytechnic). During 1979 the grazing tenants of Overton Down (F Swanton and Sons) were bought out of their tenancy by the then landowner, J V Bloomfield. A licence of Access contract for the duration of the experiment was negotiated. Three new members joined the Committee, Dr P Armitage, Dr S Hillson and Dr C Keepax. The following year the monitoring of the Overton site suffered a severe setback with the theft, on two occasions, of the meteorological station which the Nature Conservancy Council was unable to replace a second time.

After many years of meeting at the Institute of Archaeology in London the Committee changed its format in 1983, meeting near one of the earthworks, incorporating site visits and inviting specialists and other interested parties to attend. This policy was adopted to try and maintain the momentum of the Committee's work, by now a major management problem as the intervals between excavations had lengthened. It was also becoming increasingly clear that those involved had many other commitments and it was even more difficult to attract specialist work on a voluntary basis. Due to these constraints, it has proved impossible to carry through some of the suggestions made at Committee meetings although this does not rule them out in the future.

A major and ongoing problem was highlighted in 1983, that of the long-term conservation and storage of recovered buried materials and the ordering of the paper and photographic archive. At that time the Committee expressed the intention that the latter should be deposited in the National Monument Record; hopefully this aim will be fulfilled in due course. It was from 1983 that the Committee started to meet on a six-monthly basis and specialists involved with the project were also invited to attend.

It was at this time also that a link was established with a 'second generation' of experimental earthworks being constructed and monitored by the Butser Ancient Farm team (Chapter 13). Their concept, construction and monitoring arrangements differ from those of the Committee's sites, aspects which add to the diversity of experimental work which the Committee aims to foster. The director of the Butser project, Dr P J Reynolds, was co-opted on to the Committee, as was Mr A J Lawson, Director of the Trust for Wessex Archaeology.

Conforming to the principle of combining meetings and site visits, the Committee met at the Dorset Institute and visited the Wareham site in 1984. Some weeks previously Mr J Hemsley (who had rejoined the Committee in the preceeding year) had carried out an important botanical survey of the entire Overton Down site (Chapter 3) which remains one of the landmarks in the Committee's work.

In 1985 the Committee visited the Butser experimental sites in Hampshire and Sussex (Chapter 13). It was recognized that the inexorable decline in the voluntary help with specialist work available to the Committee in the past would have to be replaced by paid services and that funding would have to be sought to cover this. The Committee identified two areas which needed financial guarantee: firstly the study of previously recovered materials plus their maintenance and secondly the funding of the 1992 Overton section. It was also accepted that it would be difficult to attract funding as the Committee is independent of any one institution.

Late in the year the Committee's archive was moved from the Institute of Archaeology in London to North Farm, West Overton, Marlborough, Wiltshire, the home of the Committee secretary, Mrs G Swanton. The land upon which the Overton Earthwork is situated had changed ownership, now belonging to Mr Robert Sangster.

In 1987 the Overton site was declared a Site of Special Scientific Interest together with large portions of Overton and Fyfield Downs, the upshot being that the Committee has to apply to the National Nature Conservancy Council – now English Nature – to section its own earthwork. Professor Richard Atkinson, one of the founder members of the Committee, resigned through ill health.

By 1988 it was becoming clear that there was gathering interest in the Committee's work as the end of the 'longue durée' of the sixteen years between excavations came in sight. Members were being requested to give lectures (K Crabtree (1990) in Denmark; P J Fowler (1989 the Beatrice de Cardi lecture), the British Association for the Advancement of Science visited the Overton site and the Committee received the photographic archive of the BBC Rushmore Iron Age Village site. At the annual meeting in April it was decided to approach Dr Martin Bell regarding the direction of the 1992 (Overton) and 1996 (Wareham) sections. Accordingly he attended the September 1989 meeting at Overton and was invited to join the Committee. With the 1992 section in mind, names of others who might be co-opted on to the Committee were suggested and members who were no longer able to attend resigned. Professor B Proudfoot, an original member, rejoined the Committee as the British Association for the Advancement of Science nominee. The Committee visited Dr A Whittle's excavations at Millbarrow (Whittle 1994, 9 and 34) where the buried turflines in the ditch provided interesting parallels to the Overton Down Earthwork.

1989–90 involved the inception of a project design for the 1992 Overton section, for which it was recognized that application for substantial funding would be necessary. A research design was prepared and was the subject of widespread consultation with a range of specialists. Invitations were inserted in the *Newsletter of the Association for Environmental Archaeology* and the *Science-Based Archaeology Newsletter* for specialists with an interest in aspects of the the experiment to become involved. The 32 year section took place in July 1992 and many of the specialists participated or visited. On 17 March 1993 a progress meeting was held at the Institute of Archaeology, London. Specialists presented progress reports on their work and discussed the ways in which their various contributions could be integrated. Integration of the 1992 report was further facilitated by the exchange of draft contributions. A meeting at the Institute of Archaeology on 12 September 1994 began to formulate the research design for the Wareham 1996 excavation.

2 Background, Overton
by Peter Fowler and Gillian Swanton

2.1 Introduction

The Overton Down Earthwork is fully described in terms of its concept, design and construction in 1960 in Jewell 1963. Early results are discussed in Jewell and Dimbleby 1966. Here, we summarize some of the main points from its early years and deal with the monitoring, including excavation in 1968 and 1976, of a dynamic experiment over its first 30 years or so ie 1960–1990. The 32nd year excavation in 1992 is dealt with below in Chapter 7.

2.2 The historical background

Between 1960 and 1964 three excavations took place: March 1961, September 1962 and July 1964 (Jewell and Dimbleby 1966). The initial investigation, at six months, studied only the accumulation of sediment in the ditch. The site was inspected in September 1961, about a year after construction. The subsequent two- and four-year sections (Fig 7.3) were traverses through both bank and ditch and required the construction of a scaffolding framework to provide datum lines for recording purposes and to act as working platforms from which people could operate in restricted conditions, while keeping damage to the site to a minimum. This practice has continued throughout the lifetime of the experiment.

To take account of the potential instability of the bank shortly after construction, the width of the early cuttings was greater that the spaces set aside for later investigation. The excavations were carried out using standard archaeological equipment of trowels, brushes, buckets and barrows. During the 1962 excavation the original template used to refine the ditch shape was replaced in the cut section to demonstrate the alteration to its profile.

The excavations were carried out by members of the Committee together with student volunteers. In both 1962 and 1964 the work was supervised by R J C Atkinson and both excavations were completed in six days. The excavation team was backed up by specialists dealing with the buried materials. In 1964 they were invited to visit the excavation to view the conditions under which 'their' materials had been interred. During this period the earthwork was being inspected on a fairly regular basis. Measurements were taken in March 1963 and photographic records were made by Committee members and interested visitors. These early years of the Committee's work involved more than the monitoring of the Overton Down site. By the end of July 1963 a second earthwork had been planned and built at Morden Bog, near Wareham, Dorset. That same year the first

monograph was published (Jewell 1963). Plans were also being laid for a third earthwork to be built in contrasting conditions; the options being discussed ranged from lowland clays to highland zone conditions.

The 'infancy' of the Overton site was also monitored by the (then) Nature Conservancy Wardens of the Fyfield Down National Nature Reserve. Their interest and their observational abilities added an extra dimension to the recording of the earthwork, especially of the early changes. They provided information which would otherwise have been unavailable to the Committee, eg diary comments including the appearance of floral species and the effects of extreme weather. In the latter category, for example, interesting observations remark on the erosion of the site during the severe winters of 1961/2 and 1962/3 (p 12).

2.3 Summary of results 1960–67

The following is a summary of observations and of data from the Overton Down Earthwork 1960–67. It includes a digest of the excavation results in Jewell and Dimbleby 1966.

The presence of the separating berm maintained the mutually exclusive development of the bank and ditch. Dramatic physical changes nevertheless took place, the most striking being the alteration in the ditch profile. Erosion began immediately, taking place summer and winter when respectively fine and coarse bands of scree formed in the angles between floor and sides. The angle of repose was at first 35–38°; by the time of the 4th year section (Fig 2.2) the two deposits of scree had met and covered the ditch floor and the scree rested at the shallower angle of 32°. Although the middle strip of the floor remained exposed for three to four years it did not suffer much visible frost damage (though in 1968 and subsequent sections it was observed to have 'lifted' (p 72).

The erosion taking place above the redeposited scree undercut the turf at the upper ditch edges. Bound together by roots it overhung the sides, the first pieces breaking off in July 1962 after very heavy rain (Jewell and Dimbleby 1966, plate 24.3). This event initiated the colonization of the ditch from the existing adjacent flora, the process being markedly assisted when turves came to rest root-down, allowing mature plants to continue growing *in situ*. The descent of turf into the ditch was accelerated during the hard winter of 1962–3 when the weight of snow caused large strips of vegetation to break off (Fig 2.1).

9

Figure 2.1 General view of Overton Down Experimental Earthwork , 21 March, 1964

Figure 2.2 Overton Down section of the ditch from the south-east, July 1964

Figure 2.3   The Overton Down Earthwork in 1984

Conversely, the deep snow cover protected the ditch from potentially severe erosion.

Changes taking place to the bank were less obvious. By September 1962 a lateral spread of *c* 0.23m (*c* 9in) along the long sides had taken place and by 1964 the crest had sunk *c* 0.165m (*c* 6.5in) from its original height due to consolidation of the bank material and compression of the turf core. The 1962 and 1964 sections showed that the profiles of the component layers were becoming rounded as the bank settled and the distortion of the polythene tubes indicated that downward movement of material had taken place. This occurred more rapidly up to the 1962 section than between then and that in 1964.

Study of the bank indicated that the surface material was being broken up by physical and chemical weathering and that flint withstood these processes for longer than chalk. Disintegration and downward movement of material led to a tendency for larger lumps of flint and chalk to accumulate at the base of the bank. In addition, calcium carbonate released during chemical weathering was redeposited, thereby binding chalk fragments together. By 1964 the bank surface also carried wind-blown organic material which, together with the moisture retained in the aggregated chalk particles, formed the rudimentary environment for plant colonization.

The buried materials were examined by specialists though reports are not available for all categories. Results show that vigorous aerobic biological activity was taking place even deep beneath the bank in the turf stack. The buried materials were subject to bacterial and fungal growth and timber samples were affected by aerobic wood-rot. Worm activity appeared to be low in the first two years but by the time of the 1964 section there was evidence of their movement throughout the bank and their presence had encouraged moles to follow, penetrating at least 1.83m (6ft) into the bank.

The relocation of growing plants into the ditch from its edges formed the main means of vegetational colonization during the first four years. Taking advantage of topsoil that had trickled into the ditch, half a dozen downland species established themselves from seed. The unstable scree slopes did not provide favourable conditions for plant growth and any plants attempting to grow were rapidly buried by fresh scree falls. Grass seedlings began to grow on the bank in the first spring (1961) but failed to develop. Around the fringes of the bank established plants pushed through the sparse chalk cover, their growth encouraged by mole activity disturbing and mixing soil and chalk but the dry conditions of the bank deterred any other permanent plant growth. Blue-green algae became established below the bank surface during and after 1962.

Even after only four years the experiment was illustrating that natural processes and agencies could substantially affect archaeological evidence. Mole activity on soil and objects, earthworms transporting material through differing layers, the transport of artefacts of varying ages into the ditch bottom *via* turf roots: all these events cause the 'corruption' of data and show that caution must be exercised when using the position of objects interpretively, especially for dating purposes.

2.4   The photographic record

The photographic record is housed at North Farm, West Overton, Marlborough. It is varied in its extent and coverage, has been built up from many sources and the historical material has the potential of being extended still further in addition to the ongoing monitoring programme. The period of construction and the early years of the earthwork are well covered in black and white and in colour transparency. The building stages, buried materials and methods employed are illustrated and the first sections are recorded, including microphotography of the buried materials recovered during excavation.

Between 1964 and 1976 the archive is less extensive although records exist for most years, with pictures being taken by individual Committee members when they visited the site. The bulk of the record for this period and for later years is on colour slide, although there is good black and white cover for the 1968 section. The 1976 section was reasonably well covered despite trouble with one of the cameras: fortunately several people took photographic records. Following the section a programme of regular monitoring took place, monthly at first, and once the recent cutting had stabilized, several times a year both by the secretary who lives nearby and by other Committee members who were paying the site more regular visits on Committee and other business.

2.5   The setting

Physically the setting of the earthwork (Fig 2.3) has not changed since its construction. It still lies on open grass downland within a rabbit-proof, fenced enclosure. Race-horse training has returned as an adjacent land-use. In conservation terms, however, the setting is now significantly different. In general

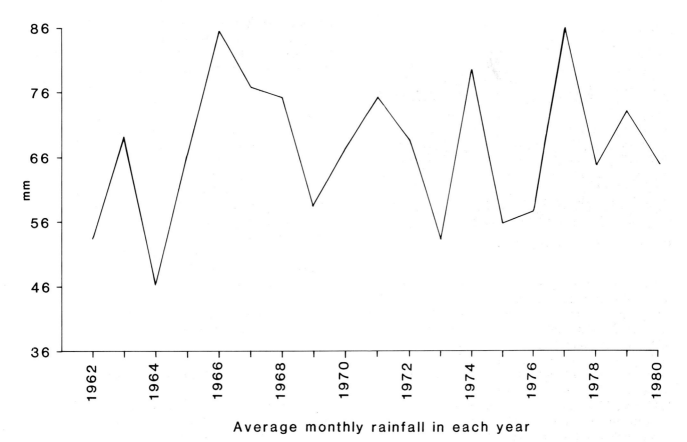

Figure 2.4   Overton Down rainfall graph

terms, the scientific value of Fyfield and Overton Downs has increased relatively as, until very recently, intensive arable farming of the Marlborough Downs continued. Archaeological studies of the Downs and the Avebury area in particular have experienced a renaissance and a better understanding of the paleo-environment and of local cultural changes is now enjoyed.

The earthwork itself is a Site of Special Scientific Interest in the National Nature Reserve and it now lies within the area designated as the Avebury World Heritage Site (co-designated with Stonehenge and its environs). A management plan for that World Heritage Site is currently being developed by interested parties, one of which, the National Trust, has now become a major landholder immediately to the west of Overton Down.

2.6   The weather

The Meteorological Office holds rainfall figures from January 1962 to September 1980 inclusive. At first these were recorded daily but the records are weekly for the bulk of the nineteen years. Repeated damage to and theft of the equipment put an end to the exercise in 1980, though it is perhaps doubtful, given the changes occurring in the National Nature Conservancy Council and the role of its field staff, whether regular monitoring could have been sustained anyway.

The readings were taken by the Wardens of the Fyfield Down National Nature Reserve. Where additional comments exist they seem to reflect, not unnaturally, the interests of the individuals rather than systematic observations.

Figure 2.4 shows, not the variation in total annual rainfall but the variation year by year of the average monthly rainfall. Over the eighteen years 1962–1979 inclusive, only two, 1966 and 1977, were substantially above the annual average (Fig 2.4) The only significant 'wet' or 'dry' phase was in 1966–72 when six of the nine 'above average rainfall' years occurred, in two groups of three years broken only by one 'below average rainfall' year, 1969. July emerges as the driest month overall, followed by April. 1964 was the driest year, 1977 the wettest. The latter succeeded the 'great drought' years of 1975 and 1976. They are only the fourth and fifth driest years but are distinguished not so much by their dryness as their being the only successive years of similar rainfall of any amount.

In other words, the measurements tend to show a consistent pattern of variability from year to year. They do not, of course, show individual events which have certainly been significant in the earthwork's life. The oscillatory pattern of annual rainfall is probably similar to fluctuations in temperature and both have almost certainly been influential in the earthwork's history. The temperature in the ditch, for example, has varied between extremes (for central southern England, that is, from a recorded mid 20's F in December to an estimated 80° F in July) and has undoubtedly directly affected the ditch sides and the nature of the infills (Crabtree p 39).

Some of these 'weather events' are recorded in the Warden's diary or elsewhere. For example:

1961
Nov   26: Walls and floor of ditch coated with ice
Dec   9: Collapse of frozen surface, some of material, chalk plus soil, came to rest in middle of ditch floor
       23: First signs of undercutting in ditch
       31: Heavy snowfall
1962
Jan   1: Six foot drifts at Down Barn
       5: Thaw. Heavy falls of chalk from walls [of ditch]. Surface water covering ditch floor
       9: Earth from overhanging turf falling on surface of new chalk heaped at base of wall [ditch side]
       11: Severe gale, chalk fragments from bank blown up to 24 yd [22m] eastwards
Jul   Heavy rain am, first turf slides into ditch pm (Jewell and Dimbleby 1966, plate 24:2)
1963
Feb   7: Ditch completely filled with snow
Mar   8: Eight to nine hundredweight of earth had collapsed into the ditch, most of this from the east face
       20: Turf overhanging ditch – 12–14 inches (c 0.32m) have been severed by mole runs.

Examples early in the history of the earthwork are chosen for they also illustrate the dynamic state of the earthwork as it went through a rapid series of changes which seem to be directly related to localized weather occurrences. The immediate results of these events were recorded in 1962 and 1964 (Jewell and Dimbleby 1966) and their longer-term consequences were apparent in 1968 and indeed later, for they literally set the shape of things to come.

It must be stressed, however, that such dramatic happenings of, and attributable to, the local weather were not confined to the early years. While long-term trends have clearly influenced developments at the earthwork, particular events have probably frequently had immediate effects. We infer that because so often something 'different' seems to happen when the Committee is in occupation. In 1976, for example, independently reflecting the observation above about the 1975–6 annual rainfall, a note recorded during

the sixteenth year excavation in July observed 'Very dry conditions have prevailed for over a year . . . and near drought conditions exist . . . The ditch fill especially seems to have virtually no moisture content – it falls away very easily and is difficult to retain in vertical section.' Both the bank and the ditch sections were difficult to retain in 1992 for exactly the opposite reason – a torrential and thunderous downpour (see below p 85).

2.7 The coin experiment

After much discussion in the late 1970s, the Committee decided to allow an additional experiment to be built into the Overton Down Earthwork. This was contrary to its general earthwork management policy but it could not see that any interference with the existing experiments would be incurred. Furthermore, as was the case in allowing glass to be inserted into the Wareham Earthwork (below p 222), it appreciated that an opportunity had arisen to generate more data without disturbing existing arrangements.

The form of the experiment, proposed by Professor Richard Atkinson, was that mint-condition coins should be inserted into the bank and along the outer edge of the ditch to monitor soil movement. They were to be placed vertically on edge parallel to the long axis of the monument at a depth of about 50mm (2in), at which level they would be most sensitive to soil movement. Any evidence of wear patterns on the coin surfaces would be a bonus to the primary objective. The proposals were subsequently modified slightly by a decision to position the ditch coins on the inner rather than outer side. Coins were to be placed in both excavated and unexcavated zones.

The experiment began on 23rd March 1979 when two rows of coins were placed as follows:

(1) along the south-west facing slope of the bank 0.914m (3ft) from the central steel tubes: 1p pieces, minted 1978;
(2) an identical line, 2.13m (7ft) from the central steel tubes: halfpennies, minted 1976.

Curiously, despite the best efforts of the bank (Lloyds, Swindon), it was impossible to acquire freshly-minted 1979 coins at the time. Coin-recovery in 1992, the first occasion for doing so, is detailed below (p 80).

3 The vegetation of the Overton site 1969–1992
by J H Hemsley

3.1 Editorial note

The key to the Overton Down vegetational record is the work of J H Hemsley periodically over nearly 40 years. Here, the first new substantial item is his 1985 report of his detailed 1984 survey of the earthwork and its immediate surrounds. This is to be compared with his first report in Jewell 1963, 70–72, though his text relates his 1984 results to his surveys of 1960, 1962 and 1966. His 1992 results, another major report, complete this section, thereby treating the floral aspect of this experiment in one thematic chapter.

Within this thematic treatment, we have appended at the end of the chapter, after the Hemsley *oeuvre*, some other vegetational notes. These are primarily to illustrate the nature of some of the archival material. We would add that probably a considerable amount of perhaps unsystematic floral data could be gleaned by examining from a botanical point of view the thousands of photographs and particularly colour slides, in the archive. Most were of course taken for archaeological and structural record purposes.

The survey of 1984 comprised the whole earthwork (Fig 3.1) with a particularly detailed survey of the bank vegetation (Fig 3.2). The enclosure and the surrounding grassland were also surveyed. The 1992 survey (p 19) was a detailed survey of the trench to be excavated (Fig 3.4) and a sketch plan of vegetation within the enclosure (Fig 3.3).

Latin names in usage at the time have been retained, but Table 3.3 includes new names and the Latin and common names of the plants discussed.

3.2 Vegetation survey 1984

A preliminary site examination of the vegetative cover was made in July 1960, immediately before construction, the results of this are given in the publication 'Experimental Earthwork on Overton Down' (Jewell 1963, 70–72). Following this, a detailed recording of the invading vegetation was made in July 1962 and in June 1966 further brief notes were made relating to the two main slopes but not the ends. In July 1984, following a suggestion by the Committee, a recording was carried out covering the earthwork banks in detail and additional notes etc made of the vegetation of the ditch, enclosure and nearby grassland. This contribution is chiefly concerned with these 1984 results.

Since construction the bank appears to have sunk a little. The north-east face now seems to be less steep and the berm between the south-west facing slope and the ditch has virtually disappeared. Within the enclosure there have been considerable changes in the character of the vegetation, due not only to the construction of the bank and ditch structure and exposure of new chalky material, but also to the effects of fencing and exclusion of grazing stock. At the same time, responding to agricultural management, the grassland adjacent has also changed, with the result that the composition as shown in the original site recording could not now be found.

The four sections – banks, ditch, enclosure and adjacent grassland – are dealt with briefly in the following account.

Earthwork and its banks

The overall picture is summarized in Figure 3.2 which shows the distribution of the two main grasses, red fescue (*Festuca rubra*) and sheep's fescue (*Festuca ovina*). While *Festuca rubra*, with a number of associates, had developed into a dense and virtually continuous cover along the less droughty lower slopes, *Festuca ovina*, able to tolerate generally drier conditions, had formed a mosaic of broken patchy cover with some smaller open bare places along the higher part, especially nearer the northern end of the south-west facing bank. In some places, however, associated with the permanent marker poles, a 'top-knot' of taller *Festuca rubra* had appeared. This grass had also occupied two very distinct bands across the earthwork, marking the positions of earlier excavations (1968, 1976).

The extent of *Festuca rubra* cover was a little more extensive on the north-east facing slope reaching heights on the bank of 1.0 – 2.75m (c 3ft 3in – 9ft) while only 0.75 – 2.25m (c 2ft 6in – 7ft 4in) on south-west aspect. There was also a north-west/south-east trend apparent on both banks, with the greater *Festuca rubra* cover on the south-east parts of the earthwork. This gradient was reflected markedly at the two ends, where at the south-east there was considerably more *Festuca rubra*, with this grass covering much of the face.

A list of 42 plants has been recorded, with some species restricted to certain sections. The tall coarse false oat (*Arrhenatherum elatius*) occurred principally on the north-west end but there were some smaller, less vigorous, patches elsewhere. As might be expected, the smaller, less competitive and drought-tolerant calcicole, cat's tail (*Phleum bertolonii*) occurred in the patchy *Festuca ovina* zone, especially along the ridge in barish places. Among the other larger and more vigorous species were

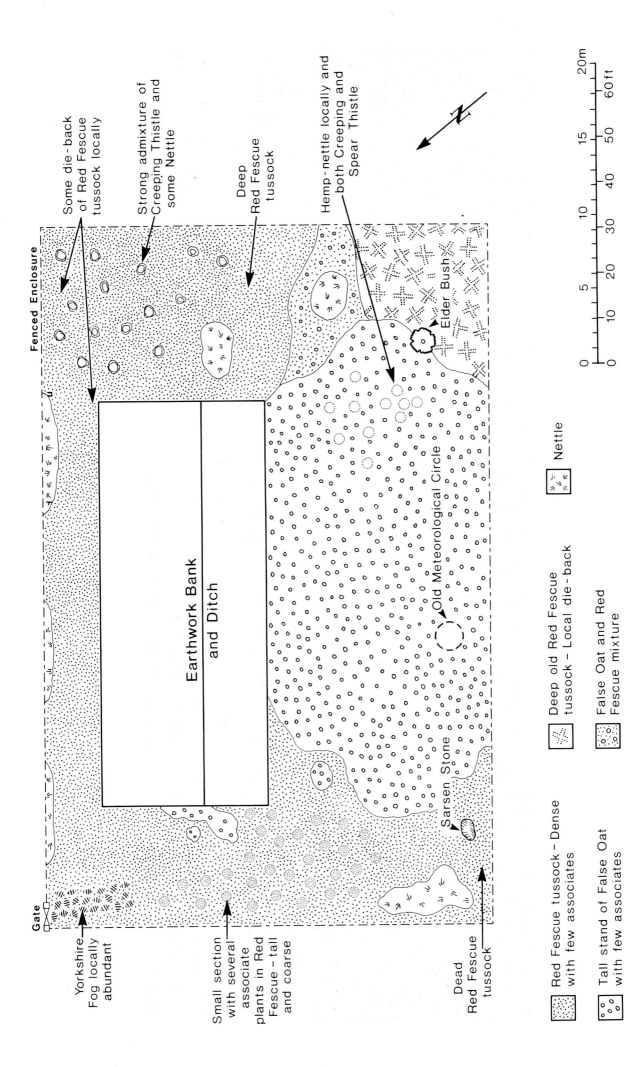

Fenced Enclosure

Some die-back
of Red Fescue
tussock locally

Strong admixture of
Creeping Thistle and
some Nettle

Deep
Red Fescue
tussock

Hemp-nettle locally and
both Creeping and
Spear Thistle

Gate

Yorkshire
Fog locally
abundant

Small section
with several
associate
plants in Red
Fescue - tall
and coarse

Earthwork Bank

and Ditch

Elder Bush

Old Meteorological Circle

Sarsen Stone

Dead
Red Fescue
tussock

0   5   10   15   20m
0   10   20   30   40   50   60ft

N

Red Fescue tussock - Dense
with few associates

Deep old Red Fescue
tussock - Local die-back

Nettle

Tall stand of False Oat
with few associates

False Oat and Red
Fescue mixture

Figure 3.1 Overton Down Earthwork enclosure, vegetation 1984

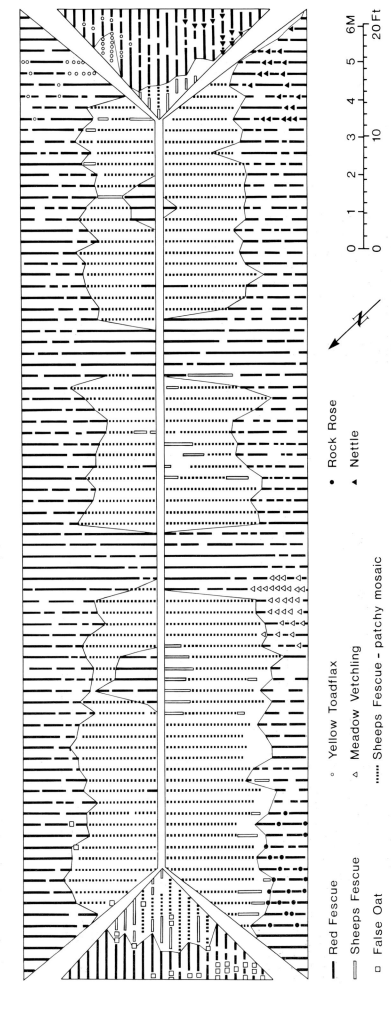

Red Fescue   ∘ Yellow Toadflax   • Rock Rose

Sheeps Fescue   ▵ Meadow Vetchling   ▴ Nettle

□ False Oat   ⋯ Sheeps Fescue – patchy mosaic

Figure 3.2 Overton Down Earthwork bank, main vegetation cover, June–July 1984. Selected associates only are included

nettle (*Urtica dioica*), well established on the south-eastern end, and yellow toadflax (*Linaria vulgaris*). Also on this end but a little higher on the bank, scattered ragwort (*Senecio jacobaea*) and thistles, both lanceolate (*Carduus lanceolatus*) and nodding (*Carduus nutans*) occurred plus a large patch of meadow vetchling (*Lathyrus pratensis*) low down on the south-west facing slope. Another species, not recorded in the earlier survey, devil's bit scabious (*Succisa pratensis*) somewhat unexpectedly had become firmly established, mainly in the westerly parts.

The number of plants showing a strong affinity for highly calcareous conditions makes a significant contribution to the total listing. Among these should be mentioned salad burnet (*Poterium sanguisorba*), small scabious (*Scabiosa columbaria*), wild thyme (*Thymus drucei*), dwarf thistle (*Cirsium acaulon*), hoary plantain (*Plantago media*), cat's ear (*Leontodon hispidus*), squinancywort (*Asperula cynanchica*), rock-rose (*Helianthemum chamaecistus*), crested hair grass (*Koeleria cristata*) and the oat-grasses (*Helictotrichon pubescens* and *H. pratense*). Among these salad burnet, squinancywort and rock-rose, along with the highly tolerant mouse-ear hawkweed (*Hieracium pilosella*), showed a marked preference for the warmer south-west facing slope. In contrast, other less demanding species in terms of base-rich habitat, eg harebell (*Campanula rotundifolia*) and yellow bedstraw (*Galium verum*), seem to have grown better on the cooler north-east slope. The small scabious (*Scabiosa columbaria*) was generally distributed in the matrix of open *Festuca ovina* but in places was noteworthy for the presence of many very small and under-developed plantlets.

Of the 34 species listed in the 1960 preliminary recording 25 can now be accounted for on the earthwork structure. An additional 11 species are now present. Several of these are 'opportunists,' eg sow-thistle (*Sonchus oleraceus*), black medick (*Medicago lupulina*) and spear thistle (*Carduus lanceolatus*), quickly able to colonize bare ground and open places. Others, eg meadow vetchling (*Lathyrus pratensis*), germander speedwell (*Veronica chamaedrys*), meadow buttercup (*Ranunculus acris*) and devil's bit scabious (*Succisa pratensis*) are widespread in meadows with a wide range of pH tolerance and a higher moisture regime.

An analysis of the relative cover values, based upon the records obtained, suggested that a little under half of the earthwork surface area carried a *Festuca rubra* cover, whilst more than one-third was recorded as *Festuca ovina* either continuous or, for the greater part, as a patchy mosaic with interspaced bare ground. In addition to these two main categories, the group of 40 flowering plants (excluding the two grasses above) occupied about one-sixth of the area. Table 3.1 shows the relative abundance of these and this can be compared with the 1960 data.

Red fescue (*Festuca rubra*) heads both tables and Yorkshire fog (*Holcus lanatus*), along with ribwort plantain (*Plantago lanceolata*), salad burnet (*Poterium sanguisorba*) and bird's foot trefoil (*Lotus corniculatus*) continue to hold places in the top ten. Species which seem to be providing a greater cover are small scabious (*Scabiosa columbaria*), harebell (*Campanula rotundifolia*), mouse-ear hawkweed (*Hieracium pilosella*) and rock-rose (*Helianthemum chamaecistus*), the latter albeit confined to one largish patch.

Among the apparent losses and absences from the 1960 list two species, quaking-grass (*Briza media*) and eye-bright (*Euphrasia nemorosa*) can be accounted for. The former, although not recorded on the banks, occurs adjacent to the south-east approach to the ditch. The latter was seen on the earthwork (frequent) in August 1985 but not recorded in 1984. One of the most striking changes has been the great drop in the bent grass (*Agrostis stolonifera*). This was not recorded on the earthwork, nor does it appear to be present nearby. Other grasses, sweet vernal (*Anthoxanthum odoratum*) and crested dog's tail (*Cynosurus cristatus*) have not been seen on the bank but may well linger on in the dense tall turf nearby, though they were not noted there in 1984. Neither would possess any great competitive capacity in the face of the coarse fescue tussock or tall false-oat grass stands which now occupy most of this area.

The rare frog orchid (*Coeloglossum viride*) was not recorded either within the enclosure nor in grassland adjacent and may have been lost.

The ditch vegetation

The ditch, which began to receive material including blocks of turf breaking away and slipping down from the margins at an early stage, is now well vegetated. A strong growth of grasses along with associated herbs covered the south-west side and floor, with a less robust but more diversified growth along the side below the earthwork. The two ends, with relatively gentle slopes, remained semi-open, showing little soil accumulation and carrying a thin, droughty, cover of plants.

In general, the side of the ditch below the berm carried a tufty fescue/salad burnet cover, with the greater amount of fescue towards the south-east end though a few small barish patches still remain. The salad burnet appeared to be more abundant here than on the earthwork above. At the north-western end a fringe of rock-rose (*Helianthemum chamaecistus*), continuous with that on the earthwork bank adjoining, was a conspicuous feature. The vegetation, well-established along this side, shared many species in common with the south-west face of the earthwork above. These include ribwort and hoary plantain (*Plantago lanceolata* and *P. media*), yellow bedstraw (*Galium verum*), small scabious (*Scabiosa columbaria*), purging flax (*Linum catharticum*), bird's foot trefoil (*Lotus corniculatus*), red clover (*Trifolium pratense*), lesser yellow trefoil (*Trifolium*

Table 3.1 Plants on the earthwork banks, 1984

Species	SW bank	NE bank	NW end	SE end	Total
Festuca rubra	4340	6131	632	905	12008
Festuca ovina including patchy mosaic	4908	3517	421	115	8961
sub-total					20969
Holcus lanatus	591	215	6	31	843
Plantago lanceolata	180	83	11	12	286
Scabiosa columbaria	124	145	2	6	277
Rumex acetosa	81	119	6	68	274
Arrhenatherum elatius	125	18	128	0	271
Phleum bertolonii	49	187	0	7	243
Poterium sanguisorba	186	20	0	0	206
Lathyrus pratensis	202	0	0	0	202
Lotus corniculatus	128	70	0	0	198
Urtica dioica	109	0	0	70	179
Linaria vulgaris	1	58	0	110	169
Campanula rotundifolia	26	126	12	4	168
Helianthemum chamaecistus	109	0	0	0	109
Galium verum	13	87	6	0	106
Thymus drucei	88	6	0	6	100
Dactylis glomerata	90	2	0	0	92
Hieracium pilosella	65	0	0	0	65
Succisa pratensis	44	10	3	0	57
Trisetum flavescens	24	6	0	0	30
Helictotrichon pratense	19	4	0	0	23
Helictotrichon pubescens	19	4	0	0	23
Asperula cynanchica	22	0	0	0	22
Plantago media	14	8	0	0	22
Leontodon hispidus	15	5	0	0	20
Koeleria cristata	17	2	0	0	19
Cirsium acaulon	16	2	0	0	18
Leontodon autumnalis	2	15	0	0	17
Veronica chamaedrys	4	13	0	0	17
Senecio jacobaea	9	2	2	0	13
Carduus lanceolatus	0	7	0	4	11
Carduus nutans	0	10	0	0	10
Medicago lupulina	8	0	0	2	10
Ranunculus acris	3	4	0	0	7
Cerastium	5	0	0	0	5
Sonchus oleraceus	0	4	0	0	4
Linum catharticum	3	0	0	0	3
Trifolium pratense	1	0	2	0	3
Ranunculus bulbosus	1	1	0	0	2
Crataegus monogyna (seedling)	1	0	0	0	1
Trifolium dubium	1	0	0	0	1
subtotal					4126
Moss	0	38	0	0	38
Dead tussock	0	50	0	0	50
Bare surface	40	0	26	22	88
Full total					25271

dubium), sorrel (*Rumex acetosa*), wild thyme (*Thymus drucei*), mouse-ear hawkweed (*Hieracium pilosella*) and the grasses Yorkshire fog (*Holcus lanatus*), cat's tail (*Phleum bertolonii*), crested hair-grass (*Koeleria cristata*), the oat grass (*Helictotrichon pratense*) and yellow oat (*Trisetum flavescens*).

The cooler, moister, west side of the ditch was very well covered with taller *Festuca rubra* and abundant *Poterium sanguisorba*. The false oat (*Arrhenatherum elatius*), continuous with the adjoining tall coarse stand, occurred locally and there was an abundant cover of moss in places as a layer beneath the grasses. Devil's bit scabious (*Succisa pratensis*) was frequent but the floristic diversity in general was much less than on the warmer south-west facing side of the ditch. Other species listed on this damper side included Yorkshire fog (*Holcus lanatus*), small scabious (*Scabiosa columbaria*), the plantains (*Plantago lanceolata* and *P. media*) and sorrel (*Rumex acetosa*).

In the bottom of the ditch, now narrowing due to infill, a grassy cover of mainly *Festuca rubra* was recorded. Other grasses were cocksfoot (*Dactylis glomerata*) and false oat (*Arrhenatherum elatius*), both rather infrequent here. A small patch of self-heal (*Prunella vulgaris*), not seen elsewhere, was also recorded.

At the ditch ends, as stated earlier, very little infill has taken place, with the surfaces remaining rather open and with comparatively little vigour in the plant growth. Small tufts of *Festuca ovina* and patchy *Thymus drucei* were the main species, along with quaking grass (*Briza media*). The most notable species however, was horse-shoe vetch (*Hippocrepis comosa*), of which a large patch near the north-west corner was the only record for the site. None of this desirable plant was seen on the earthwork banks, where it might be anticipated perhaps in the future. Also near the north-west corner was a solitary small seedling oak, a few centimetres high.

The enclosure

Following the erection of the fence and the exclusion of stock the response has been characterized by the development of a rank coarse grassland of mainly two species, red fescue (*Festuca rubra*) and false oat (*Arrhenatherum elatius*). Although both species have formed an underlying dense loose mattress of dead material, the tussocky nature of old red fescue contrasted with the more even, continuous stand of false oat. The red fescue mattress was commonly 0.20–0.30m in depth, with a maximum of 0.35m between the ditch and the south-east fence-line. The false oat, somewhat less dense, with depths of 0.1–0.20m, was at its most vigorous between the ditch and the elder bush, where a 0.25m lower loose accumulation was recorded. Along with these two grasses, nettle (*Urtica dioica*) had become established in several places, some associated with the fence-line. Latterly, both creeping thistle (*Cirsium*

arvense) and spear thistle (*Carduus lanceolatus*) have invaded the south-east sector and now threaten to take-over this corner, along with nettle, displacing the deep red fescue tussock which is showing signs of die-back in places. A solitary elder (*Sambucus nigra*), had become well-established in the south-east sector, representing the only successful colonization of a woody species to date. The distribution of this main plant cover is shown in Figure 3.1.

A small area in the north-west section continues to support some taller, more robust associates. In this section, with fairly coarse red fescue, Yorkshire fog (*Holcus lanatus*), salad burnet (*Poterium sanguisorba*), ribwort plantain (*Plantago lanceolata*), yellow bedstraw (*Galium verum*), sorrel (*Rumex acetosa*), a few emergent stems of knapweed (*Centaurea nigra*) and devil's bit scabious (*Succisa pratensis*) were noted, along with the grasses yellow oat (*Trisetum flavescens*), oat grass (*Helictotrichon pratense*) and meadow grass (*Poa pratensis* subsp. *angustifolia*). A small patch of rock-rose (*Helianthemum chamaecistus*) was noted near the north-west corner of the ditch. This section represents an attenuated version of the original sward structure but seems now to be threatened by further extension of false oat and nettle, which are both adjacent. It may have retained a slightly more species-rich character due to an earlier phase when there was frequent visitation and hence trampling between the gateway and the meteorological recording site within the enclosure.

A very small patch of bent grass (*Agrostis canina*) was noted near the south-east corner of the ditch, in dense red fescue and it is possible that some may be present in the slightly more species-rich section mentioned above. Yorkshire fog (*Holcus lanatus*) was noted in a strip near the gateway.

The great contrast between the present tall coarse species-poor stand of two species, red fescue and false oat, and the plant list recorded in 1960 should be noted. Also the phenomenon of the apparent transposition of a species-rich flora between the former semi-natural grassland and an artificially created structure within a twenty-four year period could offer an interesting example leading towards further thought on chalk grassland conservation.

Adjacent grassland

The grazed grassland adjoining the earthwork enclosure was examined briefly and some notes made of the composition. A closed turf with some herbaceous associates, and as noted in the 1960 account, small scattered patches of soil disturbance, probably the effect of mole activity, was the chief impression. Few herbs were flowering and the sward height generally was in the order of 30–50mm, having some of the appearance of an agriculturally improved grassland, eg in colour and the obvious presence of rye-grass and white clover.

The plant list was as follows:

Grasses
Rye grass (*Lolium perenne*) a
Meadow grass (*Poa pratensis*) a
Yorkshire fog (*Holcus lanatus*) f
Crested dog's tail (*Cynosurus cristatus*) a
Yellow oat (*Trisetum flavescens*) f
Cat's tail (*Phleum bertolonii*) o

Herbs
Meadow buttercup (*Ranunculus acris*) o
Bulbous buttercup (*Ranunculus bulbosus*) f
Shepherd's purse (*Capsella bursa-pastoris*) o
Lesser stitchwort (*Stellaria graminea*) r
Mouse-eared chickweed (*Cerastium* sp.) r
White clover (*Trifolium repens*) a
Red clover (*Trifolium pratense*) r
Bird's foot trefoil (*Lotus corniculatus*) r
Yellow bedstraw (*Galium verum*) o
Creeping thistle (*Cirsium arvense*) o
Spear thistle (*Carduus lanceolatus*) f
Nodding thistle (*Carduus nutans*) r
Nettle (*Urtica dioica*) o
Sorrel (*Rumex acetosa*) a
Ribwort plantain (*Plantago lanceolata*) o

a =abundant
f = frequent
o = occasional
r = rare

The list was made within a distance of about 10m (32ft–33ft) around the fenceline. It was noted that the sorrel (*Rumex acetosa*) was absent from a zone of about 25m (*c* 81ft) near the north-west end of the enclosure. At the fenceline, nettle was present in strips mainly along the north-east side and also at the north-west corner. Red fescue appeared along the fenceline, with a coarse, strong growth inside, and elsewhere in the general vicinity this grass could be seen associated with scattered sarsen stones, with the bent grass (*Agrostis canina*). Small patches with disturbed soil seemed to be the main niche for seedling spear thistle and also shepherd's purse and mouse-eared chickweed.

Comparison between this list and the earlier 1960 record, which reflects changes in composition of what originally was a reasonably uniform site, shows substantial loss of herb associates, especially those of a more calcicolous character. In species numbers a drop from 34 to 21 has been recorded, with only 12 of the latter in the original list.

The appearance of undesirable weed species, notably creeping and spear thistles and nettle, is a striking change, as is also the substantial increase in the higher nutrient demanding species, ie rye-grass, meadow grass and creeping white clover. Loss of the typical chalk flora associates, eg squinancywort, rock-rose, small scabious and dwarf thistle, has been a marked feature. Like the enclosure, but for quite different reasons, the result has been a migration and interchange between the semi-natural grassland and the artificially introduced structure, with the latter now providing the species-rich refuge.

Additional observations

It would appear that although small, the enclosure is providing refuge for certain fauna in an otherwise large expanse of grazed grassland.

The following wildlife has been recorded:

Common hare (several) and fox (1 only), open downland near enclosure.
Meadow pipit, nest with eggs, north-west corner of ditch in red fescue tussock (16.06.84). Skylark frequent near enclosure (July 1984).
Common lizard, in deep red fescue tussock, north-east side of enclosure (01.07.84)
Shelter and warmth and a greater range of food plants in the ditch and banks undoubtedly make an attractive butterfly habitat. Small copper, ditch end (01.07.84); meadow brown, several in tall grassland near ditch (June 1984); small tortoise-shell, about 50 in total, mainly SW side of bank and ditch (June–July 1984); common blue, several on bank and ditch (June 1984); small skipper, four, in and near ditch (01.07.84); marsh fritillary, one only in ditch (17.06.84). Burnet moth caterpillars on *Lotus corniculatus* (June 1984); cinnabar, few (30.06.84 and 01.07.84)

Also noted was the very extensive pattern of small mammal runs under the dense red fescue tussocks and in the tall false oat cover.

3.3 Vegetation survey 1992

Prior to the July 1992 section and as part of the project, a further botanical recording of vegetation cover in the vicinity of the 'dig' was made on 20 June, a little in advance of the main work.

Since the last recording in 1984, a time interval of eight years has seen changes in the pattern of cover perhaps to a greater degree than might have been anticipated. A preliminary visual inspection gave the impression of increasing bare ground on the ridge and higher bank, on both faces, especially towards the south-east end, where there had been a marked increase in drought tolerant species such as wild thyme and rough hawkbit.

The finer detail emerging from the transect recording has confirmed this trend and also pointed to a number of other changes here. Together they emphasise the continuing dynamic state of cover. Species fluctuate significantly in abundance and the edge of taller, more robust red fescue has continued to advance at a gentle rate upslope, mainly on the south-west face.

The main changes have been shown in Figure 3.4. The effect of an earlier section, made before the 1984 recording, can clearly be seen as a red fescue strip across the bank. It is assumed that the 'backfill' here resulted in a mixing of chalk and other soils of higher nutrient status. This was quickly re-colonized by the

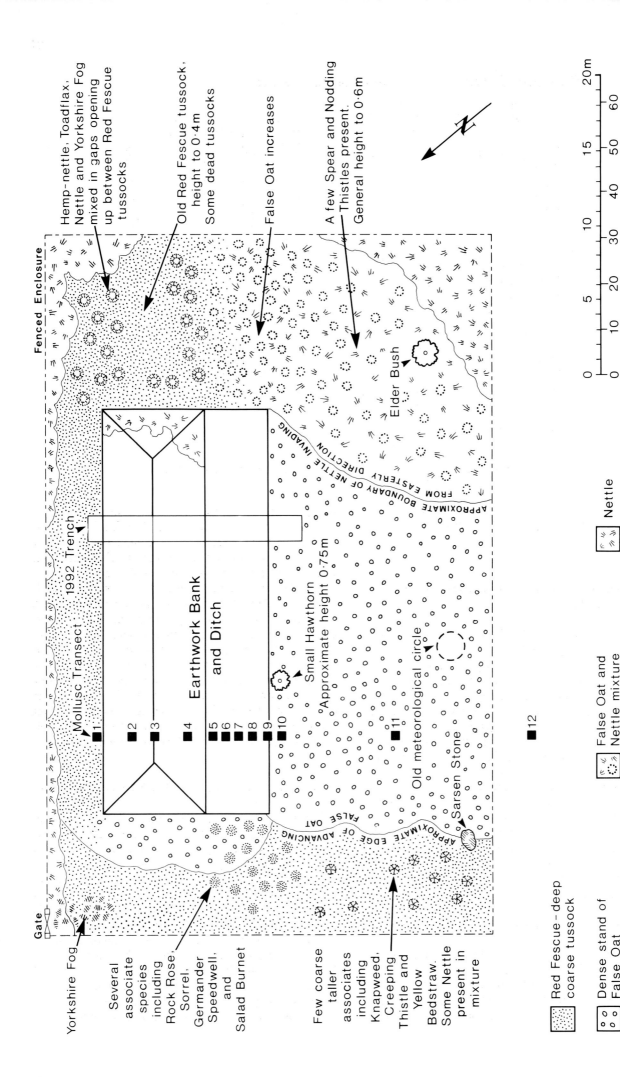

Figure 3.3 Overton Down Earthwork enclosure vegetation, 1992

Fenced Enclosure

Hemp-nettle, Toadflax,
Nettle and Yorkshire Fog
mixed in gaps opening
up between Red Fescue
tussocks

Old Red Fescue tussock,
height to 0·4m
Some dead tussocks

False Oat increases

A few Spear and Nodding
Thistles present.
General height to 0·6m

Gate

Mollusc Transect   1992 Trench

Earthwork Bank   and Ditch

APPROXIMATE BOUNDARY OF NETTLE INVADING
FROM EASTERLY DIRECTION

Elder Bush

Small Hawthorn
Approximate height 0·75m

Old meteorological circle

Sarsen Stone

APPROXIMATE EDGE OF ADVANCING FALSE OAT

Yorkshire Fog

Several
associate
species
including
Rock Rose,
Sorrel,
Germander
Speedwell,
and
Salad Burnet

Few coarse
taller
associates
including
Knapweed,
Creeping
Thistle and
Yellow
Bedstraw.
Some Nettle
present in
mixture

■1 ■2 ■3 ■4 ■5 ■6 ■7 ■8 ■9 ■10   ■11

■12

0   5   10   15   20m
0   10   20   30   40   50   60

N

Red Fescue - deep
coarse tussock

Dense stand of
False Oat

False Oat and
Nettle mixture

Nettle

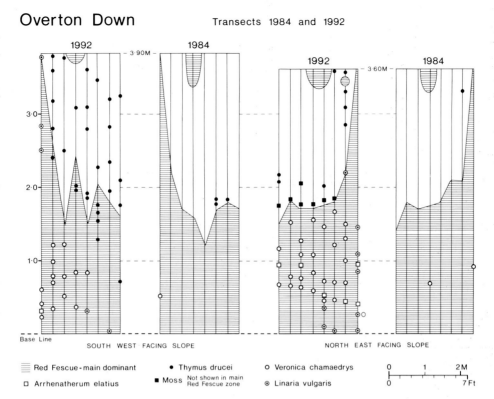

Figure 3.4 *Overton Down Earthwork vegetation transects, 1984 and 1992*

more demanding red fescue, which established an overwhelming dominance as a result of the earlier disturbance.

1. Red fescue on the two slopes, south-west and north-east facing

Eight transects at *c* 0.3m (1ft) intervals are compared for the two recordings, 1984 and 1992 in Fig 3.4. The south-west facing slope shows a greater shift of the red fescue/sheep's fescue boundary than the north-east slope, the latter having changed comparatively little. In both cases, however, there has been a small advance upslope, averaging about 0.2m (*c* 8in) for the south-west slope with development of a marked irregularity and perhaps little more than 50mm (*c* 2in) for the north-east slope.

In both cases, despite the apparent gains upslope, there has been a decrease in overall cover with diversification of the hitherto mainly red fescue/Yorkshire fog-dominated community and broad-leaves entering on an increasing scale. Reference to the full transect data, Table 3.2, shows that both these grasses appear to have declined, the latter very considerably on the south-west facing slope. Replacement broad-leaved species differ in their abundance depending on the two aspects of the bank involved.

On the warmer, and presumably drier, south-west facing slope, ribwort plantain, salad burnet and rough hawkbit, along with wild thyme and purging flax in smaller quantity, all show an increasing presence. In contrast, however, on the cooler and damper north-east facing slope, yellow bedstraw, false oat grass and the moss *Pseudoscleropodium purum* are the main replacement species. The latter forms a well-defined narrow strip in the transition zone between red fescue and sheep's fescue.

The largest increase overall however, on both slopes, has been shown by germander speedwell. It appears to have made very significant gains, especially on the south-west slope where it had been recorded at the minimal cover index value of 1 in 1984 as opposed to a value of 47 in 1992. Transect locations for germander speedwell along with other chosen examples: false oat grass (*Arrhenatherum elatius*), wild thyme (*Thymus drucei*), yellow toadflax (*Linaria vulgaris*) and moss are shown in Fig 3.4, contrasting the 1984 and 1992 performances.

2. Upper parts of the bank with sheep's fescue

The main change in the upper part of both slopes has been the emergence of a sharper distinction between bare ground and the grass/broad-leaved plant cover. In 1984 the greater part carried an intimate mixture of grass and a great number of small plantlets, little more than seedlings, including rough hawkbit, small scabious and ribwort plantain within a close mosaic of bare places. The only practicable way of recording this was under the heading of 'patchy sheep's fescue'.

The situation in 1992 proved to be simpler, with both grasses and the several associated broad-leaved herbs on the whole more clearly defined within a more precise pattern of open bare ground.

As with the red fescue cover on the lower bank, the

Table 3.2 Plants of the earthwork bank, 1992 (1984 figures in brackets)

Species	SW bank		NE bank		Total	
Festuca rubra	428	(494)	424	(605)	852	(1099)
Festuca ovina (incl. patchy mosaic)	193	(502)	210	(469)	403	(971)
Thymus drucei	109	(20)	32	(2)	141	(22)
Veronica chamaedrys	47	(1)	67	(5)	114	(6)
Leontodon hispidus	91	(4)	17	(4)	108	(8)
Plantago lanceolata	46	(13)	6	(15)	52	(28)
Galium verum	0	(0)	44	(8)	44	(8)
Poterium sanguisorba	37	(12)	7	(2)	44	(14)
Linaria vulgaris	12	(0)	28	(0)	40	(0)
Linum catharticum	30	(0)	8	(0)	38	(0)
Campanula rotundifolia	23	(17)	5	(16)	28	(33)
Arrhenatherum elatius	4	(0)	23	(0)	27	(0)
Rumex acetosa	5	(14)	14	(12)	19	(26)
Holcus lanatus	2	(123)	15	(18)	17	(141)
Taraxacum officinale agg	2	(0)	14	(0)	16	(0)
Hieracium pilosella	4	(0)	10	(0)	14	(0)
Phleum pratense subsp. *bertolonii*	4	(7)	10	(22)	14	(29)
Scabiosa columbaria	4	(8)	3	(2)	7	(10)
Koeleria cristata	2	(0)	3	(0)	5	(0)
Plantago media	0	(0)	5	(0)	5	(0)
Medicago lupulina	5	(0)	0	(0)	5	(0)
Lotus corniculatus	4	(0)	0	(1)	4	(1)
Avenula pubescens	4	(0)	0	(0)	4	(0)
Cirsium vulgare	4	(0)	0	(0)	4	(0)
Asperula cynanchica	4	(0)	0	(0)	4	(0)
Trisetum flavescens	3	(0)	0	(6)	3	(6)
Euphrasia nemorosa	0	(0)	2	(0)	2	(0)
Cirsium arvense	0	(0)	2	(0)	2	(0)
Senecio jacobaea	2	(0)	0	(0)	2	(0)
Crepis capillaris	0	(0)	2	(0)	2	(0)
Moss	3	(0)	86	(0)	89	(0)
Bare surface	139	(4)	106	(0)	245	(4)
				Total	2354	(2406)

extent of sheep's fescue may have declined since 1984. Some indication may be gained by addition of the three cover index values for 1992: sheep's fescue, patchy sheep's fescue and bare ground for both slopes. This gives a total index of 648 as against the comparable figure of 975 for 1984, showing a decline of 33.5%. Some of this loss is probably reflected in the development of open bare places, now more prominent than in 1984.

Substantial increases in the broad-leaved species wild thyme, rough hawkbit and purging flax on both south-west and north-east facing slopes have been recorded. The spread of the former on the cooler north-east facing slope is particularly noteworthy, suggesting a phase of warmer and drier conditions in latter years.

3. *Other comments on plant presence*

One new record for the earthwork bank was obtained from the upper section of the north-east facing slope.

A single plant, eyebright (*Euphrasia nemorosa*), was noted.

There were also several other species in the section covered in 1992, not recorded there in 1984 but present elsewhere on the earthwork at the time. Among these were short-term opportunists such as spear thistle, ragwort, and black medick. Others, such as squinancywort, false oat, crested hair grass, hoary plantain and mouse-eared hawkweed could become more permanent members of the plant community. The latter, a plant of dry, open habitats like wild thyme, is perhaps responding to the generally more open and dry conditions now prevailing on the upper slope.

Conversely there have been a few declines among the broad-leaved plants and grasses, including the once more prominent small scabious, Yorkshire fog and smaller cat's tail grasses and harebell. There are, however, no losses to be reported from the section recorded.

4. General observations and summary of results

The main trends as shown by transect recordings for 1992 (Fig 3.4) may be summarized as follows:

a) The taller coarse red fescue grass has made modest gains on the south-west slope but has shown little change on the cooler and damper north-east face. It has declined in cover, along with its former associate, Yorkshire fog. At the same time there has been an increase in broad-leaved components, principally germander speedwell, yellow bedstraw and salad burnet.

b) In the upper parts of both south-west and north-east facing slopes there appears to have been an increase in bare ground with conditions generally favouring such plants as wild thyme which shows a notable increase, as shown in Fig 3.4. Increasing species diversity has been shown and, like the lower red fescue zone, a number of species have appeared which were not recorded here in 1984. All but one, eyebright (*Euphrasia nemorosa*), were, however, to be seen on other parts of the earthwork at the time of the 1984 recording.

c) The appearance of false oat grass, chiefly on the north-east facing slope, is of note. This taller coarse species, which had already gained dominance over many parts of the enclosure and spread outwards from the north-west end of the bank, is also prominent along the lower parts of the south-west facing slope. If it continues to be successful in making further gains, especially on the cooler and damper north-east facing slope, there could be a fundamental change in the vegetative cover over the years to come.

d) The results of the 1992 recording, limited to a small section only, suggests that, although the main overall pattern of the two predominant fescue grasses has been maintained, there have been substantial changes in other component species during the eight years since 1984, which have brought about increasing diversification in the plant cover. At the same time there is evidence of a phase of increasing aridity affecting the upper parts of both south-west and north-east facing slopes.

The ditch vegetation

As in 1984, notes were made on the condition of the ditch vegetation generally. These form the basis of the following brief account.

The two sides have continued to show a sharp distinction; both are well vegetated with the exception of a few small bare places on the south-west facing side. The cooler and damper side (north-east facing) carries a vigorous growth of mainly red fescue/salad burnet mixture with false oat both lining the ditch edge and also forming larger invasive patches well down the sides in at least three places. There has also been a deep, dense build-up of mosses at the base of this cover and the fringe of rock-rose at the north-west end appears to have extended a little down the ditch side.

In contrast, the warmer south-west facing slope, at the foot of the earthwork, supports a wide range of chalk-loving species, sharing many in common with the earthwork bank above. These have been listed in the 1984 report (see above p 16). The bottom of the ditch has developed a deeper, well-vegetated mixture of mainly red fescue now joined by salad burnet. False oat has made some gains here and at one place has formed a patch continuous with that along the damper cooler side.

Perhaps the most noteworthy change over the eight years has been the development of cover at the two ends where there was much bare chalk in 1984. At the south-east end, although some small bare places still remain, a close, species-rich cover may now be seen. The following species were recorded: Bird's foot trefoil (*Lotus corniculatus*), red clover (*Trifolium pratense*), black medick (*Medicago lupulina*), hoary plantain (*Plantago media*), purging flax (*Linum catharticum*), wild thyme (*Thymus drucei*), mouse-ear hawkweed (*Hieracium pilosella*), sheep's fescue (*Festuca ovina*), quaking grass (*Briza media*) and smaller cat's tail (*Phleum nodosum* subsp. *bertolonii*).

Similarly, at the north-west end there is now very little bare ground. A low dense cover of chalk-loving species has now developed to an even greater degree than on the 'eastern' end above. Rock-rose was noted here and the patch of horseshoe vetch, commented upon in the 1984 report, has now increased in extent perhaps covering upwards of 3m² (c 10.5 yd²), spreading a little both sideways and into the ditch from the north-west corner.

The enclosure

The current situation has been summarized in Fig 3.3, which should be compared with Fig 3.1 taken from the 1984 report. Several trends, well in train at the earlier stages, have continued without serious intervention and have largely concerned three species: false oat, red fescue and nettle. Red fescue has declined overall, giving way to false oat and nettle in a number of places.

In the north-eastern sector nettle has increased, gaining dominance in the corner and along the fence-line. It is also well-established in the older tussock where gaps are increasingly appearing due to the collapse of the moribund red fescue. It has also invaded the 'eastern' end of the earthwork bank where the Committee has attempted to control further inroads. Yellow toadflax, Yorkshire fog and hemp nettle also occur in these gaps.

Moving in a southerly direction, false oat increasingly enters the community and this grass, along with nettle, now appears to have established dominance in the former red fescue tussock near the elder bush, with a dense stand of nettle only at the extreme corner. A few spear and nodding thistle are the main associates.

The extensive stand of 'pure' false oat occupying the larger 'frontal' area has made some further limited gains in a westerly direction, having now reached the sarsen stone. The presence of a small hawthorn, now about 0.75m in height (c 2ft 5in), should be noted. Also in this more westerly section there has been an extension of false oat at the expense of red fescue at the western margin of the earthwork and ditch. In this section, however, the remaining coarse red fescue tussock continues to support a mixture of a few taller herbs such as knapweed, with a few chalk-loving species nearer the western end of the ditch, notably salad burnet and rock-rose. There is some scattered nettle in this sector but as yet this aggressive species seems not to have achieved the success seen elsewhere.

Lastly, along the narrow strip 'northwards' of the earthwork, a deep coarse red fescue tussock continues to survive with very few associates but nettle is present along the fence-line and appears to be making some gains, especially at the western end near the gate.

3.4 Note on the recording method

The following note was added to the 1992 report to provide details of the method used and to show how index values were obtained for comparison of results arising from the 1984 and 1992 surveys. Equipment used was that readily to hand, hence the mixture of both metric and imperial measures. Both are provided in the text.

Four corner positions were established by examination of the earthwork topography in 1984 and base-lines set up using these for markers. A 100ft (c 30m) tape was then placed at the foot of the south-west facing slope, along the base-line, to provide a series of 1ft (c 30cm) intervals between corner markers. Two painted ranging poles, placed end-to-end to form a 4m (c 13ft) long 'vertical' transect were laid carefully on the slope face, resting on the vegetation, at right angles to the base-tape. Species presence and identity, bare ground etc, was recorded along the western side of the 'transect'; only plants touching and in very close proximity to the edge of a pole were recorded. A metre (c 3ft 3in) rule, in conjunction with the painted divisions of a survey pole, was used to obtain finer measurements and the readings transposed in detail on to squared graph paper, a one-tenth of an inch square (c 3mm) equalling 25mm (c 1in) of transect length.

This procedure was repeated for the two main faces and two ends of the bank, resulting in 216 transects in total and hence a reasonably detailed 'picture' of the vegetational cover was built up, the 1ft (c 30cm) – spaced transects being close enough, for example, to show the main red fescue/sheep's fescue boundary, one of the bank's more conspicuous features (Fig 3.2).

A smaller-scale recording was carried out in 1992 using a similar procedure. In order to obtain as near a repeat as possible, however, base-lines were fixed by direct measurement from the earthwork crest, taking one of the permanent metal poles as a fixed point. Using the 1984 transect lengths, 3.80m (c 12ft 5in) and 3.60m (c 11ft 9in) for the south-west and north-east slopes respectively, these lengths were taken from a known metal pole and relationship with its appropriate 1984 transect position, hence setting up the 1992 transect lines as closely as possible to those done in 1984. Data obtained from the recording were used to provide a set of cover index values for all species encountered by addition of one tenth of an inch (c 3mm) square entries (equal to 25mm or 1inch of 'vertical' occupancy), as appropriate. The actual figures obtained, although of limited importance in themselves, do provide a very useful basis for comparison and a detailed guide to the performance and changing scene relating to the range of species and cover on the bank.

To take a few examples, the cover index for wild thyme, as shown by the 1992 limited section recording, has risen from 20 to 109 on the south-west facing slope and from 2 to 32 on the north-east slope. This suggests a total increase from 22 to 141, or nearly a 7-fold rise in the index value. Being based on direct 'vertical' cover measurement, this can reasonably be interpreted as a 7-fold increase in wild thyme on the part of the bank, assuming that the clumps are roughly circular in shape. On the other hand, sorrel has shown little change, declining only from 26 to 19. False oat, which was not present in 1984, now appears with a cover index value of 27, the main presence being on the cooler north-east facing slope.

It should be possible to use this simple quantitive approach in a repetitive manner at any time in the future to record vegetation on the earthwork, giving satisfactory results, both in terms of relative abundance or otherwise, of species present as well as predicting likely further changes in the pattern of overall cover.

Table 3.3 Plants mentioned in the vegetation report

Agrostis canina	velvet bent grass
Agrostis stolonifera	creeping bent grass
Anthoxanthum odoratum	sweet vernal
Arrhenatherum elatius	false oat grass
Asperula cynanchica	squinancywort
Avenula pubescens	downy oat grass
Briza media	quaking grass
Capsella bursa-pastoris	shepherd's purse
Campanula rotundifolia	harebell
Carduus lanceolatus	spear thistle [*Cirsium vulgare*]
Carduus nutans	nodding thistle
Centaurea nigra	knapweed
Cerastium spp.	mouse-ear chickweed
Cirsium acaulon	dwarf thistle
Cirsium arvense	creeping thistle
Cirsium vulgare	spear thistle
Coeloglossum viride	frog orchid
Crataegus monogyna	hawthorn
Crepis capillaris	smooth hawk's beard
Cynosurus cristatus	crested dog's tail
Dactylis glomerata	cocksfoot
Euphrasia nemorosa	eyebright
Festuca ovina	sheep's fescue
Festuca rubra	red fescue
Galium verum	yellow bedstraw
Helianthemum chamaecistus	rock-rose [*Helianthemum nummularium*]
Helictotrichon pratense	meadow oat grass [*Avenula pratensis*]
Helictotrichon pubescens	downy oat grass [*Avenula pubescens*]
Hieracium pilosella	mouse-ear hawkweed
Hippocrepis comosa	horse-shoe vetch
Holcus lanatus	Yorkshire fog
Koeleria cristata	crested hair grass [*Koeleria macrantha*]
Lathyrus pratensis	meadow vetchling
Leontodon autumnalis	autumn hawkbit
Leontodon hispidus	cat's ear
Linaria vulgaris	yellow toadflax
Linum catharticum	purging flax
Lolium perenne	rye grass
Lotus corniculatus	bird's foot trefoil
Medicago lupulina	black medick
Phleum nodosum bertolonii	lesser cat's tail [*Phleum pratense* subsp *bertolonii*]
Phleum pratense	timothy grass
Plantago lanceolata	ribwort plantain
Plantago media	hoary plantain
Poa pratensis	meadow grass
Poterium sanguisorba	salad burnet [*Sanguisorba minor*]
Prunella vulgaris	self-heal
Pseudoscleropodium purum	moss spp.
Rumex acetosa	sorrel
Ranunculus acris	meadow buttercup
Ranunculus bulbosus	bulbous buttercup
Sambucus nigra	elder
Scabiosa columbaria	chalk scabious
Senecio jacobaea	ragwort
Sonchus oleraceus	sow thistle
Stellaria graminea	lesser stitchwort
Succisa pratensis	devil's bit scabious
Taraxacum officinale	dandelion
Trifolium dubium	lesser yellow trefoil
Trifolium pratense	red clover
Trifolium repens	white clover
Trisetum flavescens	yellow oat
Thymus drucei	wild thyme [*Thymus praecox*]
Urtica dioica	nettle
Veronica chamaedrys	germander speedwell

Latin names in common usage at the time of recording have been retained. More recent ones are given in square brackets

3.5 Two exemplars from the project archive

(i) *Descriptions based on extracts by the Honorary Secretary from notes made during Committee site visits*

These were compiled by the Honorary Secretary from various Committee sources.

It was noted in January 1978 that moss was becoming well-established on the shady, north-facing side of the ditch. In March that year, on the same side of the ditch, the moss was noticeably binding the surface material at the site of the 1976 cutting. Nevertheless, slumping and weathering were still visible in the area of backfilling.

The following winter (1978–9) was particularly harsh with long periods of frost and north-easterly winds. By March 1979 the latter had battered and sculpted the grass on and around the earthwork bank giving it a 'choppy sea' appearance. Within the previous twelve months, despite the weather, the vegetation had progressed markedly up the west end of the bank. With the exception of the 1976 scar, there was little chalk showing in the ditch. A hawthorn bush, hardly more than a sapling, was discovered growing to the south of the ditch edge.

In the early 1980s a serious thistle problem developed in the grassland surrounding the earthwork enclosure. This expansion was probably due to the changes in grazing and fertilizer policies on the part of the landowner. Recently a positive thistle control programme has been instigated. This, however, is not without its problems due to the protected species growing on the Nature Reserve.

In 1988 the Committee noted the presence of nettles within the enclosure south east of the elder tree and that the false oat population south of the earthwork had altered little in relation to the red fescue since 1984. The hawthorn south of the ditch, now nine years old, had reached nearly half a metre in height. On the bank grasses were spreading out from cutting infills (the 1964, 1968 and 1976 trenches were backfilled with mixed material). Long grasses made the 1964 and 1976 cuttings very prominent. On the south west side of the bank a lot of comminuted chalk was showing between little tussocks of grass on the upper half almost all the way along, while the lower part is more or less continuously covered with thickly matted grass and moss

(ii) *The conservation status of the site*

The following note is based on the official National Nature Conservancy Council ('English Nature') description of Fyfield and Overton Downs. The natural history interest of the area was originally seen to be 'as one of the principal areas in the southern group of geomorphic sites . . . a geological monument'. 247 hectares of the Downs became a National Nature Reserve in 1956 as 'one of the finest remaining tracts of unclaimed chalk downland in

England.' During the 1960s the area became recognized as an outstanding site for lichens, adding another biological dimension to the reservation's conservation status . . . in 1989 it was recognized that the acrocarpus moss communities on the sarsen stones, though less extensive, have a similar conservation status to that of the lichen flora.'

The Site of Special Scientific Interest (SSSI) citation, paras 1–2, is worth quoting nearly in full for it summarizes the significance of the area of the Overton Down Earthwork. 'The [SSSI] site is notified for both its geomorphological and biological interest. Geomorphologically, Fyfield Down displays the best assemblage of sarsen stones in Britain and also shows periglacial features of considerable importance. The sarsen stones support a nationally important lichen flora, which is of outstanding biological interest. Moreover, it is considered one of the best examples of this lichen community in north-west Europe. The sarsens are set within semi-natural grassland and scrub of botanical interest . . . [They] are important in the study of denudation chronology and palaeoenvironmental history of southern England, and for comparative studies in north-west Europe.'

The spirit of that passage, and to a considerable extent its actual words, closely reflect the Experimental Earthwork Committee's thinking.

4 The 1968 Overton excavation (8th year)
by Peter Fowler

4.1 Introduction

The excavation was carried out on time between 26–29 July, 1968 (Fig 4. 1–3), under the direction of Peter Jewell (PAJ) and Peter Fowler (PJF). In practice, however, PAJ was not able to contribute as intended and much of the on-site work, and its consequences, fell unexpectedly on the co-director. On site, PJF was ably helped in particular by Sue Dunstone (full-time recorder) and Elizabeth Fowler who, between them, undertook much of the metrical and graphic recording. Dr Keith Crabtree personally excavated and recorded the ditch. The late Phil Porter, assistant to Professor G W Dimbleby (who was unable to attend), attended to the collection of environmental and other samples.

PJF had, by 1968, over ten years experience of directing archaeological excavations but was something of a novice with regard to experimental earthworks. He had helped in minor ways during the construction of the Overton Down and Wareham Earthworks and had assisted during the Overton Down cuttings of 1962 and 1964. In 1968, therefore, he simply applied the basic methodology that he had observed during those earlier sections. There was a conscious attempt *not* to innovate, and a deliberate attempt to replicate as far as possible the methodology and types of observations previously made (Jewell and Dimbleby 1966). In particular, the method of excavation, including the use of a scaffold framework, was as far as possible exactly that described in Jewell and Dimbleby 1966, 313–14. It was believed that consistency in such things was the key to successful long-term experiment and, to a degree, of itself validated the 'science' of the experiment. The field exercise was arranged in the light of previous experience to take place over one weekend, with the entire team of volunteers assembling on the Friday and departing on the Monday. The assumption that this was appropriate can be seen now to stem as much from attitudes towards this research – 'I can only stay till Sunday evening at latest because I have to be back at work on Monday morning', – as from a serious underestimate of what was actually involved. Naively, nevertheless, the 1968 excavation was planned, and certainly carried out, on the basis of what had been rather than what should now be.

It was an occasion very much organized from and by the Department of Extra-Mural Studies (as it was then called), University of Bristol, where PJF was then based. Most of the assistants on site were extra-mural students, trained by PJF and/or experienced 'diggers'. Outstanding contributions, in excavating and then refilling the cutting over only four days, were made in particular by the Dunstone brothers (Peter and John), the late John Thompson and Stephen Green. While speed should not have been necessary, some of the work was indeed hurried, especially at the end: for the record, 79 objects were three-dimensionally logged during the excavation on the Saturday and Sunday, all the buried materials were removed by Sunday evening, the section drawing was completed on Monday morning, and, absorbing a maximum of 25 man-hours for the task, 7 people neatly refilled the excavation in the afternoon. In all the 'team' numbered 16, with various Committee members, experts and others visiting and sometimes helping. Professor R J C Atkinson, designer of the earthwork, visited on the Sunday morning. Everybody involved on site was a volunteer and no-one was paid, then or later. The cost of hiring the 'hut etc.' was, incidentally, £6 (cf the figures for

Figure 4.1 The Overton Down Earthwork from the north west before excavation, 1968

Figure 4.2 Overton Down, the ditch and berm from the south-east before excavation, 1968

Figure 4.3 Overton Down, north side of the bank from the north-east, on the line of the 1968 excavation

1992, below p 231, neatly exemplifying a 'culture shift' within a generation).

At the end, the site book observes: '2 people need to be on levelling more or less full-time. Four days is the minimum to do the work including time for setting up and dismantling camp. It would probably be worthwhile setting aside a full week for the 16 year section in 1976 since this time, with virtually all the excavation being done on the Saturday and Sunday, it was rather rushed and some things were done inadequately or not at all eg study of worm castings.'

The mistake in not allowing enough time we have consciously sought to avoid on each subsequent occasion, but in both 1976 and 1992 we again failed to get it right (p 231). As the earthwork has 'shrunk', and as the amount and type of data needing to be recorded to ever higher standards have expanded, the amount of time necessary for an apparently simple field exercise has increased out of all proportion to early expectations of the time requirement.

Nevertheless, despite the wisdom of hindsight, in 1968 the on-site logistics, recording, especially of the earthwork itself, and retrieval of buried materials were reasonably well-covered. The 'success' of the exercise as part of a long-term experiment, however, depended very much on the distribution to laboratories and experts of the buried materials for appropriate examination. As previously, this function was the responsibility of Committee member L Biek (Ancient Monuments Laboratory, then in the Ministry of Public Building and Works).

The excavation was geared to recovering all the buried materials by the Sunday. This was duly achieved and they were collected as arranged. Sadly it has to be recorded that that was the last time most of them were seen, either at all or until the late 1970s (p 55) or until 1992 (p 52).

Dr Susan Limbrey, while on the staff of the AM Laboratory and also, in a private capacity, responsible as a Committee member for the 1976 buried materials, tried to find earlier materials in the Laboratory, trace those that might have been distributed, and correlate such reports as had been produced. During the 1980s her successor, both in the AM Laboratory and as 'science co-ordinator' for the Committee, Dr C Keepax, attempted to do likewise, as subsequently did others; but it was only in 1992 that these efforts bore significant fruit (p 52).

The results of Dr Limbrey's efforts were embodied in her original report on the 1976 buried materials which also included, wherever possible, information from 1968 (p 55). However inadequate, some sort of report on the 1968 buried materials has now been sketched together and includes some of Dr Limbrey's data and observations from her 1976 report.

Some of the 1968 buried material has in fact now (1992–3) been retrieved, and is stored with the archive at North Farm. A catalogue of it (by Dr S Hillson) has been prepared. Its recovery is unfortunately too late, however, for adequate assessment and examination to meet the deadline for this Report. It would in any case be pointless now, 25 years after its retrieval, to submit it to most of the routine tests applied in 1964 and 1976. Nevertheless we draw attention to a scientific potential that may exist in a range of materials assembled in 1960, buried for eight years, exposed to air and light in 1968, and then boxed for 24 years before reboxing after identification.

4.2 The bank and berm

Early in July a 'great storm' occurred locally. Some 50mm (2in) of rain fell during the storm and 90mm (3.5in) altogether during the same week. There was, however, no observable gullying on the bank surface as a result of this or, for that matter, of similar weather occurences previously. Albeit a negative observation, it contrasts markedly with experience at the Wareham Earthwork (p 209).

This description works from north-east (right) to south-west (left on Fig 4.4) and, unless otherwise stated, refers to the section face as drawn through Pole VI on the north-west side of the excavated cutting.

The Pole itself, our datum in the vertical as well as horizontal planes, was not actually vertical: it was tilted slightly (c 0.5 degrees) downhill. This in practice resulted in its being out of true by only marginally over half its own diameter, and probably represents a constructional or instrumental error rather than a shift of the bank sufficiently strong to bend a steel tube. It was recorded in 1960 that it had 'proved a difficult and time-consuming task to set them [the tubes] in perfect alignment' (Jewell 1963, 32).

The objects retrieved are dealt with together in Section 6.4 and 6.5 below.

Live fauna, notably beetles, worms, centipedes and pupae, were noted during the excavation; very sparsely in the bank and not at all numerously in the ditch. No specimens were kept, however, and no full record made.

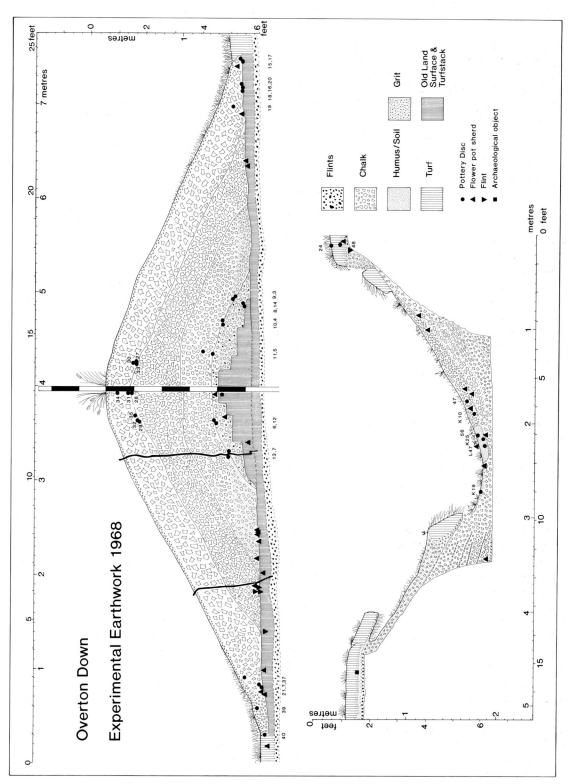

Figure 4.4 Overton Down, excavated section 1968. Bank section right side = north-east, ditch section left side = south-west

The bank: rear and centre

The trench was taken only 0.30m (1ft) beyond the north-east bottom edge of the bank. The original basal corner of outer layers E/F was clearly defined 90mm (4.5in) below the present ground surface outside the back of the earthwork. The material of this post-constructional rise in the level of the present surface was entirely humic/organic ie it contained no chalk material from the bank itself. It was not occasioned, therefore, by an accumulation from above, for example by slippage of material from the back of the bank as has happened at Wareham (p 209); nor did it seem to be the result of faunal perturbation (= hyper-active moles) as observed over the years at the front of the bank (p 32). Either the existing surface layer of 1960 had accumulated from below up against the bank or, as seems more likely, the sheer weight of the bank has pressed its bulk down into, and compressed, what became the buried ground surface on which it was built in July, 1960.

This north-east rear of the bank (Fig 4.3) possessed two other features which were recorded, one floristic, the other physical. On its surface, vegetation stretched 0.89m (2ft 9in) up its lowest portion rising from the junction with the thick grasses of the present surface (the flora included a few thistles, though none was present on the transect represented by the section line). Above that was a band 0.97m (3ft 2in) wide of thin vegetation. There was no vegetation further up ie on the line sectioned. The highest *c* 1.52m (5ft) of the bank, almost exactly its upper half, was bare chalk. This surface was weathered, the original loose-fitting, medium/large chalk lumps having apparently broken down. This superficial appearance was misleading, however, since, here on the northern slope and indeed throughout, break-down was no more than 50mm (2in) thick. Below that, the chalk of layers E/F was unaffected. Nevertheless, a 50mm (2in) thick 'weathered' layer, almost crust-like in texture and consisting of many flakes and slivers of chalk, characterized the rear surface of the bank. The blue/green algae noted in 1964 under the top of the bank were by 1968 much less obvious. One worm was found in the top of the bank.

The original flat shape of the bank top was still clearly present, though the shoulders at its edges were slightly rounded. The top surface of the bank however, was some 0.30m (1ft) lower than its original position (cf drop of 0.16m (6.5in) in 1964 after four years, Jewell and Dimbleby 1966, 319). It had originally been at the intersection of the black and white 0.30m (1ft) divisions about 0.41m (16in) below the tops of the central steel tubes (as shown in Jewell 1963, Fig 16) and it was by 1968 roughly a 0.30m (1ft) division below that along the whole bank length.

This drop was reflected inside the bank. The upper curve of the next layer down, D, which had originally been pointed at its top and was clearly depicted by Criggion basalt roadstone chippings (Jewell 1963, 37), had dropped by some 0.27m (10.5in) at its centre,

despite its appearance of 'clinging' to Pole VI. From there its surface fell away in both directions, gradually for a few centimetres and then more steeply though obviously, since its top was lower and its bases fixed, at a slightly less steep angle than in 1960.

Below D the morphological change was slight. The horizontal top surface at the centre of layer C remained *in situ* complete with its Pyx granite roadstone chippings and its 'shoulders' to north-east and south-west. It had, nevertheless, dropped 0.19m (7.5in) without loosing its shape. For a description of change in its make-up, see below.

Similarly the chalk of layer B piled over the turf stack (see below) had kept its profile without great change. Its central, upper horizontal surface – the interface with the bottom of Layer C – would, however, have been difficult to detect without the blue Penlee chippings placed on top of it, despite what should have been a clear physical and coloura-tion distinction between them (cf Jewell 1963, 34). The top of layer B had, in fact, been affected by weather and working conditions during construction (*op cit*) and, subsequently, layer C itself had become partly discoloured. The distinction between the layers had therefore become less clear-cut.

The surface defined by the chippings had dropped by some 0.20m (8in), about the same as the surface of layer C. Nevertheless, that Layer B had kept its shape, whatever the change in relative levels, was demonstrated by the find-spots of the pottery discs: they were still on, or only fractionally above or below, B's upper surface.

The big visible change was internal rather than morphological. The chalk across the base of Layer C both fore and aft of Pole VI, but not into Layer D, was brown-stained and apparently 'rotting'; the same appearance was present in the immediately con-tiguous chalk of Layer B on either side of the turf stack but only up to a level coincident with its top ie not up to the top of Layer B itself. The colour and, to a certain extent, physical changes appeared to result from the lateral transport of humic material, pre-sumably by worms, out from the turf core into its chalk environs.

The turf stack (Fig 4.5)

The flat top and the three steps on each side of the turf stack were clearly detectable. As excavated, however, the profile to each side of Pole VI was different and the steps in each profile were different from each other. Furthermore, none of the original divisions between the turves was visible, ie no turf lines were apparent to represent what had been thick grass on the tops of the turves when buried. Nor was there a clear-cut distinction between the base of the stack and the ground surface buried beneath it, ie no eight-year-old 'old land surface' was visible to the naked eye.

Figure 4.5   Overton Down, section through the bank, north-west side from the south-west 1968

The front of the bank, and the berm

In general, after only eight years, absolute and relative changes in the physical relationships between bank front, berm, and ditch had become significant and, probably, crucial. Changes in this critical area had been noted early and observed especially carefully; they are reported up to 1964 in Jewell and Dimbleby 1966, 313–24 and especially 318–19.

Of particular interest was the fact that after eight years the angle of the bank front and the inner ditch fill had become not only comparable but in line ie as the angle of the bank front had declined, so had the angle of the ditch fill risen. The latter had become almost an exact projection of the former, broken only by the 'knob', as seen in section, of the remains of the berm. The point is obscured visually on Figure 4.4 by the need to break the section graphically for presentation purposes; but see the smaller-scale profiles on Figure 14.2.

Two vertical plastic tubes had been built into the forward slope of the bank, respectively 0.61m (2ft) and 2.06m (6ft 9in) south-west of Pole VI (Jewell 1963, fig 30, where the caption corrects the graphic inaccuracy). They were intended to measure possible lateral movement at right angles to the long axis of the earthwork. In 1968 the more easterly, longer and inner tube was virtually upright, showing only the slightest of shifts downhill except at its very top which was bent and displaced by c 50mm (2in). At its base, however, the tube had been bent 50mm (2in) southwards too, so the superficial movement was in fact slight. Nevertheless, what the tube showed in its contortions in planes in addition to that of the section was evidence for considerable internal and presumably localized pressures, probably within a slight downhill 'bulk movement.'

The other, shorter, lower and more south westerly plastic tube had very definitely moved downhill. Difficult to explain was that its lowest 0.13m (5in), still firmly fixed into its peg at base, had moved up to 50mm (2in) sideways at the surface of the buried land surface. This observation, and the record of it in the field, was made quite independently of the statement in Jewell and Dimbleby 1966, 319, that 'the base of the outer polythene tube appeared to have moved bodily towards the ditch for a distance of 4 inches. This movement is difficult to explain, even by the action of moles.' Bell also independently recorded the same phenomenon in 1992 (p 73).

This displacement is indeed difficult to explain. What was found could be explained this way. The displacement is extremely unlikely to have occurred

Figure 4.6   Overton Down, north-west section of ditch infill from south east, 1968

during construction. Some lateral movement, soon after construction, has therefore to be postulated. Perhaps this was in the basal bulk of the bank, thereby pushing the tube sideways through the subsoil, rather than in the topsoil itself. That the movement was not long after 1960 was suggested by the observation of the distinctly different, straight-line displacement of the upper length of the tube, seemingly caused by movement with the bulk of the bank in Layers D and E/F. The very top of the tube was sharply bent downhill, indicating considerable surface movement.

That such had indeed occurred had been observed from the early days of the experiment, and specifically in the 1962 and 1964 sections (Jewell and Dimbleby 1966, 319). The toe of Layer E/F was clearly defined in section, both by the marked interface between its medium/large loose chalk lumps and the 'triangle' (in section) of fine fragmented chalk in front of it; and by the cluster of pottery discs (see 6.4.1 below).

On top of this presumably weathered material from the first years of the bank's surface was a slight 'hump' of markedly humic material, interpreted from previous observations as the remains of the line of mole-heaps formed along the base of the bank at the back of the berm. The brief history of this development is well-observed. By September 1962 'grasses were beginning to grow through this recently deposited rubble [from the bank]. A number of mole-hills had also contributed to the accumulation of new material at the tails of the bank . . . '. By July 1964 'the tails of the slope were becoming stabilized by a vigorous growth of grasses, itself doubtless encouraged by the soil deposited there by moles . . . the upper margin of the grass-fringe acted as a barrier to the downwards slip of the superficial layer . . . leading to the formation of a distinct hump . . . ' (Jewell and Dimbleby 1966, 318–19, 340).

Vegetation from the supplemented berm climbed up the foot of the bank's front but only for c 0.61m (2ft). Conversely, some 2.74m (9ft) of exposed bank front, upwards from the vegetation edge to the shoulder of the level top, was bare chalk.

The berm itself, originally 1.22m (4ft) wide, was now 0.61m (2ft) wide at the 1968 ground surface, but

0.41m (1ft 4in) of its inner width was superficially invisible beneath the two deposits just described ie some 0.20m (8in) of berm, by definition from its outer, ditch edge, had disappeared, neatly at an average rate of 25mm (1in) *per annum* (but in practice the ditch edge fell off not as a smooth average trend but in chunks, as shown in Jewell and Dimbleby 1966, Pl. XXIII, nos 2 and 3, respectively looking south-east and north-west).

The remains of the original berm surface, in a similar fashion to the 1960 ground surface at the rear (above p 30), was 76mm (3in) below the surface at the present inner angle between berm and bank; though here the difference was probably due more to post-construction deposition from weathering and animal activity than sinkage.

The 1960 buried land surface (Fig 4.5)

No major morphological changes were observed; essentially the 1960 ground surface preserved its slight, even slope to the south-west. Slight undulations at the rearward junctions with Layers C and D may have been due to the decomposition of different thicknesses of grass or animal activity, but were not thought to be significant. The slight dip in the buried surface at its junction with the very front of Layer E/F was probably the result of humus removal for redeposition above by moles. Otherwise, the buried topsoil was consistently a few inches slimmer compared to its thickness in 1960, but remained a well-sorted humus with a clear, consistent 'B' horizon of flints characteristically 50–75mm (2–3in) above the surface of bedrock chalk.

4.3   The ditch (Fig 4.6)

By 1968 a distinct vegetational pattern was apparent in the ditch. Its inner, south west-facing side was markedly less well-colonized than the opposite, north east-facing side. The latter may well enjoy less direct sunlight but it has its back to the prevailing wind and the bank protects it from the rarer but colder north-easterlies. The ditch infill was in general clearly attracting colonizing plants as well as developing a vegetation cover from and out of the turves fallen from the upper ditch edges. At the time of the excavation, however, ragwort was absent, a relief since its presence along the ditch bottom a year earlier had aroused fears of the 'wrong' sort of colonization (ragwort, *Senecio jacobaea*, is a proscribed plant in England).

At the upper, inner ditch side, the section was dominated by a large turf which had recently fallen the short distance from its original position at the edge of the berm. It lay turf upwards and still alive, at the top of the long slope to the ditch bottom, now pitched at an angle of some 35°. Above it was a 'gap' loosely filled with humus and stained chalk lumps plus a medium-sized flint from the 'B' horizon; below, tufts of grass were growing on the humus 'leaking' out from the bottom of the turf. All the rest of the way down the slope to an earlier turf near the ditch bottom was very thin, sparse scattered vegetation struggling to establish itself in the relatively hostile environment of a still partly unstable but now cementing surface of a matrix of light grey, fine chalk particles.

That chalk fill had accumulated against the back of a turf which had slid all the way down the surface of earlier infill, probably during the winter of 1965–66. That interpretation is made on the basis of the five bands of 'humic stained wedges' containing finer chalk particles (see Crabtree below) representing with a fair degree of certainty the 'summer infills' of the earlier years (represented by broken lines/dots on the section drawing Fig 4.4). If, as seems likely, the turf was in position by the spring of 1966, then the build-up of 0.15–0.23m (6–9in) of scree behind it over some 18 months until our interruption of the process in July, 1968, gives some indication of the order of movement and instability. The turf itself was clearly recognizable as such but was losing both its shape and structure: it was becoming a 'humic feature'. Its upper, outer point was at the lowest point of the ditch infill, a full 0.30m (1ft) further from the inner ditch basal angle than the outer one ie the centre of the fill after 8 years was 0.15m (6in) off-centre outwards from the centre of the ditch bottom as cut.

Immediately south-west, the lower, outer slope was thinly covered with small plants – *Festuca*, plantain and scabious. They were growing on a thin layer of humus which had fallen from the large overhanging turf above and trickled over the chalk infill on the ditch bottom. The turf itself, of the same date or one year later (1967?) than its counterpart on the inner scree, was still in good shape with its vegetation flourishing. The fact that it had tipped meant that it had provided even more of an obstacle to subsequent infill, so a marked layer of fresh, medium-sized rubble had built up behind it, probably in 1.5 years at most. On top of this was thinly-scattered vegetation, of 1968 and, at most, 1967 vintage. This continued back up the slope almost to the top, outer edge of the ditch; but in between, just below the latter and at the top of the infill, was the most active zone of erosion which was still mobile. The large turf shown overhanging this zone on the section (Fig 4.4) was transposed from the other side of the cutting. It was the equivalent of that already described two-thirds of the way down the infill.

A few worms were found in the turf and soil deposits in the ditch bottom. They had presumably travelled down in the turves from the upper ditch edge rather than journeyed down deliberately to occupy the humus of the disintegrating turves. Some may, of course, have fallen accidentally from the same level. One worm, which clearly had propelled itself to the spot, occurred in the outer angle of the ditch bottom where there was no humus.

The profile of the ditch had changed considerably, especially in its upper half. Before excavation, it was noted that the different angles of rest of the slopes of the ditch's inner and outer infills were apparent (the difference is partly obscured on the drawn section, Figure 4.4, by the large turf on the outer slope).

In general, after excavation, it was also apparent in both plan and section that the bottom of the ditch lacked evidence of weathering towards both basal inner and outer angles. This confirmed that the infill in the first winters was sufficiently quick, thick and extensive along the whole ditch (not just on the lines of the 1962 and 1964 cuttings, Jewell and Dimbleby 1966, 314–18) to protect the chalk exposed by the excavation of the ditch bottom. The point was emphasized by the repeated observation that the weathered centre of the ditch bottom had 'lifted' slightly so that the width of the bottom was convex (p 72).

These changes and the infilled material have already been described and discussed in Crabtree's (1971) paper on the 'Geomorphology of the Ditch Section'. Its published Abstract reads:

The ditch section of the Overton Down Experimental Earthwork provides a dated record of the degradation of two free faces with opposing aspects . . . and a record of the geomorphology of the ditch section is given. A detailed description and mechanical analysis of the ditch deposits is given as a basis for a discussion of the processes leading to asymmetrical infilling. The significance of falling turves in breaking the stratigraphy of the deposits is noted.

Crabtree's main points were:

(1) the general appearance of the ditch was very similar to that in 1964.
(2) particle size analysis showed that:
   i) infilling had occurred slightly asymmetrically: overall the south-west facing, inner slope retreated and became shallower in angle more rapidly than the outer one facing north-east.
   ii) particle size differed with aspect: the south-west facing slope, ie the ditch's inner side, in general had the finer material and lower angle of rest
   iii) the rate of accumulation had varied over time
(3) a slight narrowing of the basal width of the ditch might be due to some expansion of the *in situ* chalk following excavation of the ditch
(4) fallen turves prevented normal sequential accumulation down slope from the resting site of the turf
(5) 'The complexity of the stratigraphy after only eight years suggests the need for extensive excavations of archaeological sites if stratigraphy is to plan [sic – play?] a major part in interpretation' (p 244).

Dr Crabtree continues his involvement with the developing geomorphology of the ditch below in Section 5.4 with a full report on his examination of the 1976 (p 39) and 1992 (p 90) excavations.

5 The 1976 Overton excavation (16th year)
by Peter Fowler

5.1 Introduction
by PJF and Gillian Swanton

The excavation (Fig 5.1–2) was carried out on time in fine weather, on 14–19 July, 1976. The advice of 1968 was taken (above p 28) and six days were allowed for the work. This was almost adequate.

Procedures were almost exactly the same as previously, with the all-important development that this time two distinguished environmental archaeologists were on-site as part of the team (shown in action in Fowler 1977, p 73, Pl III.2). In the same book, Pl IV.2, (a) and (b), are two good photographs of the earthwork and its excavation in 1976. As well as examining the buried materials and their contexts *in situ*, Drs Evans and Limbrey were also looking for and at buried floral and faunal evidence as the excavation proceeded. Nevertheless, though excavation involved sampling and indeed removing the entire contexts as well as the buried materials themselves, 'scientific' work was still envisaged as primarily taking place post-excavation in an off-site, permanent laboratory (cf the 1992 on-site laboratory, below p 69).

Though still primitive by the standards of the 1990s, the 1976 exercise was significant in the evolution of the concept and methodology of the experiment. Perhaps rather belatedly, the excavation was executed not only, indeed not even primarily, as a routine, standardized exercise to expose a section and uncover and lift some objects; rather was it now envisaged as a temporary exposure for recording purposes of a series of processes. It was accepted that methodology could not continue to be rigidly applied only as it had existed in the experiment's own history (cf above p 27). It had to adjust to those processes and any changes they had brought about; it had to recognize laboratory requirements as well as those in the field; and, where relevant, it had to adjust to shifts in archaeological and conservation thinking.

Though not perhaps a very scientific thing to say, it also had to adjust to – perhaps 'inevitably reflected' would be more accurate – the greater experience of the director and his team compared to 1968. Several of those involved had worked together, or at least within a familiar 'West Country'/Bristol-Birmingham mode, for a decade or more, bringing insights

Figure 5.1 The Overton Down Earthwork from the north-west before excavation, 1976

Figure 5.2 Overton Down vegetation on inner face of ditch on line of 1976 section

and needs across a range of experiences from the rough demands of multi-period salvage excavation almost invariably on hostile subsoils to the intellectual complexities of early Medieval Somerset. In other words, over and above the different academic perspectives of a decade by 1976 well into the so-called 'New Archaeology', the personal and intellectual 'baggage' brought to the Overton Down Earthwork by those involved in guiding and exploiting the 16th year excavation was very different from the Wessex-centred prehistoric backgrounds of those who set it up in 1960.

Personnel

Compared to 1968, the field team was smaller, with only a dozen, invited and experienced people actually working full-time on site. Some were selected students but most were specialists who dug, rather than mere diggers who were cleared out of the way when a context or artefact required an expert inspection. This arrangement reflected the director's experience at Cadbury Congresbury earlier in the 1970s (Rahtz *et al* 1992). The team also contained a much stronger Committee membership than 1968 when, unexpect-

edly but in practice, PJF had rather been left alone to get on with it. Now, an element of continuity from 1968 and earlier was also a source of strength. PJF directed operations, supported by Professor Peter Jewell (and daughter Vanessa). At the core of the operation were Mike Batt, who had helped in 1968, and Agnes, his wife. Above all, the team was scientifically better informed. Drs Susan Limbrey and John G Evans between them took all responsibility for the buried materials. Phillip Porter again looked after environmental sampling for Professor Dimbleby, and Dr Keith Crabtree again worked in the ditch. Gillian Swanton, by then already Committee Secretary, was one of three full-time recorders with Jenny Britnell and Elizabeth Fowler.

Presumably reflecting this configuration of full-time, skilled specialists, 132 'finds' were recorded three-dimensionally (cf 79 in 1968). The recovery rate was quantitatively much improved, but a qualitatively better record was also generated. In other words, not least in learning from 1968 (above p 28), the longer time allowed for the excavation, the management structure and a skilled crew proved very effective (while rather embarrassingly giving the lie to earlier, misconceived attempts at 'objectivity'). The quality of the record clearly reflects the quality of the resources applied to it, a lesson which was well-learned and to the forefront of the collective Committee mind in planning the next, 32-year excavation (below p 66). Visitors included the earthwork's designer, Professor R J C Atkinson, and his wife, Hester.

Appendix

It is scientifically necessary, however unscientific and painful the memory of the circumstances, to record a modern burial in the earthwork. The director's dog, Barny, a teenaged, pedigree Golden Retriever, was mortally injured when run over on the site by a landrover during the excavation (the pelvis was crushed and the dog had to be put down). No-one could think of a scientific objection to burying a canine corpse in a 'dead' part of the earthwork; and, sentimental though it may be, it seemed appropriate to bury beneath a now scientifically-inert slice of experimental bank a dog which had posed as a puppy for photographs on its top when it stood gleaming and white.

The corpse was laid out in the fully excavated trench, head to the north-east, legs to the south-east, back against Pole VII, on the surface of the chalk subsoil, covered by an old carpet. It is just conceivable that, one day, any remains might be of scientific value. A dog who was a brilliant field archaeologist would appreciate that.

5.2 The bank (Fig 5.3–4)

The bank was now 1.52m (5ft) high, its top having dropped exactly 0.3m (1ft) since its construction in

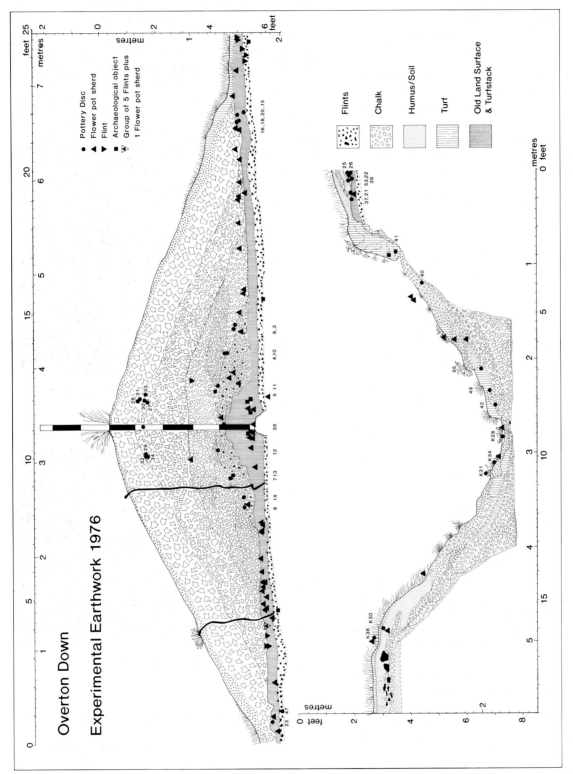

Figure 5.3 Overton Down, excavated section, 1976. Bank section right side = north-east; ditch section left side = south west

1960. Its extent north-east of the central pole was 3.5m (11ft 6in) to a basal angle between its rear slope and the then existing ground surface at a point 77mm (3in) above the 1960 surface. The front slope of the bank met the truncated remains of the berm, still at the 1960 surface level, 3.8m (12ft 6in) south-west and forward of the central pole. The berm itself was 0.3m (1ft) wide at most, its forward edge even on that narrow width sloping downwards into the ditch top.

Internally, the turf stack (Fig 5.5) was still clearly defined in profile (except at its lower level on the north-east where possible animal disturbance had occurred) to a maximum height of some 0.25m (10in), 0.12–0.28m (5–11in) lower than its original height (Jewell 1963, 34). Yet it had not spread laterally: its south-west edge touched the polythene tube on construction (*ibid*) and still did so. Its individual turves had almost completely lost their macro-visual identity. Skilled excavation allowed most to be separated off, however, because it was possible to detect the thin slits which had originally existed between them vertically. It was impossible to lift them as separate turves, however, since each consisted of crumbly soil, apparently much-worked and in any case no longer held together by roots. Furthermore, there was no macroscopically visible remains of the grass on the turves, upright or inverted (Jewell 1963, 34 and fig 20), nor of the grassy 'old land surface' of 1960.

Though there was no trace to the naked eye of the 1960 grass surface buried by the turf stack and then the rest of the bank, the humus beneath that turf line buried then was clearly distinguished from the bank material, forming a sharply differentiated 'buried soil.' Its top was below the 1976 ground level to the rear, as noted above (p 30), probably as the result of compaction from the weight upon it rather than the development of a new surface on upturned soil at the rear basal angle. On the other hand, at its forward end towards the berm and ditch, its surface was much disturbed beneath layer E/F, where animal activity had long been noted. This almost certainly accounts for the interleaving of humic material and chalk in the junction area of former land surface, front bank slope and berm; yet the berm surface was only 20–30mm (an inch or so) higher than the general level of the surface buried beneath the bank.

The 'buried soil' beneath the bank was mostly 0.1–0.14m (4–6in) thick above a clearly defined A/C-horizon characteristically 50–75mm (2–3in) thick. It consisted of small chalk roundels ('split peas') with, most obviously, thickly concentrated flints immediately above the subsoil surface. Many were flakes and most seemed to lie horizontally, forming when exposed in plan what appeared almost like a 'flint pavement'. In other words, a characteristic chalk downland soil profile existed and, apart from a certain amount of compaction, and localized animal activity ascribable to the earthwork's construction here, it had not drastically changed over 16

Figure 5.4 Overton Down, section through the bank from the south-west, 1976

Figure 5.5 Overton Down, the rear of the turf stack, 1976

years; nor would one have expected it to have done so (cf Jewell 1963, 62–63).

The four layers (B, C, D, and E/F) within the bank were still clearly distinguishable. Equally, they had not apparently suffered dramatic change except that all had dropped from their original heights. Layer B had kept its profile overall, as marked by Penlee chippings, though it had shrunk to a maximum height of 0.36m (1ft 2in) at its flat top above the original level of the 1960 ground surface (at the

Figure 5.6   Overton Down, inner plastic tube through front of bank, 1976

bottom of the lowest black interval on the scale of the central post). Its make-up contained a markedly flinty component in its south-west half, over a particularly well-preserved profile of the turf stack.

The flat top of layer C was some 0.25m (10in) lower than its original height, though it did not appear to have spread laterally. Reduction is likely to have come therefore from compaction and, probably more significantly, from slumping following compression of the turf stack. A 'lobe' of what at the time was identified as worm-cast material ie humus grains between, and humic-stained, chalk lumps, appeared in section roughly level with the top of layer B north-east of the central pole (cf p 76 for observations on this point in 1992).

South west of the central pole, three zones of change were defined in the matrix of layer C:

(1) from the old land surface upwards, what appeared like a dump of humic, rounded medium (15–30mm across) chalk rubble
(2) above (1) was clean material with sparse worm-casts
(3) above (2) was a lens of loose rubble with worm-casts (a smaller equivalent of the wormed material, described above, in a comparable situation in relation to layer B which was originally highly humic, Jewell 1963, 34).

The pointed top of layer D, marked by grey-green Criggion chippings (Jewell 1963, 37), was clearly defined and only slightly rounded; but it was some 0.25m (10in) below its original height (which, to give a vivid illustration of the drop, was almost exactly where the top of the bank itself had fallen to by 1976; another way of expressing it is that layer D at its apex had dropped the whole thickness of layer E/F). Yet internally the only sign of change was some cementing of chalk lumps in the north-east facing half: no significant compaction had occurred.

Furthermore, the width of the bank as defined by layer D hardly seemed to have changed: the positions of its outside base angles with the (now) buried ground surface were about the same as originally. Yet some change was indicated, for at each such angle a few chippings lay on the ground surface, suggesting slippage down the bank faces and/or some animal disturbance along the outer edges of the layer (as happened visibly on the bank's outside front edge). Furthermore, the dropping of the highest point of this and other layers, while the outside limits remained more or less stationary, meant that the outer faces of the layers, here notably layer D, became shorter, as well as of a lower pitch (cf Jewell 1963, 38).

Layer E/F had lost its originally sharply-defined flat top, its shoulders having rounded almost certainly as a result of weathering and erosion. The bank-top itself had dropped as much as 0.3m (1ft), so the angles of slope on both sides had obviously become less steep. It was difficult to see clear evidence for downward drift of even surface material, yet a thin 'skin' of finely cemented material had formed on the surface and, sporadically, in the matrix of large to very large chalk blocks and flint nodules from the lowest levels of the ditch (cf Jewell 1963, 37)

Editorial note: a problem in the record came to light in dealing with the measurements of Layer E/F here. Jewell (1963, 38, Fig 31(a) and Table 4) purport to give measurements for each section from the top of each pole; yet these do not square with the positions of each layer as shown, finished, in the published Plates (Jewell 1963, figs 12, 13, 14, 15, 16, 19b, 20, 21 and 22). They all show key detail of layer tops in relation to the scales on the steel posts (and comparable photographs exist in the archive). All the above measurements about layer droppage are, therefore, scaled from the photographs working UP from the base of the lowest black interval at the intersection with the 1960 ground surface. They are not, therefore, precise; and, it must be stressed, as absolute measurements they are not made from the the top of each pole as given in Table 4.

The two polythene tubes in the front slope of the bank indicated considerable internal pressures as well as some forward, downward movement. The inner, longer one (Fig 5.6) remained more or less upright, though with undulations, for much of its length, being only 50mm (2in) out of vertical overall near its top; but the top few centimetres themselves were bent downhill quite markedly, suggesting considerable downward pressure at the surface, presumably by superficial erosion products.

The bottom of the tube was even more dramatic: the top of the nail itself on which the tube was fastened had moved 50mm (2in) south-west, though fortunately the point of the nail remained *in situ*. Nevertheless a violent movement was suggested, perhaps from direct contact with a mole and/or the weakening of the humic matrix of the buried soil through the decay of the root mat. Immediately above the displaced nail-head, the tube itself then twisted round on itself horizontally both along the section line for about 50mm (2in) and also north-west into the section face for some 70mm (2.75in). It behaved similarly in the lens of worm-cast material in layer C already noted (above p 38).

The lower, shorter tube (Fig 5.7) showed less violent perturbations but had moved overall towards the ditch, again with the point of its nail-base remaining *in situ*. Its top end was 0.12m (5in) out of vertical, again showing the sharp downward bend in its last few centimetres. They protruded through a layer of tiny compacted cemented slivers, apparently the same material (the result of the same process of chemical weathering and calcium carbonate deposition?) which occupied the spaces between chalk lumps of Layer E/F in between the two polythene tubes.

The lower tube's top also marked a patch of *Galium* sp. some 0.76m (2ft 6in) above the upper limit of continuous vegetation. This edge was about 99mm (3ft 3in) above the basal angle with the ledge of the remaining berm; the equivalent point on the rear was about 1.22m (4ft) up the slope. The whole of the rest of the bank was bare chalk or sporadically occupied by thin, patchy vegetation. The most vigorous tuft, of *Festuca rubra*, was around the central steel post, a feature all along the top of the earthwork by 1976.

Figure 5.7 Overton Down, outer plastic tube through front of bank, 1976

5.3 The ditch (Figs 5.3, 5.8–9)

The ditch infill was much more complex than in 1968, with some of the detail of eight years previously now fading or disappeared. This was especially so with the annual 'grey wedges' in the basal angles, representing summer deposits, and with the remains of turves which had fallen in, say, the first ten years.

Details of the infill itself are given below in 5.4, and of the distribution of pottery in 6.4.2 and 6.5.2. The significant general point to make about the vegetation on the line of the section is that it was now sparse only on the upper slope of the inner, south-west facing side. Above that was overhanging turf (as shown on the section drawing) or a zone of still active erosion, while below it was patchily vigorous growth, especially on fallen turves, and, on the ditch bottom itself, a more or less continuous cover of such as plantains. In contrast, on the south-east side of the cutting, the section of the inner half of the ditch was quite different. There, the top of the ditch had weathered further back, undercutting the berm right back to the 1961–63 molehills (above, p 32). As a result, and with the presence of disintegrating turves, an almost continuous layer of humus, as much as 0.15m (6in) thick, covered the inner slope of the ditch fill from the inner edge of the berm to the bottom of the ditch, a distance of some 3.35m (11ft).

On the outer ditch side, the top was nearly 0.9m (3ft) out from its original position. A large chunk of turf had flopped on to the top of the infill on the section line. As its disintegration began, humus was being released to trickle down on top of and behind earlier turves in more advanced states of disintegration. With such a relatively large amount of humus present, and flora still growing on the slipped turves, the vegetation across the slope was well-established and was distributed 'thick and continuous' in the words of the original field record.

5.4 Geomorphology of the ditch infill by K Crabtree

The overall morphology of the ditch infill is shown in the context of the whole earthwork in Figure 5.3. Erosion back from the free faces of the ditch itself occurred in the first few years of the experiment (Jewell and Dimbleby 1966; Crabtree 1971). The free

Figure 5.8 Overton Down, north-west section, outer side of ditch fill, from south-east, 1976

Figure 5.9 Overton Down, north-west section, inner side of ditch fill, from south-east, 1976

Table 5.1 Values in cubic feet per foot of section, 1968 and 1976

	1968			1976		
	NE facing	SW facing	Total	NE facing	SW facing	Total
Volume eroded	5.402	4.612	10.014	6.519	5.566	12.085
Volume deposited	7.935	7.671	15.606	9.932	8.098	18.022
Expansion factor	1.469	1.663	1.558	1.523	1.455	1.492

face had been completely consumed by 1968 and only occasional exposures of the free face might have occurred 1968–76, when turves fell in, dragging considerable subsoil and weathered chalk with them. The 1976 section showed an overall increase in the width of the upper part of the ditch. Little change had occurred in the profile of the south-west facing slope, but the north-east facing slope had continued to weather back and the total infill on it had increased.

An earlier comment (Crabtree 1971) about the importance of fallen turves in preventing normal sequential accumulation down slope from the resting site of the turf until overtopped by debris was still relevant in 1976. This phenomenon had resulted in an admixture of organic material, and coarse and fine debris along the length of the infill, creating very real sampling and comparison problems. This should be remembered when considering the particle size data and infilling calculations. The turves also served as a colonization base from which vegetation had spread, in turn affecting the trapping of down-slope moving talus.

Table 5.1 records comparative figures for the volumes of material eroded and deposited per 0.3m (1ft) cross section of ditch margin taken from the cross-profiles on the two sides of the ditch for 1968 and 1976 sections. The figures include turves and organic matter.

The expansion factors are generally lower than those for scree build-up during the first four years (Jewell and Dimbleby 1966, 317). Comminution and compaction since initial deposition resulted in this lower figure, and the change from 1.558 in 1968 to 1.492 in 1976 is regarded as an indication of this change in particle size and packing. By 1976, some debris from the bank construction may have been included in the infill material of the south-west facing slope because erosion back of the top of the ditch's inner side had almost consumed the berm, thereby allowing eroded material from the bank direct access to the ditch. This may lead to some increased infill relative to erosion and so to an apparent increase on that face in the expansion factor in the future. The present asymmetry of the infill may also change.

In situ weathering of the chalk bedrock was clearly visible on the north-east facing side of the ditch. This layer of weathering of the chalk is indicated on Fig 5.3; no similar layer was noted on the opposite face. Swelling of the bedrock surface due to water seepage

and occasional desiccation, plus root penetration and possibly some chemical action, might be responsible for this *in situ* weathering. Its virtual absence from the opposite face may be explained by differing hydrology and micro-climatology, and proximity to (the shelter of) the bank.

Samples similar to, but generally larger than, those taken in 1968 were taken from the infill. Stratification there was not as distinctive as in 1968, probably as a result of two processes. Earthworm activity had led to a much greater mixing in of the organic layers noted in 1968; and water percolation and a decrease in particle size leading to compaction had also increased the mixing of organic and mineral material. This relative lack of stratification made sampling more difficult as clear horizons were not present.

Samples of *c* 2kg in weight were taken from four depths on each of the two sides of the ditch. Samples A–D were taken at base line 1.8m (6ft 9in) along the ditch, and at *c* 0.18m (6in) depths down the profile. Samples E–H were taken at base lines 3.96m (13ft) along the ditch and at similar depths as A–D. Sample J was a single bulk sample from the centre of the ditch. Samples were taken and gently hand-sieved as the 1968 samples had been (Crabtree 1971, 240), using the same mesh sizes to allow comparison with the earlier data sets. The results of these analyses are given in Table 5.2.

Particle size distribution within the infill differed markedly between the two sides of the ditch. The A–D samples showed larger proportions of the coarser-sized fragments (greater than 10mm (⅜in)) than the E–H samples. The upper samples of both profiles show an increasing number of fine-grained particles. This was as expected, since only when the free face was exposed in the first few years was there any supply of coarse blocks. In later years, fine material from the upper soil horizons, plus *in situ* weathering of the chalk debris, led to finer particles in the surface horizons.

Samples taken in 1968 (5 per profile) were not strictly comparable with those in 1976 (4 per profile) so, rather than try to compare individual samples, the results have been blocked up (Table 5.3).

The figures show an increase in finer particles, especially in the north-east facing side infill, and a very marked decrease in the coarser material ie greater than 20mm (¾in). These data indicate both *in situ* comminution of the original infill chalk blocks

Table 5.2 Analysis of size of particles, ditch infill, 1976

	gm	%	Cum. %	gm	%	Cum. %	gm	%	Cum. %
Sample Code		A			B			C	
> 1½″	143.9	7.9	7.9	84.1	3.7	3.7	367.7	16.0	16.0
¾″–1½″	50.6	2.8	10.7	466.6	20.6	24.3	636.4	27.7	43.7
⅜″–¾″	390.8	21.5	32.2	406.6	18.0	42.3	641.8	27.9	71.6
3/16″–⅜″	549.2	30.2	62.4	835.7	37.0	79.3	320.7	14.0	85.6
< 3/16″	683.3	37.6	100	467.9	20.7	100	331.0	14.4	100
Total	1817.8			2260.8			2297.6		
Sample Code		D			E			F	
> 1½″	136.5	6.0	6.0	0	–	–	0	–	–
¾″–1½″	809.8	35.2	41.2	73.2	4.4	4.4	108.5	5.7	5.7
⅜″–¾″	630.1	27.4	68.6	278.0	16.8	21.2	348.0	18.3	24.0
3/16″–⅜″	361.7	15.7	84.3	261.7	15.8	37.0	421.4	22.2	46.2
< 3/16″	361.5	15.7	100	1042.8	63.0	100	1021.4	53.8	100
Total	2299.5			1655.9			1889.2		
Sample Code		G			H			J	
> 1½″	0	–	–	77.7	3.6	3.6	125.2	10.3	10.3
¾″–1½″	127.7	5.2	5.2	182.4	8.5	12.1	90.7	7.4	17.7
⅜″–¾″	435.4	17.7	22.9	583.5	27.3	39.4	349.0	28.6	46.3
3/16″–⅜″	671.6	27.3	50.2	467.5	21.9	61.3	267.1	21.9	68.2
< 3/16″	1229.1	49.9	100.1	824.0	38.6	99.9	386.6	31.7	99.9
Total	2483.8			2135.1			1218.6		

Table 5.3 Gross particle size distribution, ditch infill, 1968 and 1976

	SW facing side				NE facing side			
	1968 A–E		1976 A–D		1968 F–J		1976 E–H	
	g	%	g	%	g	%	g	%
>1½″	774	15.4	731	8.4	1380	21.9	78	1.0
¾″–1½″	995	19.0	1963	22.6	1747	27.7	492	6.0
⅜″–¾″	1119	22.3	2069	23.8	1364	21.7	1645	20.1
3/16″–⅜″	900	17.9	2067	23.8	612	9.7	1822	22.3
<3/16″	1271	25.3	1844	21.3	1197	19.0	4127	50.6

and reduction in supply to only fine material over the eight years 1968–76.

The data should not be over-interpreted in view of the stochastic nature of the infall of turves with their large quantities of fine material attached. Nevertheless, though the decrease in particle size is as expected, its very rapid rate of change seems remarkable.

6 Artefacts and buried materials, 1968 and 1976

by Peter Fowler, Geoffrey Dimbleby and Susan Limbrey

6.1 Introduction

'Finds', as defined in a normal excavation report, have not previously been considered in detail in reports on the Experimental Earthwork Project. Nevertheless, in each section cut through the Overton Down and Morden Bog Earthworks, artefacts have been recovered. We are distinguishing them here from the 'buried materials'.

The latter are objects and materials buried by the Committee with the intention that they should be retrieved. That is, at both Overton and Morden in 1960 and 1963 respectively, materials and objects were buried in known positions along the lines of the pre-planned cuttings (for Overton, see Fig 7.3) so that specific items from known contexts could be retrieved. Other material was scattered around the area of the two earthworks beforehand, mainly to simulate pre-construction activity. This was not precisely located but the hope was that some of it would be retrieved. This has proved to be the case. In addition, particularly at Overton Down where the earthwork lies in the middle of an evolved, much-used relict landscape, excavation of the earthwork has incidentally produced a scatter of pre-1960 archaeological evidence, mainly prehistoric and Roman (Fowler, forthcoming).

Materials from both 1968 and 1976 are dealt with in this chapter. Section 6.5 affords separate treatment for each year to the buried materials from those two years, ie materials deliberately inserted into the earthwork to study for their own intrinsic qualities; while sections 6.2–4 deal with materials involved in the experiment principally as markers in the study of morphological change. The first 'marker' discussed, *Lycopodium* spores, was not, however, an artefact, nor was it meant to simulate human activity; but it is common to both earthworks throughout the experiment.

6.2 *Lycopodium* spores 1968 and 1976 by G W Dimbleby

Lycopodium spores were applied to the original, ie the then-existing, ground surface before the earthwork was built in 1960 in order to simulate deposited pollen (Jewell 1963, 67). The changes in vertical distribution of the spores during the first four years were reported (Jewell and Dimbleby 1966, 335–36), and here the results from 1962 and 1964 are included for comparison in the graphical presentation of the results from 1968 and 1976.

For each sample five microscope slides were counted and the total number of spores recorded for each sample. As previously, the percentages are based on the sum of the totals of all the samples in each series. The three series were also as before, ie:

(1) Beneath Layer A (the turf stack)
(2) Under Layer C (the chalk bank)
(3) Under Layers E/F, at the edge of the bank

The graphs are presented comparatively for each series. As indicated in the 1966 report (Jewell and Dimbleby), there are differences between the three series, herewith discussed separately.

Series 1 (beneath the turf stack)

The 1962 results showed little movement of the spores beneath the turf stack but a strong upward movement was recorded in 1964. Subsequent analyses, however, suggested that this 1964 distribution was anomalous; it is possible that the sampling line struck an earthworm burrow, so giving an exaggerated concentration of spores above the buried surface. Apart from this one aberrant series, the picture is fairly consistent, with high percentages persisting in the surface of the soil (Fig 6.1). There was little downward movement, and hardly more evidence of upward movement. As noted in Jewell and Dimbleby 1966, 338–39, earthworms were certainly active in the turf stack in 1964, but from these data it appeared that significant activity did not extend more than 25mm (1in) above or below the buried land surface. Presumably the earthworms were confining their feeding and casting to this narrow zone.

Series 2 (beneath the chalk bank)

In 1968 and 1976 sampling was extended upwards with samples being taken at 0.15–0.12m (6–5in) and 0.23–0.20m (9–8in) above the original land surface. The trends observed in the first four years had continued, with spores being transported both upwards and downwards (Fig 6.2). The downward movement had not changed markedly and no penetration below 0.15m (6in) was recorded. On the other hand, upward movement had shown a considerable development since 1964. This shows particularly in the 1968 graph, though again this may be an exaggeration due to local conditions at the sampling point. The 1976 curve, however, also shows a noticeable consolidation above the buried land surface as compared with 1964. The conclusion seems inescapable that the earthworms feeding in the humus of the

43

44

SERIES 1 (A)

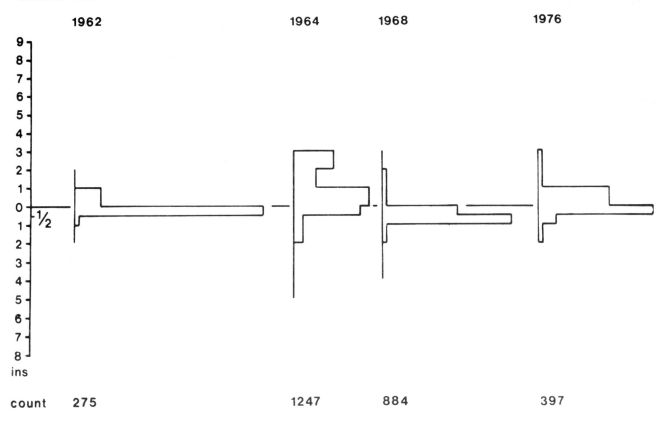

Figure 6.1 *Lycopodium spores, Series 1, 1962–76*

SERIES 2 (C)

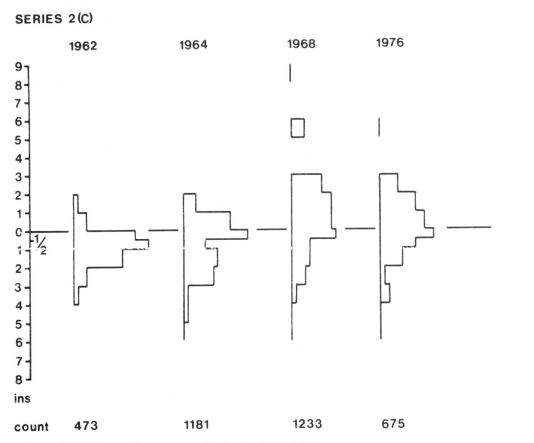

Figure 6.2 *Lycopodium spores, Series 2, 1962–1976*

SERIES 3 (E/F)

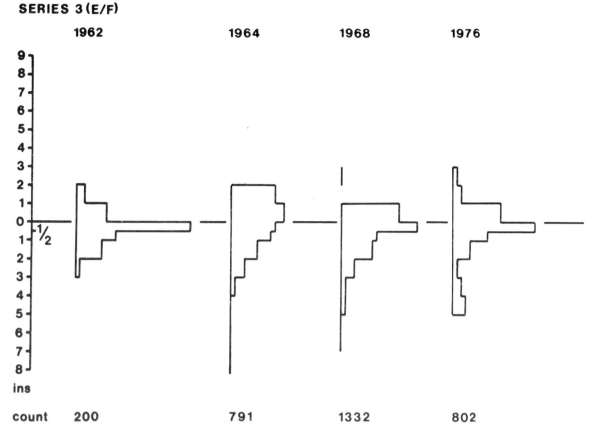

Figure 6.3 Lycopodium spores, Series 3, 1962–1976

'old' land surface were moving upwards and casting in the interstices of the chalk rubble above.

Series 3 (edge of bank)

A little chalk material lay on top of the old land surface at the edge of the bank. It was not, however, possible to sample more than 75mm (3in) above the original surface. This series (Fig 6.3) again showed a marked upward movement, but it is mainly confined to the sample 25–0mm (1–0in), perhaps because above this the influence of the surface of the bank discouraged casting. This presumably would be so if the earthworms concerned were not surface casters.

Downward movement seemed to be more marked in this series than in either of the other two. It is not possible to say how much of this is due to earthworm activity and how much to downwash, but at this point the old land surface was nearest to the bank surface and might therefore be expected to be more strongly influenced by percolating water.

General

The condition of the *Lycopodium* spores remained good after 16 years in an aerated and microbiologically active soil. This observation may have some relevance to the length of time which pollen grains remain recognizable in such a soil. It will be instruc-

tive to see whether there has been any observable deterioration in the condition of the spores by the time of the next section in another 16 years (below p 129).

6.3 Ceramics and their experimental roles in the Overton Down Earthwork

In an attempt to clarify a fairly complex situation, this note spells out the types and purposes of ceramics used in the Overton Down Experimental Earthwork.

The earthwork includes four separate types of ceramic (here numbered 1–4). They are being used in four different experiments (here W–Z). The suite of ceramic complexity can be summarized thus:

Sherd type	Experiment
1: 'Hodges-sherds'	W: to study physical change in the sherds themselves X: chemical change in the sherds themselves
2: flower-pot sherds	Y: to mimic pre-earthwork conditions
3: baked clay roundels	Z: to indicate morphological changes in the earthwork a: numbered b: unnumbered
4: baked clay triangles	Z: to indicate morphological changes in the earthwork

Sherd type 2 was derived from modern flower-pot, broken into sherds which were then scattered across the site before construction began. The other three types, 1, 3 and 4, were specially fabricated in 1959–60 for the purposes of the experiment.

Sherd type 1: The 'Hodges-sherds' were specifically to monitor Experiment W physical, and Experiment X chemical change in the sherds themselves. The sherds which were 'intended to be similar to the fabric of most prehistoric pottery' (Jewell 1963, 49).

A 'number' of these experimental sherds were produced for burial in the earthwork (though Jewell 1963 does not specify their number or location). They were made and apparently buried very much as a sub-experiment by Dr Henry Hodges (then a colleague of Dr Ian Cornwall at the Institute of Archaeology, London University) to 'determine the cause of physical decay' and 'to examine possible chemical alteration to the material'. The Committee has no evidence that Hodges himself subsequently showed any further interest in the experiment, certainly after 1962.

Jewell and Dimbleby (1966, 335), record: 'The sherds recovered [but they do not say where] in the 1962 section showed no detectable chemical or physical change, despite the fact that they were buried in a calcareous medium. Those recovered in 1964 still await examination, but even four years is probably too short a time to produce measurable results.'

Presumably the reference to burial in a 'calcareous medium' means the sherds' locus was in the chalk environment only. This inference is strengthened by their absence from Jewell 1963, fig 25, captioned, 'Placing materials for burial on the turf.' Yet we now have a record in the Archive of 1976 of 'potsherds from upper and lower positions.'

The Archive does not apparently contain any 'Hodges-sherds' retrieved in 1964 or 1968, nor those recorded in Jewell (1963, 49), as 'kept as controls for later examination'. Such are not included in the list of 'Original materials' present in the Archive, July 1992, though we do possess some 1976 sherds. These last have not, however, been examined in terms of the original intention (above).

The two other experiments using ceramics were to monitor change in the earthwork, not change in the baked clays. The sherds were, and are, merely markers, of no intended intrinsic interest as pottery:

Sherd type 2: 'pieces of broken flower-pot [were scattered] over the site' (Jewell 1963, 32), their function explained on p 22–3 as (Experiment Y) 'to characterize "pre-earthwork" conditions' . . . 'broken flower-pot to mimic "pre-earthwork" pottery'

Sherd type 3: baked clay roundels which come in two significantly different forms for the purposes of Experiment Z, 'The placing of pottery pieces' . . . 'in an identical manner in each of the six future trench sections' (Jewell 1963, 40, 42).

Type 3a, the commonest, was numbered before firing, but, in addition, similar unnumbered roundels, type 3b, were placed along the top of the bank (Jewell 1963, 42).

Sherd type 4: baked clay triangles, incised with a letter and a number before firing and then placed specifically on the outside edge of the ditch as another part of Experiment Z.

Figure 24 in Jewell 1963 has the caption: 'Close-up of pottery discs and pieces of flower-pot'. Up to a point, this is correct as far as it goes, covering sherd types 2 and 3a; but since the three roundels shown are all numbered (type 3a), it does not actually show the ceramic range utilized in the experiment. It contains no sherd types 1, 3b or 4.

Only the 'Hodges-sherds' (type 1) are, strictly speaking, 'buried materials' in the sense that the intended experiment concerned changes in the sherds themselves; but the two experiments (W, X) they were meant to carry have so far proved abortive.

The other three ceramic types (2, 3, 4), in contrast, have proved an extremely valuable mechanism in indicating morphological change (experiments Y and Z), the main thrust of the experiment in its founders' minds. Some concern was expressed at an early stage about the amount of disruption being caused to this aspect of the experiment by casual visitors picking up and throwing potsherds around (Jewell and Dimbleby 1966, 337). Clearly this happened, and undoubtedly some sherds did disappear or have been found in potentially misleading situations; but, over the three decades, the threat has reduced to minimal significance. Presumably fewer sherds have been visible on the surface to the casual visitor as the earthwork has settled down after the flurry of activity in its early years; but, more significantly, the sheer number of sherds found in 'correct' or 'theoretically acceptable' positions over five excavations has more than offset the interpretative liabilities of 'lost' ie unrecovered, sherds and a relatively few 'rogue' sherds.

Though the flower-pot sherds (2) and roundels/triangles (3,4) were not supposed to have any intrinsic interest, all those recovered in 1968, 1976 and 1992 are in the Archive (and, unlike many excavations, the exact provenance of each sherd is known).

6.4 Pottery discs, potsherds and flints

This is the first detailed report and consideration of pottery discs placed in the Overton Down Earthwork. Their anticipated role and their careful coding and placing, are reasonably described in Jewell 1963 (though not with sufficient precision to locate precisely the 1960 position of each). Section 6.3 above summarizes all the types of ceramic and their purposes in the Overton Down Earthwork in an attempt to clarify the role of ceramics there overall.

The presence and careful placing of pottery discs was envisaged as a key mechanism in achieving one of the primary objectives of the Project, that is to study morphological change (Jewell 1963, 40–42). While some observations are made, Jewell and

Dimbleby (1966, 340–41) give no systematic account of this part of the experiment up to 1964.

6.4.1 1968 Excavation (Fig 4.4)

The following numbered pottery discs were buried on or in the bank and berm in 1960 along the line of the eight-year cutting. The numbers of all pottery discs intended to be recovered in 1968 were prefaced D, except those on the outside of the ditch, which were prefaced K.

Here, to aid clarity, the numbers of those recovered from the bank/berm are printed in bold; those found in the ditch are starred*.

	Original location
1,2	on top of turf stack
3,4,5,8,10,11	on top of Layer B (rear)
6,7,9,12,13,14	on top Layer B (front)
15,16,17,18,19,20	beneath rear of Layer E/F
21,22,23,**24**,*25*,26:	beneath front of Layer E/F
27,28,29,30,31,32,33,34,35	on centre top, Layer D
36,**37**,38	angle of bank/berm
39,40,*41,42,43,44,45,46,*47	lower front, Layer E/F
48,49,50,51,52,53,54,55,*56	in berm

Comment: 38 out of 56 discs were retrieved, a recovery rate of 68%. Expressed the other way round, however, the implications could be a little alarming from an archaeological point of view: a reasonably competent, very simple excavation to find a known type of virtually indestructible artefact placed in known numbers in known positions failed, only eight years after their burial, to find 32% of them. A one-third 'cultural loss' within a decade might well give food for thought.

The eighteen pottery discs which were not found were numbered (prefaced D) and originally located as follows:

2	from on top of the turf stack
22,23,26	from beneath the front of Layer E/F
36,38	from the angle of the bank and berm
42,43,44,45,46	from on the lower front surface of Layer E/F/
49,50,51,52,53,54,55	from in the berm

How D2 was missed is difficult to understand. All the others, it must be emphasized, were with slight variations positioned in what turned out to be, especially in the first four years, the zone of great animal activity along the front of the bank and its intersection with the berm. One or two might conceivably have been missed in excavation but the great majority of these missing discs were definitely not in the 1968 cutting. Discs 47 and 56 (which were both on the south-east side of the cutting), had both been originally placed in the critical bank front berm zone; and ended up low in the ditch, probably in the 3–7 year time bracket. They probably indicate fairly clearly what happened to their missing partners. Animals, especially moles, disturbed them so that either they were disposed of on one or other side of the cutting or they were exposed on the surface and probably most were dispersed thence through human agency.

Nine pottery discs, K19–27, had been inserted in 1960 into the turf along the outer (south-west) edge of the ditch. Two, *K19 and *K25, were found. K19 was in a 'classic' position for a (simulated) pre-construction phase, though perhaps a little worrying if it really had been, because it could relate to activity very much earlier than the earthwork. It had come down with (after being under cut by erosion of?) chalk rubble from the top of the outer ditch side, probably in the second or third winter. The other, K25, is misleadingly represented in the section drawing since it was not in the turf which had slid down from the berm but about a metre away on the other side of the cutting. It lay in chalk rubble on top of primary, somewhat humic (at that point) infill slightly off-centre, indicating perhaps an asymmetry in the profile of the ditch surface after no more than three or four winters.

Two anomalous discs, K10 and L41, were also found in the infilling of the ditch in 1968; neither should have been there. K10 was one of the group, K10–18, placed in 1960 on the line of Section V, 1964 (see Jewell 1963, 42). In the absence of any detailed consideration of pottery discs in Jewell and Dimbleby 1963, it is not known whether K10 was found in 1964 – it would have been nice to know, if only because it falls to few sherds to be fully recorded twice in different contexts. Whether 1968 was the occasion of its second coming or not, the most likely explanation of its appearance in the 1968 cutting is that it was picked up by a casual visitor, perhaps after the 1964 excavation when it had been missed and left on the surface, and then simply lobbed along the ditch to land by chance on the line of the trench to be dug in 1968 (cf Jewell and Dimbleby 1966, 337).

L41 was the central disc of a line of three, each of which was inserted in 1960 into a slit on the outer edge of the ditch some 9m (28ft) north-west of the 1968 cutting. This line was itself one of fifteen such lines (Jewell 1963, 42 and fig 31(b)). The sherd and its identifier clearly appear on the 1968 field section drawing but no other data are available. Since its place of origin has not yet been excavated, it can only be guessed that it was thrown up on to the modern surface by a burrowing animal, picked up by persons unknown and thrown along the ditch to come to rest where it was found. Such an event is likely to have occurred between 1963 and 1967.

In addition at least three and at most six unnumbered pottery discs placed on the top of the bank would have been included in the width of the excavated trench (Jewell 1963, 42). None was found, with the possible exception of one at the front lower end of E/F, near D21 (see below).

All six pottery discs, D15–20, buried at the rear of the bank were found. Discs D15 and D17 were found as buried; but, assuming the third in the line was D16, the third disc had (been) moved 0.3m (1ft) south-west along the surface to lie close to the inner line of three (Jewell 1963, 40, fig 31 (b)). This seems unlikely, but the original record is unclear about the disposition of the numbers on the discs. It seems safer to infer that the outer trio of discs were nos D15, 17 and 19, with 19 having been displaced backwards and upwards into Layer E/F by animal action. Then nos D16, 18 and 20, which were all found close together in line on the buried surface beneath Layer E/F, can be envisaged as having been the original inner trio. This interpretation involves only one disc (D19) moving, whereas the 'obvious' assumption that the two lines consisted of nos 15, 16 and 17 (outer) and nos 18, 19 20 (inner) requires two (D16 and 19) to have moved.

No other pottery discs were associated with the buried land surface until right at the front of the bank where two lines of three discs were placed in 1960 just behind the leading edge of Layer E/F. These were numbered D21–26.

Only D21 was found *in situ*, though another one with an undecipherable number was close by and probably from the 21–26 sequence.

D24 was on the surface of the berm 0.91m (3ft) from its original position and had clearly been redeposited.

D25 was also not *in situ* but was recovered from the humus of a turf which had slid down the talus of the ditch fill to come to rest in the ditch bottom. It must have been removed from its original position to have begun its journey into the ditch, for the turf in which it rode down was not from under the front edge of Layer E/F in the bank where the disc had been placed.

Discs D22, 23, and 26 were not recovered at all.

Four other pottery discs were, however, recovered at the front of the bank. D37 had been placed with discs 36 and 38 (though we do not know in what order) along the very front edge of the bank, along the line where it formed an angle with the existing ground surface at the inner edge of the berm. D36 and 38 were not found but 37 was up near the top of Layer E/F, 0.15m (6in) back from and 0.20m (8in) higher than its original position. Presumably it had been redeposited as a result of animal activity.

D39 and 40, which were also recovered, were only two of nine discs placed in three rows up the lower slope of the bank above its front edge (another two, D41 and 47, were found in the ditch). Both D39 and 40 were lying at the base of a thin layer of humus on top of fine chalky material at the inner side of the berm. If both materials are correctly interpreted as redepositions, then D39 and 40 can be seen as having

slid down the forward slope of the bank as its outer surface crumbled and began to wash down towards the berm.

D48 was the other disc recovered in the berm area; it was one of nine, D48–56, inserted into the berm after construction of the bank (Jewell 1963, 42; D56 was found in the ditch). Seven of nine discs were not therefore found but D48 was probably *in situ* at the bottom of the trowel-gash in which it was inserted, perhaps subsequently buried a little deeper by the products of animal activity.

6.4.2 1976 Excavation: the numbered pottery discs (Fig 5.3)

All the numbered pottery discs placed in 1960 on the berm and on and in the bank where the 1976 trench was to be were in the series prefixed E. This is an ascription not used unless necessary in the following account. The nine discs placed on the outer edge of the ditch were, however, prefixed K and numbered 28–36.

Though elements in the following account are inevitably interpretative, it seems quite useful (to the writer anyway) for an archaeological eye to be intersecting after only 16 years the post-depositional life history of individual sherds which could theoretically span millennia. Even given all the 'knowns', the monitoring and that short time-span since burial, description, never mind interpretation, is already beset not only with complexity but also uncertainty. Furthermore, observation eg of disintegrating turves and banding in the ditch fills, suggested that the clarity and precision of some of the evidence available after sixteen years was disappearing and unlikely to be available to future investigators. Their interpretation was therefore likely to be less well-informed and inevitably more speculative (though probably innocently so; but that might make it more insidious).

Nevertheless, it was interesting to try to work out in some detail for each sherd in 1976, within local parameters sharply defined by time and space, how it moved from its place of burial to its place of discovery. The interest is, of course, not only in reconstructing the individual ceramic trails as such but in trying to look through them at the mechanics of physical change in the earthwork. Several interpretive options already existed in 1968, certainly by 1976, for most sherds were no longer in their original position. It might well be queried, therefore, what hope for sherds already buried for centuries if not thousands of years when they are excavated? One answer suggested below is that the length of time, in centuries and longer, may not always be the critical factor.

Indeed, at a more general level, there seems to be an implication in these data and interpretations from the eight and sixteen year examinations that, for some sherds at least and those were often the significantly-located ones, the great journey of their life-time was already over. Certainly an impression here is that, without some major, earth-shaking cataclysm such as a volcano or earthquake, a significant proportion of the significant movement leading to redeposition of actual and simulated 'finds' earlier than and contemporary with construction had occurred within the first sixteen years of the earthwork's life. For some, the excitement was probably over in the first decade. These remarks based on observations up to 1976 should be compared with the data and interpretation sixteen years later when 32 years had elapsed (below p 79).

In the ditch

E40, 41, 42: all came from the three rows, made up of nine discs (E39–47), placed on the lower front surface of the bank just above the berm. Rate of recovery: 3 out of 9

E40: recovered from a relatively 'late' layer (?1968–76 and therefore 8–16 years old) of small chalk lumps and chalky soil accumulated against the back of a turf which had slid down from the berm but had become suspended on top of earlier infill. The exact original position of the disc is uncertain but it is likely to have been in the lowest line of three on the bank's front, and therefore most unlikely to have arrived at its position as found without intervention. Its original position, about 0.3m (1ft) up the slope of the bank front above its junction with the berm, is fairly accurately indicated by the find-spot of E37 (see below), almost certainly still *in situ* and one of the three discs along that junction. It is suggested that E40 was upcast by mole activity during the early years of the experiment and moved outwards on to the berm, either by the upcasting process itself or by that plus subsequent erosion moving soil towards the outer edge of the already eroding berm. From there it could have been dragged down by a sliding turf, being deposited en route; or fallen towards or into its position as found during erosion of the soil and/or upper, inner ditch edge following the collapse of the turf (which was probably the third or fourth to slide down on this section of the berm).

E41: almost certainly originally alongside E40 above in the lowest row on the bank front, its position as found strongly supports the last interpretation about E40 ie that it had been moved outwards on to the berm (at a guess through mole activity), become buried and then fallen over the inner ditch edge with the collapse of a turf, coming to rest in the concavity caused by the erosion of the upper ditch side. Had the 1976 excavation not intercepted its journey, it would almost certainly have moved to (though not necessarily finally come to rest in) a position above but stratigraphically similar to that of E40, probably within a few years rather than decades. Its context as found was very transient.

E42: was also right in the bottom of a turf, among the grass roots, but one which had slid into the ditch at a much earlier stage (estimated as within the first five years and probably within the third and fifth years, 1963–5). It was on top of a loosely-packed but fairly homogeneous layer of medium chalk rubble without humus, clearly weathering material from the ditch sides, probably in the second and/or third winters. The disc must therefore, like E41 and 42, have been moved from its original position, probably in the second row up from the bank front above the berm, in order to be in a position to move down with an 'early' turf. Moles are again suggested as the explanation, one which nevertheless requires the disc to have been moved a metre or even more out on to the berm from its original position so that it could glissade so rapidly into a low, near-central position in the ditch infill.

E48, 49 and E55: came from the three rows, made up of nine discs (E48–56), each of which was inserted into a gash made into the berm with a trowel (the depth is therefore likely to have been *c* 0.1m (4in), given that a worn 130mm (5–6in) mason's pointing trowel was very much the archaeologist's basic hand-tool at the time). Recovery rate: 3 out of 9.

E48: despite its precarious position towards the lower end of a turf overhanging the undercut inner ditch edge, this disc is almost certainly in its original position in that turf, ie it was one of the discs inserted in a gash into the berm. If so, then E48 was one of the front row nearest the ditch edge about 1m (1ft 3in) in front of the discs at the bank/berm junction; as it was still about that distance by direct measurement from E37 as found. Vertically, however, it had dropped some 0.2m (8in) from its original position. If its journey had not been intercepted in 1976, it might well have dropped on to the infill surface and conceivably rolled all the way down to the bottom of the ditch to rest by flowerpot [28] (for explanation of this numbering, see below p 50).

E49: almost certainly originally beside E48 in the front row of discs on the berm, appeared to have reached its position as found only 0.23m (9in) from the ditch bottom by coming down with the 'second wave' of turves to descend into the ditch in this particular section. This would accord with E42 (above) having come down with the first turf, one which can be envisaged as from the leading edge of the berm. Its fall would have exposed a new edge just in front of the leading line of discs on the berm (E48–50, as can now be inferred; meaning, if so, that the second line on the berm comprised nos 51–53 and the inner line 54–56, see below).

E55: came from the berm, probably from the row nearest the bank bottom. Although its depth is approximately accurate and its relative position probably correct, its exact location in the horizontal dimension was not recorded ie the disc had been disturbed during excavation before it was spotted; but not, it is believed, seriously.

K28, K30, K31, K34, K36: all five came from the nine discs (K28–36) placed in three rows of three on the outer edge of the ditch. It is inferred that the three nearest the ditch edge were nos 28–30, the middle row nos 31–33, and the back line nos 34–36.

They also were inserted into trowel-gashes and laid horizontally. Recovery 5 out of 9.

K28: with virtual certainty, this disc had been in the front row nearest the outer edge of the ditch, descending to its low, central position in the ditch with the 'second wave' of turves which glissaded over the first ones and the accumulated infill behind them, probably in the fourth to sixth years (1964–66).

K30: was in an overhanging, undercut turf, almost certainly in its original position in that turf. It was, however, a few tens of mm lower relative to that position because its humic matrix was beginning to sag into the undercut below. Despite the inference above about the placing of the discs, the position of E30 would be best explained if it had been in the middle row.

K31: appears to be floating in air only because it occurred in a turf sticking up above the surface of the ditch infill as drawn along the north-west section of the excavation (the disc was 0.30m (1ft) south-east of the section). As one of the secondary, if not tertiary, falls of turf from the outer lip of the ditch, this context would accord with the disc having been placed in the middle row (above).

K34: was on the top of the latest ditch infill and appeared to have been trapped by plantain and other secondary vegetation growing on it. It can only recently have arrived there, probably within the previous five years and possibly much more recently ie it probably fell 11 years or more into the experiment. If it did indeed come from the back row on the outer ditch edge, a large amount of turf (cf position of K36) must have fallen away from the outer edge of the ditch on the south-east side of the trench (the disc was 1.14m (3ft 9in) south-east of the drawn section).

K36: was still, in effect, in its original position in the long grass as one of the three discs forming the back row of three *c* 0.82m (2ft 8in) back from the outer edge of the ditch. It had, however, presumably dropped a few tens of mm. as the ground beneath it had slumped slightly into the undercut of the top of the ditch side.

Flower pot sherds in the ditch
(described from inner side to outer)

Ten flower pot sherds were recovered from the ditch, five from each of its inner and outer halves. They were part of a scatter, strewn on the surface before work began on site in 1960, which was meant to represent contemporary 'occupation' though stratigraphically 'pre-construction'. Their original positions are not known individually, of course, but in that their distribution is throughout in 'secondary' contexts the record of them is satisfactory. On the other hand, despite the Committee's mono-explanatory intention, all the flower pot sherds recorded could theoretically have represented activity at any time before the earthwork's construction, and yet they all found their way into the ditch within sixteen years of that construction.

The sherds were not individually numbered so the number used here in brackets thus [ ] is that of the site excavation register number, preserved in the catalogue in the Archive (see above p 7).

Sherds [12], [14] and [15], which appear to float in mid-air on Fig 5.3, were found towards the south-east side of the cutting in the very top of the ditch fill. They could either have been left behind as a turf skidded or rolled down the scree or, more probably, had slid to their positions fairly recently as erosion of the top of the ditch side continued. This process itself was continuing to erode the underneath of the topsoil on the berm in which the sherds would have been enclosed. If they had remained actually on the surface of the berm, which seems unlikely after all the activity there, they could have course have tipped to their present position as the turf of the berm sagged and then drooped downwards.

Sherd [18] belongs to a slightly earlier phase (one or two years?) of deposition, being in the layer of small chalk rubble on which the above three sherds rested.

Sherd [50] was stratigraphically in a still earlier layer of collapse from the inner ditch side, an accumulation of compact small chalk roundels behind 'secondary' turves and later than discs E42 and 49.

Sherd [28] was in the humus of the (by now squashed) turf which had presumably transported it from the already collapsed edge of the ditch's outer lip into the centre of the infill only 0.12m (4in) above the original ditch bottom. The context is not 'primary' in a strict sense (though it could count as such on a 'real' archaeological site of some antiquity) because its turf lies on chalk rubble which had itself piled up over the top of the first turves, and they themselves appeared to have slid down on top of the rubble infill of the first two or three winters. Nevertheless, this particular flower pot sherd, on the grass surface when the earthwork was built, almost certainly reached its position within six years of that construction.

Sherd [23] (which had been broken – by frost?) was probably deposited about the same time or even a bit earlier – it might have been in the layer over which the turf carrying [28] slid. Sherd [10] was essentially still *in situ* but falling with its turf; and though much higher up, [40] was in a similar situation. [61] lay essentially where it had been dropped, lifted if anything by the growth of the thick grass mat rather than being pulled down into the topsoil by earthworms.

Bank and berm junction

At the junction of the front of the bank and the inner edge of the berm a row of three discs had been placed (E36–38).

E37: found in what appeared to be its original, undisturbed position (probably the middle disc in the row) exactly as depicted in the manual (Jewell 1963, fig 31(b)). If so, its position provides the location of the original front of the bank and inner edge of the berm, indicating that only 76mm (3in) of the original, 1.22m (4ft) wide berm remained at the level of the original (1960) ground surface. The other two discs were not found, presumably because they had been disturbed like the discs above them.

Under the bank twelve pottery discs had originally been placed on the 1960 ground surface before the bank was completed. Layer E/F covered six (E21–26) in two rows of three, parallel with and immediately behind the front edge of the bank; and a similar arrangement of six discs (E15–20) in two rows of three in a similar position at the rear of the bank.

At the front of the bank, of nos E21–26 all were found except 24. E21 was recovered very close to and perhaps even at its original position but an apparent error in the record places some doubt on its depth. Nos 22, 25 and 26 were more or less in the correct positions. Close to them, however, were nos 39, which had moved from the bank's lower outer surface down on to the buried surface beneath the bank, and 53 which had 'jumped' up and inwards from its position on the berm. This last movement was almost certainly the result of mole activity early (first to third years?) in the earthwork's history. E23 was 20 cm (7in) further back under the bank pressed into the surface of the buried surface in an area of (mole?) disturbance.

E47 was even further back and deeper, right at the base of the flint layer characterizing the bottom of the topsoil in this area. This pottery disc had originally been placed on the outside front slope of the bank. Again in the first year or two after construction, it may have slid down to the base of the bank – as marked in 1976 by E37 (see above), then been moved back along through the disturbed area, and eventually been moved further by the upheaval represented in section by the unevenness of the buried surface above it and around disc 23. Its newly created context of 1968 ± eight years was analogous to that of a prehistoric flint blade, [122] in an apparently undisturbed position almost 1m (3ft 3in) further along the buried ground surface, and to that of sherds of Romano-British pottery [116, 132] respectively c 1.20m (4ft) east of the central pole and at the far north east end of the section.

Of the six pottery discs buried under layer E/F at the rear tail of the bank, four were found. Three (E16, 18 and 20) were in disturbed soil but lay close to their original positions where they had formed the inner row, probably better protected than the outer but from which no 20 had been moved outwards. They were now just into rather than on the buried surface (cf. Jewell 1963, 40). Of the outer row, no 15 alone had survived and that just above the flint 'A/C' horizon at a level some 76mm (3in) lower than that at which it had been placed. Clearly there had been some faunal activity along this rear edge of the bank.

An irregular but apparently non-random scatter of flower pot sherds also occurred within the length of the buried soil. Some two dozen occurred beneath the front half of the bank; only four beneath the rear half. Most were a few tens of mm below the buried surface beneath the forward half of the bank, but beneath its rear half about twelve (excluding the four actually in the buried soil) were similarly a few tens of mm above the observed surface. Given the supposedly random nature of the flower pot scatter, the phenomenon here observed for the first time should have some significance. Perhaps active moles drew the sherds down under the front half and active worms cast them up beneath the rear half; but if so, why?

Underneath the central turf stack, where by 1976 no surface to the buried soil was any longer apparent to the naked eye, the level of the surface appeared nevertheless to be indicated fairly clearly by the uppermost potsherds ([115,114, and 96] plus shells [124 and 125]).

Flints under the bank

Flints 71–80 and A8 were buried on the ground surface by layer D of the front (southern) half of the bank. This statement contradicts that in our basic manual (Jewell 1963, 49) where, beneath Table 8, it is stated that 'c/t refers to the ground surface below the chalk of layer E/F on the northern side of the bank.'

The evidence on which the contradiction here is based that flints 72, 76, and 73, and a cluster of 60, 71, 74, 79, 80, and A8, all occurred on, or just in, the surface of the buried soil immediately west of the outer, vertical plastic tube through the lower, front or southern half of the bank (above p 38). There is no such tube through the rear (northern) half of the bank. In any case the position of the flints was exactly that shown in Jewell 1963, Pl. VII, Fig 26.

Of eleven flints supposedly placed beneath E/F but actually beneath layer D, seven (71, 72, 73, 74, 76, 79, 80) were recovered plus flint 60 which should have been placed in the line of the 1968 trench (no wonder we did not find it!). What happened to flints 75, 77 and 78 is unknown: it is surprising and disappointing that we did not recover them. Were they in fact all placed?

The manual also records (Jewell 1963, 49) that flints were 'tucked into the base of the vegetation . . . at six points (1ft [0.3m]) to the north of the bank'; and that in the case of section VII (1976) they were numbered 151–160 and A16. We found A16 (together with 158) about 1m (not 1ft) north of the edge of the bank and at about the right level, but recovered only nos 152, 156 and 158 of the ten supposedly placed much nearer the bank toe. The first two were respectively on and in the flint 'B' horizon. Again, it is disappointing that seven flints should not have been retrieved, though in fact their presence or absence is not crucial to any part of the experiment. No reason for their incorporation in the work is given in Jewell 1963, and they showed no significant change 32 years after burial.

One stray flint, A7, was recorded in the bank,

0.13m (5in) below the flat top of layer C. This context presumably explains why it was not picked up, as it should have been, along with the other flints among the 'buried materials' placed in 'the chalk environment' between layers C and D (Jewell 1963, 49). The flint prefixed 'A' was the one placed slightly apart from the others in each deposit (Jewell 1963, fig 32 and Table 8) and in this case it seems to have become detached in the horizontal dimension from the group of flints numbered 81–90 with which it was, at least presumably, laid out. It may have been displaced when the bulk of layer D was heaped on C or subsequently disturbed by isolated animal activity in the bank; but probably it simply dropped relative to the other flints through localized, differential movement (compaction, collapse?) in the bank material. The fact that it was initially missed shows, incidentally, how carefully the excavators skimmed down to the level of the buried materials and then removed them before proceeding lower.

On the bank, three unnumbered discs were placed on the flat top (layer E/F) (Jewell 1963, fig 31 (b)). None of these was found.

In the bank, nine pottery discs (E27–35) were placed in three rows of three along and to either side of the pointed top of layer D. All nine were recovered. This unusual occurence allows two inferences. The first is that all the discs were placed as stated, implying that elsewhere, where not all are recovered, the explanation lies in disturbance and/or faulty recovery techniques rather than incompetent construction. The second is that here, and by implication elsewhere, no particular order or system was followed in placing the discs in a logical pattern.

Here it is quite clear from the three dimensional record that discs 29, 32 and 34 formed the southerly row and were found more or less as placed, c 0.37m (1ft 2in) apart. On the northern side, disc 33 was in situ, it being deducible that its two companions were one of 30 or 31 in the middle and one of 27 or 28 at the north west end of the row (they were probably 31 and 28). Disc 35 was clearly one of the central row and at its south-east end; its probable companions were 30 and 27 and were certainly one of either 30/31 and 27/28.

Another twelve discs were placed in two rows of six on the surfaces on either side of the bank of earth and flint (layer B) covering the central turf core (Jewell 1963, Pl VI, fig 21). Their numbering was, however, not given, but it was possible to establish what it had been from the recovery of all twelve discs. The result is detailed here for future reference: no-one might recover the full suite of discs again but, in any case, no-one need re-establish again their original disposition.

On the slope facing the ditch, the six discs recovered were numbered E6, 7, 8, 12, 13 and 14, an enumeration betraying a pattern – two groups of three sequential numbers, – and one which quickly fell into shape: two rows north west–south east across the bank, the more northerly 3–8, the other 9–14. In fact it is easy to deduce from the record that

nos 6–8 constituted the south-west end of the row nearer the section, lying in the order 6, 7, 8 from top to lower part of the bank. In fact, the discs were virtually *in situ*.

The more southerly row was clearly likewise 12, 13, 14, the first being *in situ* and nos 13 and 14 being recorded as 'on B/C' although their absolute measurements make them appear to be in layer B in section.

Similarly, on the northerly slope of layer B, the row nearer the section line was 5, 4, 3 from top to bottom, the more southerly row being 11, 10, 9 from top to bottom. All six discs were recorded as lying 'on B/C' and it seems that they had hardly moved at all over sixteen years.

Two pottery discs were originally placed on the flat top of the turf stack at the core of the bank. Both (E1 and 2) were found *in situ* even though the top of the turf stack had dropped by some 0.25m (10in) from its original height (cf Pl II, fig 12, showing the top of the stack about 0.50m (1ft 8in) up the central post, with its 1976 top c 0.26m (10in) above the base of the post).

Flower pot sherds in the bank

The great bulk of the bank contained no artefacts at all but a few potsherds are worth comment. Half a dozen were incorporated in layer B, having been scraped up with the topsoil from the top of the ditch line used to cover the turf stack. There were none in layers C and D, though a few at the base of both in the rear half seemed to have been worked up by faunal action from the buried surface. One [54], on the C/D interface, is a little difficult to explain: perhaps it arrived there with 'tidying up' material as the ditch and/or bank was being trimmed (great play is made of this aspect of construction in Jewell 1963, eg p 36).

The general distribution of potsherds throughout the earthwork is what one might expect from pre-construction debris. Such an observation, however, says nothing here, or in general, about the chronological length of 'pre-construction' or the absolute date when 'pre-' ended. That we can give an answer of sorts in this particular case, by pointing to a small Beaker cemetery adjacent (Fowler 1967, 18–19, 30–31, 32; Fowler 1968, 109) and good documentary evidence for the moment when 'pre-' became 'now' (Jewell 1963), equally says nothing about any theoretical implications of these data or their accompanying observations from the experimental earthwork.

6.5 The buried materials

6.5.1 *The Archive*

The least satisfactory aspect of the Committee's activities has always been the failure adequately to cope with the buried materials. Now, however, stimulated by the 1992 excavation at Overton Down,

NE

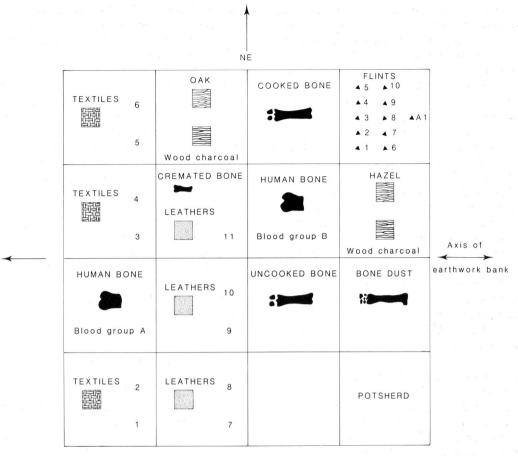

Figure 6.4   *Plan of buried materials in the chalk environment, as found 1976*

as full an archive of and about the buried materials as can reasonably be hoped for exists at North Farm, West Overton, Wiltshire. It includes buried materials from both Overton Down and Wareham Earthworks. The following section refers only to buried materials at Overton Down.

Material from 1960

Among the Archive's contents are the rest of the rawhide left after samples had been taken for burial in July, 1960. There are spare samples of each of the leathers buried. The Archive also includes the remaining wool samples after the specimens for burial had been removed in 1960, plus some spare samples. Spare samples and off-cuts of linen and cotton also exist.

Exhumed material

Chalk and turf environments are the terms used throughout to indicate the two contexts in which material (Fig 1.4 and 1.5) intended for recovery was buried in the bank (cf 'Upper Level (Chalk)' and 'Lower Level (Turf)' in Jewell and Dimbleby 1966, 326). The chalk environment was on top of layer C,

sealed by layer D; the turf environment was on the 1960 ground surface beneath the turf stack (see Jewell 1963, fig 30).The Archive includes material from both contexts. Undated but probably from 1962, for example, are wool samples of both types from both chalk and turf environments; and fibres from wool samples. There is also an undated wool sample from the chalk environment. Probably from 1964 are samples of chalk from which the wool samples in the chalk environment were lifted; the chalk lumps have fragments of wool adhering.

All the wool samples from 1968 exist, though a report on them, if ever made, has not been identified. All the textile samples from 1976 also exist.

Reports of the samples recovered after two and four years (1962 and 1964) are given in Jewell and Dimbleby (1966, 327–29, Tables VI–VIII). For the eight year excavation (1968), a written and photographic field record made at the time of the samples' excavation in the chalk environment is the basis for a report deriving from visual inspection (below) but almost no data exist from the turf environment. Worse, no post-excavation reports are available from 1968 (see above p 28). Post-excavation study of the material recovered after sixteen years (1976) (Fig 6.4) was carried out, however, thoroughly and promptly, by Dr. Susan Limbrey. Her report and discussion follow (below p 55). Some observations,

Figure 6.5   Buried materials in chalk environment, 1968

principally from microphotographs, about 1968 material have been extracted from her report and placed into the section immediately below.

6.5.2   Buried materials 1968

Editorial note: the following section derives from an only slightly-edited transcription of notes in the site-book (made by Sue Dunstone and PJF). The notes were made at the time while looking at the materials as they were exposed in the chalk environment. With them is a 'general note' (here put first) written at the end of the excavation and after removal of the materials. This section also includes some observations by Dr. Susan Limbrey.

Excavation of the buried materials (Figs 6.5–7) was technically careful but conceptually crude and simplistic by the standards of only a decade later. Each object was exposed and then lifted up by itself, whole and entire if possible, for removal from the site by L Biek. Each object was therefore unthinkingly removed from its context, which was simply trowelled away in order to recover the object itself. This after all was the stated purpose of this part of the experiment ie innocently, but unambiguously from the perspective of the 1990s, the methodology of 1968 was that of antiquarianism in environmental archaeology. The need to remove the material in context became only too apparent during the 'eight-year' excavation in 1972 at the Morden Bog Earthwork (Evans and Limbrey 1974).

In the chalk environment, the general level of the buried materials was 1.60m (5ft 4in) below the top of Pole VI. After lifting each object, evidence of earthworm activity could be seen. Darkish worm casts were present under each piece of organic material, whereas they were absent under the flints. Leathers 7, 8 and 9 had left conspicuous dark brown stain marks on the underlying lumps of chalk whereas leathers 10 and 11 had not obviously stained the chalk.

Photographs of the eight year excavation show that wool samples were also recovered from the turf environment, though the two and four year reports indicated no recovery of either from that context (Jewell and Dimbleby 1966, 328, Note (g)). This suggests failure of sample placing in 1960 or of recovery techniques in 1962 and 1964, or greater excavation expertise in 1968.

**Notes on each of the specimens among the buried materials in the chalk environment
(with some notes from the turf environment)**

Textile 1: cotton loomstate plain cloth   Sample was not detected and has apparently completely disappeared. No staining of the chalk was noted.

Textile 2: cotton khaki dyed twill cloth   Top layer partly disintegrated but other layers were well-preserved. Weave clear. Colour: khaki.

Textile 3: woollen contrast cloth   Coarse woven cloth black in colour, well-preserved but easily broken. Photographs of the 1968 excavation show that sample 3 retained areas of well-preserved fabric while in other areas degradation of the white warp threads was in progress
[Turf environment: photographs of the eight-year samples show areas of weave structure well-preserved and areas where white warp threads have been much reduced].

Textile 4: worsted gaberdine   Well-preserved finely woven, khaki colour with patchy discolouration. Top layer begining to disintegrate. Photographs show areas of well-preserved weave structure but also an area of severe damage developing into a hole.
[Turf environment: photographs show area of well-preserved weave structure, but threads appear somewhat thinned. A microphotograph of fibres showed some fibres with scale structure preserved but much surface damage and longitudinal striation].

Textile 5: linen half-bleached   Beginning to disintegrate. Folded layers sticking together. Khaki colour.

Textile 6: linen half-bleached   Similar to 5. Khaki colour, whole folded square still intact.

Leather 7: oak-bark-tanned sole leather   Well-preserved dark green/brown colour. Chalk sticking firmly to surface.

Leather 8: modern extract-tanned sole leather   Well-preserved. Appears swollen. Chalk sticking strongly to surface.

Leather 9: modern upper leather of 'semi-chrome' type   Well-preserved. Dark colour. Appears shrunken.

Figure 6.6 Buried materials in the chalk environment, 1968: cloth and leather

Leather 10: modern heavy upper leather Well-preserved. Reddish/brown colour. Not obviously shrunken.

Leather 11: modern upper leather of 'chrome-retanned' type Well-preserved, dark colour, somewhat shrunken.

Cremated bone Five small pieces 20–30 mm. in length and a few fragments. Bone structure obvious and easily detected.
    Note: the 1968 cremated bone is not yet included in the Archive, though that now contains the 1976 material from both chalk and turf environments (below, p 65).

Cooked bone Scapula – well-preserved

Uncooked bone Well-preserved

Human bone (Blood group A) Bone firm and in good condition; four empty fly pupae cases were beneath it. Polythene bag intact.

Human bone (Blood group AB) Well-preserved; polythene bag intact

Human bone (Blood group B) Well-preserved; polythene bag not found

Bone dust A spread of greyish dust covering a circular area c 0.1m (4in) in diameter was observed but might well have been missed if not being looked for.
    Note: recovery and examination of the 'bone dust' has not been successful. There was no report for 1964 (Jewell and Dimbleby 1966, 335)

Oak Billets appear well-preserved. Wood fragile and partly decayed. The charcoal is firm and apparently little altered.

Hazel Billets (Fig 6.7): in good shape and apparently better preserved than oak. Charcoal well-preserved.

Figure 6.7 Buried materials in the chalk environment, 1968: hazel billets

Note: both the hazel and oak billets were rotted on the underside and intact on the upper side.

Potsherd Lying very near the bone dust, its position may have been shifted when buried. Cracked in excavation, but otherwise hard.

Flints All 11 pieces were readily found with the black unpatinated surfaces still looking extremely fresh.

6.5.3 The buried materials 1976
by Susan Limbrey

Editorial note: the following is academically and scientifically a report by Dr Susan Limbrey, essentially based on her study of the buried materials recovered in 1976. In her report, completed in the early 1980s, she included references wherever possible to, and any information about, buried materials recovered in 1968. As explained elsewhere (p 28), at the time of her work the '1968 buried materials' seemed an almost total write-off so her inclusion of such scraps of information as could be gathered together was very much a salvage operation. That basically still remains the situation but, during preparations for the 1992 excavation and this report, some further information and some of the actual material was recovered. Specific 1968 data in Dr Limbrey's report have therefore been extracted and placed above in section 6.5.2. The editors wish to make it absolutely clear, however, that the following report is to all intents and purposes that of Dr Limbrey whose text, long-prepared, has been respected as far as possible. Editorial additions to her text are in italic in parentheses.

Details of the materials buried in the earthwork are given in Jewell 1963 and reports on the condition of most of them after two and four years burial are given

56

in Jewell and Dimbleby 1966. Reports are not available for any except the leather samples of those recovered after eight years. Some reports are still wanting for the sixteen year samples (*ie when SL was writing* c *1980*), and for these field observations only are included here (*plus, now, some details in italic*). A complete series of reports exists only for the leather samples, and these show the least alteration of any of the materials.

During the (*eight (1968) and*) sixteen year excavation (1976), it became apparent that there had been some initial misplacing and omission of items of the buried materials (in 1960). Furthermore, some failure of recovery at the earlier excavations (1962, 1964) is suspected from the condition of the equivalent samples as found in 1968 and 1976 eg wool samples 3 and 4 not found in 1962/4 were understandably assumed to have degraded completely, yet their equivalents were retrieved in 1968 and 1976 during what was consciously more meticulous excavation (p 35). Clearly 'survival' as recorded is as much a function of excavation technique as actual survival. These factors render the reports even less complete, invalidating some of the conclusions drawn in the earlier report (Jewell and Dimbleby 1966).

The materials are identified here by sample numbers and descriptions as in Jewell 1963, fig 32 (*but the actual disposition of the material as found is shown schematically here in Fig 6.4*). In the discussion which follows, materials buried within the bank are designated *chalk environment* and those beneath the turf stack *turf environment* (cf above p 3).

The materials were buried in environments of potentially high organic activity, with no limitation of soil animal and micro-organism populations by their environment. Degradation could be expected to proceed rapidly except where inhibited by the chemical condition of the samples themselves. The materials were not sterile when buried and would therefore have carried a casual burden of micro-organisms, and probably also small animals such as mites. In the turf of the rendzina soil a very high population and wide species range of organisms would have been available to utilize various components of the materials; in the chalk environment the population would have been lower and more restricted initially, so it would have taken longer for the organisms capable of utilizing the materials to become established. As retrieved during excavation at the height of the 1976 drought, the samples in both turf and chalk environments were moist enough to sustain biological activity, the fine porosity of the chalk retaining moisture very effectively. It is unlikely therefore that dryness has at any time seriously inhibited the degradation of the materials. There was no evidence that anaerobic conditions had become established anywhere in the buried soil or buried materials.

The differing conditions of the various materials as found reflected three factors: firstly, the resistance of their structural components to digestion; secondly, the inhibition of organic attack due to the tanning of leathers and the dyes present in some of the textiles; and thirdly, the lower population of degrading organisms in the chalk environment compared to that of the turf.

Even after sixteen years, animal and micro-organism attack on the leather samples was still strongly inhibited by tannins; little difference was apparent between the various tannins used. No untanned skin was buried in this earthwork (cf Hillson below p 218).

The undyed cotton samples were attacked more rapidly from an early stage than the dyed ones, and had gone completely by 1976. In contrast, the dyed ones retained considerable structure in the chalk environment.

The half-bleached linen had proved more resistant than the undyed cotton, but it was not clear whether the bleaching process inhibits decay by rendering the soluble components less readily assimilable or whether the thicker cellulose of the linen fibres is responsible for longer resistance.

Of the wool samples, the inhibitory effect of the dye was apparent in the better preservation of the dyed weft compared to the undyed warp of the woollen contrast cloth. The worsted cloth had proved less resistant. This may have been, on the one hand, either because its dye was more fugitive, as indicated by its considerable colour changes, or was less concentrated than the black dye of the contrast cloth; or, on the other hand, because the contrast cloth had much thicker thread, the sheer bulk of its material providing protection. The wool fibres are fine in both cases. The folded textiles had themselves provided considerable protection to their inner layers. Furthermore, in the chalk environment, some protection was also provided by the placing of a flat-based chalk block upon each sample (*as noted during excavation, a detail going a little further than Jewell 1963, 43*) before the looser rubble of the bank was heaped up.

Degradation of the textiles begins with loss of soluble components, resulting in weakness and brittleness of cotton and linen fibres and weakness of wool. It is often, though not always, associated with structural changes visible microscopically: transverse cracking and longitudinal striation, the latter eventually developing into fibrillation. Bacterial attack on fibres was detectable; the cells were barely resolvable under light microscope but the mottled appearance their presence produces was associated with loss of material from fibre surfaces. In none of the samples was this mode of attack intense or widespread. The surviving cotton sample and the woollen contrast cloth showed little trace of fungal activity, fungi presumably having been inhibited by the dyes. The worsted sample, however, was affected by fungi, in spite of its perhaps more fugitive and certainly less intense dye, and the linen samples showed considerable fungal colonization.

In the absence of fungal attack, comminution and digestion by soil animals has been the most important mode of degradation of the textiles. Concentrations of mite faecal pellets were associated with areas of loss of weave structure and the breaking of fibres into short lengths. No fibre fragments were detectable in these faecal materials, indicating that the animals had digested the cellulose and keratin. Faecal pellets of larger animals, cylindrical and probably of small worms, occurred in some areas; one large nematode was found.

Members of the Microbiology Department, Birmingham University, took samples from the buried materials and their surroundings during the excavation. Culture of the samples yielded large numbers of identifiable organisms, all common. In the absence of an initial record of the soil and samples' populations, no significance could be attached to this result. Where fungal structures were observed during examination of the fabrics, comments on their nature are included in the reports (below p 59). A number of soil animals, mostly mites, were found during examination but, as with micro-organisms, presence does not necessarily imply responsibility for degradation.

Too few animals were found to account for the amount of faecal material. Those noted could have been present by chance on the materials when buried, might have been passers-by rather than residents at the time of retrieval, or could have been introduced while the samples were being handled in the field or laboratory. Collection of soil animals from the samples at the time of recovery by soil extraction techniques would have been preferable to hunting for them under the microscope after the samples had been dried and stored. The individuals were difficult to find and the smaller ones were only detected if they happened to be present in the very small quantities of fibre or residue used for microscope slide preparation. The problem of resolving the conflicting needs of minimal handling and contamination of the recovered samples on the one hand, and maximum information extraction on the other, is considerable.

Leathers

Visual descriptions are given in Jewell and Dimbleby (1966, 330, Table IX) for the two and four year samples; no visual descriptions are available for the eight year samples (but now see above p 54). Description of the sixteen year samples follows. A report of measured parameters was provided by the British Leather Manufacturers' Association.

Leathers were all buried with their grain surfaces uppermost. In the chalk environment, the upper surfaces as found were partly covered by a wash of fine powdery chalk and had chalk lumps adhering. There was some bending and indentation of the leathers to accommodate plastically to the surroundings. Some chalky wormcasts adhered to the leathers, and, in the cases of samples 7 and 8 but not 9, 10 and 11, the adherent chalk was stained. The colour of 7 and 8 was blotchy, whereas it was uniform and unchanged in 9, 10 and 11. Surfaces of 7, 8 and 9 were matt, 10 and 11 glossy. Lower surfaces had adherent chalk lumps which, on being pulled away, left a chalky deposit. In the cases of 7 and 8, the subjacent chalk was heavily stained and the flesh surface of the leather blotchy in colour. On 8 there was a dark brown deposit over much of the surface, its absence negatively outlining the shape of each chalk lump around its contact area with the leather. Sample 7 had dark brown arthropod faecal material adhering; the leather surface was very dark brown in the centre where the surface was good but had a lighter colour and a roughened texture towards the edges. This was the only part of any sample in which macroscopic structural damage was visible.

In the turf environment all samples had much adherent plant material on both their surfaces, with some corresponding indentation. Colour of all the upper surfaces was uniform, with the gloss retained; the black colour of sample 11 had taken on a blue sheen. Lower surfaces were more variable in colour but without the strong blotching of samples 7 and 8 seen in the chalk environment. There was no visible evidence of tannin staining of adjacent material.

The condition of all the leathers after sixteen years remained remarkably good, and very similar to the condition reported after four years (*and, as observed in the field, after eight years, above p 54*). Measured parameters confirmed this, showing little change.

The soil above and below the leathers in the turf environment showed good preservation of plant material. Below the samples were deposits of faecal material, but since the leathers, apart from sample 7 in the chalk environment, showed no evidence of animal attack the activity must be associated with the soil and its surface vegetation. By providing protection of voids from the normal soil movements which would have amalgamated the frass with the rest of the soil, the leather samples allowed it to persist as a discrete deposit.

Textiles

(*All the textile samples from 1976 exist in the Archive*).

Reports of the samples recovered after two and four years are given in Jewell and Dimbleby (1966, 327–29, Tables VI–VIII). No reports of laboratory examination of the textiles are available for the eight year excavation. Study of the materials recovered after sixteen years was carried out by the author of this report (SL).

Cotton

In the chalk environment no trace was found of sample 1, whereas the other textiles were all still present. Bearing in mind the greater degree of degradation of this undyed cotton compared with the dyed cotton (sample 2) after two and four years, (*and its absence in 1968*), it seemed likely that the sample was placed in the right position in 1960 but had by 1978 lost all recognizable structure. In the turf environment both cotton samples had already disappeared after four years (Jewell and Dimbleby 1966, 327, Note (d)).

58

Figure 6.8   Textile 2 from the chalk environment, inside layers

Wool

Both samples (3 and 4) were recovered from the chalk environment after sixteen years *(as they had been in 1968)*, but only sample 3 from the turf environment. Photographs of the eight year excavation show that wool samples were recovered from the turf environment then, though the two and four year reports indicated no recovery of either from that context (Jewell and Dimbleby 1966, 328, Note (g)). This suggests failure of either sample placing in 1960 or recovery techniques in 1962 and 1964. The early conclusions about the degradation of the wool samples (Jewell and Dimbleby 1966, 325) are therefore invalid *(but now see the 1968 notes above p 54)*.

Linen

Both linen samples (5 and 6) were recovered from the chalk environment after sixteen years (as they had been in 1968) but there was no trace of either in the turf environment (as had been the case after four years, Jewell and Dimbleby 1966, 329).

Examination of the sixteen-year samples was by low magnification to study the whole fabric and by high magnification to study the fibres and associated microscopic features. Each sample initially had six layers, being folded three times. The results were as follows:

Sample 2: cotton, khaki-dyed twill

Chalk environment (Figs 6.8–9)   The upper layer strongly adhered to the chalk block placed on it at the time of burial. The lower layer adhered less strongly to the smaller lumps of chalk below it and was very fragile and fragmentary. Both upper and lower layers were smoothed and whitened by a fine chalk deposition, but beneath this both they and the inner layers retained a uniform, apparently unchanged, khaki colour. Edges and corners were partly destroyed but the last fold was almost complete even in the outer layer. The fabric was brittle, but the weave structure was retained though broken at the edges. In one area partial breakage penetrated all layers.

Soil animals had forced their way between threads and larger animals had burrowed beneath the sample, making grooves in the chalk below. Two kinds of faecal pellet were present; light brown spheroid to ellipsoid and of the order of 20 microns, and larger, cylindrical pellets composed mainly of chalk. The former were scattered throughout the fabric and below it on the chalk, with local concentrations in areas of greatest damage. The larger pellets were scattered on the surfaces of the fabric and in the grooves in the chalk. No fibre residues were detectable in the brown pellets; the larger cylindrical pellets, occasionally entirely brown, contained the smaller brown ones and fungal sclerotia. One small concentration of the larger pellets was very dark and contained fibre fragments.

Figure 6.9   Textile 2 from the chalk environment (a) good preservation of an inner layer (b) flattening of weave and smearing of surface of lower layer

The fibres appeared to be in good condition and showed no fibrillation, but in areas of damage they were broken into short lengths. Breakage at point of stress where warp and weft crossed was apparent, the warp being more broken in some areas than the weft. Most of the damage, however, appeared to be due to consumption of parts of the fibres by the creatures responsible for the small faecal pellets. In areas of pellet concentration parts of the threads were missing and a scatter of short lengths of fibre occurred. Of the animals possibly responsible, only part of the leg of a mite was found.

No trace of fungal mycelium was found, suggesting persistence of fungal inhibition by the dye; but black ellipsoidal bodies, about 10–12 microns in diameter, were present. These may be fungal sclerotia, their presence suggesting that after transient fungal attack, supported by soluble components, mycelium had been consumed by the soil animals.

Sample 3: woollen contrast cloth

Chalk environment (Figs 6.10–6.11)   The upper layer adhered weakly to the chalk block placed on the sample in 1960. Edges of the sample were frayed and incomplete. Some areas of the upper and lower layers retained complete weave structure; inner

layers and the rest of the outer ones showed white warp threads, stained violet, reduced to a few threads, or completely gone. Black weft threads were much better preserved and, except at the edges, the layers could be separated. Threads had little or no strength and were much broken. Preservation tended to be somewhat better in areas in direct contact with the chalk. The chalk was stained violet where it was in contact with the fabric, with much fragmentary fibre and black faecal deposits scattered on it. Several mites were found on the fabric.

Microscopically, white warp fibres showed variable degrees of preserved scale structure; it was distinct and fresh-looking in some areas, non-existent in others. There was much evidence of longitudinal striation and fibrillation, and some loss of material from fibre surfaces. Black weft fibres had some surface damage but their scale structure was well-preserved in many cases, with less evidence of longitudinal striation and fibrillation than the warp. Brown faecal pellets occurred, with concentrations in areas of greatest damage. Traces of fine white mycelium were observed.

Turf environment   The edges of the sample were very severely damaged. The centre was strongly compacted and adhering to the soil above and below it. The layers could only be separated with difficulty.

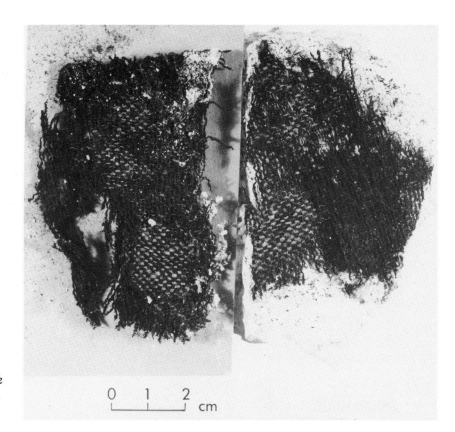

Figure 6.10 Textile 3 from the chalk
environment, upper layer lifted from
the chalk block and adhering to it

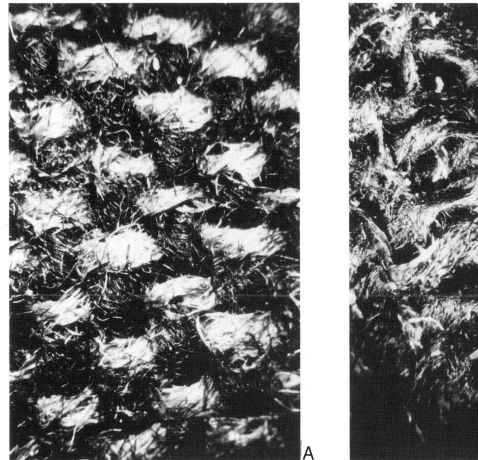

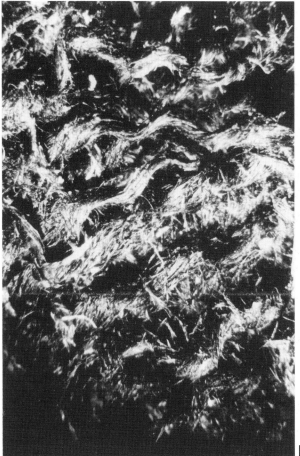

Figure 6.11 Textile 3 from the chalk environment (a) good preservation of an inner layer (b) white threads
almost gone in lower layer

White warp threads had either gone altogether or were reduced to thin, brown-stained traces of a few fibres, with no continuity between weave intersections. Black weft threads were much better preserved, retaining coherence and continuity with distinct fibres, but they were somewhat compacted with little or no strength.

Microscopically, warp fibres showed almost no scale structure, considerable longitudinal striation and some fibrillation; much faecal material was associated with them. Some weft fibres retained scale structure but others had lost it; they showed incipient longitudinal striation and frequent transverse cracking, but little fibrillation. They had much less faecal material associated with them than did the warp threads.

Traces of fungal mycelium were present in some areas. A number of large yellow masses of small ovid spores were found.

Sample 4: worsted gaberdine twill

Chalk environment (Figs 6.12–6.13) The edges were frayed and partly congealed, but most of the sample area was preserved, with the first fold preserved on

Figure 6.12 Textile 4 from the chalk environment, an inner layer

Figure 6.13 Textile 4 from the chalk environment (a) good preservation of an inner layer (b) thinning of threads in lower layer

0   1   2   cm

Figure 6.14   Textile 5 from the chalk environment, inside layer

the inner layers. A large hole, however, occupying about 30mm (1¼in), went through all layers. Colour of the fabric was variable, dark pink to fawn and olive green, with a stronger purple colour around the hole. White mycelium was visible on the under-surface at excavation.

Away from the edges of the hole the layers were separate. The upper layer was fragmentary, remaining only as a fragile web in places; it was only preserved with weave structure entire where it adhered to the chalk block placed on the sample at burial. The lower layer had large areas missing; the weave structure was represented only by sparse remaining fibres and thinned threads. Inner layers were entire apart from the hole, but have very little strength. Faecal material was scattered around damaged areas of the edges and the edges of the hole, and the adjacent chalk has much faecal material on it.

Microscopically, the fibres showed scale structure clearly, even in damaged areas, but in those area the fibres tended to be stuck together with masses of faecal material. Fibrillation and areas of longitudinal striation existed on the fibres. Two collembola were found, and scattered parts of other arthropods, probably mites.

Turf environment   No sample was recovered after sixteen years. The absence of both wool samples after four years in the turf environment suggests failure in placing the samples or in sample recovery; though the comment on sample 4 in the turf environment after two years – that it was so badly degraded that warp and weft could not be distinguished (Jewell and

Dimbleby 1966, 328) – in contrast to the photograph after eight years (above p 54), suggests there may be some variability in conditions at different points in the earthwork.

Sample 5: Half-bleached linen

Chalk environment (Figs 6.14–6.15)   The upper layer adhered to the chalk block placed on it; the lower layer adhered to the underlying chalk lumps over most of its surface. These outer layers, where preserved, adhered to the next ones in, and these latter to the inner layers, the layers only being separable in small areas, but there was no adhesion between the innermost layers themselves (*a description which, quite independently, is similar to that of 1968, above p 54*).

Much of the weave structure was gone from from the outer layers, all trace being missing in some areas, other areas were congealed into a brown mass with much black mildew present. The second layer in had weave structure preserved over most of the area. The innermost layers were entire, except for some loss of material at one corner and damage to parts of the edges, and an area of the interior where the threads are thinned, some broken, and a small area is brown and congealed. The underlying chalk had much black powdery material on it and the chalk block on top was similarly affected.

The brown congealed areas had very brittle threads which broke into a powder if disturbed. In these areas two stages of degradation were observed:

Figure 6.15 Textile 5 from the chalk environment (a) good preservation of an inner layer (b) thinned and congealed threads, brown discoloured part of an inner layer

first, thinnning of threads and the appearance of a layer of brown amorphous material obscuring the fibres; then, second, collapse of the threads so that remaining fibres appeared as a mass of short lengths in a powdery brown matrix with some dark brown mycelium and ovoid spores. In areas where weave structure was well-preserved, fibres showed much transverse cracking and longitudinal striation; there was some brown mycelium and occasional spores. In the congealed areas the remaining short fibre lengths were ragged and striated. The cast skin of a large nematode was found.

Sample 6: Half-bleached linen

Chalk environment (Figs 6.16–6.17) The sample was greatly compacted and thinned; it became very stiff on drying. Only in areas where threads were best preserved could the layers be separated, but the fibres were too brittle for the layers to be pulled apart even there. Large areas were congealed. Natural colour was retained in some areas, others being darkened, and part of the surface was obscured by black mildew. Some small areas where the weave structure had entirely gone occurred in the middle of

the sample, and parts of the edges had disintegrated. The lighter coloured congealed area showed disorganized fibre lengths; holes passed through the mass and there was a scatter of black spores and mycelium. In the darker congealed areas were more fungal structures, including sporulating mildew. There was much less brown amorphous material, of faecal origins, than in sample 5, except where weave structure had failed and a hole appeared. Holes of soil animals passed through the weave structure, rounding out the apertures between the thinned threads, and also passed through the congealed areas. A mite was found.

Areas retaining weave structure showed fibres entire, some with transverse cracking and longitudinal striation, others fibrillated. The brown amorphous material contained fibre lengths; parts of arthropods were present.

Wood billets

Field descriptions only were available for the sixteen-year samples, specialist study being in hand (*at the time of SL's report; but no report has since been forthcoming*). It was clear that the specific gravity

64

Figure 6.16 Textile 6 from the chalk environment, lower surface

determinations carried out previously were inappropriate to the present condition of the samples.

In the chalk environment the uncharred oak was entire but weak; of the charred oak only the charred surface and some partly charred adjacent material remains, as a hollow shell. The uncharred interior was completely missing, with a few worm casts in the void. The hazel billets were both entire except for some hollowing in the ends, with a deposit of faecal material indicating that arthropods had begun to eat them away. The surface of the uncharred hazel was fragile. (*Since it might seem unlikely that hazel was better preserved than oak, the point has been checked as carefully as possible. The same observation was made in 1968, above p 55, and it is also correct for 1976*).

In the turf environment the charred oak was entire except for the ends of the billet where parts of the charred surface had gone; the interior was beginning to be eaten away. Part of the surface of the uncharred oak was entire but elsewhere the segments between the rays had been attacked leaving the rays protruding. A black fungal deposit was observed on the surface. The vegetation above and below the sample was notably well-preserved.

The hazel billet was preserved only as the charred surface and immediately adjacent wood; the charred ends had gone and the interior had been reduced to a reddish brown faecal deposit. A mole hole passed right through the billet across its length and the space was filled with worm-cast soil. Of the uncharred hazel only faecal residues remained.

Bone

From the sixteen-year excavation only field descriptions and a record of superficial macroscopic examination are available. All bones were entire, with some staining and variation in residual adherence of epiphyses.

In the chalk environment the cooked bone had its epiphyses detached and there were traces of faecal deposits on the epiphyseal surfaces. Variable dark staining was concentrated in area of high nutrient supply at the diaphysis ends and there was some pink staining. A blow-fly puparium was present on the surface of the bone as exposed *in situ*.

Uncooked bone was from a more mature animal and had fused epiphyses; there was less dark

Figure 6.17 Textile 6 from the chalk environment (a) surface of lower layer flattened and smeared plus mildew (b) an area of the same surface where weave is almost obliterated, with penetration by animal holes

staining. It is likely that the difference in staining was due to the lack of high nutrient supply to the mature bone rather than to the variable of cooked or uncooked.

In the turf environment cooked bone had epiphyses fused and the entire bone was uniform in colour. Uncooked bone had epiphyses detached. The epiphyseal surface of the proximal end of the diaphysis had a hole through to the marrow cavity. The distal end had a black deposit on epiphyseal surfaces. Some fungal material was observed on retrieval *in situ*.

It should be noted for future reference that the human bone samples were buried in 1960 with paper labels attached by thin iron wire.The labels were folded in polythene. (*This fact is not recorded in Jewell 1963, 47, though it is hinted at graphically in the photograph, fig 25. Observations on the state of the bone accoutrements in 1968 occur above, p 55*).

The wire had rusted (*in 1976*), leaving stains on the bone. In future excavations when the wire has rusted completely away the cause of the stains may not be

apparent. The paper had become very fragile and the writing barely legible, while the polythene remained apparently unaltered.

Cremated bone

(*The 1976 material from chalk and turf environments is in the Archive*).

In the chalk environment the bone remained clean and retained its integrity. In the turf environment the outer table was slightly stained and the interstices of the cancellar bone were partly filled with soil. In the absence of an initial record of strength, porosity and specific gravity, it was not considered relevant to make these determinations on the recovered samples.

Fired clay ('Potsherd')

The samples are retained for future comparison.

7 Overton Down 1992 excavations (32nd year)

by Martin Bell

7.1 Introduction

A generation after the project's inception it was obviously necessary to re-evaluate its progress and its relationship to the changing research emphases within archaeology. During that period archaeological science had come of age. No longer did it depend mainly on the goodwill of people in other disciplines; archaeological science appointments had become widespread in universities and a whole series of research directions and techniques had developed which could not be foreseen in the late 1950s when the project was initiated. The question had to be asked: was it still relevant? If so, which aspects were particularly relevant and which less so than in 1960? The original conception demanded that the project be continued in a way faithful to its original design. The earlier excavations had also thrown up problems and weakness which needed to be resolved. These were identified by Evans and Limbrey (1974) and Hillson (p 224) with specific reference to the Wareham Earthwork and by Fowler (1989) in reviewing the first 30 years of the project as a whole. Needless to say, the main problem had been one of continuity; one or two of those involved have died, many have retired, still more had changed jobs and /or research interests. These difficulties had particularly affected work on the buried materials which it was generally acknowledged had been the least successful aspect of the project (Fowler 1989). It was unfortunate that this should have happened because, in parallel with the timescale of the project, conservation and material science were developing into their own distinctive and successful branches of archaeology. With hindsight we can now see that it is unfortunate that the Committee did not build on this development by recruiting material scientists as active members of the project. By the planning stage of the 1992 excavation it was appreciated that some of the changes to buried materials could be very rapid and that it was important therefore to avoid delays in getting materials analyzed. It was also important to record buried materials on excavation and an on-site laboratory was necessary for more detailed immediate recording and photography. The project was fortunate in recruiting Rob Janaway as conservationist; he took responsibility for recording and, as far as possible, stabilizing the materials following excavation.

7.2 Research design

In putting together the research design for the 32 year excavation the Committee was also anxious to build in additional objectives and studies reflecting the technical developments and changing research agenda of the subject since the late 1950s. This would be done where it was possible for additional proposals to supplement rather than eclipse the originally defined research objectives. Three main areas were defined where the project could be significantly enhanced. The first was in terms of much more detailed investigation of the buried materials by making use of recent developments in Scanning Electron Microscopy to study changes to them. Secondly it was appreciated that examination of the surface changes to the buried materials needed to be supplemented by microbiological investigation of the organisms present. The potential of this aspect had been highlighted by Dr Susan Limbrey's work (p 57) on the 1976 buried materials. Thirdly the development of archaeological soil science now made the earthwork a very valuable analogue for the investigation of changes in buried soils, both from the point of view of chemical changes and those changes which can be examined in thin section using micromorphology. That technique had, in recent years, developed into the main research technique of the geoarchaeologist. Some limited micromorphological investigation had been carried out on samples from the Wareham 1980 excavation (Macphail p 214); Overton 1992 provided the opportunity for a larger experimentally based study.

Changes in government policy meant that it was no longer possible to rely on voluntary work by government funded research laboratories. In any case it was clear from problems encountered with publication of previous excavations that prompt publication simply could not be guaranteed without adequate funding for laboratory assistance, materials etc. Thankfully the Committee was successful in obtaining funding for the 1992 stage of the project (see acknowledgements p xxii).

One of the main successes of the project in its early days was its coherence. Many of those involved were also collaborating on a range of other projects and in a way the earthworks developed as a laboratory for investigation of some of the research issues that arose. In planning the 1992 excavation the intention was to try to redevelop that early strength. We wanted to avoid the view, still entrenched in archaeology, of the 'specialist' as an outside provider of information to archaeology. What was important was to develop a team approach with a two way flow of information which would maximize opportunities for cross fertilization. One way of achieving this was by involving as many of the specialists as possible in the excavation. This would mean that people had first hand knowledge about the contexts sampled, the

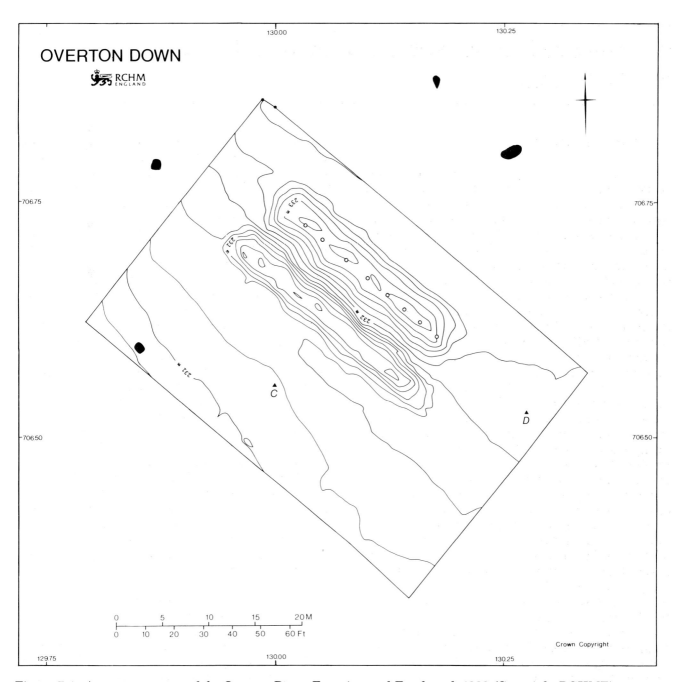

Figure 7.1 A contour survey of the Overton Down Experimental Earthwork 1992 (Copyright RCHME)

opportunity to consider research problems in the field and could begin developing a dialogue with other specialists working on cognate aspects. The proposal was to follow the excavation with a seminar exactly a year after the excavation to discuss progress and problems and help to maintain post-excavation momentum.

7.3 Methodology

The methods to be followed were laid down in outline in the handbook (Jewell 1963). The earthwork had originally been designed and built in the imperial measurement system of feet and inches (Jewell 1963). That system had been used in all the excavations up to and including the Overton 1968 and 1976

excavations (Chapters 4 and 5) and indeed Wareham 1980 (Chapter 12). The decision was made to conduct the 1992 Overton excavation using the metric system. It was decided that imperial measurements were no longer feasible in 1992 because of the scarcity of imperial equipment and the lack of familarity with the old system.

A preliminary survey of the earthwork (Fig 7.1), showing its degraded form after 32 years had been prepared and is described as follows:-

The contour survey
by Hazel Riley

The contour survey was carried out by the Royal Commission on the Historical Monuments of Eng-

Figure 7.2   Overton Down Experimental Earthwork showing the 1992 excavation

land, Salisbury office in June 1992. The area inside the perimeter fence of the earthwork was gridded out and points were surveyed at 2m intervals; the grid interval was decreased on the very steep sides of the bank and ditch. Reference was made to the survey points C and D established in 1960 (Jewell 1963, Fig 10). The data were collected via a Wild TC 1600 total station electronic theodolite and processed using the Commission's Mathshop software. The co-ordinate and height data were then processed by LMT's Digital Ground Modelling software to produce the contour diagram shown as Figure 7.1. Assistance from Nicola Smith with the fieldwork is acknowledged and Deborah Cunliffe produced the illustration.

Excavation

The excavation took place over a period of ten days between 4 July and 13 July 1992 with a team of 15 people and a varying number of specialists participating. The trench was opened up at a point 22.85m (75 feet) from the west end of the earthwork. The west edge of the trench was marked by the metal pole VIII. The location of the trench (Fig 7.2) and its relationship to the earlier earthwork excavations is shown in Figure 7.3. The trench was 15m long and 1.5m wide; it ran for 5m north of the axial line of posts

in the bank and 10m south. As previously, a scaffolding framework (Fig 7.4) was erected. This served a number of purposes. In previous years it had been devised to support planking and minimize damage when the earthwork was still in a very fragile state. Precisely located scaffolding poles also had tapes along them and provided a framework for three-dimensional recording. Also in 1992 the scaffolding provided the framework for a makeshift polythene shelter. This was important in allowing work to continue on the buried materials during rain but proved inadequate to cope with the worst weather encountered (p 85). A scaffolding framework had been employed at Overton from the time of the first bank excavation (Jewell and Dimbleby 1966; above p 27) and its value as a recording framework makes it surprising that this useful idea has not been more widely employed in the cutting of archaeological sections.

The trench was excavated entirely using trowels, hand shovels and buckets with more delicate instruments as appropriate. Spoil was temporarily dumped on corrugated iron sheeting in the north-east corner of the enclosure. At the end of the excavation the spoil was put back as closely as possible to the pre-excavation profile. As much as possible of the turf was used to prevent an accelerated erosion to the ditch and the adjacent south face of the bank. There was therefore insufficient turf to cover the lower part of the bank

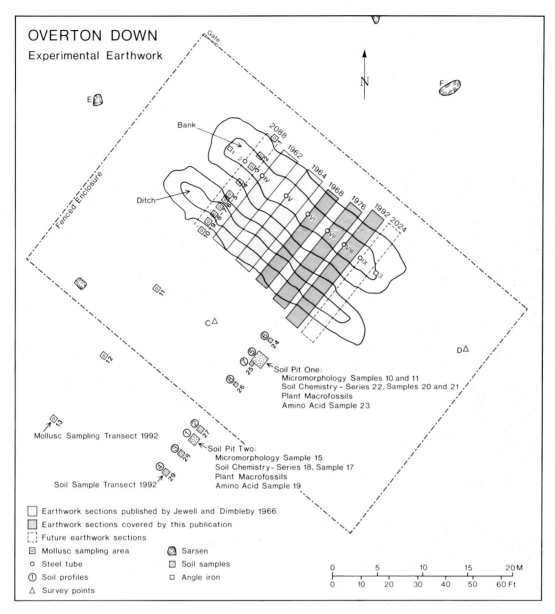

Figure 7.3 Location of the excavated sections across the Overton Down Experimental Earthwork, including the 1992 section and those proposed for 2024 and 2088

at the north end of the trench. However, it has remained stable and by 1993 was becoming colonized by vegetation.

Sieving

The sediment was dry sieved from a 0.50m wide strip on the west side of the trench, thus sampling one third of the trench. The sieve size used was 11mm (or 6mm where necessary). The sieving of 4048 litres of sediment (*c* 270 buckets) produced only two 'finds': one pottery disc H47 from the ditch, and a fragment of burnt bone, not thought to be part of the experiment and probably originating from the subsoil. The results indicate a recovery rate of around 96% for hand excavation. The sieving programme also showed that earthworms were present throughout the earthwork. The average ratio was 1 to every 18.4

litres of soil. In the upper part of the bank this ratio was fairly constant at 1 worm to every 10–20 litres. In the lower part of the bank there was more variability, with some stages in the excavation producing one worm to say 50 or more litres, others having one worm to about 10 litres. The sieving also demonstrated that fine root matter was present throughout the sediments of the bank and ditch; thus the whole monument can be seen as biologically active in terms of plant growth and fauna.

Laboratory facilities

To facilitate prompt examination of buried materials, etc immediately following excavation, a temporary field laboratory was set up at North Farm, West Overton, the home of Gillian Swanton, the Committee's Secretary. The laboratory was 2.4km from the

Figure 7.4 The final section though the Overton Earthwork in 1992 showing the ditch sediments and buried soil, and the scaffolding framework used for recording

site but with a mobile telephone and regular landrover communication this did not present problems. The laboratory was equipped with binocular microscopes including a Wild M5 enabling magnification up to 500 times and also facilitating microscopic photography. There were also computing facilities, a Macintosh Classic and Amstrad 1512, as well as facilities for basic conservation and recording.

7.4 Changes to the ditch

The 1992 section through the earthwork is shown in Figures 7.4–6. The weathered profile of the ditch has, with time, become noticeably asymmetrical. The north-east facing side has weathered back some 0.80m and is therefore less steep than the south-west facing side which has weathered back 0.60m. This probably relates to the greater susceptibility of the north-east facing side to frost weathering at a time when a free chalk face was exposed. The ditch and bank were originally separated by a berm 1.4m (4ft) wide which has proved sufficient to ensure that the bank and ditch developed almost independently of

one another. Weathering back of the ditch, and a slight spreading of the bank, has now reduced the berm to little more than a slight break of slope (Fowler p 31 and 37).

By the time of the 1992 section the ditch had been stabilized by vegetation for at least a decade. Photographs in the archive taken in 1976 are the first to show largely continuous vegetation cover with only localized erosion. By 1984 vegetation colonization was complete except for localized 'weeping' scars at the edge of the ditch. Personal observation and the photographic record suggests that the scars become vegetated after a period and their number, and the extent to which they are associated with active erosion, varies with time. Fowler (1989, 94) notes a particularly vigorous period of activity c 1985. In 1993 there were three of these scars on the south side of the ditch, one opposite pole IV, the others opposite and west of pole I (Fig 7:3). On the north side of the ditch there were seven scars along its length. The scars ranged in length from 0.35–3.2m (mean 1.4m), the average width is 0.25m and the base of the scars was between 0.20 and 0.40m (average 0.17m) below the turf surface. They all exposed the stone accumulation horizon at the base of the soil profile but only small areas of weathered chalk were exposed.

The scars are not clearly related to the locations of former trenches, indeed they are most apparent at the west end which has never been excavated. The formation process appears to involve compaction of the ditch sediments resulting in downslope movement of turves on the ditch sides and the localized pulling away of turf at the ditch edge to create an erosion scar, which may then be expanded by frost action until vegetation colonization occurs. It is noteworthy that the ditch sides as a whole show evidence of discontinuous steps as shown on the section (Fig 7.5). They are like poorly developed examples of the terracettes found on steep chalk slopes. There is debate about the role of grazing in the formation of terracettes (Jewell 1963, 81) and it is interesting that these features should be developed on this slope from which grazing animals have always been totally excluded. Apart from the localized erosion scars the only other evidence for erosion in the ditch were runs of a few chalk pieces, often associated with animal burrows. Soil was also exposed around a very large anthill on the north side of the ditch opposite pole V.

The assumption has often been that the bank has not contributed in any way to the sedimentation of the ditch. Certainly any contribution must have been very small. The berm has been continuously vegetated and regular monitoring shows that this lush growth has prevented soil eroded from the bank entering the ditch. The almost continuous profile from bank to ditch, with bank sediments present at the top of the ditch slope at c 37° does, however, suggest the possibility of some slight contribution in the form of processes related to freeze thaw, wetting and drying, and the activities of biota. This is confirmed by evidence for the movement of pottery

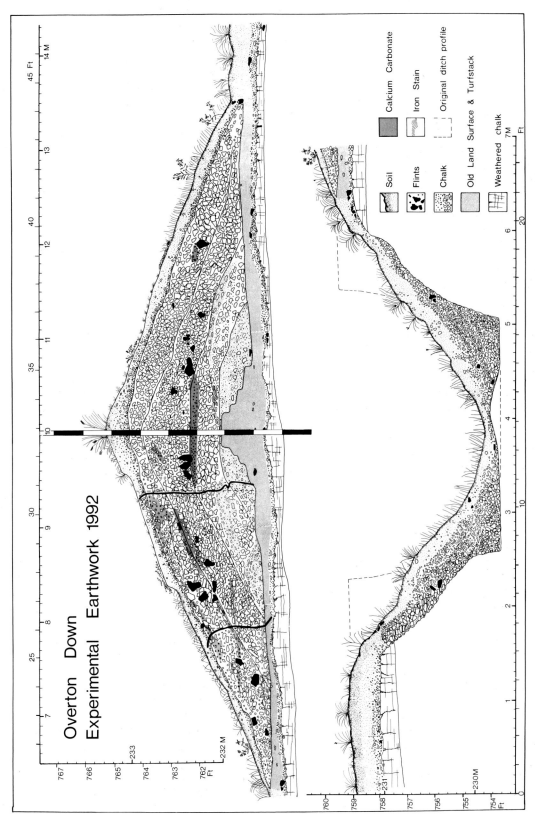

Overton Down
Experimental Earthwork 1992

Calcium Carbonate
Iron Stain
Original ditch profile

Soil
Flints
Chalk
Old Land Surface & Turfstack
Weathered chalk

Figure 7.5 Overton 1992 excavation, west section of bank and ditch. Bank section right side = north-east, ditch section left side = south-west

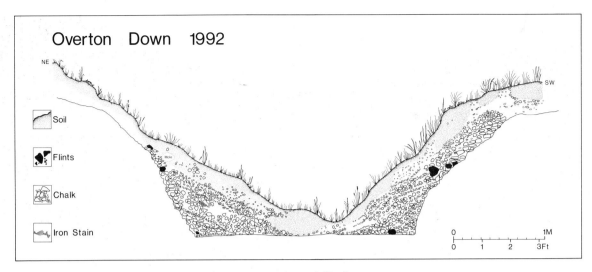

Figure 7.6 Overton 1992 excavation, east section of ditch

discs from the bank to the ditch (p 79). Crabtree (p 41) also considered that about 1976 some bank material may have entered the ditch.

The present ditch profile (Figs 7:5–6) is very different from its original sharply angular profile. On the south side a distinct break of slope remains with the original angle of the ditch side preserved where it was protected by chalk fall in the first year or two. The north side has no such distinct remnant of the original ditch wall and at this point the profile is more rounded.

On the floor of the ditch some 0.20m to north of centre was a distinct rise; it was 0.10m high on the west section (Fig 7.5), 20mm high on the east section (Fig 7.6). A slight rise of 38mm had been observed on the ditch floor during the 1976 sectioning (Fig 5:3). The most probable explanation is that the shallowly buried (c 90mm) chalk on the ditch floor has become saturated and has then periodically frozen giving rise to expansion and the observed feature. This, and the rounding of the profile of the ditch sides, shows that some post-burial change has occurred in the ditch profiles.

The section drawings (Figs 7.5 and 7.6) and Crabtree's particle size analyses (p 93) emphasize the tendency for the sediments to become finer upwards as a result both of physical weathering and increasing stability. Within the ditch sequence (Fig 7.7) there are also, however, distinct bands. Thin bands of humic silt (10YR5/3) mostly earthworm cast, with small rounded chalk granules, alternate with thicker bands comprising 80% angular chalk rubble with a loose and vacuous structure. The lowest band of chalk rubble can clearly be related to the first winter's frost weathering (Jewell and Dimbleby 1966, plate XXIV:1). Subsequent observation makes it clear that the small chalk and more humic bands represents material washed in from the soil profile during the summer whilst the coarse sediment is the product of the winter's physical weathering. The east section on the south side (Fig 7.6) showed 6 distinct fine bands, the other sections four bands. Five bands were recorded in the 1968 section. Bands were only likely to form when a free chalk face is exposed and this appears to have ceased sometime between 1965 and 1968. The bands are much less distinct than they were in earlier sections. Compaction may play a part but examination of the fine fractions suggest they had mostly passed through earthworms which accordingly seem to have blurred the banding, as the micromorphological study of Macphail and Cruise (p 106) confirms. It is also probable that once the ditch became stabilized by vegetation, well attested earthworm activity obscured some bands in the more active upper part of the profile. This banding and its significance is further discussed on p 236.

Previous sections of the ditch fill up to 1976 show very distinct individual turves in the fill, and photographs taken between 1962 (when the first turf fell: Jewell and Dimbleby 1966, plate 24.3) and 1976 demonstrate the important role these turves played in ditch sedimentation in acting as barriers to downslope movement and as nuclei of vegetation from which colonization could take place. By 1992, however, only hints of the original positions of individual turves remained (Figures 7.5–7.7). These were little festoons of small chalk pieces probably marking the base of slipped turves. In the main, however, the upper part of the ditch profile, especially on the west profile, showed a remarkably uniform earthworm sorted profile. There was an average depth of 0.12m of largely stone-free humic soil underlain by small chalk pieces.The depth of sorting after 32 years is close to the figure Darwin (1881) gives of 25–37mm (1–1.5in) per decade. On the south-west facing side the 1976 section (Figure 5:3) shows that this sorted profile had begun to form by that stage; but on the north side there was less evidence for sorting, the profile there having largely formed in the last 16 years. This suggests a high level of biological activity.

Figure 7.7   Overton 1992 west ditch section

7.5   Changes to the bank

Morphology

The bank was very carefully designed: the measurements of individual layers were precisely recorded, layers were separated by three distinctively coloured bands of stone chips. Two vertical polythene tubes were included on the south side of each bank section. This design makes it possible to estimate the extent of compaction and lateral spread which the bank has undergone.

By the 32 year section (Fig 7.5 and 7.8) the bank had settled 0.14m (5.5in), just 8% of the height of the complete earthwork. Much of the compaction apparently took place in the first 4 years. The bank had spread 0.25m (10in) on the south side but not at all on the north side. The very limited extent of lateral spread suggests little surface run-off; indeed no rills have ever been recorded on this bank, in contrast to the situation on sand bedrock at Wareham (Hillson, p 209). The polythene tubes indicate that appreciable movement of the surface layers has occurred. The south tube curves down slope some 0.23m (9in), but below 0.30m (1ft) it is in almost exactly its original position. The nail at the base appears to have been thrust out of alignment, as it had in previous sections (p 39). This is probably a consequence of compaction and thinning of the old land surface (see below). The north tube curved downslope some 80mm but 0.15m below the surface it was virtually on its original line. The base showed twists and contortions relating to compaction of Layers B and C.

Chemical and biological processes

On the surface of the bank an immature soil, of average thickness 95mm, had formed. The greatest thickness was on the crest of the bank. The soil on the north face of the bank was an average of 0.125m thick, noticeably more than the lower part of the south face, giving the impression that some erosion of the incipient soil may have occurred in that area. The soil was a light brownish grey (2.5Y 6/2); it comprised small chalk pieces, mostly less than 10mm, in a marly matrix with some humus, the whole permeated by many fine roots. A major factor in the development of this layer was the physical weathering of the chalk of Layer E/F. Vegetation colonization must also have played a part ; however, the layer is not noticeably thicker on the lower parts of the bank with greater vegetation cover, although those parts have a darker colour (7.5YR 5/2) and higher humus content. The formation processes of this soil are considered in more detail by Macphail and Cruise (p 116) and Crowther (p 105).

Near the base of the weathering horizon there was

Figure 7.8 Overton 1992 west section showing incipient soil on bank, the bank sediments (note collapse during rainstorm on left), the turf stack and the buried soil

evidence of iron deposition. On the upper part of the bank at a depth of about 0.16m the crests of chalk nodules had clear yellow-brown staining. This presumably relates to iron liberated by chemical weathering of the chalk. Other evidence of iron deposition was found in the bank, normally in association with changes of partical size, or probable changes in the water holding capacity of layers, for instance iron had accumulated just above the junction between layer E/F and the old land surface. Layers of iron accumulation are frequently encountered in association with buried soils and sediments on calcareous strata, as is further discussed by Limbrey (1975, 310).

Another result of chemical weathering of the chalk is the deposition of calcium carbonate within the bank. In places this formed a loose cement for the individual pieces of chalk rubble. It was most pronounced in Layer E/F below the incipient soil (Fig 7.5) but patches also occurred elsewhere. Where the bank was protected from percolation, for instance below leather sample 3092, its original vacuous structure was preserved; elsewhere it was partly infilled by downwashing of small chalk pieces and calcium carbonate. Jewell and Dimbleby (1966, 319) record that after only four years calcium carbonate deposition in Layers C and D was marked. The cementation of chalk sediments by calcium carbonate

is frequently encountered on archaeological sites but again it is a surprise to learn how quickly these changes occur.

Careful examination of the fine material in the interstices between the chalk lumps showed that they were generally aggregated in granules which indicated that most of the fine material within the bank interstices had been reworked by earthworms since construction. Not all of the fine material had been reworked in this way, however, because no evidence of reworking was found in Micromorphological Sample 104 (Macphail and Cruise p 102). The evidence of casts was particularly pronounced near some of the buried materials in the chalk environment. Earthworms were frequently encountered aestivating within all layers of the bank, chalk and humic alike. In nearly all buckets sieved one or two earthworms were found; regrettably these were not sampled for identification.

There was only limited evidence for disturbance of the bank by larger fauna. On the north side of the bank (at A = 2.6m) three roadstone chippings at the base of the soil on the bank had been moved at least 0.30m, presumably by moles. One Criggion basalt chip was also found at A = 9.7m at the base of the weathered incipient soil on the bank surface and at least 0.15m above the horizon on which it had been deposited. With these minor exceptions roadstone

Figure 7.9 Overton 1992. Turf stack showing intact turves

chippings still formed discrete horizons which were only blurred to the extent one would anticipate from settling and compaction. The pottery discs placed on these surfaces were similarly undisturbed (see below). The only identifiable mole runs were at the junction with the old land surface (see below) with some hints in the most humus-rich bank Layer B.

The turf stack

The originally constructed stepped stack, four turves high, was still preserved in profile (Fig 7.5). By 32 years it had compressed by 0.16m or 34% of its total thickness. Careful excavation identified the boundaries of most of the individual turves on the outer part of the turf stack (Fig 7.9). This was possible because there were cracks between them and because the bases of turves incorporated small stones from the A/C horizon (as illustrated in Jewell 1963, fig 20). The boundaries between the turf stack and Layer B, and between individual turves did, however, show signs of being blurred in places by faunal action and the turf stack was not so well preserved as at the Wareham Earthwork (eg Evans and Limbrey 1974, plate XVII). Within the turf stack the boundaries between individual turves were only hinted at in places and the impression was that the interior of the stack had been reworked by earthworms (Fig 7.10); see micromorphology report (p 101).

Figure 7.10 Overton 1992. West section of turf stack and buried soil

The old land surface

The clearly defined old land surface below the bank (Fig 7.8 and 7.11) was a very dark greyish brown (10YR8/1) with few stones overlying a 50mm thick stone accumulation horizon of rounded chalk pieces and flint resting on the weathered surface of chalk. In term of its structure it is a typical earthworm sorted chalkland soil and thus provides an ideal

Figure 7.11 Overton 1992. Bank and buried soil at A = 7.60m showing old land surface material carried up into the bank by earthworms and the location of micromorphology samples 100–102

opportunity to look at issues of medium-term diagenesis in buried soils. The stone-free horizon was an average of 0.1m thick. This compares with a 0.13m (5in) thick profile described in the manual (Jewell 1963, 62) and profiles 0.20–0.25m thick recorded in the 1992 soil pits. The soil appears to have been reduced in thickness by between about 25% and 50%. Part of this change must be the result of compression, but faunal activity also played an important part in post-burial changes to the soil.

Two very clear mole runs 50mm in diameter were encountered at the junction between the old land surface and the bank. Between 7 and 8.5m in the section (Fig 7.5) the buried soil was only 40mm thick. There was evidence of mole activity in this area and there is evidence that they have been responsible for abstracting buried soil from below the bank. During the winter of 1962–3 molehills of brown earth were recorded at the junction of the bank on the berm (Jewell and Dimbleby 1966, plate XXII:3). Despite this evidence it is clear that moles were not responsible for the wholesale reworking of the old land surface because flint group VIIIc/t on the south side of the bank was found more or less in its original

position (p 80) as were most of the buried materials below the turf stack.

The buried soil had also been modified by post-burial earthworm activity. Old land surface material had been carried up, and deposited as casts within the interstices of the chalk bank (Fig 7.11). In excavating the bank , especially between 6.5 and 8m in the basal 50–100mm of bank, an increasing proportion of aggregates of brown soil occurred between the chalk pieces. This process would also have contributed to the thinning of the buried soil. It is further discussed in the context of micromorphological evidence (Macphail and Cruise p 101) and evidence for the upward movement of *Lycopodium* spores scattered on the old ground surface (Crabtree, p 127).

It was notable that there was no clear dividing line between the old land surface and the turf stack (Fig 7.10); the same point had been observed in 1976 (p 37). Even where a precise level was actually marked by the presence of the buried materials, no associated soil change could be recognized. This made identification and recovery of the materials particularly difficult. The likely explanation is that the turf stack and the buried soil have been extensively reworked and intermixed as a result of earthworm activity, which is likely to have been particularly concentrated in the double layer of decomposing turf created by the placing of the lowest turf of the turf stack upside down (Jewell 1963, 34; Fig 25). At Wareham, by contrast, all turves were the right way up (Evans and Limbrey 1974, 175).

During the excavation of the old land surface and turf stack a careful watch was maintained for preserved vegetation. None was found in the field apart from two tiny pieces of woody, possible root, material. Subsequently laboratory analyses revealed seeds (Carruthers and Straker p 134), some of which germinated, tiny fragments of possible grasses (Hendry *et al*, p 138) and microscopic traces of plant tissue in soil thin sections (Macphail and Cruise p 99). The reports on the first four years are unfortunately silent on the extent to which plant material survived in the old land surface but at the time of the 1976 section it is clear that some did survive in contact with the leather samples (p 57) and the uncharred oak (p 64), possibly because tannins inhibited decay. There was no evidence that such preservative effects lasted until the 32nd year.

Subsoil feature

The ditch had weathered back on the north side and sectioned a small bowl-shaped feature some 0.60m in diameter and 0.22m deep. Figures 7.12 and 7.13 show a section of this feature. It underlay the old land surface and at this point was sealed by the slightly spread upper layer of the bank. It was below a particularly flinty area of the stone accumulation horizon. The feature fill was a yellowish brown (10YR 5/4) silt with 70% rounded chalk pieces. A similar

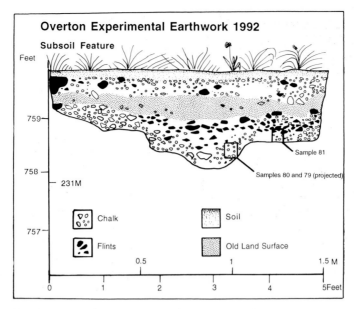

Figure 7.12 Overton 1992. Section of subsoil feature on the berm at A = 6.46m

feature was sampled on the south side of the ditch but is not shown on a section. Such features are often referred to as subsoil hollows and interpreted as a remnant of tree holes (Evans 1972, 219). Local examples are reported from Millbarrow (Whittle *et al* 1993) and valley sediments at Avebury (Evans *et al* 1993, 151). That explanation is supported by a mollusc assemblage indicating shaded conditions (Bell and Johnson p 140). Photographs in the manual confirm that small subsoil features were present

(Jewell 1963, Figures 15, 19a and b) but the text describes disturbances to the chalk surface only in terms of solution features and festooning, ie periglacial involution.

Ancient artefacts

During excavation of the 1992 section a few archaeological artefacts were found; they come principally

Figure 7.13 Overton 1992. Section of subsoil feature, also showing the stone accumulation at the base of the original profile and the soil buried below the bank spread

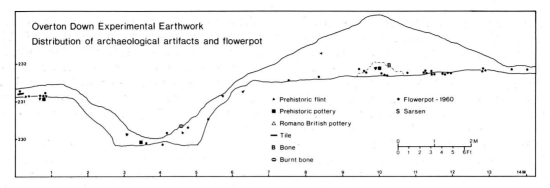

Figure 7.14 Overton 1992. The distribution of archaeological artefacts and flowerpot fragments

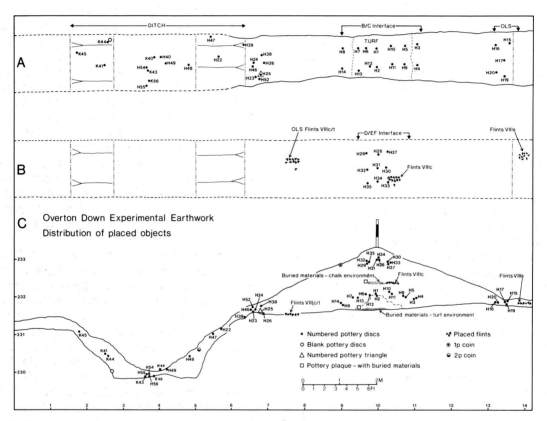

Figure 7.15 Overton 1992. The distribution of placed objects (a) the distribution of numbered pottery discs in plan, including discs below the bank and at the interface between layers B/C; (b) the distribution of flints and pottery discs at the interface between D/EF; (c) distributions in section

from the ditch and the stone accumulation at the base of the soil south of the ditch. The finds (Fig 7.14) included 13 struck flints; 1 piece of Romano-British pottery; three pieces of prehistoric pottery; one calcined bone and one unburnt bone from a turf within the turf stack. Six sherds had also been found during earthwork construction. The finds confirm evidence for prehistoric and Romano-British activity on the site, probably associated with the manuring of fields (P J Fowler pers comm). This evidence needs to be seen in the context of the major relict landscape of early field systems and associated settlements within which the earthwork sits (Fowler 1963).

7.6 Placed objects

Flower pot fragments

Prior to construction of the earthwork, pieces of broken flowerpot had been scattered over the turf in order to mimic a pre-earthwork pottery scatter (Jewell 1963, 32). Figure 7.14 shows the distribution of flowerpot recovered. Two fragments came from south of the ditch, five fragments had weathered into the ditch with topsoil, and eighteen fragments were found on, or very close to, the old land surface on which they had originally been placed. Two were in turves from the turf stack and one from the topsoil-derived Layer B. The last is explained by an account written soon after construction which notes that flowerpot was carried to each layer on the boots and buckets of diggers (Proudfoot 1961, 598). Those from the old land surface indicate that vertical movement of sherds has been very small. This contrasts with two flower pot fragments from the present day soil just north of the earthwork (Fig 7.14). These were at a depth of 0.10m (4in), very close to the depth at which flint group VIIIs was found (p 80). This burial, we can conclude, is the result of earthworm activity.

Charcoal experiment

Charcoal had been scattered on the old land surface prior to construction of the bank (Jewell 1963, 63). Charcoal was found throughout the old land surface profile providing further evidence for reworking. The laboratory investigation of this is further discussed by Moore (p 131).

Pottery discs
By M Bell and N Evans

Numbered pottery discs laid out in a predetermined pattern (Jewell 1963, Fig 31b; Fowler p 46) on various layers within the earthwork provide an excellent means of monitoring those areas which have been subject to erosion and faunal disturbance (Fig 7.15). This aspect of the experiment would have been even more useful if, within the individual groups of discs, they had been placed in a predetermined number sequence, making it possible to identify the exact spot, rather than just the group in which a disc had been placed. Two discs (H1–2) had been placed on the top of the turf stack; they were in the same horizontal position but 0.17m lower than their original position.

Twelve discs (H3–14) were placed on the sloping interface between Layers B and C; they were in place but an average of 50mm lower. Nine discs (H 27–35) were placed on the top of Layer D. They too were in the same horizontal position but an average of 0.22m lower. Six discs (H15–20) were placed on the old ground surface below bank Layer E/F on the north side. One was missing and the arrangement of the others had clearly been disturbed from its original symmetry by faunal action. Six discs (H21–26) had been placed on the old ground surface on the south side of the bank below Layer E/F. Four of these were found in roughly this position, but they were no longer symmetrically placed and there had been some faunal disturbance: one had been moved from a horizontal to a vertical orientation, another had been moved upwards slightly into the chalk of the overlying bank. This one (H25) was triangular, a type of clay object not apparently referred to in the manual (Jewell 1963). One of the six was missing, while another was found in the turf on the north side

of the ditch about 1m from its original position. One disc has moved from the bank to the ditch. The same thing was found in 1968 (p 47). This indicates there is some contribution of bank material to the ditch, although it is probable that the discs, and the missing 1992 disc, were abstracted from the old land surface by moles (see p 76) and thus reflect localized processes.

Twenty one discs (H36–56) were placed at the foot of the bank and on the berm. Two were found in chalk spread from the bank; one was on the north edge of the ditch; three from eroded sediments on the north side of the ditch; five in the ditch centre; one was found unstratified and the remaining nine were not found.

Nine discs (K37–45) were placed on the south side of the ditch, none remained *in situ*: three were found in sediments on the south side of the ditch, two in the ditch centre and four were not found.

Once the earthwork was finished at least three unnumbered discs were placed on the level top of the bank within the area of each excavation trench (Jewell 1963, Fig 31b). Only one was found and that came from the opposite (south) side of the ditch. Most probably it was picked up and thrown there by a person, or conceivably moved by animals (also discussed on p 47). What is interesting is that we can be fairly precise about the timing of this action. It was on the surface of the lowest layer of coarse chalk rubble and took place at the end of the winter or spring 1961.

Seventeen discs were not recovered, 25% of the total. Some may relate to inadequate recovery. However, only one disc was recovered from the 33% of the trench sieved, indicating that recovery was about 95%. It seems likely that the majority of the missing 17 discs had been moved to positions outside the trench; some may have been picked up by people.

The pottery disc experiment as a whole shows that there has been virtually no horizontal disturbance of material within the main body of the bank. The toe of the bank, at least 0.40m into the old land surface, emerges as an area of particular faunal disturbance, in this case due to mole activity. The fate of the discs placed on the outer bank face and the sides of the ditch emphasizes the problematic origins of material which archaeologists so often use to date ditches. Suffice it to say that some pottery discs representing a single human act of emplacement lay near the floor of the ditch, others were found within the turf covering the ditch and had clearly been eroded much more recently. What is more, these 1960 datable finds in the ditch silts lay alongside pieces of prehistoric and Romano-British pottery and flints eroded from the pre-ditch profile. Although archaeologists are well aware of this problem, this clear example may cause us to reflect on whether we give sufficient consideration to the possible origins of material which we use for dating. This point has been made a number of times since the early days of the experiment (eg Jewell and Dimbleby 1966, 340; above p 51).

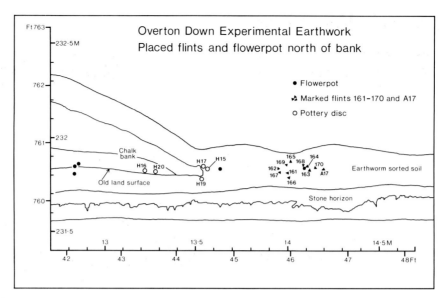

Figure 7.16 Overton 1992. Detail showing the distribution of buried objects at the edge of the bank on the north side

Coin experiment

These were inserted in the bank in 1979 (p 12). Only two coins were located in the 1993 trench (Fig 7:15) as follows:

1p 1978, in turf on top of bank A = 8.95; B = 0.64; C = 232.83

2p 1978, in turf layer in ditch A = 5.1; B = 0.3; C = 230.56 (2p coins were not apparently used in the experiment – p 12).

Flints

Three groups of worked flint were buried in each section of the earthwork (Jewell 1963, 49). Each comprised two rows of five and one separate piece with the prefix A. One group was part of the arrangement of buried materials in the chalk environment, and is considered in that context below; the other two were in contrasting contexts in the soil.

Group VIIIc/t had been tucked into the base of the vegetation on the old land surface below the bank. There is an error in the basic manual with regard to the placing of this group. It says they were placed on the north side of the bank below Layer E/F (Jewell 1963, 49). They were actually found on the south side below Layer D and Jewell (1963, Fig 26) illustrates them being placed in this position. The numbers were precisely those recorded and their arrangement (Fig 7.15) was very close to the ideal shown in Jewell 1963 Figure 32. The flints appeared to be almost exactly where they had been placed on the old land surface. This indicates that the soil at this particular spot has not been worked by moles. Some humus had, however, been moved by earthworms above the flints, but they had not been buried.

Group VIIIs had been tucked into the base of the vegetation north of the bank. This group are of particular interest because they have remained

within the active soil and have not been covered by the bank. All of the expected numbered flints were recovered, but the original neat arrangement of flints had been disrupted and they were found at depths varying between 5 and 0.12m (Fig 7.16). The average depth of burial is 0.11m and this can be attributed to surface casting by earthworms. A similar depth of burial was suggested by two flowerpot fragments (above). These results gives a figure of 35mm ($1\frac{2}{5}$in) downward movement per decade which is very close to the 25–40mm ($1-1\frac{1}{2}$in) quoted by Darwin (1881).

7.7 Buried materials in the chalk environment

This group of materials had been placed within the chalk bank between Layers C and D. The original manual (Jewell 1963, 36) states that the buried materials were placed above the layer of Pyx granite marking the boundary between the layers. What was actually found in excavation was that the buried materials had been emplaced on a layer of small chalk with much evidence of calcium carbonate deposition. They were covered by a layer of small chalk pieces, now cemented by calcium carbonate, and were 70mm below the granite chippings. The buried materials were not found in anything like such a precise arrangement as suggested by Jewell 1963, Figure 32 or plate 25. This may reflect movement during compaction and also probably some faunal disturbance. It is also possible that there was some original misplacement. Figure 7.17 shows the positions in which the buried materials were recovered, the sample numbers of the individual materials and, where possible, the locations of some samples taken in relation to the buried materials. Adjacent to each of the buried materials, samples were routinely taken for pH, humidity and one spare sample (Janaway p 147). At the level of the buried

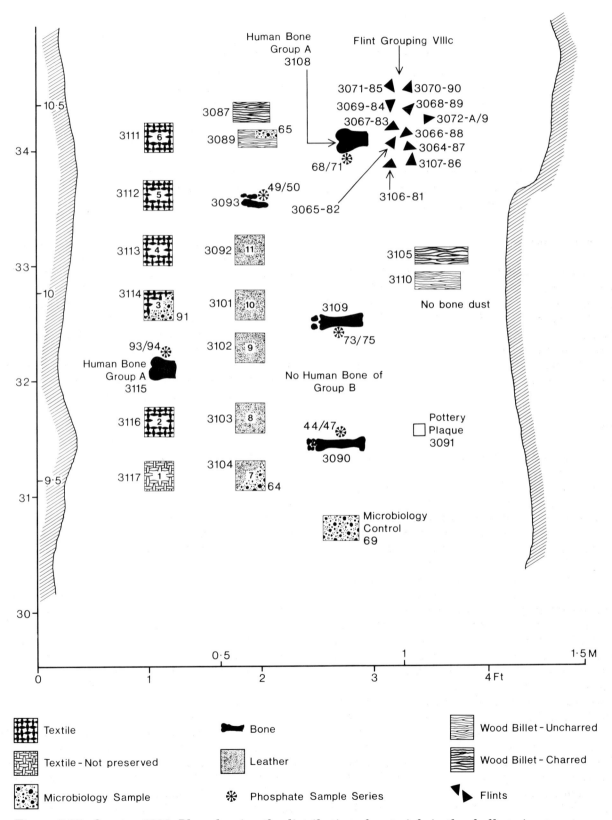

Figure 7.17 Overton 1992. Plan showing the distribution of materials in the chalk environment and their relationship with associated samples for microbiological and phosphate analysis

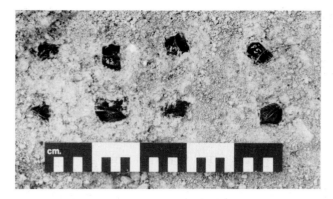

Figure 7.18 Overton 1992. The group of flints in the chalk environment showing little dislocation from the original symmetrical arrangement. Note: the photograph was taken before three of the flints were found

materials there was a distinct concentration of earthworm casts and burrows. These had also been noted under the buried objects in 1968 (Fowler p 54). Some casts were humic and brown (10YR5/3), others were calcareous and light grey (10YR 5/2). The worms had apparently been attracted by the buried materials. If, however, their presence relates to aestivation, it may be more due to microclimatic factors such as temperature, water-holding capacity or textural factors, rather than decomposition of the materials themselves. Only brief specifications for the originally buried materials are given below; for more detailed information see Jewell 1963.

Inorganic Materials

Pottery square (3091)

Recovered intact.

Flints

Flint grouping VIIIc. All the expected numbered flints were recovered and their arrangement was almost exactly that recorded by Jewell 1963, Fig 32. This is shown by Figure 7.18, which was taken before three of the flints had been found. No significant movement of the flints appears to have taken place. The flints themselves appeared black and fresh and there was no obvious sign of changes since burial.

Organic materials

Textiles

Each piece of textile had a block of chalk placed on it, which made location much easier than in the turf

Figure 7.19 Overton 1992. Textile 2 (3116) cotton khaki dyed twill cloth, from the chalk environment, in the laboratory directly after excavation.

Figure 7.20   Overton 1992. Leather samples 8 (3103), 9 (3102), and 10 (3101) in situ

environment where no chalk had been available at the time of burial.

Textile 1: Cotton loomstate plain cloth   No evidence was found of this sample, nor indeed had it survived in the 1968 and 1976 sections (p 57). Worm casts were noted in its approximate position.

Textile 2 (3116): Cotton khaki dyed twill cloth Well-preserved especially below chalk block to which it adhered. Khaki colour still present. Faunal excrement and ?eggs present on surface (Figure 7.19).

Textile 3 (3114): Woollen contrast cloth   When found this was blackened and rather friable with chalk adhering. Most of it was removed, without being uncovered, in a sterile Kubiana box for microbiological study. Other fragments were subsampled in the field for other analyses. A chalk block from this point has earthworm casts / animal excreta attached.

Textile 4 (3113): Worsted gabardine   In places this was still a discrete folded piece of cloth where protected by the overlying chalk block to which it adhered. Round the edges it was decayed.

Textile 5 (3112): Linen half-bleached   Textile adhered to chalk block.

Textile 6 (3111): Linen half-bleached   This was a decayed mass stained black in places and adhered to the overlying chalk block. An animal (?centipede) was found with the textile but escaped.

Leathers

Each piece of leather had a block of chalk on it.

Leather 7 (3104): Oak-bark-tanned sole leather   This was preserved whole with no macroscopically visible decomposition. It was placed intact in two abutting sterile Kubiena boxes and taken for microbological analysis (Sample 64).

Leather 8 (3103): Modern extract-tanned sole leather Well-preserved (Fig 7:20). Worms and worm casts were sampled in association with this specimen.

Leather 9 (3102): Modern upper leather of 'semi-chrome' type   Well-preserved (Fig 7:20). Aestivating earthworm curled up in contact with leather.

Leather 10 (3101): Modern heavy upper leather, chrome tanned, crimson colour   Well-preserved (Figure 7:20). A live animal was found on this leather ?centipede, also earthworm casts The chalk placed on top of the leather had been stained by contact.

Figure 7.21 Overton 1992. Charred oak (3087) from the chalk environment in situ

Figure 7.22 Overton 1992. Uncharred hazel (3110) from the chalk environment showing void left by wood decay

Figure 7.23 Overton 1992. Human bone (3115) originally this was from an individual named Dick. The specimen was from the chalk environment, bone intended for blood group studies with label attached by wire

Leather 11 (3092): Modern upper leather of 'chrome-retanned' type This was well-preserved. Below the leather some earthworm casts were preserved.

Wood

Oak – uncharred (3089) Wood fragment 15 by 10mm found in a void (120mm by 55mm) created by decomposition of the wooden billet. This was lifted using sterile tweezers for microbiological analysis (Sample 65). In the area between this sample and the cremated bone there was a very clear earthworm burrow with a cast lining.

Oak – charred (3087) The outer charred 'tube' was well-preserved (Fig 7:21) and within this lay some fibrous wood fragments. The tube was 105mm by 43mm externally and 30mm internally. Round the billet were a mass of earthworm casts, some were clearly humic, others calcareous.

Hazel – uncharred (3110) A void was encountered (120mm by 45mm) within which were fragments representing about one third of the original volume of the wood (Fig 7:22). The specimen was notably better preserved than the uncharred oak, as had also been noted after 16 years (p 64). The reasons for this are discussed by Blanchette (p 160). Worm activity was recorded.

Hazel – charred (3105) The charred surface was well-preserved (170 by 50mm) and within this was decayed wood, again noticeably better preserved than the oak. There was extensive evidence of worm activity in, and beneath, the billet.

**Bone
by S Hillson**

Human bone, blood group A (3115)

This bone was derived from one of two individuals, either a male aged 51 who died of lymphosarcoma or a male named Dick of unknown age (but apparently under 20: see below) who died of leukaemia. It is a human left femur, proximal end, posterior surface (sawn) with an unfused lesser trochanter. Since this fusion takes place by 20, the bone must be from the individual called Dick. Tucked into the marrow space was a small plastic bag containing a paper label rolled up and tied to the bone by steel wire passed through holes drilled in the bone (Fig 7.23). Small dark faecal pellets adhered to the bone (Fig 7.24). The bone was sampled for DNA studies but results are not yet available (see p 196).

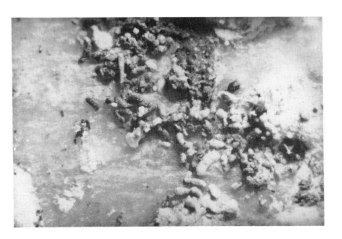

Figure 7.24 Overton 1992. Human bone (3115) from the chalk environment showing probable faecal pellets on the bone surface

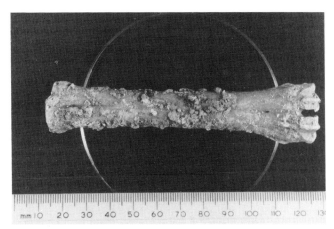

Figure 7.25 Overton 1992. Cooked bone (3090) from the chalk environment showing pellets adhering to the surface which are interpreted as the faeces of a soil animal

Human bone, blood group B

None placed in this section

Human bone, blood group AB (3108)

This bone was derived from one of two individuals, either a female aged 57 who died of left ventricular failure and hypertension, or a male named Dathan, of unknown age, who died of carcinoma of the oesophagus. It was found on the opposite side of the flint grouping (Fig 7.17) some 0.20–0.30m from where it was originally placed, implying faunal disturbance. This is puzzling, however, in view of the fact that the flints were undisturbed (see above). The sample was found with its original plastic label. It is a distal human right (?) femur separated from the rest of the bone by two cuts. Small ?faecal pellets attached to the cortical bone surfaces but not the medullary bone. Roots were present on the cortical bone. Phosphate samples (68 and 71) were taken adjacent to this bone.

Cremated bone (3093)

4.55g of bone had been originally emplaced. The weight of the material retrieved uncleaned was 5.15g. It was white (2.5Y8/10). Earthworm casts were observed under the cremated bone. A sample was taken for SEM examination (Hillson and Bond p 191).

Bone dust

None was placed in this section

Cooked bone (3090) from Soay ram

Seven bones were present: a left metacarpal and 6 associated carpals, all from one individual. Phos-phate Sample Series 44 and 47 taken from adjacent to bone. Pellets, interpreted as faeces of a soil animal, adhered to the bone in places (Fig 7.25). Samples of the bone were taken for SEM (p 180 and 187) and DNA studies (not yet completed see p 196).

Uncooked bone (3109) from Kent Cross wether

Four bones were present, a complete left metacarpal and three metacarpals from the same individual. The metacarpal had a void around the bone and extensive evidence of worm activity over the distal end. The dorsal shaft surface had scattered dark pellets adhering to it; on initial examination these were interpreted as the faecal pellets of a soil organism (Armour-Chelu and Andrews Fig 11.20). Phosphate Sample Series 73 and 75 taken adjacent to this bone. The bone was sampled for histological study (p 187); scanning electron microscopy (p 179 and 180); and DNA studies (not yet completed see p 196).

7.8 Buried materials in the turf environment

This group of buried materials was placed on the turf of the old land surface and was covered by the turf stack as shown by Jewell 1963, Figure 25. On excavation it proved impossible to recognize a clear division between the old land surface and the turf stack (p 76), this made identification of the buried material horizon difficult. Furthermore these materials were excavated under exceedingly difficult conditions. No sooner had the materials been located than heavy rain began and work could only proceed slowly under a plastic shelter. At 4–4.30pm on 11.7.92 a major thunderstorm took place. Rainfall was so heavy that the plastic shelter collapsed and there was 0.20m or more water in the trench; the sides collapsed in places as shown on Figure 7:8. The storm ended within a hour but in this time 50mm of

OVERTON DOWN 1992

Buried Materials and
Samples in Turf Environment

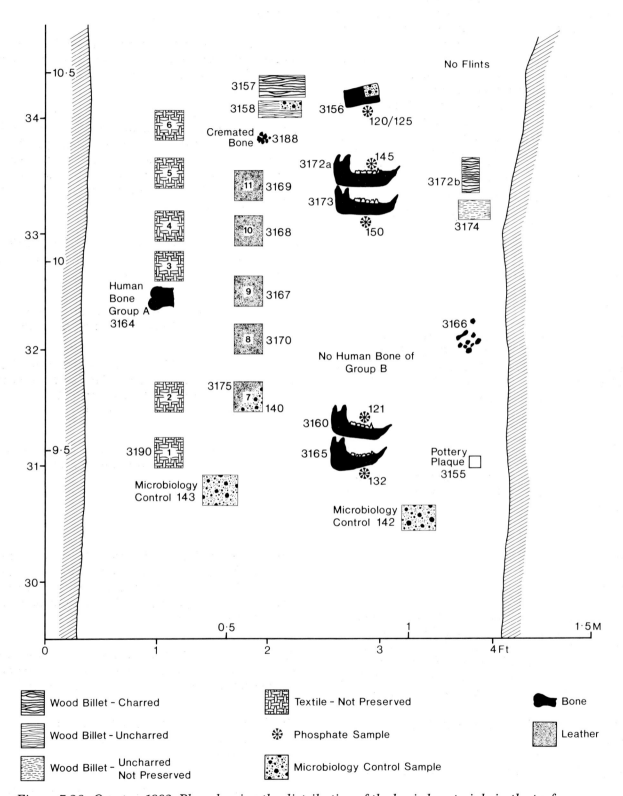

Figure 7.26 Overton 1992. Plan showing the distribution of the buried materials in the turf environment and their relationship with associated samples for microbiological and phosphate analysis

water had accumulated in a bucket. Dr T E Rogers (pers comm 28.8.92) reports that the weather station 6km to the east at Marlborough College recorded 13.6mm of rain in the 24 hours beginning 9am on 11.7.92. The weather station recorded moderate rain throughout the morning followed by a thunderstorm and very heavy rain between 1600 and 1730.

The trench was quickly cleaned up and little lasting damage was done. The storm, however, did make recovery of this group of buried materials much more difficult and it is possible that this reduced the effectiveness of recovery. To put a positive gloss on what seemed at the time a disaster, it was, in a way, a useful reminder of the effect of stochastic factors such as weather on experimental design (p 229)!

Figure 7.26 shows the positions in which the buried materials were recovered, the sample numbers of the individual materials and the locations of some of the samples taken in relation to buried materials. The identifications of the buried materials are only briefly noted below; more detailed specifications are given in Jewell 1963, 43.

Inorganic materials

Pottery square (3155)

This had been broken into two fragments but it was in the original position (as in 1968, p 55). Breakage was presumably the result of either trample after emplacement (though care was taken to avoid this) or consolidation of the bank.

Flints

No flints had been deposited in the turf environment, because at this stage they had not arrived (Jewell 1963, p49).

Organic Materials

Textiles

Textile 1: Cotton loomstate plain cloth Possible vestiges of textile were sampled (3190) from the area where Textile 1 was expected. It was sampled initially in sterile Kubiena boxes for microbiological analysis. In the event no certain textile was identified during laboratory analysis of this sample.

Textile 2: Cotton khaki dyed twill cloth No trace found.

Textile 3: Woollen contrast cloth No trace found.

Textile 4: Worsted gabardine No trace found.

Textile 5: Linen half-bleached No trace found.

Insect pupae were saved from the area where this should have been.

Textile 6: Linen half-bleached No trace found.

Leathers

The surface of several leathers displayed the hummocks of the vegetation surface on which they had been laid (Jewell 1963, Fig 25).

Leather 7 (3175): Oak-bark-tanned sole leather
This sample was taken for microbiological analysis (Sample 140). Excavated with a sterile spatula, it came out as one large solid piece and was packed in two adjacent Kubiena boxes. A control sample (143) for microbiological study was taken 0.20m south of this sample (Fig 7.26).

Leather 8 (3170): Modern extract-tanned sole leather
Found intact, dark brown colour. A living arthropod was recovered from its surface.

Leather 9 (3167): Modern upper leather of 'semi-chrome' type Found intact, brown colour.

Leather 10 (3168): Modern heavy upper leather, chrome tanned crimson colour. The bright crimson colour was preserved and on recovery the leather appeared to be in excellent condition.

Leather 11 (3169): Modern upper leather of 'chrome-retanned' type. Found intact, dark black colour.

Wood

Oak–uncharred (3158) This had rolled on top of the charred billet (3157) and the two were compressed together. The billet had fragmented into several mycelium-covered pieces, one of which was taken for microbiological study.

Oak–charred (3157) The charred surface was preserved in a compressed and broken condition. Fungal hyphae noted 10mm to the south of the wood billet.

Hazel–uncharred No trace was found of this, and indeed in the 1976 section only faecal residues had remained (p 64).

Hazel–charred (3172b) The outer charred surface was preserved but the billet was compressed and broken. On excavation it was found to be full of hyphae.

Bone
by S Hillson

Human bone, blood group A (3164).

According to the manual (Jewell 1963) this bone was either from a male aged 51 who died of lymphosarcoma or a male named Dick of unknown age who died of leukaemia. It was the posterior portion of the distal articulation of a human right femur. The distal epiphysis was fully fused onto the diaphysis and there was no sign of the fusion line in the cancellous bone. The specimen must have come from a fully mature individual. The evidence of bone 3115 from the chalk (p 84) shows that one of the individuals of blood group A was under 20; this must be the individal Dick. Bone 3164 must therefore come from the other individual aged 51. A label wrapped in a small plastic bag, and rolled up, was attached by a wire to the bone on its anterior surface. The specimen was yellowish red (5YR 5/8). When examined in the laboratory, thin layers of cortical bone had, in places, pulled away with adherent soil. Microscope examination showed that areas of cancellous bone could be seen all over the cortical bone surface, on articular surfaces and outside them, where the cortical bone had been pulled away. The area most damaged in this way was the medial condyle and epicondyle. The cut corners of the specimen were rounded and, although the cut surface of the cancellous bone was not eroded at a macroscopic level, the edges of each trabecula were rounded as well. There was no sign of the branching canals seen in specimen 3156 (below), or of hyphae or animal activity. Within the soil, there were relatively large filaments which resembled rootlets, although they did not appear to bear root hairs. There were also very fine filaments running between peds (soil structural units) which may have been fungal hyphae. An insect was found adjacent to the bone.

Human bone, blood group B

None placed in this section

Human bone, blood group AB (3156)

This specimen is either from a female aged 57 who died of left ventricular failure and hypertension or from a male named Dathan of unknown age who died of carcinoma of the oesophagus.

Human right femur, proximal end, posterior surface. The lesser trochanter was fused to the bone showing that this was from a mature individual. The specimen had been isolated from the rest of the bone by three saw cuts. This bone and its label were well-preserved. Brown fibrous material was found adhering to the bone impression. Microscope examination showed that part of the cortical bone on the posterior surface and the cut anterior surfaces was disrupted by flakes which had detached themselves

and by narrow channels which branched and anastomosed along the surface. Examination also revealed rootlets, complete with root hairs, embedded in soil adhering to the bone surface, but not apparently entering the bone surface. At the distal end a branching and anastomosing, melanomized structure was seen in one of the canals. This was tentatively interpreted as a fungal hypha and was sampled for microbiological study (p 150). Associated with this were clusters of small round, melanomized bodies also in the system of canals, possible spores and arthropod eggs were noted. In another area was a cluster of minute (*c* 40–50mm) egg-like, spherical pale bodies. Two living and moving nematode worms were seen. Several living, and also moving, microarthropods were also seen. They were about 100mm long, had 4 pairs of legs on thoracic segments, tubercles or spiracles, 8–10 segments, segmented antennae, large head, no differentiated thorax and were white all over. They may be the larvae of *Collembola*. Much of the bone surface had a striking red coloration (Munsell 2.5YR 4/6). There was a strip running along the posterior surface with little adhering soil and a pinkish white colour (7.5 YR 8/2). Sample Series 120/125 was taken for phosphates in association with this bone.

Cremated bone (3188)

The originally placed Sample 1e had weighed 4.15g.
  Pieces of cremated bone were recovered some 20–30mm long.

Bone dust (3166)

The originally placed Sample 1n had weighed 7.55g.
  A small pile of cremated bone was recovered. It comprised splinters up to 1–20mm long and white (2.5Y 8/2). Observation in the field laboratory, when the bones had not been fully excavated from the soil matrix, indicated the bone was thin cortical fragments with no sign of cancellous bone. No trace was observed of the 'crazing' typical of cremated bone. A sample was taken for SEM (Hillson and Bond p 185).

Cooked bone (3160 and 3165): a Soay ram

Left and right mandibles.
  3160 was a left mandible with a complete set of permanent teeth, fully erupted and in a stage of wear which suggests an individual around 8–10 years. Microscope examination showed that some of the cortical bone was pulling away from the underlying cancellous bone as in specimen 3164. The second permanent premolar and a bone sample were taken for SEM study (Hillson and Bond p 185), others were taken for DNA studies but that work is not complete (p 196). A microbiological control sample (142) was taken 0.20m from 3160/3165 (Fig 7.26).

Uncooked bone (3173 and 3172a): a Kent Cross wether

3172a is a left mandible with the tip of the coronoid process missing. The dentition indicated an individual aged 6–12 months. The anterior teeth had fallen out of their wide sockets and were loose in the soil. In the adhering soil small white structures which appeared to be roots were observed but were not in contact with the bone surface. Some cortical bone had pulled away from the cancellous bone underneath at the cranial end of the body (around the sockets of the anterior teeth) and on the angle of the ramus. Branching and anastomizing canals, some associated with hyphal-like bodies, were especially common on the medial surface. In the centre of the medial side of the mandibular body was a large bundle of hypha-like structures which was sampled. Moving arthropods of the type seen on specimen 3156 were common. The second deciduous premolar and bone samples were taken for SEM (p 185) and samples for DNA. Sample Series (145) was taken adjacent to the bone for phosphates (p 195).

3173 was a right sheep mandible with dentition indicating it was probably from the same individual as 3172a. Channels were common on the medial surface, especially where the ramus met the body of the mandible, some connected with canals that penetrated into the bone. Whilst these might have represented a system of canals invading the bone, it is also possible that they represent cancellous bone exposed by the falling away of its cortical covering. On excavation a mass of probable hyphae was observed below the bone. Examination in the field laboratory showed many hypha-like structures which resembled those on 3156. At one location there was a very clear fungal structure with central body and radiating hyphae. A number of live arthropods of the type described on specimen 3156 were present. There were some patches of red staining on the medial surface, more on the lateral surface. Sample Series 150 adjacent to the bone was taken for phosphates (p 195).

8 Soils and sediments from the Overton 1992 section

8.1 Introduction

During previous excavations of the Overton Earthwork some sieve analysis has been carried out on the ditch sediments (Crabtree 1971, and p 33 and 39) and, in the early years, of the surface of the bank (Jewell and Dimbleby 1966, 320). At the time of the 1992 section it was decided to carry out a more detailed study of the buried soil itself, as an analogue for the study of soils buried below archaeological monuments. The particular focus of this work was a linked programme of analysis of micromorphology and chemistry. More speculative investigations of magnetic susceptibility and amino acids were also included. Much of the sampling was carried out by Professor Bruce Proudfoot and Ms Amanda Rouse working in consultation with the specialists concerned. Figure 8.1 shows the locations of samples discussed in Chapters 8 and 9.

8.2 Particle size analysis of the ditch sediments
by K Crabtree

Samples were taken from sides of the ditch infill to compare with those taken in earlier sectionings, as reported in Jewell and Dimbleby (1966), Crabtree (1971) and Crabtree (p 39). It should be noted that strict comparison was not possible as each sectioning was unique along a line some 2 to 3m apart from the previous sectioning (Fig 7.3). The samples (Figure 8.2; Table 8.1) consisted of bag samples from the layers at the following intervals:

Table 8.1 Overton 1992. Sampling intervals for particle size analysis

North side (SW facing) below bank		South side (NE facing) opposite bank	
159A	0–0.2m	161F	0–0.2m
159B	0.2–0.39m	161G	0.2–0.32m
159C	0.39–0.53m	161H	0.32–0.46m
159D	0.53–0.62m	161I	0.46–0.54m
159E	0.62m–base	161I /Jsilt	at 0.54m
		161J	0.54–0.69m
		161 Basal silt	0.69–0.74m

Given the nature of the sediment and the size of sample required for sieving it was not possible to sample some of the individual fine layers within the ditch sediments. Mixing, attributed to earthworm activity, had been greater than in the early years, a feature noted in the 1976 sectioning. Nevertheless some gradation or banding of the infill deposits was still discernable and these have been drawn on the ditch sections (Figs 7.5–6). The samples were gently hand-sieved at field moist status through Imperial sized mesh sieves in order to compare with earlier sectioning. The results are given in Table 8.2 and on Figure 8.2. The north-east facing side had generally less material in the coarsest category and a higher proportion of fine material in virtually all samples compared with the south-west facing side. This was in contrast to the findings in 1968 (p 33), when the south-west facing slope had the finer material, but follows the 1976 pattern (p 39) with the north-east facing side having the finer material. This may be an artefact of the sampling, in that the original fines deposited in layers have become more mixed over time, making it impossible to recognize and sample the formerly distinctive horizons, and thus resulting in an overall apparent change in the proportion of fines. Rates of *in situ* weathering and comminution may also vary with aspect once the ditch infill slopes have become relatively stable. The vegetation on the south-west facing side was more varied but less lush than on the north-east facing side. In summary the last three sectionings give bulked percentage data as in Table 8.2.

The source of fines is threefold; first the original soil; secondly the breakdown of the parent chalk; and thirdly inblown dust. From the drawn cross sections it is possible to calculate the approximate volume of eroded material from each face and the amount of deposited material. The calculation is based upon cubic feet per foot of ditch face. Table 8.3 gives comparative data for 1968, 1976 and 1992, plus summed data for 1962 and 1964.

Changes in the centre point of the ditch infill, ie increased asymmetry of the ditch, may account for the apparent large difference in 1992 between the

Table 8.2 Comparative percentage data of all the ditch sediments from the last three sectionings at Overton

Measured in inches	South-west facing side			North-east facing side		
	1968	1976	1992	1968	1976	1992
>1.5	15.4	8.4	7.1	21.9	1.0	3.0
0.75–1.5	19.0	22.6	22.3	27.7	6.0	18.1
0.375–0.75	22.3	23.8	20.3	21.7	20.1	23.2
0.1875–0.375	17.9	23.8	20.2	9.7	22.3	19.5
<0.1875	25.3	21.3	30.2	19.0	50.6	36.2

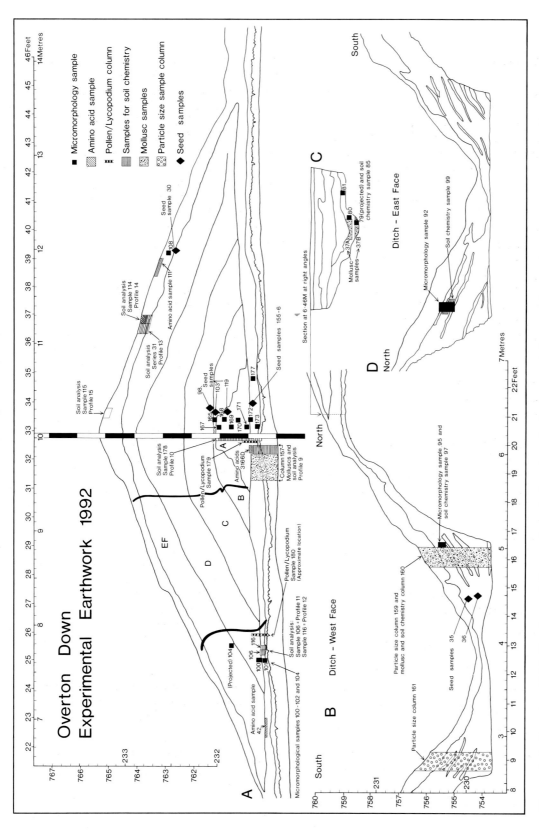

Figure 8.1 Overton 1992. Sections of the earthwork showing the location of the samples and sample series for soils, sediments and biological evidence – (A) west face of the bank (B) west face of the ditch (C) subsoil hollow (D) east face of the ditch

92

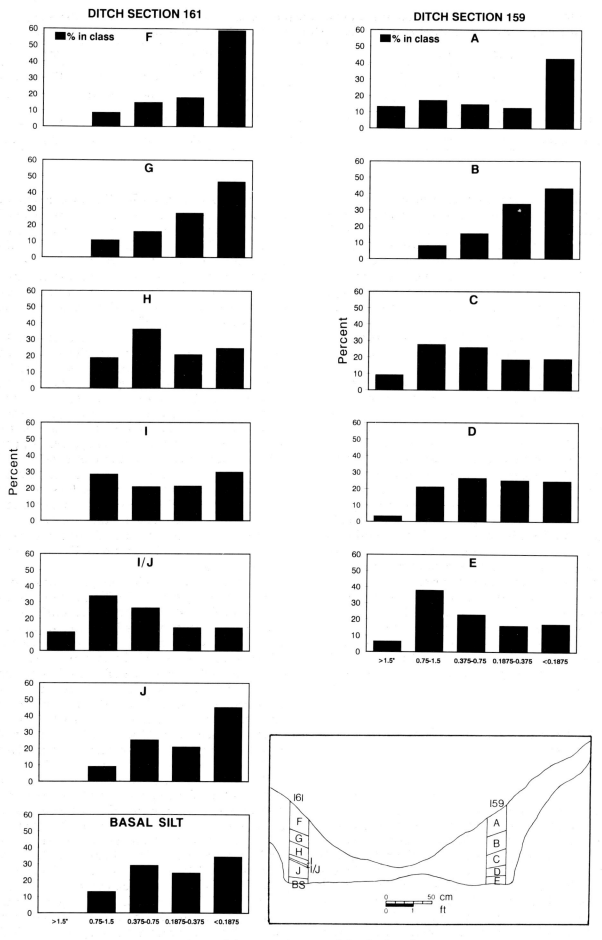

Figure 8.2 Particle size analysis of the two columns of the ditch sediments

Table 8.3 **The amount of sediment eroded and deposited and the expansion factor in the ditch section for the five sectionings at Overton. Cumulative ratios in cubic feet per foot of section**

	1962	1964	1968			1976			1992		
	Sum	Sum	NE	SW	Sum	NE	SW	Sum	NE	SW	Sum
Eroded	5.92	6.12	5.40	4.61	10.01	6.52	5.57	12.09	10.38	7.82	18.2
Deposited	9.56	11.60	7.94	7.67	15.61	9.93	8.10	18.02	10.54	12.06	22.60
Expansion factor	1.62	1.90	1.47	1.67	1.56	1.52	1.46	1.49	1.02	1.54	1.24

expansion factor north-east facing versus south-west facing side. In total the deposits in the ditch become more compact over time (expansion factors 1.90–1.24), as one would expect, with both consolidation and comminution occurring. The initial value of 1.62 may be because the material falling in the first two years differed in character and therefore packing, or because the 1962 or the 1964 ditch samples were not representative.

One also expects a general pattern of a decrease in particle size over time, as the material now being supplied to the ditch is mostly derived either from the pre-existing soil horizons or by the occasional development of temporary weathering scars (Fig 7.2) at the upper part of the ditch infill. *In situ* weathering of the infill is also occurring.

The 1992 sectioning did not reveal definite examples of fallen turves within the sediment infill. Ones which might have occurred in the earlier years and been buried by later infill material have been obliterated, presumably by earthworm activity. The base of the ditch on the section exhibited a distinctive hump just off centre and towards the south-west facing side. Some upward expansion of the ditch floor was noted in the central area in the earlier sectioning and was regarded as due to the weathering of the *in situ* ditch base, with freeze/thaw and wetting/drying occurring, especially towards the centre of the ditch base during the early years when it was exposed, prior to complete burial by the infill material. This is particularly marked on the west section drawing (Fig 7.5), although the opposite face has a very much less developed bulge (Fig 7.6).

8.3 Characterization of ditch sediments
by J Crowther

Ditches are potentially important sources of palaeoenvironmental evidence on archaeological sites in that they form very effective sediment traps in which various forms of biological evidence are often preserved. Clearly, the nature of the fill depends upon the size and characteristics of the 'catchment area' of the ditch, and whether or not the ditch has an outlet (cf defensive bank/ditch structure and drainage ditch – see discussion in Crowther 1990). In interpreting ditch sequences a distinction is often made between 'primary fill', which is dominated by

material derived from the weathering and collapse of the recently-exposed ditch sides, and 'secondary fill', which essentially originates from the surrounding catchment. The former typically comprises subsoil and weathered rock/drift, whereas the latter is predominantly topsoil from within the catchment. The ditch section at Overton Down is of interest in that it provides insight into the transition between primary and secondary fill.

Analysis was undertaken on bulk samples from each of the principal layers identified in the sediments accumulating along the north-east side of the ditch (Sample Series 160; Fig 8.1) – see also section drawing (Fig 7.5). Attention here focuses on loss-on-ignition (LOI at 375°C for 16 hrs), pH (1:2.5, water), χ and total phosphate (phosphate-P), each of which is commonly used in characterizing ditch sediments. LOI provides a relative measure of organic matter concentration. (Experimental work conducted on chalk fragments from the ditch sediments showed that there is negligible breakdown of carbonate at such a low ignition temperature). Details of the methods used and a discussion of the basic principles relating to these sediment properties is given by Crowther p 107.

The sediments below 0.35m display characteristics typical of primary chalk fill, with generally low LOI, χ and phosphate-P values and a high pH (Fig 8.3). There are, however, two distinct peaks within these basal deposits, one at the base and a second at 0.53–0.56m. It seems likely that these represent topsoil (possibly turf) which collapsed into the ditch at an early stage. If this is the origin of these particular layers, then the fact that they are not very markedly different in character from the adjacent sediments suggests that there has been considerable reworking by earthworms – evidence of which is seen in thin sections (Macphail and Cruise, p 103).

Above 0.35m the sediments clearly contain a much more substantial topsoil component. This is reflected in the marked increases in LOI (maximum, 16.9%), χ (0.202μm³μm kg⁻¹) and phosphate-P (1.16mg g⁻¹), and the decrease in pH (minimum, 7.9). The latter is attributable to the decalcified nature of the modern topsoils. By 1968 the exposed chalk of the ditch sides was buried beneath the accumulating chalk debris (primary fill), and since then all subsequent accumulation material has been topsoil and turves (Crabtree 1968). What is clear from the analytical data is that by 1992 (24 yrs later), the uppermost layer of fill is

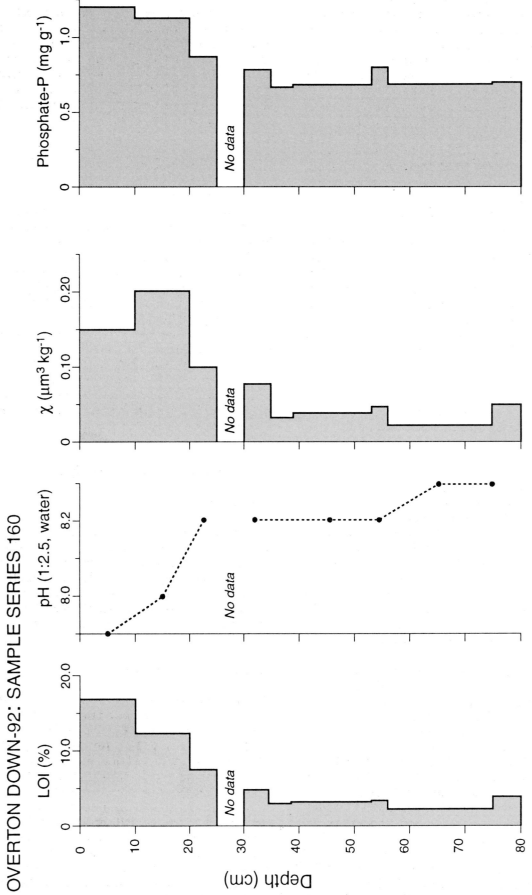

Figure 8.3 Properties of the ditch sediments in sample series 160. The properties graphed from left to right are loss-on-ignition; pH; magnetic susceptibility; and phosphate-P

very different in overall character and composition from the modern topsoil (Table 8.7). This is due to the effectiveness of earthworms in integrating the freshly-deposited, organic-rich material with the topmost layers of the primary fill.

The implication of these findings is that the chemical and magnetic properties of small *bulk* samples from the basal layers of the secondary fill of ditches cut in *this type of environment* are not representative of the contemporary topsoil material. Indeed, the ditch at Overton Down has such a very limited catchment area (effectively only the berm), with such a dense grass sward, that it seems unlikely in this case that rates of topsoil accumulation will ever exceed the rate at which earthworms are able to redistribute the debris. Here, therefore, pure secondary fill might never be identifiable within the ditch sequence. It should be emphasized, however, that many of the ditches encountered in archaeological excavations have quite extensive catchments, often including land disturbed by cultivation and/or settlements. Clearly, in these circumstances, secondary fill will accumulate much more rapidly, and the intermixing of the primary and secondary fills will tend to assume much less significance.

8.4 Soil micromorphology
by R I Macphail and G M Cruise

Introduction

Soil micromorphology, the microscopic study of undisturbed soils in thin section, is now a well established technique in archaeology (Courty *et al* 1989; Macphail *et al* 1990). Its use was initiated by Dr Ian Cornwall (1958), who applied it to numerous archaeological sites in the 1950s and 1960s. Dr Cornwall was one of the instigators of the Experimental Earthwork Project but did not apply micromorphology to this particular investigation. In Scotland, Romans and Robertson (1975, 1983) continued to develop micromorphological research in archaeology.

This is the first time that soil micromorphology has been applied to the Overton Down Experimental Earthwork but one sample was analyzed from the 16 year excavation at Wareham (Macphail p 214 and 1981; Fisher and Macphail 1985).

A literature review has shown that twenty-two archaeologically buried soils had been identified as rendzinas (Macphail 1987), indicating their importance in the past landscape of England. Some (Fussells Lodge, Wiltshire: Cornwall 1966; Windmill Hill, Wiltshire: Evans 1972) had undergone soil micromorphological investigation (Macphail 1987, 1986a). More recent excavations have permitted modern soil micromorphological investigations of Neolithic rendzinas (see Discussion). There is thus a reasonable database on archaeological rendzinas (Evans 1972, 1990; Limbrey 1975).

CD images and supporting data

Many micromorphological features are best seen in colour images and for this reason a CD of colour images has been prepared of soil thin sections and additional supporting data relating to soil analysis. In order to keep costs down the CD is not distributed with each volume but copies are obtainable from the CBA and the Committee secretary (Mrs Gillian Swanton address p xviii) at cost price.

Samples and methods

Twenty-one undisturbed samples were taken (see Figure 8.1 and Table 8.4). In the following discussion soil micromorphological samples are distinguished by a number in bold type (eg **170**); several of these sections are also illustrated by plates. Twenty were sampled in standard Kubiena boxes, approximately 75 × 63 × 37mm, in size. One sample, with the approximate dimensions of 150 × 70 × 60mm was also taken, using a cut-down fruit juice carton specifically to enclose possibly laminated ditch sediments (Sample **92**). Samples were acetone- (University of Stirling) or air- (Institut National Agronomique, Paris-Grignon) dried, prior to impregnation by resin and thin section manufacture (Guilloré 1985; Murphy 1986). For problems with loose samples and sample storage, see CD.

Soil micromorphological analysis

Description

Thin sections were described according to Bullock *et al.* (1985) and the major studies of Babel (1975) and Bal (1982) on the biological microfabrics present in humic mineral topsoils. Results from preliminary description were used to select those microfeatures that were to be estimated. See CD for soil micromorphological descriptions and colour plates.

Semi-quantitative analysis

Sixteen samples from the present day unburied soils (**10, 11, 15**), the soil formed on the bank (**108**) and the within-bank sediment (**104**) and the buried soils and bank (**100, 101, 165, 167, 168, 169, 170, 171, 172, 173, 177**) were subjected to semi-quantitative analysis. Those from the subsoil hollow (**79, 80, 81**) and the ditch fill (**92, 95**) were only described.

Thin sections were divided into 5mm squares, and amounts of void space (soil pores), chalk, flint gravel, plant residues, decalcified soil and calcareous soil were estimated as percentages of the square (CD, example of count sheet). This was to provide numerical data. In addition, types of voids (water and gas space in the soil), types of amorphous iron and manganese nodules (features of poor drainage, Fig

Table 8.4 Soil micromorphological samples

Sample no	Context	Local depth	Location
10	5009	50–120mm	Soil Pit 1; unburied soil inside experimental earthwork enclosure; from base of root mat (L: 40–60mm) through the mineral soil (Ah) to top of chalk stone line (A/C)
11	5009	90–170mm	
15	5011	10–80mm	Soil Pit 2; unburied soil outside experimental earthwork enclosure. No root mat; only mineral soil (Ah); stone line at 160mm.
81	–	0.26–0.34m	Berm of OD bank; soil (B1) overlying subsoil feature beneath stone line
80	–	0.39–0.47m	Berm of OD bank; main fill (B2) of subsoil feature
79	–	0.50–0.58m	Berm of OD bank; base (B3) of subsoil feature
92	–	0.16–0.32m	Ditch, East section.
95	–	0.23–0.31m	Ditch, West section.
100	5053	+10 / +70mm	Junction of chalk bank and buried soil
101	5015	0/ –70mm	Buried soil
104	–	0.38–0.45m	Within chalk bank
108	–	10–80mm	Modern soil (Ah) formed on surface of chalk bank (North) (below root mat)
165	–	+0.36/+0.43m	Top of turf stack and junction with chalk bank
167	–	+0.30 /+0.37m	Turf stack
168	–	+0.24 / +0.31m	Turf stack
169	–	+0.17 / +0.24m	Turf stack
170	–	+0.10 / +10.7m	Turf stack
171	–	+10 / +80mm	Turf stack
172	–	+60 / –10mm	OLS; turf stack and junction of buried soil
173	–	–20 / –90mm	Buried soil
177	–	0 / –70mm	OLS; buried soil, lateral control, 0.25m to the north of **173**
Easton Down B	–	0–70mm	Buried soil; archaeological analogue

8.8), types of excrements (faeces of invertebrates, Fig 8.14 and 8.15; see below) and types of plant residues (Figures 8.5 and 8.15) were estimated, based upon the estimation and size range schemes of Bullock *et al* (1985), studies by Babel (1975) and Bal (1982) as well as pilot investigations of the Overton Down microfabrics by the authors. Thus, for example, types of voids (Table 8.5) were estimated as being very dominant (>70%) to very few (<5%), and sizes of iron and manganese nodules and excrements were measured as micro (<100µm), meso (100–500µm) and >500µm for consistent simplicity, without using the detail of Bullock *et al* (1985). Similarly, void types were divided into spongy, planar and other. Others include, for example, packing voids around soil particles (Fig 8.6), or channels from roots and faunal burrows. These were ways of reflecting the major microfabric patterns at Overton Down. Soils with a sponge-like (Figure 8.8) appearance are typical of mull humus horizons (Babel 1975) and are hitherto referred to as spongy microfabrics (Bullock *et al*

Table 8.5 Estimation scheme for semi-quantitative analysis of types of voids and features

Table 8.5a Percentage of 5mm square

Very dominant	VD	>70%
Dominant	D	50–70%
Common	C	30–50%
Frequent	F	15–30%
Few	Fw	5–15%
Very few	VF	<5%

Table 8.5b Size of features

Micro	–	<100µm
Meso	–	100–500µm
>500µm		

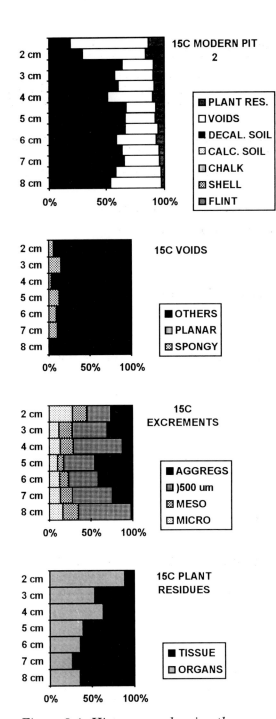

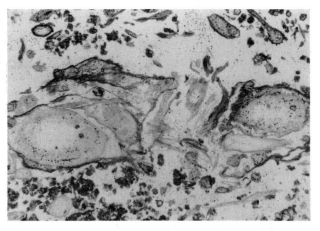

Figure 8.5 Sample 15, 15mm; heavily rooted topsoil, showing cross-sections through living roots, very open compound packing porosity, and abundant micro organic and organo-mineral excrements. Plane polarized light (PPL), frame length is 5.56mm

Figure 8.4 Histograms showing the proportions of micromorphological features in Sample 15, control soil from outside the enclosure. For location see Figure 7.3

1985). In contrast, planar voids are the fissures that are more typical of subsoil horizons, where processes such as mechanical shrink and swell are more important than biological activity. In highly biological active soils such as the rendzinas at Overton Down, all the fine soil has passed through the gut of earthworms, and the microfabrics of such soils are termed total excremental microfabrics (Courty *et al* 1989). Excrements were measured, micro-size excrements being mainly the product of small fauna such as enchytraeid worms, whereas meso-size and

>500µm-size excrements were commonly produced by earthworms. Where individual excrements could not be differentiated, because these had coalesced or become 'welded' (Bal 1982) either by earthworm reworking or through shrink and swell, excremental soil was described as 'aggregates' (Figures 8.10 and 8.11). Twelve column counts were obtained from every 5mm of depth, giving 168 column counts in all for each thin section (60mm wide and 70mm deep). These data were recorded on count sheets which have been included in the archive. It was not possible in the time available, some 12 months, to organize the use of image analysis (Murphy *et al* 1977; Delgardo and Dorronsoro 1983) or Quantimet analysis of the microfabrics, which would have speeded up counting. On the other hand it is not certain that the detail attained by the present study could be replicated by an automatic method (Murphy pers comm), but this may be tested in the future. Semi-quantitative data was incorporated into the descriptions.

Results

Selected semi-quantitative results are presented in Figures 8.4; 8.7; 8.9; and 8.13.

Modern Soil Pit 2, outside the enclosure: Sample 15

This profile (Fig 7.3) was sampled to include the heavily rooted (Fig 8.5) mineral soil downwards. Soil micromorphology showed that only decalcified soil is present (Fig 8.4: see Crowther p 108). The soil has a total excremental fabric, and roots are concentrated in the top 10mm, which has a very open compound packing porosity around crumb structures, which are porous soil aggregates produced by earthworms. Below the rooted layer fine subangular blocky structures representing soil that has coalesced through

98

wetting and drying processes, become more common (Figure 8.6). The thinnest (micro size) organo-mineral excrements are present throughout the 70mm of soil studied, although organic excrements are concentrated around the rooted layer. Typically for mull horizons (Babel 1975) and other examples of grazed rendzinas such as at Maiden Castle, Dorset (Macphail 1991), the soil is dominantly earthworm worked, whereas the thinner (micro and meso-size) excrements may derive from enchytraeid (small Annelid worms) activity associated with roots, and with the reworking of the earthworm excremental fabric. The burrowing into, and 'eating of,' earthworm excrements by enchytraeids which have a diet of fungi and bacteria (Wallwork 1976; Swift *et al* 1979) is a typical feature of mull humus rendzinas in general (Babel 1975; Bal 1982) and probably also of this soil. It must be noted that identification of these enchytraeid-like excrements has yet to be tested by field experiments. In these well-drained base-rich mull horizons as at Overton Down, however, enchytraeids will only make up a very small quantity of the biomass compared with earthworms (Wallwork 1976).

The A1h horizon of this soil can be considered the control soil for the experiment. Using the soil classification system of Avery (1990) it would be classified as a Typical Humic Rendzina, and using the system of the United States Department of Agriculture (Soil Survey Staff 1975) it would be classified as Typic Rendoll loamy skeletal, mesic soil. The main features are that it is well rooted, well drained, base-rich although decalcified, and has a stable open structure because of dominant earthworm activity.

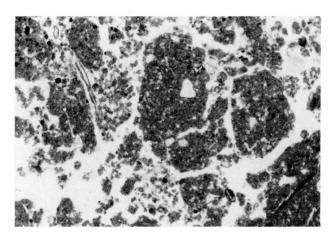

Figure 8.6 Sample 15, 60mm; total excremental fabric of open crumb and fine subangular blocky structures (aggregated earthworm excrements), with micro, meso and >500μm size organo-mineral excrements, some possibility of enchytraeids (micro-size) and root and other plant fragments. PPL, frame length is 5.56mm

Modern soil pit 1, inside the enclosure: Samples 10 and 11

The soil was sampled at the base of the 50mm thick litter mat. Typical soil diatoms (*Hantzschia amphioxys* and *Pinnularia borealis*; Nigel Cameron, pers comm) are present in this litter mat, and dark brown coloured, slowly decomposing grass stems are releasing numerous phytoliths. Below the litter mat the soil has a 60mm thick unstructured layer that contains few separate peds (soil structures). Such soil

Table 8.6 Some comparisons of void space

Depth	Bank buried soil 101	Turf stack buried soil 177	Turf stack (centre) buried soil 173/172
a) the buried soils compared with Soil Pit 2 **15** – outside enclosure			
10mm	−48.42%	−43.75%	−74.73%
20mm	−22.73%	−0.67%	−32.91%
30mm	−31.59%	−8.28%	−25.46%
40mm	+28.06%	+36.82%	+16.30%
50mm	+4.63%	+13.82%	−19.36%
60mm	+55.24%	+15.19%	−22.06%
70mm	+32.25%	−16.50%	−21.26%
average	−3.80%	−10.65%	−25.64%
b) the buried soils compared with Soil Pit 1 (**10, 11** – inside the enclosure).			
average	−14.26%	−20.37%	10
average	−14.69%	−20.76%	11
c) Pit 1 (**10, 11**) compared with Pit 2 (**15** – outside enclosure).			
average	−11.10%		

horizons are termed as massive by soil scientists. They have a homogeneous appearance and do not break apart in any preferred direction and can be best described by their porosity pattern (Courty *et al* 1989: 38, 71).

In the soil within the enclosure there is both a decrease in porosity and a change in the type of pore space, compared to the control soil (Sample **15**). The porosity of the massive soil averages 40% compared with 50–70% porosity in Sample **15**, a measured decrease in porosity of 11.10% overall (Table 8.6). The very open compound packing pores of the well structured control soil have been replaced by fine vughs (spherical to elongate irregular voids) and channels giving rise to a spongy microfabric. In addition, this massive soil contains abundant micro and meso-size iron and manganese nodules, whereas these features are quite rare outside the enclosure. Occasionally, in this massive horizon, plant remains have been (pseudomorphically) replaced by iron and manganese. Lower in the soil, the structure is coarse subangular blocky, formed of aggregated earthworm excrements down to 0.12m below the litter mat, and again this is typical of the lower part of mull rendzinas (Babel 1975).

At Overton Down, the slightly more acid (see Crowther p 113), and moist topsoil conditions within the enclosure, which have developed because of the accumulation of a litter mat, have led to a sharp decline in biological activity, especially by earthworms. Enchytraeids could be more tolerant of this new topsoil environment, and their presence may be indicated by micro and meso organo-mineral excrements loosely infilling the spongy microfabric. This microfabric may indicate that they have possibly become the dominant invertebrate fauna, a suggestion that can be readily tested by a survey of soil invertebrates within the enclosure. The slowly decomposing litter mat and associated fungal food sources are likely to have attracted such fauna as, for example, are frequently found in moist and acid moorland soils (Wallwork 1976, 149; Swift *et al* 1979). As a consequence of the litter mat holding water and the soil becoming less freely drained, possible localized waterlogged conditions (Bloomfield 1951) have ensued (see Crowther p 113), mobilizing iron and manganese at abundant anaerobic micro-sites (P E J Wiltshire, pers comm). Subsequently, iron and manganese have been deposited at aerobic sites as meso-size nodules. At the same time, grass roots, which were so numerous in the soil outside the enclosure, are few and in a mainly decomposing state. As single grass roots may live only some four years (Babel 1975)) it is probable that the compacted massive horizon has inhibited root growth, possibly because of a lack of oxygen (Wiltshire, pers comm). Evans (1990) has discussed the long term effects of 'Festuca mats' on rendzinas, leading to their decalcification, decrease in biological activity, especially that of earthworms, and the general development of poorly structured soil. These features are already apparent within the

enclosure at Overton Down where litter mat accumulation has accelerated subsequent to withdrawal of grazing.

Buried soil beneath the turf stack (Fig 7.10)

Sample **177** (buried soil), and Samples **173** and **172** (buried soil and junction with turf bank; Figures 8.7-8) show a highly reduced porosity when compared with the unburied soil (Sample **15**). In the buried soil, porosity is generally around 20–30%, decreasing to 10–15% at the top of the old land surface, whereas in the control soil, porosity averaged around 50–60% and was especially open in its highly rooted uppermost part (Fig 8.4). The deepest parts of the buried soils have a relic subangular blocky structure but most of the excrements are aggregated. In contrast, the uppermost 70mm has a massive or poorly formed fine prismatic structure, with burrowed open vughs, loosely infilled with micro and meso organo-mineral excrements (spongy microfabric; Fig 8.8). In the top 20–40mm 'ghosts' of probable grass roots occur in voids, whereas probable relic epidermal cork cells of dicotyledonous plants and other plant fragments occur as decomposing fragments which have been integrated into the soil matrix. It is also at this depth that patches of many micro to meso impregnative iron and manganese nodules, some pseudomorphic of organic matter, are concentrated. Pieces of oak charcoal, possibly scattered on the soil surface in 1960, were found worked some 5mm into the buried soil.

As a result of burial, compression and the decomposition of roots and other plant material, the soil has been transformed in character, in addition to being reduced from some 0.16m to 70–100mm in thickness. It is likely that the living population of earthworms in the buried soil was active for a time after burial (Carter 1987, 172), and this is dramatically demonstrated beneath the chalk bank (p 76) and by the movement of *Lycopodium* spores (Crabtree, p 127). These with other extant fauna comminute roots and litter, aiding their microbial decomposition, and integrate residual organic material into the aggregated excremental soil fabric. Earthworms as significant mixers of soil (Bal 1982) were probably also responsible for the incorporation of oak charcoal into the buried soil. Compression and structural transformation has led to a major decrease in porosity, and periodically very moist to anaerobic conditions (Crowther, p 115; Wiltshire p 155) have produced ubiquitous micro nodular iron and manganese formation (see enclosure soil p 113). Only in a few patches (**173**), however, has meso and compound nodular formation occurred in the buried soil.

The turf stack

In relation to Sample **172**, it was noted that the first turf, although suffering similar compaction as the

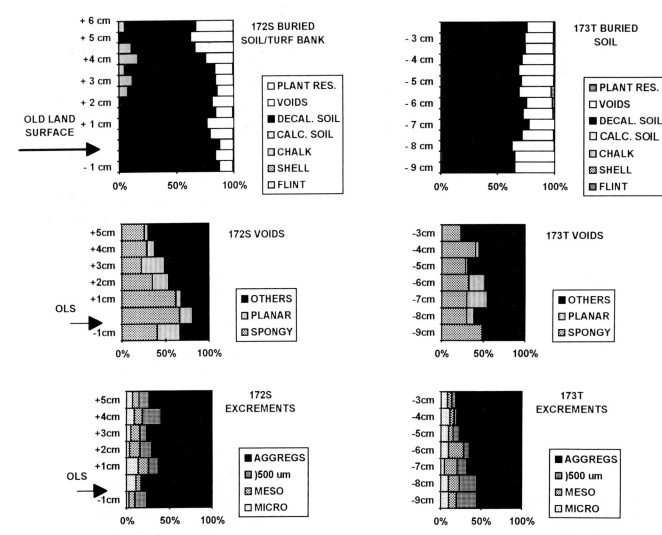

Figure 8.7 Histograms showing the proportion of micromorphological features in Samples 172 and 173 from the turf mound and old land surface buried soil. For location see Figure 8.1

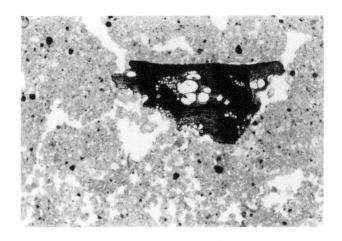

Figure 8.8 Sample 172, junction of turf stack and old land surface; probable fragment of oak charcoal, scattered on soil surface in 1960, set in a dense massive unstructured soil of compacted earthworm aggregates; dense soil has subsequently been burrowed and eaten by smaller fauna, possibly enchytraeids, producing a spongy microfabric comprising open vughs containing cylindrical micro to meso organo-mineral excrements. Occasional to many round micro iron and manganese nodules are present. PPL, frame length 5.56mm

buried soil (Fig 8.7), has better retained its fine subangular blocky structure and is only weakly massive. It is also much less reworked into a spongy microfabric. No relic organic matter of the grass and litter layers is preserved but in the lowest two thin sections (**171**, **170**; two lowest turves?) a few root remains that are probably relic of the 1960's soil, occur

in pores. Higher in the turf stack, there is little trace of roots. This preservation pattern may reflect moister conditions, more numerous anaerobic micro-sites, and hence, lower biological activity towards the junction with the old land surface, whereas more oxidizing and base-rich conditions with higher biological activity occur upwards into the turf/chalk bank (see

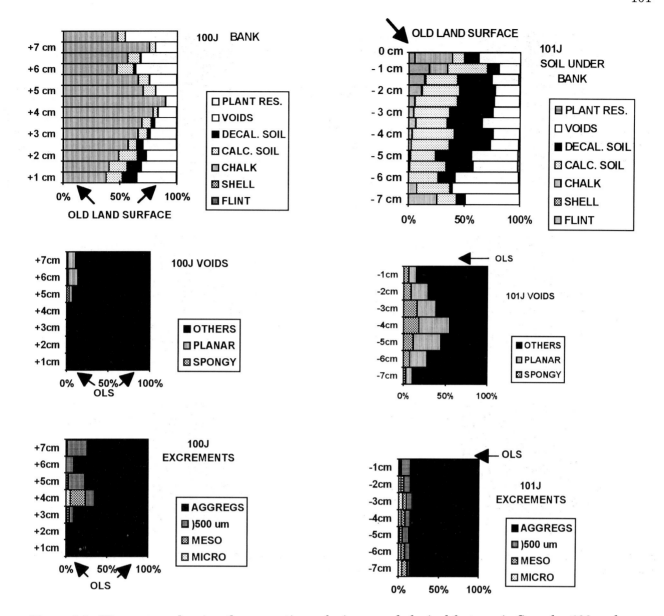

Figure 8.9   Histograms showing the proportions of micromorphological features in Samples 100 and 101 from the chalk bank and buried soil. For location see Figure 8.1

Crowther, p 115). Porosity is very low at the base of the turf stack (15–20%), and slowly increases to around 50% at the junction with the chalk bank (Samples **165**, **167**). Throughout the turf stack, fine subangular blocky structures can be well preserved or the turf soil may be transformed into a massive soil, and the last is again often well burrowed, possibly by enchytraeid worms, producing a spongy microfabric. It is possible that these massive but strongly reworked zones were once the most organic and microbially most active topmost soils of individual turves.

At the top of the turf stack, mixing by earthworms upwards and outwards into the chalk bank is evident (Samples **167**, **165**), but mixing of the chalk with the decalcified soil of the turf stack does not extend downwards into Samples **168** and **169**, for example. Although earthworm activity has been recorded within the chalk bank (Bell, p 74), parts of the chalk bank have been apparently completely unaffected by

earthworms (see below, **104**). It therefore appears quite likely that mixing of the chalk bank with the uppermost turves was limited by the extant earthworm population of the turves and buried soil. It is possible that here, and under the chalk bank (see below), earthworms were following the oxygen gradient upwards from a buried old land surface that was tending to become anaerobic at times (Wiltshire, pers comm).

The soil buried by the chalk bank (Figure 7.11)

Figure 8.9 shows clearly how chalk and fine calcareous soil has been worked all the way through the buried soil (**101**; Figures 8.10 and 8.11) by earthworms, and how decalcified soil has been worked upwards into the chalk bank (**100**). Chalk and calcareous soil from the subsoil AC horizon may also have become integrated by earthworm activity into the base of the once totally decalcified soil (**15**, **10**, **11**). At Easton Down, this mixing also occurred. The buried soil is obviously compacted upwards, but unlike the soil buried by the turf stack, there are very few micro and meso excrements, rather the soil is totally dominated by aggregated earthworm excrements. Reworking of the mainly massive soil by such fauna as enchytraeids is minimal. Relic subangular structures and root ghosts also can be recognized.

Compression

Pore space in the control soil (**15**) has been compared with that of the buried soils. Pore space in the buried soils is less than in the control soil, and has apparently decreased by average amounts of 3.8% less under the chalk bank (**101**), rising to 10.65% less (**177**) and 25.64% less (**172/173**) beneath the turf stack. These figures would be greater if space taken up with roots in the control soil had been included in the calculations of pore space. It is quite apparent that porosity is least within the soil buried by the turf stack beneath the very centre of the bank. It contains markedly less pore space compared with both the lateral control soil under the turf stack and the soil buried by the chalk bank towards the edge of the earthwork. The greatest decrease in porosity is within the top 30mm, with a very substantial decrease in porosity (by 74.73%; a compaction/porosity loss factor of *c* ×4) recorded for soil just beneath the old land surface under the centre of the turf stack. The uppermost soil horizon of the present day rendzina contains high amounts of organic matter in

excrements and root material and much of this has been lost from the buried soils and contributed to this high degree of compaction.

In summary, compression is greatest at the old land surface because, here there has been the greatest reduction in organic matter, (see Crowther, p 116), the weight of the monument is at its maximum, and here there has been the greatest amount of change in soil structure, from an open crumby soil to a massive soil, with a resulting major decrease in porosity.

Centre of bank   The bank (Sample **104**) is comprised of coarse and fine chalk, and coarse fissures between these are infilled with finer fragments, and these have been weakly cemented by micritic calcite (Fig 8.12) and inwash of clay-size chalk. The bank sediment is the result of dumping, post-depositional settling, and still later effects of physical and chemical weathering. According to this sample the centre of the bank is apparently almost completely unaffected by biological activity, except for a single rooting episode, and this interpretation was confirmed by Dr N Fedoroff. Earthworms were found within the chalk bank during the excavation (Bell, p 74), but this soil micromorphological study may suggest that many of the interstitial fillings between chalk clasts noted in the field by the authors are in reality pseudoexcrements and not of biological origin (see below), in the same way as pseudomycelia are formed chemically.

Soil formed on the bank   The heavily rooted (Fig 8.14) chalk bank material (Sample **108**) has weathered so that the finest chalk clasts and most open

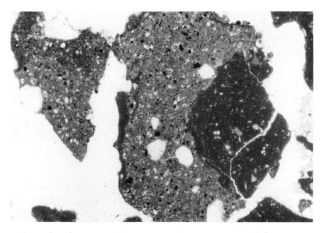

Figure 8.10 Sample 101, 20mm below old land surface; coarse earthworm excremental aggregates comprising sand-size quartz, very dark grey chalk (right centre, upper and lower right) containing fossils, black speckled humic decalcified soil and mixed calcareous humic soil (top left). The peds are separated by coarse compound packing voids. After burial earthworms mixed decalcified soil of the buried soil with chalky material from the overlying bank (cf. Figure 8.9). PPL, frame length is 5.56mm

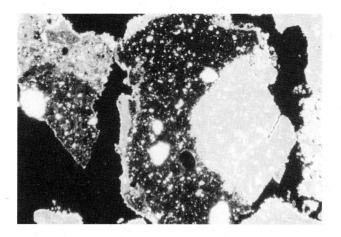

Figure 8.11   As Figure 8.10, but under crossed polarized light; the calcareous soil and chalk is a bright grey, whereas the decalcified soil is non-birefringent, but contains bright sand-size quartz and finer silt-size quartz. The largest ped may have some bright grey chalky soil adhering to it (left centre) as a result of earthworm mixing, whereas on the right some of the void space is loosely infilled by secondary micritic calcite formed from the weathering of the chalk bank material (see Figure 8.12)

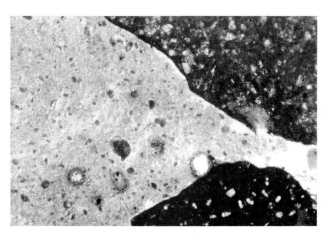

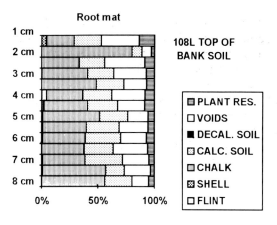

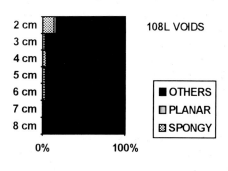

Figure 8.12 Sample 104, 400mm; very coarse simple packing porosity between large chalk clasts (right top and bottom), has become loosely infilled by fine chalk fragments as the dumped bank sediment has settled. Many of these voids have become loosely cemented by finely dusty/cloudy micritic calcite as a result of weathering (decalcification of chalk bank surface) and percolation of calcium carbonate charged water. Occasionally fine pores may develop calcitic hypocoatings (left centre), but faunal mixing appears to be absent. PPL, frame length is 3.55mm

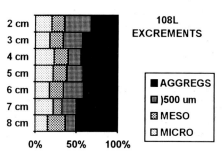

Figure 8.13 Histograms showing the proportions of micromorphological features in sample 108 from the new soil developed on the bank. For location see Figure 8.1

porosity are near the surface (Fig 8.13). Chalk has weathered into chalky soil that has been biologically mixed by fauna, and both coarse aggregates (earthworms) and micro and meso organic excrements occur down-profile, sometimes forming fine subangular blocky peds as they become 'welded' by wetting and drying phenomena (Fig 8.14). Micro organic excrements of mites, and the more coarse organic excrements (Fig 8.15) of surface feeders and primary comminuters of roots and leaves (Bal 1981), such as Isopods, larvae of insects and some Lumbricidae, are all probably present. At the surface (0–10mm) purely organic peds occur alongside strongly organic AC horizon material (mainly 0–20mm), whereas weakly humic ACu horizon soil is present throughout (mainly 20–70mm).

Ditch section Ditch fills comprise loosely packed sand to stone-size chalk with calcareous soil aggregates (earthworm casts) including abundant sand-size humic and weakly calcareous and decalcified soil clasts.

Sample **95** (0.16m below ditch surface) comes from higher up the ditch fill sequence (Fig 8.1) and when compared with sample **92** (0.23m below ditch surface) can be considered to include younger sediments. The more recent sediments appear to be more chalky in nature, although small quantities of decalcified A1h horizon material was also found. Coarse earthworm channelling and reworking of the ditch sediments is ubiquitous, and has affected the banding recognized in previous excavations (Bell 1990a; Crabtree 1990). Banding or layering is more obvious when decalcified soil is involved and least apparent

when only chalk is present. Hence banding in the more chalky Sample **95** is less discernable than in Sample **92**. Banding (see Discussion) approaches a gradient of 45° to 60° very approximately following the slope of the ditch side.

Subsoil feature The lowest part (**79**) of the hollow (Figs 7.12–13) is comprised of an earthworm-worked weathered chalk soil, and can be considered to be a long matured subsoil (AC horizon) of a woodland rendzina soil. The layer above (**80**) is more heterogeneous (Ah&A/C horizon), with a mixture of chalky subsoil, calcareous soil and decalcified soil, and probably represents the result of soil disturbance by tree throw that here may have been possibly related to clearance (Macphail and Goldberg 1990; Macphail 1992). The uppermost layer (**81**) is, in part, a rather more biologically homogenized version of the layer beneath (**80**), and results from long-term weathering of the feature. In addition, the hollow infill becomes

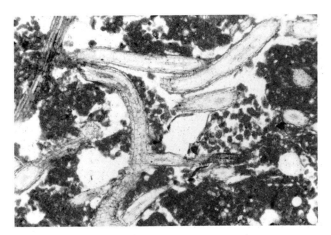

Figure 8.14 Sample 108, 50mm; a strongly interconnected living root system within the coarsely aggregated, subangular blocky chalky soil of the ACu horizon; micro organo-mineral (chalky) excrements occur within the complex packing voids and are associated with roots. PPL, frame length is 3.35mm

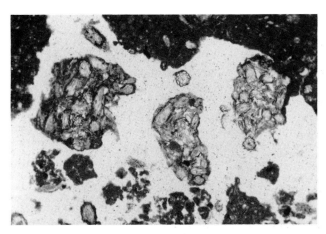

Figure 8.15 Sample 108, 20mm; large >500μm organic baccilo-cylindrical excrements of primary decomposers composed of 100–180μm lengths of root fragments occur within complex packing pores between chalk clasts and mixed humic chalky soil in the A/C horizon. Organo-mineral micro to meso excrements (bottom centre) are present along with living roots (cross-section, top centre). PPL, frame length is 3.35mm

compacted upwards, with a structural change from subangular blocky and prismatic to massive, and with chalk stones and chalky material also mixed into this uppermost horizon.

Discussion

The effects of burial on soil structure

The major effects of burial have been a decrease and change in porosity type (Figs 8.4; 8.7; 8.9), loss of organic matter such as the disappearance of roots and the reworking of the soil by buried fauna. Beneath the turf stack where the buried soil has become more acidic (see Crowther p 115), crumb and fine subangular structures have generally become transformed into a massive soil through the aggregation of micro to >500μm size excrements. The extant earthworm population may have been partially responsible for this, because, as is clearly demonstrated at the top of the turf stack and directly under the chalk bank (Fig 8.9), earthworms were initially active burrowing and mixing calcareous soil and chalk (Figures 8.10–11) with the originally decalcified buried soil (**101**) and turf stack (**165, 167**). A study of the distribution of stable soil aggregates through a recently (1947) buried rendzina at War Down, near Petersfield, Hampshire, has enabled Carter (1987: 172) to suggest, although without corroborative soil micromorphology, the possibility of post-depositional reworking of the buried soil by its buried fauna. At Overton Down, it seems possible that earthworm reworking was concentrated in the uppermost few tens of mm of the buried soil, because it was here that their food source was most plentiful. Their activities have led to the development of a

massive soil prior to possible enchytraeid reworking. Physical and chemical factors of burial would have played a part in the development of this soil, particularly compression, disappearance of much organic matter, periodic concentration of soil moisture at the old land surface, as it acted as a hydraulic break, and the development of anaerobic micro-sites. An overall effect of burial has been to change ecological conditions from a freely draining neutral to slightly alkaline soil, which is ideal for earthworms, to one which is acid and so moist at times that anaerobic micro-sites are produced and where another group of soil fauna could become dominant. This possibility is suggested by Matthew Davis, Hunting Land and Environment (pers comm). Under the developing litter mat within the enclosure (Sample **10**), a similar ecological transformation is occurring, namely a massive soil has developed, earthworms have probably died off and have been replaced by another fauna (Fig 8.8). In the turf bank buried soil the newly dominant fauna are possibly enchytraeid worms, which are probably present in the unburied rendzina (Sample **15**) outside the enclosure (see above; Babel 1975; Bal 1982), a theory that is to be tested by a survey of invertebrates. They are more tolerant of acid and very moist conditions than earthworms (Swift *et al* 1979; Wallwork 1976). The presence of fungal material beneath the turf bank, although not necessarily shown to be actively growing at the present time (Kelley and Wiltshire p 154), would also supply them with a suitable food source. Within the turf stack some layers have well preserved subangular blocky peds, whereas other layers are massive with a spongy microfabric. These two types of layers may reflect original single turves with possible enchytraeids reworking the uppermost organic horizon in each of them.

Under the chalk bank (**100, 101**) and under the chalky barrow at Easton Down (Easton Down Micromorphological Sample **B** described on Microfiche) the buried soils are calcareous (Whittle *et al* 1993). They are less affected by transformation into a massive soil and micro and meso excrements from possible enchytraeid activity are far less frequent. The higher base status of these calcareous buried soils may help to retain their structure, while the higher pH is less suitable for enchytraeids and the growth of fungi which is their main food source (Kelley and Wiltshire p 148).

The preservation of soil structures in archaeological soils varies considerably. At Silbury Hill, Wiltshire (Cornwall thin section archive; Dimbleby 1984; Macphail *et al* 1987, Figure 11) no soil structure or porosity pattern was visible because of immense compression. In contrast, at Maiden Castle, Dorset, and at Hazleton, Gloucestershire, the major microstructures of planar voids, channels and vughs with their associated textural features seem to suggest that they have been little altered and were subsoil-like in character (because of erosion; Macphail 1992) even before burial (Macphail 1990, 1991). At Hazleton there was little evidence of post-burial reworking by earthworms, probably because of a small former earthworm population. Only minor reworking by earthworms at Maiden Castle derived from surface dwelling fauna which burrowed through the overlying thin chalk bank into the buried soil. The data from Overton Down and Easton Down, indicate, on the other hand, that soils with high biological activity may be reworked by their own buried fauna.

Organic remains and ironpans

In general, biological activity is enhanced by freely draining base-rich conditions, whereas acid, wet and anaerobic conditions may inhibit microbiological processes. At Overton Down, the few root ghosts present in the buried soils may relate to very moist, periodically anaerobic conditions aiding preservation, because they are absent higher up the turf stack where the soil environment is probably more aerobic and less acidic in character, and hence more oxidizing. At Silbury Hill, extreme anaerobic conditions led to the perfect preservation of the mossy vegetation (Dimbleby 1984), whereas at Hazleton, Gloucestershire the organic matter of buried turf, including some roots, were preserved by ferruginization (Allen and Macphail 1987, Figure 2; Macphail 1986a). At the Wareham Experimental Earthwork, Dorset, lignified and other surface plant remains are well preserved by very moist, acid burial.

At Overton Down, however, it is only in a few patches (**173**) that meso and compound nodular formation (increased number of anaerobic microsites) may be thought to be incipient of iron and manganese pans although the old land surface was sampled from three areas. Nethertheless, Bell (p 74)

reports iron staining just above the layer E/F and the old land surface. Iron and iron and manganese pans are found in some archaeological buried soils (Evans 1972; Limbrey 1975; Macphail 1986b) at similar (40–60mm) depths (eg Hazleton, Gloucestershire, Macphail 1990) as the incipient iron and manganese pan was found at Overton Down. On the other hand, micro nodules, which characterize all of the buried soil microfabrics at Overton Down, are found ubiquitously in buried soils (eg Maiden Castle, Macphail 1991). At Easton Down (see Microfiche, Micromorphological Descriptions; Macphail 1993) micro nodules are present in the buried soil but no ironpan or iron and manganese pan had developed in spite of the soil having been buried since the Neolithic. Although pronounced iron banding was found in the bank (Bell p 74), paucity of iron in the soils may be an important factor in the poor development of an ironpan at Overton Down, in addition to lack of time and the maintenance of, albeit changed, soil porosity and lack of full anaerobic conditions (see above). For example, the more clay-rich soils at Hazleton developed on Oolitic Limestone are quite ferruginous with 3–4% Fe, as compared to <1.5% Fe at Overton Down (Crowther p 109). At Hazleton, both buried soil ironpans and iron and manganese pans occur (Allen and Macphail 1987, Fig 3), the last developing from the concentration of micro nodules into meso nodules, becoming a strongly impregnated compound nodular fabric (Macphail 1986a).

Turf stack

The outline of some former turves were well-preserved at Overton Down (Fig 7.9), and although turves became increasingly compressed towards the old land surface (Figs 8.7 and 8.8), their microfabrics seemed to generally reflect their original biological character (see above). Both decalcified grassland soils comparable to those at Overton Down and rendzinas with evidence of pre-burial occupation (as at Easton Down) were recognized at Earls Farm Down, Wiltshire (Cornwall thin section archive; Macphail 1987: Macphail *et al* 1987), and material from both soil types was recognized from the turf stack. In contrast, 'turf' from soils which are more poorly structured, as a result, for instance, of cultivation, or are from more acid alluvial loams, for example at Strathallan, Perthshire, have no such relic soil structures. Rather the soil has collapsed and formed many textural features (Romans and Robertson 1983; Macphail *et al* 1987, Figs 4 and 13).

Bank sediment and bank soil

The immature chalk soil would be classified according to Avery's (1990) scheme as a calcaric lithosol, according to the scheme of the United States Department of Agriculture (Soil Survey Staff 1975) as a lithic orthent and according to Babel (1975) as a protorendzina. It has a 20mm thick organic AC horizon and below, a 50mm thick chalky ACu horizon, and these have formed over the 32 year period since construction of the bank (Figs 8.14–15). An extremely heavily rooted and totally excremental fine soil is formed between dominant to very dominant chalk clasts that increase in size down profile. Possibly, excessive drainage has led to slow biological decomposition of organic matter and retarded deep biological homogenization of the soil, whereas physical (frost action) and chemical weathering are strongly in evidence (see Crowther p 116). In contrast, the bank sediment appears to be simply a deposit showing features of dumping, settling and chemical weathering (Fig 8.12), the last including the formation of a loosely infilling micritic cement. As shown at Maiden Castle and at Fort Harrouard, France (Courty *et al* 1989, Figures 14.4 e and f), the nature of bank sediment and how it weathers is strongly influenced by the material used to build the bank (see Turf Stack, above). At Overton Down, the micromorphological investigation suggests that the centre of the bank is mainly unaffected by earthworm casting although earthworms were present in the bank (see Bell p 74) (see earlier for earthworms at Maiden Castle), and only one rooting episode was noted.

Ditch sediments

Despite reworking by earthworms, bands dominated by chalk or by soil were recognizable in the ditch fills. Soil bands contain earthworm-formed aggregates of calcareous soil which include sand size humic decalcified soil. Such banding has been ascribed to winter chalk sedimentation and soil deposition in summer, which together form an annual sequence (Bell 1990a; Crabtree 1990a) and are more mature than those described by Proudfoot (1965).

The development of annual dark fine soil and chalk layers is probably not a simple result of sedimentation. Firstly, it is likely that frost action releases chalk from the ditch sides into the ditch in winter, forming a loosely packed 'talus-like' deposit. The fine humic and often decalcified and rounded sand to silt-size soil clasts are not necessarily formed *in situ* but more probably derive from turf overhanging the ditch. This soil may include individual excrements as well as smaller particles released and rounded by frost or rain splash, then translocated by wash and rolling. The resulting sediment is not particularly 'colluvial' (water transported and waterlain; Bell and Boardman 1992) in character because of rapid drainage through the coarser basal ditch sediments. Like the chalk, this soil material may also be partially deposited in the ditch over winter, but it is perhaps in the summer, when fresh plant material is available, that earthworm action mixes calcareous soil derived from the weathering chalk fill, with surface organic matter and decalcified soil. Earthworms may thus annually produce thin 'stone-free' humic soil layers and include inwashed decalcified

fine soil that may have been deposited at the same winter time as the chalk clasts. Every year, however, earthworms may mix more than one layer together through deeper burrowing.

Comparison with neolithic ditch fills from Easton Down (Macphail 1993) suggests that the present microfabric at Overton Down 1992 is an ephemeral stage in ditch soil development. At Easton Down, all decalcified soil has been totally integrated into the fine fabric of the ditch soil (time period of Neolithic to Beaker), whereas at Overton Down decalcified soil clasts are still an obvious inclusion. There is only slight evidence of fine chalky colloidal wash in the ditch fill at Overton Down, whereas very wet slaked ditch fills were noted at Millbarrow, Wiltshire (Macphail forthcoming), and at Maiden Castle, waterlain silts and anthropogenic detritus were noted towards the base of the early Iron Age ditch fill (Macphail 1991, Table 14, Figures 105d and 105e). There is also no indication at Overton Down that large amounts of decalcified soil came into the ditch through accelerated erosion as noted in Neolithic ditches at Maiden Castle and Millbarrow, or that in this part of the ditch whole turves which may well have fallen in, and have been preserved, as at Hazleton.

Thus to conclude, the ditch fills at Overton Down are useful analogues for an early ephemeral phase of ditch silting under a stabilized herbaceous vegetation (not bare soil as occurs seasonally under woodland). It is expected that long-term weathering and reworking by biological activity transforms this presently heterogeneous ditch fill soil into a homogenized calcareous AC or Bw horizon. Future workers can also compare the long term ditch fill development at Overton Down with those from antiquity (Evans 1990).

Conclusions and future work

Semi-quantitative and descriptive data on the effect of burial of rendzinas by the earthwork have been gathered together. In addition, the effect of enclosure on a previously grazed rendzina and new soil formation on the chalk bank and weathering within the chalk bank have been fully characterized using the same methods. Soil formation within a probable prehistoric subsoil hollow and formation of the ditch fills have also been investigated in detail. Findings have been compared with data from archaeological soils and their interpretation.

Future workers may wish to monitor the maturation of the chalk bank soil, and the development of the acidifying and increasingly moist soil inside the enclosure as litter continues to accumulate. The length of time for the sediment within the bank to become biologically worked, and possible increasing compaction of the buried soils, are questions that will need to be addressed. One surprise was the realization that when highly biologically active soils like the Overton Down rendzina are buried, earthworms will continue to be active, and mix buried soil with overlying bank material. Although earthworms are still present (p 69) the major episode of reworking took place at an earlier stage in the earthwork's history. The *Lycopodium* spore evidence shows, however, that a degree of reworking of the Old Land Surface has continued over the last 16 years (Crabtree p 127). Subsequent to the main period of earthworm activity the invertebrate fauna appears to have become possibly dominated by enchytraeid worms, the action of which has formed a spongy microfabric. It will be interesting to note how long this process continues and to measure the survival of this present microstructure, itself an artefact of burial. As soil development under the thick litter mat inside the enclosure is following a similar trend as that formed in the turf stack buried soils, the comparison of present day invertebrate faunas together with microbiological species and numbers outside and inside the enclosure, may help corroborate interpretations of ecological changes induced by burial. Finally, the ditch fills are described as being in an ephemeral stage in terms of archaeological timespans, and it is wondered how long it will take for these fills to become fully homogenized as in some archaeological examples.

Acknowledgements

The authors gratefully acknowledge the Science Based Archaeology Committee of the Science and Engineering Research Council and English Heritage for funding this research, which was aided by thin section manufacture at the University of Stirling and the Institut National Agronomique, Paris-Grignon. The authors thank all those involved with the project for their collaboration, aid with sampling and discussion etc. Particularly useful discussions were held with Nigel Cameron (Department of Geography, University College London), Dr J Crowther on soil chemistry, N Fedoroff (Institut National Agronomique, Paris-Grignon) on the within-bank soil thin section, Dr K. Thomas (Institute of Archaeology, University College London) on invertebrates and Ms Wiltshire on microbiology and soil ecology. John Bates is gratefully acknowledged for printing colour plates and Don Shewan (City Guidhall University) and Naomi Mott (UCL) for help with black and white versions. Alasdair Whittle is thanked for allowing his site of Easton Down to be included as a specific archaeological analogue. The Cornwall thin section archive is housed at the Institute of Archaeology, University College London.

8.5 Soil chemistry
by J Crowther

Introduction

One of the main uncertainties encountered when interpreting and making inferences from palaeosols buried beneath archaeological monuments is whether, and to what extent, the properties of soils change after burial. The rendzina soils of the chalk downlands of southern England are of considerable archaeological significance, and the Experimental Earthwork on Overton Down provides a unique opportunity to investigate the direction and rate of change in one such soil. In view of the very limited, 32-year timespan of the study, attention focused upon those properties which seemed most likely to exhibit short-term change, notably: organic matter, pH, carbonate, iron and available nutrients. The effects of burial upon χ (low frequency mass specific magnetic susceptibility) and phosphate-P (total phosphate) were also investigated. Both properties are widely used in characterizing soils on archaeological sites: the former as a means of distinguishing topsoils and subsoils, and in locating areas of burning (see reviews by Clark 1990; Scollar et al 1990); and the latter to identify areas where inputs of organic matter, including plant material, excreta and bone, have been concentrated (see Proudfoot 1976; Hamond 1983). In addition to the buried palaeosol, studies have also been made of the modern soils in the vicinity of the earthwork, and of the nature and rate of soil development on the exposed chalk of the bank. The latter aspect has practical relevance to the problems of revegetation of chalk spoil from quarrying operations and major civil engineering works, such as the Channel Tunnel (Burnham 1990). The work reported here complements the studies undertaken on soil micromorphology (by Macphail and Cruise p 95), amino acids (Beavis and Macleod p 121), and magnetic properties (Clark p 118).

Unfortunately, there is a lack of data on soil chemistry from the time of the earthwork's construction (or from previous excavations). In fact, the only known analytical data for the area are from a rendzina (here referred to as 'Profile F3') located at a similar altitude and c 100m north of the earthwork (Findlay 1960) – details in Table 8.8. Thus, whilst the essence of the project is change through time, in the case of soil chemistry there is no clear 'yardstick' against which to evaluate the 32-year data set. In these circumstances, the modern soils in the immediate vicinity must be regarded as the best available control, but this is far from ideal. Uncertainties arise as to whether in 1960 these soils were representative of those which were actually buried, and as to whether they have changed in character over the past 32 years. Moreover, from the magnetic susceptibility survey undertaken on the soils around the earthwork it appears that a band of clay-rich soil, of supposed Tertiary origin, runs through the south-western half of the enclosure, approximately parallel with the earthwork (Clark p 118). Considerable caution must therefore be exercized in interpreting the results.

Sampling design and methods

Seven soil profiles were investigated in detail: one (Profile 1/Sample Series 18) from the modern soil outside the fenced enclosure, one (5/22) from the modern soil within the enclosure, two (9/157 and 10/158) from the soil buried beneath the turf stack in the centre of the bank, two (11/106 and 12/116) from the soil buried beneath the chalk of the bank, and one (13/31) on the chalk bank. Samples of the modern soils were taken in 20mm slices down through the Ah horizon (ACu in Profile 13), whereas the buried soils were sampled in 10mm slices. Bulk samples from the Ah horizon of eight further profiles, three (Profile 2/Sample 27, 3/28 and 4/29) outside the enclosure, three (6/24, 7/25 and 8/26) inside the enclosure and two (14/114 and 15/115) on the chalk bank were also analyzed in order to provide insight into the degree of local variability in the soils. The locations of the profiles are shown in Figures 7.3 and 8.1. Samples (Table 8.9) were also taken immediately adjacent to six of the micromorphological samples studied by Macphail and Cruise (p 95). For comparative purposes, analytical work was undertaken on a profile from a nearby Late Iron Age/Romano-British lynchet investigated by Fowler and Evans (1967), and on three samples of buried palaeosols from beneath the Neolithic long barrow at Easton Down, Wiltshire, on which micromorphological work had previously been undertaken (Macphail 1993).

The methods of analysis employed are as described by Avery and Bascomb (1974), except as detailed below. LOI (loss-on-ignition) was determined by ignition at 375°C for 16 hrs (Ball 1964); phosphate-P by alkaline oxidation with NaOBr (Dick and Tabatabai 1977); extractable phosphate-P and K using standard ADAS methods (MAFF 1986); and an estimate of carbonate content using 10% HCl (Hodgson 1974). A Bartington magnetic susceptibility meter (Model MS1) was used to measure χ and χfd (frequency-dependent susceptibility). In order to minimize the errors in χfd associated with low χ samples, determinations were made on three subsamples and the mean values are presented. χfd has not been calculated for samples with χ <0.200 $\mu m^3 kg^{-1}$.

Results and discussion

1. Characteristics of soils in vicinity of earthwork

According to surveys by Findlay (1960) and Clement (1967), the soils in the immediate vicinity of the earthwork comprise rendzinas of the Icknield series (the properties and classification of rendzina soils are reviewed by Avery, 1990 Section 4.4). The drift cover in the area is very thin and patchy, and for the most part the soils directly overlie the Upper Chalk. They are characteristically shallow, organic-rich and alkaline or neutral in reaction. The following, after Dimbleby (1963a), was regarded as being a typical profile at the time the earthwork was constructed:

Depth (m)	Horizon	
0–0.025	Ah1	Mat of grass haulms and roots.
0.025–0.13	Ah2	Dark greyish brown (10YR4/2) humus horizon. Mull with good crumb structure, densely penetrated by roots. Almost stone-free.
0.13–0.15	Ah2Cu	Dense layer of small (up to 75mm long) pieces of nodular or patinated flint, coated with brown loam.
0.15–0.36	ACu	Rubble of weathered chalk with interstitial dark greyish-brown (10YR4/2) loam. Chalk fragments up to 50mm in maximum dimension, rounded at corners.

The eight profiles examined in the present study tend to have a slightly deeper Ah horizon than that described above, with depths ranging from 0.13–0.22m (Table 8.7) – presumably reflecting irregularities in the underlying chalk surface. Their texture is predominantly silty clay or silty clay loam. The high silt content (48.7–58.3%), which is typical of the Icknield series (Cope 1976, 65), is attributed to loess deposition during the Late Devensian (Catt et al 1971). Whilst the sand content is mostly low, two profiles (2 and 4) do have a relatively large sand component (22.8 and 25.5%, respectively). Interestingly, Profile F3 (Findlay 1960), which had a similarly high sand content, was also found to contain fragments of sarsen stone up to 40mm at the base of the Ah horizon. Although no such fragments were identified in the present soils, the locally higher sand contents could well be derived from weathering of sarsen stone. It should also be noted that the soils inside the enclosure have a generally higher and less variable clay content (range, 34.7–35.9%) than those outside the enclosure or beneath the bank, which is in keeping with Clark's (p 118) interpretation of the magnetic susceptibility survey.

One striking feature which emerged during sampling was that a clear layer of grass litter, c 20mm in thickness, had developed at the surface of the soil within the fenced enclosure following the cessation of grazing, and evidence suggests that this in turn has begun to affect certain soil properties. Thus, the soils outside the enclosure, despite being at a greater distance from the earthwork, must now be regarded as being most representative of those buried in 1960.

a) Modern soil outside the enclosure

The Ah horizon of this soil is rich in organic C and N, the mean concentrations being 11.0% (equivalent to c 18.9% organic matter) and 1.16%, respectively. The low C/N (range, 8.07–10.7) is indicative of a well-humified organic fraction. These figures are very similar to those recorded for Profile F3 (Table 8.8)

Table 8.7 Data for Ah horizons (sampled below root/litter mat) in immediate vicinity of earthwork

	Outside enclosure				Inside enclosure			
Profile number	1	2	3	4	5	6	7	8
Sample [or Sample Series]	[18]	27	28	29	[22]	24	25	26
Depth (m)	0.15	0.16	0.17	0.22	0.15	0.19	0.22	0.13
PARTICLE SIZE (Fine earth):								
Sand 600µm–2mm (%)	2.2	8.3	1.8	3.2	1.2	1.0	1.5	1.9
200–600µm (%)	2.6	6.9	5.4	9.1	2.0	2.1	1.9	2.9
60–200µm (%)	2.8	7.6	7.4	13.2	3.8	3.6	3.5	4.7
Silt 2–60µm (%)	56.1	54.1	53.2	48.7	58.3	57.4	57.2	54.8
Clay <2µm (%)	36.3	23.1	32.2	25.8	34.7	35.9	35.9	35.8
ORGANIC MATTER:								
LOI (%)	30.4	27.3	28.0	20.2	22.1	22.2	19.8	27.6
Organic carbon (%)	10.9	12.3	12.1	8.78	8.51	10.1	8.42	11.7
Organic nitrogen (%)	1.35	1.24	1.13	0.933	0.861	0.991	0.866	1.14
C/N ratio	8.07	9.92	10.7	9.41	9.88	10.2	9.72	10.3
pH & CARBONATE:								
pH in water (1:2.5)	6.8	7.5	6.4	6.7	6.2	6.0	6.1	6.4
pH in 0.01M $CaCl_2$	6.6	7.2	6.2	6.5	5.9	5.8	5.8	6.2
Carbonate (%)	0.5–1	1–2	<0.5	<0.5	<0.5	<0.5	<0.5	<0.5
IRON & MAGNETIC PROPERTIES:								
Pyrophosphate-ext. Fe (%)	0.076	0.071	0.085	0.064	0.099	0.102	0.084	0.077
Res. dithionite-ext. Fe (%)	1.00	0.960	1.15	1.19	1.30	1.22	1.36	1.15
χ (µm³ kg⁻¹)	0.401	0.383	0.455	0.357	0.468	0.448	0.464	0.440
χfd (%)	8.18	8.61	9.42	9.07	9.73	9.09	8.82	8.60
NUTRIENTS:								
Phosphate-P (mg g⁻¹)	2.41	2.34	2.06	1.91	1.89	1.94	1.96	1.95
Available phosphate-P (mg l⁻¹)	14.0	16.8	17.9	17.9	10.7	12.1	11.6	14.1
Available K (mg l⁻¹)	89.0	121	56.5	63.0	61.7	63.5	65.0	71.5

and other rendzinas under permanent grassland (Cope 1976, 65). As would be anticipated, organic C decreases with depth (Profile 1, Fig 8.16) as distance from the root mat/litter layer increases. As a consequence, profiles with a deeper Ah horizon tend to have a lower *overall* organic C concentration (eg profile 4, 8.78%). A similar pattern is evident in the phosphate-P data (range, 1.91–2.41mg g⁻¹), which suggests that much of the phosphate present is closely associated with the organic matter, either as part of the organic matter itself or as a result of being 'fixed' within the mineral fraction following mineralization. It should be noted that these phosphate-P concentrations are low compared with the nearby lynchet site (3.20mg g⁻¹). Whilst recent fertiliser applications may have contributed to the higher phosphate-P levels in the vicinity of the lynchet, it is

reasonable to suppose that the phosphate enrichment is partly attributable to human activity associated with former settlement (scatters of midden material, manuring practices, etc).

Perhaps the most striking feature of the four Ah horizons studied is their very wide variation in mean pH (eg 1:2.5 water, range 6.4 to 7.5), which can be directly related to the carbonate content (Table 8.7). Thus, Profile 3, with the lowest pH, is classified as being carbonate-free, whereas Profile 2, with the highest pH has an estimated 1–2% carbonate concentration in the fine-earth fraction. An even higher pH (7.7) and carbonate concentration (13.8%) was recorded by Findlay (1960) for Profile F3. Wide variations in pH and carbonate content are common in rendzina soils in southern England. Cope (1976, 65), for example, presents data for three rendzinas

Table 8.8 Data from other Ah horizons sampled for comparative purposes

Sample [or Sample Series]	Profile F3 Overton Down* –	Lynchet site, Overton Down [33]	Easton Down EDIV-2	Easton Down EDIV-3	Easton Down EDIV-4
Depth (m)	0.14–0.19	0.22	0.01–0.02	0.02–0.03	0.03–0.04
PARTICLE SIZE (Fine earth):					
Sand 60μm–2mm (%)		6.0	3.1	3.1	4.0
200–600μm (%)	27	7.7	4.2	4.2	4.7
60–200μm (%)		15.1	12.4	12.2	13.1
Silt 2–60μm (%)	51	47.6	62.2	66.2	64.2
Clay <2μm (%)	22	23.0	18.1	14.3	15.0
ORGANIC MATTER:					
LOI (%)	27.6	20.0	12.3	12.7	12.5
Organic carbon (%)	10.0	8.15	4.80	4.75	5.31
Organic nitrogen (%)	1.20	0.924	0.440	0.459	0.480
C/N ratio	8.20	8.82	10.9	10.3	11.1
pH & CARBONATE:					
pH in water (1:2.5)	7.7	7.8	8.1	8.1	8.1
pH in 0.01M $CaCl_2$ (1:2.5)		7.4	7.6	7.7	7.7
Carbonate (%)	13.8	>10	2–5	2–5	2–5
IRON & MAGNETIC PROPERTIES:					
Pyrophosphate-ext. Fe (%)		0.045	0.070	0.072	0.076
Res. dithionite-ext. Fe (%)		0.75	0.94	1.02	0.95
χ ($\mu m^3\,kg^{-1}$)		0.520	2.11	2.22	2.24
χfd (%)		10.8	13.1	13.3	13.1
NUTRIENTS:					
Phosphate-P ($mg\,g^{-1}$)		3.20	4.25	4.51	4.55
Avail phosphate-P ($mg\,l^{-1}$)		18.4	23.9	32.3	26.9
Avail K ($mg\,l^{-1}$)		91.3	47.5	50.0	55.0

* Data from Findlay (1960)

under permanent grassland in southern Wiltshire which have a pH (1:2.5 water) range from 6.5–7.8 and corresponding carbonate concentrations of 0–37%. The detailed results from Profile 1 (Fig 8.16) reveal clear evidence of leaching and decalcification in the upper part of the Ah horizon (minimum pH, 6.3). Interestingly, whilst no pH measurements were made in 1960, Dimbleby (1963b) noted the unusually good preservation of pollen in the soils adjacent to the earthwork, and according to Helmsley (1963, 71) the botanical evidence suggests 'the grassland, although underlain by chalk, to be not markedly basic in character'. Thus, despite the soil being actively worked by earthworms (Macphail and Cruise, p 97), leaching and consequent decalcification/acidification appear to be dominant pedogenic processes around the earthwork. The marked local variability of pH and carbonate content may possibly reflect the extent to which the activities of rabbits and moles have led to the incorporation of chalk fragments within the upper parts of the Ah horizon. The relatively low pH and apparently decalcified nature of some of the soils is particularly significant from the point of view of Mollusca, both in terms of habitat constraints and the preservation of shell material. It should be noted that acidification of the uppermost few tens of mm of rendzinas is not uncommon – indeed, in some areas a chalk heath vegetation is present and pH values in the range 3.5–4.5 have been recorded beneath *Calluna* (Grubb *et al* 1969; Burnham 1983).

Concentrations of pyrophosphate-extractable Fe and residual dithionite-extractable Fe average 0.074 and 1.08%, respectively. The former is thought to reflect the concentration of Fe complexed with organic matter in the soil, whereas the latter extraction provides a measure of the total amounts of poorly ordered and crystalline hydrous iron oxides. The values recorded are typical of rendzina soils. It

Table 8.9 Data for samples adjacent to thin sections

Thin section number*	10	11	15	79	92	95
Sample	20	21	17	85	99	97
PARTICLE SIZE (Fine earth):				nd	nd	nd
Sand 600μm–2mm (%)	0.7	1.6	2.2			
200–600μm (%)	1.7	2.2	2.6			
60–200μm (%)	3.0	4.6	2.8			
Silt 2–60μm (%)	57.3	59.2	56.1			
Clay <2μm (%)	37.3	32.3	36.3			
ORGANIC MATTER:						
LOI (%)	22.6	20.6	30.3	2.64	5.37	3.62
Organic carbon (%)	7.82	7.70	12.9	0.92	2.31	1.56
Organic nitrogen (%)	0.826	0.938	1.37	0.112	0.235	0.175
C/N ratio	9.46	8.21	9.42	8.21	9.83	8.91
pH & CARBONATE:						
pH in water (1:2.5)	5.7	6.6	6.4	8.2	8.2	8.2
pH in 0.01M $CaCl_2$	5.4	6.4	6.2	7.7	7.7	7.6
Carbonate (%)	<0.5	<0.5	<0.5	5–10	5–10	5–10
IRON & MAGNETIC PROPERTIES:						
Pyrophosphate-ext. Fe (%)	0.116	0.068	0.084	0.011	0.020	0.012
Res. dithionite-ext. Fe (%)	1.25	1.35	1.15	0.65	0.56	0.25
χ ($\mu m^3 kg^{-1}$)	0.463	0.472	0.442	0.105	0.087	0.036
χfd** (%)	9.71	8.88	7.26	nd	nd	nd
NUTRIENTS:						
Phosphate-P (mg g^{-1})	2.02	1.94	2.41	0.859	0.879	0.707
Avail. phosphate-P (mg l^{-1})	10.5	10.2	14.3	11.9	14.0	10.2
Avail. K (mg l^{-1})	61.5	58.0	84.0	24.0	23.5	19.0

* 15 = Ah horizon outside enclosure; 10 and 11 = Ah horizons within enclosure; 79 = ?Fossil tree hole; 97 and 99 = Soil lenses in ditch fill
** Because of errors associated with χ determinations, χfd has not been calculated for samples with χ < 0.200μm^3 kg^{-1}

should be noted that neither Fe fraction displays a clearly discernible trend down through the Ah horizon (Profile 1, Fig 8.17). Similar concentrations of residual dithionite-extractable Fe are present in the soils from the nearby lynchet and in the Easton Down samples (Table 8.8).

χ (low frequency mass specific magnetic susceptibility) largely reflects the concentration of magnetic forms of iron oxide, notably magnetite and maghaemite, in a sample. Since chalk contains relatively little magnetite, maghaemite is likely to be the principal mineral present in rendzina soils. This forms when iron compounds in the soil are subjected to alternating reduction-oxidation conditions as a result of either natural microbial activity within topsoils (Le Borgne 1955), or burning/heating under anoxic conditions (eg resulting from oxygen depletion during burning of organic matter), with subsequent cooling under oxic conditions. Very high levels of χ

enhancement can occur as a result of fire (Maher 1986; Tite and Mullins 1971). Rendzina soils of the chalk downlands generally display low background χ levels. Allen (1988), for example, reports values in the range 0.23–0.33 $\mu m^3 kg^{-1}$ for topsoils under grassland on the Sussex Downs, and regards values in excess of 0.42 $\mu m^3 kg^{-1}$ as being indicative of burning. The data from Profiles 1–4 (Table 8.7) tend to fall between these ranges, the mean figure being 0.399 $\mu m^3 kg^{-1}$ (range, 0.357–0.455 $\mu m^3 kg^{-1}$). This suggests that some burning has taken place. In fact, fine charcoal was observed in the thin sections. These results are low compared with those from the nearby lynchet (0.520 $\mu m^3 kg^{-1}$) and, most notably, with those from Easton Down (range, 2.11–2.24 $\mu m^3 kg^{-1}$), where there is much evidence of burning (Macphail 1993).

χfd (frequency dependent susceptibility) is a measure of the difference in value between χ determined at low (χ) and high frequency (χHF), expressed

112

OVERTON DOWN-92

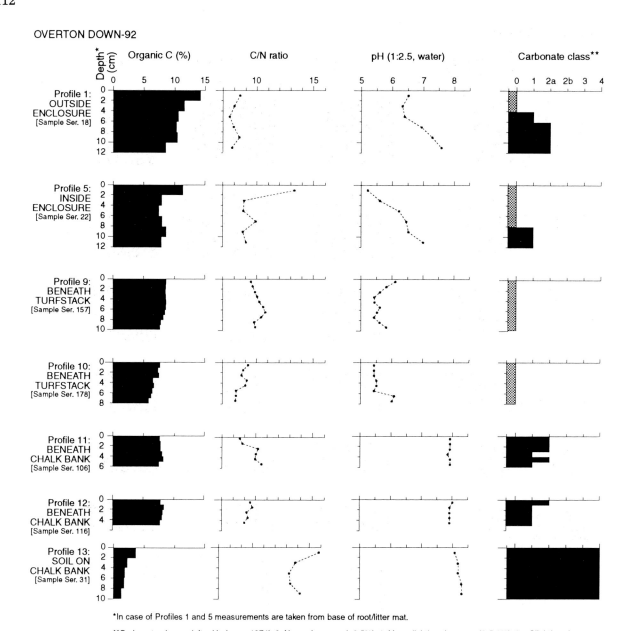

*In case of Profiles 1 and 5 measurements are taken from base of root/litter mat.

**Carbonate classes (after Hodgson, 1974): 0=Non-calcareous (<0.5%); 1=Very slightly calcareous (0.5-1%); 2a=Slightly calcareous (1-2%); 2b=Slightly calareous (2-5%); 3=Calcareous (5-10%); 4=Very calcareous (>10%)

Figure 8.16 Variations in organic matter, C/N ratio, pH and carbonate concentration down the principal soil profiles

as a percentage of the low frequency value, viz: $(\chi - \chi HF) \times 100/\chi$. This difference principally reflects the proportion of ultrafine superparamagnetic grains contributing to the susceptibility (Maher 1986; Thompson and Oldfield 1986), and these tend to form as a result of topsoil microbial activity and burning rather than being derived from primary rock minerals (Clark 1990). Values normally range between 0 and 20%. Interestingly, the χfd values at the lynchet site and Easton Down are high (10.8% and 13.1–13.3%, respectively) compared with the soils outside the enclosure (range, 8.18–9.42%). Thus, the evidence from the phosphate-P and χ data point to much lower levels of human activity in the vicinity of the earthwork than in the other two areas.

Concentrations of available phosphate-P and K

range from 14.0–17.9mg l⁻¹ and 56.5-121mg l⁻¹, respectively. As might be anticipated, these values are less than the corresponding mean figures of 22 and 138mg l⁻¹ reported by Cope (1976,140) for soils of the Icknield series on agricultural holdings – the difference presumably being due to fertilizer applications on the more intensively farmed agricultural land. By convention, available nutrients are expressed in the mg l⁻¹ dry soil volume. When expressed in the same units as phosphate-P, the range of available phosphate-P is 0.0171–0.0200mg g⁻¹ (cf. phosphate-P, 1.91–2.41mg g⁻¹). Thus, only c 1% of the total phosphate in these soils is actually available for plant uptake, the rest being 'immobilized' either within the organic fraction, or in the form of relatively insoluble phosphate compounds within the mineral fraction.

OVERTON DOWN-92

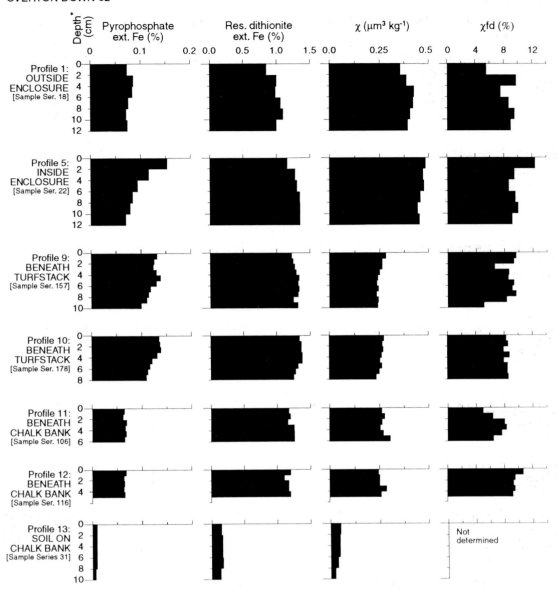

*In case of Profiles 1 and 5 measurements are taken from base of root/litter mat.

Figure 8.17 Variations in iron concentrations and magnetic properties down the principal soil profiles

b) Modern soil within the enclosure

As noted above, the soil within the enclosure is distinguished by the presence of a surface mat of grass litter. The relatively high C/N ratio of 13.3 recorded immediately below the litter/root mat in Profile 5 (Fig 8.16) reflects the incorporation of poorly decomposed litter in the topmost part of the Ah horizon. Since the litter mat inevitably tends to retain water, the upper part of the soil will increasingly be subject to waterlogging. This has reduced the stability of soil peds, leading to the formation of a relatively dense and unstructured layer, c 60mm thick, immediately below the litter mat (Macphail and Cruise, p 98). It also appears to have begun to affect other properties, especially at the very top of

the Ah horizon (Figs 8.16 and 8.17). For example, the relatively high concentration of Fe complexed with organic matter (0.153%) is indicative of slow organic decomposition under poorly aerated conditions – a finding which ties in with the abundant micro- and meso-nodules of Fe and Mn in thin sections, and the pseudomorphic replacement of plant remains by Fe and Mn (Macphail and Cruise p 99). Equally striking are the relatively high χ (0.485 $\mu m^3 kg^{-1}$) and χfd (12.2%) values at the top of the profile (Fig 8.17), which are probably attributable to alternating anoxic/oxic conditions resulting from periodic waterlogging. It should be noted that these very localized effects within individual soil profiles are independent of the broader spatial patterning of χ identified by Clark (p 118).

Table 8.10 Data for Ah horizons of soil buried beneath earthwork

	Beneath turf stack		Beneath chalk bank	
Profile number	9	10	11	12
Sample [or Sample Series]	[157]	[178]	[106]	[116]
Depth (m)	0.10	0.08	0.06	0.05
PARTICLE SIZE (Fine earth):		nd	nd	nd
Sand 600μm–2mm (%)	1.6			
200–600μm (%)	4.1			
60–200μm (%)	7.6			
Silt 2–60μm (%)	54.2			
Clay <2μm (%)	32.5			
ORGANIC MATTER:				
LOI (%)	19.0	18.9	20.0	19.9
Organic carbon (%)	8.43	6.75	7.77	7.99
Organic nitrogen (%)	0.845	0.778	0.806	0.858
C/N ratio	9.98	8.68	9.64	9.31
pH & CARBONATE:				
pH in water (1:2.5)	5.6	5.6	7.9	7.9
pH in 0.01M $CaCl_2$	5.3	5.3	7.5	7.5
Carbonate (%)	<0.5	<0.5	1–2	0.5–1
IRON & MAGNETIC PROPERTIES:				
Pyrophosphate-ext. Fe (%)	0.123	0.125	0.066	0.065
Res. dithionite-ext. Fe (%)	1.29	1.34	1.22	1.15
χ ($\mu m^3\ kg^{-1}$)	0.250	0.255	0.267	0.255
χfd (%)	8.33	8.45	7.01	9.75
NUTRIENTS:				
Phosphate-P ($mg\ g^{-1}$)	1.81	1.68	1.74	1.59
Available phosphate-P ($mg\ l^{-1}$)	10.0	9.95	13.4	13.4
Available K ($mg\ l^{-1}$)	46.5	38.4	44.5	40.7

Another contrast between the soil within the enclosure and that outside is its consistently lower pH, with values ranging from 6.0–6.4 (1:2.5, water) for the four Ah horizons (Table 8.7). In fact, at the top of Profile 5 (Fig 8.16) the pH falls as low as 5.2. This acidification probably reflects the combined effects of a reduction in the amount of physical disturbance of the soil by earthworms (Macphail and Cruise, p. 98) and rabbits (excluded from the enclosure), and an increase in the leaching potential of soil waters. The latter is attributable to three factors: (i) the development of quite an acidic surface mat; (ii) an increase in organic acid secretion by microbial activity when anoxic conditions lead to fermentation (P E J Wiltshire, pers comm); and (iii) higher carbonic acid concentrations, resulting from the impeded aeration and carbon dioxide accumulation at times of surface waterlogging.

Concentrations of phosphate-P and of available phosphate and K are generally lower within the enclosure than outside (Table 8.7). On present evidence it is impossible to establish whether variation in clay distribution and mineralogy (Clark, p 118) is an important factor. However, it should be noted that phosphate-P is more likely to be affected by variations in parent material than concentrations of *available* nutrients, which are much more dynamic in character. Indeed, the lower concentrations of available phosphate and K within the enclosure might simply be the result of nutrients becoming 'locked up' within the accumulating litter layer, combined with lower levels of microbial activity. The erection of the fence around the earthwork has thus had a significant impact upon the chemistry of the soil.

2. Soil buried beneath turf stack of bank
(Table 8.10)

The Ah horizon of the buried soil varies considerably in thickness along the 1992 section (Fig 8.1). Beneath the turf stack the range is 0.05–0.14m. Despite this variability, there is clear evidence of a general reduction in thickness (mean 0.11m; cf 0.18m outside the enclosure), and in places this exceeds 50%. Three principal processes may have contributed to this. First, the sheer weight of the overlying bank material must have caused considerable compaction, as is evidenced by the micromorphological studies (Macphail and Cruise, p 102). Secondly, the organic matter in the buried soil will have continued to decompose, albeit under poorly-aerated conditions. The difference between the mean organic C (11.0%) concentration outside the enclosure and that of the two buried profiles (7.59%) amounts to a loss of c 5.9% organic matter by weight (unfortunately, this figure cannot be used to estimate depth loss because of uncertainty about the density of the material involved). It should also be noted that 5.9% is probably an underestimate, since the data for the buried soil (unlike the modern soil) include the original root mat. The third possible mechanism involves the loss of Ah horizon material up into the overlying turf stack as a result of earthworm and mole activity. However, since there is also clear evidence of movement of material down into the buried soil (Macphail and Cruise p 101), the overall effect of earthworm activity in terms of net soil loss from the buried Ah horizon is therefore probably quite small.

As the soils would appear to have been extremely well-humified prior to burial, there was little scope for subsequent reduction in the C/N ratio. Thus, despite the overall loss of organic matter concentration since burial, the C/N ratios of Profiles 9 and 10 (9.98 and 8.68, respectively) remain well within the range recorded in the modern soils outside the enclosure. This implies therefore that there has been some loss of nitrogen from the buried soil, which is probably largely as a result of gaseous loss through denitrification – anoxic conditions supporting dentrifying bacteria will inevitably be present in such a compacted soil fabric. The phosphate-P concentration in Profiles 9 and 10 (1.81 and 1.68mg g^{-1}, respectively) is lower than that recorded in any of the modern soil profiles studied (range, 1.89–2.41mg g^{-1}). This result is somewhat unexpected in view of strength with which soils normally retain phosphate. Indeed, in view of the loss of organic matter from the buried soil, an increase in concentration might have been anticipated. Concentrations of available phosphate-P (range, 9.95–10.0mg l^{-1}) and K (38.4–46.5mg l^{-1}) are also consistently lower in the buried soil than outside the enclosure. Although the reasons for this are somewhat uncertain, it seems likely that reduced levels of both microbial activity and rates of mineralization of organic matter in the buried soil will have been contributory factors.

Both profiles are non-calcareous throughout the depth of the Ah horizon and have a mean pH (1:2.5, water) of 5.6. Close to the top of the buried soil the pH falls as low as 5.4 (ie moderately acidic). It would thus seem leaching and decalcification have continued under the turf stack. These processes will have been facilitated by the reduced levels of physical disturbance under the centre of the bank. Importantly, too, the results suggest that the alkaline water seeping through the chalk of the bank must have been been neutralized and acidified during its passage through the turf stack (which may be presumed to have been at least slightly acidic at the time of bank construction). In the case of profile 10, sampling was in fact extended up through the turf stack, and this revealed a progressive reduction in pH (1:2.5, water) from 8.1 in the chalk immediately overlying the turf stack to 5.5 at its base. The development of such acidic soil conditions in the buried soil clearly has important implications for the preservation of the material buried on the old ground surface, and of pollen and Mollusca within the buried soil. Such acidification may also lead to destabilization of soil aggregates, thereby rendering the soil more vulnerable to compaction.

Compared with the control soil outside the enclosure, the buried soil also has a higher mean concentration of pyrophosphate-extractable Fe (0.124%; cf 0.074%) and a lower mean χ (0.253µm^{3}kg^{-1}; cf 0.399 µm^{3}kg^{-1}). The difference in Fe could simply be a consequence of the more acidic and less well-aerated conditions, which tend to favour the development of Fe-organic matter complexes (as in the modern soil within the enclosure). By comparison, the reduction in χ cannot be so readily attributed to post-burial changes. One possibility might be that anaerobic conditions have led to some chemical reduction of ferric compounds (including maghaemite) to the more weakly magnetic ferrous forms (Clark 1990). However, whilst anaerobic micro-sites are likely within the buried soil (P E J Wiltshire pers comm) and moisture levels may be at or close to saturation for prolonged periods, the microbial evidence indicates the presence of aerobic micro-sites Kelley and Wiltshire p 155). Such alternating anoxic/oxic conditions might be expected to favour an increase in χ (cf modern soil within the enclosure), rather than a decrease. It seems likely therefore that the lower χ values recorded in the soil buried beneath the turf stack (and also in that buried beneath the chalk of the bank – section 3, below) reflect the fact that the bank was constructed on a strip of soil which by chance had naturally low χ levels. These observations support the findings of the more extensive magnetic susceptibility survey of the area undertaken by Clark (p 118).

3. Soil buried beneath chalk of bank
(Table 8.10)

The Ah horizon of the soil beneath the chalk has suffered a similar reduction in thickness, the mean

116

depth being 0.11m (range 0.06–0.18m). Here, as
beneath the turf stack, both compaction and loss of
organic matter through decomposition (mean organic
C, 7.88%; organic matter, c 13.6%) have undoubtedly
been important. However, in this case, movement of
soil by earthworms and moles up into the overlying
chalk has also played a significant part. Indeed, the
precise location of the old ground surface could not
be established with certainty because of the disturbance which has occurred at the chalk/soil interface.
The C/N ratio of these profiles (9.64 and 9.31,
respectively) has not changed appreciably following
burial, but there has been a clear reduction in
phosphate-P (1.74 and 1.59mg g^{-1}), available phosphate-P (both 13.4mg l^{-1}) and available K (44.5 and
40.7mg l^{-1}) – findings which replicate those from
beneath the turf stack.

The incorporation of some chalk fragments within
the upper part of the soil, combined with the seepage
of alkaline water through the soil from bank, has led
to a considerable increase in pH (1:2.5 water, mean
7.9). Conditions for molluscan preservation have
thus greatly improved over the 32 years since burial.
Importantly, too, this change in pH and calcium
concentration will have increased the stability of the
humic fraction of the soil (Avery 1990), as is perhaps
indicated by the less-massive nature of this buried
soil compared with that beneath the turf stack
(Macphail and Cruise p 104). Further evidence of the
greater structural stability of calcareous soils is
provided by morphological studies of palaeosols from
beneath the Neolithic barrow at Easton Down
(Macphail 1993). Here, the soils are calcareous
(carbonate content, c 2–5%; Table 8.8) and appear to
retain much of their original structure. Another
consequence of the increased Ca concentrations is
that some of the iron in the organic matter complexes
will have been displaced by calcium – hence the
relatively low pyrophosphate-extractable Fe concentration (mean, 0.066%). As noted above, χ (mean,
0.262µm^{3}kg^{-1}) is low compared with the control soil
outside the enclosure, and this seems likely to reflect
natural variations of χ in the vicinity of the earthwork (Clark p 118).

4. Soil development on chalk bank

The soil on the surface of the bank comprises a very
stony ACu horizon. This varies in depth (typically
from 60–110mm) and degree of development, and
profiles sampled were selected so as to represent the
range of soil present (Table 8.11). The stone content
of the three profiles ranges from 37–56% by weight,
the highest proportion in each case being small
stones (6–20mm). Quantitative analysis of thin
sections of the bank soils provides detailed insight
into their overall form and structure (Macphail and
Cruise p 102). Unless stated otherwise, the following
discussion relates only to the fine earth fraction.

Organic carbon concentrations range from 2.14–
7.00%. This amounts to c 0.94–4.41% organic matter

in the soil as a whole (ie including stones), which
represents a considerable accumulation of organic
material over 32 years on a bare chalk surface. In
fact, the more fully developed soils on the bank
already contain sufficient organic matter to be
regarded as rendzinas rather than 'raw chalk soils'
(see discussion in Smith 1980, 94). As would be
anticipated in the early stages of soil development,
the C/N ratio is relatively high (mean 14.0). Whilst
the soil remains highly calcareous, it is interesting to
note that the most organic-rich of the profiles (15)
does have a slightly lower pH (8.0) than the others,
which may reflect the beginnings of acidification and
leaching.

As would be anticipated, concentrations of pyrophosphate-extractable Fe (mean, 0.012%), residual
dithionite-extractable Fe (0.140%) and phosphate-P
(0.693mg g^{-1}), along with χ (0.051 µm^3 kg^{-1}), are
much lower than in the other soils studied. In the
case of the latter two properties, these figures
compare with mean values of 0.523mg g^{-1} and <0.010
µm^3 kg^{-1}, respectively, for samples taken from the
centre of three blocks of chalk from within the bank.
The difference recorded thus provides an indication
of the enhancement of χ and enrichment of phosphate-P which has resulted from 32 years of soil
development. The increase in χ is probably largely
the result of microbial activity, whereas that in
phosphate-P presumably reflects contributions from
atmospheric inputs (rainfall and dust) and the effects
of nutrient cycling by vegetation, whereby some
phosphate is taken up by plant roots from the
underlying chalk, and is then returned to the soil
surface in organic litter. Both properties decrease
progressively down the profile (eg χ in Fig 8.17),
which is in keeping with the above interpretations.

Whilst the concentration of available phosphate-P
(range, 18.3–24.4mg l^{-1}) is similar to that of the
modern humic rendzinas in the vicinity of the
earthwork, it should be noted that the soil on the
bank is thinner and much more stony (37–56%
stones; Table 8.11), and consequently the amount of
phosphate available to plants is correspondingly
much less. In the case of K, the actual concentration
(20.2–28.5mg l^{-1}) is much lower than in the rendzinas, and this may be a significant factor in inhibiting
vegetation growth on the chalk bank (Burnham
1990).

Implications and conclusions

As was noted in the introduction, the Overton Down
Experimental Earthwork provides unique insight
into both the direction and rate of change in soil
properties following burial, and the development of
soil on a freshly exposed chalk bank. In addition,
somewhat unexpectedly (and certainly inadvertently), the action of fencing off the earthwork has
itself led to changes in the properties of the existing
humic rendzina soils. The principal findings and
implications are as follows:

Table 8.11 Data for ACu horizons of soil on chalk bank

Profile number		13	14	15
Sample [or Sample Series]		[31]	114	115
Depth (m)		0.10	0.07	0.07
PARTICLE SIZE (Coarse fractions):				
Fine earth	<2mm	44	60	63
Very small stones	2–6mm	15	10	8
Small stones	6mm–20mm	25	23	20
Medium stones	20–60mm	16	7	9
ORGANIC MATTER:				
LOI (%)		4.44	4.59	12.8
Organic carbon (%)		2.14	2.39	7.00
Organic nitrogen (%)		0.150	0.184	0.473
C/N ratio		14.3	13.0	14.8
pH & CARBONATE:				
pH in water (1:2.5)		8.2	8.2	8.0
pH in 0.01M $CaCl_2$		7.6	7.7	7.6
Carbonate (%)		>10	>10	>10
IRON & MAGNETIC PROPERTIES:				
Pyrophosphate-ext. Fe (%)		0.008	0.008	0.021
Res. dithionite-ext. Fe (%)		0.160	0.130	0.150
χ ($\mu m^3\,kg^{-1}$)		0.039	0.046	0.068
χfd* (%)		nd	nd	nd
NUTRIENTS:				
Phosphate-P ($mg\,g^{-1}$)		0.624	0.582	0.874
Available phosphate-P ($mg\,l^{-1}$)		20.1	18.3	24.4
Available K ($mg\,l^{-1}$)		25.2	20.2	28.5

* Because of errors associated with χ determinations, χfd has not been calculated for samples with χ <0.200$\mu m^3\,kg^{-1}$

Changes in soil properties 32 years after burial

(1) As a result of the combined effects of compaction and organic decomposition, the Ah horizon has been considerably reduced in thickness, in places by more than 50%.

(2) Soil buried beneath the central turfstack has undergone further leaching and acidification, thereby favouring the preservation of pollen, organic remains, etc, but becoming progressively less suitable for mollusc preservation, and adversely affecting the stability of humic substances and soil aggregates. In contrast, the soil beneath the chalk of the bank has become more alkaline following burial.

(3) Soils buried beneath both the turf stack and the chalk of the bank show decreases in the concentrations of phosphate-P, available phosphate and K, but no significant change was recorded in C/N ratio. Lower χ values were recorded, but these are thought to be due to natural soil variations in the vicinity of the site.

(4) Soil buried beneath the turf stack also shows an increase in pyrophosphate-extractable Fe.

(5) In view of the changes recorded in certain soil properties following only 32 years of burial, it is clear that considerable caution must be exercised when interpreting similar data for buried soils from archaeological sites.

Soil development on bank after 32 years

(6) Soil on the bank comprises a very stony and highly calcareous ACu horizon, 60–110mm in depth.

(7) The organic matter content of the ACu horizon ranges from c 0.94–4.41%, and there is already very clear evidence of χ enhancement and phosphate-P enrichment in the fine earth fraction.

Effects of fencing off enclosure

(8) As a result of animals being excluded from the enclosure a substantial mat (c 20mm) of grass litter has accumulated over the soil surface, thereby increasing water retention and favouring periodic waterlogging.

(9) In turn, these conditions have led to increases in the amount of Fe complexed with organic matter, χ, χfd, and acidification; and to decreases in the concentrations of carbonate and of available phosphate-P and K.

(10) In view of the lack of soil data from the time of earthwork construction, or from previous excavations, it was initially envisaged that the soils within the enclosure would provide a reasonable basis for determining the properties of the original soils on the site (ie prior to burial). Clearly, this is not the case. Indeed, the best indication of the character of the soils buried in 1960 comes from the soils outside the enclosure. Unfortunately, these are not only further from the earthwork, but also display quite wide variability in some of the properties measured. Consequently, this somewhat limits the confidence that can be placed in data relating to change (and rates of change) in soil properties over the 32-year span of the experiment.

Acknowledgements

The author would like to thank Professor Bruce Proudfoot and Amanda Rouse for their assistance with the sampling, and Ian Clewes and John James, who undertook the analytical work. The diagrams were produced by Miles Edwards and Mark Bell. Thanks are also extended to Dr Richard Macphail and Dr Pat Wiltshire for their helpful comments on an earlier draft of this paper.

8.6 Magnetic susceptibility survey
by A J Clark

Introduction

When the experimental earthwork was constructed, archaeological prospecting was a young subject which has gained greatly in importance since then. The dominant technique has proved to be magnetometry, which is most frequently used for the mapping of former earthworks. A second magnetic technique of increasing importance is magnetic susceptibility measurement. The detection of ditches by magnetometer normally depends upon their becoming silted up with topsoil, which is usually of higher magnetic susceptibility than the lower layers, so that the ditch causes a local intensification of the earth's magnetic field seen as an 'anomaly' by the magnetometer. One of the first uses of magnetic susceptibility instruments in archaeology was to test

for a sufficient magnetic contrast between the topsoil and lower layers to produce detectable anomalies. The main mechanism of topsoil magnetic susceptibility enhancement is the concentration of original iron minerals in the soil and their conversion to the secondary ferrimagnetic oxide maghaemite (γFe_2O_3). It was realized early on that phenomena of human occupation such as burning, and a more elusive fermentation effect associated with waste decomposition, increased this effect (Mullins 1977; Tite 1972a, 1972b; Tite and Mullins 1971), and susceptibility instruments are now used for the broad definition of occupation areas, especially in large, speculative surveys such as archaeological evaluations. In contrast, where conditions are suitable, susceptibility surveys can be used for the location of individual features such as hearths that once existed only upon the surface (Clark 1990).

It seemed appropriate to include magnetic studies in the 1992 work, in case any information could be obtained about the magnetic behaviour of soil associated with earthworks, especially whether the presence of the bank and ditch had modified the magnetization of the soil or its distribution in any way likely to affect the interpretation of magnetic surveys.

The instrumentation employed for the experiment was the Bartington MS2, a system commonly used especially in Britain. It comprises a measuring instrument to which a variety of sensors can be attached for different applications. The main sensor used for this experiment was the MS2B dual-frequency laboratory sensor (36mm internal diameter; frequencies 0.43kHz and 4.3kHz), in mass-specific susceptibility (χ) mode. Comparative measurements were also made where possible with the MS2D field loop (mean diameter 185mm). This obtains much quicker readings, but is less adaptable than the MS2B, measuring volume-specific susceptibility (κ) only, and requiring fairly level and preferably vegetation-free ground; but the site provided an opportunity to test its effectiveness on downland turf and the vegetation in the enclosure under controlled conditions.

The dual-frequency facility of the MS2B gives some indication of the mineralogy of a sample by measuring its frequency dependence, a tendency to give lower apparent susceptibility at higher frequencies. This can be expressed as a percentage (%fd) by dividing the difference between the low and high frequency χ values by the low frequency value, and multiplying by 100. It results from the presence of very small superparamagnetic particles close to the stable single domain boundary, the production of which is favoured by the anthropogenic processes described above (Thompson and Oldfield, 1986). However, it has been noted that natural clay forming hilltop deposits in this part of Wiltshire shows frequency dependence values high enough to indicate that concentrations of particles in this category can occur naturally. It seems to be in soils of coarser mineralogy with naturally low frequency dependence that high values are more likely to be diagnostic of human activity.

Experiments and results

Samples from the section

The first experiment involved taking samples of topsoil at 0.5m intervals along the line of the section. The samples were extracted from either side of the trench, depending on which side the soil appeared less contaminated by chalk, etc, just below the root mat over a depth range of approximately 0.03–0.1m. Where the topsoil passed under the bank, corresponding samples were taken additionally from the soil that had begun to develop on top of the bank. Three samples were also taken from the soil included in the turf stack. Further samples were taken by coring auger at 2m intervals along the unexcavated line of the trench projected toward the south-west boundary of the enclosure. All samples were dried, pulverized with a pestle and mortar and passed through a 2mm sieve.

The graph (Fig 8.18) shows relatively low readings beneath the bank, but high readings reaching a peak in the area between the ditch and the south-west fence. These were accompanied by a small increase in percentage frequency dependence (%fd). Relatively high readings from the turf stack, derived from above the ditch, fitted in with the likelihood that the variations already existed when the earthwork was constructed; but the high readings coincided so closely with the ground within the enclosure, untouched since the construction of the earthwork, that there remained the possibility that they were either caused by some activity associated with the construction, or the fact that the ground had remained untouched and ungrazed since.

Other points are worth noting in this section: with the exception of a very high reading affected by contamination at 5m (χ = 47.9; %fd = 3.5), the ditch readings were all erratic and relatively low, due to variable admixture of chalk. The high reading at 5m proved to be due to two small dark nodules quite possibly from the Criggion basalt layer incorporated in the bank. One would only expect a positive magnetometer anomaly to develop after much more soil accumulation, which would be aided by ploughing: extant ditches tend to be hardly detectable. The peak at 12.5m seems to represent a real and very localized increase in soil susceptibility, although its low frequency dependence is anomalous and indicates that a contaminant dispersed in the soil is responsible.

The samples from the top of the bank all gave very low readings because of the large proportion of chalk in the developing soil. However, two samples from the highest part of the bank at 10m and 10.5m were measured for frequency dependence which is independent of concentration. After the larger pieces of chalk had been sieved out, the samples were bulked

together to maximize the readings. This gave a value of $5.2 \times 10^{-8\,SI/kg}$ for χ, and a frequency dependence of 7.6%, close to the average for topsoil samples.

Internal control transect

This was laid out parallel to the baseline of the 1992 section and 12.8m (42ft) from it. The zero was on the top of the bank halfway between markers 2 and IV, and readings ran from 10m, clear of the ditch, to the south-west fence of the enclosure. In this and the second control transect, as in the extension to the section, samples were taken at 2m intervals with a coring tool just below turf level. MS2D field loop measurements were also taken

A peak in readings was again observed, this time narrower and displaced about 2m further to the south-west relative to the line of the earthwork.

External control transect

This was 40m long, running south-west, parallel to the north-west fence and 8m away from it, with its zero in line with the north-east fence. It was thus parallel to the other two transects and about 21.6m from the internal control. Readings rose to a broad peak centred at about 29m. Field loop readings, which should be numerically about 80% of those obtained in the laboratory sensor, are suppressed in both the controls by the turf mat preventing proper contact with the ground; even so, the proportional variation of the readings matches that of the laboratory measurements. Thus, with a suitable correction factor, the test indicates that this type of sensor can still be used in such conditions.

A final test on the external transect was to determine the percentage conversion of iron compounds to maghaemite in six samples. This is done by heating at 650°C in reducing, followed by oxidizing, conditions to bring about the maximum possible conversion (Tite and Mullins 1971). The fractional conversion represented by the original magnetic susceptibility of the samples is then expressed as a percentage of the susceptibility of the sample after heating. On sites intensively occupied by man, the conversion tends to reach a peak, but this simple identifier of human occupation can break down where activity was relatively slight, or geological changes occur. New and so far unpublished work by the writer suggests that, in the latter case, the natural conversion tends to bear a fairly constant relationship to the maximum, so that a set of measurements across a peak will give a positive correlation coefficient. On the other hand, enhancements due to man, which upset this natural relationship, give a negative or very low correlation.

The six treated samples were from 4, 8, 12, 16, 20 and 24m along the transect, with respective conversions of 1.1, 1.2, 1.4, 1.3, 1.7 and 1.9%, approximately in proportion to the variation in original susceptibil-

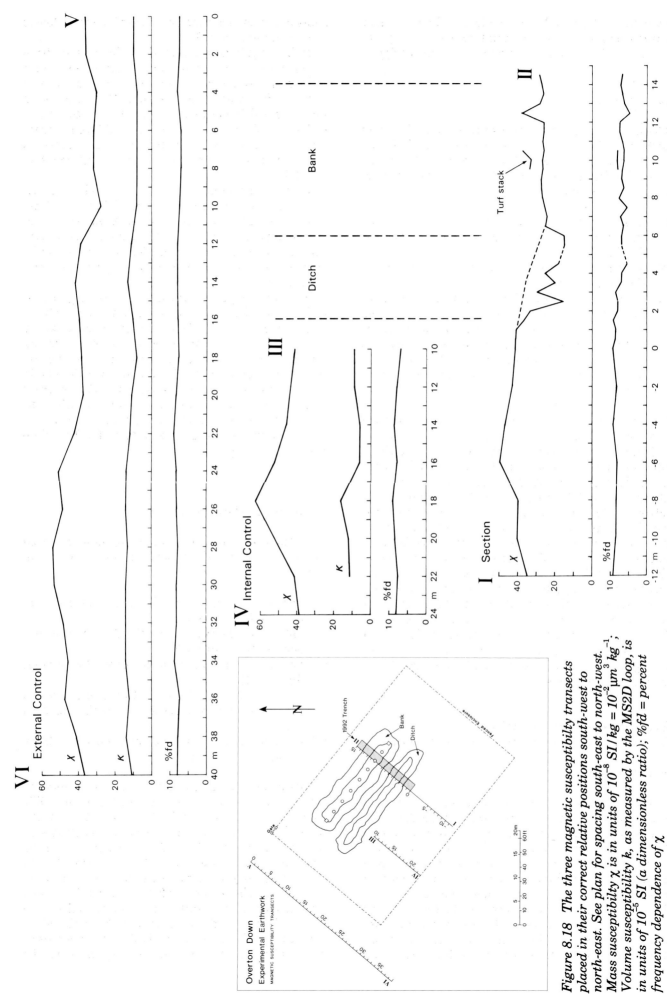

Figure 8.18 The three magnetic susceptibility transects placed in their correct relative positions south-west to north-east. See plan for spacing south-east to north-west. Mass susceptibilty χ is in units of 10^{-8} SI / kg = 10^{-2} μm^3 kg^{-1}; Volume susceptibility k, as measured by the MS2D loop, is in units of 10^{-5} SI (a dimensionless ratio); %fd = percent frequency dependence of χ

ity values. The correlation as discussed above was r = 0.73 (product moment correlation coefficient; probability >90%), a good indication of a natural origin.

Conclusion

The peaks on all three transects were in line and probably belong to the same feature, diverging from the alignment of the earthwork toward the northwest. The feature is unlikely to be a human artefact for several reasons:

(1) no sign of it was seen during construction of the earthwork, although its magnetic effect overlaps the ditch;
(2) no cultural material was found in any of the sieved samples;
(3) the magnetic susceptibility heating experiment supports a natural origin. It was also noticed that, after drying, a proportion of samples, especially those of higher susceptibility, took the form of clayey nodules so difficult to break up in the mortar that they were originally mistaken for stones.

Thus it seems that the normal chalk rendzina soil of the downland here has a varying magnetic susceptibility probably associated with a content of relatively high susceptibility clay. One linear band of this has been identified, and it is possible that many exist. Being superficial, these are unlikely to have much adverse effect on magnetometer survey, but they could be confused with man-made patterns in magnetic susceptibility surveys of small areas. In large surveys, their overall pattern would probably be distinguishable from those of settlements, which would also be expected to show as distinctive areas of higher susceptibility values. The building of the experimental earthwork has resulted in some disruption of the natural pattern, for example by the movement of soil included in the turf stack, but such changes are not likely to be easily interpretable in archaeological terms.

8.7 Amino acid studies
by John Beavis and George MacLeod

Previous work

Many measurements of amino acid concentrations in soils have been made, and reviewers of this data have generally considered that little difference can be seen between various types of soil (eg Bremner 1966; Stevenson 1982). It has now been shown that there are significant differences in amino acid composition among Bronze Age buried soils from Holne Moor, Dartmoor (Beavis 1985), between the soils within a Medieval field system and outside it, at the same site, between the surface horizons of tropical, temperate and arctic soil types, and between the surface and

sub-surface horizons of some Canadian soils (Beavis 1990, chapters 2 and 3).

Highly significant distinctions have also been found between manured and unmanured arable soils, and between grassland, woodland and arable soils of the long term Classical Experiments at Rothamsted Experimental Station, Hertfordshire; whilst grassland soils from slightly different parent materials and management regimes at Rothamsted have similar amino acid compositions (ibid, chapters 4 and 5).

Amino acid compositions of buried archaeological soils have been classified in terms of simple land use categories derived from the Rothamsted data. When corrected for age, these have been shown to compare favourably with a classification based on independent evidence for their land use prior to burial (ibid, chapter 6).

This work suggests that there may be a significant archaeological potential for soil amino acid analysis. The soils from Overton Down provide an opportunity to observe changes in amino acid composition during controlled short-term burial, during new soil formation on the earthwork bank, and among soils outside the earthwork. It is unlikely, given the current understanding of processes leading to different amino acid compositions, that the amino acids can contribute much to an interpretation of soil development at this stage.

Materials and methods

Samples came from the following locations (see Figures for details of sampling locations and procedures):

(1) unburied A horizon outside the fenced enclosure (sample 19, Figure 7.3)
(2) unburied A horizon inside the fenced enclosure (sample 23, Figure 7.3)
(3) buried A horizon beneath chalk bank (sample 42, Figure 8.1)
(4) buried A horizon beneath turf stack (sample 3166D, Figure 8.1, associated with cremated bone)
(5) unburied A horizon developing on chalk bank (sample 111, Figure 8.1)

Extraction and measurement of amino acids were carried out as previously decribed (Cheng 1975; Cheng et al 1975; Beavis 1990) apart from the following modifications. The original desalting step (demanded by the acidic buffer of the chromatograph originally used) was omitted, and prior to ion chromatography samples were taken up in a solution 0.023M in NaOH and 0.007M in $Na_2B_4O_7$ and adjusted to pH 10–12 with a few drops of 10M sodium hydroxide to suit the chromatograph employed on this occasion. This precipitated interfering cations as hydroxides which were removed by passing the solution through a 0.2µm Whatman Puradisc 25 filter. Filtered samples were stored at 0–5°C.

Amino acids were separated using a programmable Dionex Advanced Gradient pump, Rheodyne injection valve, Dionex AminoPac PA1 anion exchange column, Pye Unicam LC3-XP pump to deliver ninhydrin reagent, Dionex knitted reaction coil in a heated post-column reaction chamber, Spectra Physics SP8440 UV-VIS detector and a Spectra Physics SP4270 computing integrator.

Samples were eluted using a predetermined gradient programme supplied by Dionex for the prescribed eluants (Dionex 1990, with minor modifications). Eluant from the column was continuously reacted with ninhydrin at 130°C and the absorbance of the reaction products measured at 520nm.

Peaks on the resulting chromatograms were integrated and transformed to concentrations calibrated against standard amino acid additions included at a frequency of 1 to every 5 samples. Sample chromatogram peaks were identified visually with reference to the standard addition chromatograms. For each sample, concentrations expressed in µmol g^{-1} of soil were recorded for the following amino acids: lysine, histidine, arginine, aspartic acid, threonine, serine, glutamic acid, glycine, alanine, valine, methionine, isoleucine, leucine, tyrosine and phenylalanine.

Results

Observed concentrations in replicate extracts from the five different locations are given in Table 8.12. Discriminant functions (of which there are one less than the number of groups in the data), which are formed from a linear combination of the original variables each multiplied by an appropriate weighting, were derived from the data. The advantage of this device is that it makes use of relationships between individual variables which contribute to the discrimination sought, whilst collapsing the intangible distribution of samples in the multidimensional space of the original variables into one to three dimensions which can readily be visualized in real space.

Submitting the raw data of Table 8.12 directly to Discriminant analysis leads to a very clear separation of the groups, but is at risk of discriminating trivially on the basis of differences in overall amino acid concentration. (Such general differences between samples may be caused by differences in organic matter levels, for example.)

To eliminate this possibility the data for each sample were transformed by subtracting from each amino acid concentration the mean concentration of all amino acids for that sample. Apart from the omission of dividing the values obtained by the across-sample standard deviation, this is equivalent to 'ipsatization.' (The rationale behind the transformation is fully discussed in Beavis 1990, 86ff.) Means and standard deviations of the transformed data

along with those for similarly transformed comparative data from Rothamsted are given in Table 8.13.

A plot of individual samples on the first two Discriminant functions obtained from a five group step-wise Discriminant analysis of the Overton data is shown in Figure 8.19. Both functions are highly significant discriminators (Fn1: $p < 0.0001$; Fn2: $p < 0.005$) and the differences between the centroids are all well separated (F-ratios: $p < 0.02$), except the closest, which are the unburied soil outside the enclosure and the developing soil on the bank (F-ratio: $p = 0.06$). Little overlap among groups is shown by a classification success of 91%. Six of the original 15 amino acids (alanine, serine, valine, arginine, phenylalanine and isoleucine) were selected by the step-wise procedure to compute optimum functions.

The extent to which the Overton compositions are comparable to other grassland soils can at present be assessed only against the Rothamsted data, which were obtained in a similar way, because it is clear that results are to some extent method dependent. Combining the Overton and Rothamsted grassland data (samples collected in 1959 and 1964, and measured in 1986 as described in Beavis 1990) and performing a similar statistical analysis produces Figure 8.20. In this eight group case the first five Discriminant functions are all highly significant (and so the visual impression of discrimination between groups is impaired by the use of the first two functions only in Figure 8.20). Differences between centroids are highly significant (F-ratio: $p < 0.0001$) in all cases except between the Rothamsted groups, where the fertilized and unfertilized Park Grass soils are indistinguishable (F-ratio: $p = 0.60$); and Wilderness grass is only just distinguishable from fertilized Park Grass (F-ratio: $p = 0.06$). Classification success is 90% which confirms that the two-dimensional representation is rather misleading. GLU and MET were the only amino acids not included in this step-wise selection.

Least significant difference tests based on univariate analysis of variance on the ipsatized Overton data give the following significant ($p = 0.05$) differences between samples:

(1) the soil outside the enclosure has a relatively lower concentration (more negative mean distance) than the soil buried beneath turf of valine, methionine, isoleucine and phenylalanine (though phenylalanine does not meet the requirement of homogeneity of variance);

(2) the soil outside the enclosure has relatively lower concentration than the soil developing on the bank of valine, methionine, isoleucine, leucine and tyrosine;

(3) the soil outside the enclosure has a relatively lower concentration than the soil buried beneath chalk of isoleucine and leucine;

(4) the soil buried beneath chalk has a relatively lower concentration than the soil developing on the bank of valine;

Table 8.12 Amino acid composition in μmol/g of soil from Overton Down

Location	Lysine	Histidine	Arginine	Aspartic acid	Threonine	Serine	Glutamic acid	Glycine	Alanine	Valine	Methionine	Isoleucine	Leucine	Tyrosine	Phenylalanine
1	8.18	27.36	8.15	51.70	26.04	30.56	30.08	32.41	25.83	0.00	0.00	2.28	7.40	0.00	12.78
1	3.98	3.59	3.14	12.03	31.29	3.41	18.03	2.84	12.31	3.97	0.00	2.79	4.54	1.94	2.46
1	18.23	12.68	11.68	54.17	24.60	31.25	30.4	31.25	34.14	4.68	0.00	4.48	9.68	1.64	5.48
1	37.40	14.23	15.42	97.02	21.46	52.84	56.65	52.84	30.67	6.43	0.00	4.43	9.49	0.00	6.26
2	23.97	11.77	9.25	36.80	58.07	0.00	17.58	0.00	33.41	3.94	0.00	1.17	4.95	0.00	3.18
2	4.68	1.33	2.63	82.19	24.42	0.00	101.49	0.00	26.21	0.00	0.00	0.00	5.63	0.00	2.93
2	1.68	7.99	2.17	10.56	14.71	0.00	12.31	0.00	5.92	0.00	0.00	0.31	1.16	2.43	2.12
2	6.44	11.15	6.57	18.15	22.94	0.00	24.79	0.00	26.20	5.60	0.00	4.11	4.69	6.46	5.27
2	3.13	7.40	4.02	20.21	29.03	0.00	11.22	0.00	33.64	0.00	0.00	2.51	4.08	2.66	2.78
3	16.71	13.53	5.81	45.55	25.95	38.31	25.78	40.63	25.65	0.00	0.00	17.03	16.91	0.00	6.67
3	9.04	8.13	4.98	39.92	17.04	1.90	21.93	2.02	16.88	0.00	0.00	3.93	7.23	0.00	6.11
3	9.14	8.42	3.83	18.77	15.99	6.15	18.21	6.15	18.24	0.00	0.00	4.54	3.35	7.55	5.09
3	11.38	3.62	4.84	22.74	11.31	16.81	17.83	16.94	11.50	0.21	0.00	2.50	4.23	0.28	2.34
3	9.39	8.35	8.38	44.63	15.75	24.17	63.40	25.13	21.96	0.00	3.06	7.28	10.48	17.06	8.96
4	7.75	5.60	6.32	34.00	11.99	1.96	31.32	2.56	17.72	5.16	10.49	9.00	4.64	5.38	34.59
4	4.80	3.49	3.97	13.13	6.80	10.66	9.85	10.66	9.65	7.34	1.86	4.34	5.53	2.49	3.62
4	10.61	5.15	6.41	50.60	19.68	30.61	45.73	30.61	28.07	7.00	0.00	6.57	8.95	0.73	5.81
4	6.18	15.59	4.31	24.72	12.16	15.40	13.57	17.95	14.12	8.19	1.59	4.27	5.27	7.37	7.91
5	4.02	2.37	2.65	31.56	4.82	1.49	49.62	1.94	7.13	4.00	1.02	3.61	3.82	1.27	4.54
5	5.32	6.48	5.40	14.34	5.35	7.01	14.35	7.53	7.60	7.34	5.28	6.36	7.07	4.69	5.82
5	3.41	1.77	1.38	11.48	5.11	6.01	8.29	7.00	5.89	3.52	0.00	2.24	4.32	0.35	2.68
5	3.06	1.09	1.40	10.26	2.82	5.15	9.23	5.00	4.50	3.82	0.00	3.32	3.80	0.00	2.91

Key to location:
1 = Overton unburied outside enclosure [(sample 19) – context 5011]
2 = Overton unburied inside enclosure [(sample 23) – context 5009]
3 = Overton buried beneath chalk bank (sample 42)
4 = Overton buried beneath turf stack (sample 3166D) – assoc with piece of cremated human bone
5 = Overton developing on bank (sample 111)

124

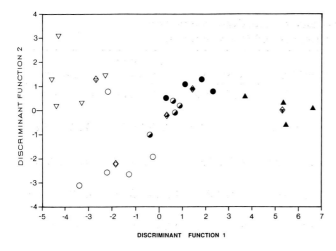

Figure 8.19 Discriminant analysis of amino acid concentrations in A horizons of soil from Overton Down

(5) the soil inside the enclosure has a relatively higher concentration (more positive mean distance) than the soil developing on the bank and both buried soils of threonine and alanine (though neither meets the requirement of homogeneity of variance);

(6) the soil inside the enclosure has a relatively lower concentration than the soil outside the enclosure and both buried soils of serine and glycine.

Discussion

The main features of the results are the large differences in fingerprint between each of the Overton locations, and between Overton and Rothamsted.

It is well known that Discriminant analysis can produce over-optimistic distinctions between groups. In the earlier work on the Rothamsted soils methods of internally validating Discriminant analyses were employed, but there is no justification for using these here, as the differences between the Overton groups is large enough to dispel any doubt that they are real. The small number of individuals in each Overton group may contribute to the low level of overlap between groups, but the variation within each group is high, and this will tend to make the groups less easy to distinguish.

From Figure 8.19, it is clear that the modern soils at Overton are more similar to each other than they are to the buried soils. The two buried soils are also very different from each other, and this may clearly reflect the different conditions of burial. In the earlier work on buried soils relatively small corrections for

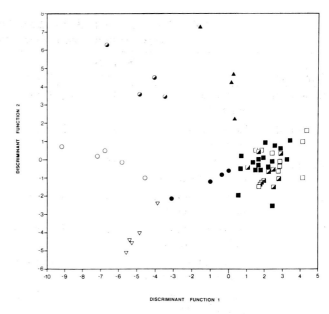

Figure 8.20 Discriminant analysis of grasslands from Rothamstead and Overton Down

the effects of age were required. These results suggest that large changes have occurred rapidly in the buried soils. This is consistent with the evidence from other studies (see above) which suggest that there was still considerable biological activity in the buried soils. If, however, this is the cause of the differences, it might be difficult to reconcile with earlier results which seem to suggest that an imprint of land use is readily retained.

On the other hand these results are encouraging because they may show that differences in pH, redox potential and biological activity are insufficient to destroy the main imprint of the site as mature grazed grassland. In Figure 8.20, although the differences between Overton and Rothamsted grassland fingerprints is large, the unburied soils from Overton lie closest to those from Rothamsted, as might be expected.

It is natural to ask in what way the fingerprints differ between the various groups distinguished in these results, but it is not possible to give a direct answer to this question. The fundamental reason for using Discriminant analysis is that univariate analysis of variance could not convincingly distinguish between soils with different amino acid compositions, but the penalty for optimizing discrimination is the creation of composite variables that have no correspondence to reality. It would be possible to draw attention to the largest Discriminant function

125

Table 8.13 Means and standard deviations of normalized amino acid concentrations of soils from Rothamstead and Overton Down

Location		Sample size	Lysine	Histidine	Arginine	Aspartic acid	Threonine
Rothamstead	Park Grass unfertilised	10	-1.06 ± 0.89	-3.75 ± 0.70	-4.19 ± 0.84	5.42 ± 1.08	-0.50 ± 0.57
Rothamstead	Park Grass fertilised	10	-0.83 ± 0.45	-2.27 ± 1.00	-3.49 ± 0.90	3.40 ± 0.92	-0.25 ± 0.82
Rothamstead	Broadbank Wilderness grass	18	-1.24 ± 0.63	-3.25 ± 0.80	-2.72 ± 1.07	5.01 ± 1.12	-0.20 ± 0.59
1	Overton unburied outside enclosure	4	-0.52 ± 8.24	-3.01 ± 9.44	-7.87 ± 3.32	36.26 ± 26.61	8.37 ± 12.23
2	Overton unburied inside enclosure	5	-2.42 ± 8.14	-2.47 ± 7.57	-5.47 ± 4.94	23.18 ± 24.47	19.43 ± 14.84
3	Overton buried beneath chalk bank	5	-1.31 ± 4.22	-4.10 ± 3.77	-6.94 ± 4.01	21.82 ± 8.88	4.70 ± 4.34
4	Overton buried beneath turf stack	4	-4.36 ± 1.97	-4.21 ± 7.16	-6.44 ± 3.32	18.92 ± 11.46	0.96 ± 1.40
5	Overton developing on bank	4	-1.94 ± 1.64	-2.97 ± 2.11	-3.19 ± 1.66	11.02 ± 8.20	-1.37 ± 1.82

Location		Sample size	Serine	Glutamic acid	Glycine	Alanine	Valine
Rothamstead	Park Grass unfertilised	10	-0.15 ± 0.43	0.87 ± 0.50	4.72 ± 2.02	3.84 ± 1.41	-0.04 ± 0.53
Rothamstead	Park Grass fertilised	10	-0.27 ± 0.85	0.39 ± 0.96	4.05 ± 1.25	1.92 ± 1.65	-0.57 ± 0.66
Rothamstead	Broadbank Wilderness grass	18	0.12 ± 0.91	0.99 ± 0.79	4.94 ± 1.61	2.14 ± 0.90	-0.68 ± 1.54
1	Overton unburied outside enclosure	4	12.04 ± 12.10	16.22 ± 8.97	12.36 ± 12.44	8.27 ± 5.43	-13.70 ± 7.61
2	Overton unburied inside enclosure	5	-10.40 ± 4.92	23.08 ± 34.79	-10.40 ± 4.9	14.68 ± 9.25	-8.49 ± 5.26
3	Overton buried beneath chalk bank	5	4.96 ± 10.43	16.92 ± 16.10	5.67 ± 11.27	6.34 ± 2.76	-12.46 ± 5.28
4	Overton buried beneath turf stack	4	2.96 ± 10.00	13.42 ± 12.52	3.75 ± 9.96	5.69 ± 3.63	-4.77 ± 4.90
5	Overton developing on bank	4	-0.98 ± 3.97	14.48 ± 17.96	$-.053 \pm 4.00$	0.39 ± 1.16	-1.22 ± 2.05

Location		Sample size	Methionine	Isoleucine	Leucine	Tyrosine	Phenylalanine
Rothamstead	Park Grass unfertilised	10	-4.54 ± 0.81	-2.81 ± 0.59	-1.38 ± 0.53	3.41 ± 1.21	-0.28 ± 0.95
Rothamstead	Park Grass fertilised	10	-3.82 ± 0.82	-2.40 ± 1.08	-1.58 ± 1.06	5.19 ± 1.13	0.55 ± 2.08
Rothamstead	Broadbank Wilderness grass	18	-3.76 ± 0.83	-2.53 ± 0.72	-1.42 ± 0.64	2.97 ± 2.15	-0.38 ± 1.44
1	Overton unburied outside enclosure	4	-17.47 ± 8.15	-13.98 ± 7.51	-9.69 ± 6.16	-16.58 ± 8.95	-10.73 ± 7.70
2	Overton unburied inside enclosure	5	-10.40 ± 4.92	-8.78 ± 5.57	-6.30 ± 3.46	-8.09 ± 6.71	-7.74 ± 4.86
3	Overton buried beneath chalk bank	5	-11.89 ± 4.59	-5.45 ± 3.35	-4.07 ± 2.34	-7.53 ± 7.34	-6.67 ± 3.76
4	Overton buried beneath turf stack	4	-8.21 ± 6.58	-5.65 ± 3.67	-5.60 ± 3.32	-7.70 ± 6.03	1.29 ± 14.39
5	Overton developing on bank	4	-4.32 ± 2.16	-2.01 ± 1.87	-1.14 ± 2.20	-4.32 ± 1.87	-1.91 ± 1.25

coefficients in an attempt to suggest which amino acids were the most influential in the separation produced by that function. But this can be misleading, as it ignores the fact that the whole of the composite variable is required for the full efficiency of the separation to be realized. To ensure an answer to this question which is strictly meaningful in terms of individual amino acid differences, procedures based on univariate analysis of variance must be used, though it may not be possible to fully reconcile conclusions based on the two approaches.

The results of the univariate analysis of variance suggest that the soils outside and inside the enclosure are the most distinctive, whereas the Discriminant analysis pointed to the buried soils as the most distinctive. It must be emphasized that this is not a contradiction, but a consequence of the univariate analyses ignoring covariance and the Discriminant analysis using it.

It is possible that these two statistical options are selectively picking out similar variations. Univariate analysis of variance may be more clearly reflecting the decrease in pH and biological activity within the fenced area induced by higher moisture retention caused by litter mat formation over the last 32 years

(Crowther p 113; Macphail and Cruise p 99). On the other hand Discriminant analysis may be grouping the chalk buried soil with the more strongly transformed turf bank soil. The latter, for example, has become acidic, anerobic at times, and has developed a whole new microstructure reflecting compaction, major loss of organic matter and a newly dominant biota. At the present time there is insufficient comparative data, or theoretical treatment to support further attempts at interpretation of the amino acid data.

The large difference between Overton and Rothamstead soils is interesting, but it is not justifiable to attempt an explanation in terms of factors such as soil type and land use at this stage, as further work is required to eliminate completely the possibility that it is due to the small differences in extraction and measurement procedures.

This note of caution should not detract from the value of the Overton data. These clearly demonstrate the existence of what appears to be treatment and diagenetic related patterning, which should provide an incentive to develop this application of archaeological soil analysis with the aim of interpreting this potentially important source of information.

9 Biological evidence in the old land surface and ditch of the Overton 1992 section

9.1 Introduction

During the excavation of previous sections, work on biological evidence had been restricted to study of the movement of *Lycopodium* spores scattered as markers on the old land surface. In the years since the experiment was set up, the study of palaeoenvironmental evidence contained in buried soils has become an increasingly important aspect of archaeological research. Geoffrey Dimbleby (1962), one of the project's founders, pioneered the study of pollen from archaeological buried soils in Britain, and J G Evans (1972) pioneered the study of molluscan evidence from buried soils on chalk and limestone. Such investigations have played a leading role in documenting how people have transformed landscapes and in identifying particular patterns of human activity carried out immediately before the construction of monuments, especially the great ritual monuments on the Wessex chalk. Concern has grown that we do not know enough about how this palaeoenvironmental aspect of the archaeological record forms. Four key questions relevant to the earthwork are: (1) to what extent is biological evidence preserved in a stratified form; (2) to what extent does post-burial alteration of that record occur as the result of faunal agency, chemical change, differential decay etc; (3) when various sources of biological evidence are associated in a buried soil horizon can we assume their original association; (4) to what extent do biological particles of different sizes and materials move and decay differentially?

The extent of the contribution which the Earthwork Project makes to these issues varies according to the source of evidence and the extent of our knowledge about pre-burial biota. The best evidence concerns *Lycopodium* spores and pollen for which Dimbleby (1963) carefully tailored the experiment to address questions of pollen movement in chalk soils. In relation to seeds we have the pre-construction botanical survey, but there was no investigation of the seeds themselves in the originally buried turf. For molluscan studies we have no record of Mollusca prior to the 1992 section and indeed it turned out that conditions for molluscan life and preservation were poor in many contexts. Perhaps in the future the earthwork may provide a suitable context in which to address similar problems in relation to such evidence as insects, mites and other soil animals, phytoliths, etc.

9.2 *Lycopodium* spores
by K Crabtree

Professor Dimbleby had the buried land surface 'dusted' with *Lycopodium* spores before the construc-tion of the bank (Jewell and Dimbleby 1966). The aim was to study movement of the spores and their degree of preservation. Reports on the *Lycopodium* experiment for the first four years can be found in Jewell and Dimbleby 1966 and for the 1968 and 1976 excavation in Dimbleby page 43.

For the 1992 excavation, two monoliths were taken; Monolith 180 from beneath the margins of the bank across the buried land surface/chalk rubble boundary (corresponding to Series 2 in Jewell and Dimbleby 1966) and Monolith 179 from the turf stack, again crossing the old land surface. The locations of both and their relationship to other samples are shown on Figure 8.1. Serial samples were taken at 10mm or 20mm intervals from the monoliths and prepared for pollen analysis. Samples were first decalcified with dilute hydrochloric acid, before treatment with dilute caustic potash, followed by cold hydrofluoric acid for 24–48 hours and finally acetolysis before mounting in glycerol jelly. The volume of sample taken and the amount of glycerol jelly used were kept constant and counts of *Lycopodium* spores on the slides were made under low power with a total of 30 or 45 traverses per slide. The numbers recorded are therefore an approximate indication of the numbers per unit volume. The actual numbers counted per set number of traverses are recorded on Table 9.1 and graphically portrayed in Figures 9.1 and 9.2.

Discussion

Chalk bank/buried soil interface; Monolith 180

Lycopodium spores had been scattered on the old land surface which was plainly visible at the zero datum. With no subsequent movement one would expect a high concentration at the −10 to 0mm level and virtually none above and below. In practice it is clear from the amount of fine soil material which now occurs between the interstices of the chalk rubble above the old land surface that movement upward of material has occurred. That this contained the *Lycopodium* spores is evidenced by the counts, with considerable numbers being found at least 90mm above the buried surface. The difficulty of sampling in the chalk rubble made it impossible to take samples of less than 20mm thick in the rubble. The variation between 16 and 35 spores per 45 traverses is not regarded as significant and there is virtually uniform upward movement of the soil and its contained spores from the buried land surface at least 90mm up into the chalk rubble.

OVERTON DOWN BANK
LYCOPODIUM SPORES

Depth in mm

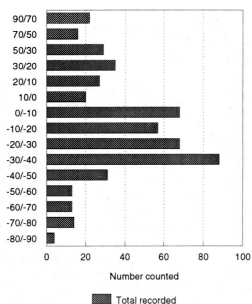

Number counted

▓ Total recorded

Nos of spores per 45 traverses

Figure 9.1 Numbers of Lycopodium spores in the old land surface and the overlying chalk bank. Sample Series 180

OVERTON DOWN STACK
LYCOPODIUM SPORES

Depth in mm

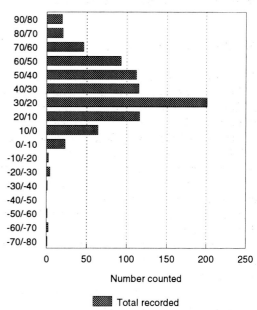

Number counted

▓ Total recorded

Nos per 30 traverses

Figure 9.2 Numbers of Lycopodium spores in the old land surface and the overlying turf stack. Sample Series 179

Table 9.1 *Lycopodium* spore counts

Chalk bank/buried soil Monolith 180		Turf stack/buried soil Monolith 179	
Sample depth	45 traverses	Sample depth	30 traverses
70–90 mm	22	80–90 mm	19
		70–80 mm	20
50–70 mm	16	60–70 mm	46
		50–60 mm	93
30–50 mm	29	40–50 mm	112
		30–40 mm	115
20–30 mm	35	20–30 mm	201
10–20 mm	27	10–20 mm	116
0–10 mm	20	0–10 mm	64
Buried land surface		Buried land surface	
–10–0 mm	68	–10–0 mm	23
–20–10 mm	57	–20–10 mm	2
–30–20 mm	68	–30–20 mm	4
–40–30 mm	88	–40–30 mm	1
–50–40 mm	31	–50–40 mm	0
–60–50 mm	13	–60–50 mm	1
–70–60 mm	13	–70–60 mm	2
–80–70 mm	14	–80–70 mm	1
–90–80 mm	4		

The extent of downward movement of *Lycopodium* spores was particularly surprising. The peak spores per 45 traverses was found 30–40mm below the buried land surface and then there is a fall off to just 4 by 90mm. Assuming the movement is due to faunal activity in the buried land surface then it is demonstrated that particulate matter is being mixed in the whole upper 90mm of the buried soil, with at least the upper 40mm or so almost homogensied in terms of the inclusion of the *Lycopodium* spores. This has occurred in 32 years.

Turf stack/buried soil interface; Monolith 179

The zero datum for the stack was based upon the field record and was marked on the side of the monolith tin. In the tin it was not possible to distinguish any buried surface; the brown organo-mineral horizon of the original soil and the buried turves of the turf stack had blended into a uniform looking layer. Difficulty had been experienced in defining the old land surface in the field (p 76). From the *Lycopodium* data one may doubt whether the marked junction of the buried land surface and the turf stack had been correctly identified. The high number of spores in the 20–30mm level suggests that this was the original surface level. If this was so, then the movement of spores down profile is of the order of 30mm with very small numbers being moved down 100mm. There is a clear distance decay, unlike beneath the chalk bank where homogenization of the upper 40mm of the buried soil was suggested. Movement upwards again shows something of a decay declining to about 10% of the number by 60mm above the peak value.

Results from earlier excavations

The samples beneath the chalk bank in the 1962 and 1964 excavations showed considerable movement both up and down profile. Maximum concentration remained at the old land surface but considerable numbers had moved up 25mm and down 100mm. By 1976 the maximum depth recorded by Dimbleby for penetration was 150mm (6in) while upward extension was greater and considerable numbers of spores were to be found above the old buried surface.

In the case of the turf stack, by 1964 movement down was slight but movement upwards was considerable over the first 70mm. By 1976 Dimbleby (p 43) notes that the 1964 upward movement appeared anomalous possibly due to a specific earthworm burrow and cast. In general, the 1968 and 1976 samples showed that most activity had occurred within 25mm of the original land surface with little further upward or downward movement. The results for 1992 show that activity in the stack has been over a wider band, but is still concentrated over c 60mm. Assuming the field recognition of the buried land surface was out by 20mm then movement down is concentrated in 20mm and movement up over c 40mm.

Implications for palynology of buried land surfaces

Even when a biologically active soil is buried there will be a period of movement and mixing of the buried soil by earthworm or other faunal activity. This will affect the fine material and included pollen and spores. This mixing may occur in an upward direction and, although here only positively recorded over a distance of 90mm, it is suspected that it does extend higher into the chalk rubble bank where there was also evidence of earthworm casts. It also, perhaps more surprisingly, occurs in a downward direction, producing an almost uniform spore content over 40mm and a fall off, but still a presence, down to 90mm. This would suggest that the amount of movement and mixing in such sites is considerable and that interpretation of pollen and spore or any other biological or mineral remains in buried soils or overlying sediments should be interpreted in this light.

Where overlain by a turf layer then biological activity penetrating those layers may take longer, but it has clearly occurred in the 32 years since burial as evidenced by both upward and downward movement of *Lycopodium* spores. The preservation of the

Lycopodium spores is still extremely good after 32 years in an aerated and biologically quite active but buried soil. This is in keeping with the occurrence of pollen in the soil, although that pollen does vary in preservation.

9.3 Pollen analysis of the old land surface
by K Crabtree

Prior to construction of the earthwork Dimbleby (1963) had carried out pollen analyses of the soil. In 1992 samples were prepared for pollen analysis as described in the preceding *Lycopodium* report. Given the character of the material, varying from compact soil to stony overburden, it was not possible to carry out quantitative preparation of the material, hence only relative counts were possible. Pollen was generally sparse and poorly preserved, making counting difficult. The population recorded could be largely residual and undoubtedly shows a bias towards the pollen types which are more easily recognizable in spite of degradation. On all slides, 20 to 50 traverses were recorded, but these only produced counts of 34 to 67 land pollen in the case of the Monolith 180 below the chalk bank, and 48 to 113 in the case of Monolith 179 below the turf stack. Data for the two series are given in Table 9.2 as the counts are too small for percentage diagrams.

Monolith 180 below chalk bank

Gramineae make up about 35–55% of all pollen recorded. Compositae (mostly *Taraxacum* type) make up 20–25% and *Plantago lanceolata* 2–15%. The presence of *Pinus* in most samples and of *Picea* in two probably represents pollen inputs of the post pine and spruce plantations of the late 19th century onwards. Fern spores may be residual but the presence of *Pteridium* spores, a feature noted by Dimbleby (1963), suggests a more recent Pteridophyte flora. This might represent a short period when the soils were sufficiently decalcified in their surface layers to encourage bracken. This was probably just prior to creation of the earthwork enclosure.

The pollen assemblage throughout the profile is essentially homogenized. Given the earthworm activity since burial of the old land surface such homogenization was largely expected. It does demonstrate the amount of mixing which has occurred in the 32 years since Dimbleby's original pollen profile was taken.

Monolith 179: below turf stack

More pollen was present as the section consisted of the buried soil and the original turves which made up the stack. The pollen present was of similar composition to that beneath the bank, and was

Table 9.2 Soil pollen analyses of Monoliths 179 and 180

Monolith 180: below chalk bank

Sample depth mm	20/30	10/20	0/10	−10/0	−20/−10	−30/−20	−40/−30	−50/−40
Pinus		3	2	7	2	1	6	3
Picea					2		2	
Quercus								1
Ulmus						1		
Gramineae	22	21	12	27	24	22	27	23
Cyperaceae	2	10	1	3	8	1	4	1
Caryophyllaceae				1				
Chenopodiaceae							1	
Compositae *Aster* type	2	2	1	1	4	5	1	3
Taraxacum type	10	22	7	8	11	5	12	10
Geraniaceae		1						
Lotus type							1	
Plantago lanceolata	3	7	9	8	1	2	5	4
Plantago media type		1		1	1			
Galium type	5	1		1				1
Filicales		9	3	7	4	4	6	3
Polypodium		1			2		2	1
Pteridium	1	3		4	1		1	1
TOTAL LAND POLLEN	45	67	34	58	53	38	59	46

Monolith 179 below turf stack

Sample depth mm	70/80	50/60	30/40	10/20	−10/0	−20/−30	−40/−50
Pinus	4	4	4	5	3	3	4
Picea					1		
Betula	2						
Quercus		1	1		2		
Alnus				1			
Corylus				2			
Gramineae	25	74	66	62	32	41	20
Cerealia	1						
Cyperaceae	2	2	4	4	2	2	2
Caryophyllaceae		1					
Chenopodiaceae						1	
Compositae *Arctium* type		1					
Aster type	5	4	2	3	5	4	3
Cirsium type		1					
Taraxacum type	13	9	13	12	15	11	17
Cruciferae		1			1		
Leguminosae					1	1	
Plantago lanceolata	13	15	12	18	13	17	2
Plantago media type			2				
Polygala	1	1	1				
Galium type	1		1				
Sanguisorba minor		1					
Ranunculaceae		2	3			1	
Thalictrum			1	2	1		
Filicales	2	3	1	5	3	4	2
Polypodium	1		1		1	1	4
Pteridium	1	7	2	3		3	
TOTAL LAND POLLEN	67	113	111	109	82	81	48

dominated by Gramineae pollen. Compositae and *Plantago lanceolata* are frequent with values up to 40% for Compositae (mostly *Taraxacum* type) at −40 to −50mm. This may be a preservation factor with only resistant and easily recognizable grains at this depth. From the *Lycopodium* spore evidence there was very little downward movement of spores below *c* 10mm beneath the stack, and hence we assume little or no post-1960 earthworm mixing of the lower part of the original soil profile. However percolation of base rich water draining through the chalk bank above the turf stack may have altered the chemical and biological environment of the pre-1960 pollen profile in the soil, leading to a less favourable environment for preservation. Slides below *c* 50mm were virtually devoid of pollen.

Only occasional pollen grains of some of the current chalk grassland herbs were present. Examples are the *Galium* type, the *Sanguisorba minor*, the Geraniaceae and the *Thalictrum*. In general very few tree pollen types were recorded suggesting that all the pollen present may represent relatively recent inputs and not residual assemblages from a pre-forest clearance phase. This would be in keeping with a view that it is only in a recent grassland phase that the soil has become acidic enough to preserve much of the pollen. The *Lycopodium* spores are still excellently preserved after 32 years while the pollen is much less well preserved. *Lycopodium* spores have a very high sporopollenin content (about three times that of most pollen) and so resist oxidation and corrosion better than pollen (Havinga 1967).

The size of the spores and pollen are similar and one would therefore expect similar behaviour as far as post-burial movement is concerned. However the spores were dusted on the surface whereas the pollen would have been present through the upper few millimetres of the soil, perhaps with maximum concentration close to the surface. Secondly the pollen would already have been bonded within the humic material while the spores were initially unbonded.

9.4 Microscopic charcoal
by Jenny Moore

Prior to construction of the earthwork in 1960, various materials were scattered over the site, in order to characterize, as far as possible, 'pre-earthwork' conditions. Included in this material was granulated charcoal, intended to mimic that carried from fires, and deposited on a land surface (Jewell 1963), and *Lycopodium* spores, designed to simulate recent pollen rain on the surface. The objective was to examine the movement of these materials within the soil after the building of the bank (Jewell 1963, 23).

The charcoal used was purchased in bulk from a local hardware shop, and consisted of large lumps of various species, which were not identified. The charcoal lumps were reduced in a large mortar until they passed through a 2mm sieve and the dust fraction was removed by passing through a 0.3mm sieve. The charcoal and *Lycopodium* spores appear to have been scattered over the surface simultaneously. There is no indication of the quantity of charcoal dispersed over the surface, although the *Lycopodium* spores are recorded as being applied at the rate of 125g to the area of each future bank section (Jewell 1963, Appendix 3).

Initial examination of the soils for pollen, before construction, revealed particles of finely comminuted charcoal in the soil profiles (Dimbleby 1963a, 63). The charcoal was reported as being up to 50μ (0.050mm) and showed no structure recognizable as being derived from wood. It was concluded that this charcoal derived from grass fires, as opposed to forest fires. The charcoal concentration was greatest through the mull humus horizon, but continued to be present down the profile, declining in quantity as the proportion of chalk increased (Dimbleby 1963a, 63).

During the excavations in 1962 and 1964, a series of soil samples were taken for analysis of *Lycopodium* spores and charcoal. The original intention had been to record the presence of charcoal in the microscopic preparations used for pollen analysis. However, because of the presence of ancient charcoal in the profile, no attempt was made at charcoal analysis from the 1962–1976 excavations of the earthwork (Jewell and Dimbleby 1966, 336).

In archaeology and palaeoecology, considerable significance is attached to the presence of microscopic charcoal in a profile, and interpretation of charcoal layers can range from postulating human firing of the landscape to natural conflagrations characterizing climatic change. However, such elucidations often assume that once charcoal reaches a depositional environment, it remains fixed at that level and survives in a relatively unaltered state. Microscopic charcoal and pollen concentrations are interpreted in comparison to each other, but this disregards the fact that pollen dispersal is a regular occurrence, while fire events are irregular and unpredictable. There is a tacit assumption that charcoal and pollen behave in a similar way, once they reach a depositional environment, but this has not been established.

The stability of microscopic charcoal in soil, and the assumption that if charcoal does move in a profile, it is in a similar way to pollen, are two aspects of current research being undertaken by the author at the University of Sheffield. The 1960 experimental design at Overton Down clearly offered the potential to extend this research. The bank and berm had been seeded with charcoal fragments and pollen at a known time, which would allow determination of the movement potential of both materials through the profile, after 32 years. In addition, the uncertainties created by the finely comminuted archaeological charcoal already present in the soil, could be addressed.

During the 1992 excavation, two monoliths (179 and 180) were taken, to provide material for pollen

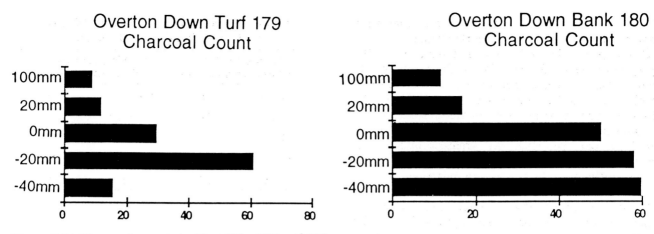

Figure 9.3 Charcoal counts in Monoliths 179 and 180

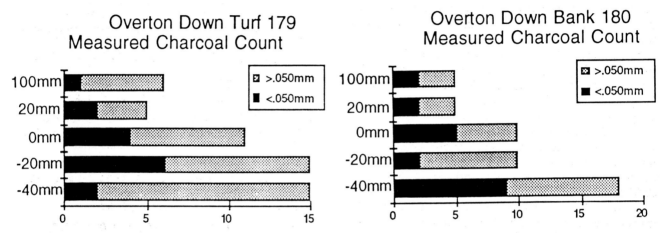

Figure 9.4 Measured charcoals in Monolith 179 and 180

analysis, by Dr Keith Crabtree (p 127). The monoliths were subsequently sampled and analyzed for charcoal by the author. The samples were taken at 20mm intervals below the old land surface, and at a greater interval above the old land surface. Standard pollen preparation procedures were used (Faegri and Iversen 1989) and the volume of samples was kept constant. Slides were prepared using silicon fluid on mounts 76mm × 26mm, with cover slips 22mm × 50mm. Counts were made using an Olympus BH-2 microscope with a ×10 eye piece and 40× objective (with graticule). The eye piece graticule was calibrated with one eye piece unit = 5.3766×10^{-3}mm.

Each fragment of charcoal was counted over 50 fields of view. The results are presented in Figure 9.3. In an additional count, measurement of charcoal fragments over 0.027mm on the longest axis (Swain 1973) was recorded and these results are set out in Figure 9.4. In each of the graphs, 0mm is the old land surface, and + mm designates distances above this level, – mm depth below.

Discussion

At Overton Down, the soil already contained finely comminuted charcoal (Dimbleby 1963). However, the distributed charcoal was known to have a size range of not greater than 2mm and not less than 0.3mm (Jewell 1963, Appendix C). Accordingly, in addition to an overall count over 50 fields of view, a count of measured charcoal particles could effectively refine the results, potentially eliminating the distorting factor of the fine archaeological charcoal. The arbitrary size range chosen was a count of all particles of, or greater, than 0.027mm. As the archaeological charcoal was noted to be up to 50μ (0.050mm) in size, the size range was divided at this point into fragments >0.050mm and <0.050mm. The sampling interval was chosen on the basis of obtaining an indication of the potential distribution in each profile.

For the purpose of this study, it is assumed charcoal fragments and pollen were distributed on the old land surface simultaneously. Jewell and Dimbleby (1966) indicate that charcoal was dispersed to represent an occupational deposit. If this is correct, then it could be anticipated that a charcoal layer would be visible in examining the profile. However, this was not the case. Charcoal was not visually evident either in the monoliths or in any of the samples taken. This was taken as an indication that there had been disturbance of the charcoal layer.

On the assumption that charcoal and pollen move in a profile in a similar way, the concentration of microscopic charcoal should be akin to that of pollen.

The results of the charcoal count and measured charcoal count are discussed on this basis.

Crabtree (p 127) predicted that the pattern of the *Lycopodium* spore distribution in the profile would show a high concentration at the −10mm to 0mm level with virtually none above and below this. The charcoal count over 50 fields of view, from the turf stack/buried soil profile (179) (Fig 9.3), follows the predicted pattern, with the greatest quantity of charcoal present at 0mm and −20mm, decreasing significantly at −40mm, but in addition there is movement up the profile. The chalk bank/buried soil (180) shows significant movement down the profile, which does not decrease with depth, although the pattern of movement up the profile is similar to the turf stack. Whilst in the turf stack, the downward movement of charcoal is as predicted for pollen; in the chalk bank, deposition is increasing down the profile.

In the turf stack, the measured count of fragments <0.050mm (Fig 9.4) shows a similar pattern to the overall count. As particles in this size range are most likely to be from the added charcoal, this supports the pattern of movement in the profile indicated by the overall count. However, the chalk bank distribution is not so clear. Although there is a similar distribution of particles <0.050mm above the old land surface (0mm), below the old land surface, particles <0.050mm do not consistently increase with depth.

The distribution of charcoal fragments originally scattered within the turf stack shows no similarity with the observed distribution of *Lycopodium* spores below the old land surface (Crabtree p 127). The charcoal fragments have followed the predicted pattern of movement for pollen, but the *Lycopodium* spores have not. However, above the old land surface, there are similarities in the pattern of movement. In the chalk bank, above the old land surface the distributions of spores and charcoal are similar. Below the old land surface, the overall charcoal count shows the same distribution pattern as the spores, with the greatest quantity at −40mm, but the measured charcoal count does not show as strong a correlation down the profile.

Conclusions

The analysis of microscopic charcoal and interpretation of the results are very much in the preliminary stages, but are of sufficient interest to warrant more detailed investigation.

In the environment of the Overton Down Earthwork, a charcoal layer cannot be seen as a discrete entity. Within the 32 years of the experiment, there has been notable movement of charcoal both up and down the profile, but the changes in the concentrations of charcoal with depth, are of particular interest. These observations suggest that investigations which do not pay adequate attention to the taphonomy of charcoal may reach erroneous conclusions. For example, if the bank profile was sampled

Table 9.3 Charcoal counts over 50 fields of view in Monoliths 179 and 180

Monolith 179 Turf stack/buried soil		Monolith 180 Chalk bank/buried soil	
+100mm	9	+100mm	12
+20mm	12	+20mm	17
0mm	30	0mm	50
−20mm	61	−20mm	58
−40mm	16	−40mm	60

Table 9.4 Charcoal particles measured (mm) over 50 fields of view in Monoliths 179 and 180

Monolith 179 Turf stack/buried soil	Monolith 180 Chalk bank/buried soil
+100mm 0.027, 0.032, 0.038, 0.043, 0.043	+100mm 0.043, 0.048, 0.048 0.054, 0.054, 0.075
+20mm 0.027, 0.027, 0.032, 0.059, 0.091	+20mm 0.038, 0.038, 0.043, 0.075, 0.081
0mm 0.027, 0.032, 0.032, 0.038, 0.038, 0.038, 0.038, 0.054, 0.054, 0.054	0mm 0.027, 0.027, 0.038, 0.043, 0.043, 0.054 , 0.059, 0.059, 0.081, 0.086, 0.134
−20mm 0.027, 0.027, 0.027, 0.032, 0.032, 0.038, 0.038, 0.043, 0.054, 0.075, 0.086, 0.097, 0.183	−20mm 0.027, 0.027, 0.038, 0.038, 0.038, 0.043, 0.043, 0.048, 0.048, 0.059, 0.065, 0.097
−40mm 0.027, 0.027, 0.027, 0.027, 0.027, 0.032, 0.032, 0.032, 0.032, 0.038, 0.043, 0.043, 0.070	−40mm 0.027, 0.027, 0.027, 0.027, 0.032, 0.032, 0.038, 0.038, 0.043, 0.043, 0.054, 0.059, 0.059, 0.059, 0.065, 0.070, 0.081, 0.081, 0.134, 0.140

for archaeological or 'environmental' evidence, there is the potential for a 'fire event' being identified as having taken place at −40mm in the profile, whereas it had actually occurred at 0mm. The 'fire event' would then be erroneously interpreted as having occurred at this level, which could in turn could lead to misinterpretations of an environmental episode or human interaction with the landscape.

Whilst there are some similarities, charcoal and pollen may not necessarily move in this depositional environment in exactly the same way. The work at Overton Down has shown that upward, as well as downward, movement of these materials can take place in a profile, and is linked to the soil micromorphological evidence for post-depositional soil reworking, particularly by earthworms (Macphail and Cruise p 99).

A qualification should be placed on the results of the present charcoal analysis. The quantity of charcoal present over 50 fields of view is small and may not be representative. The simple method of using a measured count of charcoal particles may not necessarily be effective in excluding ancient charcoal.

Experimental work currently being undertaken by the author at the University of Sheffield should enhance understanding of the movement potential of both charcoal and pollen in a soil profile.

9.5 Seed flora studies of the buried soil, bank, ditch fills and modern soil pits
by Wendy Carruthers and Vanessa Straker

When the Overton Down Experimental Earthwork Project was initiated in 1960, fruits and seeds were not included amongst the buried materials and a study of the seed flora of the soil to be buried was not carried out. Since then, advances in the study of plant macrofossils have demonstrated that the examination of the seeds present in modern and buried soils can contribute towards archaeobotanical interpretation in the ways discussed below.

Where the terms 'seed' and 'survival' are used in this report, they refer to the physical remains of this part of a plant and do not imply any retention of viability. The term 'seed flora' is used to cover all detectable seeds in the soil (see Cappers 1993), as distinct from the term 'seed bank' used in the report by Hendry *et al* (p 138) which includes only viable seeds.

Species composition of seed flora in relation to current and past vegetation records

When a soil becomes preserved by burial the seed flora within that soil may also be preserved under certain circumstances. Waterlogging of deposits resulting in a decrease in microbial decay of organic material is probably the main cause, but preservation by mineralization has also been observed, in a Late Bronze Age midden at Potterne (Carruthers 1986). At Silbury Hill, plant macrofossils and insects were preserved on the old land surface as a result of very deep burial (M Robinson, pers comm).

In order to assist in the interpretation of such samples a study of seed flora composition in relation to the past and present vegetation is of great value. The existence of botanical surveys at Overton Down covering the past 32 years (Hemsley 1963 and Chapter 3) is of particular importance to this study.

Survival of seeds in biologically active soils and the movement of seeds through the soil

Where old land surfaces have become buried but have not been subjected to waterlogging or mineralization, un-charred plant macrofossils are generally believed to be lost gradually through predation and microbiological decay. However, reports of uncharred seeds being recovered from archaeobotanical samples from biologically active soils have long been

noted, and Atkinson (1957) drew attention to the role that earthworms could play in the alteration of archaeological stratigraphy and burial of small objects. For many years such seeds have been dismissed as modern contaminants which may have worked their way down the soil profile through root or worm action, or may have been collected by rodents (Keepax 1977). Although this may account for many uncharred seeds, particularly where fresh looking embryos are observed, radiocarbon dating of blackberry seeds from Worcester Deansway (Moffett 1991) has demonstrated that uncharred seeds may survive for many centuries. On other occasions, fruits and seeds that appeared to be archaeological, such as a grape pip recovered from stratified deposits at Flagstones, Dorchester, have turned out to be modern intrusions (Straker, unpubl). The Overton Down Experimental Earthwork provides an opportunity to examine seed mobility. The vegetation surveys from 1960 show which taxa were present at the outset of the experiment and when certain species became established.

Although this study is related to the work carried out by Hendry *et al* (p 138) on viability in the relatively recently buried Overton Down seeds, archaeological seeds are not usually thought to be viable but often survive in the soil as empty seed cases. Therefore, where references are made to the 'seed flora' in this report, all identifiable fruits and seeds are included, regardless of whether or not they are viable. The viability tests do, however, provide interesting comparative information on the longevity of certain taxa. Information on the movement of other artefacts and ecofacts through the soil, for example charcoal (p 131) and pollen (p 127), are also of relevance to this study.

Methods and results

Two shallow 1m^2 soil pits were cut into the modern land surface by the authors. The pits were aligned with the section through the mound and ditch (see Fig 7.3). Soil Pit 1 was located inside the fence 15–16m south of the bank axis, and Soil Pit 2 was outside the fence 26.3–27.3m south of the bank axis. Samples 6 and 7 consist of the top 0.03–0.1m and 0.1–0.17m in Soil Pit 1, and samples 8 and 9 from Soil Pit 2 are the top 0.05–0.1m and 0.1–0.15m respectively. The depth of both trenches was restricted to the 'A' horizon. The thickness of the herbage on the surface determined the depth of the upper sample in each pit, and 6 and 8, and 7 and 9 are considered to be equivalents.

Other samples were collected from the incipient soil on the bank layer E/F (30); the upper ditch silts (35 and 36); bank layers C (98) and B (103); the turf stack (119) and the old land surface (155 and 156).

Samples 30, 35, 36, 98 and 103 were dry sieved on site through a 6mm mesh and then they, and the rest of the bulk samples, were processed by sieving in a flotation tank. The flots were retained on a 250 micron sieve and residues on a 500 micron mesh. The subsamples, that were sent to Sheffield for viability tests (Hendry *et al*, p 138), were only treated with cold water and not allowed to soak before sieving. The residues and flots were air-dried and the residues were scanned by eye for plant macrofossils. The flots were sorted under a binocular microscope. The modern samples (6–9) produced a very large volume of floating material in comparison with those from buried contexts, emphasising the reduction in fibrous plant material in 32 years.

Identification was carried out using low power binocular microscopy, with reference being made to comparative collections and the vegetation surveys by Hemsley (p 13). The results are presented in Table 9.5. With some taxonomic groups the identification of fruits and seeds to species level is difficult, but where the floristic surveys provided species identifications that fitted in with the seed morphology, the identifications were denoted as cf. Insects and worm cocoons were also present, but were excluded from this study.

Discussion

Species composition

By comparing the species composition of the seed flora samples to the lists of taxa obtained through the botanical surveys it is possible to see how closely changes in the vegetation are mirrored by changes in the seed flora.

Comparison between the old land surface and turf stack samples and the 1960 survey

The samples produced 12 taxa in common with the 1960 vegetation survey (Hemsley 1963) but it was not possible to use statistics to investigate whether the old land surface and turf stack samples were more similar to the first survey than the 1992 survey, owing to insufficient data. The 12 taxa are listed below:

> *Festuca rubra*
> *Carex flacca*
> *Ranunculus bulbosus*
> *Thymus drucei*
> *Rumex acetosa*
> *Cerastium* sp.
> *Linum catharticum*
> *Scabiosa columbaria*
> *Campanula rotundifolia*
> *Arrhenatherum elatius*
> *Euphrasia* sp.
> *Cirsium* sp.

No taxa were found to be present in the old land surface and 1960 survey but absent from the recent survey, ie there was no evidence from the seed study

of taxa that had become extinct due to changes in the management of the land.

Taxa present in the 1992 survey and modern soil but not in the old land surface or turf stack or 1960 survey, ie recent colonizers

Although no taxa fall into this category, elderberry (*Sambucus nigra*) was not recorded on the site in 1960 but was present in the old land surface and turf stack samples and was recorded in the 1984 survey. This could suggest movement of elder seeds through the profile from the new colonizer, perhaps in rodent burrows. However, it is likely that elder seeds would have been brought continually onto the site by birds, even before the establishment of the earthwork, and so would have been present in the seed flora at the time of construction. The fencing off of the earthwork would have prevented seedlings from being grazed, enabling the elder tree to become established.

Taxa in the surveys but not in the seed flora

64% of the taxa recorded in the botanical surveys were not represented in the seed flora. There are several possible ways to explain these absences, all of which need to be taken into account by archaeobotanists when interpreting assemblages:

(1) Sampling; small sample size and limited area of samples.
(2) Dispersal strategies; these differ depending on the taxon, eg some plants produce large numbers of small, short-lived, widely dispersed seeds, and others produce a few large seeds that fall close to the plant. Dispersal by birds and livestock is a further factor. Therefore the chances of recovering some taxa in the small soil samples examined are greater than for others.
(3) Predation and decay of fruits and seeds; these factors are perhaps of greatest interest to archaeobotanists, as they are subjects in need of further research. Of particular note is the relatively low recovery of grass seeds (family Gramineae) from the buried layers in comparison with the botanical surveys. This is likely to be due to both predation by rodents and birds and also rapid microbiological decay, as the seed coats of grasses are not particularly thickened. It is interesting to note that Gramineae are also relatively infrequently preserved in waterlogged and mineralized archaeobotanical samples. However, a number of grasses are included in the list of taxa forming long-term (> 4 years) seed flora given in Hendry *et al* (p 139). Another family of plants that is often poorly represented in waterlogged and mineralized archaeobotanical samples, which is missing from the seed flora samples is the legumes (Leguminosae). This may be due to the fact that some seeds in this family

Table 9.5 Plant remains

	Pit 1		Pit 2		Bank layer E/F soil	Ditch	Ditch	Bank layer C	Bank layer B	Turf stack	Old land surface	Old land surface
Samples	30–100 mm	100–170 mm	50–100 mm	100–150 mm								
Taxa	6	7	8	9	30	35	36	98	103	119	155	156
Arenaria serpyllifolia L. (thyme-leaved sandwort)	30	14	20	602	3		2		8	47	5	10
Arrhenatherum elatius (L.) Beauv. ex J&C Presl. (false oat-grass florets)	39	80										
Atriplex patula/prostrata (orache)	3	1								2		
Betula sp. (birch)				1								
Campanula rotundifolia L. (harebell)					24			1		119		
Carex cf. flacca Schreber (carnation-grass)	3	5		2						5	7	4
Cerastium sp. (mouse-ear chickweed)	1		1	5						5		5
Cirsium/Carduus sp. (thistle)	46	14	388	36	15	1						
cf. Euphrasia sp. (eyebright)		1			4		1					
Festuca rubra cf. rubra (red fescue florets)	81	54	20									
Galeopsis tetrahit L (common hemp-nettle)	291	25	2		1							
Galium cf verum L. (cf. lady's bedstraw)	1											
Gramineae (grass florets)	7											
Leontodon cf. hispidus L. (cf.rough hawkbit)					1							
Linaria vulgaris Miller (common toadflax)					6							
Linum catharticum L. (purging flax)	6	4			2			1		3	4	3
Poa sp. (poa grass)								1				
Ranunculus acris/repens/bulbosus (buttercup)	2	3	101	6								
Ranunculus cf. acris L. (cf. meadow buttercup)								1				
Rubus idaeus L. (raspberry)	2	1										
Rumex acetosa L. (sorrel, + perianths)	8	2			1							
Rumex cf. acetosa L. (cf. sorrel, nutlets only)	33	9			4			1				
Sagina sp. (pearlwort)										1		
Sambucus nigra L. (elder)	36	10	9	18			1			29	9	18
Scabiosa columbaria L. (small scabious)	1			1	1						1	1
Sonchus asper (L.) Hill (spiny sow-thistle)										1		
Succisa pratensis Moench (devil's-bit scabious)									1	1		
cf. Thymus drucei Ronn. (cf. wild thyme)									1	2		1
Urtica dioica L. (stinging nettle)			19	26		8			1			
Viola cf. arvensis Murray (cf. field pansy)										1	1	
Unidentified taxa	2			3	3			2		1	1	
TOTAL	594	223	560	700	65	9	4	8	10	97	27	43
VOLUME SIEVED (LITRES)	14	14	14	14	10	3	5.5	9	5	25	14	14
SEEDS PER LITRE	42.4	15.9	40	50	6.5	3	0.7	0.9	2	3.9	1.9	3.1
carbonised Hordeum sp.									1			
charcoal fragments	+				+			+	++	+	+	+

+ = trace, ++ = several fragments

have a particularly high nitrogen content which is attractive to both predators and microbes (P Wiltshire, pers comm).

Taxa in the seed flora but not in the surveys

Possible reasons for this are summarized below:

(1) As noted above for elder, seeds may be brought onto the site but conditions might be unsuitable for the plants to become established, perhaps due to grazing or ecological factors such as competition and light intensity. Examples of this could be the raspberry seeds (*Rubus idaeus*), which were probably brought onto the site by birds, and the birch seed (*Betula* sp.), which may have been wind-dispersed from some distance.

(2) Plants may be growing in the locality that did not fall within the area of botanical survey. An example of this must be the thyme-leaved sandwort (*Arenaria serpyllifolia*), since the seeds were numerous in many of the samples. This small plant is an early colonizer of bare soil and hence it produces large numbers of small seeds. However, it was recorded in greatest numbers in the lower spit of the sample taken from outside the enclosure and was also quite frequent in the turf stack sample. This suggests that its establishment is not necessarily associated with the disturbance caused by the building of the earthwork, but that grazing provided a sufficiently open sward for it to become established. Hemsley (1963) noted the presence of scattered areas of animal disturbance on the site which would provide bare ground suitable for colonization by this species. It could be suggested that, being a very small seed (< 1mm), it had trickled down the soil profile to the turf stack and old land surface. However, very few sandwort seeds were present in the intervening mound samples.

The ditch samples

Samples 35 and 36 were taken from the upper layers of the ditch fill (Fig 8.1) and contained very few recognizable macrofossils, the commonest being nettles in sample 35, the upper sample. No samples were taken from the lower chalk fill which was assumed to contain few seeds (the early silting included chalk rubble weathered from the unprotected ditch sides before vegetation became established). These results suggest that seeds that become incorporated in dry aerobic ditch fills, that accumulate slowly through natural silting processes in a high pH environment such as chalk, may be more vulnerable to decomposition and predation. However, it should be noted that both soil samples were small, and further research is needed on this type of deposit.

Survival and movement through the soil

By comparing the number of seeds per litre found in the modern soil samples with the figures for the old land surface and turf stack it is possible to see that the seed flora has probably been reduced to *c* 1/10th of its original level after 32 years of burial. As discussed above, some taxa will be less likely to survive due to differential predation and decay and it is notable that the tough-coated seed of elder, which is often found uncharred in archaeobotanical samples, is present in roughly the same number of seeds per litre in the buried samples as in the modern samples. Before conclusions can be drawn, however, about the survival of certain seeds over this period of time it is important to address the question of possible movement of modern seeds down through the soil profile.

The results from the analysis of the distribution of *Lycopodium* spores that were scattered on the surface before burial in 1960, have shown that the spores moved both downwards and upwards into the mound (Crabtree p 127). Unfortunately, no exotic experimental seeds were distributed at the time of burial, so it is not possible to be absolutely certain that the seeds found in the old land surface and turf stack were present as the original seed flora. However, even with the small amount of data gathered during the 1992 excavations, several factors suggest that the quantities of seeds being transported down the profile have not been great. One indicator is the relatively low frequency of seeds found in the chalk mound samples, which would have been fairly sterile at the time of construction and have remained so.

Another way of examining this question is to see whether seeds from recently arrived taxa have become incorporated into the mound and buried soils. The increase in nettles (*Urtica dioica*) noted by Hemsley (p 24) is reflected in the seed flora of the modern soil and ditch but only one seed was found in a mound sample and none in the buried soils. This suggests that changes in the flora are fairly rapidly reflected in the modern seed flora and that there has been relatively little movement of at least this species through the soil. Similarly, hemp nettle (*Galeopsis tetrahit*) was not noted in earlier botanical surveys but was present in 1992 in the north-eastern sector of the enclosure (Hemsley p 24). It is notable that this taxon only occurs in the modern soil samples apart from a single seed in the bank sample 30. Large numbers were recovered from sample 6, the upper spit of Soil Pit 1 inside the enclosure.

Small fragments of charcoal were found in some of the flots. These were mostly in the lower mound sample (103), immediately above the turf stack, and could have originated from the charcoal that was buried on the soil surface in 1960 (Moore p 131). However, the charcoal could also have been present in the soil before burial, as the recovery of a charred barley grain from the same sample suggests that archaeological deposits were present before the experiment started, and charcoal fragments are ubiquitous in archaeological contexts.

One further piece of evidence to suggest that seeds had not been carried down through the profile was obtained from the viability tests (Hendry *et al*, p 139). Hendry reports that only 6 species were found to be viable in the buried soils and none of these were considered to be short-lived taxa. Therefore, all of the seeds could have survived the 32 years of burial rather than been carried down by soil fauna. Hendry points out that the paucity of germinating seeds in the buried soils demonstrates how active the decomposition organisms have been in the Overton soils. However, the results presented here have shown that, although decomposition has obviously affected the soft internal structures of the seed, the seed coats of quite a range of species (14 taxa) have survived.

Recommendations for future analyses

The lessons learned in this study have enabled us to make recommendations for improved sampling and recovery on similar projects. It would be useful to consider implementing them when the Wareham Earthwork is sectioned in 1996.

(1) Although the modern soil samples were more than adequate in size, larger soil samples from the buried soils and sediments should be taken in the future, if at all possible, so that sufficient data is recovered for statistical analysis. This will be even more necessary as time progresses, since the number of seeds surviving in the buried soils is likely to decline.

(2) Closer sampling, for example through ditch fills, may help to study the movement of seeds through the sediments. As it may be difficult to obtain sufficiently large samples, it would probably be necessary to use the samples collected for other specialist studies once they had been finished with. Co-ordination of sample processing methods at the outset would then be essential. Similarly, soil samples from the seed persistence (viability) tests could be used for seed flora studies. It would be useful if these soil samples could be returned to the archaeobotanists for processing, once all germination has taken place. This would enable identification of the taxa which were present but did not germinate.

(3) The report on seed persistence suggests that in future years it will not be necessary to use seeds recovered from the sieving programme for persistence tests. This will save processing time, as these samples were difficult to process because they could not be soaked prior to sieving.

(4) It would be useful if, in future years, the botanical survey was carried out along the same transect as the seed sampling and for it to extended outside the enclosure to cover the sampling of the modern soil. This will enable the

seed results to be more closely related to the vegetation studies.

Acknowledgements

We are grateful to Elaine Jewkes and Tertia Barnett for help with sample processing and Lisa Moffett for permission to quote from AM Laboratory Report 123/91.

9.6 Seed persistence and plant decomposition after soil burial for 32 years
by G A F Hendry, S R Band and K Thompson

Introduction

Authenticated examples of seeds surviving in soils for 80 to 100 years are known for a small number of species from a limited number of soil types (eg Darlington and Steinbauer 1961; Kivilaan and Bandurski 1981). However, the opportunity to assess with any chronological accuracy the longevity of seeds buried in soils remains an all too rare event. The Overton Down Project provides one of the few accurately datable sources of buried seeds on a calcareous grassland plant community, in western Europe. Apart from any value of the seed study to archaeology, precisely datable information on long-term seed decay and persistence *under natural conditions* has a wider significance to ecology, agriculture, horticulture and forestry where persistent buried seed banks may wholly determine the future composition of vegetation following major soil disturbance (Hendry *et al* 1995). The value of the project to plant sciences will become even more apparent at future excavations.

Methods

Five soil samples with a total surface area of about 0.4m^2 were recovered from within a single area of about 1m^2 scraped from 0–100mm below the original land surface. In the laboratory these samples were broken up and layered to a depth of 10mm over acid-washed sand and maintained in a moist condition under a 16 hour day, at an irradiance of 150 umol m^{-2} s^{-1} at temperatures of 22°day/15°night, simulating warm spring conditions. At four-week intervals the soil samples were thoroughly mixed and reincubated twice following removal and identification of all germinating plants. In a separate investigation samples of seeds and other similar sized structures were prepared from the same soils by sieving (samples prepared by Wendy Carruthers and Vanessa Straker) and were similarly exposed to germination-favourable conditions (and are described below as sieved samples).

Results and discussion

In unsieved soil samples, six species, out of 34 recorded in 1960 (Hemsley 1960), were present on the old land surface as viable seeds (Table 9.6). Five of the six species which did survive burial are strongly suspected (from laboratory experimentation) or suspected with less certainty (from field observation) to form long-persistent buried seed banks. None of the species suspected *not* to form persistent seed banks was recovered in the buried soils. Our concern was that earthworm and other seed-consuming and excreting soil-dwelling animals might have brought down viable but short-lived seeds to the original land surface. The complete absence of any such seeds suggests that this movement, at least of *viable* seeds, did not occur to a detectable extent. The only species recovered in which long-term seed persistence is not well documented was *Carex flacca*. Data for this species, while extensive, are contradictory and its present classification as having short-term persistence is a compromise. The findings here suggest that this classification should now be revised.

Several species known to form long-term persistent seed banks were apparently absent from the soil. The well-known small-scale patchiness of seeds in the soil (Thompson 1986), combined with the rather small area of soil sampled, almost certainly account for their apparent absence. The appearance of *Agrostis capillaris* buried seeds, but its absence from the vegetation records of 1960, is not entirely surprising; the closely grazed conditions of 1960 had largely suppressed flower initiation at the time of the 1960 survey (J Hemsley, pers comm) and so probably obscured its presence within the dominant *A. stolonifera*.

Viable seeds were found in only three of the five samples available for study. We have no explanation for the apparent absence of viable seeds in samples 149 and 151, though the context of both samples (buried below a carbonized hazel billet and an uncooked sheep's mandible respectively) may have influenced seed longevity by altering the soil chemistry, though this was not immediately apparent from the soil reaction, the mean pH being 6.3 in both samples.

In a separate experiment using seeds sieved from the same original land surface, despite the presence of a considerable number of seed or seed-like structures, unexpectedly no germination occurred. In contrast, similar sieve-treated samples derived from the mound surface, and therefore most likely of recent origin, did contain viable seeds of the relatively short-lived *Festuca rubra* and two species not present in the 1960 survey *Poa trivialis* and *Arenaria serpyllifolia*. The conclusion is that the technique of sieving, while not appearing to damage the seeds, offers no advantage over the method described above of germinating from unsieved soils in seed viability and persistence studies.

The archaeological significance of dead seeds recovered from excavations is well documented, but the

Table 9.6 Vegetation of Overton Down as recorded in 1960 by Hemsley (1963)

Species recorded in 1960	Viable seeds present in 1993 – no per m² soil
Forming long-term (>4 years) persistent seed banks	
Ranunculus bulbosus	5.0
Cerastium fontanum	–
Linum catharticum	–
Trifolium repens	–
Trifolium pratense	–
Lotus corniculatus	–
Plantago lanceolata	–
Plantago media	–
Thymus praecox	–
Campanula rotundifolia	7.5
Luzula campestris	12.5
Holcus lanatus	2.5
Phleum pratense	–
Agrostis stolonifera	–
Agrostis capillaris*	5.0
Forming short-term (1–4 years) seed banks	
Helianthemum nummularium	–
Rumex acetosa	–
Scabiosa columbaria	–
Hieraceum pilosella	–
Carex flacca	2.5
Anthoxanthum odoratum	–
Forming transient (<1 year) seed banks	
Galium verum	–
Cirsium acaule	–
Festuca rubra	–
Cynosurus cristatus	–
Briza media	–
Avenula pratensis	–
Avenula pubescens	–
Arrhenatherum elatius	–
Koeleria macrantha	–
Trisetum flavescens	–
Information on seed persistence uncertain	
Sanguisorba minor	–
Asperula cynanchica	–
Euphrasia nemorosa	–
Coeloglossum viride	–

Ranked by ability to form persistent seed banks (seed bank data from unpublished European data base of K Thompson and J P Baker) together with the results of germination tests; expressed as number of seedlings per square hectare of exposed soil surface.
* This species was not recorded in the 1960 survey

significance of living seeds is limited since few, if any, seeds can survive for archaeological periods of time, other than in extreme (and largely non-European) environments. Odum (1985) germinated seeds in soils excavated from beneath dated buildings in Denmark, and claimed to have recovered viable seeds up to 1750 years old. Although the species found are generally believed to be long-lived, such great ages for living seeds are not widely accepted.

In all samples examined here, the only non-seed macroscopic plant tissues seen with any frequency were occasional orange-brown fragments up to 10–15mm in length which appeared to be the remains of sclerotic, linearly arranged, cells forming flattened fibres not exceeding 100μm width, sometimes further grouped as bundles. Traces of a compressed annular structure were occasionally present on the inside of the bundles. Our conclusion is that these were relatively degradation-resistant fragments of monocotyledonous plant vascular tissue, probably of a grass, possibly *Festuca rubra*.

Overall, the paucity of germinating seeds and the extremely limited amount of macroscopic plant remains visible in the samples confirms that the Overton soils have supported active decomposition. In non-woody plant tissues, decomposition processes would have begun at the onset of senescence (that is immediately prior to death) (Hendry *et al*, 1987), whether natural (as at autumn) or artificially induced (as on burial). The agents of decomposition would include in sequence: internal auto-degradative enzymic processes possibly lasting for days, coupled with or followed shortly by decomposition through senescence-activated leaf and root saprophytic (that is non-pathogenic decomposing) fungi and bacteria already in place on and in the plant tissue *before* burial and probably active for some weeks thereafter. Decomposition by macro-fauna (such as earthworms and moles), and the soil micro-flora (soil-borne bacterial and fungal decomposers) will have become increasingly important components of plant decomposition processes over a period of weeks or months. Purely chemical decomposition through oxidation will also have occurred in these well-aerated soils with an even longer time-span. The activity of each of the decomposition components, severally and sequentially, appears to have been to degrade much the greater part of soft plant tissues at Overton. Although the high pH of the soils may have tended to favour bacterial over fungal decomposition, the well-drained soils and moderate rainfall at the site (750–900mm year^{-1}) appear to have ensured active decomposition of the non-woody buried plant tissues, probably largely complete within the first year of burial. As none of the vascular plant species reported as being present in 1960 have particularly long-lived aerial parts it must be no surprise that such little identifiable macro-plant tissues have been found 32 years later. Conditions which might have slowed down natural decomposition (low pH, water-logging, low temperatures, high temperature sterilization following fire or high pressure from deep burial) are absent from this site, though present in other nearby locations of archaeological interest (eg Hendry 1989).

Acknowledgement

The continued support of the Natural Environment Research Council is acknowledged.

9.7 Land molluscs
by M Bell and S Johnson

Prior to the 1992 Overton excavation no previous work had been undertaken on the molluscs. The 1992 research design proposed a limited study of molluscs from the 1960 buried soil, since it had formed under known vegetation conditions and would thus represent a useful modern analogue which might help refine interpretation of archaeological mollusc assemblages. Molluscs were also examined from two sub-soil features and from the ditch. A comparative study of the living Mollusca of the site is discussed by A Rouse (p 142).

Old land surface

A series of 17 samples was taken from the old land surface (Figure 8.1: Column 157), at 10mm intervals for the top 100mm and below this at 20mm intervals. There were no molluscs at all in the top 120mm and below this just one fragment of *Pomatias elegans* and two fragments of *Pupilla muscorum*. The lack of molluscs is attributed to the effects of decalcification which was attested by the soil studies (p 115). Decalcification had not been anticipated in advance of the excavation, and is not recorded in the manual (Jewell 1963) or first report (Jewell and Dimbleby 1966).

Sub-soil hollows

Weathering back of the ditch had revealed subsoil features on the north (Figures 7.12–13; 8.1) and south sides. Molluscs were abundant in the samples taken from both features (Table 9.7). The five samples analysed were similar: *Discus rotundatus* predominated and the other abundant species are those encountered in damp, shaded and generally wooded situations. *Ena montana* and *Vertigo pusilla* tend to be characteristic of old woodland (Evans 1972, 165 and 141) and have become rare with later Holocene clearance. The samples contain a few *Pupilla muscorum* and *Vallonia costata* which may indicate the presence of openings within woodland. The mollusc assemblage is in agreement with the usual interpretation of such features as fossil tree-holes relating to a period of former woodland cover on the chalk. Similar features have previously been reported locally from below a lynchet on Fyfield Down (Evans 1972, Fig 120).

Table 9.7 Land Mollusca from the subsoil features 37A top and 37B bottom, and 89A top, 89B middle and 89C base; also from column 160 in the ditch. Samples 0.80–0m depth

Species	37A	37B	89A	89B	89C	80–75	75–56	56–53	53–39	39–35	35–30	25–20	20–10	10–0	Sieving	Modern transect
Soil wt in kg	2	2	1	1	1	0.65	1	0.5	1	1	1	1	1	1		
Pomatias elegans	27	62	12	9	16	+		+		1		+	+	+	+	–
Carychium tridentatum	35	41	2	3	1											–
Cochlicopa lubrica														1		+
Cochlicopa sp	11	13	3	2												–
Vertigo pygmaea													1	1		–
Vertigo pusilla		1														–
Vertigo spp	3	2														–
Pupilla muscorum	2	2	4	3	2						1		1		+	+
Lauria cylindracea		1														–
Vallonia costata					+											–
Vallonia excentrica	3			2												–
Vallonia spp			2		3											–
Acanthinula aculeata	13	5														–
Ena montana	4	1	1	1												—
Ena obscura		2	1		1											–
Punctum pygmaeum	1	1											1	5		–
Discus rotundatus	218	229	21	35	29				+		1	+				–
Vitrina pellucida		4			1								1	2		+
Vitrea crystallina		2														–
Vitrea contracta	13	10			1							1	1	1		+
Vitrea spp		12														+
Nesovitrea hammonis													10	19	+	+
Aegopinella pura	15	12														–
Aegopinella nitidula	14	2														–
Oxychilus cellarius	39	66	6	8	11										+	–
Limacidae	42	21	1	6	2								1	4		+
Euconulus fulvus		1														–
Cochlodina laminata	6		1													–
Clausilia bidentata	34															–
Clausiliidae	19	45	10	12	14											–
Helicella itala													+		+	+
Trichia striolata	4	4														–
Trichia hispida	22	10	5	4	4						1	5	7	33	+	+
Helicigona lapicida	1	1	+	+												–
Cepaea nemoralis																+
Cepaea hortensis																–
Cepaea spp	31	26	13	5	3								1	11	+	+
TOTAL SHELLS	560	576	82	90	88	0	0	0	0	1	3	6	24	77		

The two right-hand columns record the presence (+) or absence (–) of taxa in samples from *in situ* sieving (5mm) mesh and in the modern mollusc survey reported by A Rouse.

Ditch

Nine samples were taken in Column 160 from the ditch (Fig 8.1). The basal four samples produced no apices, not surprisingly because we know that this fill accumulated very rapidly. In the next 5 samples the numbers increased to the surface:1; 3; 6; 24; 77. The few shells of *Discus* and *Pomatias* were weathered and clearly eroded from the subsoil features (see above) in the ditch edge, but the contribution of these reworked shells was surprisingly small given the numbers of molluscs in subsoil features in the ditch edge. The predominant species in the ditch are *Nesovitrea hammonis* and *Trichia hispida*.

A record was made of the extent to which the periostracum (protein coating) survived on shells. The consensus has been that this is lost within a year of death (Evans 1972; Carter 1990). 31 shells (40%) in the top sample had the periostracum intact and in 75% half or more of its area was preserved. At 10–20cm 4 shells (17%) had the periostracum intact and 30% had at least 50% preserved. Below 0.2m one shell had an intact periostracum and one other had 50% survival.

The high proportion of shells with surviving periostracum needs to be explained. It could be that molluscs have only recently become abundant on the site, as unfortunately no earlier records were made. It could indicate that molluscs have only a very short mean residence time in these sediments, something like 2.3 years at the surface and 6 years at 0.1–0.25m. We should also consider the possibility that the periostracum survives for longer than conventionally suggested. Two shells with surviving periostracum below 0.2m may indicate a degree of incorporation of recently dead molluscs, mechanisms for which have been reviewed by Carter (1990). Assuming that the periostracum has a comparable survival time in different species, then the *Nesovitrea hammonis*, *Punctum pygmeaum* and *Cepaea* are all very recent, whereas a larger number of the *Trichia hispida* had less or no periostracum surviving and are likely to be older.

Conclusions

The assemblage makes interesting comparison with the transect survey of modern Mollusca (Rouse below). The ditch column confirms Rouse's observation that some characteristic molluscs of open chalk downland are absent: the Vallonias, *Cernuella virgata* and *Candidula intersecta*. Column 160 adds two species, *Vertigo pygmaea* and *Punctum pygmaeum*, both of which had periostracum surviving. *Helicella itala* was only represented by one non-apical fragment in the ditch, although it was frequent in the transect and in samples from on-site sieving (mesh size 5mm) designed to detect artifacts and larger biota.

Evidence from the transect and the column reflects a restricted fauna. The earthwork appears to have created an island of molluscan life, and to some

extent preservation, in the middle of an unfavourable decalcified grassland soil. This highlights spatial contrasts of molluscan assemblage over short distances in chalk grassland as noted by Rouse and Evans (1994) at Maiden Castle, where diversity correlated strongly with levels of calcium. At Overton only selected species of open downland are present. They accompany other species more generally associated with rather damper shaded situations, here provided by lush ungrazed vegetation in the ditch and around the earthwork. Some of these, *Nesovitrea hammonis*, *Vitrina pellucida* and *Punctum pygmaeum* , have been found elsewhere to characterize secondary ditch fills (Evans 1972, 196).

The recent Mollusca in the ditch are almost certainly separated by many millennia from those in the subsoil hollows which reflect a period of former woodland cover. Between these two periods there is a long hiatus in the mollusc evidence. Such hiatuses are encountered elsewhere in stable soils, for instance on chalk in the fills of Neolithic ditches (Evans 1990) and at Winterbourne Steepleton, Dorset (Bell *et al.* 1990) and on limestone at Condicote (Bell 1983) and Hazleton, Gloucestershire (Bell 1990b). These gaps in the mollusc sequence are presumably due to a combination of conditions unsuitable for the incorporation and preservation of mollusc shells and conditions at the time which were unsuitable for mollusc life, as seems to be the case today in the grassland surrounding the Overton Earthwork. The presence of such hiatuses reinforces concerns that even within seemingly continuous mollusc sequences there may be episodes when, for reasons of vegetation or land-use, stable conditions obtained, little calcium was liberated and molluscs declined in numbers or were not preserved.

The limited molluscan evidence from the earthwork supports the more extensive studies of Evans (1990) and Rouse and Evans (1994) in showing that molluscan life and preservation is closely related to calcium and the character of vegetation cover. This evidence also provides a measure of support for Carter's (1990) conclusion that mollusc diagrams from palaeosols may not represent continuous sequences, but rather some discrete episodes, of varying duration, when conditions were suitable for preservation. It follows that episodes of disturbance, such as that which created the earthwork, are more likely to register in terms of a surviving mollusc record than episodes characterized by certain forms of long-term stability.

9.8 Modern molluscs
by Amanda Rouse

Introduction

An investigation into the present-day molluscan fauna at the Overton Down Experimental Earthwork was carried out along a single transect across the bank and ditch. The transect ran north-east/south-west, near the west end of the earthwork (Fig 7.3), across a section not excavated, and so undisturbed since 1960. Thirteen areas along the transect were chosen, which displayed variation of slope, aspect, soils and vegetation cover (Fig 9.5). These environmental variables were noted for each area, but not measured in a quantitative way. Eleven of the areas were within the earthwork enclosure, protected by a rabbit fence and ungrazed. In addition, two sites were outside the enclosure, to the south of the earthwork.

Further information about the vegetation of the sampled area is contained in the report by Hemsley (Chapter 3).

Sample areas

Area 1

At the bottom of the north slope of the bank, north-east facing and gently sloping. There was 100% vegetation cover of mainly grasses, up to 1m long, but mostly approximately 0.3m, tussocky and matted at the base. There were some mosses. Beneath the mat was a mixture of soil and chalk rubble.

Area 2

The north slope of the bank, and north-east facing, approximately a third of the way down from the crest. A lot of bare chalk was exposed on this upper part of the bank, mainly concreted but with some small loose rubble. Vegetation covered only about 40% of the area examined. It consisted of a variety of plants and grasses, all generally short – mostly just 10–20mm high.

Area 3

A level site on the top of the bank. There was approximately 20% vegetation cover, consisting of very small plants. The exposed chalk was concreted with a little fine chalk rubble.

Area 4

The south slope of the bank, south-west facing, approximately half way down from the crest. The vegetation, mainly of grasses was thick and matted, providing 100% cover with an average height of 0.4m. The soil beneath the vegetation mat was very chalky.

Area 5

The berm at the base of the south slope of the bank, a fairly level site. Vegetation was fairly thick and long, up to 0.5m, with a mat, and providing 100% cover. Beneath the mat the soil was dark and humic.

Area 6

The north side of the ditch, south-west facing; near the top of the ditch slope and extremely steep, with a substrate of virtual scree. The vegetation provided approximately 30% cover, of short plants and grasses, mostly only 20mm long. The soil was very stony. Vegetation on the berm at the top of the slope (Area 5) was overhanging and ensured a certain amount of shelter: the search was made on the morning of a very overcast day after rain, and, generally the ground was very wet, but Area 6 was completely dry.

Area 7

The north side of the ditch, a south-west facing slope. There was 100% vegetation cover of a diverse range of plants and grasses, generally thick and tussocky, densely matted at its base, and fairly long – up to 0.8m. Beneath the mat the soil was stony.

Area 8

The ditch bottom, a flat site. Vegetation was mostly long grasses, up to 0.9m, with a very dense undermat. It provided 100% cover. The soil beneath was stony.

Area 9

The south side of the ditch, a north-east facing slope. Vegetation provided 100% cover and was mostly grasses approximately 0.5m long. There was a very dense undermat, with soil and chalk and some mosses below.

Area 10

A virtually level site to the south of the ditch. Vegetation providing 100% cover was mainly grasses, thick and matted, up to 0.5m long, and somewhat flattened. Beneath the mat the soil was chalky.

Area 11

A level site to the south of the ditch, with 100% vegetation cover of mainly long grasses, up to 0.90m, matted at the base. The underlying soil was chalky.

Overton Down 1992   Modern Mollusca

Figure 9.5 Modern Mollusca from a transect through the experimental earthwork

A High plant diversity.

B Sparse, short vegetation.
   Much bare chalk.

C High plant diversity.

D Long vegetation and grasses.

E Scree

F Long vegetation and grasses.

G Long vegetation and grasses.
   Some thistles

H Long grasses, thistles
   and nettles

Table 9.8 Survey of modern Mollusca on the experimental earthwork

Snail Search Area	1	2	3	4	5	6	7	8	9	10	11	12	13
Cochlicopa lubrica L	–	–	–	–	–	–	–	2	–	–	1	–	–
Cochlicopa lubrica D	–	–	–	–	–	–	–	–	–	–	1	–	–
Pupilla muscorum D	2	–	–	–	–	–	–	–	–	–	–	–	–
Arion ater L	–	–	–	–	–	–	–	1	–	–	–	–	–
Arionidae L	2	–	–	–	2	–	1	2	2	1	3	–	–
Vitrea contracta D	–	–	–	–	–	–	–	1	–	–	–	–	–
Vitrina pellucida L	1	–	–	–	–	–	–	–	–	1	–	–	–
Vitrina pellucida D	–	–	–	–	–	–	–	–	–	–	1	–	–
Nesovitrea hammonis L	1	4	–	1	2	1	–	4	–	2	2	–	–
Nesovitrea hammonis D	6	–	–	4	–	–	–	6	2	1	1	–	–
Nesovitrea hammonis S	–	–	1	–	–	–	–	–	–	–	–	–	–
Limacidae L	1	–	–	–	–	–	–	1	–	–	–	1	2
Helicella itala L	–	4	9	2	6	9	–	–	–	–	–	–	–
Helicella itala D	1	10	4	4	3	8	6	1	–	–	–	–	–
Trichia hispida L	1	–	–	13	4	3	9	3	2	–	2	–	–
Trichia hispida D	52	5	–	15	11	8	45	56	15	3	16	–	–
Trichia hispida S	2	5	–	3	2	–	6	–	1	–	3	–	–
Cepaea nemoralis / sp. L	5	8	4	9	9	6	20	11	9	4	4	–	–
Cepaea nemoralis / sp. D	19	5	–	5	2	1	–	9	7	2	8	–	–

L = Live; D = Dead; S = Subfossil

Area 12

A flat area outside the enclosure, to the south of the earthwork. Vegetation provided 100% cover, consisting mainly of grasses approximately 0.20m in height, some reaching 0.40m. There were some thistles up to 0.40m high and fungi. The vegetation was matted at its base and beneath this the soil was humic. The area had recently been grazed by sheep; there were several droppings in the search site, although it appeared that grazing was far from intense. It was also probably grazed by rabbits.

Area 13

A flat area outside the enclosure, to the south of the earthwork. A thistle-free patch, though surrounded by thistles. There was 100% vegetation cover, mainly of grasses and clovers up to 0.20m long and some fungi. It was matted at its base, with humic soil underneath. The site had been grazed by sheep and, no doubt, rabbits.

Methods

In each area a careful search was made in an area of 0.5 × 0.5m. A pointed trowel was used to tease gently at plant roots, soil and chalk rubble. Plant leaves and stems, the soil or chalk surface and any cracks in the substrate were examined for snails, which were identified, recorded and released. Any that could not be identified in the field were collected and later examined under a stereo microscope before release. As well as live specimens, dead and 'subfossil' shells were also recorded – 'subfossil' being those that had lost their periostracum and colour.

Searches were made between 5.7.92 and 22.7.92. They were made at different times of the day but always when the ground was wet or damp, either early in the morning, or during, or immediately after rain.

Time restriction allowed only one search at each site chosen on the transect, so within-site variation was not observed. It is acknowledged that some specimens may have been overlooked using this method of investigation, particularly small forms. However, a survey of modern Mollusca was carried out at Maiden Castle, Dorset, where both searches were made and turves taken from the same sites along a transect; a comparison of results from the two methods of investigation suggested that even the small, dark-coloured *Vertigo pygmaea* was only slightly under-represented in the search results and no species were completely missed (Evans and Rouse 1991).

Results and discussion

The results are presented in Table 9.8 which presents live, dead and subfossil data and Figure 9.5 which presents just live and dead specimens.

Numbers were low, especially of live snails, but some points can be made.

(1) The main species present were *Helicella itala, Trichia hispida, Cepaea nemoralis, Nesovitrea hammonis* and slugs.

(2) *Helicella itala* was characteristically most abundant at the drier sites, occurring in greatest numbers in Areas 2 and 3, near the top of the bank, and Area 6, the very steep side of the ditch. In each case vegetation covered only 40% or less of the search site and there was a lot of bare chalk or stones, providing a dry microclimate.

(3) *Trichia hispida* and *Cepaea nemoralis* occurred in most areas but were considerably more abundant where vegetation was long and thick, particularly in Areas 1, 7 and 8.

(4) *Cochlicopa lubrica* appeared in low numbers in Areas 8 and 11, both flat sites with long vegetation, where the microclimate must have been dampest.

(5) Slugs were found in most of the areas examined, absent only from the slopes of the bank, Areas 2, 3 and 4, and the steep scree slope in Area 6; these sites had the driest microclimate. Slugs were the only Mollusca found outside the earthwork enclosure in Areas 12 and 13.

(6) The ditch bottom, Area 8, yielded the highest numbers and greatest diversity of Mollusca. There was 100% vegetation cover of mainly long grasses, providing a damp and sheltered microhabitat. Immediately above the soil surface the vegetation was densely matted. A similar vegetational situation was found in the rampart ditches at Maiden Castle. There, however, molluscan abundance and diversity were at their lowest, correlating strongly with low pH and calcium measurements. This was not surprising given that these banks and ditches were constructed in the late Iron Age, and the basic topography and grassland cover has remained much the same since. Paul (1978) noted that acidity was related to drainage and thus slope, and Perring (1959) found that the pH of undisturbed soils on chalk grassland correlated with angle of slope, a pH of < 6.0 being confined to the gentlest slopes. At Overton Down, however, the earthwork is only 32 years old and, presumably, the soil in the ditch bottom has not become decalcified (Crowther p 93).

(7) A single specimen of *Arianta arbustorum* (live) was spotted near the ditch bottom, amongst damp grass though away from the transect.

(8) Areas 1 and 2, the lower parts of the bank slopes, and Area 7, the southwest-facing side of the ditch, also yielded relatively high molluscan abundance and diversity. This may be in response to the high vegetational and architectural diversity at these sites.

(9) It may be considered strange that the sites outside the enclosure were so poor. *Cepaea nemoralis* was very abundant inside the enclosure (especially after rain many could be seen crawling all over and around the earthwork) yet none were seen outside the fence, despite plentiful supplies of thistles and nettles which are often favoured activity sites of this species. More decalcified soil conditions away from the earthwork is a probable explanation (Crowther p 108).

(10) The absence of a number of species of typical chalk grassland may be worthy of note: no *Vallonia excentrica, Vallonia costata, Vertigo pygmaea, Cernuella virgata, Candidula intersecta* and just two dead shells of *Pupilla muscorum*. Although the search areas were small and only 13 areas were investigated along a transect, further searching was carried out informally during the nine days of excavation, and, apart from the single *Arianta arbustorum*, the species list could not be increased further.

Conclusions

(1) There was a somewhat limited molluscan fauna. The survey method may account for the low abundance, but probably not for the low species diversity.

(2) Despite low numbers faunal differences can be related to vegetation height, structure, and surface cover, and to topography.

(3) *Helicella itala* and *Pupilla muscorum* (just two dead shells) were the only typical chalk grassland species, though *Nesovitrea hammonis, Vitrina pellucida* and *Cochlicopa lubrica* are often found in this type of habitat. The small proportion of 'open-country' or 'catholic' species from this completely open site may have implications for the interpretation of molluscan assemblages from archaeological contexts.

10 Buried materials from the Overton 1992 section

10.1 Field recovery and storage of the buried materials
by R Janaway

During the planning stage of the project it was decided that a specialized set of sample recovery and storage procedures would have to be adopted in order to minimize post-excavation deterioration and contamination of the recovered buried materials. It was soon realized that, due to the range of scientific techniques employed, care would have to be taken in order to minimize potential conflicts in sampling and storage procedures needed for the different techniques being employed on the same sample and that the normal procedures which have been adopted as good practice on most archaeological sites were not relevant at Overton. After consultation with all the specialists involved, a set of procedures for *in situ* recording, recovery, storage, handling and sampling was established for each group of materials. As a general principle, handling of the material was kept to a minimum and no chemical agents such as fungicides were added to the samples. A programme of basic recording was established in the temporary laboratory which had been set up at North Farm during the excavation. This was supplemented by further recording and basic Scanning Electron Microscopy at the Department of Archaeological Sciences at Bradford University. Most of the buried material groups were taken intact to Bradford, and, after a basic level record had been made, subsamples were sent out to the relevant specialists. The exceptions to this were the animal bone, which was recorded and sampled for analysis at North Farm by Simon Hillson, and the samples which were recovered in Kubiena boxes for microbiology. These went directly to the Microbiological Institute's laboratories at Egham. These were later processed at Bradford after the microbiological work had been completed.

The on-site procedures for organic materials which were established prevent contamination which might invalidate biochemical analysis as well as minimize post-excavation deterioration. It was clear that as soon as a sample was uncovered, it would be in a much more oxygenated environment, subject to desiccation and damage through handling and transport. In addition it would be subject to colonization by airborne micro-organism which would initiate patterns of biochemical degradation not present in the ground. In this new environment degradation would be much more rapid and steps would need to be taken in order to slow this rate down until the samples had been examined.

With the exception of the samples selected for microbiological investigation the following general principles were adopted for the organic materials (wood, leather, textile and bone):

(1) No buried materials were handled without plastic gloves, and handling was kept to minimum.
(2) Finds were wrapped in aluminium foil (which had previously had any grease etc. removed by washing in acetone) and then placed in a polythene bag.
(3) All organic finds were transferred to refrigerated storage immediately on excavation – a special refrigerator which could be powered by either gas, 12v or 240v mains electricity – had been purchased for the immediate storage and transport of the samples. It was run in 12v mode while the samples were being transported by van.
(4) Two soil samples were taken from earth in immediate contact with the object. One was for general use, the second was sealed in a plastic sample container which would enable the percentage weight loss on drying to be calculated.

Handling and sampling procedures were less rigorous for the ceramics and flint. The flint was stored in polythene bags and the ceramic wrapped in aluminium foil and stored at high relative humidity to prevent soluble salts coming out of solution on drying. Two soil samples were recoved for pH and moisture content for each flint and ceramic sample.

Materials selected for detailed microbiological investigation were cotton loomstate, oak billet and oak tanned sole leather. With the exception of the cotton sample from the turf environment, which had not survived, all were sampled from both the chalk and turf. In addition soil control samples were taken from both turf stack and chalk bank.

The basic sampling procedure consisted of driving a sterilized Kubiena box over the sample. All excavation tools were flamed and the whole procedure from the first discovery of the sample by trowelling back, to full encapsulation by the Kubiena box was carried out by two people with the greatest of speed in order to minimize contamination from airborne micro-organisms. The basic operational problem was that, in order to determine the sample's location, it was necessary to at least partially uncover it, and in doing so the risk of exposure to the airborne spores was increased. This problem would only have been alleviated by the inclusion of inert markers at a slightly higher level over the top of each sample during the construction of the earthwork.

The long-term storage procedures for each material were as outlined in (1)–(3) below:

148

Table 10.1 Moisture content of soil samples associated with buried materials in the earthwork

Soil samples assoc. with:-	% Wt loss on drying	
	Range	Mean
Pottery discs in root mat	31–47%	41.7%
Pottery discs in chalk bank	11–29%	22.5%
Buried materials in chalk	26–29%	27%
Buried materials in turf	60–70% [after storm]	64% [after storm]

Table 10.2 Summary of pH determinations for buried materials in the bank

Material and context	Range	Mean
Pottery discs etc in root mat	6.07–7.58	6.69
Pottery discs: chalk bank	7.09–7.75	7.43
Buried materials: chalk environment	6.95–7.78	7.45
Flower pot etc: old land surface	6.46–6.83	6.63 [5.3–7.5*]
Buried materials: turf environment	4.33–5.67	4.75 [5.3*]

Figures in brackets [*] are determinations by J Crowther for comparable contexts.

(1) *Textiles, leather and wood*
These samples were wrapped in aluminium foil, with soil matrix and stored at 0–4°C to minimize microbiological degradation. Temperature not to be taken below 0°C to minimize risk of ice crystal damage.

(2) *Animal bone*
The problem anticipated with degraded animal bone was to minimize changes in relative humidity and in particular to prevent the bone drying out and splitting. For this reason the bone samples for SEM, as well as subsamples for biochemical analysis, were removed by sterile hand saw in the temporary laboratory at North Farm. The samples for SEM were sent for immediate analysis and the samples for biochemistry were stored at –20°C with associated soil matrix. The bulk of the sample was wrapped in aluminium foil and stored at 0–4°C. On site, as with the other organic materials, surgical gloves were used during recovery and during subsequent handling of the bone.

(3) *Human bone*
The human bone was not targeted for morphological or microbiological study but it was stored at 20°C in order to minimize any biomolecular degradation.

While the situation with so many different specialist scientific techniques being applied to a single, small set of samples at Overton is unusual, the interesting issue to come out of the planning and application of the buried material recovery and storage programme is that, so far, standard 'finds shed' practice has lagged behind the requirements of a number of specialized techniques. Although the complete range of techniques utilized at West Overton in 1992 is probably greater than that likely to be experienced on a mainstream excavation in the foreseeable future, it did indicate that a substantial shift in emphasis in finds recovery and handling is necessary. In particular the use of handling and packaging techniques to minimize contamination needs to be examined, as well as the use of different refrigeration regimes to minimize deterioration of the samples.

10.2 Moisture content and pH within the earthwork
by R Janaway and P Maclean

Determinations were made of the moisture content of the various parts of the bank in order to relate this to biodegradation of the buried materials. Two methods were employed, one by direct measurement of weight loss on drying of small soil samples adjacent to buried materials, the other by means of an electronic humidity probe inserted into the section. This programme was disrupted by torrential rain (p 85) just as the first buried materials had been uncovered in the turf environment. As a result part of the trench flooded. Consequently there are no meaningful measurements of pre-excavation moisture content for buried materials in the turf environment and only the results from the % weight loss are presented here. A detailed report on moisture content of samples associated with the buried materials and pottery discs is in the project archive and the main results are summarized in Table 10.1.

Soil samples for pH determination were taken from adjacent to all the buried materials, pottery discs and flower pot fragments. Determinations have been made on 76 samples; a more detailed report is in the project archives and the main results are summarized in Table 10.2. Determinations were based on 10 grams of soil in a 0.01 solution of $CaCl_2$ using a Jenway 3100 pH meter.

10.3 Microbiological report
by Joan Kelley and Patricia E J Wiltshire

Introduction

In their document 'Research proposals for the 1990s' the Experimental Earthworks Committee (1992) identified the need for a more comprehensive micro-

Table 10.3 Details of samples for microbiological analysis

	IMI Sample No	Project No	Sample
		Sample list	
Chalk bank	1	69	Control 1
	2	88	Control 2
	3	65/3089	Untreated oak
	4	64/3104	Oak-tanned leather
	5	91/3114	Textile – woollen
Buried turves	6	142	Control 1
	7	143	Control 2
	8	3158	Untreated oak
	9	140/3175	Oak-tanned leather
	10	3190	Textile
	11	3156	Human bone

biological study of the buried materials from Overton Down. Although an investigation of decay was included in the initial project design (Jewell 1963) the organisms involved in bringing about the observed changes were not assessed. This was partially rectified in this study, although the limited material available did not allow a rigorous and more complete analysis of microbiological status. Accordingly, the results presented here represent a somewhat fragmented picture of the assemblages and activities of microbial communities within the earthwork. Nevertheless, useful conclusions can be drawn from the limited data obtained which may help to set the scene for future investigation.

Sampling

Site sampling was carried out between 9 and 12 July 1992. A total of eleven samples were obtained for microbiological analysis. Details of all samples are given in Table 10.3.

The materials were buried within two environments in the earthworks. One set of samples was placed in the chalk bank and the second set was sandwiched between the buried turf surface and the inverted turf stack at the centre of the bank (Jewell 1963). Samples of 'background' control soils were obtained by hammering sterile Kubiena boxes (80 × 65 × 40mm) into the exposed surfaces. The locations of samples analysed and background samples are shown on Figures 7.17 and 7.26.

Heavily degraded materials were sampled by placing a Kubiena box over the artefact and collecting both this and the surrounding soil, thus transporting it to the laboratory as a 'monolith'. Entire artefacts were excavated using sterile equipment and were transported to the laboratory in sterile universal bottles. All materials were refrigerated very soon after collection and kept at 5°C in the field laboratory. They were analysed upon receipt by the analytical laboratory and remaining material was stored at 5°C.

Chalk environment (Site 1)

Control soil 1: Sample 1(69) A Kubiena box of chalk was taken from the same level as the buried materials. The sample was obtained 0.20m away from sample 3104 (oak-tanned leather) and 0.20m away from sample 3090 (cooked sheep bone) (Fig 7.17).

Control soil 2: Sample 2 (88) A Kubiena box of chalk was taken from the same level as the buried materials 0.35m north of the flints (Fig 7.17).

Untreated oak billet: Sample 3 (65/3089) This was a clean wood fragment of approximately 15mm × 5mm found lying within the void created by decomposition of the original wooden billet. It was removed aseptically and placed in a sterile universal bottle.

Oak bark-tanned leather: Sample 4 (64/3104) This consisted of a large piece of sole leather and was removed with flamed forceps and placed within two abutting sterile Kubiena boxes. The material appeared to have retained its integrity and no obvious decomposition was observed.

Textile 3 – Woollen tweed: Sample 5 (91/3114) The fabric had blackened and had become rather friable. It was obtained by hammering a Kubiena box over the whole, so that the woollen material was embedded within chalk fill inside the box. Excess material from the edges was collected with a spatula for other analyses.

Turf environment (Site 2)

Control 1: Sample 6 (142) A Kubiena box of the old ground surface was taken from the same level as the buried material 0.20m from the pottery square 3155 and 0.20m from the animal bone 3165 (Fig 7.26).

Control 2: Sample 7 (143) This was sampled with a Kubiena box, taken as in Sample 6 (142) 0.20m from leather 3175 (Fig 7.26).

Untreated oak billet: Sample 8 (3158) This was exposed unexpectedly during excavation and was found to have fragmented into several moist pieces. A large fragment was transferred immediately to chloroform/methanol-treated aluminium foil and wrapped securely. This was subsequently transferred aseptically to a sterile universal bottle in the field laboratory. Billet fragments were sheathed in a bluish-grey weft of mycelium.

Oak bark-tanned leather: Sample 9 (140/3175)
This was obtained in exactly the same way as Sample 64/3104. It was placed in two abutting Kubiena boxes. Decomposition seems to have been minimal.

Textile: Sample 10 (3190) The material appeared to have completely decomposed. Therefore, darkened soil from the location of the original fabric was collected.

Human bone: Sample 11 (3156) There was possible fungal growth on surface and a tiny fragment of the bone was taken for microbiological study.

Methods

The eleven samples were analyzed for: (a) total viable aerobic bacterial proportions, (b) total fungal propagule counts and (c) fungal species isolated.

Spread and pour plates

Samples for bacterial analysis were pour-plated while fungal dilutions were spread-plated as this technique recovers more fungal colonies than pour-plating where reduced oxygen tensions can inhibit growth.

Portions of sample from the edge and the centre of the soil 'blocks' (Samples 1, 2, 6 and 7) were assessed separately and the mean counts taken as final results. Samples of soil from the edge of the block and from the centre were aseptically transferred to separate clean, sterile Petri dishes. The soil was crumbled and 0.1g of each was plated directly onto Rose Bengal Agar (RBA) and Malt Extract with antibiotics (MEAB) (Smith and Onions 1983). Results were expressed as the mean of fungal counts from both sampling points within each block.

For dilution plating a further 0.1g was taken as described above from each of the two areas of each sample. Each sample was placed separately into 9.9ml of sterile distilled water containing 0.05% Tween 80 as a wetting agent. The resulting suspensions were shaken for 2 minutes and allowed to settle for a further 2 minutes. For fungal counts, each suspension was serially diluted to 10^{-2}, 10^{-4} and 10^{-6}. Duplicate aliquots (0.1ml of each dilution) were spread-plated onto RBA and MEAB. For bacterial analysis, duplicate pour plates were prepared each with a further 1.0ml, using Tryptone Soya Agar (TSA) (Parkinson *et al* 1971, BS 5763 part 6 1986). Results were expressed as the mean of the counts on all four plates for each sample (ie both sampling points in duplicate).

MEAB is a general purpose mycological medium, the addition of antibiotics inhibits competing bacterial growth. The use of Rose Bengal Agar inhibits the radial growth of fungi, thus making isolation of single colonies easier. Tryptone Soya Agar was used as a good general growth and isolation medium for aerobic bacteria.

Direct plating and diluted washings

For solid samples (ie Samples 4, 5, 9 and 10), where possible, 1.0g pieces were washed in sterile distilled water and Tween 80, the washings were diluted and plated as above, while the solids were directly plated onto the two mycological media. The oak billets (Samples 3 and 8) were plated only onto RBA due to shortage of material. Only a tiny fragment of human bone (Sample 11) was available; this was plated directly onto RBA.

All plates were incubated at 30°C. The TSA plates were counted at 48 hours and checked at 7 days. RBA and MEAB plates were counted at 4 days and checked at 7 days. A temperature of 30°C was selected as a compromise for both fungi and bacteria.

Results

Table 10.4 gives the numbers of bacteria isolated on TSA (mean counts g^{-1} of sample $\times 10^4$). Also included in Table 10.4 are counts of viable colony-forming units on RBA and MEAB. Both dilution plate counts (mean number g^{-1} sample $\times 10^2$) and counts of numbers of colonies obtained from direct plating (where it was possible to count these) are shown. Table 10.5 (p 154) gives the identification of the fungi and the samples from which they were isolated.

Comments on results

Total viable counts

Samples 1–5 were collected from the chalk environment of the earthwork while Samples 6–11 were from between the turf environment. Dilution plate counts from the artefacts give the number of organisms on the sample and in adhering soil crumbs, thus giving an indication of the number and type of organisms in the immediate vicinity. Washing helps to remove soil and extraneous debris allowing outgrowth of fungi which are actually colonizing the material. Surface sterilization is also often used for this purpose. However, the material was limited and it was decided not to carry out this procedure here.

Controls

The controls from the two areas showed expected differences. Higher bacterial counts were found in the buried turves than in the chalk fill area (Table 10.4). Malt Extract Agar with antibacterial agent (MEAB) gave better recovery for counting dilution

Table 10.4 Microbial counts

Sample number	Sample	Bacteria Mean counts/g^{-1} $\times 10^4$ TSA	Fungi-colony-forming units			
			Mean counts/g^{-1}		No. colonies Direct plating	
			$\times 10^2$ RBA	$\times 10^2$ MEAB	RBA	MEAB
Chalk bank						
1	Control 1	5.3	<10.0	<10.0	12	8
2	Control 2	8.0	<10.0	0.1	5	TNTC
3	Untreated oak billet	50.0	10.0	NA	1	NA
4	Oak-tanned leather	520.0	60.0	1000.0	22	TNTC
5	Textile – woollen tweed	1400.0	1.0	0.30	14	TNTC
Buried turves						
6	Control 1	TNTC	160.0	80.0	14	TNTC
7	Control 2	360.0	<10.0	140.0	8	TNTC
8	Untreated oak billet	25.0	180.0	NA	17	NA
9	Oak-tanned leather	20.0	540.0	20.0	32	TNTC
10	Textile	40.0	55.0	1.0	24	TNTC
11	Human bone	NA	NA	NA	2	NA

TNTC = Too numerous to count; NA = Not analysed – too little material; TSA = Tryptone Soya; RBA = Rose Bengal Agar; MEAB = Malt Extract Agar with Antibiotics

plates than Rose Bengal Agar but, on the direct plates, the mycelium grew much quicker on MEAB so that colonies overgrew each other and could not be counted. Fungal counts were low in the chalk fill area (Table 10.4), and, as could be expected, counts were higher from the soil/turf area. Sample 7 (Control 2) gave a low count on RBA but this might be an anomalous result as counts on MEAB were of an order of magnitude which could be expected.

Untreated oak billets

Fungal counts from the soil/turf sample were similar to the background soil, while the addition of a carbon source/humic substances to the chalk increased counts by a factor of 10^3 over the controls on RBA. Bacterial counts were increased in the chalk by 10^{-1} and were reduced by a factor of 10^{-1} in the soil/turf site (where colonies could be counted).

No Basidiomycotina were isolated because of the small sample of wood available, and isolation techniques were thus limited. It is not possible, therefore, to comment on the role of higher fungi on the decomposition of the wood. However, SEM studies have revealed micromorphological changes in the wood which might imply activity by both Basidiomycotina and Ascomycotina/Deuteromycotina (Blanchette p 155).

Oak tanned leather

As with the billets, these samples increased fungal counts in chalk by 10^3 on RBA and by 10^5 on MEAB.

Counts from the soil/turf site were of the same order as the background counts. Bacterial counts were increased in the chalk by 10^2 but decreased by 10^{-1} in the soil site.

Textiles

Fungal counts from the area around the buried textiles increased by approximately 10^2 on average in the chalk and appeared to decrease by 10 in the soil/turf area. Bacterial counts were raised by 10^3 over the control chalk site, but were reduced by 10^{-1} in the soil.

Human bone

Only direct fungal plating was carried out due to lack of material. One fungal species was found which could have been the mycelial growth which was visible to the naked eye on exhumation.

Fungal Species

Absidia cylindrospora (Hagem)

This fungus has a worldwide distribution. It is found in various soil types, and is isolated frequently from forest soils, grassland, arable soils, fen, estuarine sediments, marsh soils, etc (Apinis 1958; Stenton 1953).

In contrast to other Mucorales it occurs at depths down to 0.60–1m in the soil (Domsch *et al* 1980). It tolerates a wide range of pH from acid to slightly alkaline, and it also tolerates high salinity (Luppi-Mosca 1960). The optimum temperature for growth is around 25°C with a maximum of 30°C. It has been reported to have amylase and protease activities. It produces phenol oxidases and can utilize lignosulphonates, humic and fulvic acids (Domsch *et al* 1980). This species was isolated from both soil control sites and also from the textile sample in the turf/soil area. It is likely to have been utilizing nutrients from the soil rather than causing decay in the textile.

Cephalotrichum stemonitis (Link)

This fungus was isolated once from one of the chalk control sites. It is common and widespread.

Chaetomium globosum (Kunze ex Fr.)

Although identified as *C. globosum*, this isolate proved to be atypical of the species. This is of interest since all the colonies isolated from the site appeared to share the same atypical characteristics. This fungus was very common, being found in all soils and on all samples. *Chaetomium* species are important agents in the decay of cotton and other cellulosic man-made materials. They are also active agents of soft rot in wood (Millner, 1975; Blanchette p 156). They occur commonly on dung and straw (Lodha 1964; Millner 1975). In general they are very important components in the decomposition of herbaceous and lignified plant matter in the soil (Domsch *et al* 1980). It might be considered worthwhile investigating this isolate further because of its ubiquity and obvious involvement in wood decay (see Blanchette p 156).

Epicoccum nigrum (Link ex Link) [Syn. *Epicoccum purpurascens* Ehrenb. ex Schlecht.]

This isolate was obtained from all samples except the oak billet and leather from the chalk site, and the human bone. This fungus has been isolated from most soil types and areas worldwide, and is mainly found in the upper 0.20m of soil. It is often considered a secondary invader of damaged plant tissue, but has also been found on mouldy paper, pulp and paper, cotton and textiles (McGinnis *et al* 1975), rotting wood (Hawksworth 1976), and insects etc. Optimum temperature for growth is in the range 23° to 28°C (Eka 1970) with minimum down to −3° or −4°C and a maximum up to 45°C (Arsvoll 1975). The pH optimum is in the range 5.0–6.0 with no growth occurring at pH 2.0 or 10.0. Cellulose decomposition has been demonstrated with relatively good growth on lignin sulphonate (Domsch *et al* 1980). Its growth has been observed to be inhibited by tannins from oak leaves (Harrison 1971). The presence of phenoloxidase has been demonstrated, thus suggesting an ability to degrade lignin. Growth has been found

to be stimulated in the presence of clay minerals (Domsch *et al* 1980).

Fusarium culmorum ([W.G.Sm.] Sacc.)

This species was isolated from only one of the control samples (7) from the turf/soil area. It is a cosmopolitan species and, on plants, causes seedling blight, root and foot rot, head blight in cereals, brown patch of turf and many more diseases (International Mycological Institute description sheet No 26).

In soils it is rarely reported in forest areas, but is frequently found in grassland and especially in arable soils (Domsch *et al* 1980). It occurs mainly in the uppermost soil layers (Apinis 1958; Warcup 1951) and more frequently in neutral or slightly alkaline soils (Brown 1958). It is one of the first colonizers of wheat straw (Chang & Hudson 1967; Lucas 1955) and its survival in straws is favoured by a high nutrient content. It is classed as a soil inhabitant with high competitive saprophytic ability (Butler 1953).

Optimal temperature for growth is 25°C with a maximum 31°C and minimum of 0°C. Optimum pH values for growth in culture are wide, between 4.8 and 8.0 (Dickinson and Boardman 1970; Ross 1960). It is a good degrader of pectin and cellulose (Flannigan 1970). The optimum temperature for cellulose decomposition is 25°C (Walsh and Stewart 1971). Lignin sulphonate can be utilized quite well. *F. culmorum* is osmotolerant (Moreau *et al* 1965) and can grow in an atmosphere with 3–7% O_2 tensions (Domsch *et al* 1980). Its appearance here is consistent with its normal habitat and degradative abilities.

Fusarium solani ([Mart.] Sacc.)

This was isolated only from the turf/soil control area. *F. solani* is a very common soil fungus; it is very frequently reported in temperate, tropical and sub-tropical soils, being very common in grassland and arable areas but more rarely isolated from forest soils (Domsch *et al* 1980). It is also found on numerous plants in both tropical and temperate regions. It has been isolated from the roots of numerous cultivated and wild plants, and is one of the first colonizers of composted grass. It is not uncommon on wood; studies on *Pinus ponderosa* buried in soils show this fungus to be one of the early colonizers (Merrill and French 1966).

The available data for soil depths show considerable divergence. There is a marked reduction in viable spore counts with depth but occurrences down to 0.80m have been documented (Apinis 1958; Guillemat and Montegut 1956). It has been shown experimentally that the fungus has an optimum pH of 7.8 (Elarosi 1957) but has a very wide tolerance range with soil pH having little effect on its occurrence; it does, however, have a high sensitivity to soil fungicides (Guillemant and Montegut 1956; Domsch

1960). The optimal temperature for linear growth is 27–31°C (Chi and Hanson 1964; Zaleski *et al* 1960).

Penicillium griseofulvum (Dierckx)

This species was found only from the chalk site, from control soil and the untreated oak billet. It is a very commonly occurring species with worldwide distribution. It plays a major role in the decay of vegetation as well as seeds, cereals, food and feedstuff (Pitt 1979). It is quite rare in forest soils but is common in most other soils. There are reports of isolations from soil depths down to 0.40m. Mycelial growth occurs in the range 4°C–35°C with the optimum at 23°C and no growth at 37°C (Mislivec *et al* 1975). Cellulose decomposition has been shown on textiles and on carboxymethyl cellulose (Marsh *et al* 1949). Lignosulphonate, fulvic and humic acids can be utilized. It can produce the mycotoxin patulin in soils which inhibits both gram positive and gram negative bacteria (Grossbard 1952).

Penicillium simplicissimum ([Oudem.] Thom)

This was found on oak tanned leather from the chalk area and the soil control from turf area. It has a worldwide distribution from a very wide range of soils and pH, with best growth over the range pH 5.8–7.4 (Domsch *et al* 1980). Limited growth occurs at 5°C with good growth at 37°C (Pitt 1973). It can utilize pectin, starch (Flanagan and Scarborough 1974), cellulose (Marsh *et al* 1949) and tannins (Crowley and Whittingham 1961). It has also been reported growing on humic acid (Flanagan and Scarborough 1974).

Penicillium thomii (Maire)

P. thomii was found on the untreated oak billet and oak tanned leather from the turf area. This species is felt to be more widely distributed in temperate rather than tropical regions.

Isolations have been obtained from uncultivated soils, very often from forest soils, grassland, heathlands, very frequently from peat bogs, rarely from cultivated land, from acid sand dunes but also typically from chalk soils (Nicholls 1956). It has also been isolated from decaying vegetable matter, cotton, timber, bird feathers, slime in paper mills and stored rice. It is claimed, somewhat contradictorily, that it is inhibited by oak leaf tannins (Harrison 1971) but can also grow on gallotanins (Lewis and Starkey 1969). Little growth occurs at 5°C and none at 37°C. Pectin is utilized (Flanagan and Scarborough 1974) and cellulose degraded (Sasaki and Sasaki 1971). Antibiotic activity against bacteria and fungi has been observed in the laboratory (Blunt and Baker 1968).

Stachybotrys atra (Corda) [Syn. *Stachybotrys chartarum* (Ehreb. ex Link) Hughes]

This was isolated from the woollen tweed excavated from the chalk fill area. It is the commonest species of its genus and has worldwide distribution. Due to abundant sporulation it is easily isolated by dilution plates, but also responds well to selective media designed for cellulolytic fungi.

It is common in hardwood and coniferous forest soils, peat, sand dunes, desert soils, saline soils etc. It is also isolated from compost and polluted waters. This species is known to be celluloytic and has been found capable of degrading filter paper, textiles, methyl cellulose and cellophane (Domsch *et al* 1980). Cellulose degradation increases with increasing availability of nitrogen (Park 1976).

S. atra causes soft rot in timber (Duncan and Eslyn 1966). Chitin and wool (Domsch *et al* 1980) can be decomposed. It has certain antagonistic activity against other fungi and *Bacillus subtilis* and is also a known mycotoxin producer (Forgacs 1972). Its isolation here from heavily degraded woollen material would indicate that it had played a major role in its decay.

This species is normally associated with upper soil layers, the maximum recorded depth being 0.20m (Guillemat and Montegut 1956). It is not markedly affected by soil pH and can occur in chalk soils (Dale 1914). It is common on rotting plant remains. Good growth occurs in the temperature range 10–37°C with the optimum between 23–27°C and the minimum between 2–7°C (Domsch *et al* 1980). It grows within the pH range 3.6–7.7 (Butt and Ghaffar 1974).

Talaromyces stipitatus ([Thom] C.R. Benjamin)

This species was found only on oak-tanned leather from the turf site. It is isolated relatively rarely, but from a variety of sources (Pitt 1979), eg rotting wood, diseased flowers, soil, bark of dead *Pinus virginiana*. It is likely to have been isolated from the soil rather than the leather itself.

Trichoderma sp. (Pers. Ex Fr.)

This fungus was isolated from the untreated oak billet and the textile from the turf/soil site. Like *Chaetomium globosum* it proved to be atypical and, in this case, has not been identified to species level. Without complete identification it is not possible to give in-depth information. However, *Trichoderma* sp. are particularly known for cellulolytic abilities and to a lesser extent some ligninolytic activity. They are very widespread in soils and are easily isolated. The two substrates here would be typical candidates for degradation by *Trichoderma* (Domsch *et al* 1980). *Trichoderme viride* is an agressive competitor; it produces viridin (a potent antifungal agent) and is capable of causing lysis of other fungal hyphae.

Table 10.5 Fungi isolated from buried materials and backgound soil

Fungal isolate	Chalk bank					Buried turves					
	1	2	3	4	5	6	7	8	9	10	11
Absidia cylindrospora		+					+				
Cephalotrichum stemonitis		+									
Chaetomium globosum	+	+	+	+	+	+	+	+	+	+	+
Epicoccum nigrum	+	+	+			+	+	+	+	+	
Fusarium culmorum							+				
Fusarium solani						+					
Penicillium griseofulvum	+		+								
Penicillium simplicissimum				+			+				
Penicillium thomii									+	+	
Stachybotrys atra					+						
Talaromyces stipitatus									+		
Trichoderma sp.								+			
Zygorhynchus moellei				+					+	+	

Zygorhynchus moellei (Vuill.)

This species was isolated from oak-tanned leather from chalk fill, oak-tanned leather from the turf site and textile from the turf site. *Z. moellei* is one of the commonest of the Mucoraceae with worldwide distribution. It has been suggested that it is isolated 'almost exclusively' from soil (Hesseltine *et al* 1959), but it has also been isolated from plant rhizospheres, wood exposed to soil, stored wheat and straw compost (Domsch *et al* 1980). Personal experience in the laboratory confirms that it has also been found on leathers and plastic materials.

Optimum growth is at 25°C with a maximum at 32°C (Zycha *et al* 1969). It will not degrade starch or cellulose (Hesseltine *et al* 1959) but will utilize pectin and hemicelluloses (Domsch *et al* 1980). It will often grow on the breakdown products of more complex molecules (eg glucose, mannose, xylose and arabinose) and it is possible that these substrates were being utilized here (Fothergill and Jones 1958).

Discussion

First, it must be remembered that due to the limited nature of the study, the results cannot be tested statistically. Also the limited media and isolation techniques employed means that the number and variety of species may have been under-represented.

Chemical analysis of the soils within the chalk bank and the turves (Crowther p 114) shows that the major difference between the two environments is in soil reaction (pH). Background phosphorus and nitrogen levels appear to differ very little between the two soils, and it is doubtful that the small observed variations could be interpreted as having a significant differential impact on microbial activity. Microorganisms respond largely to nutrient concentrations in the immediate vicinity of the cell wall; they may be considered to operate in microsites within the soil fabric, particularly where organic materials offer foci of appropriate nutrients. It is not surprising, therefore, that the buried materials do seem to have had some effect on microbial populations in the two soils.

The number of viable units obtained from the earthwork is slightly lower than would be expected for cultivated agricultural soils (Campbell 1983). However, Overton Down has supported pasture for many years so lower microbial numbers might be expected from its soils. What is of more interest is the paucity of species which have been isolated in this study; the soils within the earthwork generally supported a species-poor assemblage of fungi. The pH values for the deposit in the chalk environment were very high (above pH 8.0 in samples analyzed by Crowther and with a mean pH of 7.45 in those analyzed by Janaway and Maclean p 148) so when the pH optima for fungal isolates are inspected (see above), the small number of viable species obtained is not surprising (Campbell 1983). Furthermore, chalk is oligotrophic in terms of available nitrogen, phosphorus and other essential nutrients, and microbial activity might be confined to oases of organic debris such as those provided by the buried materials.

The low number of species in the buried turves is rather more difficult to explain. The pH in the turf layers approximate to pH 5.3 in the samples analyzed by Crowther (p 114) and those analyzed by Maclean and Janaway (p 148) had a mean pH of 4.75.

This is well within the optima for many fungal species. Macphail and Cruise (p 101) have shown the turves to be completely decalcified, presumably through leaching. It is possible, therefore, that other ions essential for microbial growth have been lost from the turf profile, so that the poor nutrient status of the soil might be contributing to the low species richness. It is interesting that in the chalk bank, the addition of degradable materials measurably increased microbial activity, creating pockets of enhanced growth. This was much less obvious in the turf/soil areas and indeed, on some occasions, counts of viable units appeared to decline. This might be expected since, although the buried material would add a source of carbon locally, it would provide little nitrogen and, indeed, might actually lock up nitrogen from its immediate surroundings.

It must be remembered that redox potential and hydrological status are important determinants in the nature of soil microbial populations. Both Macphail (p 102) and Crowther (p 117) have commented on compaction of soils both within the chalk bank and at the buried ground surface. Furthermore, Blanchette (p 156) has reported evidence of extensive activity by soft-rot fungi, and *Chaetomium*, a common soft-rot fungus was certainly ubiquitous (see Table 10.5). Soft-rot occurs in wood when constantly high moisture levels are present, and it may be assumed, therefore, that humidity was high in the buried soils.

Compaction and high moisture levels might suggest a general lowering of redox potential and, possibly, the creation of anaerobic microsites within the soil fabric. *Chaetomium* can certainly tolerate high levels of carbon dioxide – up to 40% (Domsch & Gams 1972) but, for it to be actively growing and hydrolysing cellulose, oxygen must be available. It is unlikely, therefore, that the compacted, wet soils were uniformly anaerobic.

To assess fully whether fungi are actively growing in the soil requires very specialized field techniques and observation. In most cases, the methods employed in this study made it impossible to determine whether or not the fungi were present in quiescent form. However, isolates from the samples which were plated directly after washing were probably derived from hyphae which were actively growing. It may be assumed, therefore, that isolates obtained from the untreated oak billet, oak-tanned leather, and woollen tweed from the chalk bank, and the oak-tanned leather in the buried turves, were from actively-growing hyphae. There are many abiotic and biotic factors in soils which exert fungistatic influences on both vegetative mycelium and fungal spores/resting bodies (Parkinson *et al* 1971). This means that although a large fungal flora might be isolated in any one case, it need not be actively involved in decomposition processes. It is important to note that once removed from the depositional environment, fungistatic influence may be removed. Indeed, bioturbation by, for example, soil fauna, might even operate to modify fungistasis. In this study, the experimental procedure did not allow the evaluation of these factors.

Final comments

The microbial analysis at Overton Down has shown that the buried materials themselves have had some impact on the microbial numbers within both the chalk bank and the buried turves. Most of the fungal isolates were common soil organisms and might be expected to be present in any archaeological sediment containing organic debris. However, in some instances, the buried material seems to have provided a selective 'bait' for certain fungi with specific enzyme activity (eg *Stachybotrys atra* on the woollen tweed textile). These results are encouraging and, with greater resources, a more rigorous and representative study could be undertaken in order to construct a predictive model for microbial systems in archaeological contexts.

10.4 Micromorphological aspects of wood decay
by Robert A Blanchette

Summary

Extensive degradation of hazel and oak wood was found in samples from the two buried environments. Micromorphological characteristics observed with scanning electron microscopy showed the decay was caused by fungi. A common pattern of degradation observed was an erosion of the secondary wall layers but not the compound middle lamella. This type of attack is typical of decay by soft-rot fungi, and is classified as Type 2 form of soft-rot attack. In hazel wood buried in the turf environment, cell walls contained distinct cavities representing the Type 1 form of soft-rot attack. Also in the turf covered soil, large masses of hyphae were evident in the decayed wood. The mycelia contained numerous crystalline structures containing large concentrations of calcium. These fungi appear to be white-rot Basidiomycetes. Wood that was charred had regions of carbonized cells that were not extensively colonized by fungi. These zones, however, were found to have little structural integrity and often were observed to be collapsed and fragmented. Wood adjacent to the charred zones was colonized by fungi and had advanced stages of cell wall degradation evident.

Introduction

Biological and nonbiological degradation processes result in chemical and morphological changes in wood that can be readily identified using a number of different techniques (Blanchette *et al* 1990; Eriksson *et al* 1990; Fengel 1991; Hedges *et al* 1985;

Singh 1989). Micromorphological characteristics have been found to be particularly useful for identifying degradation patterns that are unique to specific fungi or bacteria as well as to identify wood deterioration by nonbiological causes (Blanchette *et al* 1990, 1991, 1994).

Fungal degradation of wood can be divided into three broad categories, (brown-, soft- and white-rot) and defined as:-

Brown-rot: fungi in the Basidiomycotina that cause extensive depolymerization of cellulose.

Soft-rot: fungi in the Ascomycotina or Deuteromycotina that cause distinct cavities within secondary walls (Type 1) or an erosion of the secondary wall (Type 2). These fungi cause extensive cellulose and hemicellulose degradation, but may also attack and degrade some lignin.

White-rot: fungi in the Basidiomycotina that can degrade all cell wall components, including lignin. Lignin, cellulose and hemicellulose are degraded simultaneously or one component, such as lignin, may be degraded preferentially followed by a progressive attack on the other cell wall components.

Patterns of bacterial degradation can also be separated from fungal attack and several different forms of wood destroying bacteria have been identified, such as cavitation, erosion and tunnelling bacteria (Blanchette *et al* 1990; Singh 1989; Singh *et al* 1990). Usually, environments where wood is saturated with water exclude most fungi and the major decay organisms found in these situations are bacteria.

Nonbiological decay processes have not received much research attention but several recent investigations indicate that deterioration patterns are morphologically distinct from biological causes of decay (Blanchette *et al* 1991, 1994).

Buried wood samples from the Overton Down Experimental Earthworks were prepared for scanning electron microscopy to ascertain what type of decay had occurred, the organisms responsible for the attack, and the current condition of the deteriorated woods.

Materials and methods

Segments of decayed wood were obtained from the following objects:

Chalk Environment: 3087 Charred oak billet; 3089 oak billet; 3105 charred hazel billet; 3110 hazel billet.

Turf Environment: 3157 Charred oak billet; 3158 oak billet; 3172b charred hazel billet (note 3174, hazel billet, was not examined since this wood apparently was totally decomposed and not found during the excavation).

Small samples from the decayed woods were cut with a microtome, and prepared for scanning electron microscopy as previously described (Blanchette *et al* 1991). Transverse sections of the decayed wood

were photographed and used to determine the decay patterns present.

Results and discussion

All of the samples examined had evidence of fungal hyphae present within the deteriorated woods. In the charred zones of burned samples, the carbonized cells were not extensively colonized by mycelia. However, in the noncarbonized areas of these woods, fungi were prevalent and advanced stages of decay were evident. The morphological characteristics of carbonized wood cells were different from sound or fungal deteriorated wood, and they appeared to have an altered cell wall structure. The secondary cell wall layers and middle lamellae were not distinct. The cell walls were somewhat swollen and had a porous appearance (Figs 10.1A,B,D). The strength of these woody cells had been compromised as evident by the crushed and fragmented cell walls that were often observed (Figs 10.1C and E). Wood adjacent to the charred cells contained increasingly more fungal hyphae (Fig 10.1B), and was extensively degraded (Figs 10.1C and F). Cell walls of vessels and fibres of both oak and hazel wood were severely eroded with only a fragile network of middle lamellae remaining.

The two major forms of wood decay observed were a Type 2 soft-rot attack consisting of an erosion of the secondary wall layers with only a thin framework of middle lamellae left (Figs 10.2A and B), and Type 1 soft-rot attack displaying distinct cavities within secondary walls (Figs 10.2 C and D). Only samples of hazel wood were found to contain soft-rot cavities within the secondary wall layers of the cell.

An erosion form of cell wall degradation could have been caused by either soft-rot or white-rot fungi. Commonly, soft rot fungi cause a progressive thinning of cell walls in wood of angiosperms. As the decay progresses, a complete degradation of secondary walls may occur (Eriksson *et al* 1990; Nilsson *et al* 1989). The compound middle lamellae between cells, however, are not degraded and usually remain relatively unaltered. Since white-rot fungi typically degrade the entire cell wall, including the middle lamellae, the decay observed in this study most likely was due to soft-rotters.

The mycological report of microorganisms isolated from the buried wood and surrounding soil (Kelley and Wiltshire p 155) indicated that several soft rot fungi, including *Chaetomium*, were readily isolated. This report also found bacteria present within the decayed oak billet that was sampled. These bacteria were most likely soil-inhabiting organisms or bacteria capable of scavenging the fungal degraded woody cell walls. There was no micromorphological evidence for direct bacterial degradation of the wood.

In many of the extensively deteriorated wood samples of both oak and hazel, the cell walls were completely degraded and voids occurred within the wood. Cell walls in these areas were compressed and distorted and secondary changes due to other fungi,

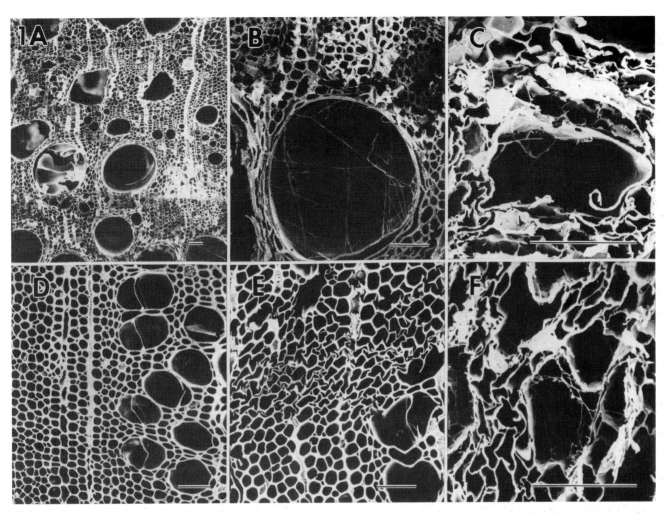

Figure 10.1 Scanning electron micrographs from transverse sections of oak billet 3087 (chalk environment) and hazel billet 3172 (turf environment). Bar = 50 μm.

A. Cells from the charred zone showing relatively intact vessels and fibres

B. Cells adjacent to the charred zone with fungal hyphae present in degraded cells

C. Collapsed and degraded cells colonized by fungal hyphae in wood a few mm away from the charred region. Vessel and fibre cells have extremely thin cell walls. Many of the cells are distorted and appear compressed

D. Charred region showing intact cells. Cell walls lack the distinct wall layers found in sound wood and have a porous appearance

E. Charred cells with little structural integrity left. Many cells appear fragmented and collapsed

F. Cells from wood a few mm away from the charred zone showing eroded and thinned vessel and fibre walls. Fungal hyphae are evident in many cells

insects and/or earthworms was evident (Fig 10.3). Wood samples from the turf environment had become colonized by hyphal aggregates. The surface of the mycelium contained large concentrations of crystalline structures that appeared as long, needle-like projections. Energy dispersive X-ray microanalyses showed these structures to consist primarily of calcium, suggesting that they are a form of calcium oxalate. Many white-rot Basidiomycotina commonly produce calcium oxalate, and white-rot fungi may be responsible for some of the erosion type of cell wall attack observed. Typically, white rot fungi are aggressive lignin degraders that attack wood in contact with or buried in soil (Blanchette 1991). Another group of fungi known to have genera that produce large amounts of oxalic acid that precipitates

in soil are ectomycorrhizal fungi and other saprophytic basidiomycetes (Cromack *et al* 1979). These hypogenous fungi, such as *Hysterangium crassum*, produce large amounts of calcium oxalates on fungal mats within the soil. The fungi observed in Figures 10.3B, C and D could be secondary colonists that are utilizing the residual fragments of decayed cell walls, or may have been actively degrading the lignified woody remains.

Although the mycological investigation (Kelley and Wiltshire p 148) did not report the presence of Basidiomycetes, these slow growing, nonsporulating organisms often need selective media to be successfully isolated from wood or soil samples (Worrall 1991). Undoubtedly, if specific procedures were used to isolate these soil colonizing Basidiomycetes, they

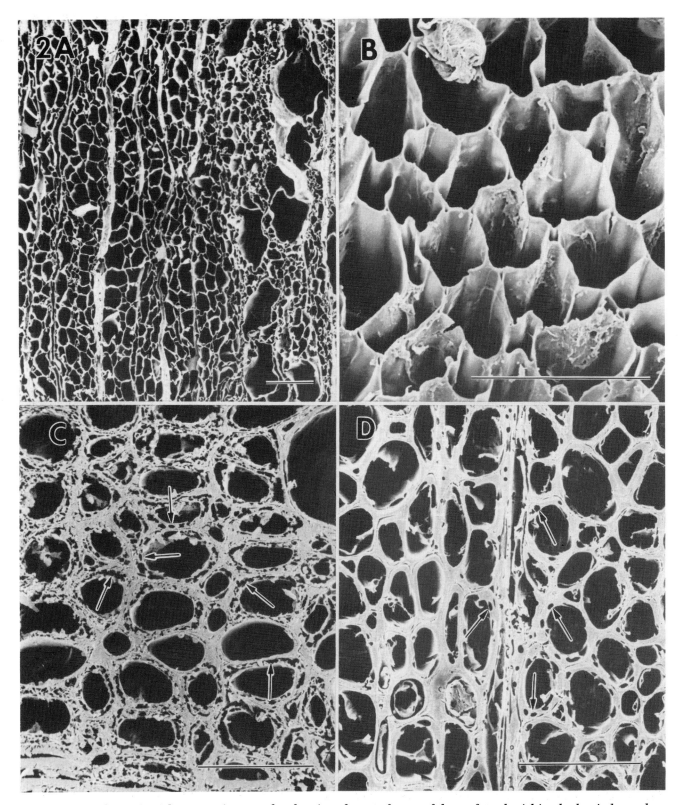

Figure 10.2. Scanning electron micrographs showing the two forms of decay found within the buried woods: eroded and thinned cell walls (A and B) typical of Type 2 soft rot, and cavities within secondary walls (C and D, arrows) typical of Type 1 soft rot attack. Bar = 50 μm. A and D. Hazel billet 3110 from the chalk environment. B. Oak billet 3089 from the chalk environment. C. Hazel billet 3172b from the turf environment

would have been isolated from the oak and hazel billets within the turf environment.

The presence of soft-rot cavities, Type 1 form of attack, in many areas of the hazel wood but not oak is a curious phenomenon. Both hazel and oak had cell walls that displayed an erosion type of attack but some cells, especially fibre cells in certain areas of the hazel billets, contained distinct cavities within

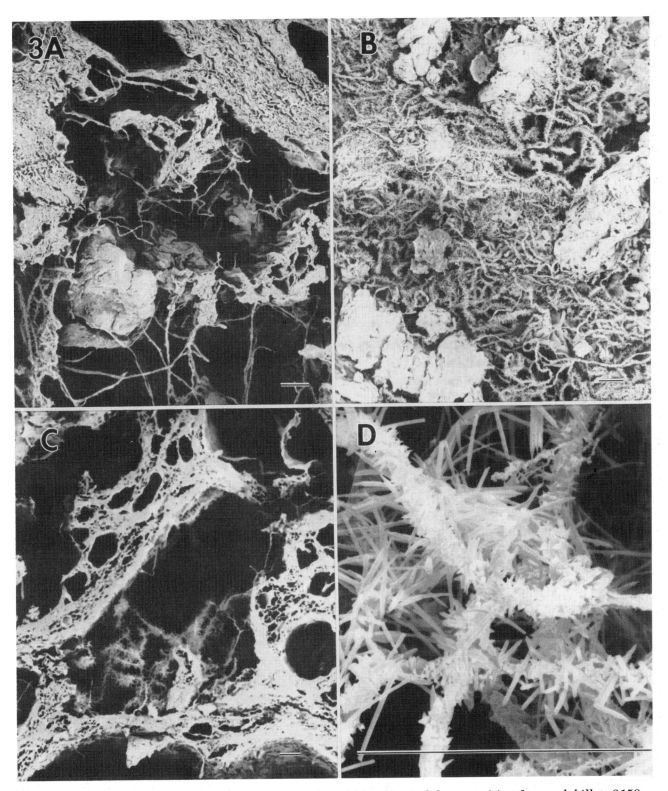

Figure 10.3 Scanning electron micrographs of regions with advanced decomposition from oak billets 3158 (A) and 3157 (C and D), and hazel billet 3172b (B) removed from the turf environment. Bar = 25 μm. A. Severely degraded wood cells appear extensively eroded with hyphae colonizing voids. B and C. Aggregates of mycelia growing within degraded cells. Voids within the decayed wood are often filled with the hyphae. Mycelial aggregates are coated with numerous needle-like crystalline structures. D. Crystalline structures on mycelia of hyphae within degraded region

the secondary walls. This may have been due to an increased resistance of the hazel wood to fungal attack resulting from differences in cell wall structure or chemical composition, or possibly due to

different types of soft-rot fungi that colonized various regions of the woods. Differences in soft rot attack have been reported in woods with increased lignin content, greater concentrations of phenolics, etc

160

Table 10.6 Textile samples recovered in 1992 and analyses undertaken

Original sample number	Material	Chalk or turf	OD 1992 sample no	Sample recovered in 1992	SEM report	Report by M Ryder	FT-IR report by S Hardman	Micro-biological report
1	cotton	chalk	–	no	–	–	–	–
2	cotton	chalk	3116	yes	+	+	+	–
3	wool	chalk	3114	yes	+	+	+	9248/5
4	worsted	chalk	3113	yes	+	+	+	–
5	linen	chalk	3112	yes	+	+	+	–
6	linen	chalk	3111	yes	+	+	+	–
1	cotton	turf	–	no	–	–	–	–
2	cotton	turf	–	no	–	–	–	–
3	wool	turf	–	no	–	–	–	–
4	worsted	turf	–	no	–	–	–	–
5	linen	turf	–	no	–	–	–	–
6	linen	turf	–	no	–	–	–	–

Samples 3162 and the microbiological sample 9248/10 were both taken from where textile samples were believed to be in the turf environment. However, neither of these samples revealed any morphologically identifiable textile remains.

(Blanchette et al 1990; Eriksson et al 1990). Gymnosperm woods, considered more resistant to attack by soft-rot fungi, usually contain the Type 1 form of decay when colonized by these fungi. Chains of conical-shaped cavities appear throughout the secondary cell walls. In transverse section, these cavities appear as circular holes. In advanced stages of decay, the entire secondary wall may appear riddled with numerous coalescing cavities as observed in many of the hazel samples examined (Fig 10.2C and D). Although additional investigation would be needed to examine the susceptibility of hazel wood to soft-rot fungi, it appears that the fibre cells of the hazel wood used in this experiment were somewhat more resistant to attack by soft-rot fungi than the oak wood. This resistance appears localized to only some of the hazel billets since one sample, 3174, was totally decayed and not recovered from the site.

Acknowledgements

The author would like to thank John Haight for his technical assistance.

10.5 Textiles
by R C Janaway

Six textile samples were buried in each environment. From each roll of cloth a sample 0.46m by 80mm (18 × 3in) was cut and then folded to form a parcel 80mm (3in) square and six layers thick. Each set of textiles consisted of two cotton, two wool and two linen samples (Jewell 1963, 44–45). Excavation in 1992 recovered five samples from the chalk environment

and no identifiable textile material from the turf stack. After excavation, all the samples (except sample 3114, Textile 3, which was sent for microbiological analysis) were photographed, and examined under a stereo and video microscope at magnifications between ×20 and ×200. Once a general description of condition had been derived, the textiles were subsampled for Scanning Electron Microscopy (R Janaway) FT-IR Microscopy (Sue Hardman) and general observation and fibre diameter measurement (Michael Ryder). Sample 3114 was later examined after its return from the microbiologists. Table 10.6 summarizes samples recovered and the analyses conducted.

Cotton Textiles

Two types of cotton textiles were buried at Overton, one undyed, the other dyed with mineral khaki dye. The khaki dye, being a mixture of iron and chromium hydroxides, would be expected to have at least a partial biocidic effect.

Textile 1 consisted of undyed cotton loomstate plain cloth, with a 12% sago starch size (Fig 10.4), while Textile 2, was cotton khaki dyed 1/4 twill (see Table 10.7 for full technical description).

Cotton fibres are derived from the seeds of plants from the genus Gossypium. The earliest archaeological evidence for cotton comes from India in the 3rd millennium BC (Barber 1990, 31) with its use not reaching the northern Mediterranean regions until the first millennium BC. While there have been numerous archaeological finds of cotton textiles from the middle east and North Africa, finds from northern Europe are rare. This is partly because dry burial

Table 10.7 Technical descriptions of textile samples buried

Sample no	Fibre type	Warp	Weft	Finish	Dye
1	Cotton loomstate plain cloth	29 threads/cm 22's (27 Tex)	28 threads/cm 20's (29.5 Tex)	sago starch	no
2	cotton khaki dyed twill cloth	37 threads/cm 11's cotton count (53 Tex)	18 threads/cm 9's cotton count (64 Tex)	–	mineral khaki (Fe/Cr hydroxides)
3	woollen contrast cloth	12's Y.S.W (161 Tex) Montevideo lambs' wool, mean fibre diameter 23.58 microns	12's Y.S.W. (161 Tex) from 64's Australian merino wool, mean fibre diameter 22.10 microns	–	undyed warp black dyed weft (chromium mordant)
4	worsted gabardine (wool)	2/48's (37 Tex) worsted counts from 64'sAustralian merino wool, mean fibre diameter 21.18 microns	2/48's (37 Tex) worsted counts from 64's Australian merino wool, mean fibre diameter 20.34 microns	–	yes (Fe/Cu mordant)
5	linen half-bleached	13 threads/cm 5's cotton count (120 Tex)	13 threads/cm 5.5's cotton count (111 Tex)	half bleached	no
6	linen half-bleached	12 threads/cm 5's cotton count (120 Tex)	13 threads/cm 7's cotton count (85 Tex)	half bleached	no

conditions favour the preservation of cotton and linen, while waterlogged deposits, which have yielded so many wool and silk textiles from northern Europe, do not generally preserve cellulose-based textiles (Jakes and Sibley 1983, 1984; Wild 1970). However, in addition to loss from the archaeological record, the use of cotton in northern Europe was limited until the development of the English cotton spinning industry in the 17th century AD. For this reason the degradation of cotton in a chalk burial environment in southern England is probably of least archaeological relevance of any textile material that could have been chosen.

The cotton fibre is a seed hair formed by the elongation of a single epidermal cell of the cotton seed. During initial growth the cell wall consists of a cuticular envelope. When elongation is almost complete, the cell wall is thickened by a secondary wall of cellulose being laid down on the inner side of the cuticle. When ripe the cotton boll bursts, the hairs dry, collapse and twist, taking the form of convoluted flattened tubes, open at the base and closed at the tip. The collapsed nature of the cell is particularly clear in the areas where it is most kinked (Fig 10.4). The principal component of cotton is cellulose, the bulk of which (95%) is located in the secondary wall (Bailey *et al* 1963, 435). The proportion of cellulose to other bio-molecules in vegetable-based textile fibres, such as cotton and flax, is much higher than in many other plant-derived materials. For instance, cellulose comprises 90–99% of cotton and flax, while wood, with significant amounts of hemicellulose and lignin, has only around a 45% cellulose content.

Cellulose is a polysaccharide formed from about 14,000 glucose residues, with the general empirical formula $(C_6H_{10}O_5)_n$, held together by oxygen bridges with beta 1,4 glucosidic bonds (Esau 1965, 49). Cellulose molecules combine in bundles of some 2,000 molecules, to form micro-fibrils (*ibid*, 48). The stability of cellulose in terms of insolubility and mechanical strength indicates that it is unlikely to be a single-chain structure, and that the chains must be interconnected in such a way that the hydrophillic groups (CH_2OH and OH) are masked. These groups take part in inter and intramolecular hydrogen bonding. The orientation of the microfibrils is different between the each layer of the primary and secondary wall (*ibid*, 53; Berkley 1948, 73–74).

In an acid environment the cellulose molecules are susceptible to hydrolysis of the glycosidic link between anomeric C1 and O. This results in a shortening of the cellulose chains and a structural weakening of the fibre (Cardamone *et al* 1991, 111).

Cellulose can oxidize at the sites of the hydroxyl

Figure 10.4 Scanning Electron Micrograph of Sample number 1, Cotton Loomstate plain cloth as buried, 200× original magnification

Figure 10.5 Macrophotograph of 3116, (sample 2) Cotton khaki dyed twill cloth from chalk environment after 32 years burial

groups on C_2 C_3 and C_6 to form oxycellulose. Cardamone *et al* (1991, 112) illustrate some of the oxidative reactions. It should be noted that these oxidative reactions can take place without hydrolysis of the glycosidic link, in which case the chain will remain intact (*ibid*, 111). The effect of oxycellulose formation is to disrupt the hydrogen-bonded molecular network, thus reducing fibre strength and opening up the fibre to further degradation.

In addition to purely chemical degradation, cellulose is readily attacked by the cellulolytic enzymes of micro-organisms. The enzymatic cleavage of cellulose is catalysed by cellulase, which in fungi consists of at least three enzymes. Firstly endo-beta–1,4 glucanases break the beta–1,4 bonds, then exo-beta–1,4 glucanases remove cellobiose units from the chain ends (cellobiose consists of two glucose units linked by a glycosidic link); finally beta-glucosidases break the glycosidic link in cellobiose to form glucose (Schlegel 1986, 407). Some fungi do not produce endo-beta–1,4 glucanases and can only degrade modified cellulose, which has already been subject to chain scission by other micro-organisms or acid hydrolysis. In well aerated soils cellulose is degraded by fungi, myxobacteria and eubacteria, while under anaerobic conditions it is bacteria of the genus *Clostridia* that predominate.

Textile 1 – Cotton loomstate plain cloth – chalk environment

After two years the sample recovered in 1962 was reported to be in a weakened condition, there were numerous holes, and evidence of bacterial and fungal damage. After 4 years the textile was in a very weak condition with extensive fibrillation at the broken fibre ends (Jewell and Dimbleby 1966, 327). This sample was not recovered in 1992 and is presumed to have totally degraded.

Textile 2 – Cotton khaki dyed twill cloth – chalk environment

The samples recovered after two and four years are both described as well preserved, with only slight staining, with some loss of strength after four years (Jewell and Dimbleby 1966, 327). By 1992 the 80mm square of Sample 3116 was still largely intact. The fibres had become brittle and were easily broken in both weave directions. Both individual fibres and the pattern of weave were still easily discernable. The colour was still a uniform light khaki, obscured by white chalk on the outermost layers, with some areas of darkened staining (Fig 10.5). When the rate of degradation of this material is compared with that of the undyed cotton, the effective bio-inhibition by the chromium hydroxides in the dye are apparent.

Video-microscope examination of the fine detail at magnifications up to 210× was hindered on the outer layers of the cloth by fine chalk particles, although the brittle nature of the yarn demonstrates that the cellulose structure has been degraded. Despite the chalk, it was possible to ascertain that the cotton fibres did retain their integrity although it was not possible to observe surface morphology. Examination of the inner layers of cloth revealed largely undamaged fibres, light green in colour with black specks randomly distributed over the fibre surface. When examined by light microscopy at a 400×, the fibres showed no evidence of fibrillation, or fungal hyphae. The black specs were identified as fungal spores. This was confirmed by SEM low magnification (Fig 10.6). Examination of the fibres by SEM at magnifications up to 1000× revealed only limited morphological changes to the fibre surfaces, without extensive fibrillation.

Woollen/worsted textiles

The woollen contrast cloth (Textile 3) consisted of a contrast 2/1 tweed with undyed warp and black dyed weft, while Textile 4 consisted of a worsted gaberdine (see Table 10.7 for full technical description). Worsted yarn is produced from long-staple wool which is combed parallel before spinning, while woollen yarn is spun from carded, non parallel wool fibre, usually of shorter staple. While the production method will affect the properties of the cloth in use, the relative degradation of these in the soil will have been more influenced by the presence, or absence, of synthetic dyes and their metal mordants (chromium in the weft of Textile 3 and copper and iron in Textile number 4).

The sheep was domesticated by about 9000 BC, although the earliest archaeological evidence for the use of wool fibres in textiles comes from North-East Iraq and dates to about 3000 BC (Barber 1990, 25). Through domestication and subsequent selective breeding the nature of the fleece has become modified; wild sheep have an outer coat of kemps (short hair-like fibres) and a sparse undercoat of fine, short stapled, wool. With domestication the woolly undercoat became denser and the kemps were largely replaced with long-staple wool. Fleece structure continued to be modified and by the Post-Medieval period there were a number of different breeds with totally different fleece characteristics in terms of length of staple, fineness of wool, amount of hair and kemp etc (Ryder and Stephenson 1968, 3–24; Ryder, 1969, 1981b, 1983, 1987a). Both the Overton samples were machine-made wool and worsted cloth manufactured from modern imported fleece types totally different from those available in prehistoric Europe, although the basic structure and chemistry of the fibres does remain largely the same. The modern

Figure 10.6 SEM micrograph of 3116, (sample 2) Cotton khaki dyed twill cloth from chalk environment after 32 years burial, 100× original magnification

synthetic dyes in the experimental samples, however, will have had an effect on their bio-degradation.

Ninety-nine percent of a wool fibre is formed from the protein keratin with 1% or less minor compounds such as fats, sterols, lipoids, as well as a very small mineral and phosphorous content (Ryder and Stephenson 1968, 313). The primary structure of keratin is in the form of a polypeptide chain of 18 different amino-acids. All amino-acids have the common basic structure of a amine and a carbonyl group, but are distinguished by different side chains. The secondary structure of keratin twists the primary chain into an alpha-helix. It is held in this position by a number of bonds: weak cross links may be formed between ionized COOH and NH_2 groups as well as hydrogen bonds between groups, while disulphide bridges form much stronger structural reinforcement of the helix. When compared to other proteins, keratin has a relatively high proportion of cystine (Ryder and Stephenson 1968, 259). This molecule is capable of forming peptide links at either end and thus has an important function in forming di-sulphide bridges which form a cross link joining two keratin chains (*ibid* 261) or between different parts of the same chain (*ibid* 318). It is thought that three molecular chains of keratin twist together to form protofibrils, and possibly eleven protofibrils group together to form the microfibril which forms the principal structural unit of wool (Ryder and Stephenson 1969, 320). The centre of the fibre consists of longitudinal corticular cells, formed from roughly cylindrical microfibrils embedded in an amorphous matrix. The exterior is covered in overlapping cuticular scales also formed from keratinaceous microfibrils.

Thus keratin is in two forms in the fibre: crystalline and amorphous. The crystalline fraction has well ordered three-dimensionally intermolecularly bonded chains which are regularly placed with respect to each other, while the amorphous fraction has more randomly arranged, randomly-linked,

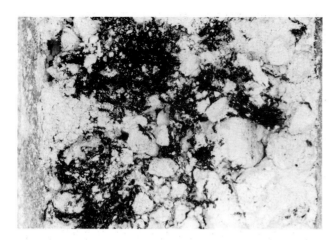

Figure 10.7 Macrophotograph of sample 3114, woollen contrast cloth (3), recovered in 1992, in Kubiena box

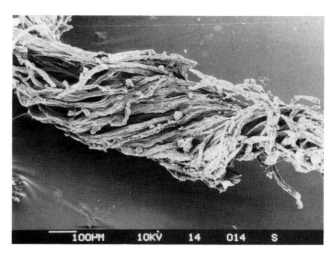

Figure 10.8 SEM micrograph of 3114 woollen contrast cloth (3), recovered in 1992, original magnification 200×

poorly packed chains. The proportion of crystalline microfibrils to amorphous material is low, which make wool a relatively weak fibre (Jakes and Sibley 1984, 21).

The degradation of wool occurs in a number of stages with the amorphous fraction being attacked much more readily than the crystalline fraction. The ion-ion and hydrogen bonds are easily broken while the peptide and disulphide bonds are much more resistant.

Wool is susceptible to alkaline attack affecting not only the weaker bonds but also the disulphide bonds and the peptide links. As temperature and pH increases the extent of the damage increases. The ion-ion forces between the carboxyl group of one amino-acid and the amine of another will be easily disrupted by the removal of a proton by the alkali. Weak alkalis will more readily attack the amorphous areas, where structure relies on ion-ion forces, rather than the crystalline regions with a higher proportion of disuphide bridges. Disulphide bridges react with weak alkali to form a new cross link based on a single sulphur atom, the lanthionine link; thus in these conditions little weakening of the fibres takes place (Jakes and Sibley 1984, 22). If wool is subject to higher concentrations of alkali or to a higher temperature, then the lanthionine link is also broken, and if the conditions are severe enough the peptide bonds can be broken. Wool is much more resistant to acids than alkalis (Cook 1988, 9). Weak acids will cause limited damage while stronger acids can hydrolyse the peptide links, disrupt the ion-ion bonds and hydrolyse some amine groups. However because the disulphide links are resistant to acid attack above about pH2, and although the peptide chains are shortened by acid hydrolysis (Jakes and Sibley 1984, 23), wool, in all but the most aggressive acid environment, will, although weakened, retain structural integrity.

Wool is subject to attack by both fungi and bacteria, which involves enzymic attack of the disulphide bond followed by hydrolysis of the peptide links (Jakes and Sibley 1984, 23) attacking both the crystalline and amorphous zones of the fibre (Cook 1988, 9). Bacteria attacking wool include *Bacillus mesentericus, B. substilis, B. cereus* and *B. putrificus*, while fungal agents include *Penicillium* sp., *Apspergillus* sp. and a number of Actinomycetes (Cook 1988, 9). Jain and Agrawal (1980) tested 34 fungi from 13 different genera for their ability to degrade keratin. There are three stages in the fungal degradation of wool when exposed to *Aspergillus* and *Penicillium* spp. Firstly there is an erosion of the surface structure, secondly swelling and production of spindle shaped cortical cell bundles, and thirdly the separation of cortical cells (Watanabe and Miyazaki 1980). However, it should be noted that fibres can still retain cuticular scales while the cortex has broken down to separating cellular units. Of the two fungal species, *Chaetomium* sp. and *Stachybotrys atia*, identified by the microbiological study of the woollen cloth sample from the chalk environment, the former is normally associated with decay of cellulitic materials while the latter is associated with the decay of wool (see p 155).

Textile 3: woollen contrast cloth (tweed) – chalk environment

From the first excavation in 1962, it became clear that the presence of the chromium mordant had resulted in slightly more degradation of undyed warp than dyed weft. There was some loss of scale margins and a few holes in the cloth. Bacteria and fungal mycelium were present. By 1964 there were holes in comparatively large areas of the cloth and the warp was very weak (Jewell and Dimbleby, 1966, 328). On excavation in 1992 the warp had completely decayed leaving only fragments of the black dyed weft. The bulk of the Sample (3114) was sent for micro-biological investigation. Because of this, some compromises were necessary in the sampling procedure; as soon as

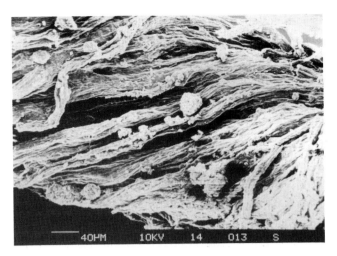

Figure 10.9 SEM micrograph of 3114 woollen contrast cloth (3), recovered in 1992, showing heavily degraded fibres and fungal colonies, original magnification 1000×

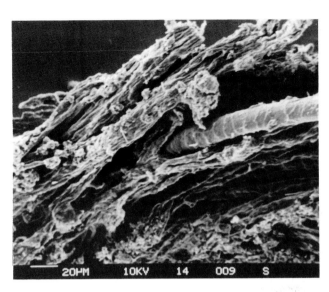

Figure 10.10 SEM micrograph of 3114 woollen contrast cloth (3) recovered in 1992, showing single fibre with cuticular scales intact, surrounded by much more heavily degraded fibres, original magnification 1000×

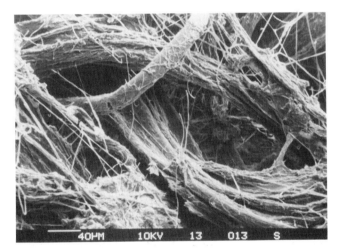

Figure 10.11 SEM micrograph of 3113 worsted gaberdine (4) recovered in 1992, showing hyphal growth over fibre surfaces, original magnification 500×

the sample position was identified, a Kubiena box was hammered over the spot, with good accuracy such that only a few strands of yarn were left outside. These were taken for immediate morphological study. When the bulk of the sample was returned from the International Mycological Institute, it was photographed (Fig 10.7) and examined using a deep-field video-microscope. All the sample is in the form of a black, compressed mat of material. While the black, dyed weft is morphologically distinct, with the yarn and fibre clearly recognizable, there is no trace of the undyed warp. The sample is very fragmentary, consisting of loose black threads. The yarn is brittle and has broken down into lengths of 4–20mm. Examination by SEM and high power light microscopy revealed considerable degradation of the individual fibres (Fig 10.8). These had little mechanical strength, and while some still retained their cuticular scales (Fig 10.9) many were severely modi-

fied, with no original surface morphology, and consisted of degraded corticular material (Fig 10.10).

Textile 4: worsted gabardine – chalk environment

After burial for two years there was only slight damage to the textile with a few patches of green and orange staining, although both yarns had been slightly weakened. By 1964 the damage was very severe. All the fibres were badly degraded and friable with loss of cuticular scales; there were large holes, some patches of pink or green discoloration, and both yarns very weak (Jewell and Dimbleby 1966, 328). After 32 years, Sample 3113 was recovered adhering to the underside of the chalk block which had been placed on top of it during burial. There was active fungus growing on the sample, which was very fragmentary, with colour ranges from pale green, through bleached grey to red/brown. Examination by video-microscope revealed that in the red/brown areas the fibres are the most extensively degraded with heavy cortical splitting, while the pale green areas were the least degraded. Examination by SEM revealed extensive areas covered by fungal hyphae (Fig 10.11) and in certain areas the hyphal mat was so dense that it obscured the underlying fibres (Fig 10.12). The wool fibres from this sample are not as badly degraded as in the case of the weft yarn from Sample 3114. Many more have retained their cuticular scales and there is less splitting down of the material from the cortex (Fig 10.13). In general the yarn from 3113 is less friable than 3114. The fungal activity is different between the two; 3113 had an actively growing fungal mat covering areas of the textile surface, and individual hyphae can be seen on

Figure 10.12   SEM micrograph of 3113 worsted gaberdine (4) recovered in 1992, hyphal mat obscuring fabric surface, original magnification 500×

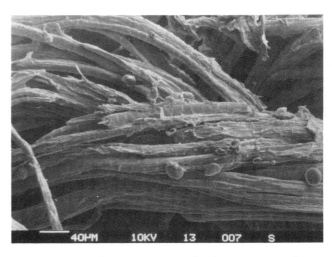

Figure 10.13   SEM micrograph of 3113 worsted gaberdine (4) recovered in 1992, showing breakdown of individual fibres and fungal spores, original magnification 500×

the fibre surfaces (Fig 10.11), while 3114 had different colonies (Fig 10.9).

Linen Textiles

Textiles made from plant stem (bast) fibres are probably the earliest known with flax fibres being identified from Nahal Hemar in the Judaean Desert, dating from the seventh millennium BC and from Çatal Hüyük in Anatolia from *c* 5000 BC (Barber 1990, 11). While there is good evidence for the use of other bast fibres in antiquity, such as hemp and nettle (Barber 1990, 15–19; Hald 1942), linen textiles have been used throughout the Middle East and Europe from the Neolithic onwards (Barber 1990, 12). Bast fibres are obtained from the stems of dicotyledonous plants. They consist of elongated, thick walled single cells with tapering closed tips. These cell (ultimates) are 'cemented' together end to end and side to side forming bundles along the stem of the plant. The number of fibre bundles in each stem range from 15 to 40 with each bundle containing 12 to 40 ultimate fibres (Textile Institute 1970, 16). They are removed by the processes of retting, that is a process of partial maceration to weaken, and then remove by combing, the non-fibrous stem material. The cell walls have extensive secondary thickening, which in flax accounts for 90% of the cross sectional area (Esau 1965, 209). Unlike cotton, whose cell walls are composed of over 95% cellulose, flax has significant amounts of hemicellulose (*c* 15.4–16.7%) pectin (1.8–3.8 %) and lignin (2.0–2.5%), as well as 68.6% cellulose (Florian 1987, 30). The flax cell wall is composed of three layers, in which the cellulose microfibrils are laid down in a spiral, which is reversed for each layer (Roelofsen 1951, 412–418). The fibrils in flax are more orientated in relation to the fibre axis than is the case with cotton. This confers higher strength and rigidity on

the bast fibre (Cardamone *et al* 1991, 115). Flax microfibrils are embedded in a matrix of hemicellulose, pectin and lignin. Morphological changes that occur in degraded flax fibres include a break up of the gross structure into individual fibrils (Cook 1988, 8).

Textile 5: linen half-bleached – chalk environment

The sample recovered in 1962 showed little evidence of damage on outer layers although there was black/brown and grey staining. The inner layers were in good condition. Although there was evidence for considerable bacterial growth, no fungal hyphae were present. By 1964 there had been a partial breakdown of outer layers, and the sample was a pale brown colour with black staining on the outer layers. Examination of the fibres revealed fibrillation, structural weakness, and there was evidence of bacteria but no fungal activity (Jewell and Dimbleby 1966, 329). Sample 3112, recovered in 1992, consisted of a largely intact fragment of cloth, with a well defined weave and fibre morphology. There had been loss of the outer cloth layers, the remains of which were black in colour and less well morphologically defined than the inner layers, which were off white in colour with dark patches. There had been a loss of fabric from the edges so that it was no longer an 80mm square. It was stuck to the underside of the chalk block which had been placed over the sample (Fig 10.14). The black areas were extensively colonized by fungal hyphae, some with fruiting bodies, which obscured the underlying fabric (Figs 10.15–16). Where the fibres were more visible there was evidence that they were fibrillating and structurally weak, having a tendency to break into short lengths (Fig 10.17). Even in the areas that were not as heavily colonized by fungi, individual fungal hyphae were visible.

Figure 10.14 Macrophotograph of sample 3112 linen half-bleached (5) recovered in 1992

Figure 10.15 SEM micrograph of 3112 linen half-bleached (5) recovered in 1992, hyphal mat obscuring fabric surface, original magnification 100×

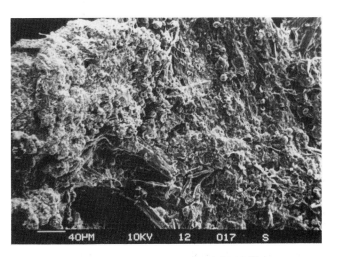

Figure 10.16 SEM micrograph of 3112 linen half-bleached (5) recovered in 1992, hyphal mat obscuring fabric surface, original magnification 500×

Figure 10.17 SEM micrograph of 3112 linen half-bleached (5) recovered in 1992, original magnification 500×

Textile 6: linen half-bleached – chalk environment

After two years this sample was more degraded than sample 5, especially in the outer layers, although the inner ones were in fairly good condition. However the sample recovered in 1964 was less degraded than the equivalent sample of Textile 5. This reversal of results demonstrates the danger in a lack of replication of samples from the same burial environment in the same year, a basic methodological flaw with the buried materials programme. Sample 3111 recovered in 1992 was very degraded, much more than 3112, fragmentary with dark coloration (Fig 10.18). The sample was adhering to the underside of the chalk block which had been placed over it. Most of textile was black in colour with some light brown areas. Examination under video-microscope revealed that the black areas were very degraded so that both the individual fibres and the weave pattern in

general were indiscernible. The light brown areas are less degraded with the weave pattern less obscured. Examination by SEM revealed some remaining fibres in a dense matt of fungal mycelium (Fig 10.19) which in places had a large number of fruiting bodies (Fig 10.20).

Turf Environment

In 1962 the textiles recovered from turf were confined to the wool/worsted materials (Textiles 3 and 4) and the half-bleached linen (Textile 6) (Jewell and Dimbleby 1966, 328). The wool/worsted materials, being keratinaceous rather than cellulosic, would be expected to be more resistant to all except extremely alkaline burial conditions (Jakes and Sibley 1984). By 1964 only the worsted gaberdine sample was detected in the turf. In 1992 it was not possible to

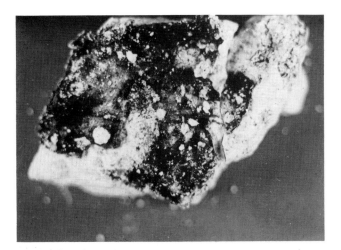

Figure 10.18 Macrophotograph of sample 3111 linen half-bleached (6) recovered in 1992

Figure 10.19 SEM micrograph of 3111 linen half-bleached (6) recovered in 1992, hyphal mat obscuring fabric surface, original magnification 500×

detect, with certainty, any textile material from the turf environment. One sample (3162) was recovered as it was initially thought to be very degraded textile material; however, subsequent examination by both low power and scanning electron microscopy revealed highly degraded vegetable material from the decaying turf.

The lack of textile materials from the turf environment can partially be explained by the lower pH, but higher moisture and organic content. This would promote hydrolysis of cellulosic material, and, while a depression of fungal growth in this environment is not surprising, greater bacterial activity would be expected. This is borne out by the microbiological control samples (see p 150). Degradation would have been promoted in the turf environment from the start by a higher and more diverse population of microorganisms.

In addition to the turf being a poor burial environment for textile materials, the heavy rain and subsequent flooding of the trench during the recovery programme (p 85) further hindered location. Even without these difficulties the location by eye of degraded textile remains from damp loam is liable to be problematic because of the close similarity in colour and texture of the degraded samples and the soil matrix.

Conclusions

Textile material would not be expected to survive in a chalk bank over archaeological timescales, so these results are of limited use to the study of archaeological textiles. They have, however, greater applicability to the excavated recovery of burial remains over shorter timescales, the subject of forensic archaeology (Hunter *et al* forthcoming).

Glossary of textile terms

Tex: international unit of measurement expressing the size of textile materials of all kinds. It indicates the weight in grams of 1000 metres of thread (Burnham 1981, 31).

Staple: Textile fibres of short length are known as staple fibres. Used particularly in regard to length and fineness, for instance, long staple wool, fine staple cotton (Burnham 1981, 134).

Woollen Yarn: a yarn made from carded rather than combed wool fibres, the fibres are not parallel before spinning; these are generally softer, more elastic than worsted yarns.

Worsted: a smooth, strong thread spun from wool fibres, usually long staple, which have been laid parallel by combing (Burnham 1981, 192).

10.6 The textiles and their fibres
by Michael L Ryder

Introduction

The present report covers the integrity of the cloth and yarns plus the measurement of fibre diameter using a technique used with archaeological remains (Ryder 1961; 1963). The specifications of the original fibres and fabrics are only of significance to modern textile machinery: they have little relevance to archaeological material. A quantitative investigation was made of the extent to which the weave might have changed during burial and the extent to which spinning twist could still be discerned. With the plant fibres, flax and cotton, the mean fibre diameter is the main parameter. With wool, the mean diameter is less important archaeologically than the fibre diameter distribution. This defines fleece type, which varies greatly in wool, whereas plant fibres apparently show little variation. The integrity of individual

Figure 10.20 SEM micrograph of 3111 linen half-bleached (6) recovered in 1992, hyphal mat obscuring fabric surface, original magnification 500×

fibres is covered in greater detail by Janaway (above) using the Scanning Electron Microscope and by Hardman (below) using spectrographic analysis.

Material and methods

No textiles were recovered from the turf environment bank. The excavated material all came from the chalk environment and it was surprising that the wool as well as the plant fibres had survived in the chalk. The excavated cloth samples were received and yarn sub-samples were mounted for microscopic examination before the unburied control samples were received. Gross observations were made at the time of sampling, on the weave, yarn count per unit length and width of the cloth, yarn thickness and spinning twist (whether S or Z, Barber 1991, 65). The same observations were later made 'blind' on the unburied material.

The yarn count of the buried material was made with a light-weight mm scale and converted to inches, for comparison with the values given with the original cloth specification. For the unburied controls the standard yarn-count instrument was used, which incorporates a lens and allows one to count the number of yarns per inch. Fibre diameter measurements were made on whole mounts of the fibres (100 fibres in each sample) using the standard international Wool Textile Organisation method with a projection microscope at a magnification of 500×. Only intact fibres were measured. The results are recorded as a histogram giving the fibre diameter distribution, which defines the fleece type of sheep and has enabled a scheme for the evolution of different fleeces to be formulated (Ryder 1969; 1983). The method is now being applied to plant fibres (Ryder and Gabra-Sanders 1987; Ryder 1993a). The difficulty of separating the plant fibres from the yarn (and the wool fibres from the worsted yarn) meant

that it was only easy to measure their diameter where they projected from the cut ends of the yarns. Within the yarn they formed a solid mass in which it was difficult to get the fibre edges into focus.

In the past only a standard deviation of the mean has been calculated, since the main comparison was made on fibre diameter distributions. To allow more precise comparisons of mean fibre diameters in the present study, confidence limits were calculated by dividing the sd by the square root (10) of the number observations (100) and multiplying by two.

In archaeological material where the warp and the weft are not known, the two yarns are designated (a) and (b). In the present study, because there was in general no yarn marker, it was not possible to match up the buried yarns with the control yarns. In Table 10.8 therefore the yarns are listed in pairs with separate identification letters because there is no way of telling which yarn of the buried pair corresponds to which yarn of the control pair. Fibre diameter measurements falling outside the main range are listed separately. The differences in the measurements of the controls from those in the original specifications can be explained by observer and instrument differences.

Gross observations

It was usually possible to discern the spinning twist of the yarns as easily in the samples as in the controls, and as expected there had been no modification. In this section the order in which the textiles are described is simplest fibres first followed by those of more complex character.

Textile 6 – 3111 (Linen half-bleached)

This appeared as a grey-black sheet, the original weave not being evident. The edge appeared 'fuzzy' under a lens and a few fibres were visible when a fragment was crushed onto a slide.

Textile 5 – 3112 (Linen half-bleached)

This still had the creamy colour of flax fibre, except where stained black on one side and encrusted with chalk on the other. The plain weave remained clear; the relative looseness of the weave was already evident in the unburied material, but one system of yarns was finer (0.25mm) and more tightly spun and so presumed to be the warp, while the more loosely-spun presumed weft was 0.5mm thick. The thickness of each yarn, however, varied along the length, and in parts the yarns appeared to comprise alternate thick and thin yarns. Each system (warp and weft) had 31 yarns per inch, which compared with later counts in the control material of 32 'warp' yarns (the same as the specification) and 36 'weft' yarns per inch (compared with 34, Jewell 1963, 44). This suggested

Table 10.8 Textile fibre diameter measurements (in microns)

Sample	Diameter range	Mean ± s.d.	Confidence limits	Mode
Linen cloth (flax fibre) (5) buried (12)				
yarn (a)	6–34, 40 46	14.12 ± 5.5	± 1.20	14
yarn (b)	8–24	14.51 ± 4.33	± 0.96	16
Linen cloth (flax fibre) (5) control				
yarn (c)	8–28	15.47 ± 4.13	± 0.81	16
yarn (d)	8–32,36	15.58 ± 5.25	± 1.05	16
Linen cloth (flax fibre) (6) buried (11): too few fibres.				
Linen cloth (flax fibre) (6) control				
yarn (a)	8–26	15.52 ± 4.15	± 0.83	16
yarn (b)	8–26	14.81 ± 4.07	± 0.81	16
Cotton (2) buried (16)				
yarn (a)	8–20, 22	12.38 ± 3.1	only 47 fibres ± 0.91	12
yarn (b)	8–20	13.81 ± 3.5	only 65 fibres ± 0.87	12
Cotton (2) control				
yarn (a)	8–24	13.35 ± 3.3	100 fibres ± 0.66	12
yarn (b)	8–20, 24	13.54 ± 3.4	± 0.68	12
Cotton (1) control (no buried sample received)				
yarn (a)	8–22, 26	13.86 ± 3.9	± 0.78	12
yarn (b)	8–22	13.60 ± 3.4	± 0.69	12
Woollen (3) buried (14)				
dyed (a)	8–30, 38	17.30 ± 5.14	± 1.28	16
weft (b)	8–28	16.08 ± 4.39	± 0.88	16
Woollen (3) control				
weft	12–28	19.08 ± 4.19	± 0.84	16
suppliers specification		22.10	no other details given	
warp	12–38, 42, 44, 48	23.83 ± 6.71	± 1.34	22
suppliers specification		23.58	no other details given	
Wool worsted (4) buried (13)				
yarn (a)	8–36, 40	18.30 ± 6.12	± 1.22	16
yarn (b)	8–30	16.70 ± 4.35	± 0.87	16
Wool worsted (4) control				
yarn (c)	12–32	19.74 ± 4.67	± 0.93	16
yarn (d)	14–30	19.64 ± 3.78	± 0.76	18
yarn (e)	suppliers specification	21.18	no other details given	
yarn (f)	suppliers specification	20.34	no other details given	

that the weave had become more open with burial, and visual comparison with the control confirmed this.

Textile 2 – 3116 (Cotton khaki dyed twill/cloth)

This sample had become only slightly paler than the control, and one side had a deposition of chalk. The integrity of the cloth had been maintained. It was impossible to distinguish the warp from the weft, but each system had 48 yarns per inch. This compared with 44 and 48 in the different systems of the control, which suggests slight shrinkage of the buried material in one direction. It is odd that, while the weft count specification is given as 45, the warp count is given as 93 (Jewell 1963, 44). One wonders whether this is a misprint for 43. The fine yarns were only about 0.1mm thick, as in the control.

Textile 3 – 3114 (Woollen contrast cloth (tweed))

This was black, which made it appear like the archaeological remains of wool textiles, but it was in an even worse condition since the cloth had disintegrated into the constituent yarns. These were about 0.5mm thick compared with 1mm in the control. At this stage it appeared that the black colour made it impossible to distinguish what had been the undyed warp from the dark blue weft. One yarn appeared to be finer and straighter than the other and so on mounting was presumed to be the warp, although each yarn in the control cloth was later found to be wavy. Microscopic examination of the buried material showed that each yarn was dyed; the undyed warp had not survived. Limbrey's examination of the 1976 samples (p 59) showed that the dyed wool yarn was less decayed than the undyed one. Unlike the worsted yarns (below), the mounted yarn disintegrated into the constituent fibres on the slides.

Textile 4 – 3113 (Worsted – gabardine (wool))

The original light brown colour had not changed greatly. The cloth had become darker around the edges but was paler within the fold, and more so on the undersurface, partly due to chalk deposition. There was also a green stain, presumably from metal on the undersurface. Comparison with the control showed that, except at the edges, the integrity of the cloth had been maintained, although the buried sample had some wrinkling. It was impossible to make a thread count on either this or the control, owing to the tight 'herring-bone' twill weave. One yarn system had yarns 0.1mm thick, while the other was only half this thickness. The possibility of plying was supported by the control, in which dark and light yarns appeared to have been plied together.

Microscopic observations and measurements

Textile 5 – 3112 (Linen half-bleached cloth (flax fibre))

The fibres in the present buried material appeared colourless as in the controls, although some had a yellow-brown discolouration. The periodic nodes (cross striations) were far less clear than in the controls. Otherwise the only hint of decay in these two yarns, was an apparent longitudinal splitting of some fibres. This must be checked with the SEM, however, since longitudinal striations are normal in flax and indicate incomplete retting. Indeed some of the control fibres appear to have been incompletely retted. Otherwise the control 'ultimates' (single cells) had few longitudinal striations and few of them had a central lumen.

Reported mean fibre diameters of flax can vary according to the extent to which the retting has split the fibre bundle into the individual ultimates: these only should be measured. The fibre diameter measurements are shown in Table 10.8. It is noteworthy that the modes were nearly all the same. Although the mean fibre diameters in the buried flax were lower than those of the controls, the differences are only of the order of 1 micron, which is equivalent to the experimental error. If the confidence limits are added to the means of the buried yarns, the values approximate more closely to those of the controls; and if the confidence limits are deducted from the control means the values approximate more closely to those of the buried material.

Textile 6 – 3111 (Linen half-bleached cloth (flax fibre))

Fewer fibres were evident in this buried sample. Some colourless ultimates were seen protruding from masses of brown debris, but too few measurements could be made to allow a satisfactory mean to be calculated. There were many apparent 'spores' elliptical in shape, 10 microns long by 6 microns wide.

Textile 2 – 3116 (Cotton khaki dyed twill/cloth)

Cotton fibres are single cell seed hairs. The buried fibres appeared colourless under the microscope and no different from those of the control. Since cotton has been encountered in only Post-Medieval oriental carpets, there is no experience of the form of decay likely to occur in buried samples. There was a filamentous mass of presumably fungal hyphae, and brown 'spores' ranging from 14 to 30 microns in diameter were observed. The fibre diameter measurements are shown in Table 10.8 and considering that the experimental error of the mean is nearly 1 micron, these show remarkable consistency notably between the different control cloths and between their yarns. It is noteworthy that the modes were all the same. Although buried yarn (a) has a lower mean fibre diameter than both of the control yarns, yarn (b) has a higher mean diameter than both of the controls. From these similarities and the confidence limits there does not appear to have been any change of fibre diameter through burial, and the most likely explanation of the observed small differences is the small sample size of the buried material.

Textile 3 – 3114 (Woollen contrast cloth (tweed))

Since yarn sub-sample (a) as well as yarn sub-sample (b) was dyed it seems that only the weft remained. Different forms of decay were evident. Some fibres had frayed into the constituent cortical cells, which is a common form of disintegration. None of the thin, flat cells (scales) of the outer cuticle were seen. The SEM may indicate what has happened to them. It is not usually easy to see these on the surface of intact fibres under the light microscope, but scale edges were very obvious in the control fibres. Other fibres showed a smooth constriction; no examples of what appears to be a 'bite out of' the fibre were seen. Others had the stepwise breakage thought to occur along the boundary between the ortho- and para-cortex forming the bulk of the fibre. This was described by Whiteley (1964) in the Iron Age wool of Ryder (1961). It has been most recently described in some Roman wool by Ryder (1993b). In yet other fibres the stepwise breakage was concentric so that the diameter was suddenly reduced from 20 micron to 16 microns.

The diameter measurements are shown in Table 10.8. Wool is much more variable than either flax or cotton (illustrated by the inclusion of coarser fibres in the warp control) and this explains why the repeat measurements are apparently not as close. However, the confidence limits indicate that the repeat buried weft measurements are within the limits of experimental error.

When the confidence limits are taken into account to consider the apparent lower mean diameter in the buried samples compared with the control, it is clear that any reduction is only of the order of 1 micron and could be explained by the loss of cuticular scales. The diameter distribution shows a shift to finer fibres in the buried material, but the mode is the same at 16 microns.

Textile 4 – 3113 (Worsted gabardine (wool))

Although some fibres had lost their colour, the dye was, on the whole, as clearly visible as in the control fibres, whereas it is rare to see dye in archaeological specimens. Burial had not obscured the well-known phenomenon in which dye is taken up more readily on one side (the ortho-cortex) than the other (Ryder and Stephenson 1968, 296). No cuticular scales were visible on either the buried or control fibres. None of the general degradation was observed in which fibres

are seen to disintegrate into their constituent cortical cells. However, some fibre ends had frayed into the cortical cells and others had tapered down to a single cortical cell. Smooth constrictions, which are not unknown in wool and which might be thought to indicate degradation, were seen in the controls. One or two fibres had the 'bite-out' form of decay. Other tests might be able to clarify whether this is due to tiny animals or to micro-organisms. Some apparent fungal spores, 26 microns in diameter, were observed on some fibres. These were the same colour as the light brown dye of the fabric – was this coincidence or could the dye have been absorbed from the fibre in some way?

Although the buried samples had a finer lower limit to the distribution (Table 10.8), as with the woollen, the mode was the same and the mean was only about 1 micron lower, ie within the range of experimental error.

Discussion

1. Choice of the cloth

It is unfortunate that in all instances modern, machine-made fabrics were used. Only the linen cloth was of the kind encountered on prehistoric sites. Cotton is not known in Britain before the Middle Ages. Each wool cloth was made from an inappropriate, imported fleece type unknown in prehistory, and the gaberdine was made using the modern worsted process. One could argue that this is providing information for use by the archaeologists of the future, but it would have been more informative to have used hand spun and woven wool cloths made with primitive fleeces, having a natural pigment (Ryder 1990).

Most prehistoric wools (eg Bronze Age Soay) had at least some natural pigment and it would have been interesting to note the effect of burial on this. Non-pigmented wools (eg Iron Age Shetland) could have been included and dyed with plant dyes. It would have been useful to include silk (known from Roman times), and other natural plant fibres such as hemp. Since the different yarns in archaeological material are investigated separately (often having a different fibre or fleece type) a marker to indicate which was the warp and which was the weft should have been included – they might have shown differential decay. In only the woollen cloth was there a marker (dyed weft).

2. The general conditions of textile preservation and survival

In outline the conditions under which textiles may be preserved are: (a) freezing as in Siberia (Ryder 1961; 1974); (b) desiccation as in Sudan (Ryder 1984); (c) salting as in the mines at Hallstatt (Ryder 1992a); (d) association with metal (Janaway 1983);

(e) waterlogging, eg Bronze Age Denmark (Ryder 1988) and Medieval Britain (Ryder 1981a). The type of fibre preserved in these conditions is thought to depend on the pH, with protein fibres being preserved in acid conditions and plant fibres in alkaline conditions. There are inexplicable exceptions and the present experiment has highlighted the variable and fortuitous nature of preservation (Limbrey p 55).

3. The nature of textile decay

So that the findings from this experiment can be related to actual textile remains, it will be useful to outline past observations. It is also important to distinguish the damage that can result from the wear of a textile, from that occurring during burial. I have never observed wear or decay in flax and cotton. With wool, fibre damage takes two forms: (1) garment wear results in 'flexing' damage in which a fibre appears bent and split to reveal the cortical cells, but it not actually broken; (2) carpet wear results in 'abrasion' damage in which the ends of the fibres appear smooth and rounded and there is no fraying into the cortical cells (Ryder 1987b).

Burial degeneration of wool takes at least three forms, all of which have been observed in the present investigation: (1) fibre breakage, which can be (a) 'clean' across the fibre, (b) step-wise (Whiteley 1964; Ryder 1993b) and (c) concentric; (2) fraying or splitting into the cortical cells – the use of the SEM in the present study revealed the extent to which thin outer cuticle has decayed by the time that separation of the cortical cells became evident (p 165); (3) decay which appears exactly like the 'bite out' of a fibre resulting from it being eaten by moth lavae. The present study has confirmed that this can occur during burial, suggesting that such damage in archaeological material is not necessarily due to moth damage.

4. Textiles from the 1992 excavation

It was remarkable that the wool as well as the plant fibres had survived in the chalk; the expectation was that the wool keratin would have been attacked by the alkali of the chalk. Most of the textile samples were well preserved. This leads to two comments based on my study of hundreds of textile remains: (1) if a sample has survived for a few years it could well survive very many years. Whether or not a textile survives is largely determined by the initial burial conditions; (2) survival tends to be an all or nothing effect – surviving textiles with degraded fibres are uncommon. In the earthwork most samples were preserved in the chalk environment (pH 8.2), whereas nothing was found in the turf environment (pH 5.6). Kelley and Wiltshire (p 150) found more microbiological activity in the soil than the chalk, which could explain the lack of survival in the soil.

The insolubility and relative dryness of the calcium carbonate of the chalk might have prevented any alkali from reaching the wool. It is noteworthy, however, that protein does not survive on chalk sites.

As in the earlier excavations (Jewell and Dimbleby 1966; Limbrey p 58), folding the cloth was an important factor in preserving those parts of the inside. It is unusual to see dye in prehistoric textiles so it is unfortunate therefore that synthetic dye was used in the samples. Not only does this appear to have survived better than natural dye, but it seems to have preserved the wool. However, a 32 year survival is still only a short time compared with most archaeological material.

There appeared to be little change in overall dimensions. Yarn counts suggested slight expansion of the linen cloth and slight shrinkage of the cotton cloth. It was not possible to make yarn counts on the wool fabrics. The woollen cloth had disintegrated and the weave of the worsted cloth was so tight as to preclude a count even in the control. Some of the buried yarns appeared to be thinner than in the controls, particularly those in the woollen cloth. As expected, there had been no modification of the spinning twist.

The different forms of decay observed previously in archaeological material were seen – nothing new was observed. Because wool has a cellular structure, it showed more disintegration than the single cells comprising the plant fibres. This is presumably the 'fibrillation' observed by Janaway in his report (p 166). Whereas I selected the best-preserved parts to measure, Janaway probably chose the less well-preserved parts to look at the nature of the decay.

Although the wool as well as the plant fibres each had hints of a slight fall in mean fibre diameter, more samples would have to be measured and the data subjected to statistical analysis to prove such a decrease. One might expect that finer fibres would decay more readily, but the decreased mean was associated with an increase in the proportion of finer fibres, the mode remaining the same. Where differential decay has been observed previously it has occurred in the coarsest, heavily medullated (and therefore brittle) hairy fibres, of a fleece which has had the effect of increasing the proportion of fine fibres (Ryder 1993a). The omission of any hairy fleeces from this experiment precluded an investigation of this phenomenon.

If the changes in dimensions should prove to be real, they would not cause an error in the identification of fleece type because this is made on the shape of the distribution. There is strong evidence that the diameter of flax and wool does not change with burial since flax values have remained the same since earliest times (Ryder and Gabra-Sanders 1987) and wool fibres of the same category eg fine and medium, have the same diameter throughout history.

The fact that wool fibre remains can exhibit physical integrity yet show changes in chemical structure, points the way to future work on all the samples retrieved to date. Ryder (1992b) reviewed unpublished work on archaeological remains of wool by R C Marshall of Melbourne. Variations in the electrophoretic mobility of the high-sulphur proteins of wool occur between sheep (Marshall and Gillespie 1989) and the analyses by Marshall were carried out in answer to my wish to exploit this to study breed origins and sheep history. Gillespie (1970) had found that mammoth hair 32,000 years old retained the characteristic ordered structure of keratin; but whereas the high-sulphur proteins of modern elephant hair gave several bands in starch-gel electrophoresis, the mammoth hair gave an unresolved, diffuse smear. He suggested that these changes had been caused by limited proteolysis.

The archaeological remains of wool available are not more than 4000 years old, and this suggested two possibilities: (a) that less degradation would have occurred in these than in the mammoth hair so that there might be some resolution of the electrophoretic mobilities, and (b) that if the amount of degradation precluded characterization, it might nevertheless provide a method of dating hair and wool remains. I was able to supply R C Marshall with 12 samples of archaeological material ranging in age from over 3000 years to 600 years. Two-dimensional electrophoresis of the solubilized proteins was used. The electrophoretic patterns of the ancient wools were very different from those of modern wools in that there were no typical low-sulphur or high-sulphur proteins. All the samples had material of low molecular weight.

The patterns almost certainly reflect changes with time as a result of contact with soil. Electrophoresis therefore appears to be unsuitable for the genetic characterization of old wool samples. But the amount and type of degradation can be described and it is just possible that this might provide the basis for a method of dating.

10.7 Infrared analysis of textile samples
by Susan Hardman

Samples received from Rob Janaway were as follows. All samples were from the chalk environment (none being recovered from the turf environment).

Control Sample 1	– Cotton loomstate Plain cloth
Sample	– Sample not received
Control Sample 2	– Cotton Khaki dyed Twill cloth
Sample 3116	– Cotton Khaki dyed Twill cloth
Control Sample 3	– Woollen Contrast cloth (Tweed) (White Warp and Dark Navy Weft)
Sample 3114	– Woollen Contrast cloth (Tweed) – (Dark Navy fibre only)
Control Sample 4	– Worsted Gaberdine Twill
Sample 3113	– Worsted Gaberdine Twill
Control Sample 5	– Linen Half Bleached
Sample 3112	– Linen Half Bleached
Control Sample 6	– Linen Half Bleached
Sample 3111	– Linen Half Bleached

The extent to which a textile survives a given burial environment involves many parameters. These include the chemistry of the textile itself and the use of dyes and mordants, soil type, drainage, pH, microbiology and burial context (for example the presence of metal artifacts, a coffin etc).

The results of such variations have been directly reflected in the Overton Down experiment, in the first instance by the survival of the textile samples in the chalk environment and their complete destruction in the turf environment. The preservative effect of chromium has also been clearly demonstrated, the metal ions acting as a biocide.

Samples were analysed using Fourier transform infrared (FT-IR) microscopy, the basic principle being that molecules show characteristic absorption bands in the IR region of the electromagnetic spectrum. An IR spectrum of a given compound will therefore provide information concerning molecular structure, groups present and molecular symmetry. The speed and accuracy of data collection is increased by the Fourier transform process; this coupled with the microscope (which allows the IR beam to be focused on an area as small as $10\mu m \times 10\mu m$) permits a single fibre to be analysed with minimal sample preparation.

Fibres samples were selected for analysis using a ×30 magnification optical microscope. To prevent diffraction of the IR beam, the sample was gently flattened with a small roller before being transferred to a potassium bromide disc on the FT-IR microscope sample stage. Once focused, the area for analysis was selected by means of shutters both above and below the sample plane. The infrared beam was then transmitted through the sample and onto the detector. Any absorptions by molecules in the sample are recorded on the plotted spectrum as a decrease in the % transmittance.

Figure 10.21 shows three IR linen spectra obtained from:

(1) an untreated, linen half-bleached control fibre.
(2) a linen half-bleached fibre from sample 3112.
(3) a linen half-bleached fibre from sample 3111.

Linen is a cellulosic fibre obtained from the stem of the flax plant. Being a cellulosic fibre, it is primarily composed of a polymer of β-anhydroglucose units joined together via an ether link (Fig 10.22). Breakdown of the polymer can occur in both acid and alkaline environments by hydrolytic and or oxidative attack, resulting in the destruction of the chain and opening of the ring by the conversion of the hydroxyl groups to carbonyl functionalities. This is observed in the spectra of both experimental linen samples by the appearance of a band at $17.35 cm^{-1}$ which is attributed to carboxyl carbonyl (Yang and Freeman 1991). The intensity of the peak in the spectrum of linen sample 3111 also indicates that this has been degraded to a greater extent than 3112. Most of the other differences between these and the reference spectra can be attributed to the chalk itself.

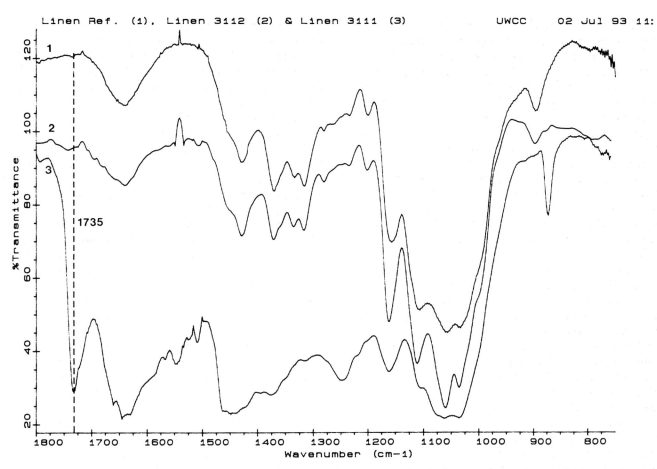

Figure 10.21 Infrared analysis of textiles (1) Linen reference sample; (2) Linen sample 3112; (3) Linen sample 3111

The variation in preservation of these two apparently identical samples placed side by side in the experimental earthwork was noted in the earlier excavations and serves to highlight how localized attack can be (Jewell and Dimbleby 1966). Comparison of the two linen reference spectra indicated no obvious variation in their structure (the inference being that the differences could be attributed to the degree of bleaching), although a more detailed chemical analysis might reveal otherwise. At this stage, however, localized microbial attack would be the favoured answer.

Although cotton is also a cellulose fibre, the spectrum of the khaki-dyed cotton showed minimal breakdown compared to the linen samples. This can be attributed to the chromium present in the dye

(khaki being essentially a mineral dye of iron and chromium hydroxides).

Protein fibres such as wool are essentially a complex polymer of amino acids joined together via peptide links. Their exact composition varies not only from breed to breed but also from sheep to sheep. Like cellulose fibres, protein fibres are susceptible to attack in acid and alkaline environments. However they are more likely to survive in acidic conditions as the reactive disulphide bonds found in wool are more resistant to attack. Given the alkaline conditions produced in the chalk environment (approximate pH = 8) one would have predicted degradation of the wool fibres. In reality the limited extent to which this occurred only serves to highlight the complex nature of fibre survival.

In the woollen contrast cloth (tweed) sample the preservative effects of chromium were again emphasized with the survival of the chrome dyed fibres and the complete loss of the undyed ones. The dark navy fibres showing little change in either colour or IR spectrum.

In contrast to the loss of the undyed tweed fibres, the undyed worsted gaberdine had survived well. The spectrum of the twill fabric showed little change except for a slight oxidation of the disulphide bonds indicated at $10.40 cm^{-1}$ due to the formation of cysteic acid ($-SO_3^-$). Why this untreated wool fabric should survive while the undyed fibres of the woollen

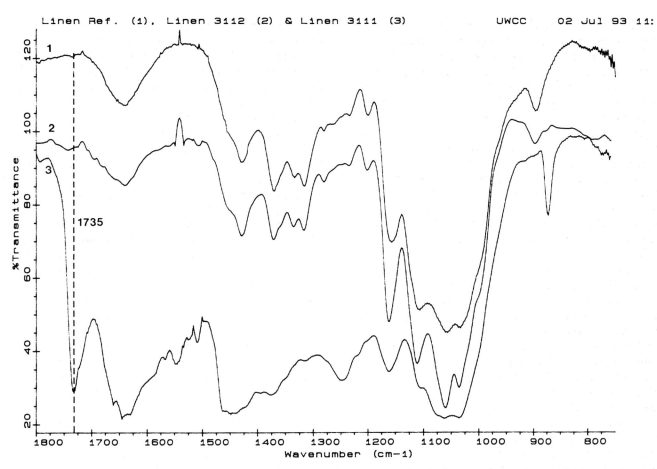

Figure 10.22 Diagram to illustrate that cellulose consists of repeating units of cellobiose (DP = 2n + 2)

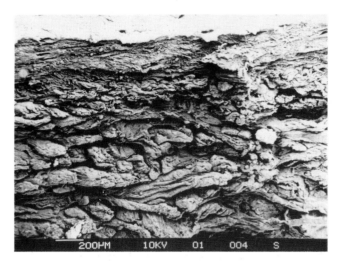

Figure 10.24 *SEM micrograph of Leather Sample 10 (3101) from the chalk environment in section*

Figure 10.23 *Leather Sample 9 (3167) from the turf environment*

contrast cloth (tweed) did not is not entirely clear. One important factor is undoubtedly the tighter spin and weave of the worsted gaberdine. This reduces the surface area accessible for microbial attack and also restricts the percolation of groundwater through the fabric.

In summary, this study has shown that where fibres have survived they have done so with minimal degradation. This can be attributed to a number of factors including a relatively dry, well drained burial environment, and the tightness of the spin and weave of the fibres and fabrics. The preservative effects of metal ions such as chronium have also been clearly demonstrated in the woollen contrast cloth (tweed) and cotton khaki dyed twill cloth samples. However, it should be remembered that chromium is not representative of dye materials used by prehistoric communities as it was first used in textile manufacture during the 1800s.

10.8 Leather samples
by Glynis Edwards

The buried samples which had been tanned using modern methods, the chrome tanned upper leathers (9–11) and the modern extract tanned leather (8), were in a good state of preservation (Fig 10.23). In the case of the chrome tanned leathers it is felt that the chrome has prevented deterioration by having a bacteriostatic effect. This type of preservation has been observed in archaeological deposits where organic materials have been buried in close contact with copper alloy artefacts (Edwards 1989, 5). The potential of the mineral preservation of organic

materials may not have been realized fully at the time of the construction of the earthwork. The British Leather Manufacturers Research Association suggested the inclusion of these leathers tanned by modern methods (Jewell 1960, 45). The leathers were unused and had suffered no damage from wear and this may have contributed to the clarity of the grain pattern on all the samples. Scanning Electron Micrographs of two of the leather samples are shown in Figure 10.24 (Leather 10 – chalk) and Figure 10.25 (Leather 11 – turf).

The oak-bark tanned leather (7) was examined after microbiological investigation; it too had suffered minimal deterioration. The most noticeable feature was that the samples from both environments had darkened considerably, much more than any of the other buried leathers. This blackening of the material has been observed on archaeological leather which has been preserved by contact with copper corrosion products. The modern extract tanned leather (8) had darkened slightly more than the chrome tanned material and the sample from the chalk environment (3103) had a mottled appearance.

Leather samples 8–11 were all kept damp wrapped in aluminium foil and stored in a refrigerator. When they were examined at the School of Archaeological Sciences, University of Bradford there was no appreciable difference in flexibility between samples from the chalk and from the turf environment. The thinner upper leathers had maintained their flexibility particularly well. The modern extract tanned leather (8) was thicker and correspondingly less flexible while the oak tanned leather (7), which had been allowed to dry, was rigid, though this was also a much thicker leather.

Two of the thinner upper leathers, 9 (3102) from the chalk and 11 (3169) from the turf, were showing signs of delamination, the former on one edge with a loosening of the fibres on the other edges, while the latter shows it on all edges. One other sample which has loose fibres on the edges is leather 9 (3167) from the turf. The flesh side of leather 10 (3101) from the chalk is showing a slight break-up with loose fibres.

The grain surfaces are all very well preserved, the only example of deterioration being on leather 7 (3104) from the chalk where there are cracks appearing in this surface which follow the cracking of the chalk. There has been slight surface loss on the grain side on two other samples from the chalk environment, leather 8 (3103) and leather 9 (3102), as a result of chalk adhering strongly to the surface. Some samples also have impressions in the surface from the surrounding soil, clearly shown in leather 8 from both chalk and turf (3103 and 3170) and leather 10 (3168) and leather 11 (3169) from the turf. All the samples from the chalk environment have traces of chalk adhering to them while those from the turf have a fine silty soil and compressed vegetable material. There was no vegetable material on leather 7 (3175) from the turf but this may be a result of microbiological sampling.

The most fugitive dye was in the crimson dyed upper leather 10 (3101) where it could be seen to have leached into the surrounding chalk on site. The sample from the turf (3168) had also suffered a colour loss. The other coloured leathers have become dull and Leather 9 has darkened, but they do not appear to have suffered a major colour loss, although Leather 11 (3092) was observed to be covered with a piece of stained chalk.

As there had been no significant deterioration, it was decided to record any changes that had occurred by comparing sub-samples of the buried material with samples of unburied material from the site archive. The flesh and grain side, a fresh cut section of both materials, and the exposed edge of the buried samples were photographically recorded in colour. The fresh cut sections of the sub-samples made it possible to see how far any staining had penetrated into the leather and it was also possible to see any changes in both grain and flesh sides.

The sub-samples were stored in alcohol, and these were allowed to dry slowly before photography. The fugitive dye from leather 10 was evident in the alcohol in both the chalk and turf examples. After drying it could be seen that the thinner upper leathers from the chalk environment had distorted more than those from the turf.

The oak-bark tanned leather 7 showed the most colour change and the dark brown staining could be seen to have penetrated right through the section. The sample from the turf environment (3175) is slightly darker on both grain and flesh sides than the sample from the chalk (3104). The sections appear to be stained to the same extent.

The modern extract tanned sole leather 8 has no staining in the section, rather a slight dulling of the colour. There has been a slight darkening of both grain and flesh side; in this case the sample from the chalk environment (3103) being darker than that from the turf (3170).

The semi-chrome tanned leather 9 has slight

Figure 10.25   SEM micrograph of Leather Sample 11 (3169) from the turf environment in section

staining visible in the section, more on the sample from the turf environment (3167). The grain side has darkened in both cases and is now black rather than brown in colour. The flesh side on the sample from the chalk environment (3102) is more stained than that from the turf (3167), which shows very little change when compared to the unburied material.

The unburied sample of the chrome tanned leather 10 has a slight blue tinge in the centre of the section which has disappeared from the sections of the buried samples. The chalk on 3101 has become stained blue apparently from this colourant. The centre of the section of the sample from the turf (3168) has been stained by the fugitive crimson dye. The colour loss on the grain side can be seen on both samples, while the flesh side is more stained on the sample from the turf. The slight staining on the flesh side of the sample from the chalk possibly being more of the fugitive dye. The exposed edge in this latter sample is also stained red.

The chrome re-tanned leather 11 has no staining visible in the section on both samples and the three distinct layers seen in the unburied material are still clear. There has been a slight colour loss on the grain side, more on that from the chalk (3092) while the flesh side on this sample is more stained than that from the turf (3169) which has very little staining.

There is no consistent pattern of changes to the buried samples in either environment. The only difference in the preservation of the leather between the two environments is the slight physical damage to some of the samples from the chalk which is not evident on any from the turf. The leather which has undergone the most change is the oak bark tanned material (leather 7) which is the probably bears the closest resemblance to leather generally found in archaeological contexts.

A full description of the condition of the leathers, together with a photographic archive showing their condition as a whole and in section, is in the project archive.

11 Studies of the buried bone from the Overton 1992 excavation

11.1 Introduction

This aspect of the project was coordinated on site and in the field laboratory by Dr Simon Hillson, whose description of the complete bones, as recovered, has been outlined in Chapter 7 (p 84–85 and p 88–89). That chapter also describes the sub-sampling of bones in the field laboratory for more detailed analytical investigations, the results of which are presented in this chapter. The two final contributions, which concern DNA, are reports on the philosophy and aims of work in progress rather than results. This is because the investigation of ancient biomolecules is undergoing very active research at the time of writing, and appropriate techniques are being developed. It was regarded as premature to produce results for this publication, and the results, when available, will be published elsewhere. For the same reason, a report is not included on the originally planned aspect of the experiment which involved placing human bone of known blood group in the earthwork (Jewell 1963, 47). On this aspect Dr Robert Sockel, Consultant Haematologist with the blood transfusion service at Sheffield, and the DNA specialists have advised that better techniques are being developed. We hope it may be possible to publish aspects of this additional work with the reports of the 1995 excavations at Wareham.

11.2 Surface modification of bone
by Miranda Armour-Chelu and Peter Andrews

Introduction

This study describes the surface modifications observed from two sheep metacarpals buried for 32 years in the chalk bank. Modifications identified included cutmarks associated with the butchery of the sheep prior to burial, and damage caused by physical and biological agencies during burial. Interdisciplinary studies of buried bones, where the local depositional environment is known, can supply useful analogues for reconstructing the taphonomic history of faunal assemblages retrieved from archaeological and palaeontological sites (Andrews 1995). Furthermore, research upon bones of known depositional history is of potential value to DNA, blood grouping and isotope studies, where the original biological signal has been altered by diagenetic effects.

Material and methods

The buried bone samples included elements derived from human cadavers and two, domestic, sheep skeletons (*Ovies aries*), of known breed and sex

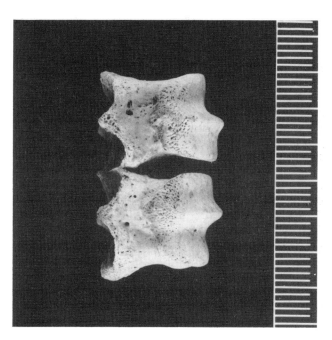

Figure 11.1 Juvenile sheep metacarpal, specimen 3109, anterior aspect

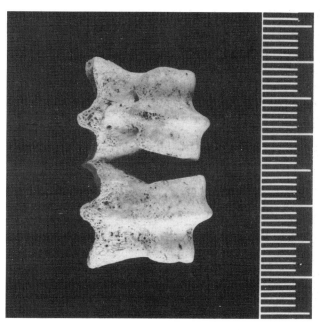

Figure 11.2 Juvenile sheep metacarpal, specimen 3109, posterior aspect

(Jewell 1963). One of the sheep skeletons was derived from a juvenile, Kent Cross wether (3109) and the second skeleton was from a mature, Soay ram (3090). The bones from the Soay ram were boiled for approximately one hour before they were buried.

The sheep metacarpals were buried in layer C of the bank, at a depth of 1.5m (4ft 11.5in) (Jewell 1963). This layer was composed of chalk and flint rubble with individual lumps ranging from 50 to 80mm (2–3in) in size. Weathering of the bank occurred almost immediately after construction which reduced the average size of its constituent chalk lumps, and there was also incipient soil formation (Jewell and Dimbleby 1966). The pH value of the chalk substrate surrounding the metacarpals was found to be 8.3 at the time of excavation.

The metacarpals were excavated on 10 July, 1992 and appeared to be in their original position as recorded by Jewell (1963). The juvenile metacarpal (3109) was lying with the posterior surface uppermost, whereas the mature metacarpal (3090) was lying with the anterior surface uppermost. The metacarpals were removed to the on-site laboratory immediately after excavation, where they were examined with a low powered binocular microscope. Details of the condition of the metacarpals were recorded by Hillson (p 85), prior to sub-sampling of the bones for histological, DNA, blood grouping and SEM studies.

The material examined for this study comprised a left, juvenile, sheep metacarpal epiphysis (3109) (Figs 11.1 and 11.2), and a left, mature, sheep metacarpal distal shaft and epiphysis (3090) (Figs 11.3 and 11.4). These were not cleaned to avoid inadvertently removing extraneous objects adhering to the surface of the bones. However, prior to SEM analyses, it was necessary to place the bones in a dessicator where they were dried over silica gel at a low vacuum. Specific gravity determinations after drying gave results of 0.49 for specimen 3109 and 1.20 for specimen 3090. The bones were examined using a ISI–60A scanning electron microscope (SEM), housed within the Electron Microscope Unit at the Natural History Museum, London. Preparation of the bones for analyses at higher magnification entailed sputter coating of both specimens with carbon and these were then examined with a Hitachi S2500 SEM.

Pre-burial modifications

Before burial the sheep skeletons were disarticulated and defleshed with a steel knife; this was the sole implement used in the butchery of the carcasses (Jewell 1963). Cutmarks caused by butchery were observed from both metacarpals. A group of five cutmarks, orientated transversely to the long axis of the bone, on the anterior aspect (Fig 11.5), were recorded from the epiphysis proximal to the medial condyle of specimen 3109. Figure 11.6 shows a detail of two of these cutmarks taken at the most distal point along the epiphysis. These cutmarks have a deep, V-shaped transverse section and the cutmark on the left of Figure 11.6 contains a thin splice of bone. These features appear to comprise some of the morphological attributes of cutmarks (Shipman 1981), but are not the sole criteria that can be used to differentiate between marks created by butchery or carnivore damage (Lee Lyman 1987).

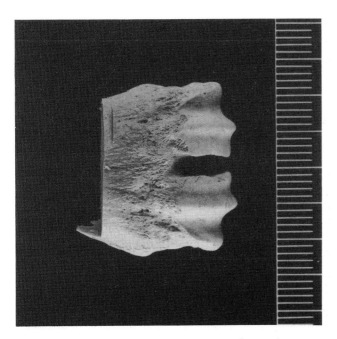

Figure 11.3 Mature sheep metacarpal, specimen 3090, anterior aspect

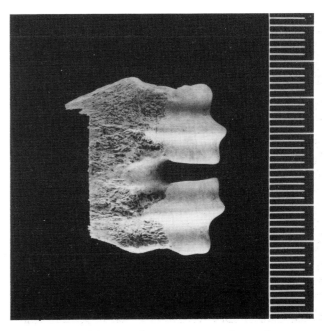

Figure 11.4 Mature sheep metacarpal, specimen 3090, posterior aspect

Four short cutmarks were present upon the keel of the medial condyle on the anterior side of specimen 3090 (Fig 11.7). These ran transversely to the long axis of the bone and were probably caused by disarticulating the metacarpal from the first phalanges.

Modifications incurred during burial

Abrasions or scrapes were present upon the anterior aspect of the articular surface of the mature metacarpal. These abrasions were shallow with multiple striations and either occur singly or superimposed upon each other. Figure 11.8 shows an example of two associated abrasions upon the keel of the lateral condyle. Figure 11.9 shows that these do not share the same orientation. The first abrasion runs transversely to the long axis of the bone, whereas the second abrasion is approximately parallel to the long axis of the bone. Small holes within the abrasions, probably fungal damage (see below), demonstrate that these modifications did not occur after excavation. It is not possible to establish exactly when these abrasions occurred but they probably date to the time when the bones were buried in the bank.

Although some sharp object is implicated in creation of these abrasions, modification by butchery has been rejected as they do not show the deep 'V' shaped profile characteristic of cutmarks created by metal tools. The morphology and multiple orientation of these abrasions is most closely matched by trampling damage (Andrews and Cook 1985). However, this can be discounted as the bones were not subjected to subaerial exposure prior to burial. It seems likely that these abrasions occurred due to contact between the bone and the chalk and flint rubble. In this context it seems significant that the abrasions occurred on the uppermost surface of the bone which is where the chalk and flint would settle during the compaction and consolidation of the bank. Measurements taken along the crest of the bank show that it had sunk by 0.15m four years after construction (Jewell and Dimbleby 1966), which suggests that there was considerable internal movement of the chalk and flint substrate.

At the macroscopic level both metacarpals appeared well preserved, although the surface of the bone of the juvenile metacarpal (3109) had a lower specific gravity and notably porous appearance compared to the mature specimen. Bone loss was evident from the epiphyseal margin and across the articular surface of the condyle. Figure 11.10 shows loss of compact bone from around the epiphyseal margin with exposure of cancellous tissue. A similar pattern of bone loss was observed from the margin of the condyle (Fig 11.11) with the anterior side more severely affected. Severe loss of bone was also observed along the keel of the condyle, particularly along the lateral condyle on the posterior side (Figs 11.12 and 11.13). The bone from the articular surface of the adult specimen (3090) was better preserved

and this differential pattern of bone loss can be attributed to the relative strength of juvenile and mature bone (Gordon and Buikstra 1981). Maximum bone loss occurred upon the keel and distal portion of the condyle and along the epiphyseal margin of the epiphysis. These are the weakest areas of the condyle with the greatest proportion of surface area exposed. It has not been possible to identify how this damage was caused but it seems probable that leaching and/or the effects of rain water percolating through the bank were responsible.

Cracks were present across the articular surface of the condyle of specimen 3090, the mature metacarpal, and these had conjoined to form a mosaic pattern (Fig 11.7). These cracks largely occurred before burial or whilst the bone was buried within the bank as they were visible at the time of excavation. No cracking was visible on the immature specimen, 3109. Conditions after excavation are known to have contributed in a minor way to the development of these cracks. Two days after excavation the metacarpals were taken to the Natural History Museum, London, and stored within a drawer with no control for humidity or temperature. Both metacarpals were examined repeatedly under the SEM which involved drying the bones in a dessicator. Comparisons of SEM photographs taken throughout 1992–93 showed that one of these cracks had elongated by 55 microns.

The origin of these cracks is unknown although it seems possible that they may be related to stresses caused by bone expansion and contraction whilst buried. Specimen 3090 was cooked, whereas 3109 was not, and this may also have contributed to the presence of cracking. Relative humidity affects bone weight as was demonstrated by the repeated weighing of the specimens before and after examination in the SEM. It was found that the mature matacarpal sustained an average weight loss of 5% and the juvenile metacarpal lost 10% after drying in the vacuum chamber of the SEM. It seems likely that the greater weight loss in the juvenile metacarpal may be accounted for by the more porous nature of the bone. Porous bones can absorb more moisture from the atmosphere and this is indicated by greater weight loss and gain. Behrensmeyer (1978) has observed that fluctuations in soil moisture and temperature are significant in the destruction of bone in arid environments although this is unlikely to occur to the same extent in temperate climates.

The fact that these cracks are restricted to the articular surface suggests that there are histological differences between the bone of the articular surface and shaft area. Bell (1990) noted microscopic cracks encircling osteons in samples of modern and archaeological bone and considered that these respected natural cleavages within the bone.

The epiphysis of the juvenile metacarpal and distal shaft area of the mature metacarpal showed extensive loss of outer compact bone. In the juvenile specimen, bone loss was especially apparent from

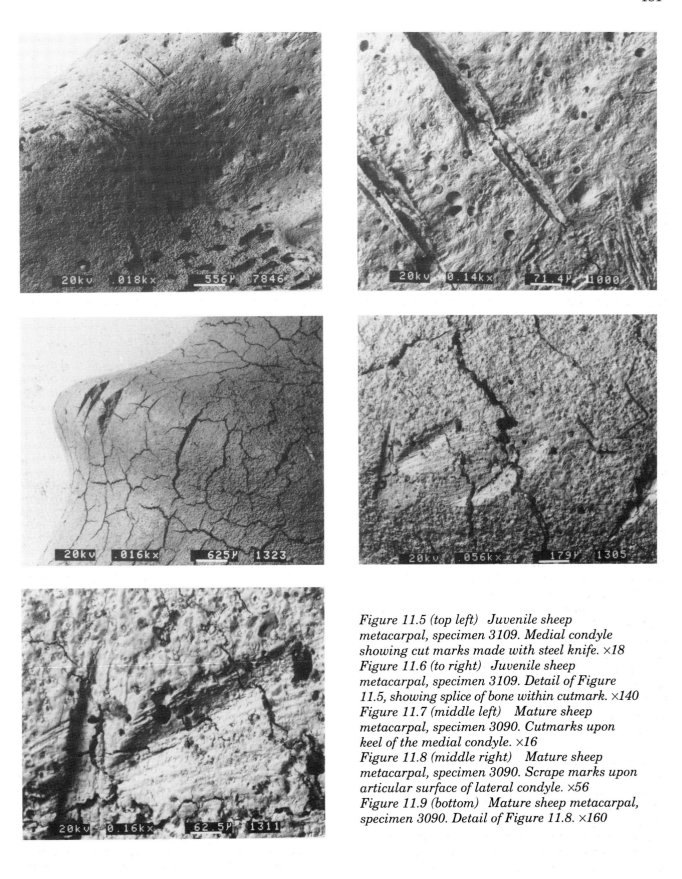

Figure 11.5 (top left) Juvenile sheep
metacarpal, specimen 3109. Medial condyle
showing cut marks made with steel knife. ×18
Figure 11.6 (to right) Juvenile sheep
metacarpal, specimen 3109. Detail of Figure
11.5, showing splice of bone within cutmark. ×140
Figure 11.7 (middle left) Mature sheep
metacarpal, specimen 3090. Cutmarks upon
keel of the medial condyle. ×16
Figure 11.8 (middle right) Mature sheep
metacarpal, specimen 3090. Scrape marks upon
articular surface of lateral condyle. ×56
Figure 11.9 (bottom) Mature sheep metacarpal,
specimen 3090. Detail of Figure 11.8. ×160

around the epiphyseal margin (Fig 11.14), and
vascular canals. The pattern of bone loss was not
visible at the macroscopic level but at higher magnifications innumerable channels etched into the bone
were seen (Figs 11.15 and 11.16). The width of the
channels is of the order of six microns and individual
channels have coalesced giving a scalloped appearance to the surface of the bone. Channelling of bone
on the juvenile metacarpal was seen across the
compact bone around the ephipyseal margin and

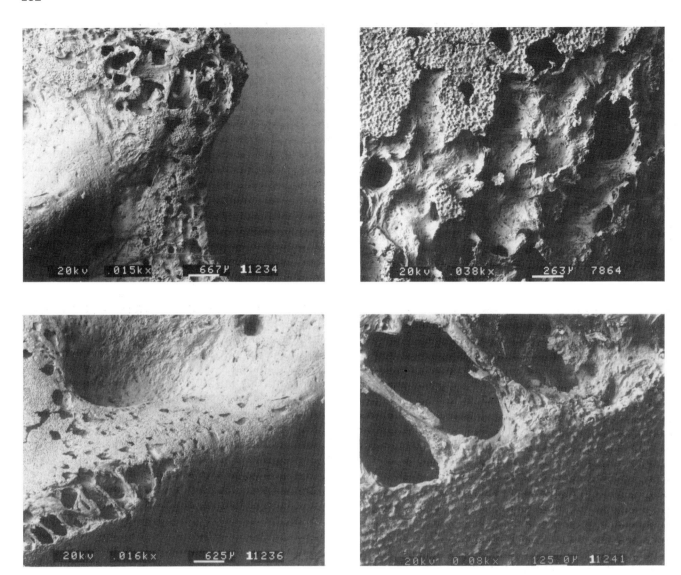

Figure 11.10 (top left)   Juvenile sheep metacarpal, specimen 3109. Bone loss along epiphyseal margin. ×15
Figure 11.11 (top right)   Juvenile sheep metacarpal, specimen 3109. Loss of compact bone from condyle. ×38
Figure 11.12 (bottom left)   Juvenile sheep metacarpal, specimen 3109. Bone loss along keel of condyle. ×16
Figure 11.13 (bottom right)   Juvenile sheep metacarpal, specimen 3109. Detail of Figure 11.12. ×80

from the cancellous bone underlying the compact bone of the articular surface of the condyle. Almost all of the compact bone from the distal shaft of the adult metacarpal had been lost as a consequence of channelling.

The dissolution of the bone by channelling is attributed to the action of saprophytic fungi. Luxuriant growth of fungal mycelium around the bones was observed during the excavation and some hyphae were still present upon specimen 3109 after placement in the SEM (Fig 11.17). Fungal hyphae were also observed growing along the surface of the bone and penetrating vascular canals, while fungal spores were seen on the anterior aspect of specimen 3109.

One of the interesting features of the damage caused by fungal channelling is that it is spatially discrete. Figure 11.18 shows that the division between bone damaged by channelling is quite marked, with the articular surface of the condyle unaffected,

whereas the surface of the compact bone covering the shaft has been almost totally destroyed. This suggests that structural differences between the articular surface of the condyle and non-articular surfaces have played a determining role in the destruction of bone by fungi.

One further modification observed from the surface of both metacarpals was the presence of 'cuffs' of bone surrounding the rim of vascular canals (Fig 11.19). These are identified as hypermineralized rims formed by the redeposition of dissolved hydroxyapatite (Hackett 1981; Piepenbrink 1989). This interpretation is supported by electron probe analysis which showed that the chemical composition of these rims is indistinguishable from the surrounding bone (Williams pers comm). It is possible that these cuffs were produced as a consequence of fungal action (Piepenbrink 1989), but micro-organisms such as bacteria could also be implicated.

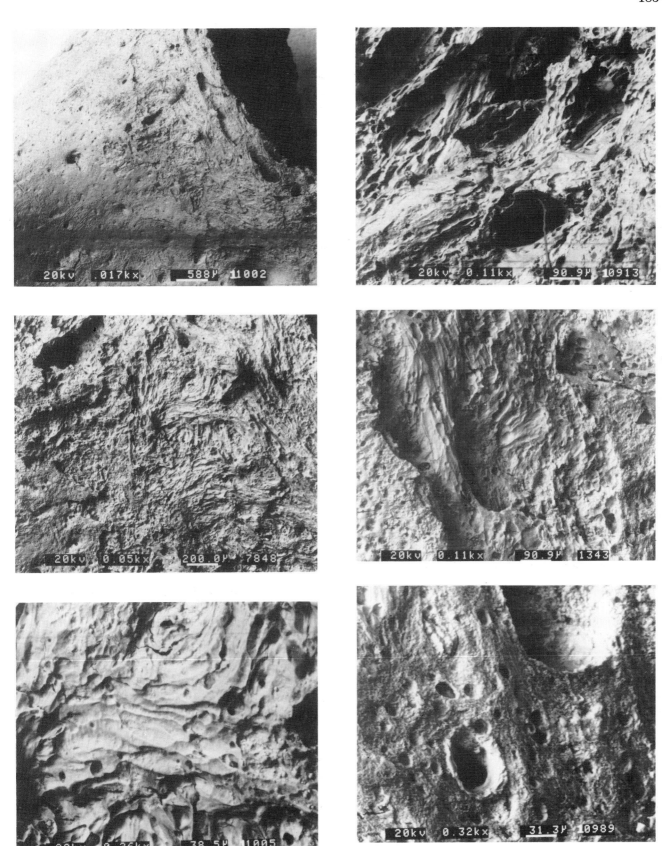

Figure 11.14 Juvenile sheep metacarpal, specimen 3109. Bone loss around epiphyseal margin. ×17
Figure 11.15 Juvenile sheep metacarpal, specimen 3109. Channelling caused by fungal hyphae. ×50
Figure 11.16 Juvenile sheep metacarpal, specimen 3109. Detail of Figure 11.15. ×260

Figure 11.17 Mature sheep metacarpal, specimen 3090. Fungal hyphae penetrating cancellous bone. ×110
Figure 11.18 Mature sheep metacarpal, specimen 3090. Differential preservation of bone from the articular surface and shaft. ×110
Figure 11.19 Juvenile sheep metacarpal, specimen 3109. Hypermineralized rim. ×320

184

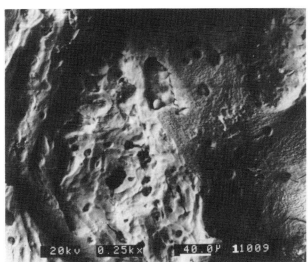

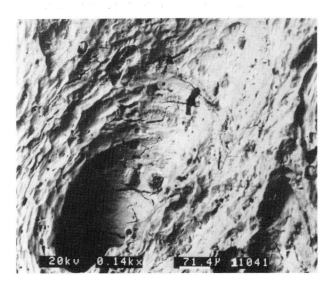

Extraneous objects adhering to the surface of the metacarpals

Faecal pellets were present upon the surface of both metacarpals and these measured approximately 60 microns in length. Figure 11.20 shows a group of faecal pellets upon the anterior aspect of the epiphysis of the juvenile metacarpal. These pellets could not be identified but it seems possible that they were deposited by arthropods, such as mites, as these were observed crawling over the surface of the bone at the time of excavation.

Numerous eggs were observed adhering to the surface of specimens 3109 and 3090 and these had an average length of 12 microns (Fig 11.21). These have not been identified.

Aggregates of crystals, generally spherical in form and measuring between 20 to 40 microns were common upon the surface of both metacarpals and could also be seen within vascular canals (Figs 11.22 and 11.23). Crystal aggregates have been recorded from the surface and intracortical areas of bone and may be the waste products of invading organisms or secondary minerals formed during bone diagensis (Molleson 1990). The mineral composition of these crystals was not uniform, which could suggest that they are of non-biological origin (Williams pers comm).

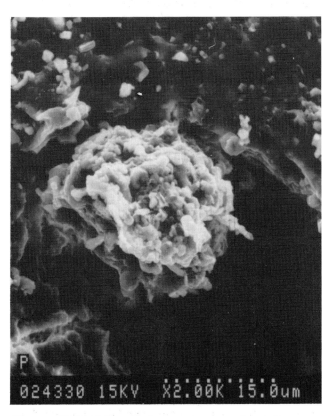

Figure 11.20 Juvenile sheep metacarpal, specimen 3109. Faecal pellets. ×100
Figure 11.21 Juvenile sheep metacarpal, specimen 3109. Egg. ×250
Figure 11.22 Mature sheep metacarpal, specimen 3090. Crystal aggregates in vascular canal. ×140

Figure 11.23 Mature sheep metacarpal, specimen 3090. Crystal aggregate. ×2000

Discussion

Analyses of the two sheep metacarpals recovered from the 1992 excavation at Overton Down has shown that there was extensive surface modification to the surface of the bones caused by physical and biological agencies. Physical processes included abrasions probably caused by the consolidation of the chalk and flint substrate, cracking of bone due to changes in relative humidity and temperature and bone loss caused by leaching or percolation. Modifications, attributed to biological agencies, included cutmarks caused by humans, and channelling formed by the action of saprophytic fungi. All of these modifications were superficial, and there was no breakage or major damage apparent from SEM analysis.

Bone loss is apparently correlated both with developmental age and histological structure of the sample bones. The degree of surface modification on specimen 3109 is low for an immature bone, and specifically it is less than was observed on the mature bone specimen 3090. Since immature bones have low specific gravity, are less ossified and are relatively porous, they generally become modified within a few years when exposed to surface weathering. On the other hand, in bones located in acid conditions, surface loss is greater in mature bones because of their greater mineralization. This suggests that the greater surface modification of specimen 3090 can be attributed to acid attack, although there is the additional factor for this specimen of it having been cooked. It is not known what long term effects this may have had. Damage on both bones is mainly present on the side of the bone facing up after burial, and this further suggests that the modification has been caused by percolating water. It is also concentrated on the articular surface and epiphysis, both of which project above the general level of bone and are therefore more exposed to the effects of the environment.

Certain patterns of bone loss or alteration seem to be linked to histological structure. Cracking of bone was only visible on the articular surface of the mature condyle, and channelling damage caused by fungi was confined to the non-articular surface of the metacarpals. This supports the findings of Hanson and Buistra (1987) who have shown that secondary Haversian bone is mechanically weaker than interstitial and circumferential lamellar bone.

The conditions of burial within the earthwork at Overton Down replicate those found in many prehistoric earthworks on the chalk downland of southern England. The results of this study suggest that the local environment of the chalk bank was not favourable for bone preservation and that the metacarpals would not survive long at the present rate of destruction. It can be predicted that the level of damage after another 32 or even 64 years would not be substantially greater than it is at present, but the longer term survival of the bones in these conditions is poor. Faunal assemblages retrieved from comparable sites appear to have suffered extensive loss of weak or susceptible bone and this limits their value for palaeoenvironmental or palaeodietary studies.

Acknowledgements

We are very grateful for help from Sue Barnes, Chris Jones, Louise Jones, Pat Hart and Nick Hayes in the SEM Unit (Natural History Museum, London), and Phil Crabbe of the Photographic Unit (National History Museum, London). John Spratt kindly assisted with the preparation of samples and Terry Williams undertook the electron microprobe analyses. Special thanks are due to Simon Hillson, Theya Molleson and Terry Williams for discussing and improving the content of this report.

11.3 A Scanning Electron Microscope study of bone, cement, dentine and enamel
by Simon Hillson and Sandra Bond

Specimens examined

The cooked (3090) and uncooked (3109) sheep metapodials from the chalk environment were sectioned approximately at mid-shaft. A complete slice some 1–2mm thick was taken.

The cooked (3160) and uncooked (3173) sheep mandibles from the turf environment were sectioned at roughly the middle of the ramus. Again a complete slice some 1–2mm thick was removed. In addition, the loose second deciduous premolar of 3173, and second permanent premolar of 3160 were removed complete. For the purposes of later discussion it should be emphasized that the uncooked specimen (3173) represented a much less mature animal than the cooked specimen (3160).

Small fragments of burned human bone were also collected, from the chalk environment (3093) and the turf environment (3166). In both cases small fragments of cortical bone were simply lifted out with forceps.

Sectioning was carried out with a clean, flamed, hacksaw blade at the same time as samples were taken for biochemical analysis. The specimens destined for microscopic study were immediately placed in sealed bottles of 70% ethanol, which is the normal procedure for histological samples of bone (Boyde et al 1986).

Methods of specimen preparation and microscopy

The specimens were all embedded in polymethylmethacrylate, using a procedure derived from that outlined in Bell (1990) and Boyde et al (1986). The specimens were dehydrated in a series of alcohols to absolute ethanol and were then left in methylmethacrylate monomer (from which the stabilizer had been washed) with 5% styrene monomer. A catalyst was then added (0.2% 2,2′ azo bis methylproprionitrile) and the mixture polymerized at 32°C. The solidified blocks were cut on a Buehler Isomet slow speed saw, using a wafering blade. The cut surface was then polished on a series of silicon carbide abrasive papers and finally on diamond laps down to 1mm grade. At each stage, as little polishing as possible was carried out in order to reduce the amount of surface relief produced on the specimen, as features of different hardness were abraded. For similar reasons, the abrasive papers were placed upon hard surfaces and the diamond laps were based on thin plastic sheets mounted on steel discs.

The technique used for examination was Scanning Electron Microscopy. For a general text on the method see Goldstein et al (1992). The polished surfaces were coated with carbon. They were then examined in a Hitachi S570 scanning electron microscope equipped with a 4 segment solid state backscattered electron detector (K E Developments). The microscope was operated at an accelerating voltage of 20 kV and the backscattered (BSE) detector was operated in two modes by appropriate switching of its four segments. In compositional mode it could be used to emphasize contrasts of atomic number and density within the specimen in a very thin layer (1μm or so thick) at the polished section surface. The BSE signal, however, is also affected by any slight surface undulations, so to check for this effect, the detector was also switched into topographical mode for each position of examination. All photographic images thus came in pairs with a compositional and a topographic version.

Rationale for BSE examination of bone and dental tissues

The method first proposed by Boyde and Jones (1983) is based upon the density differences which are found in bone and other mineralized tissues (Boyde et al 1986). The more heavily mineralized parts generate a higher BSE signal and thus appear brighter in the image which is produced. This effect is enhanced because such areas are also more resistant to the effect of polishing and therefore tend to stand up slightly higher than the surrounding less heavily mineralized material. This has an additional effect in the compositional mode of detector operation and is distinguishable in the topographic mode. These contrasts not only allow the characteristic features of each mineralized tissue's structure to be made out, but also allow diagenetic effects to be detected (Bell 1990; Bell et al, 1991). Demineralization by microorganisms and other soil forming processes can readily be seen, as can the secondary deposition of minerals, out of solution from the ground water which percolated through the specimen.

BSE imaging is therefore the method of choice for assessing the overall amount of tissue disruption by diagenetic effects. It has the added advantage that it only requires polished surfaces to be prepared. For archaeological material, it is much more difficult to prepare reliably the thin sections which are needed for transmitted light microscopy.

Features of bone

Scattered through the bone are osteocyte lacunae, which are the spaces occupied in life by flattened cells some 20μm long, 10μm wide and 5μm thick. Radiating out from the floor and roof of these lacunae are tiny tunnels known as canaliculae. All these are either present as spaces, or filled with polymethylmethacrylate resin in the preparation technique described above, and so are seen as dark features in BSE images. The dominant features of mature bone are concentric layered features known as osteones, which have a central canal surrounded by bone lamellae. Osteones are typically 100–300μm in diameter. The central canal is usually occupied by resin and thus shows as dark in the BSE image. The layering of the lamellae is also frequently visible and this is due, not so much to differences between lamellae in their density, but to differences in the orientation of collagen fibres in the different layers. This causes a differential pattern of wear when the surface is polished and some lamellae stand up slightly higher than others, giving rise to topographic effects which are visible in both forms of BSE image. Also visible are fragments of earlier osteones which have been cut into by the formation of new osteones. These are called interstitial lamellae. Finally, near the surface of the bone, circumferential lamella bone is laid down without following the concentric osteone pattern. In later adult life, this is disrupted by the cutting of new osteones into it. Once again, the different directions of collagen fibres within the lamellae gives rise to topographic contrast, even when there is little density contrast within an area of bone. When an osteone or an area of circumferential lamella bone is formed it is not immediately fully mineralized and the process of maturation takes some months. In any one field of view, there are therefore also density contrasts between different osteones, interstitial lamellae, and circumferential lamella bone units which reflect how recently they were formed.

Bell (1990; Bell et al 1991) carried out BSE examination of both archaeological bone specimens, and bone specimens from a general anatomy department collection which had been handled for some years by students. In both cases, large areas of circumferential lamella bone had apparently fractured away. The archaeological specimens were further marked by irregular foci of changed density, each between 20–150μm across. These were delimited by a clear boundary of increased density but, within this, they were highly variable. Some were very dense, perhaps from the secondary deposition of

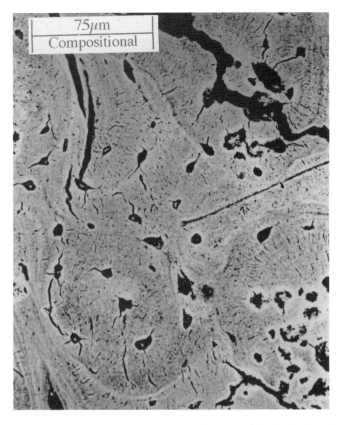
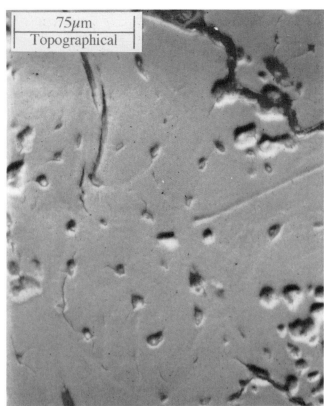

Figure 11.24 Uncooked sheep metacarpal shaft (3109) from the chalk environment. Field of view is deep within the layer of cortex

Note: Figures 11.24–11.38. All pictures were taken in a Hitachi S570 Scanning Electron Microscope, operated in backscattered electron mode. Each figure consists of a pair of photographs, the left hand picture being taken in compositional mode and the right hand in topographic mode

minerals from groundwater, whilst others had a much lower density than the surrounding bone. The areas immediately underlying the bone surfaces were particularly affected in this way, but the canals at the centre of osteones often acted as additional centres for these changes. In some cases large areas of unaltered bone could be seen in between patches of the foci, but many specimens showed almost total disruption of structure. Another effect seen both in the modern and archaeological specimens was cracking. This may have been an artefact of the specimen preparation procedure, but in the archaeological material the foci often appeared to be related to the crack lines. It may well be that they are formed as part of the process of diagenetic change in bone.

Uncooked bone specimens from Overton Down

The section of sheep metacarpal shaft (3109) from the chalk environment showed large areas of unaltered cortical bone (Fig 11.24). There was, however, extensive cracking right through the thickness of cortical bone and even in the centre there were scattered foci of altered density. At the surface (Fig 11.25), large areas of circumferential lamella bone had been lost, and there was a higher concentration of foci of

changed density, which were frequently associated with cracking.

The sheep mandible ramus section (3173) from the turf environment showed much less alteration to the interior part of the cortical bone (Fig 11.26). There was, however, a certain amount of cracking. Even an area of delicate plexiform bone (Fig 11.27), which represented new growth at the posterior border of the ramus, was unaltered internally. At the surface (Fig 11.28), the circumferential lamella bone, which would be expected away from the rapidly growing border, was not present and there were scattered areas of foci of changed density. All in all, however, this specimen was rather less affected than 3109.

Cooked bone specimens from Overton Down

The sheep metacarpal from the chalk environment (3090) showed very little alteration to its internal structure, with very clear osteones, lamellae and osteocyte lacunae. There was, however, very extensive cracking along lines of weakness. At the surface (Fig 11.30) there was little evidence of circumferential lamella bone and there were scattered areas of foci of changed density. There was also cracking, particularly running between the foci.

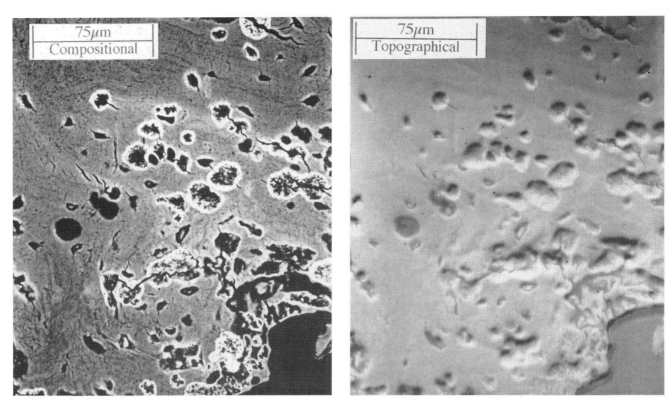

Figure 11.25 Uncooked sheep metacarpal shaft (3109) from the chalk environment. Field of view is at the outside of the cortex, with the boundary between the bone and the resin in which the specimen is mounted at the bottom right corner

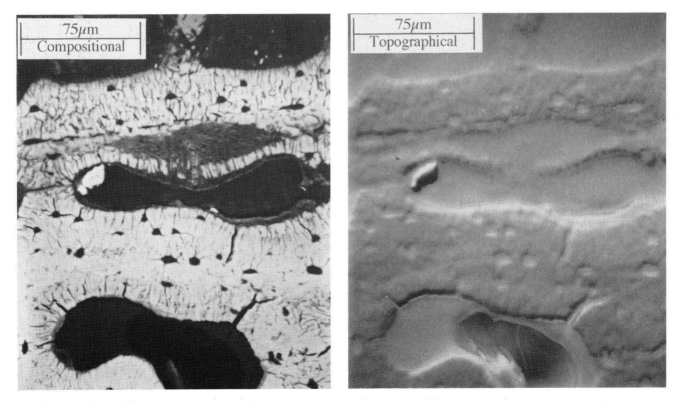

Figure 11.26 Sheep mandible ramus (3173) from the turf environment. Field of view is deep within the compact cortical part of the bone

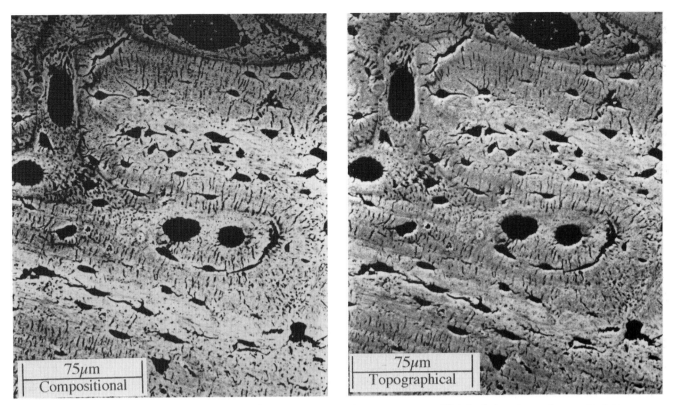

Figure 11.27 Sheep mandible ramus (3173) from the turf environment. Field of view is at the posterior border of the ramus, and shows an area of plexiform bone, of a type which is common in mid-sized mammals such as sheep

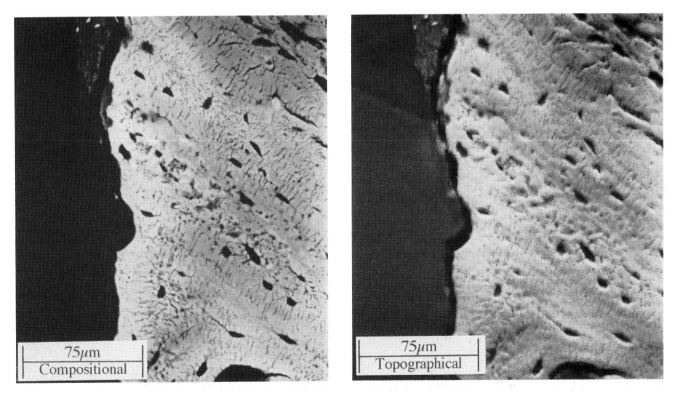

Figure 11.28 Sheep mandible ramus (3173) from the turf environment. Field of view is at the outer edge of the compact cortical bone, and the dark area on the left hand side of the pictures represents the embedding medium

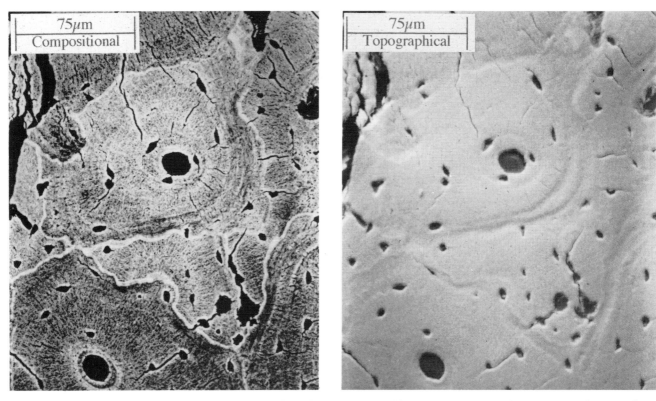

Figure 11.29 Cooked sheep metacarpal shaft (3090) from the chalk environment. Field of view is deep in the layer of cortex

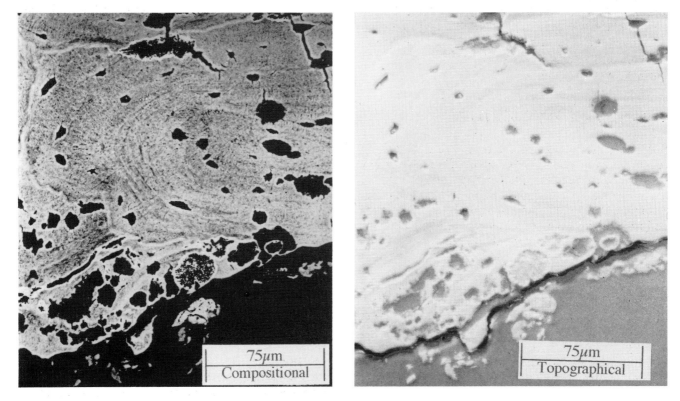

Figure 11.30 Cooked sheep metacarpal shaft (3090) from the chalk environment. Field of view is at the edge of the cortex and the dark area in the lower quarter of the pictures is the embedding resin

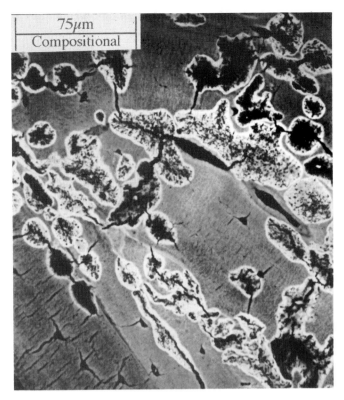
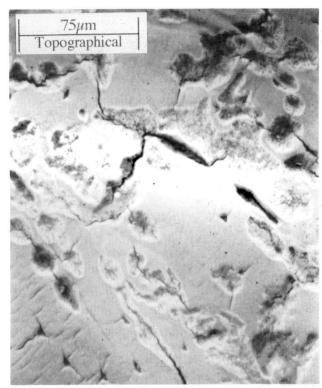

Figure 11.31 Cooked sheep mandible ramus (3160) from the buried soil. Field of view includes both deep and surface areas of cortex, with the surface of the bone in the bottom left corner

The section of mandible ramus from the turf environment (3160) was much more strongly affected by foci of altered density, which appeared particularly to follow a network of cracks (Fig 11.31). In this specimen there were larger areas of circumferential lamella bone at the surface (Fig 11.32) than 3090 and there were still areas of little altered bone in between the disrupted regions.

Burned bone from Overton Down

Both specimens (Fig 11.33 and 11.34) had been considerably altered by the process of burning, which produced a rather granular texture throughout. The appearance fits well with the experimental results of Shipman *et al* (1984), who suggested that recrystallization and sintering of mineral crystals lead to the formation of a roughened texture. Some elements of normal structure, however, could be made out in both specimens from Overton Down, including the outlines of osteones, canals and even osteocyte lacunae. Neither the specimens from the chalk (3093) nor the turf (3166) environments showed much evidence of post-burial alteration. There were no foci of altered density, although there was some cracking which might have occurred during the process of burning as well as during burial or preparation.

Dental tissues from Overton Down

The second deciduous premolar from the uncooked sheep mandible in the soil environment (3173) showed very few changes which could be ascribed to diagenesis. The enamel was unaltered, as was the dentine – even next to the pulp chamber and root canals (Fig 11.35). The cement showed none (Fig 11.36) of the foci of changed density which were seen in the bone and would be expected in cement (Bell *et al* 1991). In some areas voids were present in the cement, but these had an entirely different appearance and their origin is unclear.

The second permanent premolar from the cooked mandible (3160) was much more affected, with cracking and areas of changed density in dentine and cement (Fig 11.37 and 11.38). These were concentrated in the root, but did spread under the crown, next to the enamel dentine junction.

Discussion

The internal disruption described above matches the surface observations made of 3090 and 3109 by Armour-Chelu and Andrews (p 180). They note both cracking (particularly on articular surfaces), and channelling which they link to the action of fungi which were present at the bone surface. Both specimens showed extensive cracking when examined in section and the foci of changed density seen with BSE are consistent with the finding of destructive activity at the surface. Even in 32 years, however, the process has not penetrated very deeply into the compact bone of the metapodial shaft. Normal bone histology is well preserved inside. The

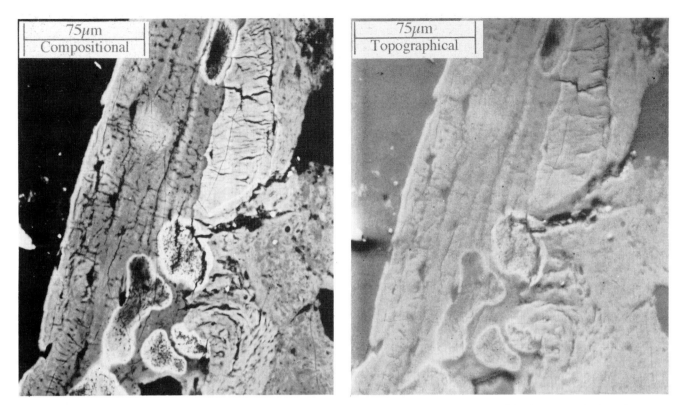

Figure 11.32   Cooked sheep mandible ramus (3160) from the turf environment. Field of view includes the outer edge of the cortex, with the dark area on the left of the photographs representing the embedding resin

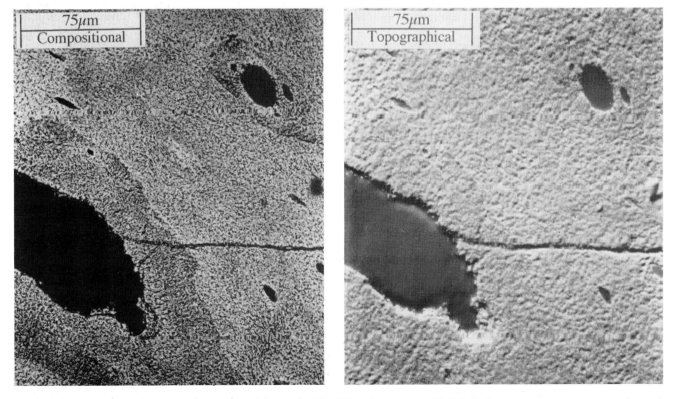

Figure 11.33   Burned human bone (3093) from the chalk environment. Field of view represents an area deep within the bone fragment

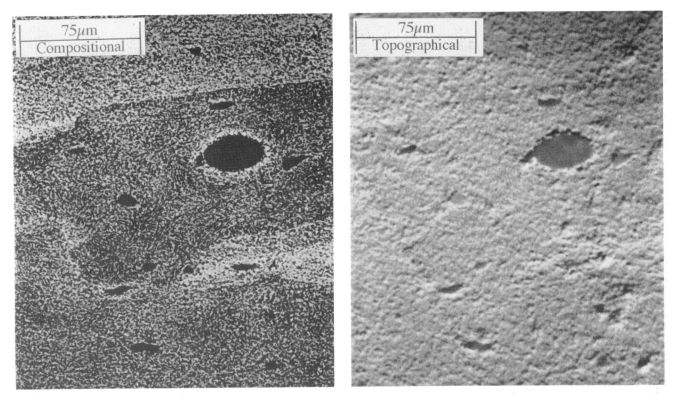

Figure 11.34 Burned human bone from the turf environment (3166). Field of view represents an area deep within the bone fragment

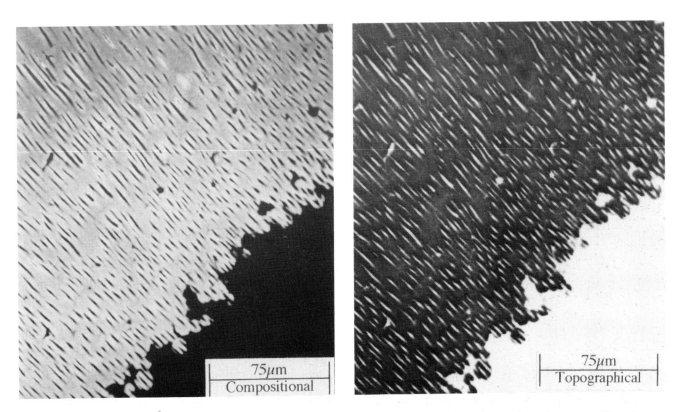

Figure 11.35 Second permanent premolar from the sheep mandible (3173) in the turf environment. Dentine occupies the left two-thirds of the field of view. The dark material is resin occupying the tooth's pulp chamber. The boundary represents the growing dentine edge

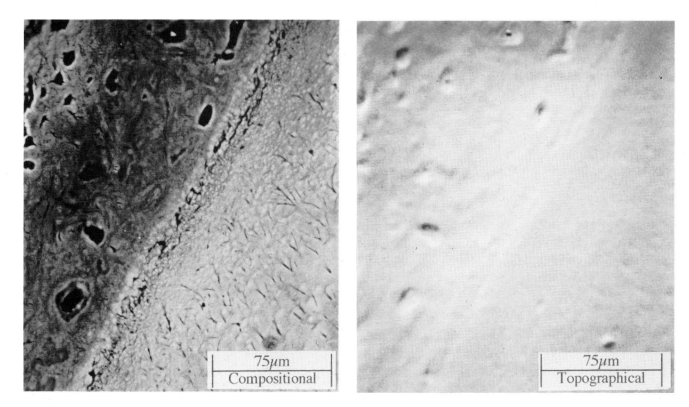

Figure 11.36 *Second permanent premolar from the sheep mandible (3173) in the turf environment. Cement occupies the top left half of the field of view, and dentine the lower right. The cement is slightly less dense than dentine and thus shows as darker*

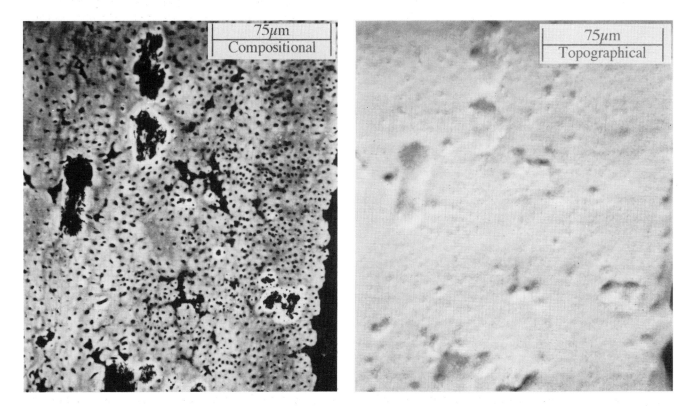

Figure 11.37 *Second permanent molar from the cooked sheep mandible (3160) in the turf environment. Dentine occupies most of the field of view, with its growing edge on the right*

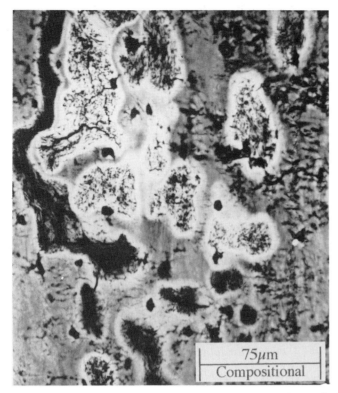 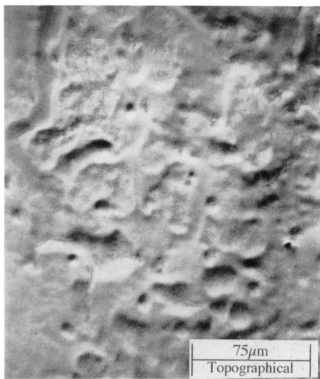

Figure 11.38 Second permanent molar from the cooked sheep mandible (3160) in the turf environment. Field of view shows cement

effect on the more thinly covered cancellous bone of the distal end may have been much more severe, but this has not yet been examined.

The effect of cooking on diagenesis is unclear. In the chalk environment, the uncooked specimen (3109) was more severely affected than the cooked (3090), but there was not a great difference between the two. In the turf environment, it is the cooked specimen (3160) that is more severely affected than the uncooked (3173). At present, therefore, it could not be argued that cooking has any effect one way or the other.

The general impression is that all specimens are to some extent affected by both cracking and alterations which may be due to the action of microorganisms. These organisms are still active and viable (see Kelley & Wiltshire, p 148), but it is unclear whether or not they will induce extensive further changes.

11.4 Phosphate migration around buried bones
by J Crowther

Of all soil chemical properties, total phosphate (phosphate-P) is the one which has perhaps been used most widely in archaeological site investigation (see Proudfoot 1976; Hamond 1983; Gurney 1985). Phosphates are significant in that: (i) they occur in all organic matter, including plant material, excreta and bone; and (ii) they tend to become 'fixed' in the form of relatively insoluble compounds within the mineral fraction of the soil as they are released

during organic decomposition. As a consequence, former patterns of human activity across an archaeological site may remain detectable for up to several millennia. Since bones are particularly phosphate-rich, comprising typically c 60% of the mineral hydroxyapatite [$Ca_5(PO_4)_3OH$], the technique has often be applied in the study of inhumation sites (eg Keeley *et al* 1977; Crowther 1992) and cremation sites (eg Crowther 1993). Whilst the chemistry of soil fixation is well-understood, little is known about the actual rate at which soil in the immediate vicinity of buried bone becomes enriched in phosphate, both in terms of the concentrations reached and the distance over which the effect of phosphate enrichment can be detected. The objective of the present study was therefore to determine phosphate-P concentrations in the chalk rubble and soil immediately surrounding some of the buried bones. The work has added interest because of the detailed SEM work on surface modification of two of the bones undertaken by Armour-Chelu and Andrews (p 178).

In all, 10 bones were investigated: 5 from within the chalk environment and 5 from the turf environment. In each case small bulk samples of rubble/soil were taken in 5 or 10mm slices (depending upon ease of sampling) along lines extending horizontally, or vertically downwards, from the bone. Phosphate-P was determined by alkaline oxidation with NaOBr using the method described by Dick and Tabatabai (1977).

The two environments in which the bones were buried are very different, and this has important implications in terms of both the weathering of hydroxyapatite and subsequent phosphate migration. On theoretical grounds, conditions within the chalk of the bank would appear to be particularly unfavourable for both processes, for three reasons. First, the chalk matrix and groundwaters seeping through it are alkaline (pH of chalk, 1:2.5 water = 8.3) and calcium-rich. Under these circumstances, hydroxyapatite has a low solubility (Lindsay 1979). Moreover, relatively insoluble calcium phosphates will tend to form around the edges of the bone and within the adjacent soil, thereby 'stabilizing' the bone (White and Hannus 1983) and reducing the rate of phosphate diffusion through the soil. Secondly, because of the general lack of organic material within the chalk, the level and range of microbial activity is likely to be somewhat limited – micro-organisms being important agencies in dissolving phosphate through the secretion of acids. Thirdly, whilst earthworm casts were found in association with the bones within the bank (p 85), it does seem likely that earthworm activity will be more limited here than on the old land surface, thereby restricting the redistribution of any phosphate which is chemically or physically released from the bone.

By comparison, conditions on the old ground surface would appear to be much more favourable for the release and movement of phosphate. The soil is decalcified and has a pH of 5.4–6.1 – conditions in which hydroxyapatite is much more soluble (Lindsay 1979) and which are optimum for phosphate diffusion within the soil (Brady 1974). Also, there are larger and more active microbial and earthworm populations.

The analytical results are generally in keeping with the principles outlined above. In the case of the chalk bank (Fig 11.39), four of the sites (bone 3115 being the exception) show detectable signs of phosphate-P enrichment against background concentrations of c 0.4–0.7mg g^{-1}. Bone 3108 displayed the highest level of enrichment, with concentrations of 1.26 and 0.924mg g^{-1}, respectively, at distances of 0–10 and 10–20mm. From the SEM studies (p 178), abrasion of the bone during compaction of the chalk and flint rubble, and dissolution by saprophytic fungi are identified as the two principal agencies responsible for the release of phosphate from the bone. In relation to the latter of these, it should be noted that the micro-environment within bones might be much more acidic than the surrounding soil as a result of hydrogen ions released directly and indirectly, via carbon dioxide, during microbial decomposition of collagen – the principal organic component of bones (White and Hannus 1983). It should also be noted that recent work on bone from the British Camp shell midden on San Juan Island, Washington, USA has suggested that, contrary to normal expectations, substantial weathering of bone specimens is detectable in deposits with pH ≥ 8.4 (Linse 1992). Thus, some migration of phosphate is detectable within the chalk bank, and this is in keeping with other findings. For the most part, however, it is limited in both magnitude (typically

c 0.2–0.3mg g^{-1}) and extent (rarely extending beyond 10mm from the bone).

In contrast, the soils of the old ground surface show much higher levels of phosphate-P enrichment (Fig 11.40). In some cases, concentrations in excess of 3.0mg g^{-1} (cf. background concentrations of c 2.0mg g^{-1}) were recorded in samples closest to the bone, and generally there is evidence of enhanced phosphate at 10–20mm. The horizontal transect sampled from bone 3160 is particularly interesting in that it passes through bone 3165. Here, high levels of phosphate-P are present between the two bones (minimum, 2.66mg g^{-1}), despite the bones being 50mm apart.

The above results show that even in a chalk downland environment, where conditions are generally considered favourable for bone preservation, migration of phosphate from buried bones is clearly detectable after 32 years of burial, not only on the old ground surface, but also within the chalk bank. In due course, the 1995 Wareham Excavation will provide interesting comparative data. In this much more acidic environment, no visible traces of the buried bones were found in the previous (16 year) excavation (p 222), and it will be an extremely valuable test of phosphate analysis to see whether the former presence of bones remains detectable after 32 years and, if so, what degree of phosphate migration is evident.

11.5 A note on work in progress on the DNA content and other diagenetic aspects of Overton Down bone
by R E M Hedges, M B Richards and B C Sykes

Introduction

The purpose of this note is to place on record studies which are still in their preliminary state, and cannot be completed in time for publication. We invite enquiries at any time concerning this work, and plan to publish the results when completed (for example in *Journal of Archaeological Science*).

DNA studies

We plan to quantify the abundance of *amplifiable* indigenous DNA (Richards *et al* forthcoming). Although indigenous DNA has been unambiguously detected in a range of archaeological bone, its quantitation is not straightforward, but should, we believe, be done on such 'reference' material as Overton Down. Most detected ancient DNA from bone has been from mitochondria, since in living tissues mtDNA is present in about 1000 times the amount of nuclear DNA. Usually a length of about 200 base pairs of mtDNA is chosen for amplification, as in general it appears that longer lengths do not

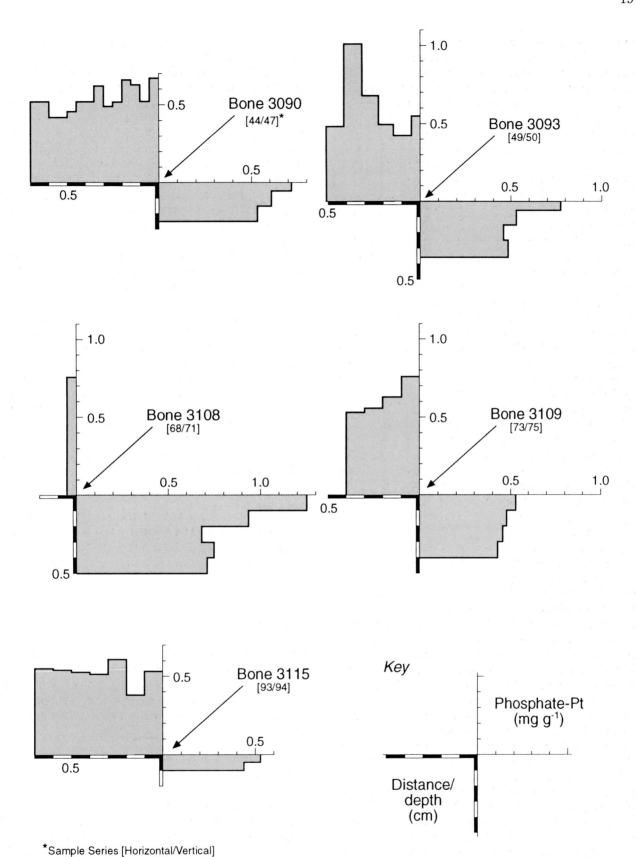

*Sample Series [Horizontal/Vertical]

Figure 11.39 Vertical and horizontal phosphate migration from bones in the chalk environment

198

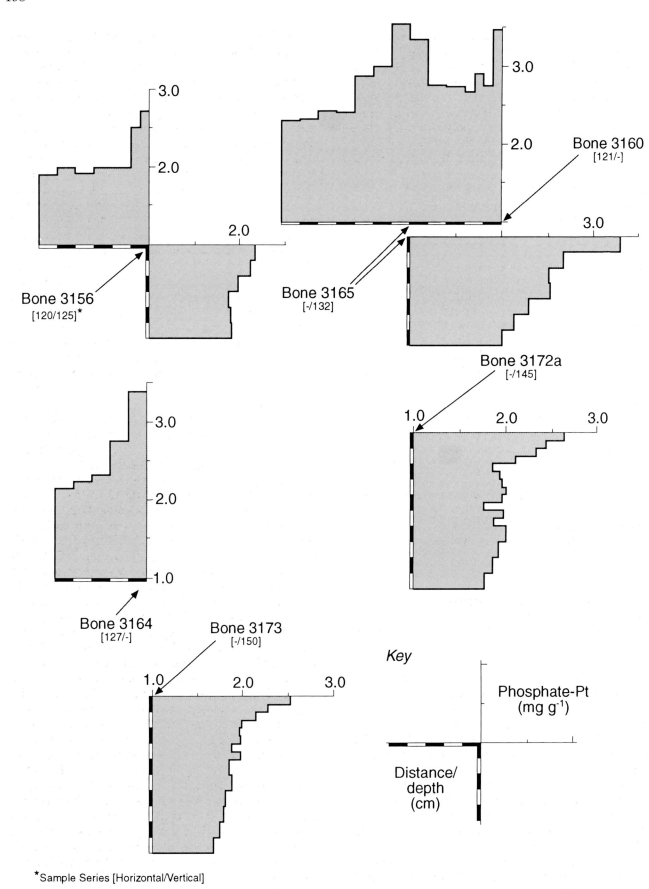

Bone 3156
[120/125]*

Bone 3160
[121/-]

Bone 3165
[-/132]

Bone 3172a
[-/145]

Bone 3164
[127/-]

Bone 3173
[-/150]

Key

Phosphate-Pt
(mg g⁻¹)

Distance/
depth
(cm)

*Sample Series [Horizontal/Vertical]

Figure 11.40 Vertical and horizontal phosphate migration from bones in the turf environment

survive intact. Given the recent age of the Overton Down material, we might well expect longer lengths to survive in this case, and we shall be investigating this. Furthermore, it may well be possible to quantify nuclear DNA survival. Nuclear DNA contains many single copy sequences of genetic interest, for example sex-specific genes and highly polymorphic regions (VNTRs), and knowledge of the extent to which nuclear DNA is recoverable after 32 years of burial will be very valuable.

A second aspect of this work is to quantify the degree of human contamination (if any) of the excavated animal bone.

Diagenetic studies

We are measuring the surviving DNA (which we expect to be more abundant than from longer buried archaeological material) as part of a larger study which seeks to relate the quantity of residual DNA to other diagenetic parameters of bone (Hedges *et al* forthcoming). In particular, we shall relate the DNA to the extent of micromorphological destruction due to microbiological attack, to levels of surviving collagen, and to such physical parameters as porosity change and crystallinity change and put this into the context of other archaeological bone data. Very little is known at present as to how well correlated these changes are.

A related area of study is to understand how the degree of diagenetic change in bone is related to the local hydrological conditions (Hedges and Millard 1995), although these are not well documented for Overton Down.

11.6 Chemical structure of DNA in bone from Overton Down
by Terence A Brown, Kerry O'Donoghue and Keri A Brown

The existence of preserved (or 'ancient') DNA in archaeological bones, first reported by Hagelberg *et al* (1989) and subsequently confirmed by a variety of other research groups (eg Horai *et al* 1989; Hänni *et al* 1990; Thuesen and Engberg 1990; Williams *et al* 1990), has generated a great deal of interest, as it has opened up the possibility of applying genetic techniques to the direct examination of a widespread and plentiful archaeological resource. Already there have been demonstrations of the potential of ancient bone DNA in sex determination (Hummel and Herrmann 1991), population studies (Horai *et al* 1991; Hagelberg and Clegg 1993) and kinship analysis (Hagelberg *et al* 1991) in projects directly or indirectly relevant to archaeology.

Although remarkable progress is being made in the genetic analysis of ancient DNA, these investigations are being carried out against a background of uncertainty regarding the physical and chemical nature of the material being analysed. This uncer-

tainty is so great that a leading DNA biochemist has expressed doubt over the veracity of certain spectacular reports of ancient DNA in palaeontological fossils (Lindahl 1993). The scepticism arises from the difficulties in rationalizing the demonstrations of DNA in an ever-increasing range of archaeological and palaeontological material with our knowledge of the rate of degradation of DNA in aqueous solution (reviewed by Lindahl 1993), the latter suggesting that after a few thousand years any DNA preserved in a bone or other fossil should be too degraded to yield meaningful genetic information. The simplest resolution of this dilemma is to assume that in a fossil the degradation of DNA can be slowed down, because of protective effects conferred by the microenvironment within which the DNA is contained. Dehydrated and/or oxygen-free conditions could conceivably protect DNA from degradation, as could absorption of the molecules onto an inorganic matrix, such as could occur in bone. However, these suggestions are purely speculative and the limited amount of relevant experimental evidence suggests that on their own they would be insufficient to cause more than a one-half reduction in the rate of DNA degradation (Lindahl 1993).

These questions are important as the chemical state of ancient DNA has a direct bearing on the degree of confidence that can be assigned to the genetic studies. The genetic information that enables us to study populations, kinship, etc, is contained in the sequence of monomeric units (called 'nucleotides') in the polymeric DNA molecule. There are four different nucleotides, generally referred to by the abbreviations A, T, G and C. A DNA molecule with the nucleotide sequence ATGGGATACCAATAG possesses a genetic meaning that is quite different from a molecule of sequence ATGGGATAACAATAG, in the same way that COM*M*UTER has a different meaning to COM*P*UTER in the English language. When we carry out an experiment to read a nucleotide sequence it is therefore critically important that our techniques provide us with the correct sequence and not one in which letters have been left out or changed. The problem with ancient DNA is that the degradative processes predicted from chemical studies would result in changes that would cause misreadings when the DNA is analysed by nucleotide sequencing techniques. The sources of two types of error are shown in Figure 11.41. In example (b) the distinguishing chemical component (the 'base') of one of the nucleotides has become detached, resulting in a letter being inserted at random during the reading process. High temperatures and/or acidic conditions result in loss of bases, especially A and G, from DNA in aqueous solutions, with a slow rate of detachment occurring even at ambient temperatures. Over the years the accumulation of this type of damage would result in ancient DNA molecules in which a high proportion of the letters are missing, and which would therefore be read incorrectly during the sequencing procedure. Heat, as well as oxidation and radiation, can also result in the second type of

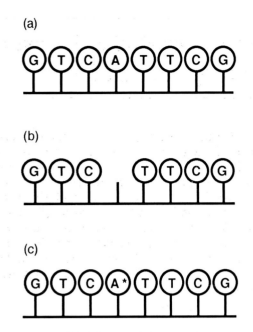

(a)

(b)

(c)

Figure 11.41 Two sources of error that may arise during nucleotide sequence analysis as a result of chemical damage to the ancient DNA being studied. The original, undamaged DNA molecule is shown in part (a). In (b) a nucleotide base has become detached; the sequencing procedure will insert an A, T, G or C at random at this position. In (c) a nucleotide base has become modified to a related chemical version, designated here as A*; depending on the chemical nature of the modification, this nucleotide may still be read as A, or may be misread as one of the other nucleotides

error shown in Figure 11.41 (c). Here the base remains attached but has become modified into a different chemical structure. The sequencing technique may read this modified base correctly (eg A* read as A) but more frequently the modification will result in a misreading; for example, the heat-induced removal of the -NH₂ group from C results in this nucleotide being read as T.

An extreme view would be that, because of these factors, all nucleotide sequences obtained from ancient DNA are uncertain and that hypotheses based on these sequences are of questionable validity. In fact most ancient sequences do appear to make genetic

sense, suggesting that the extreme view is unwarranted, but this does not lessen the desirability of a more complete understanding of the chemical nature of ancient DNA. So far there have been only three reports in which the chemical state of ancient DNA has been investigated (Pääbo 1989; Golenberg 1991; Rollo *et al* 1993), and each of these has utilized a technique – high performance liquid chromatography (HPLC) – that is not entirely suitable for the task. HPLC enables the extent of damage present in a DNA sample to be assessed, but does not allow the chemical nature of the damage to be determined with precision. Importantly, it is very difficult by HPLC to identify the second type of damage shown in Figure 11.41 – modification of the nucleotide base. The identification of these modifications is the most important objective as they may enable us to determine which environmental factors are important in diagenesis of preserved DNA, and possibly to speculate about the nature of any protection provided by the fossil microenvironment.

In our project we are using gas chromatography linked with mass spectrometry (GC-MS) to study the chemical nature of ancient DNA. GC-MS is a more sensitive and informative technique than HPLC, and should enable us to make reliable identifications of modified nucleotides present in ancient material. However, the technique has not been routinely applied to DNA, and so the first year of our project has been devoted to developing the necessary procedures. The value of the Overton Down bones in our study lies with the wealth of information that is available about the soil chemistry and microbiology of the site and the changes occurring in these bones as revealed by taphonomic and other studies. This information will provide the framework against which we will attempt to deduce the causes of any nucleotide modifications that we detect in the bone samples. Our results, when available, will be published in the archaeological literature.

Acknowledgements

We are indebted to Dr Richard Evershed of the University of Bristol for his assistance in this project. The research is supported by a grant from the NERC.

12 The earthwork on Morden Bog, Wareham, Dorset 1972 (10th year) – 1990 (27th year) *by S W Hillson*

12.1 Introduction

The experimental bank and ditch at Morden Bog near Wareham in Dorset was built in 1963 and has since been excavated at intervals. This report by the Experimental Earthwork Committee covers the last excavation in 1980 and subsequent analyses of sediments, soils and buried materials. The results are discussed in relation to Bronze Age earthworks on the heathlands of southeast England.

This is the Committee's second report on the Morden Bog Experimental Earthwork. The first (Evans & Limbrey, 1974) dealt with the earthwork's construction (Fig 12.1), with the excavations carried out between 1964 and 1972, and with the examination of buried materials recovered from these excavations. The earthwork consists of a 28m (92ft) bank running parallel with a 29.26m (96ft) ditch, built between 7 and 29 July 1963 in the Morden Bog

National Nature Reserve, 4.8km (3 miles) north-north-west of Wareham, Dorset. The long axis of both bank and ditch was north-north-west / south-south-east (157° true). Heathland vegetation characterizes the site, overlying a typical podzol of the better drained part of the Sollom 2 Association (Findlay *et al* 1984). The bank was constructed mainly of materials taken from the podzol soil profile during the excavation of the ditch, and built up into four contrasting layers, separated by three thin marker layers of roadstone chippings.

12.2 Current vegetation and management of the site

The site has been visited regularly since 1972, both by Committee members and by students of the Dorset Institute of Higher Education (now

Figure 12.1 Experimental Earthwork at Wareham as constructed July 1963

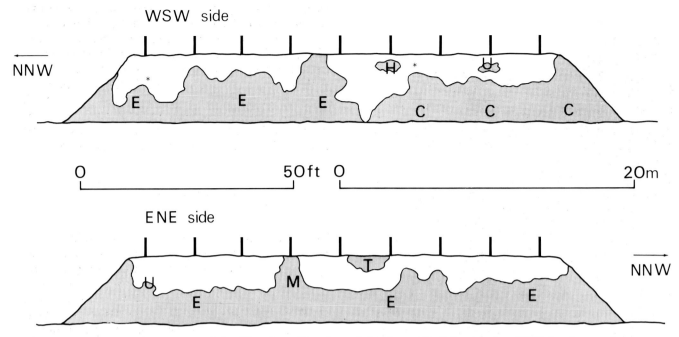

Figure 12.2 *Vegetation survey of the Wareham Earthwork bank on 23rd September 1987 (re-drawn from field notes by Mr J Hemsley). The west-south-west and east-north-east sides are shown in elevation. Vegetated areas are shaded and the unshaded area denotes an unvegetated sandy surface. Key:*
* – *isolated pine* Pinus sylvestris *seedling*
U – *dwarf gorse* Ulex minor
C – *strong growing fringe of heather* Calluna vulgaris *overhanging dwarf gorse*
M – *purple moor grass* Molinia caerulea *mainly at this point*
E – *good cover with mixed bell heather* Erica cinerea, *heather, some purple moor grass and bristle bent grass* Agrostis curtisii
T – *topknot with dwarf gorse, bell heather, bristle bent grass and pine seedling*
H – *heather*

Bournemouth University). A detailed survey of the vegetation cover was carried out by Mr J Hemsley during a Committee meeting at the site on 23 September 1987 and is incorporated here, together with his elevation views of the bank (Fig 12.2). In assessing the results of the survey it should be recalled that, when built 24 years previously, both bank and ditch had bare and sandy surfaces, and the area within which they were constructed had been cleared of vegetation down to the soil surface.

The vegetation of the bank
by J Hemsley

The south-south-east end of the bank carried a full cover of a mixed heath sub-shrub character which would, in some regards, be difficult to distinguish from 'semi-natural' stands of similar vegetation within the general vicinity. Few species were present, with heather (*Calluna vulgaris*) contributing about 30% of the cover, and bell-heather (*Erica cinerea*) 35%, dwarf gorse (*Ulex minor*) 20% and the bristle bent grass (*Agrostis curtisii*) 15%. The well-grown plants of heather, height to 0.50–0.60m, were notably inclined in a down-slope direction. Dwarf gorse, up to about 0.50m in height, was flowering

profusely. A pine (*Pinus sylvestris*) seedling had established itself near the foot of the slope. In general, this plant community made up a mixed mosaic, with no strong trend of segregation due to the slope. The plants were well-grown and healthy, and had formed a reasonably tight closed cover over the entire bank.

The west-south-west side of the bank had a good cover of mixed heathland sub-shrubs along with some grasses, covering up to 60% of the slope, with the greater density in the lower parts. The upper parts however, and most of the earthwork crest, remained bare with a sandy surface. In places, for example nearer the south-east end, there were numerous small scattered seedlings and plantlets which ultimately might develop into part of an established cover, depending upon future seasons and the effects of drought. Also in this section were two larger, discrete clumps of well-established heather and dwarf gorse, along with a larger pine seedling. The general mixed mosaic of heather, bell-heather and dwarf gorse contained both bristle bent grass and purple moor grass (*Molinia caerulea*), along with pine seedlings. A notable feature was the vigour of both the heather and the bell-heather. The former, especially towards the foot of the slope and the old berm, had achieved heights (perhaps better

Figure 12.3 View of the ditch at the time of the Wareham excavation in 1980, showing the vegetation of the ditch floor and the condition of the sides

expressed as lengths, for these plants leant heavily downslope towards the ditch) of up to 1m with thick woody basal stems over 20mm in diameter. Another feature of the woody cover was the manner in which rank heather had overtopped and virtually suppressed dwarf gorse along the upper edge of the ditch. Much of the gorse was still present as a dead layer under heather, its weakly prostrate form having been unable to survive the dense canopy of dominating heather fringing and overhanging the entire length of the ditch margin.

The north-north-west end of the bank had a complete cover mainly of heather, but with some bell-heather, with a canopy height of up to 0.6m. Two pine seedlings were found there along with a single frond of bracken at the extreme north corner. Unlike other aspects of the bank, there was no dwarf gorse, but this plant did occur immediately around the corner on the west-south-west side.

The east-north-east side of the bank, like its counterpart to the west-south-west, had developed a good sub-shrub cover occupying 50% or a little more of the surface in the lower parts. The main species were heather and bell-heather, bristle bent grass and some purple moor grass, mostly confined to one small area. Pine seedlings were frequent and dwarf gorse, al-

though present throughout, was relatively scarce compared with the west-south-west side. Some of the wet-loving cross-leaved heath (*Erica tetralix*) occured along the foot of the bank. As with the west-south-west facing slope, the growth of heather was robust, with occasional plants up to 1m in height. The more general size range, however, was around 0.5–0.6m. A small discrete patch of mixed dwarf gorse, bristle bent grass, bell-heather and some pine seedlings occurred high on the bank in a roughly central position.

The vegetation of the ditch
by J Hemsley

The ditch bottom was fairly well vegetated (Fig 12.3), with some places patchy and the constituent cover species generally somewhat lacking in vigour. The chief plants here were heather, bristle bent grass, purple moor grass and cross-leaved heath. The northern half seemed generally a little more 'grassy' and, about two-thirds of the way along in a north-west/south-east direction, two small willows (probably *Salix atrocinerea*) were noted. Birch seedlings (*Betula pendula*) were noted about half-way along the ditch bottom, with frequent pine, the density of the latter being up to 10 per 90cm^2 (square yard). Parts of the ditch surface carried an algal slime, dry at the time of the visit, which indicated standing water in winter. Mosses and lichens were plentiful throughout, with one of the heathland *Cladonia* species conspicuous. The north-east side of the ditch, flanking the earthwork bank, was now a small 'clifflet', heavily overhung with heather, over dead or moribund dwarf gorse. It seemed very dry and would be protected by the thatching effect of the top over-cover. On the west-south-west side of the ditch the overhang of sub-shrubs, mainly heather, was far less vigorous. Some bell-heather and dwarf gorse also formed a part of this fringe. This was a remnant along the edge of the original heather sub-shrub cover and closely reflected the age and structure of the now over-mature (in terms of the cycle of heathland management by burning) heath nearby, with abundance of lichen and with individual heather plants opening in the centre, some showing collapse and others dying-out or dead. The sloping ramp at the south-south-east end of the ditch carried a weakish lichen cover on sand, bordered by mixed heather and bell-heather. At the north-north-west end, there was a weakish cover of heather, dwarf gorse, bell-heather and a few pine seedlings occupying about half the area. Otherwise, the north-north-west end ramp was also largely open, sandy with a thin lichen cover.

Relationship with general heathland flora
by J Hemsley

The general flora of the area around the site contained little other than what could be seen on the

Figure 12.4 General view of the Wareham 1980 excavation looking to the north

earthwork itself, but there were more fronds of bracken (*Pteridium aquilinum*) not far away from the north-east corner. Also not far from the north-north-west end were a few of the larger European gorse (*Ulex europaeus*). It is a little surprising that none of this invasive species appears to have been on the earthwork, for both this and the bracken could pose some threat of future invasion. Pine seedlings were frequently found. As with much of the heathland, the larger of these (about 0.8–0.9m in height near the earthwork) could form a complete tall woody cover within a relatively few years. New seed apparently arrives from old stands of 'mother' trees west and north-west of the heath in a regular succession.

One of the most notable features of the plant cover of the Wareham Earthwork in 1987 was the great similarity in higher plant species (few in the acidic and nutrient-poor habitat) between the disturbed site of the earthwork and its undisturbed surroundings. So closely did the composition and structure of the earthwork's south-south-east end mirror that of

parts of the heathland nearby, that it could well escape notice as a relatively recent disturbance to the underlying soils. The general vigour of heather, especially along the foot of the west-south-west side of the bank, seemed to exceed almost anything to be observed in the undisturbed heathland of the surrounding area. This effect was probably due to a rise in nutrient levels brought about by additional soil depths and decaying vegetation within the bank structure, perhaps small, but of significance under the conditions of lowland heath and the poor soils of the Wareham area. There may also possibly have been an increase in summer moisture, especially under drought conditions, due to the earth pile and its effect. The manner in which heather had gained supremacy over dwarf gorse along the lower fringe of the bank was a striking feature. The dwarf gorse seemed variable in its stature, depending upon locality, but the low-growing and semi-prostrate version in the Morden Bog area seemed to have been particularly ill-equipped to cope with the prevailing pattern of heather competition. The distribution of the grasses on the site tended to reflect the position and timing of the latest excavation. The bristle bent, in particular, is one of the early heathland colonists in south-west England and establishes relatively quickly, in advance of other plants over the first few years after disturbance.

So far as has been possible, the Committee has left the earthwork and its surrounding area of heathland to develop in its own way. There have, however, been a number of management issues. A certain amount of human disturbance has been noted, from walkers and others. This has now been minimized by the locking of gates along the access road. There has also been disturbance by deer, whose tracks are frequently seen on the bare sand which remains at the top of the bank. A larger issue, however, was control of the spread of pine seedlings. The heathland conservation programme in any case demands the removal of pine seedlings, and the Committee has

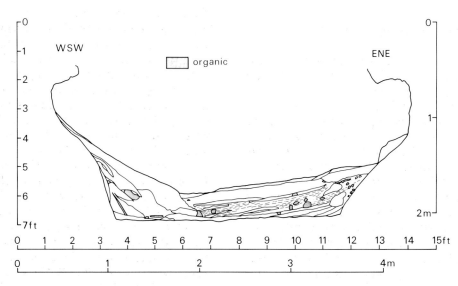

Figure 12.5 Wareham ditch section 1980

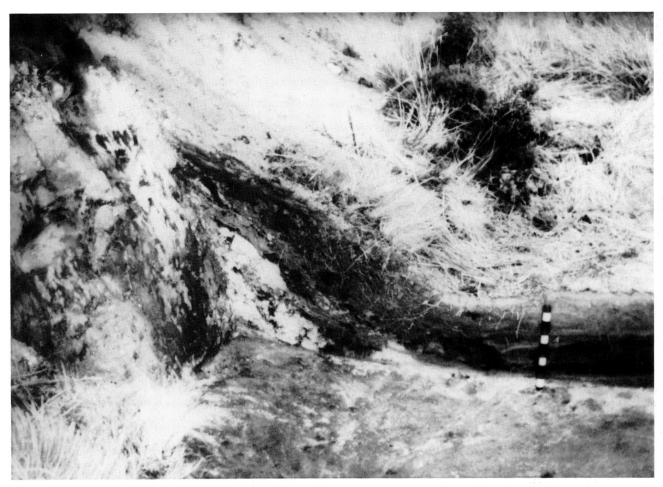

Figure 12.6 Wareham ditch cutting 1980, north-north-west section, showing fill of the ditch floor

felt that the experiment requires a maintenance of vegetation around the site, as far as possible, in a similar state to that which existed when the earthwork was built. A stand of pine trees around or over the site would very greatly alter the effects of climate, erosion and soil development. Pine seedlings have therefore been removed from the earthwork and surrounding area.

12.3 Excavation programme

As originally planned, sections were to be cut through the bank and ditch 1, 2, 4, 8, 16, 32, 64 and 128 years after the building of the earthwork. The actual programme has departed from this to some extent (Table 1.1). The report presented here outlines the results of the 1980 excavation and compares them with previous findings. The excavation (Fig 12.4) was carried out under difficult conditions by Professor P J Fowler, Mrs Gillian Swanton and Dr Carole Keepax. Further difficulties, like those described by Evans and Limbrey (1974) have persisted and the Committee has decided to publish all results currently available, even though some specialist studies on the buried materials have still not been received.

For consistency with previous reports on both Morden Bog and the Committee's other experimental

earthwork at Overton Down (Jewell, 1963; Jewell and Dimbleby, 1966), measurements of plans, sections and descriptions of the earthwork are given in metric with imperial measures in brackets.

12.4 The development of the ditch section

The original ditch section (Fig 14.1) was 1.75m (5ft 9in) deep, 3.05m (10ft) wide at the top and 2.44m (8ft) wide across the flat bottom. It had steep sides, sloping down at 79° from horizontal, which met the bottom to form a sharp angle. By the time of the 1972 section, approximately 0.23m (9in) of sediment had accumulated in the middle of the ditch and 0.46m (1ft 6in) by the sides. These deposits buried the flat bottom, sharp angles and base of the sides. The surface of the deposits formed a smooth curve in section and clumps of vegetation grew almost continuously along the deepest part of the ditch. The sides had been undercut by almost 0.91m (3ft), whilst the original cut edge of the topsoil was preserved and a mat of humic material, held together by living vegetation, was starting to overhang the ditch. At its widest point, between the undercut sides, the ditch was now just over 3.66m (12ft) wide.

By the time of the 1980 section (Figs 12.6–7), a

206

Figure 12.7 Wareham ditch cutting 1980, eastern end of the north-north-west section, showing overhanging mat of vegetation

further 25–50mm (1–2in) of sediment had accumulated in the middle of the ditch, with up to a further 0.15m (6in) in some parts of the ditch near the sides. Vegetation was now well established along the bottom, although unstable areas at the side were still not colonized by plants. Further undercutting of the sides (Fig 12.7) had taken place and, at its widest point in the section, the ditch was now some 3.8m (12ft 6in) wide. The overhanging mat of heather and gorse now grew luxuriantly and, in places along the north-east side, joined up with the plants in the bottom of the ditch to form a superficially continuous cover with the bare sand face of the undercut hidden behind it.

Geomorphology of the ditch
by K Crabtree

This report should be read in conjunction with the previous geomorphology report in Evans and Limbrey (1974, 177).

Samples were taken from the ditch infill for particle size analysis in a similar sequence to those taken in earlier years. For details of the method see Evans and Limbrey (1974). The samples are contigu-

ous, and were taken as columns from the east-north-east side, the centre and the west-south-west side of the ditch infill at intervals which varied according to the visible layering of the deposits. The columns were taken as follows:

E series – between 0.457m (1ft 6in) and 0.61m (2ft) from the east-north-east ditch edge
C series – between 1.066m (3ft 6in) and 1.219m (4ft) from the east-north-east edge
W series – between 0.457m (1ft 6in) and 0.61m (2ft) from the west-south-west edge.

Each sample was air dried and treated with 20 vol hydrogen peroxide solution to remove organic matter and then dispersed in Calgon and sodium bicarbonate solution, according to British Standard 1377 (1961). The mixture was wet sieved through a British Standard sieve No 200 (mesh 75μm or 0.003in) and the residue dried and then dry sieved on a Pascall shaker for 15 minutes using sieves of mesh sizes 2.4mm (0.094in), 600μm (0.024in), 210μm (0.008in), 75μm (0.003in) and a collecting pan. The fines were made up into a suspension of 1 litre and a hydrometer was used to determine the specific gravity of the suspension at fixed time intervals. Only the data for the coarse sieving plus total fines are included in Table 12.1.

Samples E9, C17 and W27 are essentially the parent materials of the soil at their respective sites. This parent material is very variable, with W27 having a very large percentage of fines present and a much lower coarse sand fraction compared with E9 and C17. The seam of pipe clay outcropping at the ditch base accounts for such a big difference. See Evans and Limbrey (1974) for comments on the problems imposed by the original site chosen for the earthwork.

The 1980 section of the ditch was less influenced than the 1972 section (Evans and Limbrey, 1974) by the pipe clay in that the percentage of fines, in all but the W27 parent material, was generally less than 20%, whereas in 1972 most samples had 20% to 60% fines less than 75μm. Conversely, much higher proportions of sand were present in 1980, with 25–50% greater than 600μm compared to the 1972 record of 10–40%. These contrasts are regarded as largely derived from the parent material. Of significance is the increased fine clay in the upper samples of the column taken from the centre of the ditch, where clay rose to 21% at 0.10–0.17m (4–6.5in) and to 13.9% at 0–40mm (0–1.5in). This concentration of fine clay is in part a consequence of the occasional presence of standing water in the base of the ditch and, in part, a cause of that standing water.

These findings have not altered the suggested sequence of infilling outlined in Evans and Limbrey (1974). The initial winter would have seen coarse blocks falling in and building up at the sides of the ditch, while finer sands and clays were spread across the ditch floor. Within about 3 years a veneer of material extended across the whole of the ditch and,

Table 12.1 Wareham, sieve analysis of the ditch sediments

Sample	Depth (in)	Character	2.4mm	600μm	210μm	75μm	<75μm
E1	0.0–1.0	Light sand	–	41.0	45.2	4.7	9.1
E2	1.0–3.5	Dark sand	0.1	32.7	53.2	5.4	8.5
E3	3.5–5.5	Dark sand	–	36.2	50.9	4.3	8.6
E4	5.5–6.75	Light sand	–	25.8	61.8	5.4	7.1
E5	6.75–10.25	Dark sand	–	21.1	63.7	6.7	8.5
E6	10.25–11.5	Light sand	–	32.3	53.1	5.9	8.7
E7	11.5–13.0	Dark sand	0.4	8.6	74.6	10.8	5.7
E8	13.0–14.5	Yellow sand	–	31.1	41.2	4.3	23.4
E9	14.5+	Parent mat.	0.1	46.1	27.3	9.1	17.5
C10	0.0–1.5	Yellow sand	0.1	25.3	60.4	1.3	13.9
C11	1.5–4.0	Grey sand	0.4	44.7	42.9	2.5	9.5
C12	4.0–6.5	Grey sand	0.1	33.5	43.8	1.7	21.0
C13	6.5–7.5	Light sand	–	23.4	60.9	10.2	5.5
C14	7.5–10.0	Dark sand	–	50.6	38.7	4.2	6.5
C15	10.0–11.5	Dark sand	0.1	51.0	39.3	4.7	5.0
C16	11.5–12.5	Light sand	–	43.5	44.3	3.0	9.1
C17	12.5+	Parent mat.	–	41.5	34.7	2.5	21.3
W20	0.0–1.5	Turf	1.6	28.9	55.9	2.7	11.0
W21	1.5–5.0	Grey sand	0.1	30.2	58.8	3.4	7.4
W22	5.0–9.5	Grey sand	0.1	26.7	60.4	3.6	9.2
W23	9.5–12.0	Organic	–	33.0	53.0	3.6	10.4
W24	12.0–13.5	Clay/organic	0.1	31.3	50.2	3.1	15.4
W25	13.5–15.25	Organic	–	43.1	45.7	4.2	6.9
W26	15.25–16.0	Light sand	0.4	48.7	37.0	1.6	12.7
W27	16.0+	Parent mat.	0.2	24.2	12.2	2.8	60.6

Figures are % retained in each sieve mesh size

as the free face of the sides became partly consumed, the supply of material decreased. The surface vegetation held the ditch edges firm for a long period, until undermining resulted in the falling-in of turves which then acted as pockets of organic material within the ditch fill, when the turves became buried by later debris. In many cases, they also acted as sites for the spread of vegetation which acted as a barrier against material slipping further into the ditch. Over time, the ditch face supplied material more slowly to the ditch sediments as the angle of the face decreased and it became partly protected from weathering by the overhanging gorse and heather. Unlike at Overton Down on the chalklands (Crabtree 1971; 1990), the free face at Wareham was still present at 1980, as the angle of rest of the material in the ditch was lower and the total infill less. Some of the current erosion might have been caused by animals running along the gap between the overhanging vegetation and the ditch walls.

The outlines of ditch sections from all five excava-tions are superimposed over one another in Figure 12.8. From these, an estimate of the approximate volume of infilling per 0.30m (1ft) cross section of ditch margin can be calculated (Table 12.2). These are crude estimates, produced from the data of different sections. The trend, as expected after the second year, has been for a decreasing infill rate as the free face became consumed and buried, and the ditch sediments underwent some compaction. It is expected that infilling will continue as long as some free face exists, and also possibly by spillage from the bank into the ditch as erosion of the bank continues and the original berm becomes buried by bank material. The previous excavations themselves led to greater erosion of the bank and ditch sides, and this has supplied more material to the ditch sediments.

From the superimposed cross sections (Fig 12.8) the progressive erosion, particularly of the east-north-east ditch side, can be seen to have produced a considerable overhang. The 1980 section ditch over-hang was poised for collapse prior to sectioning. In

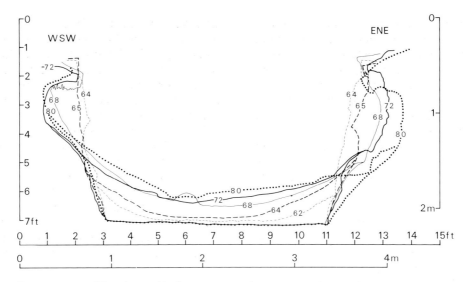

Figure 12.8 Wareham ditch section outlines superimposed for 1964, 1965, 1967, 1972 and 1980

addition, the 1980 outline demonstrates the relatively low angle of rest and the eccentric position of the low point in the ditch infill. The west–south-west side of the ditch was less undermined and had a thinner turf overhang. The ditch infill on this side rested at a slightly steeper angle than the opposite face. This asymmetry can also be seen in Figure 12.5, with greater erosion and infill on the east-north-east side (the east side below and in Table 12.3) and less on the west-south-west side (the west side below and in Table 12.3). A fuller discussion of the asymmetry is given in Crabtree (1990) and in Evans and Limbrey (1974). The approximate volumes of material eroded and deposited per 0.30m (1ft) of ditch section on the two faces of the ditch are given in Table 12.3. Although the figures are crudely obtained from the drawings, the expansion factor shows a surprising increase compared to the 1972 figure of 1.24 for the total expansion factor. One would have expected compaction to lead to a decrease in the factor over time and it is suggested that the increased amount of turves included in later falls might be causing the factor to rise.

The laminations which were very clear in 1972 were still distinct in the 1980 section (Fig 12.5). The low biological activity of the acid sands at Morden Bog and the slow percolation of water through the sands has enabled the inherent banding of the

deposits in relation to their depositional sequence to be retained. Given the stochastic nature of the fall of turves, the ponding up of water and the deposition of fine clays, it is unlikely that the laminae are of a very regular periodicity.

12.5 The development of the bank

The changing bank stratigraphy

When built (Fig 12.1), the bank was 1.524m (5ft) high, 5.994m (19ft 8in) wide at the base with a 0.61m (2ft) wide horizontal strip at its apex. Its sides sloped down from the horizontal at a regular 30°. The west south-west edge of the bank was separated by a 1.219m (4ft) berm from the edge of the ditch. At the core of the bank was a stack of 0. 31m (1ft) square turves, laid right way up in four layers to a height of *c* 0.39m (1ft 3.5in). These turves were gathered from the area to be excavated for the ditch. The turf stack was covered with a layer (called Layer B) of bleached sand and flints from the Ea (A2) horizon of the soil, coated with a marker layer of roadstone chippings, reaching 0.48m (1ft 7in) above the buried ground surface at its flat-topped apex and extending 2.337m (7ft 8in) across its base. Over this again was Layer C, containing largely grey and black sand from the

<table>
<tr><th colspan="3">Table 12.2 Wareham, rates of ditch erosion and deposition</th></tr>
<tr><th>Date</th><th>Cubic feet/foot</th><th>Cubic feet/foot/year</th></tr>
<tr><td>1964</td><td>1.65</td><td>1.65</td></tr>
<tr><td>1965</td><td>4.04</td><td>2.02</td></tr>
<tr><td>1968</td><td>8.67</td><td>1.73</td></tr>
<tr><td>1972</td><td>9.56</td><td>1.06</td></tr>
<tr><td>1980</td><td>13.1</td><td>0.77</td></tr>
</table>

<table>
<tr><th colspan="4">Table 12.3 Wareham, balance of erosion and deposition in the ditch by 1980</th></tr>
<tr><th></th><th>W side</th><th>E side</th><th>Total</th></tr>
<tr><td>Amount eroded</td><td>3.52cu ft</td><td>5.84cu ft</td><td>9.36cu ft</td></tr>
<tr><td>Amount deposited</td><td>5.6cu ft</td><td>7.53cu ft</td><td>13.13cu ft</td></tr>
<tr><td>Expansion factor</td><td>1.59</td><td>1.29</td><td>1.4</td></tr>
</table>

Bh/Fe horizon of the soil and again covered by a thin marker layer of roadstone chippings. The flat apex of Layer C reached a height of 0.74m (2ft 5in) above the original ground surface and the bank at this stage was 3.556m (11ft 8in) wide at the base. Over Layer C, a mixed layer of material from the subsoil was laid down and coated with the third thin marker layer of roadstone chippings. The flat apex of this Layer D rose to 1.194m (3ft 11in) above the buried ground surface and was 4.775m (15ft 8in) wide at its base. The outer layer of the bank (Layer E/F) was composed of mixed material derived from trimming the ditch.

By 1972 (Fig 12.9), the bare sand of the upper part of the bank was extensively rilled, and fans of re-deposited material extended over the original west south-west edge and across the 1.14m (3ft 9in) berm almost to the ditch edge, as well as some 1.372m (4ft 6in) out beyond the original east north-east edge of the bank (Fig 12.10). A luxuriant growth of heather and grasses characterized the berm and lower slopes and vegetation, mainly clumps of grasses, had also colonized higher parts of the slope, well above the fans of re-deposited material. Evans and Limbrey (1974) suggested that the plants growing on the fans and along the ditch edge were trapping material and preventing it from spreading into the ditch. Overall, the height of the bank above the old ground surface had been reduced to 1.303m (4ft 3in). The height of the turf stack had reduced to 0.23m (9in) above the old ground surface, the top of Layer B to 0.37m (1ft 3in), Layer C to 0.62m (2ft 1in), and Layer D to 1.064m (3ft 6in).

The 1980 bank section (Figure 12.9) is compared with the 1972 section in Figure 12.11. Its height above the old ground surface had been reduced to 1.14m (3ft 9in) and erosion had greatly thinned Layer E/F at its apex. This layer had been lost entirely on the west-south-west side, exposing part of Layer D. The fans of re-deposited material on the east-north-east side of the bank extended out for about the same distance as in the 1972 section, but were a little more thickly developed. On the west south-west side, thick fans of re-deposited material extended right across the berm to the edge of the ditch. Vegetation had by now colonized most of the lower slopes of the bank, with some clumps of grass and other plants towards the top of the bank.

The measurements given in Table 12.4 were scaled from the bank sections drawn at the five excavations (Fig 12.11). The heights given are the maximum vertical distance between the apex of each layer and the surviving traces of the buried ground surface. The layer thicknesses given are the differences between the heights of the tops of the layers. These figures must all be regarded as approximate, and have been rounded off to the nearest inch and the nearest centimetre respectively. The overall height of the bank decreased quite steadily over the 17 year period since construction. This must be due partly to erosion and partly to compaction and sideways slip of the bank deposits. The heights and thicknesses of

all layers (except layer D) inside the bank decreased sharply during the first year after construction. Following this, layers B and C have fluctuated around constant thickness, whilst layer D and the turf stack have shown sustained decreases. The total thickness of turf stack, layers B, C and D at the centre line of the bank was decreasing by around 45mm (1.8in) per year up to 1965, 6.7mm (0.25in) per year by 1968, 5mm (0.2in) per year by 1972 and 3.8mm (0.15in) per year by 1980. Overall, by 1980, around 13% of the starting height had been lost. These changes are from within the bank, ignoring the erosion of layer E/F, and must have been due to compaction and slip alone. To all intents and purposes, therefore, the bank appears to have undergone most of its compaction within the first 2 or 3 years.

Markers within the bank

Flexible polythene tubes were built vertically into the bank at four positions in each plane of section. Horizontal spreading of material in the bank was demonstrated by the sections for 1964, 1965, 1968 and 1972 (Fig 14.1), where the tubes were recovered and had been pulled sideways by the lateral movement of material, particularly in the outermost layers. Unfortunately, only two tubes were discovered during the 1980 excavation, and the upper parts of both were clearly out of position, due to disturbance (Fig 12.9).

When the bank was constructed, 56 numbered pottery discs were incorporated at various points in the layer sequence at each of the areas to be uncovered by future sections. The discs for the 1972 section all had the prefix D and for the 1980 section, the prefix E. Their arrangement was the same in each section, as described in Evans and Limbrey (1974) and shown in Figure 12.12. In each section two discs (1–2) were placed along the top of the turf stack, twelve discs (3–14) on the apex and upper sides of Layer B, and nine discs (27–35) on the flat top of Layer D. Six discs (15–20) were placed on the old ground surface under Layer E/F on the east-north-east side and six discs (21–26) on the old ground surface under Layer E/F on the west-south-west side. Nine discs (36–38, 43–45 and 50–52) were placed on top of the lower slopes of the west-south-west side of the bank, three discs (39, 46 and 53) along the very west-south-west edge of the bank, and nine discs (40–42, 47–49 and 54–56) on the surface of the berm.

These discs seem to have been displaced remarkably little from their original position in relation to the layers during 17 years of compaction, erosion and deposition. In the 1972 section (Fig 12.9) all the discs recovered from the turf stack, top of Layer B, top of Layer D and from underneath Layer E/F on the east-north-east side, had stayed approximately in position. At the same time, there appears to have been some disturbance on the lower west-south-west slope and the original edge of the bank was not easy to identify. One disc was preserved clearly *in situ*

210

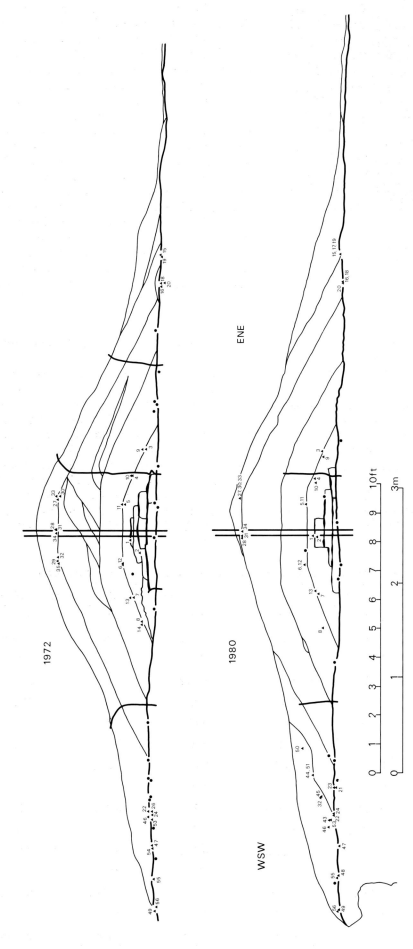

Figure 12.9 Bank sections for 1972 and 1980. Positions of numbered pottery discs and flower pot fragments projected onto plane of section. Circular dots = flower pot fragments. Triangles = numbered pottery discs

Figure 12.10 The north-north-west end of the Wareham bank in 1980, showing fans of re-deposited material, and colonization by vegetation

very little from their original positions. The three discs (E29, E32 and E35) which had originally formed the west-south-west edge of the group of nine on the top of Layer D (Fig 12.12) had been lost in the 1980 section where Layer E/F had been eroded away to expose them. There was less disruption on the lower west-south-west slope and the discs placed on the surface of slope and berm were only partially disturbed. Although the whole north-north-west line of seven discs (E36-E42) had been lost, most of the others were in place – including those on the slope of the bank. Only one of the highest (E43) had been displaced down into the re-deposited material over the berm. Disruptive effects of erosion therefore seem to have been rather variable in the lower slope of the bank. The process of deposition must also be very gentle in some areas, particularly over the berm, or the vegetation's stabilizing effect must have held the discs in position, as well as trapping the sediments.

under Layer E/F at this point. Three more from the same series (D22, D24 and D26) were still in position near where they had originally been placed just under the bank edge. Two out of three discs originally placed on the surface, along the edge of the bank (D53 and D46), were preserved nearby and again seem not to have moved much. Those placed on the berm itself were also still approximately in position but, by contrast, none of the discs originally placed on the lower slope of the bank above was recovered. Recovery of the discs was more complete (Fig 12.9) in the 1980 excavation. The discs under Layer E/F, on the turf stack, and on Layers B and D had again moved

Buried soils within and under the bank

Soils (Fig 12.13) were sealed into the bank at the time of construction in two ways. Firstly, the old ground surface, cleared of vegetation, was buried by the bank. Secondly, the turf stack at the centre of the bank was built with turves taken from the top of the area excavated for the ditch. Four layers of turves were laid in the stack right way up. In a heathland podzol of the Sollom 2 Association (Findlay *et al*, 1984), the uppermost horizon under the main root mat of the grass is a highly organic layer here denoted *Ah*. Underneath this is a leached horizon,

Table 12.4 Wareham, heights and thicknesses of layers at the centre of the bank

	As built in 1963	1964 Section	1965 Section	1968 Section	1972 Section	1980 Section
Bank top height	5′ 1.52m	4′ 10″ 1.48m	4′ 9″ 1.45m	4′ 3″ 1.29m	4′ 3″ 1.3m	3′ 9″ 1.14m
Layer D top height	3′ 11″ 1.19m	3′ 7″ 1.09m	3′ 7″ 1.1m	3′ 6″ 1.08m	3′ 6″ 1.06m	3′ 5″ 1.03m
Layer D thickness	1′ 6″ 0.45m	1′ 6″ 0.44m	1′ 6″ 0.45m	1′ 5″ 0.45m	1′ 5″ 0.44m	1′ 4″ 0.4m
Layer C top height	2′ 5″ 0.74m	2′ 1″ 0.65m	2′ 1″ 0.65m	2′ 1″ 0.63m	2′ 1″ 0.62m	2′ 1″ 0.63m
Layer C thickness	10″ 0.26m	9″ 0.24m	10″ 0.26m	11″ 0.27m	10″ 0.25m	11″ 0.29m
Layer B top height	1′ 7″ 0.48m	1′ 4″ 0.41m	1′ 3″ 0.39m	1′ 2″ 0.36m	1′ 3″ 0.37m	1′ 2″ 0.34m
Layer B thickness	4″ 0.09m	3″ 0.09m	2″ 0.06m	2″ 0.05m	3″ 0.07m	3″ 0.07m
Turf stack height	1′ 3″ 0.39m	1′ 1″ 0.32m	1′ 1″ 0.33m	1′ 0.31m	1′ 0.3m	11″ 0.27m

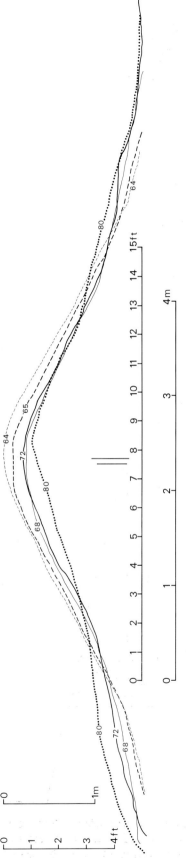

Figure 12.11 Bank section outlines superimposed, for 1964, 1965, 1968, 1972 and 1980. Line of old ground surface omitted for clarity, but base of central pole indicated

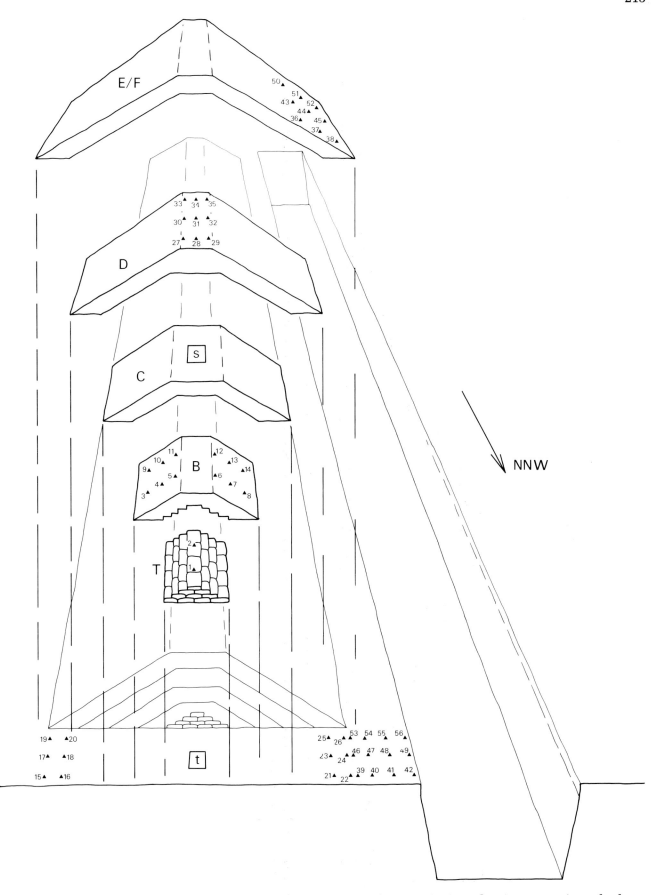

Figure 12.12 Exploded view of the bank at a point destined for later sectioning, showing approximately the original positions of the pottery discs and buried materials. The drawing shows Layers E/F, D, C, B and the Turf Bank removed one-by-one. Triangles = numbered pottery discs; S = buried materials in sand environment; T = buried materials in turf environment

Figure 12.13 The bank section in 1980, showing the buried soil

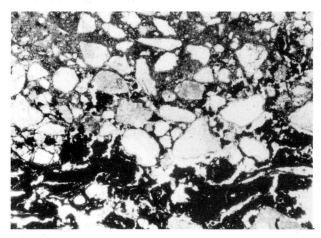

Figure 12.14 Photomicrograph of the buried soil. Plane polarized light. Field width 5.56mm. The field of view is at the upper boundary of the buried H horizon, with abundant (black) amorphous organic matter, and shows the base of the overlying mineral (sand and grey silty soil) Ah horizon of the lowermost turf of the turf stack. The latter turf is clearly right way up. The buried H horizon appears to have been compressed by 2–3 times. It is possible that buried soil fauna have mixed some amorphous organic matter into the sands at the base of the overlying turf

denoted *Ea*, which is particularly deep in heathland podzols. Evans and Limbrey (1974) termed the Ah horizon A1, and the Ea horizon A2. During the excavation of 1980, Mr N. Syers collected a single small soil monolith which included material from the lowest turf of the turf stack in the bank and the uppermost horizon of buried soil at the old ground surface. The monolith included only the lower part of the lowest turf, comprising the Ah and uppermost Ea horizons of the original soil, and the uppermost part of the buried soil profile – the buried Ah horizon (denoted *b Ah* here) of the same soil. Dr R I Macphail prepared thin sections (Figure 12.14) from this monolith and, in addition, took samples to determine weight loss on ignition and to appraise iron content, to be analysed for organic carbon and alkali soluble humus, and sent to the Soil Survey of England and Wales Laboratory at Rothamstead, where pyrophosphate and sodium dithionite extractable iron were measured.

Soil micromorphology
by R Macphail

The thin sections were described using a 1100 point count after Bullock (1974) and Bullock and Murphy (1979).

Table 12.5 Micromorphological data for 1980 Wareham soil monolith

Horizon	% Mineral Grain	% Void	% Organic Matter		
			Strongly decomposed	Moderately decomposed	Lightly decomposed
Ah/Ea	65	17	16.0	0.9	0.6
b Ah	38	16	24.0	15.5	3.3

Table 12.6 Chemical data for 1980 Wareham soil monolith

Horizon	pH	% Organic Carbon	% Loss on ignition	% Alkali soluble humus	Humus as % of Organic Carbon	%Pyro- phosphate extractable iron	% Sodium dithionite extractable iron
Ah/Ea	5.0	3.88	6.75	0.51	13.1	0.3	0.1
b Ah	4.8	7.41	17.68	0.85	11.5	0.3	0.0

Percentages are calculated out of total weight

Micromorphological description for lower part of lowest turf in bank turf stack, Ah/Ea

Homogenous; fine granular (faecal pellets); 17% macrovoids; simple packing voids, some compound packing voids; orthovughs; 65% mineral material; quartz; medium sand; fine sand; coarse silt present; subangular to subrounded; moderately well sorted; no clay; 16% strongly decomposed, 0.9% moderately decomposed, and 0.6% little decomposed organic matter; root fragments; granular to intertextic.

Micromorphological description of old ground surface buried turf, b Ah

Extraneous silasepic material may have been present and was taken to be evidence of introduced material, perhaps from someone's shoe. Fine subangular blocky, fine granular (faecal pellets); platy in H zone; 16% macrovoids; compound and simple packing voids; mainly orthovughs; no channels; 38% mineral material; 24% strongly decomposed, 15.5% moderately decomposed and 3.3% little decomposed organic matter (root fragments); 4% carbonized plant fragments (charcoal); mite droppings 60–100μm; organic material not strongly decomposed was often porous; of plant material, bark and epidermal cells present, inner cells becoming humified; elsewhere phloem still present; agglomeroplasmic to weakly porphyroskelic. The b Ah horizon comprised three layers:

Ah layer. 1.2mm thick; organic matter mainly strongly decomposed; rather dense fabric
H layer. 1.6–3.6mm thick; organic matter little to moderately decomposed; little mineral material, and a concentration of root fragments and charcoal
Ah layer. 3mm or more thick; organic matter moderately to strongly decomposed.

Interpretation of soil chemistry and micromorphology

The layering within the b Ah horizon may be due to deposition of material eroded from the surface of neighbouring soils. Both the buried old ground surface turf and the lowest turf of the rampart turf stack exhibited compression, by approximately two to three times when compared with a podzol in its non-buried state. As at the Bronze Age cemetery at West Heath, Sussex (Macphail, 1981a), the degree of compression declined up the monolith. There was a sharp discrepency in organic matter content (see Table 12.5) between the b Ah and Ah/Ea horizons. This would be expected in a normal podzol profile. Nevertheless, they both had very low iron contents, generally with most of the iron in the mobile (Fe ext.) pyrophosphate extractable form. This suggests that there had been little breakdown of organic complexing agents under conditions of burial except in the bank, where the environment may have been more oxygenated.

If the percentage of alkali soluble humus (as compared with organic carbon content) is a measure of humification, then only 11–13% humification was apparent in the turves. This lack of organic breakdown was also apparent in thin section, where much organic material was only moderately or lightly decomposed – that is, plant material was still recognizable (see micromorphological description above). Organic matter decomposition, as investigated by Babel (1981), allowed recognition of 'browning' as the major mechanism of organic matter decay at Wareham. Parenchymatous tissue was brownish, with brownish spheres along cell walls. Other parenchymatous cells were seen perfectly preserved, as were lignified epidermal cells of (?Calluna) roots. Fungae were not identified, although are certain to have been present, and 'blackening' (Babel, 1981) and other melanotic alterations (Dinc et al, 1976) which are commonly related to fungal activity (Miedema, Wageningen, pers comm) seemed poorly expressed.

The nature of the organic fabric may be compared with turves from the West Heath cemetery (Macphail, 1981a) (c 3000 BP), which were from humus-iron podzols developed on the Cretaceous Lower Greensand. Here, humification was greater at 20–24% and compression was more distinct; six times that of an unburied podzol in the buried soil profile, decreasing to three or four times in the base of the turf stack. There were practically no identifiable plant remains – that is, 100% of the organic matter was 'strongly decomposed' in the terms of Table 12.5. Mite excrements, which are common at Wareham, were either welded or so altered as to be unidentifiable at West Heath. Lastly, at West Heath the major characteristic of organic decomposition was 'blackening'. Indeed, at Wareham the Ah horizon was clearly visible in the buried turf, while this horizon was only barely visible at West Heath. Charcoal was characteristic of turf at Wareham, whereas it was only apparent in floated samples from West Heath.

These differences between Wareham and West Heath can be attributed to time. Under the acid heath conditions at West Heath, organic decomposition led to rather little oxidization and mineralization of organic matter (turves from this site still contained 3.78–4.73% organic carbon). Instead, organic matter alteration was most important with 'welding', 'blackening', compression and some humification. In contrast, on base-rich substrates such as Sproxton Bronze Age (1550 BC) barrow on Jurassic Limestone parent material, organic matter in relic turves was very greatly mineralized and oxidized (Macphail 1979). Preservation is variable, however, even in acid conditions and at the Bronze Age Saddlesborough Reave, Dartmoor (Macphail 1981b), peaty layers were preserved with none of the alteration shown at West Heath.

12.6 Archaeological applications of ditch and bank studies

The most common ancient monuments on the heathlands of South and Southeast England are Bronze Age round barrows. Many have been excavated, from the earliest days of archaeology (Hutchins 1767). Typically, they do not yield many artefacts or human remains but it has long been recognized that, in the conditions of the heathland podzols, the organic remnants of ancient soils are preserved both underneath the barrow mounds and within the sediments of mounds and ditches. A heathland barrow excavation, therefore, often yields more of interest from a geomorphological and pedological point of view than from a more culturally-based archaeological point of view. The earliest studies included those of Professor F E Zeuner (Piggott 1941) and Dr I W Cornwall (Ashbee 1953; Case 1952; Cornwall 1953). Subsequently Professor G W Dimbleby (Ashbee &

Dimbleby 1959; Ashbee and Dimbleby 1976; Dimbleby 1962, 1985) found that pollen was preserved amongst the ancient soil remains. More recently, Dr R G Scaife has continued this palynological work and Dr R I Macphail has studied the micromorphology of the buried soils (Macphail 1986b; 1987; Scaife and Macphail 1983; Drewett 1975, 1985, 1989). Professor Dimbleby and Dr Cornwall were both much involved in the early organization of the Experimental Earthworks project (Professor Dimbleby was the first chairman of the Committee) and the Wareham Earthwork arose largely out of the questions posed by barrow excavations on which they and Dr P Ashbee (another former secretary of the Committee) had worked.

In spite of its bank and ditch plan, the Wareham Earthwork does incorporate the main structural elements of many heathland barrows: a buried ground surface, a turf stack covered by a sand and gravel mound, a narrow berm and a ditch. Evidence for a turf stack comes in the form of irregular, dark and humic stripes within a barrow mound. These are taken to represent the Ah horizon of a soil, together with the broken down organic matter of the plants and root mat that originally held the turves together. The paler stripes in between are taken to be the top of an underlying eluvial horizon from the soil. These interpretations can be confirmed by pollen analysis when the sequence of change in the pollen spectrum down through the buried ground surface is matched in the dark and pale stripes. It is even possible to determine whether the turves were laid down inverted or the right way up (Ashbee and Dimbleby 1976; Drewett 1985). In some cases, such as Phase I of Barrow III at West Heath in Sussex (Drewett 1976), the mound seems to have consisted entirely of a turf stack. At most sites, however, the central turf stack is covered with sand, gravel and clay – as at Moor Green in Hampshire (Ashbee and Dimbleby 1976), and Portesham (Thompson and Ashbee 1957), Arne (Wainwright 1966) and Poole (Case 1952) in Dorset. In some barrows, excavation produced no evidence of a turf stack as at Canford Heath (Ashbee 1953), which is near to Poole and at Chick's Hill, East Stoke, in Dorset (Ashbee and Dimbleby 1959). The Chick's Hill barrow mound had, however, been much altered by later podzolization and it was not even possible to see the buried ground surface in the mound section – it could only be detected through pollen analysis. It is clear (Limbrey 1975) that soils and turves may be considerably altered under conditions of burial and, at some sites, it may not be possible to tell whether or not the mound was constructed of turves at all. The turf stack in the Wareham Earthwork therefore provides an opportunity to observe the complex issues involved. It was built only from turves gathered during the excavation of the ditch. This resulted in a low and narrow stack, four turves high, at the very core of the bank. The 29.261m (96ft) long by 3.048m (10ft) wide ditch produced a 89.24m² (960ft²) area of turf. The turves were 102mm (4in) thick and the total volume of turf was therefore originally around 9.061m³ (320ft³). Allowing for the 13% of compaction, which has reduced the average thickness of turves to 88mm (3.48in), the total volume of turf at 1980 would be in the order of 7.883m³ (278ft³). These figures highlight the very large numbers of turves included in many Bronze Age barrows, which must have required wide areas of ground to be stripped (Drewett 1976; 1985), well over and above the area of the surrounding ditch. In at least one case (Drewett 1989) this is thought to have produced a detectable environmental impact. Once buried in the Wareham bank, the main change in the turf stack has been compaction. The rate of compaction slowed very rapidly during the first eight years and, since 1968, has changed relatively little. Humification seems also to have proceeded throughout at a slow rate. In 1980, each turf was still readily distinguishable in three dimensions and, at a microscopic scale, still showed many recognizable plant remains and faecal pellets characteristic of the unaltered soil.

The bank as a whole is nearing stability. Most changes due to compaction occurred during the first few years and, although there has been erosion by fan formation, it will not be many more years before a stable vegetation cover reaches to the top. Sideways slip of the bank sediments, as monitored by the plastic tubes, has not been marked, but has been more noticeable in the outermost layers. It has not greatly disturbed the buried layering inside. Fans of eroded material from the bank covered the soil surface and associated vegetation of the berm with little disturbance, over most of its width, by 1968. The ditch sides eroded very rapidly at first, but erosion and infill are now proceeding slowly and a vigorous growth of vegetation is firmly established on the deposits in the bottom. Full stability awaits the collapse of the overhanging mat of vegetation at the sides, although it is not yet clear how long this will take. The mat has appeared precarious since 1968, but is still in place at the time of writing. When it finally does collapse, the line of the soil which extends under the buried berm and joins the buried soil surface under the bank, will curve down into the ditch. Further erosion may then occur at the base of the bank sides, and the berm, for so long protected by its covering, may finally be disturbed. The deep, flat-bottomed design of the Wareham ditch was dictated by the previous earthwork at Overton, but is not very common at round barrow sites. When present, however, as at West Heath (Drewett 1976), the profile and lines of infill are very similar. The Wareham Earthwork is demonstrating how long it may take for such structures to stabilise fully, and the critical role of the rapidly re-established heathland vegetation.

12.7 Buried materials

The samples of material and the details of their burial are described in Jewell (1963) and Evans and Limbrey (1974). Two sets of buried materials were buried at each plane of section (Fig 12.12), one on the old ground surface under the turf stack and one on the flat top of Layer C, under the thin marker layer of roadstone chippings. Following the convention of Evans and Limbrey (1974) the burial environment of the samples on the old ground surface is called here the *turf environment*, whilst that of the samples on top of Layer C is called the *sand environment*.

Wool
following a report by H M Appleyard

Samples of two types of woollen cloth were buried in each environment. The samples were folded in four, with a halfpenny placed on one corner and a steel disc on the opposite corner.

Textile 1: woollen contrast cloth

This is a woollen spun fabric, in which the yarns have a softer twist and a more open weave than the gaberdine (below). It is the same fabric as Textile 3 at Overton Down (Jewell, 1963; Evans & Limbrey, 1974). Originally, it was thought that the experiment might show differences in preservation between the two fabrics, but this appears not to be the case. The main difference in preservation is between the dyed yarn in the contrast cloth, as against the undyed or lightly dyed fibres.

In the *turf environment*, the sample of this cloth showed large areas where the warp and weft had broken down completely, and other areas where only the undyed yarns had broken down. There was a general discolouration, with some green staining on one corner, representing the copper coin. Where the steel disc had been there was strong iron staining around and immediately under the disc, decreasing in each layer of the folded cloth. Some of the weft fibres had very clear scale structure, but there was considerable bacterial degradation and fibrillation. The warp fibres were in much worse condition than those in the weft – almost all showing signs of bacterial degradation and also with much more fibrillation, some fibres being almost completely broken down. In the green stained area, the fibres were well preserved with good scale structure, but there were a few fibres showing some bacterial damage and some partial fibrillation. Under the steel disc, the sample was badly iron stained, the fibres were very broken up and it was virtually impossible to see any structure. Fibres from the lowest folds of fabric beneath the disc showed much less staining, but the undyed fibres were almost all completely broken down. The dyed fibres in this region were much better preserved, with some scale structure visible.

In the *sand environment* most of the undyed warp had disintegrated, whilst the dyed warp had again suffered much less. There were copper stains immediately under the copper coin, but not on the other surfaces. The fabric in these areas was comparatively strong. Under the steel disc, the iron stain persisted through all the folds of fabric. The fibres from the weft were in general quite well preserved considering the state of the fabric. There was some bacterial damage and a little fibrillation, and there were also some features which resembled the bites of insect larvae. The warp fibres were stained a reddish colour. All were badly degraded, with much fibrillation. Under the copper coin, both warp and weft fibres were relatively well preserved in comparison with the rest of the fabric, but there were the beginnings of fibrillation in the undyed fibres. Under the steel disc there was severe iron staining, but the fibres were still better preserved than in the fabric outside it – again the dyed fibres fared better than the undyed.

Textile 2: worsted gaberdine

This worsted spun, more tightly woven fabric is the same as Textile 4 at Overton Down (Jewell 1963; Evans and Limbrey 1974). From the *turf environment*, this fabric sample was badly discoloured, especially on the outer surfaces, and very weak. The inner folds showed some areas of pink stain, presumably due to colour producing bacteria. In the outer layer, it was difficult to separate out any single fibre pieces. There was much bacterial damage on all fibres, with various stages of fibrillation, and little sign of normal microscopic surface structure. Below the steel disc, the folds could not be separated and the fibres showed similar poor preservation, with the addition of strong iron staining.

From the *sand environment* the gaberdine sample was stained almost magenta all over, except for the copper stain immediately under the coin and to a lesser exent on the next layer. The fibres in the sample were very weak and difficult to separate, with some bacterial degradation and fibrillation, but also some fibres whose scale structure was clear. Under the copper coin, there was still much bacterial degradation, but in general the fibres were better preserved than in other areas. Under the steel disc there was severe iron staining of all four layers and almost all the fibres had disintegrated.

Fungal mycelia were absent from all the woollen fabric samples recovered in 1980. This is in direct contrast to the samples from previous excavations.

Linen and rope

Linen and rope specimens were retrieved by Dr Carole Keepax from both the turf and sand environments in soil blocks which remained unopened until 1986 when they were each excavated to extract material for specialists to examine. It was noted at this time that some drying and colour changes had occurred since excavation. The specialist's report is not yet available, but the following comments have been compiled from Dr Keepax's notes and photographs.

Linen (unbleached)

In both the *turf* and *sand environments*, recognizable textile was only preserved under and around the halfpenny. In the *sand environment* there was also some evidence of altered fibres adhering to the corroded steel disc but, in the *turf environment*, the steel disc was missing.

Rope

Flax and hemp rope were preserved in both *turf* and *sand environments*. The soil blocks from the *turf environment* were still intact and were left undisturbed for specialist investigation. The soil blocks from the *sand environment* had disintegrated and the remains of both flax and hemp ropes were preserved, particularly where they were in contact with the halfpenny.

Leather and hide

The two types of leather buried at Wareham, oak-bark tanned heavy sole leather and red chrome tanned upper leather, are believed to be the same as Leather Specimens 7 and 10 at Overton Down (Jewell 1963). This is not stated in the first Wareham report (Evans & Limbrey 1974), but a recent examination of the original samples held in the archive strongly suggests that this is the case. The hide, an uncured goatskin, was a new addition to the Wareham project. The samples were retrieved in 1980 from the excavation in blocks, and were removed from their matrix in 1987 by Dr Keepax. The following descriptions have been compiled from Dr Keepax's notes and photographs.

Descriptions

Leather 1: oak-bark tanned sole leather In both *sand* and *turf environment*, the square of leather was still apparently intact, sharp-edged and glossy in appearance. In the *sand environment*, there was some staining under both copper and iron discs, but neither adhered to the leather.

Leather 2: red chrome upper leather From both *sand* and *turf environments*, the square of leather appeared well preserved to the eye. It was glossy and retained its red colour. There was some staining under the metal discs – the iron discs adhered to the leather in both samples, but the copper disc adhered only in the sand environment.

Raw goatskin 3: (i) Buried hair side up From the *sand environment*, the goatskin was preserved only as a patchy layer of hair. These hair fibres were best preserved under the copper disc (where they were stained green). The iron disc was heavily corroded

Table 12.7 Chemical analysis of leather samples from Wareham

Sample	Oak-bark tanned sole (turf)	Oak-bark tanned sole (sand)	Red chrome upper (turf)	Red chrome upper (sand)
% moisture	14.0	14.0	14.0	14.0
% protein	45.5	48.6	65.5	67.3
% grease	1.5	0.6	0.5	0.5
% chromic oxide	0.0	0.0	3.3	4.7
% mineral tan	0.0	0.0	8.3	11.8
% total ash	4.5	6.8	4.6	6.3
% total ash – chromic	4.5	6.8	1.3	1.6
% water solubles	0.2	0.1	0.13	0.25
% SAWS	0.1	0.0	0.06	0.05
% organic water sols	0.1	0.1	0.1	0.2
% bound organics	34.4	29.9	10.3	4.3

Analyses reported by C N Calnan
% Moisture – leather analyses are usually calculated to 14% moisture, which corresponds approximately to leather in an equilibrium of 60% relative humidity and 20°C.
% Protein – Kjeldahl extracted nitrogen, multiplied by a factor of 5.62 to convert it to hide substance of 'leather protein'.
% Grease – fats and other material extracted by dichlormethane.
% Chromic oxide – the tanning agent in chrome-tanned leather, determined by chemical analysis.
% Mineral tan – tanning material in the form of basic chromium sulphate, determined by multiplying the figure for chromic oxide by a factor of 2.5.
% Total ash – the residue left from burning leather in an open crucible at 800°C after sulphating. It includes mineral salts such as sodium chloride, sodium sulphate and calcium chloride, as well as the chromic oxide.
% Total ash less chromic oxide – all the mineral salts (water soluble and water insoluble), less the chromic oxide.
% Water solubles – the quantity of soluble mineral salts, and soluble organic material (tannins and other material) which is extracted by water.
% SAWS – Sulphated Ash of Water Solubles. The dried, water extracted material is sulphated and then ashed at 800°C. It is a measure of the soluble mineral salts.
% Organic water solubles – % SAWS subtracted from % water solubles. A measure of the soluble organic (vegetable) tannins.
% Bound organics – a measure of the non-soluble organic (ie. vegetable) tannins bound into the leather. Defined as the percentage remaining after subtracting % moisture, % protein, % grease, % total ash less chromic oxide, % organic water solubles, and % mineral tan all from 100. Described as % fixed tan in (Jewell 1963).

and orange stained fibres were preserved underneath and adjacent to it. From the *turf environment*, the hair was also preserved as a fibrous layer, but this was more tenuous and the fibres were only well preserved under the copper disc. Underneath the heavily corroded iron disc, no fibres were apparent.

Raw goatskin 3: (ii) Buried hair side down From the *sand environment*, the goatskin was again preserved as a patchy layer of hair. The copper disc had been displaced, but its outline was visible on the fibres. The corroded remains of the iron disc formed a mass which included hair fibres. From the *turf environment*, as above, the hair layer was considerably more tenuous, with green stained fibres under the copper disc.

Chemical analyses

Dr Keepax sent the specimens to The Leather Conservation Centre for analysis. Samples for these analyses were taken wherever possible from outside the area of contact with the iron and copper discs. The goatskin specimens were too poorly preserved for analysis and so results are available only for the sole and upper leather (Table 12.7). A much more limited analysis was carried out on the original specimens (Jewell 1963) and in 1968, and those results which are comparable are summarized in Table 12.8. The following comments were compiled using notes and advice from Dr C Calnan, Head of Conservation and Research at The Leather Conservation Centre.

Following the standard practice for leather analyses, all the samples were brought to a moisture content of 14% in the laboratory in order to maintain comparability. The protein content (the so-called 'hide substance') of both leathers appears to have been preserved little changed in both the *turf* and *the sand environment*, whilst the fatty content (% grease) decreased. For the oak-bark tanned sole leather, this decrease was more marked in the sand environment than in the turf. Water soluble mineral salts and organic material might be expected to be lost rapidly and, in the oak-bark tanned leather, a marked decrease occurred in % water solubles. A figure was unfortunately not recorded in the original analysis of the chrome tanned leather (Jewell 1963), but the 1980 analyses again show low percentages.

220

**Table 12.8 Comparison of leather analyses from original specimens,
1968 excavation and 1980 excavation at Wareham**

Sample	Original leather analysis[1]	1968 excavation (turf)[2]	1968 excavation (sand)[2]	1980 excavation (turf)	1980 excavation (sand)
Oak-bark tanned sole leather					
% moisture	14.0	14.0	14.0	14.0	14.0
% protein	43.4	48.2	51.2	45.5	48.6
% grease	2.2	1.4	0.7	1.5	0.6
% chromic oxide	–	–	–	0.0	0.0
% mineral tan	–	–	–	0.0	0.0
% total ash	–	–	–	4.5	6.8
% total ash less chromic oxide	–	–	–	4.5	6.8
% water solubles	9.8	0.5	0.6	0.2	0.1
% water insoluble ash	0.3	2.7	2.1	4.4	6.8
% bound organics	30.2	33.2	31.4	34.4	29.9
Degree of tannage	69.6	68.9	61.3	75.6	61.5
Red chrome tanned upper leather					
% moisture	14.0	14.0	14.0	14.0	14.0
% protein	70.9	–	–	65.6	67.3
% grease	3.4	–	–	0.5	0.5
% chromic oxide	4.2	4.01	4.69	3.3	4.7
% mineral tan	10.5	10.03	11.73	8.3	11.8
% total ash	5.4	–	–	4.6	6.3
% total ash less chromic oxide	1.2	–	–	1.3	1.6
% water solubles	–	–	–	0.13	0.25
% water insoluble ash	–	5.5	6.2	4.54	6.25

% Water Insoluble Ash – the percentage of the mineral component which is not soluble in water, usually taken to be an indication of added filler such as kaolin. Calculated by subtracting % SAWS from % total ash.
Degree of tannage – % bound organics, divided by % protein, multiplied by 100.
[1] Figures from (Jewell 1963).
[2] Figures from a report by British Leather Manufacturers' Research Association, Egham, Surrey, dated 20 November 1968.
A dash (–) means that the component was not determined.

The tanning material in the leather is shown in the figures for % mineral tan (chromium sulphate) and % bound organics (vegetable tannins). In the oak-bark tanned sole leather, it is to be expected that % bound organics will be high and that mineral tan will be 0%, because only vegetable tannins are used to produce this type of leather. It is usual to express this as a percentage of the % protein, a figure known as Degree of Tannage. The Degree of Tannage in the original analysis was almost 70% and both the 1968 and the 1980 analyses produced figures at about this level. The figures for the sand environment were slightly lower than those for the turf.

The other leather samples are described (Jewell 1963) as 'chrome tanned leather' and, as such, high levels for % mineral tan and very low levels for %

bound organics would be expected. Indeed, neither the original nor the 1968 analyses included a figure for % bound organics, but the 1980 analysis showed bound organics present suggesting that the original sample had some vegetable tan treatment. If so, it is better described as either a 'chrome retan' or a 'semichrome' type of leather. The reported figures unfortunately do not allow any comparison with the original sample. The figures for mineral tan can, however, be compared and show similar levels in the original, 1968 and 1980 analyses. The figures for the sand environment are slightly higher than those for the turf.

The figures for water insoluble ash are difficult to interpret. Presence of a non-soluble mineral component normally suggests that the leather has been 'loaded' or 'weighted' with a filler such as kaolin. This is not an uncommon practice as it improves wear and adds weight (sole leather was sold by weight). The water insoluble ash figure in the original analysis of the oak-bark tanned leather was low, but it was higher in 1972 and higher still in 1980. One explanation for this might be that the amount of filler varied over the leather sheet. It is also possible that mineral material has been deposited in the leather from the soil and is difficult to remove by the normal cleaning procedures. If podzolic leaching were still active, then translocated sesquioxides of iron and aluminium could possibly be precipitated onto any kaolin clay which was present. In the case of the chrome tanned leather, however, the figures were similar for both the 1968 and 1980 analyses, although it was not possible to derive a figure for water insoluble ash from the original analysis.

Wood billets
by J Hather

This examination was carried out in 1991 and, in spite of careful packaging, it seems that there were changes to at least some of the billets during the period of storage.

The billets of Oak (*Quercus* sp.) and Hazel (*Corylus avellana*), were 100mm long, with a circular transverse section 40mm in diameter, when originally buried. The tissue was sap wood and cut from living trees during the previous twelve months prior to burial. The bark of all specimens had been removed. Half of the billets were 'charred' in a muffle furnace, to carbonize the outer tissues to a depth of one eighth of an inch (Jewell 1963).

The billets excavated in 1980 were examined, using both incident light microscopy and Scanning Electron Microscopy, to determine the nature and extent of decay. On previous occasions (Evans and Limbrey 1974) the density of the remaining wood was determined. This was not included in the present report for the following reasons:

(a) The density of three out of the eight billets was not measured in the 1972 material, presumably due to poor preservation. It would only have been measurable in three billets from the 1980 excavation.
(b) It was considered likely that the long period of storage would have greatly affected density.
(c) It was felt that a detailed histological examination would yield useful results in addition to a similar assessment of loss of bulk.

(1) Oak billets

Turf environment: uncharred   Only about 1–2% of the original bulk survived, consisting of fragments of highly degraded secondary xylem. Both lignified and unlignified cell walls persisted and were identifiable, but all were highly degraded. The tissue was clearly identifiable as wood, but not to the level of species, genus or even family.

Turf environment: charred   Only the outer charred tissues survived and, of these, only some 25% remained. The uncharred tissues had either degraded completely or had not been recovered. The charred tissues consisted of almost two complete years' growth and were clearly identifiable to genus.

Sand environment: uncharred   Very well preserved secondary tissues were present. They were clearly identifiable to genus.

Sand environment: charred   Approximately 90% of the charred outer tissues were preserved, with a slim central tract of highly degraded uncharred tissue no more than 5–7mm across. Both outer charred and inner uncharred tissues were identifiable to the level of genus.

(2) Hazel billets

Turf environment: uncharred   A few fragments of dry, highly degraded secondary tissue remained, perhaps 1–2% of the original bulk. The tissue was clearly identifiable as wood but not to the level of species, genus or even family. Dr Keepax had noted that decay was much further advanced than at the time of excavation.

Turf environment: charred   A few fragments of charred secondary tissues remained, representing approximately 5% of their estimated original bulk. These consisted of almost two complete years' growth and were clearly identifiable to genus.

Sand environment: uncharred   The billet was waterlogged, and preserved almost complete. All tissues were well preserved and were clearly identifiable to the level of species. There was a marked outer dark deteriorated region approximately 250μm across, probably related to the waterlogging.

Sand environment: charred   The billet was almost complete and in a dried condition. All tissues were present – the outer tissues being charred and the internal tissues uncharred. Clearly identifiable to the level of species.

(3) General points

Only one of the four charred billets, hazel from the sand environment, was sufficiently sealed by the charred tissues to prevent the decay of the uncharred internal tissues. In this specimen, all the tissues survived intact. The uncharred tissues inside the charred oak billet from the sand environment had decayed partially, and had been lost completely in both charred billets from the turf environment.

222

Both of the uncharred billets from the sand environment survived intact, with practically no decay of any of the tissues. This was despite the dry nature of the oak billet and the waterlogged nature of the hazel billet. It is possible, however, that this reflects conditions of post-excavation storage. The uncharred billets from the turf environment were almost completely decayed leaving, in both cases, only a thin strand of degraded tissue. Neither would have been identifiable if excavated in this condition. The remains of all the other billets, both charred and uncharred, would have been readily identifiable at least to genus.

The turf environment promoted a greater degree of decay than the sand environment. Both charred and uncharred hazel billets, and the uncharred oak billet in the sand environment survived with once living tissues of the ray and axial parenchyma undamaged. This suggests that the billets had been allowed to dry out after being cut from the living trees, prior to burial. If the tissues had been buried in a fresh state it is likely that there would have been a much greater degree of microbial damage visible in these unlignified tissues.

The results presented here confirm those of Evans and Limbrey (1974), covering the excavations of 1964, 1965, 1968, and 1972. The state of decay of the billets recovered from these previous excavations was quantified by a measurement of density. Whilst density was not measured for the 1980 billets, the pattern of decay follows the general pattern of the previous analyses. That is, greater deterioration in the organic rich conditions of the turf environment and a lesser degree of decay in the mineral rich sand environment.

The contrast between the sand and turf environments should provide good conditions under which to examine differential preservation. As originally proposed, however, the questions that are being investigated in this experiment are unclear. If the question is to determine whether the deterioration of the billets is of a nature that would still allow identification, then the studies on the billets excavated between 1964 and 1972 are inappropriate. Density determinations simply indicate that the wood samples have decayed. If the question is whether the decay of wood differs with environment and the presence or absence of a charred surface, then both the density determinations and the histological examination described here can be of value.

The following points are raised as suggestions for future projects:

(1) Incorporation of both softwoods and hardwoods.
(2) Use of specimens of varying sizes to represent both twig wood and mature wood, sapwood and heartwood.
(3) Placing the wood specimens both horizontally and vertically within the earthwork to examine the possibility of differing rates of decay for posts, as opposed to horizontal structural timbers.

(4) Incorporation of fully charred tissues as well as partially and uncharred samples.
(5) Incorporation of both fresh and dried tissues.

Animal bone

Neither the cooked nor the uncooked animal bone samples was preserved in either the turf or the sand environment in 1980. In 1972, this material survived to some extent in the turf environment.

Cremated human bone and human blood

No trace of the cremated bone or foam rubber cubes soaked in blood was found in either environment. Samples were taken, but did not yield any results, as had been the case with the 1972 excavation.

Glass

The original samples of nine different types of glass were provided by W W Fletcher, of the British Glass Industry Research Association in Sheffield. It was realized that the acid soil at Morden Bog was unlikely to produce much change in the samples, and a further experimental mound was built in 1970, on carboniferous limestone at Ballidon, in Derbyshire (Fletcher 1972). Similar glass samples were buried at Ballidon and retrieved at intervals of 1 year (1971), 2 years (1972), 8 years (1978), 9 years (1979) and 16 years (1986). Professor R.G. Newton, who continued the work of reporting on the Wareham material, did so by comparing it with the results from Ballidon. All the material available was examined in March 1980 and reported in Newton (1981). Further reports on the Ballidon experiment include Newton (1985) and (1988), and the experiment is also mentioned in Newton and Davison (1989), which includes a relevant discussion of the effects of humid atmospheres on glass. The Morden Bog samples were much less altered than those from Ballidon, and the 1980 samples had not changed materially from the state reported for 1972 (Evans and Limbrey, 1974). Professor Newton has, however, commented additionally that, overall, the *turf environment* samples from Morden Bog were more altered than the *sand environment* samples, probably because the turf environment might remain moist, or at least have a higher humidity, for longer periods each year, than in the sand environment.

Fired clay

Neither of the two samples was recovered from the turf environment, but both were preserved in the sand environment. This is the same result as for the 1972 excavation. Their position was known and they were carefully looked for in both excavations, but there was no sign of them.

Flints

Samples were recovered, but no specialist reports are yet available.

Halfpennies and steel discs

Samples were recovered, but no specialist reports are yet available.

Lycopodium spores

Samples were taken and stored, but these subsequently disappeared without trace (see below).

12.8 Archaeological applications of the buried materials

As described above, the most common ancient monuments on the heathlands are Bronze Age round barrows and one of the characteristics of such barrow excavations is the paucity of artefactual evidence and of human remains. In some cases, such as barrows IX and X at Beaulieu in Hampshire (Piggott 1941), barrows I, II and VII at West Heath in Sussex (Drewett 1985; 1976) and barrow 2 at Kinson (Knocker 1959), nothing at all was found inside or under the barrow mound, so that it might not have been interpreted as a funerary monument had it not been in the company of other barrows that did contain burials.

Human remains could either be from an inhumation burial or a cremation. An inhumation may have been laid straight into a pit, or be contained in a coffin. A cremation can show varying degrees of fragmentation, ranging from very fine fragments to large and readily recognizable bone elements. Some cremations were placed in a pottery urn before burial and some straight into a pit. Some of the heathland barrows, such as Worgret (Wainwright 1966) and Poole II (Case 1952), have produced no human remains, even though they yielded other finds such as pottery and charcoal. At others, the remains from the primary burial are missing, but those of the secondary burial have survived – as at Kinson 3 (Knocker 1959) and Portesham (Thompson and Ashbee 1957). At further barrows, such as Knighton in Dorset (Petersen 1981), there is preservation of cremated human bone in both primary and secondary burials. There are many reasons why human remains may be missing – they may not have been buried there or they may have been subsequently removed – but the acid and well-drained nature of many heathland soils would in any case be expected to destroy them. Differences between cremations and inhumations might be expected – at sites in upland Wales, with similarly acid soils, calcined bone often survives when uncalcined bone does not (M Bell, pers comm). At Wareham, no trace of either uncooked, cooked or cremated bone was present after 17 years of burial. Even in soils of the same Soil Series, however, human remains may be very differently preserved. One of the classic 'monoxylous' oak coffin burials came from the King's Barrow at Stoborough (Hutchins 1767; Ashbee 1960), some two miles from the Wareham Earthwork and on the same Sollom 2 Soil Association (Findlay et al 1984) as the Wareham Earthwork. It contained the bones (somewhat stained and softened) of an inhumation, which was wrapped in hides. Local factors such as drainage, the construction of the mound, and the oak coffin itself, must have had a controlling effect.

Charcoal is perhaps the most consistent find underneath the heathland barrows. Identifications vary, but the commonest is from oak, followed by alder, hazel, birch, pine and willow. The coffin at Stoborough is one of just a very few finds of uncharred oak. The Wareham experiment might, in retrospect, have more usefully included more completely charred pieces and a wider range of trees, but it nevertheless demonstrates a rapid breakdown of uncharred wood in the turf environment. By contrast the charred outer layers have remained relatively intact.

Pottery, particularly in the form of burial urns, is also a common find in barrows on the heathlands, but it is far from universal, even when there are human remains preserved as at Poole I in Dorset (Case 1952) and Beaulieu in Hampshire (Piggott 1941). The fired clay buried in the Wareham bank was produced in a laboratory at a low firing temperature thought to be representative of prehistoric pottery in Britain (Jewell 1963). After just nine years in the bank, no trace of these samples could be found in the sand environment, in spite of particular care in looking for them. They were, however, preserved intact in the turf environment. This implies that the preservation of pottery may vary markedly over a small area in heathland soil conditions – so that a lack of pottery in an excavation does not necessarily imply that none was buried in the first place. This is of critical importance to any suggestion that the highland zone is aceramic in prehistory.

Other materials are rare in heathland barrows. A piece of iron was found at Poole I in Dorset (Case 1952) and an amber necklace in barrow VI at Beaulieu in Hampshire (Piggott 1941). The oak coffin in the King's Barrow at Stoborough (above) provides what may be a unique example of the preservation of hides (reported as 'deer skins', with some hair intact). The rapid disintegration of all except the hair of the goatskins in both sand and turf environments of the Wareham experiment underlines the exceptional conditions that must have prevailed at Stoborough.

12.9 Suggestions for further planning

The pattern of difficulties discussed in the conclusion of the Committee's first Morden Bog report (Evans and Limbrey 1974) has continued. The 1980 section was again late, although only by one year. Some of the original specialists, although officially retired now, again produced their reports rapidly. In other cases, new specialists had to be found and it was difficult to maintain continuity. With the pollen samples, changes in staff and building work resulted in loss of samples. Analysis of the buried materials have thus proved the most difficult part of the project to sustain. One difficult issue is the preservation of the materials in their original state and as excavated. Evans and Limbrey (1974) had already recommended that provision be made for this and, although it is regrettable that these recommendations were not carried out, there are formidable financial and organizational problems to be solved in order to ensure the continuity of preservation over so long a period. The resolution of these problems must clearly be one of the Committee's priorities before the next Wareham excavation takes place in 1996. Since 1992, the Experimental Earthworks Committee has gathered together materials, samples and correspondence for the first time under the care of the Secretary, Mrs Gillian Swanton, at North Farm, Overton, near the Overton Down Earthwork. This material had been widely scattered amongst many people, including former chairmen, secretaries and specialists, and the work of tracing it is still continuing. Recent research in the archive has already yielded much useful information about the buried materials and it is hoped that this approach will ease some of the problems associated with the buried materials in the future.

If further experimental earthworks are to be constructed, a great deal more might be accomplished without the disruptive effects of excavation. Regular surveying using modern techniques could establish the changing outlines of the earthwork, ditch erosion and fill almost as effectively as repeated excavation could. Vegetation surveys could be carried out at the same time. In relatively fine grained material, as at Morden Bog, the main features of changing stratigraphy could also be established by coring. Samples for sedimentological analysis could be extracted at the same time. The only compelling reason to excavate is the recovery of buried materials. Again, given the necessary precision of deposition, or the leaving of suitable markers, it might be possible to recover these by coring. Surveying methods are now precise enough to allow this type of work, so long as very strong and immovable base stations can be established around the site.

13 Experimental domestic octagonal earthworks
by Peter J Reynolds

Complementary to the major long-term experimental earthworks at Overton and Wareham, a series of short-term experimental earthworks have been built under the combined aegis of the Earthworks Committee and the Butser Ancient Farm (Reynolds 1989). This series was inspired by a small pilot earthwork built at the demonstration area of the Ancient Farm in 1976 (Figure 13.1). The purpose of the pilot earthwork was twofold. First, the aim was to create a simulated farmstead bounded by a simple ditch and bank surmounted by a fence to be the primary focus of the demonstration area. It was based upon an Iron Age enclosure, rectangular in plan, at Steeple Langford in Dorset for no other reason than the nature of the terrain of the demonstration area which would only allow a rectangular plan. Secondly, the construction of the enclosure allowed a very simple observational experiment of the erosion and revegetation cycles of the ditch and bank against a daily recorded history of the weather.

The scale of the earthwork was deliberately chosen to typify the usual boundary ditch, and generally hypothesized bank, found around prehistoric settlements especially those of the Iron Age. The ditch profile was a 'V' section 1.5m deep and 1.5m across with a 300m wide berm separating the inner face of the ditch from a dump bank. The turf from the surface of the ditch was used to construct two turf walls two metres apart and 300mm high to contain the bank. A simple wattle fence was built on top of the bank. The geology comprised a 300mm deep soil layer of friable rendzina, clay with flints and chalk granules directly onto middle chalk.

Within seven years the bank and ditch had been virtually revegetated with erosion occurring only in discrete areas. The plant recolonization had significantly affected the erosion patterns to the extent that the deposition of material into the ditch bottom was positively skewed. The rapid growth of plant material from the berm and turf retaining wall had created a barrier to erosion from the bank and in autumn had provided a protective curtain to the

Figure 13.1 Butser Demonstration Area, Hampshire, Experimental Earthwork. Section cut after 6 years showing alternating bands of chalky sediment and fine soil. The bank is on the right. Scale 50mm units (Photo P J Reynolds)

Figure 13.2 An aerial view of the experimental octagonal earthwork at the Science Museum, Wroughton, Wiltshire (Photo Butser Ancient Farm Project)

upper inner face of the ditch. No such growth or protection was afforded to the outer ditch face which eroded more quickly. Sections cut across the north, east and south arms of this earthwork in 1983 (Fig 13.1) clearly showed the asymmetric nature of the layers and further indicated some three identifiable layers of eroded material per annum. It was also observed that the erosion sequence gradually undermined the rootbonded topsoil for some four years until this, too, fell into the ditch forming a characteristic 'dark' layer subsequently covered by more chalk layers being eroded after their exposure. This fall of topsoil with its seedbank created an acceleration and diversification of the plant regrowth coinciding with an almost natural angle of rest for the ditch sides. This regrowth was, in major part, responsible for the final phase of revegetation and stabilization of the ditch. Once stabilization had occurred the ditch was still one metre deep and a perfectly effective barrier to stock, especially cattle.

The pilot experiment provided such unexpected and contrary results that it was decided to implement a series of earthworks on different rock types in order to discover if this erosion pattern was consistent and whether the revegetation cycle, along with the local climate, held the key to understanding the deposition of layers within 'domestic' scale earthworks.

Given the premise that vegetation was critical, an octagonal design was adopted for the earthworks (Fig 13.2) with each arm of the octagon being opposed to a major point of the compass. In addition the design of each arm was altered to incorporate variables in bank construction. In the pilot earthwork the bank had played such an insignificant role as to pose key questions of validation. Three methods of bank construction were adopted. Assuming the ditch is dug from grassland, the surface turf from the ditch can become a retaining turf wall set either on the inner edge of the ditch or 300mm back allowing the presence of a berm; it can become the core of the bank being simply the first phase of digging and therefore the bottom-most element of the bank; it can be stripped off and set on one side until ditch and bank are completed and then laid over the surface of the bank and thus immediately arrest any erosion from the bank into the ditch. In this way each arm offered six variables, the three types of bank construction with and without a berm, each major variable occupying a four metre length while the minor, arguably the least likely variable of the turf covered bank, spanning the change from berm to no berm. This, in turn, allowed three transects per major variable to be used, avoiding any interference from the adjacent variable.

To date four experimental earthworks (Figure 1.1) following this design have been built respectively on Lower Chalk (Wroughton, Wiltshire 1986 – Figure 13.2), Middle Chalk (Little Butser, Hampshire 1985), Upper Chalk (Bascomb, Hampshire 1991) and aeolian drift over clay (Fishbourne, Sussex 1986). Each earthwork has an associated daily reporting meteorological station. The focus is upon the sequence and abundance of revegetation and the erosion within the ditches. Excavation of sections across each variable is planned once complete stabilization has been reached, which includes the stabilization of plant species. The data comprises an annual mapping of plant vegetation across the outer face of the bank and the inner and outer faces of the ditch along with occasional recording of physical sections.

The early phases of the Wroughton and Fishbourne earthworks have been published as specialist reports from the Ancient Farm but the principle of publishing prime data to allow subsequent reworking and analysis has forced a re-evaluation of this approach. It is now planned to publish the vegetation surveys and physical surveys for each earthwork on computer discs with regular updates through time.

One further earthwork built under the aegis of Butser Ancient Farm and the University of Barcelona has been constructed at the research site of L'Esquerda near the city of Vic in Catalonia, north-east Spain. The design of this earthwork has been modified to include only four major points of the compass (N.E.S.W.) and therefore comprises just two arms, each divided to face opposite ways. Again the variables have been reduced to two per element, the bank having a turf retaining wall throughout but with bermed and bermless halves. This earthwork is a major element of a programme examining post-depositional processes.

Emerging from this series of experimental earthworks are a number of immediate observations. Such a ditch and bank, the bank being a physical expression of the material capacity of the ditch, cannot be regarded as any kind of significant military installation. They do form extremely effective livestock fences which they traditionally became in later periods. It would further appear that the original scale of the ditch was adopted in the full knowledge and expectation of erosion taking place. The final revegetated and stabilized state would still be a perfectly adequate barrier or fence and would require only the minimum of maintenance. Similarly the erosion pattern suggests the ideal bank construction employs a berm which in due course erodes away, but there is no subsequent undermining of the banks. Specifically a great deal has been learned about the sequence of plant recolonization on the different soil types not least the rapidity of occupation. The major *lacuna* in the series is an experimental earthwork built on a sand site.

The final objective of all these earthworks is to provide a set of *cognita comparanda* for field archaeologists to use in analysing the physical excavated evidence from ditch sections. In conclusion, the motivation for this series of earthworks derived from a section cut across the ditch of the pilot earthwork, the traditional analysis of which would firmly place the bank on the wrong side of the ditch.

14 Discussion and conclusions *by Martin Bell*
(including comments by members of the project)

14.1 Historical context

When the project was set up in the late 1950s archaeology was emerging from a period of relatively isolated introspection, reflecting the decimating effects of two world wars and a long period of preoccupation with artefact typology and the development of excavation method. The subject had to some extent been liberated from its typological preoccupation by the discovery of radiocarbon dating in 1948. That also helped to re-establish the links between archaeology and the sciences, and engendered interdisciplinary research which the project's founders did much to encourage. In acknowledgement of their contribution we publish photographs of several of the project's founders in the frontispiece to this report.

Insights into the philosophical positions of those who set the experiment up are provided by their writings and lectures at the time and here it is profitable to return briefly to some of the themes identified in the preface. The experiment was first suggested at the British Association Darwin centenary meeting in 1958. A paper was given at that meeting by Peter Jewell (1958), a zoologist by training who had helped on a number of excavations. That paper, and recent reappraisal of its theme (Jewell 1993), provide valuable insights into the context of the experiment and the inspirational role of Darwin's work, and particularly his earthworm experiments (Darwin 1881). Jewell particularly emphasized the long-term nature of the experiments conducted by Darwin over 40 years and then subsequently taken up by Sir Arthur Keith (1942), giving a total timescale of 100 years. The archaeologist Richard Atkinson (1957) had also made great use of Darwin's work in considering the effects of earthworms on sites, notably Stonehenge.

In an introductory chapter of the original project manual the archaeologist Paul Ashbee (1963) situated the project in the historical context of interdisciplinary research concerned with the relationship between people and the natural world. He wrote (1963, 17): ' the tendency has been to think on the one hand of man and man's work and on the other of nature and nature's work as well as the effects of nature as though they were in some way separate'. It is clear that in contrast the project's originators were moving towards a more integrated ecological approach.

Particularly useful statements of the founders' philosophies are contained in inaugural lectures given by two of them. Richard Atkinson's (1960) inaugural lecture at Cardiff was *Archaeology, History and Science*. In acknowledging that his own background was not in science, he delivered a plea for archaeologists to 'train upon the problems of man's history the full armament of his science'. He argued that a reluctance to experiment is one of the ways in which current archaeological practice was unscientific and acknowledged that the initiative to make the earthworks came from scientists rather than from within archaeology.

Geoffrey Dimbleby (1965), in his inaugural lecture for the Chair of Human Environment at the Institute of Archaeology, London, approached the issue from the different perspective of a training in botany and forestry. Dimbleby always labelled himself an ecologist. His particular contribution was to highlight the role of past communities in the development of present-day environment types, particularly the origins of British heathland and moorland (Dimbleby 1962; 1977; 1985). Issues raised by that research, some of it in collaboration with Paul Ashbee, were responsible for the siting of the Wareham Earthwork on heathland. In his inaugural lecture, Dimbleby (1965) wrote; ' it should be apparent that in biology and in the field sciences, in particular, a study of the parameter time is an essential part of the whole study.' The paper highlights the difficulties with the ecological concept of climax in situations of significant human impact and emphasizes the importance of the time dimension in the study of ecological succession (see also p 231). It is argued that time tended to be a blind spot for ecologists and that archaeologists destroy information relevant to ecological history without understanding its significance. The lecture makes clear that, for Dimbleby, as for many subsequent environmental archaeologists, these were not peripheral issues; the time dimension was an essential perspective to the study of present-day environmental concerns.

Other leading founders of the experiment included Ian Cornwall and Bruce Proudfoot. Cornwall had contributed to the development of scientific approaches in archaeology through work on animal bones (Cornwall 1956) and soils (Cornwall 1958) and was mainly responsible for the work study aspects of the experiment, ie the calculation of the number of person hours involved in constructing earthworks (p 244). Proudfoot was a geographer by training from the Belfast school which had a history of research in archaeology, folk studies and anthropology. His PhD was in historical geography and archaeology (Proudfoot 1957). He published a series of articles making the case for experiment in archaeology which drew on the earthwork project (Proudfoot 1961, 1965a and b, 1967). Proudfoot was particularly responsible for work on geomorphological aspects of the earthwork's weathering. Thirty-two years after the original construction of the Overton Earthwork, we are delighted to report that Bruce Proudfoot played a leading role in the excavation of the 1992 section and that Peter Jewell was also able to visit, and both of them (frontispiece) have guided us in bringing this latest phase of the work to publication.

The experiment's relationship to broader trends in the history and philosophy of science also needs consideration. Related issues concerning cultural aspects of environmental science have recently been reviewed by Simmons (1993). The foundations of the experiment were empirical. They were based on careful observation and recording, and the search for regularity and pattern. This normative reasoning is concerned with the prediction of what ought to happen given certain known conditions. The approach would now be described as essentially positivist, with pattern recognition leading to generalization and perhaps to the formulation of law-like statements. Underlying positivist reasoning is perhaps most clearly suggested by the meticulous description of the meals consumed by those who constructed the Overton Earthwork (Jewell 1963, 94). Today this detail is mainly interesting for its insight into dietary change and the three substantial meals a day considered normal a generation ago. Why this information was originally given is not specified in the manual. It may reflect normative assumptions that precise definition of all the parameters would itself define the outcome, in this case presumably of the work rate experiment (see p 244). Two of the founders have also provided retrospective comments on why the dietary information was included. Bruce Proudfoot (pers comm 19.7.94) writes 'actual details of human food consumption . . . were rare, so that any reconstruction of dietary requirements starts from an imperfect data base, a problem BP and PJ had faced in trying to get from animal bones recovered in excavations, to early diets, to early land-use practices.' Interestingly Peter Jewell (pers comm 14.7.94) emphasizes a different point: 'part of our reason for doing this was to be provocatively unconventional and try to say that one should record these personal things for the sake of future historians of science'.

At no point do the experiment's publications specify that the definition of laws was an objective. Perhaps that reflects a recognition by the originators of the problematic nature of law definition in the historical sciences, archaeology and ecology. In any case the recognition of pattern and regularity does not necessarily presuppose the existence of underlying laws.

The experiment situates itself philosophically within an hypothetico-deductive methodology. Ashbee and Cornwall (1961, 130) describe excavation as 'a means of investigating the truth of an hypothesis by excavation.' Coles (1979, 33) describes testing as a basic principle behind experimental archaeology. The basic manual outlines a number of hypotheses which the experiment was designed to test, for example, geomorphological aspects of the bank and ditch. One great strength of the experiment can be seen as the very clear statement of methodology and objectives in the handbook (Jewell 1963). This is a model which surely deserves to be followed. Thirty-four years after the construction of the first earthwork, it is still a rarity for an excavation report to contain a statement of how the work was done. Yet it is only in the context of that information, warts and all, that it is possible to make a sensible evaluation of the results.

At the time of the project's formulation the emphasis in science was very much on the search for order, pattern and regularity. In ecology the preoccupation was with concepts of balance, equilibrium, succession and climax. Dimbleby's (1965) inaugural lecture had made some critical observations about these concepts in making the case for greater consideration of the time dimension and the effect of people (see also Dimbleby 1977). That view prefigures recent dynamic views of ecosystems which are seen as non-predictable and constantly subject to changes of various magnitudes – the role of chaos (Worster 1990).

It is perhaps paradoxical that a dynamic view of ecosystems has significant implications for a long-term experiment such as the earthworks. Ingersoll and Macdonald (1977, xv) once described the earthwork project as a tightly controlled laboratory situation and it may appear so by comparison with other archaeological endeavours. It would, however, be wrong to envisage the experiment gradually unfolding within a basically stable environment. We need to give adequate emphasis to chance factors which could conceivably have given rise to differing results from those which have been observed. An example of the possible effects of stochastic factors concerns the relationship between weather conditions and geomorphological processes in the early years of the experiment. At Overton the first two winters were relatively mild, yet even so, more sedimentation occurred than during the third very cold winter. We can only speculate about how the ditch profile and sedimentary sequence may have differed if the extreme winter had taken place in the first year, before any of the ditch side was protected by sediment. We may similarly speculate what the effects of the catastrophic storm which occurred during the 1992 Overton excavation would have been had it impacted on a newly constructed and entirely unvegetated monument in 1960. As it was, in 1992 it disrupted the recovery of buried materials in the turf environment. Also possibly relevant is the key role which seems to have been played at Overton by fluctuating populations of earthworms and moles recorded, but not quantified, by Jewell and Dimbleby (1966, 338). Fluctuating numbers may relate to a range of factors: the opportunities provided by the earthwork itself; the timescales of population change; the availability of suitably adapted organisms for colonization; chance factors such as weather patterns. Any one of these may have facilitated the build-up of population levels at particular stages of the earthwork's life. It is not difficult to hypothesize a situation where, if other conditions had obtained, the extent of reworking of the old land surface could have been very different; indeed evidence is reviewed below which indicates that some essentially similar buried prehistoric soils experienced much less evidence of biological reworking than the Overton Earthwork (p 237).

During the early years of the Overton experiment (but not at Wareham) an attempt was made to monitor the most obvious stochastic factor by inclusion of a weather station in the earthwork enclosure. More or less regular recording was maintained by the Nature Reserve warden from 1962 to 1980 until the equipment was twice vandalized (see p 11). So far as we are aware, no attempt was ever made at analysis of the weather station data, comparing it for instance with the ditch weathering sequence. The data are available and this could prove an interesting exercise for the first few years when most of the weathering took place. Originally it was also proposed to include a lysimeter to monitor hydrology within the bank. The plan had to be abandoned because of the difficulty of making regular readings (Jewell 1963, 23). Those data would have been useful in monitoring the environment of the buried materials, particularly in the context of bone chemistry which is relevant to current interests in DNA (R Hedges pers comm).

Stochastic factors may also have impacted on individual sections of the earthwork to varying extents. This challenges the underlying assumption that each successive section of the earthwork represents an essentially repeatable experiment in time series. Although it will often be the case that time is the key variable other factors will, in some instances, have a greater influence. Localized effects will be produced in the ditch by particular patterns of turf fall or in the old land surface by contrasting levels of faunal activity. It is also likely that differing microenvironments and populations of microorganisms within the earthwork may have facilitated the decay of buried materials in some sections but not others; some possible examples are considered in the section on buried materials.

14.2 Issues of timescale

Despite the issues created by changing ideas and research agendas the continuing relevance of the project is highlighted by the question of timescales. Archaeological observations about natural processes affecting sites and artifact scatters are often very short-term, limited perhaps to a single field season, a research programme lasting a few seasons and only rarely extending over a professional career of perhaps 30 to 40 years. We also draw on knowledge written down by previous generations, as the earthwork project drew on observations of 19th century natural historians, particularly Darwin (Jewell 1958). Even so, logic suggests that our individually

limited timescale of environmental knowledge must weaken the hypotheses which we can develop. This problem is seldom very directly acknowledged, at least in the archaeological literature. One of the strengths of the earthwork project is that it is a medium-term experiment, demanding cooperative effort across the generations and helping to bridge the gap between our own short-term contemporary observations and the much longer timescales with which we, as archaeologists, are dealing.

The question must be asked, never the less, how relevant are medium-term observations to the mainly long-term issues with which archaeology is concerned? The earthwork evidence suggests they are more relevant than might at first have been expected. Many of the changes documented take place more or less at an exponentially decreasing rate. This was appreciated at the outset and that was the rationale behind the geometric progression of excavation intervals: 2; 4; 8; 16; 32; 64 and 128 years (Proudfoot 1961). Change is rapid at first then gradually a greater degree of equilibrium is attained. The timescale of that process varies from one type of study, or class of buried material, to another. However, with just 25% of the experimental timescale gone many aspects of the experiment have already produced a range of worthwhile observations. There are 32 years now before the next planned section at Overton so it is as well that we have taken stock and provided a detailed account of results for the next generation of excavators on the earthworks and elsewhere.

The experiment is not situated in an unchanging context. It is affected both by episodic environmental processes and by changing research agendas. What could not be envisaged was how the emphasis of the experiment would change even in the first 32 years. At the time of original construction perhaps the greatest archaeological interest was in the time and motion studies concerning the use of prehistoric tools and their implications for the time and resources required to construct prehistoric monuments (see p 244). A preliminary account of this aspect was promptly published by Ashbee and Cornwall (1961). Up to about the first decade the key results concerned the sedimentation of the ditch and the rapid stabilization after 8 to 10 years of the Overton Earthwork and the more gradual stabilization at Wareham. From 16 to 32 years comparative vegetation changes on the earthwork and outside the enclosure have been of particular interest (see Chapter 3). At the 32 year section some of the most important aspects concerned analytical investigation of the buried soil using micromorphology and chemistry and also the application of Scanning Electron Microscopy and many other techniques to the buried materials. The buried materials had until this stage been a somewhat neglected and secondary aspect of the experiment. In the future we may anticipate, for instance, that there will be further work on the diagenesis of bone and its relationship to DNA studies. It is a tribute to the careful way in which the project was originally conceived and executed that 32 years after the original construction of the earthworks they are still providing fresh opportunities for investigations unforeseen at the time of their original design.

The changing emphasis of the experiment itself reflects change on various overlapping timescales. Most obviously they are a reflection of the various stages in the earthworks' life, such as the natural sequence of sedimentation and vegetation colonization. They also reflect changing research agendas, improved recovery techniques (p 56) and technological advance giving rise to the greater availability and variety of microscopes (particularly SEM) and other analytical equipment.

Changing research agendas are also related to the chance availability of individuals. Hence the limited vegetational record, for example, between about 1962 and 1984 when, in part, Jim Hemsley worked abroad. Other similar discontinuities in the project occurred in the 1960s and 1970s when, for a time, Peter Jewell worked in Nigeria and Bruce Proudfoot in Canada.

Early sections of the earthworks had been cut in a single long weekend but at Overton in 1992 the aim was to carry out a more detailed programme of work. Eight days were allowed with an average team of 15. This was insufficient and long hours had to be worked. Some aspects suffered, particularly the buried materials in the turf environment, which were lifted under bad weather conditions, and some of the final sampling could not be done as slowly and carefully as we would have wished. The work would have been better done over 2 weeks. Relative expenditure of person hours gives some idea of how the project's brief has expanded over the last 32 years. Figures in Jewell (1963) indicate that original construction of the Overton Earthwork in 1960 took about 1155 person hours. The excavation in 1992 of just 7% of the earthwork's length took about 1215 person hours. Comparative costs tell a comparable story, of inflation, the increasing professionalization of archaeology and the project's expanding brief. Earthwork construction at Overton in 1960, together with photography, cost £323, while the 1992 excavation cost about £5000 with an additional £21000 for post-excavation aspects.

14.3 Vegetation history – Overton Down

Fyfield and Overton Downs became a National Nature Reserve in 1956. The Nature Conservancy annual report (1956) describes it as 'one of the finest tracts of chalk downland in England.' Palaeoenvironmental research around Avebury indicates that chalk grassland communities are of considerable antiquity; some were well established during the Neolithic (Evans *et al* 1993). On Fyfield and Overton Downs the higher downland may have been continuously grazed grassland since at least the Bronze Age

and the lower slopes have probably been continuously grazed since abandonment of the excellently preserved field systems in the Romano-British and Medieval periods (Bowen and Fowler 1962; Fowler 1963, 1967 and forthcoming). The original designation of the Downs by the Nature Conservancy was for geological reasons as they contained the best preserved concentration of sarsen stones; these are relics of Tertiary strata which have come to occupy their present positions as a result of Pleistocene periglacial processes. In the 1960s it was recognized that the sarsens themselves also supported a nationally important lichen flora.

The chalk grassland itself has recently been described as 'prime downland' (Gillam 1993) which is increasingly threatened by agricultural changes. Smith (1980, 476) was less complimentary, describing it as species-poor *Festuca rubra* chalk grassland. Even so, the Wiltshire Biological Survey records the existence of some species of at least county rarity on Overton and Fyfield Downs. The 1km square within which the earthwork lies has 47 species described as less common (S Scott-White pers comm). For the earthwork site itself we have Jim Hemsley's 1960 vegetation record prior to construction (Hemsley 1963) followed by notes of the invading vegetation in 1962 and 1966, detailed survey of the earthwork and enclosure in 1984 and a further survey of the enclosure in 1992 with more detailed survey of the 1992 trench area (Hemsley p 19).

Chalk grassland was once widespread and was once thought to be a natural climax on droughty soils. It was later realized that if grazing by domestic animals and rabbits was excluded then trees could colonize (Tansley 1968). The erection of a rabbit proof fence round the earthwork is, in effect, one of many replications of ecological experiments designed to prove this point, although its original purpose was to prevent disturbance by animals. The invasion of some areas of chalk grassland by trees and scrub following post World War II reductions in grazing and rabbit populations demonstrates that chalk is capable of supporting woodland, and there is also much palaeoenvironmental evidence for climax woodland (Evans 1972). In the Avebury area much of the woodland was cleared in the later Neolithic and early Bronze Age (Evans *et al* 1993, 188). Various sources of evidence agree therefore that the grassland community is a plagioclimax maintained by the biotic factor of grazing (Gillam 1993).

It is noteworthy that after 32 years of excluded grazing there has been so little invasion of woody species at Overton. By 1979 one hawthorn was established and there was a hawthorn seedling and two oak seedlings; a single elder bush was established by 1984. The paucity of trees may result from a lack of seed and it also seems probable that the development of a very thick turf mat has made the grassland highly resistant to invasion (Smith 1980, 328). Small mammals may also play a greater role than generally appreciated in preventing regeneration by eating young seedlings (Smith 1980, 329). In

September 1993 the litter layer in red fescue tussocks to the north of the earthwork was covered in animal runs perhaps relating to vole activity.

The earthwork was constructed in an area of grassland which has been continuously grazed by sheep and occasionally cattle since designation as a Nature Reserve (Hemsley 1963). Throughout the 1960s mixed grazing by sheep and cattle took place, then from c 1972 the sheep were replaced by more intensive cattle grazing (G Swanton pers comm). Jim Hemsley (pers comm 26.7.94) describes the main changes as follows:

'Over the 24 year period (1960–1984) there was a significant reduction in species diversity in the grassland adjacent to the earthwork study enclosure, with only 12 of the original 34 species being recorded in 1984. There now existed a species-poor sward predominantly of red fescue and rye-grass. Within the fenced enclosure, in parts not affected by earthwork construction, and where ecological changes have taken place on a more magnified scale due to complete exclusion of grazing stock, the tall red fescue and false oat grassland has developed a thick litter layer and there are now large tussocks of red fescue. The key factors involved in these changes probably relate to cattle grazing and higher levels of nutrient outside the fence-line and stock exclusion within the enclosure The decimation of a once very abundant rabbit population on the Down (King and Sheail 1970), following myxomatosis in 1954, may also have contributed to these changes.'

In the 1990s rabbits are again abundant. It is also possible that fertilizer applications from 1979 to 1992 contributed to the changes observed.

Ecological changes comparable with those at Overton have been documented following the exclusion of grazing and mowing at Swyncombe, Oxfordshire (Smith 1980, 183). On that site the litter layer proved very resistant to decomposition until invasion by nettles. Similarly at Overton between 1984 and 1992 there is evidence of nettle invasion of moribund fescue tussocks and also an increase in false oat.

It seems probable that the changes in the grass sward have contributed to the development of surprisingly low pH levels within the enclosure (Crowther p 114). Reduced sheep and rabbit activity may also mean that there was a reduction in the liberation of chalk onto the surface; this had been a prominent feature of some heavily grazed chalk grassland before myxomatosis (Tansley 1968, 69). Despite low pH within the enclosure the earthwork itself has created conditions suitable for several plants with a strong affinity for high levels of calcium. Of the 34 species originally recorded on the site of the experiment 25 are now found on the earthwork. As species richness has declined in the grassland surrounding the National Nature Reserve so it has increased on the earthwork. It will be interesting to see what further changes result from an agreement reached in 1993 by English Nature to end the fertilizing of grassland on the National Nature Reserve which includes the earthwork.

In the context of vegetational change it is also relevant to return to the linked themes of chance and timescale (p 229). Hemsley (p 22) has documented a reduction of ground cover between 1984 and 1992 on the short section of bank recorded before the 1992 excavation, associated with an increased proportion of drought tolerant species, which seems most likely to relate to climatic factors. Unfortunately the weather station ceased operation before this. There is also the issue of disturbance, its frequency and the ability of plants to respond to changes. Key factors here include the ability of seeds to arrive from elsewhere and the timescale of seed bank viability. Seed numbers in the buried and unburied profiles indicate that only about 10% of seeds survive (Carruthers and Straker p 137) and the germination experiment shows that six species buried in the old ground surface were still capable of germination after 32 years (Hendry et al p 138). All have very resistant seed coats and would be some of the species most readily on hand to colonize after disturbance.

14.4 Comparison of vegetation history at Overton and Wareham

The evidence available at present for Wareham is presented on pp 202–5. One essential difference between the two earthworks is that Wareham has never been surrounded by a fence so that we cannot observe the effects of excluded grazing which has been of such interest in terms of the soil and vegetation studies at Overton. Indeed the Wareham earthwork has become very much part of the surrounding heath, apart from the bank top which is still partly unvegetated. The ditch has comparable plant communities to the wetter areas of the surrounding heath.

14.5 The experiment's contribution to conservation issues

Archaeology does not form a part of the designation of National Nature Reserves or SSSIs but the two interests are closely linked at Overton, as so often elsewhere (Fowler 1968; Bell and Walker 1992, Chapter 8; Macinnes and Wickham-Jones 1992). The archaeologically derived palaeoenvironmental record summarized above (p 231), makes it clear that the Nature Reserve is a relic chalk grassland of considerable antiquity, the field systems are among the best preserved and most intensively studied, the sarsens have in some cases been used to make field boundaries and other archaeological features, and some of them were used in the Neolithic as axe-sharpening stones (Fowler and Sharp 1990, 192).

The documented vegetational changes at Overton are clearly relevant to the development of conservation strategies. This newly created habitat has acquired a floristic composition in some ways comparable with that of old grassland in just 24 years. This is at variance with the view that species-rich grassland takes centuries to form (Gillam 1993) although much could depend on scale and the nature of disturbance. The experiment shows that disturbance, at least of a specific and spatially limited type, can help to maintain diversity in chalk grassland. The botanical observations over 32 years highlight the value of knowledge of the time dimension to the development of conservation strategies. In this context it is interesting that a small experimental round barrow has recently been constructed in Monkton Nature Reserve, Thanet, jointly for archaeological reasons and to investigate the effects of disturbance factors on plants and animals (Jay 1993).

14.6 Comparison of the buried soils and turf stacks

The Wareham Earthwork buries an acid humus / iron podzol, the Overton Earthwork a rendzina profile. The original soil surface at Wareham, still sharply defined on photos from the 1972 and 1980 sections, even below the turf stack (Evans and Limbrey 1974, Plate 17), shows no indications of the mixing at this boundary which was such a feature of the Overton Earthwork (p 76). Each individual turf of the turf stack was also very clearly defined by comparison with Overton (see Figures 7.9 and 7.10). After 17 years plant material was still recognizable in the Wareham soil, whereas at Overton traces of plant material were only found on the leather at 16 years and only vestigial traces remained in soil samples after 32 years. Pottery discs on the old ground surface at Wareham had also undergone little movement (p 209) by comparison with Overton, where some of those on the ditch side had been moved by moles (p 79). The only possible evidence noted of faunal activity within the bank at Wareham was the absence of one of the placed steel discs (p 218) and the presence of arthropod faecal pellet residues from the decomposition of rope (Evans and Limbrey 1974, 191). In the Wareham ditch faunal activity was noted behind the vegetation curtain overhanging the ditch. Generally, however, there was a very much lower level of faunal reworking and biological activity in the more acid Wareham soils. The main change in the Wareham soil had been compaction, partly brought about by a reduction in void spaces from c. 50–60% to 16% (Scaife and Macphail 1983; Fisher and Macphail 1985). Compaction was mainly in the first two years and it has remained relatively stable since the eight year stage. At Overton the main change to the morphology of the earthwork was compression of the turf stack and the overlying topsoil (B). This occurred mainly during the first four years or so (Fig 14.2). The Overton buried soil has also become very thin in places because some soil has been abstracted by moles and some has been moved upward into the bank by earthworms. It is noteworthy that the upward

reworking of more shallowly buried soils had been predicted by Atkinson (1957), prior to the experiment, on the basis of his observations at Stonehenge.

Micromorphological and chemical analysis was first carried out on the Wareham buried soil from the 17 year section. This was partly to facilitate comparison of this 17 year old buried soil and turf stack with essentially comparable features preserved in the cores of Bronze Age round barrows (Scaife and Macphail 1983). That demonstrated the potential of analytical work on the earthwork buried soils. When the time came to excavate the 32 year section at Overton a more ambitious programme of micromorphological and linked chemical analysis was planned. Soil micromorphology had, by this stage, developed into an important technique in archaeology (Courty *et al* 1989) but interpretations were often hampered by a limited knowledge of processes occurring after burial. The extent of earthworm reworking of the buried soil at Overton is remarkable and evidenced both by the visible signs of upward topsoil movement into the interstices of the bank (Figure 7.11) and by Dimbleby's (p 43) and Crabtree's (p 127) evidence for the movement of *Lycopodium* spores both upwards and downwards. Macphail and Cruise (p 101) also postulate, on the basis of micromorphological evidence, a subsequent phase of reworking by enchytraeid worms.

14.7 Comparison of the banks

The development of the two earthworks is illustrated in two comparative diagrams: Figure 14.1 which shows Wareham over 17 years and Figure 14.2 which shows Overton over 32 years. The two earthwork banks have adopted very contrasting profiles. Overton has a steeper bank in comparison with the low spread bank of Wareham. The reason is the smaller particle size and consequent lower angle of rest of the Wareham sediments. The Overton earthwork has not spread at all to the north and only some 0.3m to the south whereas the Wareham Earthwork has spread 0.9m to the south and 1.3m to the north. This contrast is emphasized by the greater downslope curvature of the upper part of the polythene tubes in the Wareham bank indicating slope processes operating on the surface of that bank.

There is a marked contrast in the extent to which the two earthworks have stabilized over the experimental period. After 5 months the Wareham bank was found to be deeply gullied, some gullies subsequently filling with wind-blown sediment. No gullies ever developed on the more permeable Overton bank. The latter also vegetated and stabilized more quickly, within about 15 years (Fowler 1989, 94). Although on parts of the bank top there was still only a patchy vegetation cover after 32 years there is no evidence of active erosion and the bank surface is a compacted ACu horizon representing the early stages of soil formation (p 116). By contrast, after 31 years, the upper part of the Wareham bank is more sparsely

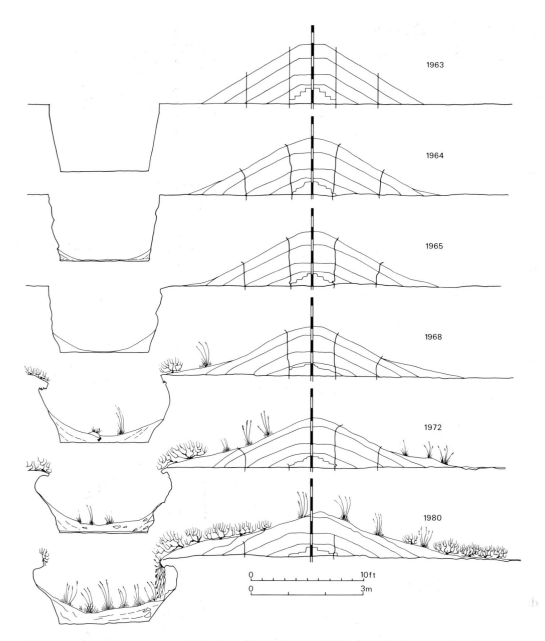

1963

1964

1965

1968

1972

1980

0 _____ 10ft
0 _____ 3m

Figure 14.1 The section of Wareham Experimental Earthwork showing its changing profile betwen 1963 and 1980

vegetated and, despite evidence for the formation of a surface 'crust', there are also signs of active erosion: coarser particles, such as the roadstone chips, tend to be left on little pedestals reflecting perhaps the effect of deflation or rainsplash. In making these comparisons between the two banks, a note of caution should be introduced. The Overton Earthwork is surrounded by a rabbit proof fence which does not exist at Wareham. During some Committee visits to Wareham deer footprints have been much in evidence on the upper part of the bank and this may have acted to prevent vegetation colonization, thereby favouring continued erosion. Even so, the main differences can confidently be attributed to the contrasting sediment types and vegetation of the two sites.

14.8 Comparison of the ditches

Ditches form one of the most common features on archaeological sites. They form traps for many of the artefacts which we recover, so it is clearly important to think about how ditch sediments form and how the artefacts relate to the timescale of ditch sedimentation. One early result of the experiment was to emphasize that material of widely differing dates can easily become associated in the primary fill of a ditch (eg Figs 7.14–15). The earthwork experiments showed how rapidly primary ditch silts form. The experiment facilitated the definition of a three-fold sequence of ditch sedimentation: primary (physical weathering), secondary (stability and soil development) and tertiary (overploughing and colluviation). This sequence is outlined by Evans (1972), Limbrey

235

OVERTON DOWN
Experimental Earthwork

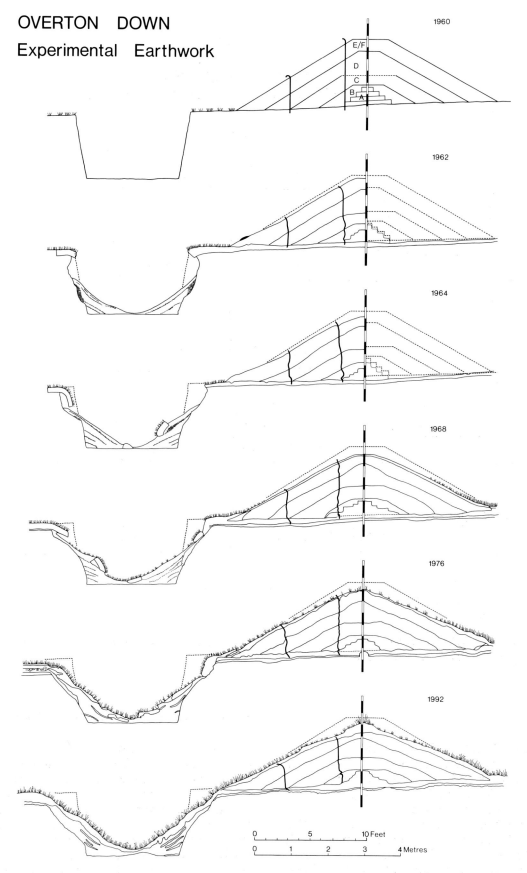

1960

1962

1964

1968

1976

1992

0   5   10 Feet
0   1   2   3   4 Metres

Figure 14.2 The section of Overton Down Experimental Earthwork showing its changing profile between 1960 and 1992. Note: For 1962 and 1964 the bank section to the right of the central pole shows the original profile in dotted form. No section of this part of the bank is available for these two years

(1975) and Proudfoot (1965). Identification of this basic pattern should help to save some inessential description of ditch sediments in excavation reports and enable archaeologists to focus more specifically on those anomalous contexts where human agency has produced a different pattern.

The virtual stability of the Overton ditch by vegetation after about a decade contrasts with the Wareham ditch which still has exposed parent material faces after 31 years, albeit under overhanging vegetation, and partly maintained by rodent runs. The stability of the V-profile Overton ditch suggests that some totally sedimented ditches encountered archaeologically may have been deliberately backfilled. Clearly, however, the width of the berm is a key factor. We also need to consider the likelihood that many archaeological examples were in situations with a greater concentration of disturbance and grazing than has obtained in the somewhat protected environment of the Overton Earthwork enclosure, where even the Committee tend to avoid walking on the earthwork during their twice yearly visits! Another factor which needs to be considered is the local topography and catchment area of individual ditches. We should also remember that the rapid stabilization of the Overton Earthwork may not be typical of the chalkland as a whole. Indeed (Reynolds 1989,19) records significant differences in the rates of vegetation colonization and erosion on Upper, Middle and Bottom Chalk. Reynolds (p 225) further emphasizes that vegetation is a key factor in the pattern of ditch sedimentation. The tendency for luxuriant vegetation to develop on a berm prevents material entering the ditch from the bank and can in fact lead to greater erosion of the less protected ditch side opposite the bank as happened at the Butser Demonstration Area Earthwork.

One consequence of the reduced stability and greater spread of the Wareham bank is that it has made a more significant contribution of sediment to the ditch than is the case at Overton where the contribution is very slight, and probably largely related to localized faunal disturbance (p 70).

During the early years it was noticed that the Overton ditch showed a distinctive sequence of bands of coarse chalk separated by small chalk and soil. These could be interpreted respectively as winter and summer increments (Jewell and Dimbleby 1966; Crabtree 1971). Similar evidence for banding has been recorded in the ditch of the Butser Demonstration area (Bell 1990a; Reynolds p 225). In the early years at Overton the banding was very distinct (Jewell and Dimbleby 1966, Plate 24:3). Between four and six bands remained in various faces of the 1992 section but they were less distinct than previously and there was evidence that they had been blurred by faunal reworking of the ditch sediments and by pedogenesis (p 72). Macphail and Cruise (p 106) consider the effects of faunal agency on the formation of these bands. It is also possible that individual bands could result from brief erosion events, ie storms, or that the pattern of banding could be affected by turf falls. In view of the 1992 evidence that bands may become blurred and their numbers reduced, the evidence of banding should not be pushed too far. Nonetheless comparable evidence of banding survives in the fills of prehistoric ditches on several sites (Bell 1990a). This has the potential to provide a precise timescale for artefact deposition and other activities in the first decade or so after construction of a large earthwork. For instance, in the Overton 1992 section there was evidence that a pottery disc had been moved, probably by human agency, from the bank top to the opposite side of the ditch. The stratigraphic position of this disc shows precisely when this action took place: in winter or spring 1961. Recognition of such banding might facilitate the detection of episodic, perhaps seasonal, patterns of structured deposition in ditches such as those around causewayed enclosures. Evidence of banding is for instance suggested by some of the ditch sections at Hambledon Hill (Mercer 1980, Figure 15b) and the potential is further underlined by an often reproduced photograph of a human skull in a Hambledon Hill ditch on a thin layer of sediment (Mercer 1980, Figure 18). Evidence for pairs of apparently annual bands in the ditch of Coneybury Henge has enabled a timescale for the primary silt to be suggested as probably less than a decade which, when taken in conjunction with the mollusc evidence, indicated that the henge was built in a small clearing which regenerated within about a decade (Bell 1990a). At Wilsford Shaft alternating coarse and fine bands in the upper fill (Bell 1989, 74) have been interpreted as annual pairs; these have been used to suggest a hypothetical timescale for sedimentation of very roughly 150 years which is in broad agreement with the radiocarbon evidence.

Fine clay banding was observed in the Wareham ditch: seven bands were recorded at the 9 year stage. Evans and Limbrey (1974, 179) considered the possibility that these were annual, perhaps the result of the ditch holding water in winter. However, Crabtree (p 208) felt that it was unlikely that they were of regular periodicity given the various stochastic factors involved.

Aspect and microclimatic effects are important influences on erosion (eg Smith 1980, 79) and probably account for the asymmetric profile of both the Overton and Wareham ditches (eg Figs 14.1 and 14.2). This question has been more specifically addressed by the Octagonal Earthworks Programme (Reynolds p 225) and recently by the reconstruction of a barrow on chalk at Monkton Nature Reserve Thanet, Kent (Jay 1993).

14.9 Earthworms and soil fauna

On the acid soil at Wareham there was little evidence for faunal disturbance and earthworm activity, virtually no movement of *Lycopodium* spores had taken place between construction and 1972 (the 1980 samples were lost). By contrast at Overton there were many signs of faunal changes. Locally, moles had burrowed into the Old Land Surface and abstracted soil, and earthworms seem to have re-worked most of the fine sediment in the buried soil and bank over the last 32 years. Their activities had obliterated any clear boundary between the old land surface and the turf stack, making it difficult to define the surface on which the lower group of buried materials had been placed. Old land surface material had been moved by earthworms into the base of the bank and the *Lycopodium* spore evidence of Dimbleby (p 43) and Crabtree (p 127) confirms the existence of upward and downward movement from the old land surface. Richard Macphail writes that in 1992 soil micromorphological evidence suggests that earthworms are not so active now; more in evidence is the activity of enchytraeids which may reflect chemical changes to the buried soil.

Even in the bank at Overton the impression during the 1992 excavation was that, in the interstices between chalk lumps, most of the finer chalk particles were in globular aggregates which were interpreted as the result of earthworm activity. The impression was that, in 32 years, virtually all the fine bank sediment had passed through the guts of earthworms and this view was shared by Peter Jewell who examined the evidence in the field. At least one earthworm was found in most buckets of sediment sieved. The hypothesis of large-scale earthworm reworking of the fines is not, however, supported by Micromorphological Sample 104 which showed that area to be unaffected by earthworms, as Macphail and Cruise argue on p 102. Either that single sample is atypical, or field impressions have exaggerated the extent of earthworm activity. Macphail and Cruise (p 102) suggest the aggregates are pseudoexcrements produced by some non-biological process. This is a question which could be taken further in the future because there are samples of globular aggregates in the project archive.

At Overton a distinct concentration of earthworm casts was noted in 1968 (p 54) and 1992 (p 82) around many of the buried materials in the chalk environment. Earthworm activity was confirmed by the discovery of aestivating worms in contact with some of the buried materials. There was no obvious sign that earthworms were feeding on the buried materials; they could have been feeding on fungi or other organisms involved in decomposition (Edwards and Lofty 1977). It seems more probable that they were attracted by a more favourable, eg moister, microenvironment created by the buried materials.

A key factor in the diagenesis of this buried soil seems to have been mole and earthworm activity. Both these creatures seem from the records (Jewell and Dimbleby 1966, 339; above p 229) to have undergone a linked population explosion in 1962–3. This may be plausibly linked with a particular stage in the decomposition of buried vegetation and also perhaps with the timescale necessary for the build-up of populations in a favourable habitat. A further variable is climate, and it is a matter for speculation

whether the archaeological record would be significantly different had climatic conditions at this stage been inimical to the growth of earthworm or mole numbers. In demonstrating the role which earthworms have played in transforming the Overton Earthwork the experiment has come full circle back to its original inspiration in the work of Charles Darwin.

14.10 Biological evidence

At Wareham some plant material was still recognizable in the turves at the 16 year stage (p 215). At Overton plant material on the old land surface only survived at 16 years above and below the leathers (Limbrey p 57), presumably because tannins had inhibited decay. By the 32 year stage at Overton no macroscopically visible plant material remained on the old landsurface. Small fragments of possible grass were found in the preparations for seed studies (Hendry et al p 140) and traces were observed in the micromorphological sections (Macphail and Cruise p 99). The seeds of many species were well preserved (Carruthers and Straker p 134); indeed six species remained viable (Hendry et al p 138). The experiment has made a worthwhile contribution to previously limited knowledge of seed viability which is of significance in studies of ecological change.

The *Lycopodium* evidence from Wareham indicates that no significant faunal reworking has taken place. In that situation it is likely that the soil and pollen stratigraphy reflects the ecological history of the site. This is an hypothesis which can be further tested during the 1995 excavation. The extensive evidence for faunal reworking in the Overton soil highlights a factor which needs to be considered in the interpretation of all buried soils and their associated biota. This point has been argued previously by Carter (1990) who predicted some reworking of buried soils and also suggested that successive mollusc assemblages in old land surfaces could be of very different ages, those in the stone-free horizon representing decades immediately prior to burial, whereas those in the stone accumulation zone could include a significant residual element. The extent of biological activity revealed in the Overton Down buried soil also has implications for the investigations of a range of properties of buried soils as noted in relation to amino acid studies by Beavis and Macleod (p 124).

The extensive reworking seen at Overton does not, however, seem to apply everywhere. Some old land surfaces on chalk in the Avebury area clearly preserve good palaeoenvironmental sequences in an apparently stratified form, as illustrated by the old land surfaces below long barrows at South Street (Ashbee et al 1979) and Easton Down (Whittle et al 1993). Both soils have a thin earthworm-sorted surface, clearly succeeding cultivation at South Street, and the soils at both sites preserve well-stratified molluscan sequences. Photographs of South Street (Ashbee et al 1979, Plate 35b) show an exceptionally clearly-defined old land surface with no evidence of blurring by earthworm activity. At Easton Down, however, a photograph of the buried soil (Whittle 1993, Fig 5) hints at some upward movement of soil material into the bank as at Overton (Fig 7:11). Richard Macphail (pers comm) reports that on this site the buried soil was mixed, but he feels it is unclear whether this is the result of Neolithic agriculture or post-burial changes. It appears that significant differences in the extent of reworking exist, even between individual sites in the Avebury area; these might reflect a range of factors affecting earthworm population dynamics.

At Overton there was unfortunately no opportunity to investigate the effects of reworking on land mollusc sequences because the old land surface was found to be decalcified and virtually no molluscs survived except in the very much earlier subsoil hollow at the base of the profile (p 140). This evidence, however, serves to remind us that decalcification arising from periods of stability, or particular vegetational changes such as the development of a thick turf mat, can produce conditions which are poor for both mollusc life and survival. Evans (1990) has developed a similar point in relation to the sequences from prehistoric ditches and at Avebury has shown evidence for the successive decalcification and calcification of a buried soil (Evans et al 1993, 176). At Overton, Rouse's (p 142) evidence suggests that molluscs are today rare except in the calcium-rich conditions engendered by the earthwork itself. This suggests that particular vegetation episodes may engender conditions which result in hiatuses in molluscan sequences, which in some cases may only be detected by a combination of palaeoenvironmental approaches.

14.11 The buried materials

The approach to the buried materials has changed dramatically during the project's life. Peter Jewell (pers comm 14.7.94) writes:

'The original idea and intention was to provide a set of references for *field excavators* to help them make reliable interpretations. The inclusion of buried materials and their subsequent examination was an afterthought.'

Even then, during the planning stage, the emphasis was more on the recovery and interpretation of the buried materials in the field, rather than on the laboratory investigations of the materials which have become such an important aspect of the project today. This helps to explain why, during the early decades, the buried materials proved to be the most problematic aspect of the project (Evans and Limbrey 1974; Fowler 1989, 92). The record of observations in the field are not always as complete as required and some materials were lost, for example all the buried materials from Wareham 1965 except for the wood. Comparability between individual sections is made

more difficult because of variations and improvements in recovery techniques (p 56). Difficulties were also experienced in obtaining reports from specialists. Dr Limbrey's record of the buried materials from Overton 1976 (p 55) represented an important step forward. During the 1992 Overton excavation, one objective was a more detailed analytical approach to the buried materials, which was made possible by funding from the Science Based Archaeology Committee of the Science and Engineering Research Council (now part of the Natural Environment Research Council) and English Heritage.

Despite problems with the buried materials aspects, much worthwhile information is available from earlier years and some consistent patterns emerge. To help clarify these, evidence for preservation on the two sites is summarized graphically in Figures 14:3–4. Preservation is categorized on a scale of 0–4 : 4 = well preserved; 3 = localized degradation; 2 = general degradation; 1 = traces only; 0 = no trace. Inevitably the classification is somewhat subjective but it does help to identify the main trends and the chief contrasts, both between the different burial environments (turf and bank) and the Overton and Wareham sites.

Overton buried materials

The preservation of organics is much poorer in the more biologically active turf than the chalk environments.

Textiles

In the turf, Textile 1, cotton loomstate plain cloth, and Textile 2, cotton khaki dyed twill cloth, were not recovered, even in the first section after 2 years. The linen textiles were represented by traces up to, but not beyond the two year section. The wools survived rather longer. Textile 3, woollen contrast cloth, was present in a degraded form up to 16 years. Despite careful searching no trace remained of any textiles in the 32 year section. In the chalk environment, Textile 1, cotton loomstate plain cloth, only survived to the 4 year section but the khaki was still well preserved after 32 years. Both wool textiles survived in a fragmentary condition up to 32 years and the linens were also present in a degraded form. Chalk blocks placed on the surfaces of textiles to hold them in place had clearly helped to protect the underlying textiles in the chalk environment.

Leather

These survived very well in both burial environments and all samples were recovered with little macroscopically visible deterioration after 32 years.

239

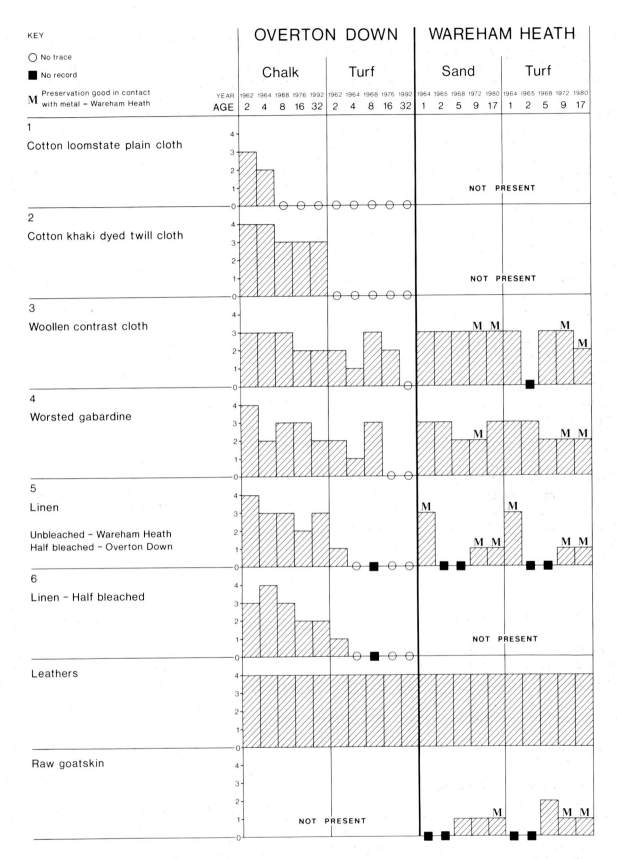

Figure 14.3 Diagram summarizing the preservation of buried materials (textiles, leather and goatskin) in the earthworks on a scale of 0–4. 4 = well preserved; 3 = local degradation; 2 = general degradation; 1 = traces only; 0 = no trace

240

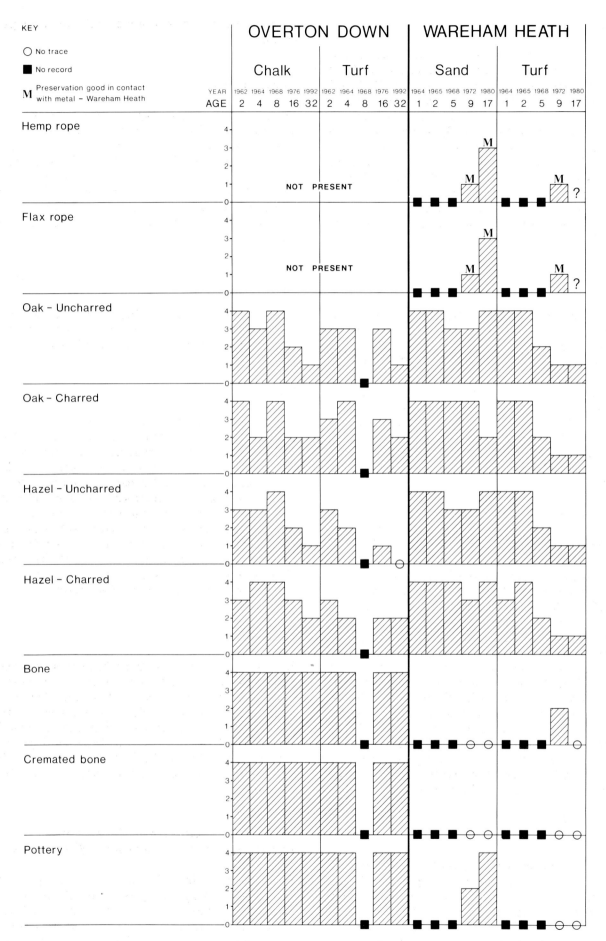

Figure 14.4 Diagram summarizing the preservation of buried materials (rope, wood, bone and pottery) in the earthworks on a scale of 0–4. 4 = well preserved; 3 = local degradation; 2 = general degradation; 1 = traces only; 0 = no trace

Wood

All woods were intact up to the 8 year section in the chalk environment but there is no information about this stage from the turf. At the 16 year stage the hazel in the turf environment was more degraded than in the chalk and conversely the oak was more degraded in the chalk than in the turf. By 32 years no trace remained of the uncharred hazel and of the other woods only fragments or 'charcoal tubes' remained. In the chalk environment at both the 16 and 32 year stages hazel was better preserved than oak. Blanchette suggests (p 160) that the fibre cells of hazel may be more resistant to soft rot fungi than those of oak.

Bone

All the bones survived in both the turf and chalk environments up to the 32 year stage when, on excavation, preservation appeared to be very good. Scanning Electron Microscope examination has, however, produced evidence of significant post-burial modification including cracking and dissolution by saprotrophic fungi and percolating water (Armour-Chelu and Andrews p 185). The results of phosphate analysis confirm the effects of dissolution and indicate that it is occurring to a greater extent in the lower pH turf environment (Crowther p 195).

Wareham buried materials

Here the record only relates to the first 17 years, since the 32 year section will not be cut until 1996. The buried materials record is less complete for the early years than at Overton. A smaller range of textiles and leathers was buried at Wareham but additional objects included goatskin and ropes of hemp and flax. On each organic material a halfpenny and a steel disc were placed making possible consideration of the effects of metal corrosion products on preservation. By the 5 year stage it was clear that preservation was greater below the metals and by the 9 year stage some organics were only preserved where they were in contact with metal. This clearly relates to the well-known decay-inhibiting properties of copper and indicates iron decay products are having a similar effect. Preservation was generally better in the sand than in the turf environment.

Textiles

In the turf environment, the woollen contrast cloth survived in a partly decayed form up to the 17 year stage as did the worsted gaberdine. Linen only survived in contact with the metals. In the sand environment a similar picture obtains. It would be expected that materials such as linen and hemp, which are largely composed of cellulose, would not survive long in acid environments (R. Janaway pers comm).

Leather and hide

Leather survived well in both environments at the 17 year stage but there was evidence that in the more freely draining sand environment it was being detanned more rapidly than in the turf where, unlike the other organics, it was better preserved. Of the goat hide the skin had decayed by the fifth year except where it was in contact with the metals but in all cases a deposit of hairs remained in the 17 year section.

Rope

The first records relate to the 9 year excavation by which time the rope was only preserved in contact with the metal discs, similarly after 17 years.

Wood

Changes in wood density over the first 9 years bring out interesting contrasts (Evans and Limbrey 1974, Table 2). Only slight reductions in density are apparent in the one and two year sections. After that in the sand environment density gradually reduces. By the 17 year stage the uncharred oak and hazel samples were still well preserved, the charred hazel likewise; the charred oak was not so well preserved. In contrast each of the wood samples from the turf shows a sudden reduction in density at the 5 year stage and only residues and fragmentary 'charcoal tubes' remained in the 9 and 17 year sections.

Bone

In the 9 and 17 year sections bone was no longer preserved in the sand environment at Wareham. Even cremated bone appeared to have been lost which is a surprise in view, for instance, of the survival of cremated bone from Iron Age contexts in acid soils of Wales (Austin *et al* 1986; Gilchrist and Mytum 1986). In the turf environment bone did survive but dissolution of the upper surfaces had occurred.

14.12 Comparison between buried materials at Overton and Wareham

Burial contexts in both earthworks are generally aerobic and have probably remained damp but not waterlogged since construction. It is noted (p 56) that even at the height of the 1976 drought the Overton buried materials were still damp enough to sustain biological activity. Evans and Limbrey (1974) noted the possibility of some anaerobism in the turf at Wareham.

The Wareham site has lower pH values, in the range 4.5–5.1 in both environments, compared to Overton, with 5.5 from the turf environment, and 7.5 in the chalk environment. The contrast between the pHs of the two old ground surfaces is probably less than would have been expected by the project's founders. The extent of decalcification at Overton does not seem to have been recognized until 1992; furthermore the process has probably increased over the last 32 years. Figures 14.3 and 14.4 show that, as a generalization, the decay of organics is occurring at a comparable rate in the two earthworks, although there are also some interesting contrasts.

In making comparison between preservation at the two sites we must note that the inclusion of coins and steel disc on the Wareham organics has introduced a variable not present at Overton, but one can assume that areas of textile not underneath metals share equivalent conditions with Overton. Even a difference in the number of layers of textile, 6 at Overton and 4 at Wareham, could prove to be significant, because it is clear that inner layers tend to be better preserved.

Up to the 32 year stage at Overton and the 17 year stage at Wareham preservation of organic samples is generally better in the bank environment, which in both cases is better drained and more aerobic than in the turf. The probable explanation is the higher rates of biological activity in the turf environments. Microbiological study of the Overton 32 year section showed that both bacterial and fungal counts were higher in the turf than in the chalk environments (Kelley and Wiltshire p 148). It is suggested that fungal activity may have been supressed in the chalk environment by high pH and a paucity of nutrients. The only cases from the two sites where preservation seems to have been better in the turf seem to relate to processes involving dissolution at Wareham where bone was lost and leather more leached in the more freely draining sand environment.

Other aspects of preservation reveal major contrasts between the two earthworks. All the bone samples were well-preserved in both environments at Overton but at Wareham all the bone, cooked, uncooked and cremated, had vanished by the 17 year stage. Even at Overton the amount of damage to the bone, apparently as a result of fungal activity, suggests that *if* the present rate of damage continues the bone is unlikely to survive over archaeologically relevant timescales (Armour-Chelu and Andrews p 185). This indicates that we need to give greater consideration to the possibility of spatial contrasts in bone preservation even on those sites where, generally speaking, conditions for preservation appear to be good.

Pottery was well-preserved at Overton but at Wareham was only preserved in the sand environment and had vanished in the turf after just 9 years or less. The apparent speed of pottery destruction at Wareham is remarkable and must go some way towards explaining the paucity of poorly fired prehistoric pottery on acid and upland soils. This makes the identification of aceramic cultures in the west and north of Britain more open to debate.

Charred and uncharred wood billets had been included in the earthworks to establish whether the traditional practice of charring the ends of posts before putting them in the ground aids preservation. The results suggest that, generally speaking, it has little effect. Tubes of charcoal were all that remained after 16 and 17 years respectively. However, in one instance at Wareham, Hather (p 221) suggests that charring had created a sufficient seal to prevent decay.

14.13 Ongoing analysis

With an 128 year project a published report is inevitably an interim statement, which we hope will stimulate further thought and additional investigations. DNA studies are one aspect of the Overton 1992 excavation on which it has only been possible to include an outline of what members of the team hope to do (Hedges *et al* p 196; Brown *et al* p 199). That subject is undergoing a phase of very rapid development stimulated by the Natural Environment Research Council Ancient Biomolecules Initiative. The indications are that the Overton bone samples, of known age, origin and with fairly precisely defined environmental contexts, will be important for the investigation of the survival of DNA sequences in buried bone. The appropriate methods are being developed and the results will be published elsewhere. With the bone and the organic materials, in particular, we have ensured that only a small proportion has been sacrificed for the analyses reported here; much of the original sample is refrigerated and available for future analysis.

With the earlier excavations at both earthworks analytical studies of the buried materials were much more limited. Many of the samples are still available in the project's archive. They have generally been kept in a dry but not refrigerated condition. It is inevitable therefore that changes have taken place since excavation and any future analysis should be planned with this in mind. The archive also contains reference specimens of the originally buried materials. The Committee, through its secretary Mrs G Swanton, would be interested to receive research proposals from specialists interested in carrying out further research on any of the buried materials in the archive.

The potential should also be explored for non-destructive monitoring (Hillson p 224) of changes to the earthworks eg by very detailed contouring or perhaps geophysics.

It should also be noted that within the earthwork there are baulks between the designated sections (Figure 7.3) which could be used for limited studies of the buried soils and their contained biota etc between those years predetermined for experimental sections, if that were necessary in order to address particular research problems.

14.14 Problems with the experiment

With a long-term project it is important to keep the research difficulties and strengths clearly in view. The following points are put forward because they need to be considered in interpreting the results and in planning further additional studies. The points are, of course, made with hindsight. Their recognition does not detract from the pioneering and far-sighted achievement of those who set up the experiment, but they nonetheless identify serious issues concerned with long-term experiments in the context of technical developments and changes of research agenda. These issues reflect back to the significance of timescale in archaeological research discussed above (p 230).

(1) Problems of continuity. It is far from ideal that the results of four separate experimental stages have been brought together in one publication, although this has given us the opportunity to review the progress of the project as a whole. In the future it is important that a prompt programme of publication is maintained in order that an effective dialogue is achieved between the experiment and field archaeological practice.

(2) Limited financial support until Overton 1992 made it very difficult to make progress, particularly with regard to the buried materials.

(3) It is difficult to take account of the role of chance and chaos in interpreting the results of such an experiment.

(4) The lack of replication of samples within an individual section was a basic methodological flaw, as Janaway notes (p 167). Pat Wiltshire also comments that the earthwork as a whole is unique and without replicates which can be used to test hypotheses. It should be noted, however, that chance variations in a whole range of environmental conditions such as faunal activity mean that the concept of a replicate in this context is somewhat problematic.

(5) The buried materials were said to be similar to those used in prehistoric times (Jewell 1963, 43). That applies to most inorganic materials (with the exception of the choice of metal alloys used at Wareham), but not the organic materials, many of which had been treated in ways which differ significantly from prehistoric practice. Ryder (p 172) remarks on the inappropriateness of the wool types used. Of the leathers, only the oak-bark tanned example is directly archaeologically relevant and textile preservation seems to be very much related to the presence, absence and nature of dyes such as the modern chromium based khaki which probably has a greater preservative effect than the dyes and mordants which were used in antiquity (R Janaway pers comm).

(6) The purpose behind incorporating particular materials in the earthwork is sometimes not all that clearly specified. Hather (p 222) makes this point with regard to the wood but in this case Blanchette's work (p 155) has been able to go beyond what could originally be envisaged. In other cases, such as the flints or the changes to the discs, we have discussed suitable analytical approaches with colleagues but come to the conclusion that we have not been able to identify meaningful tests which can be applied to them at this stage. They remain in the archive for possible future study.

(7) Each section cannot be seen as a perfect replica in a time series. Each will have its own unique properties of, for example, chemistry or post-burial faunal history which may, or may not, have a significant influence on the outcome of the experiment. Similarly, each of the buried material samples (Janaway p 167) and the contexts in which they are placed will not be perfect replicates. Two linens of very similar specification (Jewell 1963, 45) were found in the chalk environment at Overton to be in one case largely intact and in the other case very degraded (see Janaway, p 166; Hardman, p 175). At Overton the worsted gaberdine in the chalk environment was found to be very degraded in the 4 year section but well preserved in the 8 year section. Of the two oak samples from the chalk environment in the Overton 1976 section the uncharred example was intact and the charred example just a charcoal tube. Evans and Limbrey (1974, 188) also suggest that a distinctive pattern of staining on the worsted gabardine from the sand environment in the Wareham 9 year section was probably caused by an 'attacking substance' on the surface on which it was placed.

(8) Grazing animals are excluded from Overton but not Wareham, where deer activity is quite frequent on the bank.

(9) Interpretation of current analyses is sometimes hampered by a lack of background information at the time of construction. For instance, we have to rely on data from surrounding present soils for comparison with the analytical properties of the buried soil, but at Overton there is clear evidence for significant vegetation and probably soil change since the beginning of the experiment, arising primarily from the exclusion of grazing within the fenced enclosure. This makes these modern comparanda of doubtful validity (Crowther p 118).

(10) The 1992 Overton Excavation was a conscious attempt to tackle some of the identified shortcomings of previous stages of the project. Even so it has its own weaknesses which need to be identified because this will help future generations to do better and because they have an

impact on the results. Two of the main short-comings were:- (a) Insufficient time was allowed (p 231) and (b) No survey was conducted of the fauna encountered within the earthwork and specifically the earthworms were not identified.

(11) The experiments are limited to chalk and sand geologies where most excavation was taking place in the 1950s and 1960s. Since then excavation has expanded on to a much wider range of other geologies. The octagonal earthworks have helped to address this issue with the Fishbourne Earthwork on brickearth and the Little Butser Earthwork on Middle Chalk (Reynolds p 225). More distantly, in Germany an earthwork of somewhat comparable shape, replicating the Neolithic Michelsberg earthwork, was constructed in 1970 on loess and lava strata at Mayen, Eifel (Luning 1971).

14.15 Merits of the experiment

It is not necessary to specify these in as much detail as the problems. We hope the benefits are apparent from the volume as a whole. Even so it may be helpful to specify some general points:

(1) From the beginning the project had clearly stated aims and method.
(2) The project helped to make experimental methodology an accepted part of archaeological practice.
(3) The interdisciplinary approach is relevant to a range of disciplines concerned with change over time.
(4) The project helped the development of a team approach to the application of science in archaeology. From the beginning specialists worked on the site providing the opportunity to appreciate the contexts from which samples were derived.
(5) The experiment is a welcome attempt to address issues of medium-term change.
(6) The care with which the experiment was set up makes it possible to use the site for a range of studies which were not originally foreseen.

14.16 Work study

An oft-quoted aspect of the experiments at Overton and Wareham concerns work rates: the person-hours taken to construct a given volume of earthwork using prehistoric tool types (Overton: Jewell 1963, 50; Wareham: Evans and Limbrey 1974, 199). On the basis of the Overton experiment it was, for example, suggested that a small barrow could have been made by 10 people in a week and the Dorset Cursus took about 100 people 740 days (Ashbee and Cornwall 1961, 130). Atkinson (1961, 295) refined the calculations by proposing a formula which took account of the size of monuments and the distance from ditch to

bank/ mound. This was applied by Ashbee (1966) to calculate the person-hours represented by construction of Fussell's Lodge Long Barrow. Calculations based on Atkinson's formula also formed a key element in an influential paper by Renfrew (1973) which considered the person-hours involved in the construction of prehistoric monuments as evidence of social structure and its changing nature in the Neolithic and Bronze Age. The earthwork evidence was also used by Startin (1982) to calculate the person hours involved in the construction of a range of Neolithic to Iron Age monuments. It can be seen therefore that the work rate experiment has played an important part in helping to put prehistoric monuments in some sort of perspective in terms of relative human effort.

In using the Overton and Wareham evidence it should, however, be appreciated that the figures for volumes of sediment per unit time are based on fairly small-scale, short-term tests. The distance between the bottom of the ditch and the top of the bank was short but the work became markedly more strenuous as the height increased (B. Proudfoot pers comm). It was also appreciated at the time by Ashbee and Cornwall (1961, 130) that we cannot necessarily replicate prehistoric tool use and work rates (Reynolds 1981, 97). Furthermore it is increasingly being recognized that human actions are context specific rather than law-like. We cannot replicate the attitudes of past communities to time, materials or knowledge, any more than we can hope to replicate the particular patterns of climate or weather which obtained in the past. It also needs to be borne in mind that figures derived from Overton and Wareham may not be applicable to other bedrocks, as the differences in hundredweights per person-hour dug emphasise: 4.4 at Overton; 7 at Wareham.

These comments are not intended to dismiss the results of the work rate experiment. For the most part they are the best data we have. In applying figures we do, however, need to take full account of the theoretical issues involved and the necessary relationship between the scale of the experiment and the reliability of the interpretations of which it forms the basis.

14.17 Experiment and the study of formation processes in archaeology

Overviews of experimental archaeology are provided by Coles (1973 and 1979) supplemented by edited volumes summarizing the results of individual projects, for example Ingersoll et al (1977) and Robinson (1990), both of which, as it happens, contain progress reports on the Experimental Earthworks (in the former, a reprint of Jewell and Dimbleby (1966); in the latter, a review paper by Crabtree 1990). The majority of archaeological experiments have been relatively small-scale and short-term and have addressed particular research problems which arose in the course of larger projects. Many have been concerned with how to make artefacts or carry out particular tasks. An influential pioneering experiment was that conducted in the Draved forest, Denmark, between 1953 and 1955 (Steensberg 1979). The results have dominated interpretations of Neolithic agriculture in northern and western Europe for 40 years. Considering the dominance of the model erected upon it, the experiment was actually fairly short-term and small-scale and was conducted on soils which were probably significantly less fertile than most of those cultivated in the Neolithic. This re-emphasizes a point made above in relation to the work study concerning the relationship between the scale of an experiment and the reliability of the results obtained. Where environmental factors are a key variable, as in experiments on crop growing, ditch weathering or vegetation colonization, the timescale also needs to take account of the natural variation of environmental phenomena through time: both predictable cyclical change and stochastic events. Where the results of an experiment turn out to be central to the formulation of wider models, then those results should be the subject of regular critical examination and testing.

Probably the most influential experiments have been those of a particularly ambitious long-term nature. Lejre Research Centre, Denmark, is focussed on a reconstructed Iron Age village and opened in 1965 (Hansen 1982). Butser Iron Age Farm Project in Hampshire was founded about 1972 (Reynolds 1979); it has produced experimental data for around twenty years. So powerful are the images presented by Lejre and Butser that they have tended to dominate perception of the periods in question and of experimental archaeology by the general public and archaeologists alike.

The Experimental Earthworks are rather different from the average archaeological experiment. For one thing the proposed timescale is far longer than any other archaeological experiment. The problems which that has created will be obvious to any reader of this monograph. We hope that we have also demonstrated why archaeology needs to concern itself with medium-term change and to focus on issues of perception and its relationship to timescale (Bell in prep).

The earthworks also differ from conventional experiments because they are not an attempt to recreate any specific type of prehistoric monument. There had been the idea at the beginning of constructing something like a Bronze Age barrow (Jewell 1993, 109), but that was abandoned in favour of a more abstract creation, designed to address the problems of earthworks and buried materials in general. This has the disadvantage of not conveying to the general public a clear visual idea of what one aspect of the past was like, and it could also be criticized as a somewhat dehumanized piece of archaeological research. Conversely we would argue that the originators of the earthworks were refreshingly honest in having somewhat circumscribed and generally clearly defined objectives.

This brings us to the question: what are the legitimate objectives and aspirations of experiment in archaeology? Ascher (1961) quoted in Coles (1979) describes experiments as a way of testing beliefs about past cultural behaviour. That is questionable, because of the completely different social, and often environmental, context of past actions. Experiment does, however, play an important part in helping us to appreciate the limitations on actions imposed by the physical properties of raw materials. To do this we need to reacquire more or less lost skills. Equally important is the role which experiment plays in studying how the archaeological record is formed and transformed through time by a combination of natural factors and human agency. As Reynolds (1981, 98) has said of the Butser experiment: 'the Ancient Farm is a laboratory from which will emerge the boundaries of probability rather than an historically true ... and proved record'. The question arises, how central is the study of formation processes to modern archaeology which is increasingly, and rightly, preoccupied with social theory (Shanks and Tilley 1987)? In other words, is the experiment an outmoded exercise in processual archaeology? In addressing this question we are in a way reflecting back to the theme of Atkinson's (1960) inaugural lecture on 'Archaeology, History and Science'. Atkinson wrote: 'Archaeologists are seen as only writing history in the broadest possible sense because we cannot distinguish individuals and the timespans we can recognize are often enormously greater than the human life.' Archaeologists have very similar objectives to historians and make use of similar bodies of social theory. Nevertheless, archaeology approaches the past using different sources of evidence from history. It does so primarily through material culture and the information people leave in the way they transform their environment and create landscapes, rather than primarily through written or oral sources, which are none-the-less very important to the archaeologist. Given that the source material of much archaeology is very different from that of history it is important for archaeology to develop its own theoretical perspectives and methods appropriate to the particulars of its main source material, the archaeological record and its changing nature over long timescales. In the context of the recent development of interest in archaeological formation processes (Schiffer 1987) the earthwork experiment was in some ways a generation ahead of its time. Atkinson (1957, 219) had argued that archaeologists had not given enough attention to 'the processes of formation of the sites which they dig.' Thirty seven years later it is clear that the study of formation processes is necessarily a central aspect of the development of increasingly sophisticated interpretations of artifact patterning and palaeoenvironmental evidence.

In the introduction to both this volume and this chapter we reviewed the historical context of the experiment, and discussed some philosophical issues concerned with time and chance which it raises. The direct question arises: is an experiment formulated in the intellectual climate of the 1950s still relevant

246

today? We hope that the results presented in this volume demonstrate that it is. Its contribution is highlighted by the opportunities afforded for addressing a range of issues not originally foreseen at the time of the project's design. The experiment also acts as a sort of open air laboratory in which successive generations of archaeologists can think through issues of formation processes and the timescales of change and help to build a bridge between individual short-term observations and archaeological time.

Acknowledgements

I am grateful to the following who, whilst they may not agree with all the sentiments expressed, kindly commented on an earlier draft of this concluding chapter and often provided additional comments: Keith Crabtree; John Crowther; Peter Fowler; Jim Hemsley; Simon Hillson; Rob Janaway; Peter Jewell; Richard Macphail; Bruce Proudfoot; Michael Ryder; Gill Swanton and Pat Wiltshire.

Bibliography

Aldhouse-Green, S, 1994 Obituary: Professor Richard Atkinson. *The Independent* 17.10.94, 14

Allcroft, A Hadrian, 1908 *Earthworks of England,* London, Macmillan

Allen, M J, 1988 Archaeological and environmental aspects of colluviation in south-east England, in Groenman-van Waateringe, W and Robinson, M (eds) *Man-made soils BAR IS410* (Oxford, Brit Archaeological Rep), 67–92

Allen, M J & Macphail, R I, 1987 Micromorphology and magnetic susceptibility studies: their combined role in interpreting archaeological soils and sediments, in Fedoroff, N, Bresson, N L & Courty, M A (eds) *Soil Micromorphology* (Plaisir; Association Française pour Etude du Sol), 669–676

Andrews, P, 1995 Experiments in Taphonomy, in Hedges, R and van Klinken G-J (eds) Proceedings of the Oxford Bone Diagenesis Workshop, *Journal of Archaeological Science* **22**, 147–153

Andrews, P & Cook, J, 1985 Natural modifications to bones in a temperate setting, *Man* **20**, 675–691

Apinis, A E, 1958 Distribution of microfungi in soil. Profiles of certain alluvial grasslands, *Angewandte Pflanzensoziologie* **15**, 83–90

Arsvoll, K, 1975 Fungi causing winter damage on cultivated grasses in Norway, *Norges Landbruk hogskole Foringsforsokense Beretning* **54**, 641–664

Ascher, R, 1961 Experimental archaeology, *American Anthropologist*, **63**, 793–816

Ashbee, P, 1953 The excavation of a round barrow on Canford Heath, Dorset, 1951, *Proceedings of the Dorset Natural History and Archaeological Society,* **76**, 39–50

Ashbee, P, 1960 *The Bronze Age Round Barrow in Britain* (London, Phoenix House)

Ashbee, P, 1966 The Fussell's Lodge Long Barrow Excavations 1957, *Archaeologia,* **100,** 1–80

Ashbee, P, 1972 Field archaeology: its origins and development, in Fowler, P.J. (ed) *Archaeology and the Landscape,* London, J Baker, 38–74

Ashbee, P & Cornwall, I W, 1961 An experiment in field archaeology, *Antiquity* **35**, 129–134

Ashbee, P & Dimbleby, G W, 1959 The excavation of a round barrow on Chick's Hill, East Stoke Parish, Dorset, *Proceedings of the Dorset Natural History and Archaeological Society* **80**, 146–159

Ashbee, P & Dimbleby, G W, 1976 The Moor Green barrow, West End, Hampshire: excavations, 1961, *Proceedings of the Hampshire Field Club and Archaeological Society* **31**, 5–18

Ashbee, P, Smith, I F & Evans, J G, 1979 Excavation of three long barrows near Avebury, Wiltshire, *Proceedings of the Prehistoric Society* **45**, 207–300

Atkinson, R J C, 1956 *Stonehenge: Archaeology and Interpretation* (London, Hamish Hamilton)

Atkinson, R J C, 1957 Worms and Weathering, *Antiquity* **31**, 219–233

Atkinson, R J C, 1960 *Archaeology, History and Science* Inaugural lecture (Cardiff, University of Wales Press)

Atkinson, R J C, 1961 Neolithic engineering, *Antiquity,* **35**, 292–299

Austin, D , Bell, M G, Burnham, B C & Young, R, 1986 *The Caer Cadwgan Project: Interim Report for 1985* (Lampeter, University of Wales)

Avery, B W, 1990 *Soils of the British Isles* (Wallingford, Commonwealth Agriculture Bureau International)

Avery, B W & Bascomb, C L, 1974 (eds) Soil Survey Laboratory Methods *Soil Survey Technical Monograph* **6** (Harpenden, Soil Survey of England and Wales)

Babel, U, 1975 Micromorphology of soil organic matter, in Geiseking, J E (ed) *Soil components, 1: organic components* (New York, Springer-Verlag), 369–473

Babel, U, 1981 Alteration of plant material, in Bullock P & Murphy C (eds) *Proceedings IVth International Working Meeting on Soil Micromorphology,* London, 369–473

Bailey, T L W, Tripp, V W & Moore, A T, 1963 Cotton and other Vegetable Fibres, in Hearle, J W S & Peters, R H (eds) *Fibre Structure* (London, Butterworths for The Textile Institute), 422–454

Bal, L, 1982 *Zoological Ripening of Soils,* Agricultural Research Reports **850** (Pudoc, Wageningen, Centre for Agricultural Publications and Documentation)

Ball, D F, 1964 Loss-on-ignition as an estimate of organic matter and organic carbon in non-calcareous soils, *Journal of Soil Science* **15**, 84–92

Barber, E J W, 1990 *Prehistoric Textiles* (Princeton University Press)

Barker, C.T, 1985 The Long Mounds of the Avebury Region, *Wiltshire Archaeological and Natural History Magazine,* **79,** 7–38

Beavis, J, 1985 Amino acids in buried soils, in Fieller, N R J, Gilbertson, D D & Ralph, N G A (eds) *Palaeoenvironmental Investigations,* BAR

248

IS 258 (Oxford, Brit Archaeological Rep), 113–124

Beavis, J, 1990 *The effects of land use burial on the amino acid composition of soil* (University of Reading, PhD Thesis)

Behrensmeyer, A K, 1978 Taphonomic and ecological information from bone weathering, *Palaeobiology* 4, 150–162

Bell, L S, 1990 Palaeopathology and diagenesis: an SEM evaluation of structural changes using backscattered electronic imaging, *Journal of Archaeological Science* 17, 85–102

Bell, L S, Boyde, A B & Jones, S J, 1991 Diagenetic alteration to teeth *in situ* illustrated by backscattered electron imaging, *Scanning* 13, 173–183

Bell, M G, 1989 The environmental material from the shaft's fill, in Ashbee, P, Bell, M & Proudfoot, E, *Wilsford Shaft: Excavations 1960–62* (English Heritage Archaeological Report 11: London, HBMC), 72–75

Bell, M G, 1990a Sedimentation rates in the primary fills of chalk cut features, in Robinson, D (ed) *Experiment and Reconstruction in Environmental Archaeology* (Oxford, Oxbow Books), 237–248

Bell, M G, 1990b The land molluscs, in Saville, A, *Hazleton North, Gloucestershire, 1979–82: the excavation of a Neolithic long cairn of the Cotswold-Severn group* (London, English Heritage Archaeological Report 13), 219–222

Bell, M G, in preparation Perception and the timescale of environmental change

Bell, M G & Boardman, J (eds) 1992 *Past and Present Soil Erosion* (Oxford, Oxbow Books)

Bell, M G & Walker, M J C 1992 *Late Quaternary Environmental Change : Physical and human perspectives* (Harlow, Longmans)

Bell, M G, Watson, N, & Jones, J, 1990 The land molluscs from Winterbourne Steepleton, Dorset, in Woodward, P *The Dorset Ridgeway* (Dorchester, Dorset Natural History and Archaeological Society Monograph 8), 114–117

Berkley, E E, 1948 Cotton – a versatile textile fibre, *Textile Research Journal* 18:2, 71–88

Blanchette, R A, 1991 Delignification by wood-decay fungi, *Annual Review of Phytopathology* 29, 381–398

Blanchette, R A, Cease, K R, Abad, A R, Burnes, T A & Obst, J R, 1991 Ultrastructural characterization of wood from Tertiary fossil forests in the Canadian Arctic, *Canadian Journal of Botany* 69, 560–568

Blanchette, R A, Haight, J E, Koestler, R J, Hatchfield, P B & Arnold, D, 1994 Assessment of deterioration in archaeological wood from ancient Egypt, *Journal of the American Institute of Conservation* 33, 55–70

Blanchette, R A, Nilsson, T, Daniel, G & Abad, A, 1990 Biological degradation of wood, in Rowell, R M & Barbour, R J (eds) Archaeological Wood: Properties, Chemistry and Preservation,

Advances in Chemistry, 225 (Washington, American Chemical Society), 141–174

Blunt, F L & Baker, G E, 1968 Antimycotic activity of fungi isolated from Hawaiian soils, *Mycologia* 60, 559–570

Bloomfield, C, 1951 Experiments on the mechanism of gley formation, *Journal of Soil Science* 2, 196–211

Bowen, H C, 1961 *Ancient fields; a tentative analysis of vanishing earthworks and landscapes* (London, British Association for the Advancement of Science)

Bowen, H C & Fowler, P J, 1962 The archaeology of Fyfield and Overton Downs, *Wiltshire Archaeological Magazine* 58, 98–115

Boyde, A & Jones, S L, 1983 Backscattered electron imaging of dental tissues, *Anatomy and Embryology* 5, 145–150

Boyde, A & Jones, S L, 1984 Back-scattered electron imaging of skeletal tissues, *Metabolic Bone Disease and Related Research* 5, 145–150

Boyde, A, Maconnachie, E, Reid, S A, Delling, G & Mundy, G R, 1986 Scanning electron microscopy in bone pathology: a review of methods, potential and applications, *Scanning Microscopy* 4, 1537–1554

Brady, N C, 1974 *The Nature and Properties of Soils* (New York, Macmillan)

Bremner, J M, 1966 in McLaren, A D & Petersen, G H (eds) *Soil Biochemistry* (New York, Marcel Dekker)

British Standards Institution, 1961 British Standard Number 1377. *Methods for Soil Testing*

Brown, J C, 1958 Soil fungi of some British sand dunes in relation to soil type and succession, *Journal of Ecology* 46, 641–664

Bullock, P, 1974 Micromorphology, in Avery, B W & Bascombe C L (eds) *Soil Survey Laboratory Methods* (Harpenden, Soil Survey Technical Monograph 6), 70–83

Bullock, P & Murphy, C P, 1979 Evolution of a palaeo-argillic brown earth (paleudalf) from Oxfordshire, England, *Geoderma,* 22, 225–252

Bullock, P, Fedoroff, N, Jongerius, A, Stoops, G J & Tursina, T, 1985 *Handbook for soil thin section description* (Wolverhampton, Waine Research Publishers)

Burnham, D K, 1981 *A Textile Terminology* (London, Routledge)

Burnham, C P,1983 Soil profiles on Lullington Heath, Sussex, in Burnham, C P (ed) Soils of the Heathlands and Chalklands, *SEESOIL: Journal of South-East England Soils Discussion Group* 1, 172–177

Burnham, C P, 1990 Chalk and chalk debris as a medium for plant growth, with particular reference to Channel Tunnel spoil, *Soil Use and Management* 6, 131–6

Butler, F C, 1953 Saprophytic behaviour of some cereal root rot fungi 1. Saprophytic colonisation of wheat straw, *Annals of Applied Biology* **40**, 284–297

Butt, Z L & Ghaffar, A, 1974 Effects of certain physico-chemical factors on growth and antifungal property of *Stachybotrys atra*, *Zeitschrift für Pfanzenkrankheiten und Pfanzenschut* **71**, 463–466

Campbell, R, 1983 *Microbial Ecology* (Oxford, Blackwell Scientific Publications)

Cappers, R J T, 1993 Seed dispersal by water: a contribution to the interpretation of seed assemblages, *Vegetation History and Archaeobotany* **2**, 173–186

Cardamone, J M , Keister, K M & Osareh, A H, 1991 Degradation and Conservation of Cellulosics and Esters, in Allen, N S, Edge, M & Horie, C V (eds) *Polymers in Conservation* (London, Royal Society Chemistry), 108–124

Carruthers, W J, 1986 The late Bronze Age midden at Potterne, *Circaea* **4** (1), 16–17

Carson, R, 1965 *Silent Spring* (London, Penguin)

Carter, S P, 1987 *The reconstruction of land-snail death assemblages,* Unpublished PhD Thesis, (London, Institute of Archaeology, University of London)

Carter, S P, 1990 The stratification and taphonomy of shells in calcareous soils: implications for land snail analysis in archaeology, *Journal of Archaeological Science*, **17**, 495–507

Case, H, 1952 The Excavation of Two Round Barrows at Poole, Dorset, *Proceedings of the Prehistoric Society*, **9**, 148–159

Catt, J A, Corbett, W M, Hodge, C A H, Madgett, P A, Tatler, W & Weir, A H, 1971 Loess in the soils of North Norfolk, *Journal of Soil Science* **22**, 444–52

Chang, Y & Hudson, H J, 1967 The fungi of wheat straw compost 1. Ecological studies, *Transactions of the British Mycological Society* **50**, 649–666

Cheng, C-N, 1975 Extracting and desalting amino acids from soils and sediments: evaluation of methods, *Soil Biology and Biochemistry* **7**, 319–322

Cheng, C-N, Shufeldt, R C & Stevenson, F J, 1975 Amino acid analysis of soils and sediments: extracting and desalting, *Soil Biology and Biochemistry* **7**, 143–151

Chi, C C & Hanson, E W, 1964 Relation of temperature, pH and nutrient to growth and sporulation of *Fusarium* sp. from Red Clover, *Phytopathology* **54**, 1053–1058

Clark, A J, 1990 *Seeing beneath the soil* (London, Batsford)

Clark, J G D, Godwin, H & Clifford, M H, 1935 Report on recent excavations at Peacock's Farm, Shippea Hill, Cambridgeshire, *Antiquaries Journal*, **15**, 284–319

Clement, D W, 1967 *A soil survey of Fyfield Down Nature Reserve,* Unpublished report

Coles, J M, 1973 *Archaeology by Experiment* (London, Hutchinson)

Coles, J M, 1979 *Experimental Archaeology* (London, Academic Press)

Cook, B, 1988 Fibre damage in archaeological textiles, in O'Connor, S A & Brooks, M M *Archaeological Textiles* (London, United Kingdom Institute for Conservation, Occasional Paper **10**), 5–15

Cope, D W, 1976 Soils in Wiltshire I, Sheet SU03 (Wilton), *Soil Survey Record* **32**

Cornwall, I W, 1953 Soil Science and Archaeology with illustrations from some British Bronze Age Monuments, *Proceedings of the Prehistoric Society*, **2**, 129–147

Cornwall, I W, 1956 *Bones for the archaeologist* (London, Phoenix House)

Cornwall, I W, 1958 *Soils for the archaeologist* (London, Phoenix House)

Cornwall, I W,1966 Appendix IV, in Ashbee, P (ed), The Fussell's Lodge long barrow excavations 1957 *Archaeologia* **100**, 74

Courty, M A, Goldberg, P & Macphail, R I, 1989 *Soils, Micromorphology and Archaeology* (Cambridge University Press)

Cowley, G T & Whittingham, W F, 1961 The effect of tannin on selected soil microfungi in culture, *Mycologia* **53**, 539–542

Crabtree, K, 1990 Experimental earthworks in the United Kingdom, in Robinson, D E (ed) *Experimentation and Reconstruction in Environmental Archaeology* (Oxford, Oxbow Books), 225–35

Crabtree, K, 1971 Overton Down Experimental Earthwork, Wiltshire 1968 *Proceedings of the University of Bristol Spelaeological Society* **12**, 237–244

Cromack, K, Sollins, P, Graustein, W C, Speidell, K, Todd, A W, Spycher, G, Li, C Y & Todd, R L, 1979 Calcium oxalate accumulation and soil weathering in mats of the hypogeous fungus *Hysterangium crassum*, *Soil Biology and Biochemistry* **11**, 463–468

Crowther, J, 1990 Palaeosols and sediments, in Burnham, B C & Davies, J L (eds) *Conquest, co-existence and change: recent work in Roman Wales* (*Trivium* **25**), 85–94

Crowther, J, 1992 Soil phosphorous, in Murphy, K (ed) Plas Gogerddan, Dyfed: a multi-period ritual burial site, *Archaeological Journal* **149**, 1–38 and Microfiche M1, 5–13

Crowther, J, 1993, Report on the soils and pit fills of Cairn 1, Carneddau, Powys, in Gibson, A M (ed) Excavation of two cairns and associated features at Carneddau, Carno, Powys, 1989–90, *Archaeological Journal* **150**, 1–45 and Microfiche M1 17–23

Curwen, E C, 1930 The silting of ditches in chalk, *Antiquity* **4**, 97–100

Dale, E, 1914 On the fungi of the soil, *Annals of Mycologia* **12**, 33–62

250

Darlington, H T & Steinbauer, G P, 1961 The eighty-year period for Dr. Beal's seed viability experiment, *American Journal of Botany* **48**, 321–325

Darwin, C, 1881 *The Formation of vegetable mould through the action of worms with observations on their habits* (London, Faber & Faber)

Delgardo, M & Dorronsoro, C, 1983 Image analysis, in Bullock, P and Murphy, C P (eds) *Soil micromorphology* (Berkhampstead, A B Academic Publishers), 71–86

Dick, W A & Tabatabai, M A 1977 An alkaline oxidation method for the determination of total phosphorus in soils, *Journal of the Soil Science Society of America* **41**, 511–14

Dickinson, C H & Boardman, F 1970 Physiological studies of some fungi isolated from peat, *Transactions of the British Mycological Society* **55**, 293–305

Dimbleby, G W, 1962 *The Development of British Heathlands and their soils*, Oxford Forestry Memoirs, **23**

Dimbleby, G W, 1963a Soils and soil charcoal, in Jewell, P A (ed) *The experimental earthwork on Overton Down, Wiltshire, 1960* (London, British Association for the Advancement of Science), 62–63

Dimbleby, G W, 1963b Vegetation history – pollen analysis, in Jewell, P A (ed) *The Experimental Earthwork on Overton Down, Wiltshire, 1960* (London, British Association for the Advancement of Science), 67–70

Dimbleby, G W, 1965a *Environmental Studies and archaeology*, Inaugural lecture. (London, Institute of Archaeology)

Dimbleby, G W, 1965b Overton Down Experimental Earthwork, *Antiquity* **39**, 134–136

Dimbleby, G W, 1977 *Ecology and Archaeology*. London, Edward Arnold, Institute of Biology, Studies in Biology No 77

Dimbleby, G W, 1984 Anthropogenic changes from Neolithic through Medieval times, *New Phytologist* **98**, 57–72

Dimbleby, G W, 1985 *The Palynology of Archaeological Sites* (London, Academic Press)

Dinc, U, Miedema, R, Bal, L & Pons, L J, 1976 Morphological and physico-chemical aspects of three soils developed in peat in the Netherlands and their classification, *Netherlands Journal of Agricultural Science*, **24**, 247–265

Dionex Corporation, 1990 *AminoPac Test Chromatogram,* Document **020593**, 3

Domsch, K H, 1960 Die Wirkung von Bodenfungiciden 4. Versederungen im Spektrum der Bodenpilze, *Zeitschrift für Pfanzenkrankheiten und Pfanzenschut* **67**, 129–150

Domsch, K H & Gams, W, 1972 *Fungi in Agricultural Soils* (Harlow, Longman)

Domsch, K H, Gams, W & Anderson, T-H, 1980 *Compendium of soil fungi Volumes 1&2* (London, Academic Press)

Drewett, P L, 1975 The excavation of a turf barrow at Minsted, West Sussex, 1973, *Sussex Archaeological Collections* **113**, 54–65

Drewett, P L, 1976 The excavation of four round barrows of the second millenium, B.C., at West Heath, Harting, 1973–5, *Sussex Archaeological Collections* **114**, 126–150

Drewett, P L, 1985 The excavation of barrows V–IX at West Heath, Harting, 1980, *Sussex Archaeological Collections* **123**, 35–60

Drewett, P L, 1989 Anthropogenic soil erosion in prehistoric Sussex: excavations at West Heath and Ferring, 1984, *Sussex Archaeological Collections* **127**, 11–29

Duncan, C G & Eslyn, W E, 1966 Wood decaying ascomycetes and fungi imperfecti, *Mycologia* **58**, 642–645

Edwards, C A & Lofty, J R, 1977 *Biology of Earthworms* (London, Chapman & Hall)

Edwards, G, 1989 Guidelines for dealing with material from sites where organic remains have been preserved by metal corrosion products, in Janaway, R & Scott, B (eds) *Evidence Preserved in Corrosion Products, New Fields in Artifact Studies. United Kingdom Institute for Conservation Occasional Paper* **8**, 3–7

Eka, O U, 1970 Studies of *Epicoccum nigrum* 1. Influence of environmental factors on growth and pigmentation, *West African Journal of Biological and Applied Chemistry* **13**, 3–12

Elarosi, H, 1957 Fungal associations 2. Culture studies on *Rhizoctonia solani, Fusarium solani* and other fungi and their interactions, *Annals of Botany* **21**, 569–585

Eriksson, K E, Blanchette, R A & Ander, P, 1990 *Microbial and enzymatic degradation of wood and wood components* (New York, Springer-Verlag)

Esau, K, 1965 *Plant Anatomy* 2nd Edition (New York, Wiley)

Evans, J G, 1972 *Landsnails in Archaeology* (London, Seminar Press)

Evans, J G, 1990 Notes on some Late Neolithic and Bronze Age events in long barrow ditches in southern and eastern England, *Proceedings of Prehistoric Society* **56**, 111–116

Evans, J G & Limbrey, S, 1974 The experimental earthwork on Morden Bog, Wareham, Dorset, England: 1963–1972, *Proceedings of the Prehistoric Society* **40**, 170–202

Evans, J G, Limbrey, S, Mate, I & Mount, R, 1993 An environmental history of the Upper Kennet Valley, Wiltshire, for the last 10,000 years, *Proceedings of the Prehistoric Society*, **59**, 139–195

Evans, J G & Rouse, A, 1991 The land Mollusca, in Sharples, N M *Maiden Castle excavations and field survey 1985–86* (London, English Heritage Archaeological Report), 118–125

Experimental Earthworks Committee 1992 *Research Proposals for the 1990s* (Lampeter, St David's University College)

Faegri, K, and Iversen, J 1989 (ed)*Textbook of pollen analysis,* 4th edition (revised by Faegri, K, Kuland, P E and Krzywinski, K) (London, J. Wiley & Sons)

Fengel, D, 1991 Aging and fossilization of wood and its components, *Wood Science Technology* **24,** 153–177

Findlay, D C, 1960 *Fyfield Down Nature Reserve: soil survey* (Unpublished report.)

Findlay, D C, Colborne, G J N, Cope, D W, Harrod, T R, Hogan, D V & Staines, S J *et al.,* 1984 *Soils and their use in South West England,* Soil Survey of England and Wales (Harpenden, Lawes Agricultural Trust Bulletin No **14**)

Fisher, P J & Macphail, R I, 1985 Studies of archaeological soils and deposits by micromorphological techniques, in Feiller, N, Gilbertson, D D, & Ralph, N G A (eds) *Palaeoenvironmental Investigation: Research Design, Methods and Data Analysis BAR IS258* (Oxford, British Archaeological Reports), 93–112

Flannigan, B, 1970 Degradation of aribinose and carboxymethyl cellulose by fungi isolated from barley kernels, *Transactions of the British Mycological Society* **55,** 277–281

Flanagan, P W & Scarborough, A M, 1974 Physiological groups of decomposer fungi on Tundra plants remains, in Holding, A J, Heal, O W, Maclean, S F & Flanagen, F W (eds) *Soil Organisms and Decomposition in Tundra* (Stokholm, Tundra Biome Steering Committee), 159–181

Fletcher, W W, 1972 The chemical durability of glass. A burial experiment at Ballidon in Derbyshire, *Journal of Glass Studies* **14,** 149–151

Florian, M L E, 1987 Deterioration of organic materials other than wood, in C. Pearson (ed) *The conservation of Marine Archaeological objects* (London, Butterworths)

Forgacs, J, 1972 Stachybotryotoxicosis, in Kadis, S Ciegler, A & Ajl, S J (eds) *Microbiol Toxins* (New York, Academic Press), 95–128

Forum for Archaeology in Wessex 1994 Experimental Earthworks, *C.B.A. Wessex Newsletter,* April, 4, 1994

Fothergill, P G & Jones, M, 1958 Nutritional studies of *Zygorhycus* species, *Journal of General Microbiology* **19,** 298–304

Fowler, P J, 1963 The Archaeology of Fyfield and Overton Downs, *Wiltshire Archaeological Magazine* **58,** 342–350

Fowler, P J, 1967 The Archaeology of Fyfield and Overton Downs, *Wiltshire Archaeological Magazine* **62,** 16–33

Fowler, P J, 1968 Conservation and the countryside, *Wiltshire Archaeological and Natural History Magazine* **63,** 1–11

Fowler, P J, 1977 *Approaches to Archaeology* (A & C Black)

Fowler, P J, 1984 Experimental Earthworks in England, *Bulletin of Experimental Archaeology* **5,** 24–32

Fowler, P J, 1989 The Experimental earthworks: A summary of the Project's first thirty years: The thirteenth Beatrice de Cardi Lecture, *Annual Report of the Council for British Archaeology* **39,** 83–98

Fowler, P J, Forthcoming *A Landscape Plotted and Pieced: Field Archaeology in Fyfield and Overton, Wiltshire*

Fowler, P J & Evans, J G, 1967 Plough marks, lynchets and early fields, *Antiquity **41,*** 289–301

Fowler, P J & Sharp, M, 1990 *Images of Prehistory* (Cambridge University Press), 17

Gillam, B, 1993 *The Wiltshire Flora* (Newbury: Pisces)

Gilchrist, R & Mytum, H C, 1986 Experimental archaeology and burnt bone from archaeological sites, *Circaea* **4,** 29–38

Gillespie, J M, 1970 Mammoth Hair, *Science* **170,** 1100–1102

Gingell, C, 1992 *The Marlborough Downs: A Later Bronze Age Landscape and its Origins* (Wiltshire Archaeological and Natural History Society Monograph **1**)

Godwin, H, 1978 *Fenland: its ancient past and uncertain future* (Cambridge, University Press)

Goldenberg, E M, 1991 Amplification and analysis of Miocene plant fossil DNA, *Philosophical Transactions of the Royal Society of London* Series B **333,** 419–427

Goldstein, J I, Newbury, D E, Echlin, P, Joy, D C, Romig, A D, Lyman, E, Fiori, C & Lifshin, E, 1992 *Scanning electron microscopy and X-ray microanalysis* (New York, Plenum Press)

Gordon, C G & Buikstra, J E, 1981 Soil pH, bone preservation and sampling bias at mortuary sites, *American Antiquity* **116,** 566–571

Grime, J P, Hodgson, J G & Hunt, R 1988 *Comparative Plant Ecology* (London, Unwin)

Grossbard, E, 1952 Antibiotic production by fungi on organic manures and soils, *Journal of General Microbiology* **6,** 295–310

Grubb, P J, Green, H E & Merrifield, R J C, 1969 The ecology of chalk heath: its relevance to the calcicole-calcifuge and soil acidification problems, *Journal of Ecology* **75,** 175–212

Guillemat, J & Monegut, J, 1956 Contribution à l'étude de la microflora fongique des sols cultivés, *Annales des Epiphyties* **7** (Paris), 471–540

Gurney, D A, 1985 Phosphate analysis of soils: a guide for the field archaeologist, *Institute of Field Archaeologists, Technical Paper* **3**

Guilloré, P, 1985 *Méthode de Fabrication Méchanique et en Séries des Lames Minces* (Paris, Institut National Agronomique)

Hackett, C J, 1981 Microscopical focal destruction (tunnels) in exhumed bones, *Medicine, Science, Law* **21**, 243–265

Hagelberg, E & Clegg, J B, 1993 Genetic polymorphisms in prehistoric Pacific islanders determined by analysis of ancient bone DNA, *Proceedings of the Royal Society of London* Series B **252**, 163–170

Hagelberg, E, Sykes, B & Hedges, R, 1989 Ancient bone DNA, *Nature* **342,** 485

Hagelberg, E, Gray, I C & Jefferys, A J, 1991 Identification of the skeletal remains of a murder victim by DNA analysis, *Nature* **352**, 427–429

Hald, M, 1942 The Nettle as a Culture Plant, *Folk-Liv* **6**, 28–49

Hamond, F W, 1983 Phosphate analysis of archaeological sediments, in Reeves-Smyth, T & Hamond, F W (eds) *Landscape Archaeology in Ireland BAR* **BS116** (Oxford, Brit Archaeological Rep), 47–80

Hanni, C, Laudet, V, Sakka, M, Begue, A & Stehelin, D, 1990 Amplification of mitochondrial DNA fragments from ancient human teeth and bones, *Comptes rendus de Academie des Sciences, Paris,* Series III, **310**, 365–370

Hansen, H-O, 1982 *Lejre Research Center* (Lejre, Historical-Archaeological Research Center)

Hanson, D B & Buikstra, J E, 1987 Histomorphological alteration in buried human bone from the Lower Illinois Valley: implications for palaeodietary research, *Journal of Archaeological Science* **14**, 549–563

Harrison, A F, 1971 The inhibitory effect of oak leaf litter on the growth of fungi in relation to litter decomposition, *Soil Biology and Biochemistry* **3**, 167–172

Havinga, A J, 1967 Palynology and pollen preservation, *Review Palaeobotany and Palynology* **2**, 81–98

Hawksworth, D L, 1976, The natural history of Slapton Ley Nature Reserve 10. Fungi, *Field Studies* **4**, 391–439

Hedges, J I, Cowie, G L, Ertel, J R, Barbour, R J & Hatcher, P G, 1985 Degradation of carbohydrates and lignins in buried woods, *Geochimica et Cosmochimica Acta* **49**, 701–711

Hedges, R E M, Millard, A R & Pike, A W G, 1995 Measurements and relationships of diagenetic alteration of bone from three archaeological sites, in Hedges, R and van Klinken G-J (eds) Proceedings of the Oxford Bone Diagenesis Workshop, *Journal of Archaeological Science* **22**, 201–209

Hedges, R E M & Millard, A R, 1995 Bones and groundwater: towards the modelling of diagenetic processes in Hedges, R and van Klinken G-J (eds) Proceedings of the Oxford Bone Diagenesis Workshop, *Journal of Archaeological Science* **22**, 155–164

Hemsley, J H, 1963 Present Vegetation, in Jewell, P A (ed) *The Experimental Earthwork on Overton Down Wiltshire 1960* (London, British Association for the Advancement of Science Research Committee Report), 70–73

Hendry, G A F, 1989 Biochemical Studies, in Ashbee, P, Bell, M & Proudfoot, E (eds) *Wilsford Shaft Excavations 1960–1962* (London, English Heritage Archaeological Report **11**), 96

Hendry, G A F, Houghton, J D & Brown, S, 1987 The degradation of chlorophyll – a biological enigma, *New Phytologist* **107**, 255–302

Hendry, G A F, Thompson, K and Band, S R 1995 Seed survival and persistence on a calcareous landsurface after a 32-year burial, *Journal of Vegetation Studies* **6**, 153–156

Hesseltine, C W, Benjamin, C R & Mehotra, B S, 1959 The genus *Zygorhyncus*, *Mycologia* **51**, 173–194

Hodgson, J M, (ed) 1974 *Soil Survey field handbook* (Harpenden, Soil Survey Technical Monograph **5**)

Horai, S, Hayasaka, K, Murayama, K, Wate, N, Koike, H & Nakai, N, 1989 DNA amplification from ancient human skeletal remains and their sequence analysis, *Proceedings of the Japanese Academy* **65**, 229–233

Horai, S, Kondo, R, Murayama, K, Hayashi, S, Koike, H & Nakai, N, 1991 Phylogenetic affiliation of ancient and contemporary humans inferred from mitochondrial DNA, *Philosophical Transactions of the Royal Society of London,* Series B **333**, 409–417

Hummel, S & Herrmann, B, 1991 Y-chromosome specific DNA amplified in ancient human bone, *Naturwissenschaften* **76**, 266–267

Hunter, J R, Martin, A L & Roberts, C A, forthcoming 1995 *An introduction to forensic archaeology*. London: Batsford

Hutchins, J, 1767 *Gentleman's Magazine*, 53–54

Ingersoll, D, & Macdonald, W, 1977 Introduction in Ingersoll, D, Yellen, JE & Macdonald W (eds) *Experimental Archaeology* (New York, Columbia University Press), xi-xvii

Ingersoll, D, Yellen, J E & Macdonald, W, 1977 *Experimental Archaeology* (New York, Columbia University Press)

Jain, P C & Agrawal, S C,1980 A note on the keratin decomposing capability of some fungi, *Transactions of the Mycology Society of Japan* **21**, 513–517

Jakes, K A & Sibley, L R, 1983 Survival of Cellulosic Fibres in the Archaeological Context, *Science and Archaeology* **25**, 31–38

Jakes, K A & Sibley, L R, 1984 Survival of Protein Fibres in the Archaeological Context, *Science and Archaeology* **26**, 17–27

Janaway, R C, 1983 Textile fibre characteristics preserved by metal corrosion: the potential of SEM studies, *The Conservator* **7**, 48–52

Jay, L A, 1993 Barrow Reconstruction, *Archaeologia Cantiana* **112**, 421

Jewell, P A, 1958 Natural History and Experiment in Archaeology, *Proceedings of the British Association for the Advancement of Science* **59**, 165–172

Jewell, P A, 1959 Earthworms and Archaeology, *The Times Science Review,* Winter 1959, **18**

Jewell, P A, 1961a An Experiment in Field Archaeology, *Proceedings of the British Association for Advancement of Science,* **71**, 106–109

Jewell, P A, 1961b An Experimental Earthwork on Fyfield Down, *Wiltshire Archaeological Magazine,* **58**, 38

Jewell, P A (ed) 1963 *The Experimental Earthwork at Overton Down, Wiltshire, 1960* (London, British Association for the Advancement of Science)

Jewell, P A, 1993 "Natural history and experiment in archaeology" revisited, in Clason, A, Payne, S & Uerpmann, H-P (eds) *Skeletons in her cupboard: Festschrift for Juliet Clutton-Brock* (Oxford, Oxbow Monograph **34**), 109–116

Jewell, P A & Dimbleby, G W (eds) 1966 The Experimental Earthwork on Overton Down, Wiltshire, England: the first four years, *Proceedings of the Prehistoric Society* **32**, 313–342

Keeley, H C M, Hudson, G E & Evans, J, 1977 Trace element contents of human bones in various states of preservation: 1, The soil silhouette, *Journal of Archaeological Science* **4**, 19–24

Keepax, C, 1977 Contamination of archaeological deposits by seeds of modern origin with particular reference to the use of flotation machines, *Journal of Archaeological Science* **4**, 221–229

Keith, A, 1942 A Postscript to Darwin's Formation of vegetable mould through the action of worms, *Nature* **149**, 716–720

King, N E & Sheail, J, 1970 The old rabbit warren on Fyfield Down, near Marlborough, *Wiltshire Archaeological and Natural History Magazine* **65**, 1–6

Kivilaan, A & Bandurski, R S, 1981 The one hundred-year period for Dr. Beal's seed viability experiment, *American Journal of Botany* **68**, 1290–1292

Klindt-Jensen, O, 1957 *Denmark before the Vikings* (London, Thames and Hudson)

Knocker, G M, 1959. Excavation of three round barrows at Kinson, near Bournemouth, *Proceedings of the Dorset Natural History and Archaeological Society,* **80**, 133–145

Le Borgne, 1955 Susceptibilité magnetique anormale du sol superficiel, *Annales de Géophysique,* **11**, 399–419

Lee Lyman, R, 1987 Archaeofaunas and butchery studies: a taphonomic perspective, *Advances in Archaeological Method and Theory* **10**, 249–337

Lewis, J A & Starkey, R L, 1969 Decomposition of plant tannins by some soil micro-organisms, *Soil Science* **107**, 235–241

Limbrey, S, 1975 *Soil Science and Archaeology* (London, Academic Press)

Lindahl, T, 1993 Instability and decay of the primary structure of DNA, *Nature* **362**, 709–715

Lindsay, W L, 1979 *Chemical equilibria in soils* (New York, John Wiley & Sons)

Linse, A R, 1992 Is bone safe in a shell midden? in Stein, J K, *Deciphering a shell midden* (New York, Academic Press), 327–45

Lodha, B C, 1964 Studies on coprophilous fungi 1. Chaetomium, *Journal of the Indian Botanic Society* **43**, 121–140

Lucas, R L, 1955 A comparative study of *Ophiobolus graminis* and *Fusarium culmurum* in saprophytic colonisation of wheat straw, *Annals of Applied Biology* **43**, 134–143

Luning, J, 1971 Neue grabungen im Michelsberger erdwerk in Mayen, *Germania* **49**, 212–214

Luppi-Mosca, A M, 1960 Investigaciones sobre la microflora de terrenos Espanioles, *Annales del Instituto Botanico A J Cavailles* **18**, 69–90

Macinnes, L & Wickham-Jones, R, 1992 *All Natural Things: Archaeology and the Green Debate* (Oxford, Oxbow)

Macphail, R I, 1979 Soil report on the barrow and buried soil at Sproxton, Leicestershire (London, *Ancient Monuments Laboratory Report* **2929**)

Macphail, R I, 1981a Soil report on West Heath Cemetery (1980), West Sussex I: Soils, II: Micromorphology (London, *Ancient Monuments Laboratory Report* **3586**)

Macphail, R I, 1981b Soil report on the Saddlesborough Reave at Shaugh Moor, Dartmoor, Devon, (London, *Ancient Monuments Laboratory Report* **3484**.)

Macphail, R I, 1981c Soil report on the micromorphology and the first turf of the turf stack at the Experimental Earthwork on Morden Bog, Wareham, Dorset (London, *Ancient Monument Laboratory Report* **3587**)

Macphail, R I, 1986a Soil report on Hazleton long cairn, Gloucestershire (London, *Ancient Monument Laboratory Report* **4898**)

Macphail, R I, 1986b Palaeosols in archaeology: their role in understanding Flandrian pedogenesis, in Wright, V P (ed) *Paleosols: their recognition and Interpretation* (Oxford: Blackwell Scientific Publications), 263–290

Macphail, R I, 1987 A review of soil science in archaeology in England, in Keeley, H C M (ed) *Environmental Archaeology of England: a regional review II* (London: English Heritage), 332–379

Macphail, R I, 1990 The soils in Saville, A (ed) *Hazleton North: the Excavation of a Neolithic longcairn of the Cotswold-Severn Group*

254

(London, English Heritage Archaeological Report **13**), 223–226

Macphail, R I, 1991 The archaeological soils and sediments, in Sharples, N M (ed) *Maiden Castle: excavations and field survey 1985–6* (London, English Heritage Archaeological Report **19**), 106–117

Macphail, R I, 1992 Soil micromorphological evidence of ancient soil erosion, in Bell, M & Boardman, J (eds) *Past and Present Soil Erosion* (Oxford, Oxbow Books), 197–215

Macphail, R I, 1993 Soil micromorphology, in Whittle, A, Rouse, A J & Evans, J G (eds) A Neolithic downland monument in its environment: excavations at the Easton Down long barrow, Bishops Cannings, Wiltshire, *Proceedings of Prehistoric Society* **59**, 218–219, 234–235

Macphail, R I, 1993 Micromorphological analysis of soils and sediments, in Whittle, A (ed) Excavations at Millbarrow chambered tomb, Winterbourne Monkton, north Wiltshire, *Wiltshire Archaeological Magazine* **87**, 13–15, 25–28

Macphail, R I, (In preparation) Soil micromorphology, in Whittle A (ed) *Windmill Hill Report*

Macphail, R I & Goldberg, P, 1990 The micromorphology of tree subsoil hollows: their significance to soil science and archaeology in Douglas, L A (ed) *Soil micromophology: a basic and applied science* (Amsterdam, Elsevier), 425–430

Macphail, R I, Romans, J C C & Robertson, L, 1987 The application of micromorphology to the understanding of Holocene soil in the British Isles; with special reference to cultivation, in Federoff, N, Bresson, L M & Courty, M A (eds) *Soil Micromorphology* (Plaisir, Association Français pour l'Etude du Sol), 647–656

Macphail, R I, Courty, M A & Goldberg, P, 1990 Soil micromorphology in archaeology, *Endeavour* New Series **14**, 4, 163–171

Maff, 1986 *The analysis of agricultural materials. 3rd Edition. MAFF/ADAS Reference Book* **427** (London: HMSO)

Maher, B A, 1986 Characterisation of soils by mineral magnetic measurements, *Physics of the Earth and Planetary Interiors* **42**, 76–92

Marsh, P B, Bollenbacher, K, Butler, M L & Raper, K B, 1949 The fungi concerned in fibre deterioration 2. Their ability to decompose cellulose, *Textile Research* **19**, 462–484

Marshall, R C & Gillespie, J M, 1989 Variations in the proteins of wool and hair, in Rogers, G E , Reis, P J, Ward, K A & Marshall, R C (eds) *The Biology of Wool and Hair* (London, Chapman and Hall), 117–126

McGinnis, M R, Nilson, A D & Ware, L L, 1975 Mycotic biodeterioration associated with the movement and storage of commercially

handled household goods, *Mycopathologia* **57**, 41–45

Merrill, W & French, D W, 1966 Colonisation of wood by soil fungi, *Phytopathology* **56**, 301–303

Mercer, R, 1980 *Hambledon Hill : a Neolithic Landscape* (Edinburgh, University Press)

Millner, P D, 1975 Ascomycetes of Pakistan-*Chaetomium, Biologia, Lahore* **21**, 39–73

Mislivec, P B, Dieter, C T & Bruce, V R, 1975 Effect of temperature and RH on spore germination of mycotoxic species of *Aspergillus* and *Penicillium, Mycologia* **67**, 1187–1189

Moffett, L, (unpublished) *Botanical remains from Worcester Deansway,* Ancient Monuments Laboratory Report **123/91**

Molleson, T, 1990 The accumulation of trace metals in bone during fossilisation, in Priest, N D & Van de Vyver, F L (eds) *Trace Metals and Fluoride in Bones and Teeth* (Boca Raton, CRC Press), 341–365

Moreau, C, Moreau, M & Pelhate, J, 1965 Compartement cultural de moisissures double en relation avec leur ecologie sur grains, *C R Hebd Seanc* **SD260** (Paris, Academie de Science), 1229–1322

Mullins, C E, 1977 Magnetic susceptibility of the soil and its significance in soil science – a review, *Journal of Soil Science* **28**, 223–246

Murphy, C P, Bullock, P & Turner, R H, 1977 The measurement and characterisation of voids in soil thin sections by image analysis, *Journal of Soil Science* **28**, 498–508

Murphy, C P, 1986 *Thin Section Preparation of Soils and Sediments* (Berkhamsted, A B Academic Publishers)

Nature Conservancy Council, 1956 *Seventh Annual Report of the Nature Conservancy 30.9.56* London: HMSO, **34**

Newton, R G, 1981. A summary of the progress of the Ballidon glass burial experiment, *Glass Technology* **22**, 42–45

Newton, R G, 1985 The Ballidon glass burial experiment, *Glass Technology* **26**, 293

Newton, R G, 1988 More results from the Ballidon glass burial experiment, *Glass Technology* **29**, 106–107

Newton, R G & Davison, S, 1989 *Conservation of Glass* (London, Butterworth)

Nicholls, V O, 1956 Fungi of chalk soils, *Transactions of the British Mycological Society* **39**, 233–236

Nilsson, T, Daniel, G, Kirk, T K & Obst, J R, 1989 Chemistry and microscopy of wood decay by some higher ascomycetes, *Holzforschung* **43**, 11–18

Odum S, 1965 Germination of ancient seeds, *Dansk Botanisk Archiv* **24**, 1–70

Paabo, S, 1989 Ancient DNA: extraction, characterisation, molecular cloning and enzymatic amplification, *Proceedings of the*

National Academy of Sciences, USA **86**, 1939–1943

Park, D, 1976 Nitrogen levels and cellulose decomposition by fungi, *International Biodeterioration Bulletin* **12**, 95–99

Parkinson, D, Gray, T R G & Williams, S T, 1971 Methods for studying the ecology of soil microorganisms, *International Biological Programme Handbook* **19** (Oxford, Blackwell Scientific Publications)

Paul, C R C, 1978 The ecology of Mollusca in ancient woodland: 2 Analysis of distribution and experiments in Hayley Wood, Cambs, *Journal of Conchology*, **29**, 281–294

Percival, J, 1980 *Living in the Past* (London: BBC)

Petersen, F F, 1981 *The Excavation of a Bronze Age Cemetery on Knighton Heath, Dorset* BAR **B98** (Oxford, Brit Archaeological Rep)

Piepenbrink, H, 1989 Examples of chemical change during fossilisation, *Applied Geochemistry* **4**, 273–280

Phillips, C W ed 1970 *The Fenland in Roman times, studies of a major area of peasant culture, with a gazeteer covering all known sites and finds.* London, Royal Geographical Society Research Series **5**

Piggott, C M, 1941 Excavation of Fifteen Barrows in the New Forest 1941–2, *Proceedings of the Prehistoric Society* **9**, 1–27

Pitt, J I, 1973 An appraisal of identification methods for *Penicillium* species-novel taxanomic criteria based on temperature and water relations, *Mycologia* **65**, 1135–1157

Pitt, J I, 1979 *The Genus Penicillium* (London, Academic Press)

Pitt Rivers, A H, 1898 *Excavations in Cranborne Chase* vol VI (privately printed)

Pitts, M & Whittle, A,1992 The development and date of Avebury, *Proceedings of the Prehistoric Society* **58**, 203–212

Pollard, J, 1992 The Sanctuary, Overton Hill, Wiltshire: A Re-examination, *Proceedings of the Prehistoric Society* **58**, 213–226

Proudfoot, V B, 1961 The British Association's experimental earthwork, *New Scientist* **11**, 596–598

Proudfoot, B, 1964 Experimental Earthworks in the British Isles, *Geographical Review* **54**, 584–6

Proudfoot, V B, 1965a The study of soil development from the construction and excavation of experimental earthworks, in Hallsworth, E G & Crawford, D V (eds) *Experimental Pedology* (London, Butterworths), 282–294

Proudfoot, V B, 1965b Bringing archaeology to life, *British Association for the Advancement of Science* July 1965, 125–133

Proudfoot, V B, 1967 Experiments in archaeology, *Science Journal* November 1967, vol **3**, 59–64

Proudfoot, V B, 1976 The analysis and interpretation of soil phosphorous in archaeological contexts, in Davidson, D A & Shackley, M L (eds) *Geoarchaeology* (London, Duckworth), 93–113

Pyddoke, E, 1961 *Stratification for the Archaeologist* (London, Phoenix House)

Rahtz, P, Woodward, A, Burrow, I, 1992 *Cadbury Congresbury 1968/73: a late / post-Roman hilltop settlement in Somerset,* (Oxford: British Archaeological Reports, British Series **223**)

Renfrew, C, 1973 Monuments, mobilisation and social organisation in Neolithic Wessex, in Renfrew, C, *The Explanation of Culture Change: models in Prehistory* (London, Duckworth), 539–558

Reynolds, P J, 1979 *Iron Age Farm: the Butser Experiment* (London: British Museum Publications)

Reynolds, P J, 1981 Deadstock and livestock, in Mercer, R (ed) *Farming Practice in British prehistory* (Edinburgh: University Press), 97–122

Reynolds, P J, 1985 *Research Earthworks, Wroughton, Base Data 1985* (Petersfield; Butser Ancient Farm Project Trust)

Reynolds, P J, 1986 *Butser Ancient Farm Yearbook* (Petersfield; Butser Ancient Farm Project Trust)

Reynolds, P J, 1987 *Butser Ancient Farm Yearbook* (Petersfield; Butser Ancient Farm Project Trust)

Reynolds, P J, 1988 *Butser Ancient Farm Yearbook* (Petersfield; Butser Ancient Farm Project Trust)

Reynolds, P J, 1989 Experimental Earthworks, *British Archaeology,* **14**, 16–19

Reynolds, P J & Wyman, A, 1987 *Butser Ancient Farm Meteorological Records 1987* (Petersfield, Butser Ancient Farm Project Trust)

Reynolds, P J & Wyman, A, 1988 *Butser Ancient Farm Meteorological Data 1988* (Petersfield, Butser Ancient Farm Project Trust)

Richards, M B, Sykes, B C & Hedges, R E M, 1995 Authenticating DNA extracted from ancient skeletal remains, in Hedges, R, and van Klinken, G-J (eds) Proceedings of the Oxford Bone Diagenesis Workshop, *Journal of Archaeological Science* **22**, 291–299

Robinson, D E, 1990 (ed) *Experimentation and reconstruction in Environmental Archaeology* (Oxford, Oxbow)

Roelofsen, P A, 1951 Contradictory Data on Spiral Structures in the Secondary Cell Wall of Fibres of Flax, Hemp and Ramie, *Textile Research Journal* **21:6**, 412–418

Rollo, F, Venanzi, F M & Amici, A, 1991 Nucleic acids in mummified plant seeds; biochemistry and molecular genetics of pre-Columbian maize, *Genetical Research* **58**, 193–201

Romans, J C C & Robertson, L, 1975 Soils and archaeology in Scotland, in Evans, J G, Limbrey, S & Cleere, H (eds) *The Effect of Man on the Landscape: the Highland Zone* (London, CBA Res Rep **11**), 37–39

Romans, J C C & Robertson, L, 1983 The general effects of early agriculture on the soil, in Maxwell, G S (ed) *The Impact of Aerial Reconnaissance on Archaeology* (London, CBA Res Rep **49**), 136–41

Ross, D J, 1960 Physiological studies of some common fungi from grassland soils, *New Zealand Journal of Science* **3**, 219–157

Rouse, A J & Evans, J G, 1994 Modern land Mollusca from Maiden Castle, Dorset, and their relevance to the interpretation of subfossil archaeological assemblages, *Journal of Molluscan Studies* **60**, 315–329

Ryder, M L, 1961 A specimen of Asiatic sheepskin from the 4th or 5th century BC, *Australian Journal of Science* **24**, 246–248

Ryder, M L, 1963 Remains derived from skin, in Brothwell, D R and Higgs, E S (eds) *Science in Archaeology* (London, Thames and Hudson), 529–544

Ryder, M L, 1969 Changes in the fleece of sheep following domestication, in Ucko, P J and Dimbleby, G W (eds) *The Domestication and Exploitation of Plants and Animals* (London, Duckworth), 495–521

Ryder, M L, 1974 Hair of the Mammoth, *Nature* **249**, 190–192

Ryder, M L, 1981a British Medieval sheep and their wool types, in Crossley, D W (ed) *Medieval Industry* (London, CBA Res Rep **40**), 16–28

Ryder, M L, 1981b Fleece changes in sheep, in Jones, M & Dimbleby, G W (eds) *The Environment of Man: the Iron Age to Anglo-Saxon Period BAR IS87* (Oxford, Brit Archaeological Rep), 215–229

Ryder, M L, 1983 *Sheep and Man* (London, Duckworth)

Ryder, M L, 1984 Skin, hair and cloth remains from the ancient Kerma civilisation of northern Sudan, *Journal of Archaeological Science* **11**, 477–482

Ryder, M L, 1987a The evolution of the fleece, *Scientific American* **2**, 56/1, 104

Ryder, M L, 1987b The measurement of wool fibres in yarns as an aid to defining carpet type, *Oriental Carpet and Textile Studies* **3**, 134–152

Ryder, M L, 1988 Danish Bronze Age Wools, *Danish Journal of Archaeology* **7**, 136–143

Ryder, M L, 1990 The natural pigmentation of animal textile fibres, *Textile History* **21**, 135–148

Ryder, M L, 1992a Iron Age haired animal skins from Hallstatt, Austria, *Oxford Journal of Archaeology* **11**, 55–67

Ryder, M L, 1992b The use of biochemical polymorphisms to study livestock history with particular references to sheep and wool, *Biology History* **5**, 30–39

Ryder, M L, 1993a (forthcoming) *Report on Bronze Age textile fibres from St Andrews*

Ryder, M L, 1993b The textile fibres, in Taylor, A, A Roman lead coffin with pipeclay figurines from Arrington, Cambridgeshire, *Britannia*, **24**, 191–225

Ryder, M L & Gabra-Sanders, T, 1987 A microscopic study of textiles made from plant fibres, *Oxford Journal of Archaeology* **6**, 91–108

Ryder, M L & Stephenson, S K 1968 *Wool Growth* (London, Academic Press)

Sasaki, Y & Sasaki, H, 1971 A taxanomic study on cellulose decomposing fungi, *Memoirs of the Faculty of Agriculture of Hokkaido University* **8**, 30–39

Scaife, R G & Macphail, R I, 1983 The post-Devensian development of heathland soils and vegetation, in Burnham, C P (ed) Soils of the Heathlands and Chalklands, Wye; *SEESOIL, Journal of the South East Soils Discussion Group* **1**, 70–99

Schiffer, M B, 1987 *Formation Processes of the Archaeological record* (Albuquerque, University of New Mexico Press)

Schlegel, H G, 1986 *General Microbiology* (Cambridge University Press)

Scollar, I, Tabbagh, A, Hesse, A & Herzog, I, 1990 *Archaeological prospecting and remote sensing* (Cambridge University Press)

Shanks, M & Tilley, C, 1987 *Social Theory and Archaeology* (Cambridge, Polity Press)

Shipman, P, 1981 Application of scanning electron microscopy to taphonomic problems, in Cantwell, A M E, Griffin, J B & Rothschild, N A (eds) *The Research Potential of Anthropological Museum Collections, Annals of the New York Academy of Sciences* **376**, 357–385

Shipman, P, Foster G & Schoeninger, M, 1984 Burnt bones and teeth: an experimental study of colour, morphology, crystal structure and shrinkage, *Journal of Archaeological Science* **11**, 307–325

Simmons, I G, 1993 *Interpreting Nature: Cultural constructions of the Environment* (London, Routledge)

Singh, A P, 1989 Certain aspects of bacterial degradation of *Pinus radiata* wood, *International Association of Wood Anatomists Bulletin* **10**, 405–415

Singh, A P, Nilsson, T & Daniels, G F, 1990 Bacterial attack of *Pinus sylvestris* wood under near anerobic conditions, *Journal of the Institute of Wood Science* **11**, 237–249

Smith, C J, 1980 *Ecology of the English Chalk* (London, Academic Press)

Smith, D & Onions, A H S, 1983 *The Preservation and Maintenance of Living Fungi* (Farnham Royal, Commonwealth Agricultural Bureau)

Smith, R W, 1984 The Ecology of Neolithic farming systems as exemplified by the Avebury region of Wiltshire, *Proceedings of the Prehistoric Society* **50**, 99–12

Snow C P, 1959, *The two cultures and the scientific revolution. Rede lecture* (Cambridge University Press)

Soil Survey Staff, 1975 *Soil Taxonomy: a Basic System of Soil Classification for Making and Interpreting Soil Surveys,* USDA- SCS, Agricultural Handbook **436** (Washington DC, U S Government Printing Office)

Startin, D W A, 1982 Prehistoric earthmoving, in Case, H J & Whittle, A W R (eds) *Settlement patterns in the Oxford region: Excavations at the Abingdon causewayed enclosure and other sites* (London, CBA Research Report **44**), 153–156

Steensberg, A, 1957 Some recent Danish experiments in neolithic agriculture, *Agricultural History Review* **5**, 66–73

Steensberg, A, 1979 *Draved: An experiment in Stone Age Agriculture: Burning, sowing and Harvesting* (Copenhagen, National Museum of Denmark)

Stenton, H, 1953 The soil fungi of Wicken Fen, *Transactions of the British Mycological Society* **36**, 219–257

Stevenson, F J, 1982 *Humus Chemistry* (New York, Wiley)

Straker, V (unpublished) Charred plant remains from the Dorchester by-pass sites

Sumner, J Heywood 1913 *The Ancient Earthworks of Cranborne Chase* (London, Chiswick Press, republished 1988 Gloucester, A. Sutton)

Sumner, J Heywood, 1917, *The Ancient Earthworks of the New Forest* (London, Chiswick Press)

Swain, A M, 1973 A History of Fire and Vegetation in Northeastern Minnesota as Recorded in Lake Sediments, *Quaternary Research* **3**, 383–396

Swift, M J, Heal, O W & Anderson, J M, 1979 Decomposition in terrestrial ecosystems, *Studies in Ecology* **5** (Oxford, Blackwell Scientific Publications)

Tansley, A G, 1968 *Britain's Green Mantle: Past, Present and Future* (London, Allen & Unwin)

Textile Institute, 1970 *Identification of Textile Materials* 6th edition (Manchester, Butterworths for The Textile Institute)

Thuesen, I & Engberg, J, 1990 Recovery and analysis of human genetic material from mummified tissue and bone, *Journal of Archaeological Science* **17**, 679–689

Thompson K, 1986 Small-scale heterogeneity in the seed bank of an acidic grassland, *Journal of Ecology* **74**, 733–738

Thompson, M W & Ashbee, P, 1957 Excavation of a Barrow near the Hardy Monument, Black Down, Portesham, Dorset, *Proceedings of the Prehistoric Society* **23**, 124–136

Thompson, R & Oldfield, F, 1986 *Environmental magnetism* (London, Allen & Unwin)

Tite, M S & Mullins, C, 1971 Enhancement of magnetic susceptibility of soils on archaeological sites, *Archaeometry* **13**, 209–19

Tite, M S, 1972a *Methods of Physical Examination in Archaeology* (London, Seminar Press)

Tite, M S, 1972b The influence of geology on the magnetic susceptibility of soils on archaeological sites, *Archaeometry* **14**, 229–236

Wainwright, G J, 1966 The excavation of a round barrow on Worgret Hill, Arne, Dorset, *Proceedings of the Dorset Natural History and Archaeological Society* **87**, 119–125

Wallwork, J A, 1976 *The distribution and diversity of soil fauna* (London, Academic Press)

Walsh, J H & Stewart, C S, 1971 Effect of temperature, oxygen and carbon dioxide on cellulotic activity of some fungi, *Transactions of the British Mycological Society* **57**, 75–84

Warcup, J H, 1951 Effect of partial sterilisation by steam or formalin on the fungi flora of an old forest nursey soil, *Transactions of the British Mycological Society* **34**, 520–532

Watanabe, T & Miyazaki, K, 1980 Morphological deterioration of acetate, acrylic, polyamide and polyester textiles by micro-organisms (*Appergillus* spp. and *Penicillium* spp.) *Sen-I Gakkaishi* **36**, 409–415

White, E M & Hannus, L A, 1983 Chemical weathering of bone in archaeological soils, *American Antiquity* **48**, 316–322

Whiteley, K J, 1964 Stress-strain properties of an ancient sample of wool, *Journal of the Textile Institute* **55**, 214–216

Whittle, A, 1990a A model for the Mesolithic-Neolithic transition in the upper Kennet valley, north Wiltshire, *Proceedings of the Prehistoric Society* **56**,101–110

Whittle, A, 1990b A Pre-enclosure Burial at Windmill Hill, Wiltshire *Oxford Journal of Archaeology,* **9** (1), 25–28

Whittle, A, 1993 The Neolithic of the Avebury Area: Sequence, Environment, Settlement and Monuments, *Oxford Journal of Archaeology,* **12** (1), 29–53

Whittle, A, 1994 Excavations at Millbarrow Neolithic Chambered Tomb, Winterbourne Monkton, North Wiltshire, *Wiltshire Archaeological Magazine* **87**, 1–53

Whittle, A, Rouse, A J & Evans, J G, 1993 A Neolithic downland monument in its environment: excavations at the Easton Down Long barrow, Bishops Canning, North Wiltshire, *Proceedings of the Prehistoric Society* **59**, 197–239

Wild, J P, 1970 *Textile Manufacture in the Northern Roman Provinces* (Cambridge, University Press)

Williams, S R, Longmire, J L & Beck, L A, 1990 Human DNA recovery from ancient bone, *American Journal of Anthropology* **81**, 318

Williams-Freeman, J P, 1915 *An introduction to field archaeology as illustrated by Hampshire* (London, Macmillan)

Worrall, J J, 1991 Media for selective isolation of hymenomycetes, *Mycologia* **83**, 296–302

258

Worster, D, 1990 The ecology of order and chaos, *Environmental History Review* **14**, 1–18

Yang, C Q & Freeman, J M, 1991 Photo-oxidisation of cotton cellulose studied by FT-IR photoacoustic spectroscopy, *Applied Spectroscopy* **45**, 1694–1698

Zaleski, K, Plaszczak, W & Glaser, T, 1960 Studies on the biology and pathogenicity of four *Fusarium* species from *Lupines* and of two strains of *Rhizoctonia solani* and attempts of their control in greenhouse conditions, *Prace Komisji Nauk Rolniczych i Komisji Nauk Lesnych Poznanskie Towarzystwe Przyjaciol Nauk* **5**, 1–63

Zycha, A, Siepmann R & Linneman, G, 1969 *Mucorales eine beschreibung aller gattungen und arten dieser pilzgruppe* (Lejne, J Cramer)

Index *by Susan Vaughan*

Page numbers in *italics* denote that the reference is, or includes, an illustration. Excavation dates are in **bold** type.